SOCIAL PROBLEMS

SOCIAL

PROBLEMS

Jon M. Shepard
Harwin L. Voss

Macmillan Publishing Co., Inc.
New York

Collier Macmillan Publishers
London

**To Richard Scudder and Lowell Maechtle,
who attracted us to sociology**

Copyright © 1978, Macmillan Publishing Co., Inc.

Printed in the United States of America

Macmillan Publishing Co., Inc.
866 Third Avenue, New York, New York 10022

Collier Macmillan Canada, Ltd.

Library of Congress Cataloging in Publication Data

Shepard, Jon M
  Social problems.

  Includes bibliographies and index.
  1. Sociology. 2. Social problems. I. Voss,
Harwin L., joint author. II. Title.
HM51.S517   301   77-23386
ISBN 0-02-409670-9

Printing: 1 2 3 4 5 6 7 8   Year: 8 9 0 1 2 3 4

preface

One of the goals of this text is to present readers with current perspectives on the nature and causes of social problems and possible ways of solving them. This is particularly important because social problems are often viewed by citizens in inaccurate, outdated, and nonscientific ways. In an age of rapid social change and mounting social problems, it is essential for students to become better informed about undesirable social conditions.

No one, including the authors of this text, sees social conditions without some degree of bias. One's view is influenced by his or her attitudes, values, and beliefs. Consequently, we have consciously taken an eclectic approach and included a variety of sociological perspectives. Because no single theoretical perspective can capture all aspects of a social problem, it is necessary to consider diverse views. This approach is based on the belief that a multifaceted view of any social problem is more informative than a unidimensional one.

To provide as wide a view of social problems as possible, we have examined concepts, theories, and research findings from fields other than sociology. Although the text is distinctly sociological, we also rely on other disciplines, such as anthropology, psychology, political science, and economics.

The text is divided into three major parts. In Parts I and II the focus is on problems of structure or social problems that are created by the ways in which various social structures are organized. In Part I the major theme is inequality—economic inequality, prejudice and discrimination (including sex roles), inequality in government and corporations, and educational inequality. In Part II we concentrate on those social conditions that are emerging as social problems because of shifting values in American society. The major social problems in this category involve the family, work, population, and the environment. Problems of deviance are considered in Part III. These problems involve the violation of generally accepted norms. The chapters in this section deal with crime and juvenile delinquency, drug use (including alcohol), sexual deviance, and mental illness.

Students often object to the nature of social problems courses; they say, "We know that a problem exists, but what can be done about it?" To meet this understandable and legitimate criticism, we have included a section entitled "What Can Be Done?" in each chapter. Solutions to social problems are explored in much greater depth and breadth than is the case in other textbooks. Coverage includes solutions presently in effect, solutions that may be implemented in the near future, and solutions that are not politically or socially acceptable now.

There is an unfortunate tendency to view social problems as static, unchanging conditions. Of course, in modern society, just the reverse is the case. In order to portray social problems as dynamic and changing, we have emphasized the place of values, norms, and attitudes in the creation, alteration, and handling of social problems.

We have attempted to provide a text that is intellectually thorough yet easily readable and understandable. We have avoided technical terms wherever possible and have defined and illustrated concepts that had to be included for an adequate understanding of the issue at hand. Photographs, tables, and graphs have been selected carefully to illustrate the text. Each chapter also contains several boxes with items designed to stimulate the reader's thinking on important points. Some of these items are humorous, some are poignant, some make substantive points not explicitly covered in the text, and others illustrate points discussed at some length.

We are indebted to several people for their help in the preparation of this book. T. Neal Garland contributed the chapter on the family. Both he and

Mary A. Dunbar also provided assistance in the preparation of the chapter on the political institution. Irene Hultman provided valuable editorial help, particularly during the first drafts of the manuscript. The authors are also deeply indebted to Carol Voss for her editorial assistance; privately we refer to her as the unnamed author. Ken Scott, the sociology editor at Macmillan, deserves a great deal of credit for helping us to shape the text into its present form. Although our energies may have flagged at times, his ability to offer additional critical suggestions never did.

J. M. S.
H. L. V.

contents

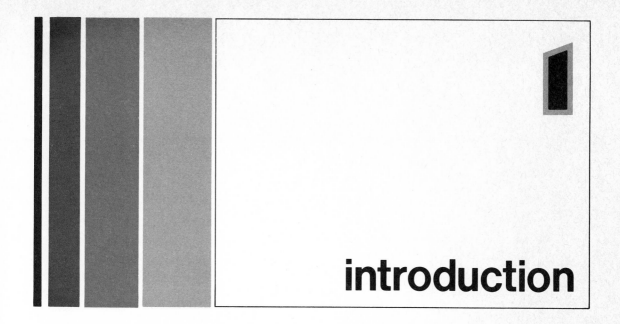

introduction

Millions of children the world over face the evening and morning with a gnawing physical hunger that is their constant companion. Men and women who prefer to work rather than receive welfare payments must often take the least desirable and lowest-paying jobs in the economy. Competent females are passed over for corporate promotion in favor of less qualified males. Men and women in large cities are afraid to walk certain streets even in broad daylight. Each of these conditions is, of course, a reflection of the larger social problems of poverty, sexism, and crime.

Although most people could identify these and many other current problems, few would be able to indicate why these conditions are considered to be social problems. Consequently, it will help in understanding the remaining chapters to elaborate on the meaning of a social problem.

WHAT IS A SOCIAL PROBLEM?

A *social problem* is any social condition that is thought either by a large proportion of a society or by powerful segments of it to be undesirable and in need of attention. This definition contains several distinct elements. Its most important aspects can be explored by answering two questions: When does a social *condition* come to be viewed as undesirable and in need of attention? Who decides when a social condition is a social problem?

When Is a Social Condition a Social Problem?

Obviously, before a social condition can become a social problem, it must exist; it must have some *objective* reality. Before there can be a problem of crime, poverty, or drug abuse, there must be criminals, poor people, and drug addicts. The mere existence of some social condition, however, does not ensure that it will be defined as undesirable and in need of change. It must be perceived by a substantial number of people as a social problem. This is the *subjective* side of a social problem. For example, at one time women and children worked incredibly long hours at hard labor for meager wages. Despite the existence of this objective condition, considerable time elapsed before it came to be viewed as an undesirable condition requiring change.

That raises further questions: How can a social condition be socially acceptable at one time and become a social problem later? Conversely, how can a social condition thought to be a severe social problem at one time be perceived as considerably less undesirable later? The answers to these related questions lie partly in the existence of values, beliefs, and attitudes, which affect people's subjective perceptions. *Values* are ideas about what is worthwhile or desirable. Patriotism, equality, and freedom are values. *Beliefs* are ideas about what is true. Beliefs do not have to be true in order to affect a person's perception of an objective situation, but they do have to be *accepted* as true. Although it was not true that ancient sailors could fall off the edge of the earth if they ventured too far out to sea, their belief that they would affected their voyages. *Attitudes* are tendencies to react favorably or unfavorably toward one's self, others, or social situations. A hatred of war, a love of children, or a lukewarm response to marriage are all attitudes.

Values, beliefs, and attitudes are interrelated. Equality is a value in American society. Two traditional beliefs related to equality have been that all Americans have an equal opportunity to be successful in life and that the unsuccessful do not have the abilities or the will to succeed. Disdain for those in poverty is a long-standing American attitude toward the poor, based on the value of equality and some associated beliefs.

Existing values, beliefs, and attitudes affect people's subjective reactions to objective social conditions. As values, beliefs, and attitudes change, it follows that ideas regarding which social conditions are social problems will also change.

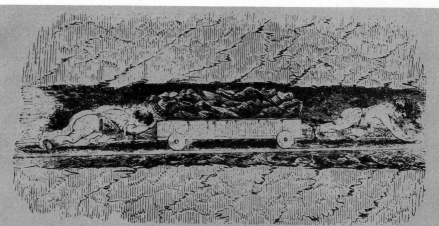

An illustration from Children's Employment Commission, *First Report of the Commissioners: Mines* (London: H. M. Stationery Office, 1842), one of the many white papers reporting the government's investigations of labor conditions in 19th-century England. The accompanying text (pp. 81–82) follows:

By far the greater number of Children and persons employed in coal-mines are engaged in propelling and drawing tubs laden with coal, from the face to the pit-eye, or the mainlevels in those pits where they have horses. This is done by placing the hands on the back of the waggon, and propelling it forward with as great velocity as the inclination of the mine, the state of the road, and the strength of the waggoner admit of. The mines in this district [Lancashire and Cheshire] are for the most part laid with rails, and the waggon runs on wheels. . . . There are, however, mines . . . where the old mode of drawing the baskets or wooden sledges (called in Lancashire 'sleds') is still retained. The drawer is in this case harnessed by means of a chain attached to the 'sled'; the other end of the chain passes between his legs, and fastens in front to a belt round the waist. When thus harnessed, and moving along on his hands and feet, the drawer drags after him the loaded basket; if he is not sufficiently strong he has a helper rather younger than himself. . . . [The figure] represents three young Children hurrying or drawing a loaded waggon of coals. The Child in front is harnessed by his belt or chain to the waggon; the two boys behind are assisting in pushing it forward. Their heads, it will be observed, are brought down to a level with the waggon, and the body almost in a horizontal position. This is done partly to avoid striking the roof, and partly to gain the advantage of the muscular action, which is greatest in that position. It will be observed the boy in front goes on his hands and feet: in that manner the whole weight of his body is in fact supported by the chain attached to the waggon and his feet, and consequently his power of drawing is greater than it would be if he crawled on his knees. These boys, by constantly pushing against the waggons, occasionally rub off the hair from the crowns of their heads so much as to make them almost bald.

The situation of women in American society is an excellent illustration of how changing values, beliefs, and attitudes can cause a social condition to be defined as a social problem. In early times, a woman was considered to be a man's property. A man's wife, like his children and servants, was essentially his slave. Such overt slavery has long since disappeared, but its influence has lingered in the form of certain values, beliefs, and attitudes. One expression of the idea that women exist to serve men was a primary emphasis on women taking care of domestic matters while men worked outside the home. Today, many women work outside the home and many men share in household chores. Another expression of the traditional inequality between men and women has been the exclusion of women from higher-level business, professional, and political positions. Values, beliefs, and attitudes about women's roles have undergone sufficient change that the exclusion of women from important occupational positions has become defined as a social problem by a significant proportion of Americans.

If changing values can cause a social condition to become a social problem, changing values can also cause an undesirable condition to become more acceptable. Pollution and environmental protection emerged as social problems during the late 1960s and early 1970s. While they are still objectively legitimate concerns, the economic recession and energy crisis of the 1970s has led many people to place pollution and the environment second to such things as employment, economic growth, and the maintenance of old and the development of new energy sources.

Sometimes a social condition can be thought to be undesirable by a significant proportion of a society but still not be defined as a social problem because there does not seem to be any way to improve the situation. Before modern medical advances, the death rate all over the world was quite high, particularly among children. That was not considered desirable, but it was not defined as a social problem because it seemed inevitable.

The possibilities that values, beliefs, and attitudes may change and that the ability to improve social conditions may increase do not always ensure that conditions will be publicly perceived as social problems. This raises a second major question: Who decides that a social condition is undesirable and in need of attention?

Who Decides That a Social Condition Is a Social Problem?

An objectively undesirable social condition does not become defined as a social problem unless either a large proportion of the population or powerful segments of a society perceive it as such. It was not the women and children in the early factories who successfully made the case that their condition was a ''social disease.'' They were not influential enough to convince others that a change was in order. More recently, some people have expressed a belief that the violence depicted on American television is an undesirable influence on children. Residents of a poor inner-city neighborhood may believe that being forced out of their homes because of urban renewal is undesirable. Any society contains many groups who consider a particular social condition to be a social problem. No condition will be perceived as a social problem, however, unless those views are shared by a significant number of people or until a situation is championed by persons in positions of power, influence, and prestige.

One way for a social condition to be considered a social problem, then, is by sheer force of numbers. If a significant number of the members of a society define a social situation as undesirable and in need of alteration because of widely shared values, beliefs, and attitudes, then it will very likely be defined as such by public figures. The current widespread concern with the rising crime rate illustrates this route.

Another way for a social condition to become a social problem is for those with influence to show concern. This can occur in two ways. A relatively small number of persuasive persons may, out of their concern for the victims of an undesirable social condition, influence those in powerful positions to recognize it as a social problem. Also, a relatively small number of rich, powerful, and prestigious persons may successfully elevate a social condition to the level of a social problem.

That these two sometimes distinct avenues may occur simultaneously was illustrated in the 1960s in the matter of poverty. Some intellectuals called the long-standing and extensive poverty existing in America to the attention of John Kennedy's advisors. Michael Harrington, now a United States Representative from Massachusetts, in his book *The Other America,* documented the vast economic gulf between the poor and the nonpoor in the affluent America of the 1960s.[1] Kennedy's advisors, who saw the 1960 West Virginia presidential primary as crucial to his election, encouraged the future president to focus attention on poverty in West Virginia and in his subsequent campaign. Poverty subsequently became a national concern.

In most societies there are conflicts in values, beliefs, and attitudes in the general population as well as among interest groups. The existence of such conflicts affects the probability that an objectively undesirable social

[1] Michael Harrington, *The Other America* (New York: Macmillan Publishing Co., Inc., 1962).

condition will become defined as a social problem and will be given the time, effort, and money needed for its change.

Value Conflicts and Social Problems

Within complex societies are individuals and groups that have different values, beliefs, and attitudes. The presence of these differences affects the likelihood that a social situation will be treated as a social problem because people view the same situation differently. Should the possession and use of marijuana be legalized or should the penalties for its sale and consumption be made stronger? Younger people are more likely to favor legalization, whereas middle-aged and older people are more likely to cite harmful effects. To further complicate the matter, both sides can cite scientific studies to support their viewpoints. There are individuals and groups in America that believe some restrictions should be placed on the sale and possession of guns. Some believe in the licensing of firearms; others are convinced that the sale of certain types of guns should be banned and that possession should be punished by law. Opponents of gun control cite the United States Constitution as their legal ground for owning guns. Such a lack of agreement makes the passage of gun control legislation difficult.

Interest Group Conflict and Social Problems

Value conflicts affect the probability of identifying and changing a specific social condition, but their impact is even greater when expressed through powerful interest groups. Advocates of the freedom to buy and use firearms (the ''gun lobby'') express their attitudes in well-organized and well-financed efforts to influence those with political power to support their position.

The efforts of the gun lobby are not simply a matter of Constitutional rights; self-interest may also be involved. Although the possession and use of guns is believed by many who support this lobby to be a basic freedom, some of its supporters have much more to preserve than their Constitutional rights. There are vast industries built on the manufacture and sale of firearms, ammunition, and a variety of accessories such as gun sights, gun magazines, hunting gear, and hunting lodges. Should the lack of gun control come to be considered a social problem, then the economic well-being of many persons who are benefiting from the unrestricted sale of guns would be threatened.

FINGERING GUN CONTROL

WASHINGTON—The House Judiciary Committee in its infinite wisdom sent the latest handgun control bill back to a subcommittee for further "revision," thus probably killing it for another year. After a committee vote of 18 to 14 to send it to the floor, the National Rifle Association put on so much pressure that three congressmen reversed their previous positions. That was the end of this year's hope for a safer and saner America.

When my friend Mindermann heard the news on the radio, he called me. "You owe me $5. I told you Congress was too yellow to pass a gun control bill."

"**THAT IS NOT** nice to say. The committee members probably voted their consciences," I said.

"Yeh, right after they got the mailgrams from the NRA. Listen, you're living in a dream world if you think Congress is ever going to pass any kind of a handgun control law."

"I can always hope," I said.

"The trouble with you bleeding hearts is that you're going about it the wrong way. You're trying to outlaw weapons that are as sacred to Americans as underarm deodorants. You have to figure out some way of letting the people keep their guns, but at the same time do no harm to anyone."

"**WHAT DO YOU** suggest, wise guy?" I asked Mindermann.

"Well, you're going to think I'm crazy, but I have an idea. You cut off everybody's trigger finger at birth."

"You are crazy."

"Hear me out. We can't do anything with the present generation, but we can save future generations from killing each other through accidents and anger and despair if you cut off everybody's trigger finger at birth."

"But you can't cut off someone's trigger finger at birth," I protested.

"**WHY NOT?** The Constitution gives everyone the right to bear arms, which is the main argument the NRA throws at us all the time. But there is nothing in the Constitution that says an American has to have 10 fingers."

"But, Mindermann," I said, "it sounds so gory."

"It's a simple operation. Any doctor can perform it. The baby would never know it. When he or she got old enough the parents could explain that, since Congress would never pass a law prohibiting the manufacture and sale of guns, the only road open to them was to pass one forbidding any American to have a trigger finger."

"**BUT THE GUN** manufacturers and the NRA would be up in arms if you tried something like that."

"Why would they? We're not saying they can't sell guns or ammunition. They can do anything they damn please."

"But what good would a gun or ammunition be if no one has a finger to squeeze the trigger?"

Mindermann said, "Now you're getting the point. Listen, I've researched this thing. I took a poll of the House Judiciary Committee and the Senate, and not one of them had any strong feeling about fingers. There is no finger lobby to speak of. In fact, all I talked to said they couldn't see any reason for their constituents to object to having one finger removed providing the government paid for it under Medicare."

"I'LL HAVE TO ADMIT it sounds simpler than trying to get a handgun control bill through Congress."

"It's the only answer to the problem," Mindermann said. "The slogan for the bill would be, 'If you can't take the trigger out of the gun, take the trigger finger out of the boy.'"

© 1976 by Art Buchwald

Public Perception of Social Problems

Public perception of a social condition as a social problem requires exposure to information about it. Today exposure is achieved chiefly through the mass media (television, radio, newspapers, films, and national magazines). Instead of experiencing a social condition personally, people form their beliefs and attitudes about social problems by reacting to the *interpretations* of media representatives. The media affect the public perception of a social condition in at least three ways. They help to expose a social problem, they may distort the objective nature of a social problem, or they may contribute to the magnitude of a recognized social problem.

Watergate and its aftermath illustrates how the media may help to expose an undesirable social condition. When the Watergate story first broke, the public was uninterested in what appeared to be an amateurish attempt to break into the national Democratic headquarters. Even after months of constant media coverage, most Americans viewed the Watergate episode as simply typical of what political parties do constantly to each other. According to a Gallup poll conducted a few months after the break-in, one half of the country had never heard of Watergate. It took over a year of concentrated media coverage before the public generally perceived the extent to which cheating, lying, "dirty tricks," misuse of federal agencies, political extortion, and law-breaking were being practiced by America's top political officials.

If the media aid in the exposure of social problems, they may also unintentionally serve to distort the real nature of social conditions. Lincoln Steffens, a muckraking journalist of the 1920s and 1930s, contended that he had created a "crime wave" simply by constantly placing reports of criminal activities on the front page of the newspaper.[2] More recently, a study examined the relationship between the reporting of crime in local newspapers and public perception of crime. The four newspapers studied reported crime in such a way that it appeared to be more widespread than justified by the official crime statistics. When a survey was conducted, it was found that the public perception of the extent of certain types of crime was closer to the amount of crime reported in the newspapers than to the officially recorded crime figures.[3] In the late 1960s it was generally believed that college campus riots and demonstrations were declining. In fact, there were more campus incidents then than at any previous time. The press had simply not given as much coverage to campus disturbances as they had in the past.

Finally, the media may actually increase the severity of an already recognized social problem. One of the recommendations of a report on the drug problem in the United States is to "stop publicizing the horrors of the 'drug menace.' "[4] The original intent of the anti-drug publicity campaign was to frighten people away from illegal drugs, but an unintended result of publicizing the drug problem has been to popularize the drugs and to make them attractive to the young.

If the media sometimes contribute significantly to the public's erroneous perception of social problems, then the media itself may constitute a social problem of some sort.[5] Public misperception of the existence and severity of a social problem makes attempts to combat the problem all the more difficult.

WHY STUDY SOCIAL PROBLEMS?

There are several reasons for studying social problems. First, it is important to become more familiar with the role of social science in understanding and

[2] Lincoln Steffens, *The Autobiography of Lincoln Steffens,* Vol. 1 (New York: Harcourt Brace Jovanovich, Inc., 1931), pp. 285–291.
[3] F. James Davis, "Crime News in Colorado Newspapers," *American Journal of Sociology,* 57 (January 1952): 325–330.
[4] Edward M. Brecher, ed., *Licit and Illicit Drugs* (Boston: Little, Brown and Company, 1972), pp. 523–524.
[5] See Robert Cirino, *Power to Persuade: Mass Media and the News* (New York: Bantam Books, Inc., 1974).

DOPE IS EXCITING!

In the past week we were entertained [on television] by seven dope discussion/documentaries, a dope agony ballet, two dope poetry readings, innumerable anti-dope commercials, and three dramatic series shows centering around junkies. Not to mention Rona Barrett revealing Hollywood's latest hophead horror, a variety show host wittily confusing grass and grass, Jim Jensen crackling gravely as he narrated the [New York Police Department's] "biggest raid of the week" bit, LeRoi Jones accusing the Pope of dealing, and countless other pieces of programs. Reds, greens, ups, downs, agony, ecstasy, sniff, smoke, mainline, degradation, or rehabilitation—you name it, we had it, as usual.

All of these items began with the assumption that since dope is an evil, its horrors must be portrayed as graphically as possible in order to educate the viewer. But the question which nobody seems to ask is just what is being taught by all this electronic moralizing—that drugs are bad, or that *Dope Is Exciting!* Like everything else on tv, dope "education" is show biz. And like all show biz, it is glamorous form first, content second. One National Football League anti-drug spot begins with exciting field action, while up tempo, big band jazz blares over. Then, as the music recedes, the camera picks out one player smashing an opposing ballcarrier and we hear his voice over: "This is Mike Reid. . . . That's the way I like to crack down. I'd like to rack up the drug traffic, too." Up jazz, building to crash climax. It's all groovy sounds and fast action, only slightly interrupted by some rich jock's [anti-drug comments]. Wham, bam, dope, man! Dope is so exciting that even the anti-dope swings.

That impression is enhanced by the fact that only beautiful, vibrant people turn to drugs on entertainment tv. Last Friday, for one example, among many, the "D.A.," a new NBC law and order hour, had a show about a junkie witness. She was, of course, young, beautiful, intelligent, and paying for her mistakes. Decadence sells better than ever these days. It makes people romantically exciting, cool, tragic and *plugged in*—beautiful people, that is.

Even documentary dope can be a gas. In Frederick Wiseman's "Hospital," shown last week on NET, a long sequence (which I am pulling out of context) shows a bad-tripping teenaged boy in the emergency room. He screams, moans, shakes, crawls in his own puke, begs the doctors not to let him die. All genuine, all riveting. Yet at the same time completely unreal, because the tv screen automatically distances us and makes it a performance—a show about a kid connecting with life in the rawest, most primal way. And again, I think that what may remain in the mind from it is the generalized excitement of that elemental connection, rather than its individual real-life horror. Because tv is not real life, and while it is surprisingly easy to ignore someone else's horror on film, it is no trick at all to get excited by it.

So there you are. A small piece of last week's junk action. Next week there will be more of the same, and more the week after, and so on, until we have theoretically been "educated" or frightened off dope—or on to it. Because if McLuhan is at all right, then some people are going about this all wrong. Maybe there is no right way to treat dope on television as it is presently constituted, but I wish to hell someone in a foundation or school somewhere would at least sit down and worry about it.

Ken Sobol, *Village Voice*, October 21, 1971. Reprinted by permission of the *Village Voice*. Copyright © the Village Voice, Inc., 1977.

combatting social problems. Second, a knowledge of social problems promotes understanding of how undesirable social conditions affect the daily lives of individuals. Third, it should be understood that although many social problems are the result of deviance, other social problems stem from conformity to social expectations.

Social Science and Social Problems

The cartoon on page 12 about the bridge that new math didn't build is humorous, partly because it represents failure on a colossal scale. More importantly, we can laugh at it because Americans are not accustomed to technological failure. Of course, our color television sets need frequent repair and our big cars produce harmful pollution. But solid-state construction is now prolonging the durability of color television sets and automakers are being forced to create pollution-reducing devices.

There is less humor in our failure to combat human problems successfully. The 1960s started with bright social promise in the form of John Kennedy's "New Frontier." Lyndon Johnson then pledged a "Great Society" and backed it with policies, programs, and money. Yet at the end of his presidency, the general judgment was that, despite some improvement, President Johnson's policies and programs, many of which were grounded in sociological and psychological theory, had not lived up to their advance notices. At least partly because of this disappointment, optimism about solving social problems has diminished markedly in the 1970s.

That the politicians' promises and visions fall short of their full realization is often taken for granted. They regularly promise more than they can be expected to deliver. A potential danger, however, is that disenchantment with the record of politicians and social scientists in dealing with social problems will lead to a public and, finally, a political rejection of such efforts.

"Well, so much for the new math." (Drawing by William O'Brian. © 1971, The New Yorker Magazine, Inc.)

If the social scientists' contributions to the handling of social problems are not to be considered worthless, it is necessary to increase public awareness of the ways in which social science can help people understand and combat social problems. Consistent with this goal, this book will explore the perspectives, concepts, and theories that sociologists use in the scientific study of social problems.

Private Troubles and Social Problems

C. Wright Mills defined the *sociological imagination* as a way of thinking that uses current and historical information to understand the impact of social events on individuals.[6] The sociological imagination emphasizes that what troubles us as individuals is intimately linked with the historical and social forces that are at work in our daily lives.

The adolescent subculture in modern society provides an example for the application of the sociological imagination.[7] An adolescent subculture is created in large part because of the changes taking place in the family and educational institutions as industrialization proceeds. In a stable, rural society, parents essentially re-create themselves and their society by socializing their children to the values, beliefs, and attitudes they learned from their own parents a generation earlier. In such a society, education is part of the same process that is involved in teaching children to walk and talk. Education is accomplished mainly at home by parents.

Industrialization leads to the transfer of education from the family to other institutions. Because modern societies change so rapidly, parents cannot afford to mold their children into mirror images. Parents represent the past; the knowledge and skills they have accumulated are often outdated in their own lifetime and do not seem highly relevant for the future their children will face. Economic specialization in industrial society makes the family incapable of preparing children for their future occupational lives. At one time, the son of a farmer could learn his future occupation by starting to work alongside his father at an early age, or the son of a carpenter could become an apprentice by his early teen-age years. Starting to work at 13 or 14 is no longer a common alternative, and parents do their work in distant places where they cannot be observed by their children. Even if children could observe their

---

[6] C. Wright Mills, *The Sociological Imagination* (New York: Oxford University Press, 1959), p. 6.
[7] James S. Coleman, *The Adolescent Society: The Social Life of the Teenager and Its Impact on Education* (New York: The Free Press, 1961), pp. 2–4, 52–57.

parents at work, the experience would have little relevance in a society in which existing occupations may either vanish or radically change in the future and new occupations constantly emerge. Children in modern societies must be trained through formal schooling so as to take advantage of the occupational opportunities available when they enter the job market.

These circumstances constitute some of the important social forces affecting today's young people. How do these circumstances become the private troubles of individuals? Children are isolated from adult society as they are set apart in school for most of their pre-adult lives. Because they are separated from the adult world for such a long time, young people are forced to depend upon each other for social life. Thus, they form what has become known as the adolescent subculture complete with some of its own values, beliefs, and attitudes. The private troubles caused members of both sexes by the emphasis on physical attractiveness and popularity is but one example of how membership in the adolescent subculture affects the lives of individuals. Emotional wounds are often inflicted upon the unattractive and unpopular during the pre-teen and teen-age years. Attitudes toward oneself and others formed during these years often last a lifetime.

It is easy to see that social forces frequently contribute to an individual's private troubles. The study of social problems should help us understand that what we think of as distant abstractions (industrialization, occupational specialization, formal education) have concrete and often painful personal consequences. Such an understanding should make an individual less vulnerable to the effects of those social forces.

TYPES OF SOCIAL PROBLEMS

Deviance and Social Problems

One major type of social problem stems from behavior that deviates from society's norms. It is not difficult to classify as social problems juvenile delinquency and crime because they involve violations of what the majority of any society believes to be "correct" and "normal" behavior. Deviant behavior seemingly is easily identified because it stands out in contrast to the behavior of most other people.

Yet, two factors make deviant behavior harder to identify than it seems on the surface. First, norms permit a certain amount of variation in behavior; the boundaries of a norm can be stretched to some degree without the result-

IS THERE LIFE AFTER HIGH SCHOOL?

All the arrogance you read about stems from those days in high school. It all stems from a desire to be nobody's fool ever again.

—BOBBY DARIN

I am totally motivated by—I call it revenge.

—NORA EPHRON

I think for a long time there was an element in everything I did of "I'll-get-you-you-bastards."

—MIKE NICHOLS

Someday, so help me, I'll be so famous none of you will ever be able to touch me again!

—RONA BARRETT

If they don't like me, someday they'll learn to respect me.

—BETTY FRIEDAN

'Cause I was a Jewish girl growing up in a Samoan neighborhood . . . I left . . . and, you know, the old story about "I'll show *them*" . . . I really felt that way and I had a lot of anger built up in me from those years.

—BETTE MIDLER

Man, those people hurt me. It makes me happy to know I'm making it and that they're still back there, plumbers and all, just like they were.

—JANIS JOPLIN

If I had been a really good-looking kid, I would have been popular with my classmates, I would have been smooth with the girls, I would have started scoring at about age 14, I would have been a big fraternity guy in college and I would have wound up selling Oldsmobiles. For sure, I wouldn't have had the bitterness and the fierce ambition I've needed in order to become a successful freelance writer.

—DAN GREENBURG

I'd love to do something about all those football players I used to envy in high school. What's with them? They sell insurance and send their kids for karate lessons every Saturday.

—ROBERT BLAKE

Thank God for the athletes and their rejection. Without them there would have been no emotional need and . . . I'd be a crackerjack salesman in the Garment District.

—MEL BROOKS

I really knew despair.

—LAUREN HUTTON

Ralph Keyes, *Playboy*, 1976

ing behavior being considered deviant. Second, deviance is a relative matter; behavior thought to be deviant in one situation may be socially acceptable in another.

The limits of socially acceptable behavior are more elastic for some individuals than for others. A driver of an automobile is supposed to come to a complete halt at a stop sign. But coming to a near stop is generally close enough for the police. Knowing how near to a full stop one must come is a matter of knowing the territory. Some police forces are strict with everyone; others reacquaint out-of-towners with enforcement of the letter of the law. There are more serious illustrations showing that the limits of socially acceptable behavior are elastic and are not the same for everyone. An unemployed man caught stealing a car may receive a longer jail sentence than a bank president who is found embezzling a large sum of money, and teen-agers are held less accountable for their crimes than adults.

Deviant behavior is a relative rather than an absolute matter. Behavior can be considered to be conforming or deviant only within a particular social context. Behavior considered deviant in one group may be acceptable and even encouraged in others. Members of a group may believe that gods live in rocks and trees and that these spirits are capable of granting them power over their enemies, the ability to heal the sick, and the foresight to predict the future. In a highly industrialized society, it is quite probable that members of such a group would be defined as psychotic and in need of immediate psychological treatment. On the other hand, among the traditional Alaskan Eskimo, people in such a group would be awarded high social status and deference. Variations in forms of marriage also illustrate the relativity of deviance. Bigamy is illegal in the United States. Yet in Arab cultures, polygyny, a plural marriage composed of one husband and two or more wives, is practiced with full social approval.

The severity of reactions to a given type of deviant behavior is also relative. In mid-eighteenth century America, the punishment for women who were divorced because of adultery was whipping, branding the letter A on their foreheads, and forcing them to wear perpetually around their necks a sign with a large A. Although adultery is still in violation of America's norms, it carries less stigma and less severe social sanctions today.

Conformity to the norms in one social group may earn intense, disapproving social pressure within another. Teen-agers, for example, are usually torn between conforming to the social demands of their peers and meeting the expectations of their parents. The possibility of being considered deviant from some group's point of view is especially likely in such a complex society as America. This is reflected in a study by Jerry Simmons, in which he asked a sample of respondents to list "things or types of persons" they thought to be deviant. He summarized the results as follows:

> The sheer range of responses predictably included homosexuals, prostitutes, drug addicts, radicals, and criminals. But it also included liars, career women, Democrats, reckless drivers, atheists, Christians, suburbanites, the retired, young folks, card players, bearded men, artists, pacifists, priests, prudes, hippies, straights, girls who wear makeup, the President, conservatives, integrationists, executives, divorcees, perverts, motorcycle gangs, smart-alec students, know-it-all professors, modern people, and Americans.[8]

Not only are definitions of deviance relative, but they also change within the same society. Homosexual organizations have made considerable efforts to eradicate the idea that homosexuality is a type of mental disorder. Their efforts were partially rewarded in 1974 when the American Psychiatric Association officially announced that homosexuality was no longer on its list of mental disorders. If the American public comes to accept this new definition, then the homosexual pressure groups will have made progress in their drive to change the public perception of homosexuality.

Thomas Szasz wants to go even further toward changing the public perception of mental illness. In fact, Szasz has called for the abandonment of the idea of mental illness.[9] It makes little sense, he contends, to refer to some people as being mentally abnormal when there exists no standards for mental normality outside some social, legal, and ethical context. Since no one is innately mentally "normal," he contends, there are no absolute standards against which to conclude that a person is mentally abnormal or "ill."

It should be noted that not all types of deviance are equally relative. Most people feel that murder is an undesirable and abnormal act. Certainly, members of a society would consider a murder more deviant than a traffic violation. There is a difference of opinion as to the appropriateness of killing another person under certain conditions, such as war, mercy killing, or capital punishment, but few members of any society would consider arbitrary and deliberate murder as normal and acceptable.

---

[8] J. L. Simmons, *Deviants* (Berkeley, Calif.: Glendessary Press, 1969), p. 3.
[9] Thomas S. Szasz, *The Myth of Mental Illness: Foundations of a Theory of Personal Conduct* (New York: Dell Publishing Company, 1961).

THE MYTH OF MENTAL ILLNESS

Far from being culture-free, . . . ''symptoms'' [of mental illness] are themselves offenses against implicit understandings of particular cultures. Every society provides its members with a set of explicit norms—understandings governing conduct with regard to such central institutions as the state, the family, and private property. Offenses against these norms have conventional names; for example, an offense against property is called ''theft,'' and an offense against sexual propriety is called ''perversion.'' As we have seen, however, the public order also is made up of countless unnamed understandings. ''Everyone knows,'' for example, that during a conversation one looks at the other's eyes or mouth, but not at his ear. For the convenience of the society, offenses against these unnamed residual understandings are usually lumped together in a miscellaneous, catchall category. If people reacting to an offense exhaust the conventional categories that might define it (e.g., theft, prostitution, and drunkenness), yet are certain that an offense has been committed, they may resort to this residual category. In earlier societies, the residual category was witchcraft, spirit possession, or possession by the devil; today, it is mental illness. The symptoms of mental illness are, therefore, violations of residual rules.

Thomas J. Sheff, ed., *Labeling Madness* (Englewood Cliffs, N.J.: Prentice-Hall, Inc., 1975), p. 7.

Problems of Structure

If problems of deviance are more dificult to pinpoint than they at first seem, what about social problems that stem from conformity to society's rules? They are considered problems of structure.[10]

The contemporary concern over the dramatic rise of population growth now occurring throughout the world illustrates the idea of problems of structure. Rapid world population growth is a relatively recent event.[11] By estimate, only 200 to 300 million persons were on the earth in 1 A.D. And it was not until 1650 that the world's population doubled to reach a half-billion. It required 16 centuries for the world's population to double the first time, but subsequent doublings have taken less and less time. The second doubling occurred 200 years later in 1850, when the world's population stood at approximately 1 billion. By 1930, only 80 years later, there was another doubling. A

---

[10] For further detail on problems of structure, see Jonathan H. Turner, *American Society: Problems of Structure* (New York: Harper & Row, Publishers 1972).

[11] Donald J. Bogue, *Principles of Demography* (New York: John Wiley & Sons, Inc., 1969), pp. 47–51.

mere 42 years later, in 1972, a fourth doubling was imminent as the world's total population had climbed to almost 4 billion.

At the present rate of growth, the world's population is expected to reach 6.5 billion by the year 2000, an addition of nearly 3 billion persons in only 28 years. If this projection becomes reality, as many people will have been added to the world's population in that 28 years as it took nearly 2,000 years to reach. Figure 1-1 illustrates graphically the spurt in the world's population since 1650. Of course, the problem is not the number of people per se but whether they can be accommodated. Can they be fed, housed, educated, and generally provided with the resources to lead what we have come to think of as a "quality" life? More fundamentally, can massive starvation on a world-wide scale be prevented?

The population explosion cannot be blamed on deviants of some kind; rather, it has occurred because parents have conformed to what has traditionally been expected of them. Until quite recently, it was thought necessary to produce a large number of children because of high infant mortality and because children's labor was an economic asset. Now, however, infant death rates have been sharply reduced, and in many countries children are no longer expected to make significant contributions to the family's economic welfare.

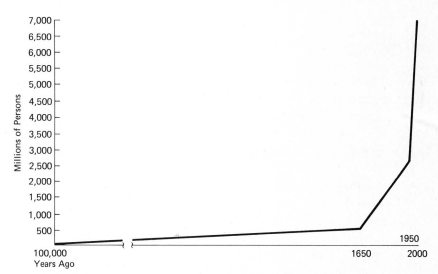

Figure 1-1. Acceleration in world population growth. [Reprinted by permission of the author and publisher from William Petersen, *Population,* 3rd ed. (New York: Macmillan Publishing Co., Inc., 1975), p. 5. Copyright© 1975, by William Petersen.]

Yet, for many, the old idea of producing large families still exists, people still conform to it, and the population swells.[12]

A second illustration of a problem of structure lies in some consequences of the rise of the nuclear family in highly industrialized societies. In modern societies, a *nuclear* type of family structure (one in which only two parents and their children live together) has replaced the traditional *extended* family structure (one composed of a married couple, their adult children, grandchildren, and other relatives living together). This change has created a problem of adjustment. For example, the extended form of family structure provided a setting for close emotional relationships with a variety of relatives beyond the parents and their children. In the home or nearby were grandparents, aunts, uncles, and cousins with whom one could interact. Also, the extended family provided some social, emotional, and economic insurance for close family members during their old age.

The nuclear structure leaves the family free to move from one place to another to take advantage of job opportunities or to meet an employer's demand that a transfer be accepted. This fits well with industrial society's need for a highly mobile labor force, but it appears to come at a substantial cost.[13] To mention only two dimensions of the problem: What are the social and psychological consequences for male children, dependent on their fathers as models for developing a masculine identity, when their fathers spend most of their time at work and may see them only on weekends? Where do elderly family members derive the social and emotional support so important to all human beings when they are isolated from their grown-up children and other relatives? Some consequences of that situation will be covered in Chapter 6 on the family.

THE DYNAMICS OF SOCIETY

This section will consider two different views of the dynamics of society. These two perspectives on the way societies work—consensus and conflict theories—are important because they lead to quite different approaches to the study of social problems.

---

[12] Of course, the Zero Population Growth movement, which has achieved some success in the United States, represents an attempt to change these values, attitudes, and beliefs.

[13] For further analysis, see Richard Flacks, *Youth and Social Change* (Chicago: Markham Publishing Company, 1971), pp. 22–34.

Consensus Theory

Consensus theory was subscribed to by nearly all modern sociologists until recently. Even though it is now being challenged by the conflict perspective, for some good reasons to be noted in the following section, it remains an influential approach to the study of social problems. A summary of the basic assumptions of the consensus and conflict theories is presented in Table 1-1.

Table 1-1. Contrasting Assumptions of Consensus and Conflict Theories

Consensus Theory	Conflict Theory
1. A society is a relatively integrated whole.	1. A society experiences inconsistency and conflict at every moment everywhere.
2. A society tends to seek relative stability or dynamic equilibrium.	2. A society is continually subjected to change at every moment everywhere.
3. Most elements of a society contribute to its well-being and survival.	3. Elements of a society tend to contribute to its change.
4. A society rests on the consensus of its members.	4. A society rests on the constraint of some of its members by others.

SOURCE: Adapted from "Toward a Theory of Social Conflict," by Ralf Dahrendorf, *Journal of Conflict Resolution,* 2 (June 1958), p. 174, by permission of the publisher, Sage Publications, Inc.

According to the first assumption of the consensus theory, the parts of a society are organized into a relatively integrated whole. A change in one part of a society will very likely lead to modifications in other parts. The reduction in family size that accompanies the shift from an agricultural to an industrial economy is an illustration. Partly because the need for a relatively large pool of farm labor (fulfilled by having many children) disappears in an industrialized, urbanized society, the average family size decreases. A major change in the economy promotes a major change in the family. Thus, particular aspects of a society can be explained through knowledge of their impact on and relationship with other aspects.

Consensus theorists realize that societies are not perfectly integrated, that conflicts and inconsistencies exist. Thus, although integration is necessary for the survival of a society, it is recognized that the actual extent of integration may vary.

A second assumption of the consensus theory is that societies tend to return to a state of equilibrium or stability after some disturbance and change.[14] It is believed that they return to a state of stability or equilibrium by absorbing and adjusting to changes within the basic framework of the original arrangement of their parts. Because a society is said to both change and maintain most of its original nature, consensus theory refers to a *dynamic equilibrium,* a constantly changing balance of the parts of a society.

The student unrest on college and university campuses in the late 1960s illustrates the concept of dynamic equilibrium. Student radicals believed that the structure of American society was so undesirable that its dismantlement was the only hope for the future. They were not successful in reaching that goal, but although American society is now operating in most ways just as it did before the "revolution," the disturbances made by those students seem to have created some changes. The students have altered the public's tendency to accept all wars as being in the national interest, their efforts have made universities and colleges more responsive to student needs, and they have made the nation aware of the importance of protecting the natural environment. These apparent changes may be of long- or short-term duration. Either way, these changes, along with others, have been absorbed into American social structures. They have not revolutionized them.

A third assumption of consensus theory is that because any society has certain functions that must be performed, many of its elements have evolved to fulfill those needs. It is for this reason that all complex societies are said to have economies, family arrangements, governments, religions, and some means for formal or informal education. It is assumed that most elements of a society contribute to its well-being and survival.

It is not assumed in the consensus theory, however, that all elements of a society make positive contributions.[15] The consequences of any part of a society may be positive or negative. In ascertaining whether the effects are positive or negative, it is essential to refer to specific parts of a society. What is negative for one part of the society may be positive for another. At the

---

[14] For example, see Wilbert E. Moore, *Social Change* (Englewood Cliffs, N.J.: Prentice-Hall, Inc., 1963), pp. 9–11.

[15] Robert K. Merton, *Social Theory and Social Structure,* rev. ed. (New York: The Free Press, 1957), pp. 19–84.

same time corrupt political machines, typical of American society in an earlier era, interfered with the operation of democratic government, they also
served human and social needs by providing jobs, education, food, and
money for the poor.

According to the fourth assumption of the consensus perspective, every
society rests on a general agreement or consensus regarding values. It is
because of this high degree of consensus and the relative permanence of values, say the consensus theorists, that social integration is achieved.

Conflict Theory

The points accented by the conflict theory are just the reverse of those emphasized by the consensus theory (see Table 1-1).[16] According to the conflict
perspective, more powerful members of a society coerce or constrain other
people to do what they (the more powerful people) want. If this is true, it
means that individuals often behave as they do because they are forced to do
so by others, rather than because of a conviction that they are following the
"right" course. According to the conflict theory, then, societies feature a
conflict of values, not, as the consensus theory would have it, a general
agreement on goals and interests.

This brings us to the center of the conflict-consensus debate. People generally do not struggle with each other when they are in agreement. Conflict
tends to arise when there is disagreement on basic values and interests. Advocates of the conflict theory believe that different segments of a society have
their special values and interests and that they compete (conflict) with other
segments for the realization of their own aims and interests. They depict
social life as a contest, with the paramount weapon being *power*—the ability
to control the behavior of others even against their wishes.[17] Interest groups
use their power to fulfill their own values and to achieve their own interests.
The American Medical Association fights against what it calls "socialized
medicine," the National Rifle Association exerts great effort to prevent restrictive gun legislation, and the oil companies attempt to retain their tax advantages. A multitude of interest groups operate at all levels of society, from

---

[16] See Ralf Dahrendorf, "Toward a Theory of Social Conflict," *Journal of Conflict Resolution,* 2 (June
1958): 174–179.
[17] Max Weber, *From Max Weber: Essays in Sociology,* translated and edited by H. H. Gerth and C.
Wright Mills (New York: Oxford University Press, 1958), p. 180.

local political elections to the White House, from Ralph Nader's Raiders to International Telephone and Telegraph (ITT).

From even this brief description of the conflict theory, it is not difficult to see how it contradicts the assumptions of the consensus theory. Since modern societies contain countless competing interest groups, they are characterized by inconsistencies in values and interests rather than by a high degree of consensus. Because there are so many conflicting groups, and because various groups are seeking their own self-interests, their activities are not necessarily geared toward the benefit of society.[18]

Consensus, Conflict, and Social Problems

Most contemporary sociologists would agree that both the consensus and conflict perspectives have validity, but there is still a tendency for individual sociologists to stress either one theory or the other. Some illustrations should help to clarify the different slant that accompanies the use of either the consensus or conflict theory in the study of social problems.

Problems of Deviance. As noted earlier, the consensus perspective emphasizes integration, stability, and general agreement on basic values and norms within a society. Consensus on the rules by which members are supposed to live and on the goals toward which they are to strive are reflected in the conformity exhibited in their behavior. When there is a breakdown of agreement on values and norms and when traditional ways of thinking and behaving are not accepted by large numbers of people, then the rate of deviant behavior increases. Logically, this would mean that deviance would rise when rapid social change is occurring or when the equilibrium of a society is upset. Thus, deviance is greater in cities than in rural areas because social change is accelerated in urban areas by extensive population growth, industrialization, and geographic mobility.[19]

Deviance from the conflict perspective appears in a quite different light. Some of those advocating the conflict perspective contend that various inter-

[18] It remains for sociologists to formulate a theory incorporating the insights contributed by each of these two theoretical perspectives. Some steps in this direction have been taken. For example, see Pierre van den Berghe, "Dialectic and Functionalism: Toward a Theoretical Synthesis," *American Sociological Review,* 28 (October 1963): 695–705.

[19] Robert E. Park, Ernest W. Burgess, and Roderick D. McKenzie, *The City* (Chicago: University of Chicago Press, 1967).

THE USES OF POVERTY: CONSENSUS AND CONFLICT

I have described thirteen of the more important functions poverty and the poor satisfy in American society, enough to support the functionalist [or consensus] thesis that poverty, like any other social phenomenon, survives in part because it is useful to society or some of its parts . . . [However,] many of the functions served by the poor could be replaced if poverty were eliminated, but almost always at higher costs to others, particularly more affluent others. Consequently, a functional analysis must conclude that poverty persists not only because it fulfills a number of positive functions but also because many of the functional alternatives to poverty would be quite dysfunctional for the affluent members of society. A functional analysis thus ultimately arrives at much the same conclusion as radical sociology, except that radical thinkers treat as manifest what I describe as latent: that social phenomena that are functional for affluent or powerful groups and dysfunctional for poor or powerless ones persist; that when the elimination of such phenomena through functional alternatives would generate dysfunctions for the affluent or powerful, they will continue to persist; and that phenomena like poverty can be eliminated only when they become dysfunctional for the affluent or powerful, or when the powerless can obtain enough power to change society.

Herbert J. Gans, "The Uses of Poverty: The Poor Pay All," *Social Policy,* 2 (July–August 1971), p. 24.

est groups compete in an effort to influence the passage and enforcement of legislation serving their interests; laws are created and enforced by those with sufficient political power. Laws, then, are said to serve the vested interests of those with the power to make and enforce them. Criminal law is depicted as the result of power politics. Those who have the least input into shaping the law are the most likely to be classified as criminals.[20]

Problems of Structure.　Problems of structure can also be examined from the consensus and conflict perspectives. The problem of poverty is a good example. According to Herbert Gans, poverty serves certain positive functions for American society.[21] Without the poor, who would buy substandard products such as day-old bread and overripe fruit, who would hire over-the-hill lawyers and doctors, where would social workers and penologists find work,

[20] For example, see George B. Vold, *Theoretical Criminology* (New York: Oxford University Press, 1958); and Richard Quinney, *The Social Reality of Crime* (Boston: Little, Brown and Company, 1970).
[21] Herbert J. Gans, "The Uses of Poverty: The Poor Pay All," *Social Policy,* 2 (July-August 1971): 20–24.

and what would the Democratic party do without this part of its constituency? This interpretation would be consistent with the consensus theory.

If taken a step further, as Gans does, it can be concluded that poverty is a social arrangement benefiting the more powerful and affluent. From a conflict perspective, of course, alterations in this social arrangement are likely to be resisted because the interests of those with influence and wealth are served by such an arrangement.

It should be apparent that either the consensus or the conflict theory may underlie the discussion of either a problem of structure or a problem of deviance. This will be the approach throughout this text even though explicit reference to one perspective or the other will not always be made.

Additional Readings

Adams, Bert N. "Coercion and Consensus Theories: Some Unresolved Issues," *American Journal of Sciology,* 71 (May 1966): 714–717.

Antonio, Robert J., and George Ritzer, eds. *Social Problems: Values and Interests in Conflict.* Boston: Allyn & Bacon, Inc., 1975.

Chambliss, William J., ed. *Sociological Readings in the Conflict Perspective.* Reading, Mass.: Addison-Wesley Publishing Co., Inc., 1972.

Coser, Lewis A. *The Functions of Social Conflict.* New York: The Free Press, 1956.

Dahrendorf, Ralf. *Class and Class Conflict in Industrial Society.* Stanford, Calif.: Stanford University Press, 1959.

Denisoff, R. Serge, and Charles H. McCaghy, eds. *Deviance, Conflict, and Criminality.* Chicago: Rand McNally College Publishing Company, 1973.

Eitzen, D. Stanley. *Social Structure and Social Problems in America.* Boston: Allyn & Bacon, Inc., 1974.

Farrell, Ronald A., and Victoria Lynn Swigert, eds. *Social Deviance.* Philadelphia: J. B. Lippincott Company, 1975.

Gibbs, Jack P., and Maynard L. Erickson. "Major Developments in the Sociological Study of Deviance," *Annual Review of Sociology,* 1, Alex Inkeles, James Coleman, and Neil Smelser, eds. Palo Alto, Calif.: Annual Reviews, Inc., 1975. Pp. 21–42.

Horton, John. "Order and Conflict Theories of Social Problems as Competing Ideologies," *American Journal of Sociology,* 71 (May 1966): 701–713.

Kohn, Melvin L. "Looking Back: A 25-Year Review and Appraisal of Social Problems Research," *Social Problems,* 24 (October 1976): 94–112.

Lenski, Gerhard E. *Power and Privilege: A Theory of Social Stratification.* New York: McGraw-Hill Book Company, 1966.

McCaghy, Charles H. *Deviant Behavior: Crime, Conflict, and Interest Groups.* New York: Macmillan Publishing Co., Inc., 1976.

Taylor, Ian, Paul Walton, and Jack Young. *The New Criminology: For a Social Theory of Deviance.* New York: Harper & Row, Publishers, 1973.

Traub, Stuart H., and Craig B. Little, eds. *Theories of Deviance.* Itasca, Ill.: F. E. Peacock Publishers, Inc., 1975.

Williams, Robin M., Jr. "Some Further Comments on Chronic Controversies," *American Journal of Sociology,* 71 (May 1966): 717–721.

part

problems of
structure:
inequality

economic inequality

THE PUBLIC VIEW OF POVERTY: HERE TODAY, GONE TOMORROW

Poverty seems to capture attention at one time and slip from view the next. Poverty, of course, has not disappeared, but the commitment to eliminate it does seem to have weakened considerably in recent years.

Until the Great Depression, the poor in America were viewed intolerantly, largely because of the attitudes toward work and the poor flowing from the Protestant Ethic:

> The Protestant Ethic postulated that a man was poor because of his own shortcomings and not because of any particular economic or social structure. Hard work, thrift, and piety were ways to end poverty. Those that were poor because they did not take this route were improvident and undeserving of help. Benjamin Franklin voiced such views in these adages: "God helps those who help themselves." "Laxness travels so slowly that Poverty soon overtakes him." "Diligence is the mother of good luck, and God gives all things to industry."[1]

The late 1920s and early 1930s brought attention to the fact that poverty need not reflect a lazy individual but, rather, a person who cannot find work in a

[1] Irving G. Wyllie, *The Self-Made Man in America* (New York: The Free Press, 1954), p. 57.

THE INVISIBLE POOR

To be sure, the other America is not impoverished in the same sense as those poor nations where millions cling to hunger as a defense against starvation. This country has escaped such extremes. That does not change the fact that tens of millions of Americans are, at this very moment, maimed in body and spirit, existing at levels beneath those necessary for human decency. If these people are not starving, they are hungry, and sometimes fat with hunger, for that is what cheap foods do. They are without adequate housing and education and medical care.

. . . There are perennial reasons that make the other America an invisible land.

Poverty is often off the beaten track. It always has been. The ordinary tourist never left the main highway, and today he rides interstate turnpikes. He does not go into the valleys of Pennsylvania where the towns look like movie sets of Wales in the thirties. He does not see the company houses in rows, the rutted roads (the poor always have bad roads whether they live in the city, in towns, or on farms), and everything is black and dirty. And even if he were to pass through such a place by accident, the tourist would not meet the unemployed men in the bar or the women coming home from a runaway sweatshop.

Michael Harrington, *The Other America* (New York: Macmillan Publishing Co., Inc., 1963), pp. 9, 11.

malfunctioning economy. Many Americans who had prided themselves on being responsible, dependable, hard-working people found themselves out of work and standing in long bread and unemployment lines. Poverty was experienced by Americans in all social classes. Under Franklin Roosevelt's New Deal, a vast array of policies and programs was directed toward helping those who were suffering economic deprivation. By the 1950s, America was hailed as the "affluent society." Concern about problems associated with affluence replaced concern about problems related to poverty as the majority of Americans enjoyed the economic prosperity that followed World War II. As John Kenneth Galbraith points out, many came to believe that poverty was no longer a major social problem.[2]

Michael Harrington's *The Other America* clearly disproved the prevailing belief that poverty was no longer a significant social problem in America.[3] To the surprise of many, Harrington documented the presence of

[2] John Kenneth Galbraith, *The Affluent Society* (Boston: Houghton Mifflin Company, 1958).

[3] Michael Harrington, *The Other America* (New York: Macmillan Publishing Co., Inc., 1963). Other factors in the revival of poverty as an important social problem in America include the civil rights movement, the politicalization of poverty in the 1960 Democratic presidential primaries, and various studies of the poor.

40 to 50 million poor people in America. Could America really have between one fifth and one fourth of its citizens living with inadequate diets and housing? Partly because of Harrington's book, this question captured public attention. Renewed interest in America's poor culminated in the Economic Opportunity Act of 1964, the strongest commitment to fighting poverty ever made by the federal government.

By the late 1960s, however, poverty had once again slipped from its place at the pinnacle of governmental priorities. President Lyndon Johnson, who liked to compare his "Great Society" to President Franklin Roosevelt's New Deal, was frustrated in his dream to make America the first society without poverty. The Vietnam War cost him the public's attention to poverty, the money needed to support poverty policies and programs, and, ultimately,

THE DISCOVERY OF HUNGER IN AMERICA

Hunger in America was conceived as a national issue in April 1967 by two northern senators in an alien rural South. On a mission guided by politics, they came to study poverty programs, but in the small Delta town of Cleveland, Mississippi, they found more than they had bargained for.

The United States Senator from New York felt his way through a dark, windowless shack, fighting nausea at the strong smell of aging mildew, sickness, and urine. In the early afternoon shadows, he saw a child sitting on the floor of a tiny back room. Barely two years old, wearing only a filthy undershirt, she sat rubbing several grains of rice round and round on the floor. The senator knelt beside her.

"Hello . . . Hi . . . Hi, baby . . ." he murmured, touching her cheeks and her hair as he would his own child's. As he sat on the dirty floor, he placed his hand gently on the child's swollen stomach. But the little girl sat as if in a trance, her sad eyes turned downward, and rubbed the gritty rice.

For five minutes he tried: talking, caressing, tickling, poking—demanding that the child respond. The baby never looked up.

The senator made his way to the front yard where Annie White, the mother of the listless girl and five other children, stood washing her family's clothes in a zinc tub. She had no money, she was saying to the other senator, couldn't afford to buy food stamps; she was feeding her family only some rice and biscuits made from leftover surplus commodities.

For a few moments Robert F. Kennedy stood alone, controlling his feelings, which were exposed to the press entourage waiting outside the house. Then he whispered to a companion, "I've seen bad things in West Virginia, but I've never seen anything like this anywhere in the United States."

Nick Kotz, *Let Them Eat Promises* (New York: Doubleday & Company, Inc., 1971), pp. 1–2.

his presidency. Although numerous welfare policies and programs are still a part of the federal government today, subsequent administrations have reduced the commitment to fight poverty.

ECONOMIC INEQUALITY IN A RICH LAND

Paul Samuelson describes the inequality of income in America in these words: "If we made an income pyramid out of a child's blocks, with each layer portraying $1,000 of income, the peak would be higher than the Eiffel Tower, but most of us would be within a yard of the ground."[4] The truth in Samuelson's statement is supported by government figures on the distribution of income (see Table 2-1). In 1972, the richest 20 per cent of American families received slightly more than 40 per cent of the nation's income before taxes, and the poorest 20 per cent controlled only about 5 per cent. Although income inequality is less today than during the Great Depression, the income gulf between the poor and nonpoor has not narrowed since the mid-1940s.[5]

Table 2-1. Share of Aggregate Income Before Taxes Received by each Fifth of Families, Ranked by Income, Selected Years, 1947–72 [Per cent]

Income Rank	1947	1950	1960	1966	1972
Total families	100.0	100.0	100.0	100.0	100.0
Lowest fifth	5.1	4.5	4.8	5.6	5.4
Second fifth	11.8	11.9	12.2	12.4	11.9
Third fifth	16.7	17.4	17.8	17.8	17.5
Fourth fifth	23.2	23.6	24.0	23.8	23.9
Highest fifth	43.3	42.7	41.3	40.5	41.4
Top 5 percent	17.5	17.3	15.9	15.6	15.9

SOURCE: *Economic Report of the President* (Washington, D.C.: U.S. Government Printing Office, 1974), p. 140.

Although these income distribution figures reveal persistent economic inequality, they do not show the full nature of the concentration of wealth in America. Whereas about 6 million families currently have annual incomes

[4] Paul A. Samuelson, *Economics,* 9th ed. (New York: McGraw-Hill Book Company, 1973), p. 84.
[5] For an analysis contending that income inequality may be decreasing, see Robert K. Merton and Robert Nisbet, *Contemporary Social Problems,* 4th ed. (New York: Harcourt Brace Jovanovich, Inc., 1976), pp. 335–337.

WHAT'S IN A BILLION?

"Billion." It's a word that is tossed about with increasing nonchalance in the matter of government finance.

But what *is* a billion dollars? How can one comprehend such a stupendous number?

Well . . . ponder this:

If, beginning with the moment Christ was born, you had begun receiving one dollar every minute of every day—twenty-four hours a day, seven days a week, without interruption . . .

. . . by the time of the Battle of Hastings in 1066 A.D.—that is, after more than a thousand years of dollar-a-minute, round-the-clock earning—you would be barely more than halfway toward having collected a billion dollars.

In fact, you would not have amassed your first billion dollars until 2:21 A.M. of April 14, 1901: very nearly two thousand years after the birth of Christ—and after the receipt of your first dollar.

And if, when that magic moment arrived, you wanted to be sure you hadn't been short-changed and began counting your dollar bills at the rate of one per second, eight hours a day, five days a week, with no vacation, it would take you one hundred and thirty-three and a half years to complete the count.

Philip M. Stern, *The Rape of the Taxpayer* (New York: Random House, Inc., 1974), p. 3.

---

under $3,000, only 3,000 families have incomes above $1 million. Similarly, less than 1 per cent of the population has an income in excess of $100,000, but almost 46 per cent of all Americans are in families with incomes below $10,000. It is simply beyond comprehension that before his death in 1976, J. Paul Getty was said to have ended each day with $300,000 more than he had at breakfast.[6] The true nature of economic inequality in America is further revealed by the facts that most of the wealth of the rich does not come from earned income (wages and salaries) and the rich are protected by tax laws written to their advantage.

Sources of Wealth of the Rich

Most of the wealth of the rich comes from dividends and capital gains rather than from wages and salaries. Those Americans with incomes over $100,000

---

[6] Philip M. Stern, *The Rape of the Taxpayer* (New York: Vintage Books, Random House, Inc., 1974), pp. 7, 9.

receive only 15 per cent of their taxable income from wages and salaries. Sixty-seven per cent of their taxable income comes from dividends and capital gains, and 13 per cent comes from small business profits. In contrast, those with incomes below $20,000 a year receive 87 per cent from wages and salaries, only 3 per cent from dividends and capital gains and 9 per cent from operating businesses.[7] It is estimated that among those with incomes exceeding $100,000, 57 per cent of total assets comes through inheritance.[8]

Wealth and the Tax Structure

Reliance on taxable income figures gives a distorted picture of the actual extent of economic inequality because of the nature of the American tax system. Theoretically, the federal income tax is progressive; that is, the higher the income, the higher the rate and amount of taxes paid. Thus, the 1976 federal income tax schedule showed tax rates ranging from 13 per cent for taxable income of $5,000 to 51 per cent for taxable income of $100,000. It is generally true that those with low income tend to pay less taxes than those with middle and high incomes. Still, because of the nature of the tax structure, high-income people, through their tax lawyers and accountants, are able to reduce the amount of taxes they pay. Philip Stern states that in 1969 there were 1,235 families with annual incomes over $100,000 who paid *no taxes whatever*. Fifty-six of those families had incomes in excess of $1 million per year.[9] And this was all legal.

The tax structure also helps the rich even when they do pay taxes. Because of existing tax loopholes, Stern points out, the percentage of income saved increases as wealth increases. For example, by employing tax loopholes, families with annual incomes between $500,000 and $1 million saved 30 per cent on their federal tax bill, compared to 1.4 per cent for those with incomes between $2,000 and $3,000 and 8.7 per cent for those in the $20,000 to $25,000 income bracket. The dollar savings difference is also astronomically greater for the rich because of their base amount. Whereas loopholes on the average saved $1,931 for those with incomes between $20,000

---

[7] Melvin M. Tumin, *Patterns of Society: Identities, Roles, and Resources* (Boston: Little, Brown and Company, 1973), p. 55.

[8] Edwin Kuh, "The Robin Hood Syndrome," *New York Times*, March 5, 1973. Quoted from Ian Robertson, ed., *Readings in Sociology: Contemporary Perspectives* (New York: Harper & Row, Publishers 1976), p. 137.

[9] Stern, *The Rape of the Taxpayer*, op. cit., p. 14.

THE ELECT AND THE DAMNED

Most Americans—citizens of the wealthiest, most powerful and most ideal-swathed country in the world—by a very wide margin own nothing more than their household goods, a few glittering gadgets such as automobiles and television sets (usually purchased on the installment plan, many at second hand) and the clothes on their backs. A horde if not a majority of Americans live in shacks, cabins, hovels, shanties, hand-me-down Victorian eyesores, rickety tenements and flaky apartment buildings—as the newspapers from time to time chortle that new Russian apartment-house construction is falling apart. (Conditions abroad, in the standard American view, are everywhere far worse than anywhere in the United States. The French, for example, could learn much about cooking from the Automat and Howard Johnson.)

At the same time, a relative handful of Americans are extravagantly endowed, like princes in the Arabian Nights tales. Their agents deafen a baffled world with a never-ceasing chant about the occult merits of private-property ownership (good for everything that ails man and thoroughly familiar to the rest of the world, not invented in the United States), and the vaulting puissance of the American owners.

Ferdinand Lundberg, *The Rich and the Super-Rich* (New York: Lyle & Stuart, Inc., 1968), p. 11.

and $25,000, those with incomes between $500,000 and $1 million saved $202,751. Those families with annual incomes of $2 million averaged tax savings of approximately $700,000.[10]

There are a variety of tax benefits enjoyed by the rich. They include the exemption of 50 per cent of the money derived from capital gains (profits from the sale of buildings, land, stocks and bonds, and so on), the exemption of 22 per cent of the income from the production of oil and gas, the exemption of interest earned from state and local government bonds, and the loopholes in estate and gift taxes.

The extent of economic inequality goes even further because of existing regressive taxes, which apply the same rates for the poor as for the rich. Examples of regressive taxes are Social Security, sales taxes, and state and local property taxes. The poor lose a larger proportion of their income when they pay at the same tax rate as the affluent. In 1968, those with incomes under $2,000 paid 27 per cent of their total income on Social Security, state, and property taxes, whereas those with incomes over $50,000 paid less than 7 per

[10] Ibid., p. 11.

IT'S NOT EASY BEING RICH

"Two years ago we went to Europe and zipped about for five weeks. Last year we were in Europe for eight weeks. We went to Istanbul and came back on a ship through the Greek islands. And I bought a fur coat in Germany. And a topaz pin in London. We mostly buy jewelry and paintings. And my husband has started collecting rare books. I adore to get new things. I'm mad about it. I've always felt this way. Probably because I'm basically a rotten capitalist. I like life to be as comfortable and beautiful as it can be. Because it makes me sweeter and everyone else around. . . . Usually we just buy things because they strike us as something we'd like to have. If it's beautiful and within our means we'll buy it. . . . I consider traveling first-class on ocean liners and staying at the best hotels in Europe a luxury of which I never tire . . . When we are in New York, which we often are, we hire a chauffeured limousine . . . The things I look forward to are trying to stay conscious and feeling alive and trying to guide my children to being conscious and feeling alive. So few people are conscious. It's hard."

Jeremy Main, "Good Living Begins at $25,000 a Year," *Fortune*, 77 (May 1968): 188.

cent. In fact, writes Stern, "according to the Census officials, in 1968 people with total earned incomes of less than $2,000—that is, less than $40 a week—were paying half of that meager privately earned income in taxes of all kinds." [11] Those earning $50,000 or more pay only 45 per cent in taxes of all kinds. Those with moderate annual incomes ($8,000 to $10,000) pay only 4 per cent less in taxes of all kinds than do those with incomes between $25,000 and $50,000.

Economic inequality clearly exists in American society. While the rich enjoy the benefits of this inequality, the poor suffer. Poverty in America persists despite the vast wealth created by the American economic system.

WHAT IS POVERTY?

On an absolute scale, being poor involves a lack of housing, food, medical care, and other necessities for maintaining life. *Absolute poverty* is usually defined as the absence of enough money to secure life's necessities. On a relative scale, it is possible to have those things required to remain alive, and even to live in reasonable physical health, and still be poor. *Relative poverty*

[11] Ibid., p. 25.

THE WELFARE AND WEALTHFARE SYSTEMS

	Wealthfare	Welfare
(1) Source of Subsidy	Market purchases by government Government price policies Government export-import policies Government tax expenditures	Federal "grants and aids," supplemented by state and county subsidies
(2) Amount of Subsidy	Unknown for government economic policies, but probably at least 50 billion 60–70 billion in tax expenditures	15–20 billion by federal, state, and local governments
(3) Recipients of Subsidy	Middle and upper income fifths; the more you make, the more you get	Bottom income fifth; the less you make, the more you get
(4) Stereotypes Associated with Recipients	Decent, hard-working people and/or clever entrepreneurs who know how to work the system	Lazy, immoral people who do not know how to manage their finances and who do not want to work
(5) Eligibility Requirements for Subsidy	Work for a large corporation which does a lot of business with government; belong to a large union or professional association; own large shares of stock in large corporations doing business with government; and have a good tax lawyer fill out complicated forms provided by government	Be close to starving; have kids; have a physical deformity; lose your job; or be old
(6) Monitoring of Recipients	Proclamations by President's Council of Economic Advisers on the "state of the economy"; spot checking by IRS	Frequent checking by "eligibility" worker who visits your home

Jonathan H. Turner and Charles E. Starns, *Inequality: Privilege and Poverty in America* (Pacific Palisades, Calif.: Goodyear Publishing Co., Inc., 1976), p. 152.

is measured by comparing the condition of those at the bottom of a society with other segments of the population. Poverty is determined by the standards that exist within a society. Thus, poverty in India may not be the same as poverty in America. Viewing poverty as a relative matter goes beyond the material dimension to consider such things as low self-esteem, limited education, restricted participation in social and leisure activities, chronic sense of failure and defeat, and a continual state of dependency.

Absolute Poverty

Poverty in America has traditionally been measured in an absolute way. Absolute measures of poverty involve an annual income level below which people are considered to be poor.

Several different measures of absolute poverty have been developed over the past few years, each yielding a different count of America's poor. In 1964, President Johnson's Council of Economic Advisors drew the poverty line at $3,000 a year for a nonfarm family of two or more, and $1,500 a year for unrelated individuals (persons who live alone or with others to whom they are not related). According to these figures, 9 million families and 5 million persons living alone were below the poverty line. This meant that a total of 35 million people were poor, or 20 per cent of all American families and 45 per cent of all unrelated persons.[12] Leon Keyserling proposed a somewhat higher standard for the poverty line, $4,000 annual income for a family of four. This standard identified 23 per cent of the American population as poor. Keyserling added another poverty category: those families whose annual income fell between $4,000 and $6,000 were considered "deprived." Another 23 per cent of the population fell into this second category.[13]

Both of these measures of poverty are misleading in that they fail to take into account important factors affecting a family's needs and costs: the number of dependents in the home, the age and sex composition of the family, its geographic location, the condition of family members' health, and the age of the head of the family.

[12] Council of Economic Advisors, *Economic Report of the President: 1964* (Washington, D.C.: U.S. Government Printing Office, 1964), pp. 62–69.

[13] Leon Keyserling et al., *Poverty and Deprivation in the United States,* Conference on Economic Progress (Washington, D.C.: U.S. Government Printing Office, 1962). As Herman Miller points out, since Keyserling's figure included noncash income, his $4,000 figure and the Council of Economic Advisor's $3,000 figure are not as different as they might seem. See Herman P. Miller, *Rich Man, Poor Man* (New York: Thomas Y. Crowell Company, 1964), p. 58.

There is one measure of absolute poverty that does provide adjustments for such factors as family size, sex of the head of the household, and place of residence. Developed by Mollie Orshansky of the Social Security Administration, this measure was originally based on an "economy" food plan, designed by the United States Department of Agriculture as nutritionally adequate for use in emergencies or temporarily when funds are low. The poverty cutoffs were based essentially on the amount of income left after allowing for the purchase of an adequate diet at minimum cost. New poverty lines were "drawn separately for each of 124 different types of families, described by the sex of the head, the total number of other adults, the number of children under age 18, and whether or not they lived on a farm." [14] Table 2-2 shows various poverty lines by family size and sex of head of household according to farm and nonfarm residence. For example, a nonfarm family of four persons with a male head and annual income below $5,040 was considered poor in 1974.

The Orshansky method of measuring poverty has at least three advantages. It provides a variety of poverty lines, based on a number of family characteristics. Also, the poverty lines can be easily adjusted to match fluctuations in the Consumer Price Index. This takes inflation into account to some

Table 2-2. Income Levels of the Poor in 1974 by Size of Family and Sex of Head, by Farm and Nonfarm Residence

| Size of Family Unit | Total | Nonfarm | | | Farm | | |
		Total	Male Head	Female Head	Total	Male Head	Female Head
1 person (unrelated individual)	$2,487	$2,495	$2,610	$2,413	$2,092	$2,158	$2,029
2 persons	3,191	3,211	3,220	3,167	2,707	2,711	2,632
3 persons	3,910	3,936	3,957	3,822	3,331	3,345	3,133
4 persons	5,008	5,038	5,040	5,014	4,302	4,303	4,262
5 persons	5,912	5,950	5,957	5,882	5,057	5,057	5,072
6 persons	6,651	6,699	6,706	6,642	5,700	5,700	5,702
7 persons or more	8,165	8,253	8,278	8,079	7,018	7,017	7,066

SOURCE: U.S. Bureau of the Census, *Current Population Reports,* Series P-60, No. 102, "Characteristics of the Population Below the Poverty Line: 1974" (Washington, D.C.: U.S. Government Printing Office, 1976), p. 146.

[14] Mollie Orshansky, "Who's Who Among the Poor: A Demographic View of Poverty," *Social Security Bulletin,* 28 (July 1965): 8.

degree. Finally, it provides a method for determining the number of persons who are below a given minimum level of income and how that number changes over time.

Despite these advantages, there are many critics of any measure of absolute poverty. To these critics, a relative approach to poverty is both more realistic and more humane.

Relative Poverty

Those who favor using a measure of relative poverty agree on at least two major criticisms of the absolute approach to poverty. An absolute measure of poverty is too static; it does not allow for changing standards about what are considered to be necessities and what are thought to be luxuries. After things formerly considered to be luxuries become widely dispersed throughout the population, they come to be viewed as "necessities." Televison sets, automobiles, and washing machines are examples. Herman Miller put it this way:

> The essential fallacy of a fixed poverty line is that it fails to recognize the relative nature of "needs". . . . Old timers may harken back to the "good old days" when people were happy without electricity, flush toilets, automobiles, and television sets; but they must also realize that, once it becomes possible for all to have these "luxuries," they will be demanded and will quickly assume the status of "needs". . . . [I]t is unrealistic in an expanding economy to think in terms of a fixed poverty line.[15]

According to this viewpoint, the poverty threshold should be raised as the standard of living in the country rises. Also, an absolute measure of poverty ignores the general distribution of income in a society.[16] Whether or not persons are poor is said to depend on the income levels of those with whom they compare themselves. A rising amount of spendable income does not make one feel less poor if the income levels of those around him are increasing at the same or a faster rate. One measure of relative poverty is a comparison of the lowest fifth of the population in terms of income with the other four-fifths. Such a measure, of course, means that a segment of the population will always be "poor" unless the total income *distribution* approaches equality.

[15] Herman P. Miller, "Changes in the Number and Composition of the Poor," in Edward C. Budd, ed., *Inequality and Poverty* (New York: Norton & Company, Inc., 1968), p. 165.
[16] Anthony Downs, "Who Are the Urban Poor?" Supplementary Paper Number 26, Committee for Economic Development, rev. ed., 1970, pp. 8–9.

THE MYTH OF THE AMERICAN ECONOMY

"The U.S. has the world's highest standard of living. It's not utopia, but in the real world, our economy is the best there is." How often have you heard these statements either as an expression of national superiority or as a defense of the status quo?

Alas, they are simply untrue. Our country has not generated the world's highest per capita GNP since the early 1950s when we were surpassed by Kuwait. More important, perhaps, is the fact that we have been surpassed, or are about to be, by a number of countries in Europe. Among industrial countries, Sweden and Switzerland can each claim to be more successful with a per capita GNP 20 per cent above ours. We have also been passed by Denmark and are about to be surpassed by Norway and West Germany. Relative to achievements in the rest of the world the U.S. economy no longer "delivers the goods."

It is still, moreover, marked by large inequalities in the distribution of economic resources. The richest 10 per cent of our households receive 26.1 per cent of our income while the poorest 10 per cent receive only 1.7 per cent. And most of this small amount comes in the form of government income transfer payments. Blacks earn 69 per cent as much as whites; women who work full time earn only 56 per cent as much as men. If we look at the distribution of physical wealth, the top 20 per cent owns 80 per cent of all that can be privately owned in the United States and the bottom 25 per cent owns nothing (many of them, in fact, have debts that exceed their assets).

The Growth of Incomes

Traditionally, the "world's highest standard of living" has been used to justify these inequalities. They may be regrettable, but they are a necessary price that must be paid for growth. After all, so the argument goes, a person near the bottom of the U.S. income distribution would be at least middle class in the rest of the world.

All of these propositions are called into question when we look at the countries that are outstripping us. With the growth of incomes in Western Europe, America's poor are no longer middle class abroad. They are poor. As we have seen, the top 10 per cent of all U.S. households receive fifteen times as much income as the bottom 10 per cent. In the industrial country with the world's highest standard of living, Sweden, the same ratio is 7. In the country with the world's highest rate of growth, Japan, the same ratio is 10. In the major country that is about to surpass us, West Germany, the same ratio is 11. The degree of inequality that exists in America (100 per cent more than that in Sweden, 50 per cent more than that in Japan, and 36 per cent more than that in West Germany) is clearly not necessary to sustain economic growth. (The U.S. does not, however, have the highest degree of inequality among industrial countries—that honor is reserved for France. We are only second.)

Rating Productivity

But our affluent competitors are interesting from another perspective. In the long run, standards of living are determined by productivity. Improvements in productivity allow us to have both more goods or services and more leisure. In this sphere the U.S. is clearly falling behind. Our competitors in Western Europe have enjoyed a sustained rate of productivity growth over the past two decades twice that of ours; Japan has achieved a rate of productivity growth three times ours. We have comforted ourselves with the idea that our poor performance could be explained by our economic leadership. Our competitors were achieving higher rates of productivity growth because they were simply adopting technologies already developed by us rather than developing new technologies themselves.

But as these countries have reached our level of productivity, their growth rate has not slowed down to ours. In the first five years of the 1970s, the level of industrial productivity rose 11 per cent more in Sweden, 17 per cent more in West Germany and 25 per cent more in Japan than in the U.S. These countries continue to outstrip us even though they have advanced to a point where they are now the leaders in industrial productivity. We are the ones with the "easy" task of adopting existing technologies.

Sometimes the poor productivity performance of the American economy is blamed on the size of the defense budget. We are using 6 to 7 per cent of our GNP for defense, West Germany and Sweden are spending only 3 per cent, and Japan only 1 per cent. There may be some truth in this argument, but military expenditures are often defended and seen by other nations as a vehicle for generating new technologies. If they are simply a negative weight slowing down economic progress, then this negative influence needs to be taken into account in setting our defense budget and in sharing defense expenditures with our allies.

The standard conservative response is to advocate the "liberation of free enterprise" and a reduction in social expenditures. Yet this is not how any of these countries have outperformed us—quite the opposite. Sweden is famous for the most comprehensive social-welfare system in the world; West Germany insists that union leaders hold places on corporate boards of directors; the Japanese Government controls and plans the economy to a degree that makes the U.S. seem like rugged free enterprise.

Expenditures and Success

"Liberating free enterprise" also runs into the facts about the U.S. economy. In the history of the United States our best decade in terms of growth in real per capita GNP (a 36 per cent increase) was that of the 1940s when the economy was run as a command (socialist) wartime economy. The second best decade (a 30 per cent increase) was that of the 1960s, with all of its social-welfare programs.

The *best* decade (a 22 per cent increase) prior to the advent of government intervention occurred between 1900 and 1910. Real per-capita growth since the advent of government intervention has been more than twice as high as it was in the days when government did not intervene or have social-welfare programs.

As both our own experience and foreign experience demonstrate, there is no conflict between social expenditures or government intervention and economic success. The lack of government planning, worker participation, and social spending may in fact be at the heart of our poor performance in recent decades. As we, and others, have shown, social reforms can be productive, as well as just, if done in the right way.

Lester C. Thurow, *Newsweek*, February 14, 1977, p. 11. Copyright 1977 by Newsweek, Inc. All rights reserved. Reprinted by permission.

WHO ARE THE POOR?

Although the *poor* in America in the mid-1970s are nearly three fourths white, the poverty rates for blacks and Spanish-speaking Americans are higher than for whites. Less than 9 per cent of the white population fall below the poverty threshold, compared to over 30 per cent among blacks and 23 per cent among Spanish-speaking persons.[17]

Blacks and Spanish-speaking individuals account for a disproportionate share of the poor. Although blacks constitute only about 11 per cent of the population, they account for around 30 per cent of the poor. Spanish-speaking Americans account for approximately 4 per cent of all Americans, but constitute 9 per cent of the poor.

There is a heavy concentration of the poor in homes without fathers. Nearly half of the poor (about 9 million persons) are members of female-headed families, while almost 90 per cent of the nonpoor are in families with a father present.

Of all those in poverty, nearly 40 per cent are children under 18 years of age. Just over 10 million of America's poor—two out of every five persons—are children less than 18 years old.

The aged account for another large segment of the poor. Approximately 15 per cent of the poor are 65 or older.

Another large segment of the poor is the disabled. The blind, deaf, crippled, and other disabled account for some 12 per cent of America's poor.

[17] U.S. Bureau of the Census, *Current Population Reports*, Series P-60, No. 102, "Characteristics of the Population Below the Poverty Line: 1974" (Washington, D.C.: U.S. Government Printing Office, 1976).

Finally, a large segment of the poor are individuals who either live alone or live with nonrelatives. Approximately 20 per cent of the poor, one out of every five, are unrelated individuals.

WHY ARE THE POOR POOR?

Social Darwinism, Individualism, and the Poor

Why is there poverty? There is a deceptively simple answer formulated long ago that still has some influence. It is an adaptation of Charles Darwin's theory of biological evolution to the social world. According to Darwin, only the fittest plants and animals survive in a particular environment. Those plants and animals that have survived carry with them physical characteristics that give them a competitive edge for continued survival. The process of natural selection ensures that the fittest survive. When applied to human society, this view, called "Social Darwinism," contends that the fittest individuals survive as a result of social selection, whereas the inferior are eliminated by the same process.

A few early sociologists advocated Social Darwinism. William Graham Sumner wrote in 1914:

> The millionaires are a product of natural selection, acting on the whole body of men to pick out those who can meet the requirement of certain work to be done. In this respect they are just like the great statesmen, or scientific men, or military men. It is because they are thus selected that wealth—both their own and that intrusted to them—aggregates under their hands. . . . They may fairly be regarded as the naturally selected agents of society for certain work. They get high wages and live in luxury, but the bargain is a good one for society. There is the intensest competition for their place and occupation. This assures us that all who are competent for this function will be employed in it. . . .[18]

Edward A. Ross, writing in the 1920s, believed that "In a really competitive society the hopelessly poor and wretched are, to a large extent, the weak and the incompetent who have accumulated at the lower end of the social scale because they or their parents have failed to meet the test of the competitive system."[19]

[18] William Graham Sumner, "The Concentration of Wealth: Its Economic Justification," in *The Challenge of Facts and Other Essays* (New Haven: Yale University Press, 1914), p. 102.
[19] Edward A. Ross, *Social Control: A Survey of the Foundations of Social Order* (New York: Macmillan Publishing Co., Inc., 1926), p. 394.

Of all those in poverty nearly 40 per cent are children under 18 years of age. (Courtesy of Joe Molnar.)

Although social scientists have long since rejected Social Darwinism, this philosophy has contributed to that part of America's basic value system that is variously labeled the work ethic, the achievement and success ideology, or the ideology of individualism. Individualism in America involves several central beliefs:

1. That each individual should work hard and strive to succeed in competition with others.
2. That those who work hard should be rewarded with success (seen as wealth, property, prestige, and power).
3. That because of widespread and equal opportunity, those who work hard will in fact be rewarded with success.

Approximately 15 per cent of the poor are 65 or older. (Courtesy of Joe Molnar.)

4. That economic failure is an individual's own fault and reveals lack of effort and other character defects.[20]

The most generally shared conception of the poor in America is based on the ideology of individualism. Joan Huber and William Form summarize this popular view of the poor:

> The opportunity to learn a trade, a skill, or profession is essentially equal because elementary and secondary schools are free. An able youth can usually obtain a scholarship to pay his way in the university or he can get a job and pay his own way—it will "make a man of him." After he has left school, a man who is willing to work can always find something to do if he looks hard enough. There are always plenty of jobs that need doing and the person who sits around doing nothing hasn't really "tried" to find work. A man who works

[20] Joe R. Feagin, *Subordinating the Poor: Welfare and American Beliefs* (Englewood Cliffs, N.J.: Prentice-Hall, Inc., 1975), pp. 91–92.

hard will "get ahead." Any man who doesn't get ahead, must be stupid, lazy, or (as the professors say) lacking the requisite need achievement.[21]

According to the ideology of individualism, then, those at the bottom are where they belong because they lack the ability, energy, and motivation to survive in a competitive social world. From this vantage point, it is the poor who are to blame for their condition—those who fail deserve to do so.

In order to test whether or not the ideology of individualism still affects the public's view of the poor, Joe Feagin conducted a nationwide survey. Respondents were asked to judge the importance of a list of "reasons some people give to explain why there are poor people" in America. Table 2-3 shows that individualistic explanations of poverty were the most popular. About half the sample judged lack of thrift, lack of effort, lack of ability, and loose morals and drunkenness—all individualistic causes—to be *very* important reasons for poverty. Much less emphasis was placed on structural explanations that find the causes of poverty in social and economic factors beyond the control of the poor. The percentage evaluating structural explanations as very important ranged from 42 per cent on the existence of low wages to 18 per cent on the exploitation of the poor by the rich. Although structural explanations for poverty have grown in importance in recent years, the individualistic interpretation remains dominant.

If the public has negative attitudes toward the poor in general, its judgment of those on welfare is even harsher. It is still widely believed in America that the poor are persons who simply prefer welfare to work. In his nationwide survey, Feagin asked the respondents to evaluate a number of statements about welfare and welfare recipients. The statement drawing the highest percentage of agreement (84 per cent) was this: "There are too many people receiving welfare money who should be working." And half of the respondents disagreed with the statement that "Most people on welfare who can work try to find jobs so they can support themselves." Like many other beliefs about welfare and the poor, both of these are incorrect.[22]

There are several reasons why the poor should not be considered as persons who prefer welfare to work. First, not all of those who are poor are on

[21] Joan Huber and William H. Form, *Income and Ideology: An Analysis of the American Political Formula* (New York: Free Press, 1973), p. 4.

[22] For rebuttals of welfare myths, see Feagin, *Subordinating the Poor,* op. cit., pp. 102–115; and *Welfare Myths vs. Facts,* U.S. Department of Health, Education, and Welfare (Washington, D.C.: U.S. Government Printing Office, 1971); and Elizabeth Herzog, "Perspectives on Poverty 3: Facts and Fictions About the Poor," *Monthly Labor Review,* 92 (February 1969): 42–49.

Table 2-3. Reasons for Poverty

Reasons for Poverty	Percentage Replying				
	Very Important	Somewhat Important	Not Important	Uncertain	Total
1. Lack of thrift and proper money management by poor people	58%	30%	11%	2%	101%*
2. Lack of effort by the poor themselves	55	33	9	3	100%
3. Lack of ability and talent among poor people	52	33	12	3	100%
4. Loose morals and drunkenness	48	31	17	4	100%
5. Sickness and physical handicaps	46	39	14	2	101%
6. Low wages in some businesses and industries	42	35	20	3	100%
7. Failure of society to provide good schools for many Americans	36	25	34	5	100%
8. Prejudice and discrimination against Negroes	33	37	26	5	101%
9. Failure of private industry to provide enough jobs	27	36	31	6	100%
10. Being taken advantage of by rich people	18	30	45	7	100%
11. Just bad luck	8	27	60	5	100%

SOURCE: Joe R. Feagin, *Subordinating the Poor: Welfare and American Beliefs,* © 1975, p. 97. Reprinted by permission of Prentice-Hall, Inc., Englewood Cliffs, New Jersey.
*Some totals do not add to exactly 100 per cent because of statistical rounding procedures.

welfare. In fact, less than half of those in poverty receive welfare payments. Second, the demographic profile of the poor given earlier reveals that the bulk of the poor do not live in families with able-bodied male heads. Third, contrary to the popular impression, a large percentage of the poor work. Over 60 per cent of the poor are employed either on a full- or part-time basis. Although one third of the poor are not employed, almost 20 per cent of this one third are either ill or disabled during this period, 1 per cent are still in school, and about 2 per cent have looked for work without success.[23] The percentages of the poor and nonpoor who are able to work but are not doing so were 12 per cent and 10 per cent, respectively. When only males are considered, 1.4 per cent of the able-bodied poor were not working, compared with 0.6 per cent of the nonpoor.[24]

Several studies challenge the belief that welfare recipients are lazy, opposed to work, and enjoying their welfare-supported existence. Two studies of welfare mothers in New York and California indicated that about three fourths preferred employment to staying at home. Most said they were not presently working because of their children, housework, bad health, or lack of skills.[25] According to Bradley Schiller, "What distinguishes the employed from the nonemployed poor at any point in time is not the work ethic, but a combination of job opportunities and demographic problems."[26] Some studies reviewed by Schiller indicate that the desire to work is more pronounced among the poor than the nonpoor. Leonard Goodwin reports that he found no difference in aspirations and desire to work between the poor and nonpoor.[27] Whether male or female, black or white, young or old, poor people appear to share in the middle-class identification of self-esteem with work and self-support. The aspirations of the poor for achievement match those of the nonpoor; both desire an adequate education and a home in a good neighborhood. If the poor seem to prefer welfare to work, Goodwin concludes, it is because of their discouraging work experiences.

Statistics also belie the belief that those on welfare are persons who could be working if they only had the desire. Of those on welfare, only about 1 per cent are able-bodied fathers (see Figure 2-1). It is estimated that 80 per cent of them desire work and half are enrolled in job training programs.[28] Ac-

[23] U.S. Bureau of the Census, "Characteristics of the Population Below the Poverty Line: 1974," op. cit., Table 4, p. 32.

[24] These figures appear in *The Poor in 1970: A Chartbook,* Office of Economic Opportunity (Washington, D.C.: U.S. Government Printing Office, 1972), pp. 30–31. Since the statistics on the poor have remained relatively stable since 1970, these figures are still accurate.

[25] Lawrence Podell, *Families on Welfare in New York City* (New York: The Center for the Study of Urban Problems, the City University of New York, n.d.); and Martin Warren and Sheldon Berkowitz, "The Employability of AFDC Mothers and Fathers," *Welfare in Review,* 7 (July–August 1969): 1–7.

[26] Bradley R. Schiller, "Empirical Studies of Welfare Dependency: A Survey," *The Journal of Human Resources,* 8 (Supplement 1973): 21.

[27] Leonard Goodwin, *Do the Poor Want to Work?: A Social-Psychological Study of Work Orientations* (Washington, D.C.: The Brookings Institution, 1972).

[28] *Welfare Myths vs. Facts,* op. cit.

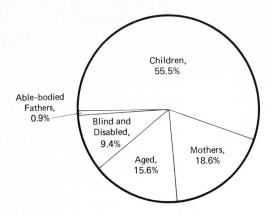

Children, 55.5%

Able-bodied Fathers, 0.9%

Blind and Disabled, 9.4%

Aged, 15.6%

Mothers, 18.6%

Figure 2-1. Federally assisted welfare population. [Adopted from *Welfare Myths vs. Facts*, U.S. Department of Health, Education, and Welfare (Washington, D.C.: U.S. Government Printing Office, 1971).]

tively seeking work is a requirement for welfare eligibility. Of the remainder on welfare, almost 10 per cent are blind or disabled, nearly 16 per cent are over 65; and over 55 per cent are children. Thus, more than 80 per cent of the poor on welfare are unable to work either because they are too young or too old or because they are blind or otherwise disabled. Most of the remaining persons on welfare are mothers with dependent children without husbands in the home.

Given the popular image of those on welfare as able-bodied loafers, it is not surprising that forcing welfare recipients to take jobs is the solution to poverty most widely endorsed by the public. (A 1972 Harris poll found that 90 per cent of Americans agreed that those on welfare should go to work.) But employment is obviously not the solution to removing people from the welfare rolls in the current economy, because the young, the elderly, and the disabled are generally unemployable in today's labor market. Even if they were able to work, their wages would be extremely low. Also, without adequate and reasonably priced day care centers for children, it is questionable that forcing welfare mothers who are without husbands to work will help much in reducing poverty. Not only might their children be less well cared for, but mothers' wages would be severely strained by child care costs.

Still, the idea that the poor are different from other people persists. For this reason, it is important to pursue the matter in greater depth.

Are the Rich and the Poor Different?

Are the rich and the poor different from each other? Consider the following two passages from American literature regarding the rich:

Let me tell you about the rich. They are different from you and me. They possess and enjoy early, and it does something to them, makes them soft where we are hard, and cynical where we are trustful, in a way that, unless you were born rich, it is difficult to understand. They think, deep in their hearts, that they are better than we are because we had to discover the compensations and refuges of life for ourselves. Even when they enter deep into our world or sink below us, they still think that they are better than we are. They are different.

F. Scott Fitzgerald
"The Rich Boy," 1926

The rich were dull and they drank too much, or they played too much backgammon. They were dull and they were repetitious. He remembered poor Julian and his romantic awe of them and how he had started a story once that began, "The very rich are different from you and me." And how someone had said to Julian, "Yes, they have more money."

Ernest Hemingway
"The Snows of Kilimanjaro," 1936

Fitzgerald is saying that the rich are really quite unlike other kinds of people, but Hemingway contends that the only thing separating the rich and the nonrich is money. Something of a parallel to this literary disagreement exists in the social science debate between two explanations for poverty, one cultural, the other situational.

The Cultural Explanation of Poverty.   There are those who contend that the poor participate in a subculture of poverty. That is, the poor are said to have evolved certain ways of thinking, feeling, and behaving that are different from those of participants in the larger culture and that are passed on from generation to generation.

Oscar Lewis, a noted anthropologist, sees the creation of a subculture among the poor as an adaptation, an attempt at self-defense on the part of people at the bottom of society.[29] A notable aspect of the subculture of poverty is identified as the absence of a success orientation. Realizing that they cannot experience success according to the terms of the larger society, states Lewis, the poor attempt to deal with feelings of discouragement and despair by creating and subscribing to values, beliefs, and attitudes better suited to their deprived condition.

An important implication of the cultural explanation is that changing the objective situation of the poor does not ensure that they will make the effort needed to get out of poverty. Their cultural traditions, originally created to

[29] Oscar Lewis, *A Study of Slum Culture: Backgrounds for La Vida* (New York: Random House, Inc., 1968), pp. 4–21.

help them cope with their social and economic hopelessness, are said to be passed from generation to generation and to persist even when the conditions that gave rise to them no longer exist. These subcultural ways of thinking, feeling, and behaving are thought to stand as a barrier to rising above poverty. Lewis is quite explicit on this point: "by school age, children of poverty are so thoroughly socialized in their subculture and so psychologically stunted that they are seldom able to capitalize on opportunities they may encounter in later life." [30]

Richard Ball also sees subcultural traits among the poor as an adaptation to the reality of living a denying and frustrating existence. [31] He contends that persons in poverty face such overwhelming problems that they build a way of life based on dependence, belligerence, and fatalistic resignation. Although the subculture that is developed does not permit the poor to deal effectively with their situation, it soothes the pain of day-to-day living and provides some relief from the discomforts of frustration. Like Lewis, Ball believes that the subculture of poverty becomes a way of life and that it endures even when the conditions that created it no longer exist.

Although recognizing the influence of a lower-class subculture, Edward Banfield argues that the primary cause of poverty is the poor's attitude toward providing for the future. According to Banfield, the poor have difficulty in imagining their future and lack the capability to make sacrifices today in order to have a better tomorrow. Their view of the world is said to be exclusively in the present time:

> the lower-class individual lives from moment to moment. If he has any awareness of a future, it is of something fixed, fated, beyond his control: things happen *to* him, he does not *make* them happen. Impulse governs his behavior, either because he cannot discipline himself to sacrifice a present for a future satisfaction or because he has no sense of the future. He is therefore radically improvident: whatever he cannot consume immediately he considers valueless. His bodily needs (especially for sex) and his taste for "action" take precedence over everything else—and certainly over any work routine. He works only as he must to stay alive, and drifts from one unskilled job to another, taking no interest in the work. [32]

[30] Ibid., p. 6. It should be noted that Lewis contends that the subculture of poverty is characteristic of only a minority of America's poor (about 20 per cent).

[31] Richard A. Ball, "A Poverty Case: The Analgesic Subculture of the Southern Appalachians," *American Sociological Review*, 33 (December 1968): 885–895.

[32] Edward C. Banfield, *The Unheavenly City: The Nature and Future of Our Urban Crisis* (Boston: Little, Brown and Company, 1970), p. 53. Banfield has attracted a number of critics. For example, see William Ryan, "Is Banfield Really Serious?" *Social Policy*, 1 (November–December 1970): 74–76; and "Banfield's Unheavenly City: A Symposium and Response," *Trans-action*, 8 (March–April 1971): 69–78.

BLAMING THE VICTIM

Blaming the Victim is, of course, quite different from old-fashioned conservative ideologies. The latter simply dismissed victims as inferior, genetically defective, or morally unfit; the emphasis is on the intrinsic, even hereditary, defect. The former shifts its emphasis to environmental causation. The old-fashioned conservative could hold firmly to the belief that the oppressed and the victimized were born that way—"that way" being defective or inadequate in character or ability. The new ideology attributes defect and inadequacy to the malignant nature of poverty, injustice, slum life, and racial difficulties. The stigma that marks the victim and accounts for his victimization is an acquired stigma, a stigma of social, rather than genetic, origin. But the stigma, the defect, the fatal difference—though derived in the past from environmental forces—is still located *within* the victim, inside his skin. With such an elegant formulation, the humanitarian can have it both ways. He can, all at the same time, concentrate his charitable interest on the defects of the victim, condemn the vague social and environmental stresses that produced the defect (some time ago), and ignore the continuing effect of victimizing social forces (right now). It is brilliant ideology for justifying a perverse form of social action designed to change, not society, as one might expect, but rather society's victim.

William Ryan. *Blaming the Victim* (New York: Random House, Inc., 1971), p. 7.

The Situational Explanation of Poverty. Those who favor a situational explanation of poverty contend that the nonpoor have social, educational, and occupational opportunities that are not available to the poor. Change this situation and the poor will also change is the message of those who support the situational explanation of poverty.

According to Lee Rainwater, the lower class only appears to have rejected middle-class values.[33] In fact, this apparent rejection serves as a camouflage for those whose life experiences have hammered home that failure is inevitable if one attempts to succeed without the necessary resources and opportunities. It follows, Rainwater asserts, that a radical change in available social and economic opportunity would reveal the true desire among lower-class persons to achieve occupational success and to live the "good life."

William Ryan views the subculture of poverty explanation as a new form of "blaming the victim," of finding the cause of poverty in the poor themselves. Whereas in the past, in the context of Social Darwinism, the poor were thought to be biologically defective, the new version locates the defects of the poor in their social environment.[34]

[33] Lee Rainwater, "The Lessons of Pruitt-Igoe," *The Public Interest,* 8 (Summer 1967): 116–126.
[34] William Ryan, *Blaming the Victim* (New York: Pantheon Books, Inc., 1971).

Which explanation of poverty, the cultural or the situational, is correct? Each of these two theories of poverty is incomplete when considered alone. They are complementary explanations that in combination increase our understanding of poverty.

A notable attempt to synthesize the cultural and situational theories of poverty has been made by Hyman Rodman. Like the culturalists, Rodman believes that lower-class values, beliefs, and attitudes help the poor adjust to their deprived and frustrating situation. But he attempts to clarify the nature of this adaptation by way of the concept of the "lower-class value stretch." According to Rodman, lower-class persons who realize the impossibility of living up to general societal goals minimize potential pain and frustration by settling for less. They do not decide that success is unimportant, just that less of it will suffice. Middle-class values are not abandoned; they are stretched to fit the lower-class condition:

> Lower class persons in close interaction with each other and faced with similar problems do not long remain in a state of mutual ignorance. They do not maintain a strong commitment to middle class values that they cannot attain, and they do not continue to respond to others in a rewarding or punishing way simply on the basis of whether these others are living up to the middle class values. A change takes place. They come to tolerate and eventually to evaluate favorably certain deviations from the middle class values. In this way they need not be continually frustrated by their failure to live up to unattainable values. The resultant is a stretched value system with a low degree of commitment to all the values within the range, including the dominant, middle class values.[35]

Those who advocate a cultural or a situational explanation of poverty do not agree on the likelihood of the poor changing if their situation improved, but they do agree that poverty is a problem of structure. Leonard Goodwin states that the philosophy of letting the poor help themselves ignores the existing barriers to continuous employment and self-support that are beyond the control of poor people. It glosses over the ways in which educational and economic structures are arranged to induce failure among the poor. Inferior education, dead-end and low-paying jobs, and discrimination cannot easily be overcome by individual motivation and hard work. These are characteristics of social structures rather than of individuals.[36] Oscar Lewis, a proponent of the cultural explanation, also sees poverty as a problem of structure:

[35] Hyman Rodman, "The Lower-Class Value Stretch," *Social Forces,* 42 (December 1963): 209.
[36] Goodwin, op. cit.

POVERTY AS A PROBLEM OF STRUCTURE

William Ryan wants us to look all around us as well as inward: he wants us to stop and think why we . . . spend so very much time talking about the "cultural deprivation" among blacks or Chicanos or Indians, about the "mark of oppression" or the psychological "disadvantage" to be found among ghetto children—and much less time trying to analyze what in our particular social and economic system makes for the very special circumstances some groups of people have to contend with: the scandalously high infant mortality rate among these people, the high unemployment rate they have to face as a fact of life, the wretched housing, insulting welfare regulations, not to mention the thoroughly discouraging schools their children must attend.

To examine some of these "structural" problems, to ask why the world's richest and most powerful nation chooses to spend 70 billion dollars a year on its armed forces, while thousands and thousands of our children grow up malnourished, get bitten by rats, suffer lead poisoning because certain buildings, thousands of them, are allowed to stand—to look at such awful paradoxes is unnerving, Dr. Ryan keeps pointing out, and so we have to do something to ease the tension. We could, of course, look at this nation very carefully. We could ask who owns what, who profits enormously from whose labor.

Robert Coles, *American Journal of Sociology*, 78 (September 1972): 448–449.

There is nothing in the concept [of the subculture of poverty] that puts the onus of poverty on the character of the poor. Nor does the concept in any way play down the exploitation and neglect suffered by the poor. Indeed, the subculture of poverty is part of the larger culture of capitalism, whose social and economic system channels wealth into the hands of a relatively small group and thereby makes for the growth of sharp class distinctions.[37]

Lewis touches on the fundamental source of poverty, whether or not participation in a subculture of poverty helps to keep the poor in poverty. The basic cause of poverty is the economic and political nature of American society.

WHAT CAN BE DONE?

Prior to the mid-1960s, poverty was not a prominent concern of the federal government. The New Deal policies and programs of the 1930s were gener-

[37] Lewis, *A Study of Slum Culture*, op. cit., p. 20.

ally conceived as short-range measures to handle the economic crisis of the Depression. The interest in poverty as a nationwide problem by Presidents John Kennedy and Lyndon Johnson, however, led the federal government to launch the broadest attempt to combat poverty ever made in America. In August 1964, after House and Senate passage, Lyndon Johnson began the War on Poverty by signing into law the Economic Opportunity Act. The government's commitment to combatting poverty from 1965 to 1972 is reflected in the money allocated to social programs for low-income persons. Total expenditures went from $6 billion in 1965 to $24.5 billion in 1972.[38]

Progress Against Poverty

The philosophy behind the Economic Opportunity Act of 1964 was to help people help themselves. The intent was to enhance the income-generating capacity of the poor. If the chains of poverty are to be broken, President Kennedy said, it must be through self-improvement rather than through temporary relief. The Economic Opportunity Act took as its primary target the young, those who were the most likely to rise out of poverty. The antipoverty programs concentrated on either providing employment or offering services that would lead to employment. Thus, almost 60 per cent of the original budget for the Economic Opportunity Act was earmarked for youth opportunity programs and the work experience program (a program of work and job training designed primarily for welfare recipients and unemployed fathers). The bulk of the remaining funds was allocated to urban and rural community action programs (33 per cent).[39]

Some changes in the social welfare policy of the federal government have occurred over the past ten years. The most significant change has been a gradual move away from manpower development and education toward cash payments, in-kind transfers (provision of goods rather than money), and direct services (legal services and medical care). Although manpower development and educational improvement are still part of the government's programs, they account for a smaller percentage of the poverty budget. In the early 1970s, AFDC (Aid to Families with Dependent Children) payments,

[38] Robert D. Plotnick and Felicity Skidmore, *Progress Against Poverty: A Review of the 1964–1974 Decade* (New York: Academic Press, Inc., 1975).

[39] Ibid., p. 6.

food stamps, and Medicaid accounted for 41 per cent of the total welfare budget, an increase of 100 per cent over 1965.[40]

What has been the progress against poverty in recent years? Whether measured in absolute terms (the federal government's fixed poverty line) or on a relative basis (as measured by comparing families with the lowest incomes to other families), poverty decreased during the 1960s but has leveled off in the 1970s.

It is clear from Figure 2-2 that according to the government's fixed standard of poverty both the number of poor people and the percentage of the total population that they represent declined between 1959 and 1969. In 1959, approximately 22 per cent of the American population (39.5 million persons) were in poverty. By 1969, that figure had dropped to about 12 per cent (25.3 million persons). The decline in poverty was relatively steady during these years when the federal government's commitment to poverty policies and programs was at its peak.

The trend toward a reduction in poverty, however, ended in 1969. By the mid-1970s, almost 25 million Americans—12 per cent of the population—remained below the official poverty line.

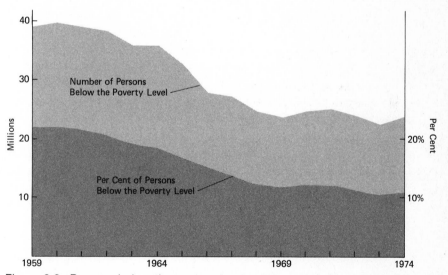

Figure 2-2. Persons below the poverty level: 1959 to 1974. [Current Population Reports, U.S. Department of Commerce (Washington, D.C.: U.S. Government Printing Office, 1976).]

[40] Ibid., p. 26.

If the fight against poverty is to gain momentum again, new strategies must be adopted by the federal government. These might include job guarantees, a guaranteed annual income, and the deliberate redistribution of income.

Guaranteed Employment

During the 1930s, the federal government assumed the responsibility of emergency employer for those who could not find work. With such programs as the Works Progress Administration (WPA), the government ensured that the unemployed had some sort of job.[41] The idea of the government as the "employer of last resort" has resurfaced in recent years. For example, the National Commission on Technology, Automation, and Economic Progress has presented a job guarantee proposal, with the federal government as the employer of last resort for the chronically unemployed as one of its central features.[42]

Although the job guarantee approach has not been used since the 1930s, criticism of it is not as widespread or vehement as that directed at either guaranteed income or income redistribution proposals.[43] This, at least in part, is because the guaranteed job approach is more consistent with the work ethic and the ideology of individualism. Still, some shortcomings of current guaranteed job proposals have been noted. In the first place, argue the critics, most proposals do not really favor changing the economy so that the government provides a large number of new jobs. Rather, most job guarantee proposals emphasize increased job training programs and federal monies to subsidize the private sector of the economy. In fact, it was just this sort of strategy that Lyndon Johnson adopted in his War on Poverty. Reliance on the private sector of the economy diminishes the government's ability to respond quickly to the changing needs of those at the bottom of the occupational structure. Providing a job right away better serves the immediate needs of the unemployed poor than do programs of job training that may require a residential move and a period of training time. Also, say the critics, even if the federal government became the employer of last resort, there is a tendency to create low-paying, temporary, dead-end jobs, or jobs that become stigmatized as welfare work.

[41] *Encyclopedia of Social Work,* Vol. II (New York: National Association of Social Workers, 1971), p. 926.

[42] National Commission on Technology, Automation, and Economic Progress, *Technology and the American Economy* (Washington, D.C.: U.S. Government Printing Office, 1966).

[43] In a 1972 survey, the Opinion Research Corporation reported that 72 per cent of the American public would favor a guaranteed job plan even if taxes were raised, but only 38 per cent would endorse a guaranteed income plan. See Feagin, *Subordinating the Poor,* op. cit., p. 136.

Guaranteed Income

A guaranteed income would provide every American with the economic resources to live in reasonable comfort, above the level of bare necessities. Although there are a variety of guaranteed income approaches, most recent proposals have been based on the *negative income tax*.[44] The basic principle in the negative income tax is that when a family's income rises above certain designated levels, the wage earner must pay a given amount of taxes to the government and when income falls below certain specified levels, the government pays the family. As income rises, the government income payment falls, but money from the government would not decrease dollar for dollar as earned income rises. A certain amount of income above the government payment could be earned without losing that same amount from the government payment. If the upper limit on a guaranteed annual income program were $5,000, for example, then a person might lose only 50 cents of every dollar earned until his or her income reached $5,000. When income reached the $5,000 upper limit, a person would begin to pay taxes at the same rate as others in that income bracket. A hypothetical illustration is supplied in Table 2-4. These figures are too low in today's economy, but they are useful for purposes of illustration.

Table 2-4. Hypothetical Illustration of a Negative Income Tax Payment Schedule

Annual Family Earnings	Cash Benefits from Government	Total Cash Income	Food Stamp Benefits	Total Income
0	$1,500	$1,500	$500	$2,000
500	1,250	1,750	425	2,225
1,000	1,000	2,000	375	2,375
1,500	750	2,250	325	2,575
2,000	500	2,500	250	2,750
2,500	250	2,750	200	2,950
3,000	0	3,000	125	3,125
3,500	0	3,500	0	3,500
4,000	0	4,000	0	4,000

SOURCE: Daniel P. Moynihan, *The Politics of a Guaranteed Income: The Nixon Administration and the Family Assistance Plan* (New York: Random House, Inc., 1973), p. 138.

[44] See David M. Gordon, "Alternative Income Maintenance Proposals," in David M. Gordon, ed., *Problems in Political Economy* (Lexington, Mass.: D. C. Heath & Company, 1971).

Almost 25 million Americans—12 per cent of the population—remain below the official poverty line. (Courtesy of Joe Molnar.)

One appealing aspect of the negative income tax is that it encourages welfare recipients to work, because they can earn certain amounts of money and still retain a given level of governmental financial aid. Nevertheless, various guaranteed income proposals have been criticized by both liberals and conservatives. Liberal critics contend that under conservative plans persons eligible for a cash benefit would be forced to exist at a standard of living below the government's current poverty line.[45] Conservative critics worry about the costs of guaranteed income programs and erosion of the work ethic. The costs of a guaranteed income system, say more conservative critics, will result in increased federal spending and taxes. So as not to undermine the work ethic, these critics advocate a strict employment requirement in any guaranteed income plan.

Two forms of negative income tax are already in effect. On January 1, 1974, the Supplemental Security Income plan (SSI), a nationwide negative income tax for the aged, blind, and disabled, went into effect. Eligibility and benefits are the same in all states. A minimum income of $2,500 for a couple

[45] For a conservative guaranteed income proposal, see Milton Friedman, *Capitalism and Freedom* (Chicago: University of Chicago Press, 1962). A more liberal plan is advocated in James Tobin, "Raising the Incomes of the Poor," in Kermit Gordon, ed., *Agenda for the Nation* (Washington, D.C.: The Brookings Institution, 1968), pp. 111 ff.

is guaranteed, and couples can earn up to $6,000 annually before all government payment stops.[46] Another type of negative income tax went into effect during 1976. First payments were based on 1975 earnings. The maximum allowance a family can receive is $400 per year. This full allowance can be obtained only by a working parent earning $4,000 a year or less. If a worker's annual income rises above $4,000, the allowance diminishes and is phased out for families earning as much as $8,000 a year. However, only the working poor can receive this benefit. Those who cannot get jobs or refuse them are specifically excluded from the program.

A guaranteed income plan does not have to be a total substitute for the present welfare system. It is now being used as a supplement. Neither should the guaranteed income approach be confused with the idea of income redistribution.

Toward Increased Income Equality

Without a doubt, traditional welfare systems have helped the poor. But the traditional approach has not eliminated poverty and was never intended to achieve income equality. This raises an important question: Should dealing with poverty involve giving the poor more money, or should poverty be viewed as a form of structural inequality requiring more radical changes? The answer depends on the objectives.

> Conventional poverty discussions are superficial because they are cast in terms of nineteenth-century concerns about pauperism and subsistence rather than in twentieth-century terms of redistribution. . . . When poverty is viewed in the stratificational perspective, it becomes clear that the goal of bringing all families up to a certain income level cloaks disagreements about the relative importance of differing, often conflicting, objectives. For example, in the objectives of efforts to change the stratificational system, is the goal a classless society with only minor differences among individuals? Or is the goal a meritocracy in which individuals have in actuality equal access to high-level jobs which are highly rewarded? Or is the target to connect an underclass, which does not improve its conditions as much as the rest of the society, into the processes which will begin to make it less distinctive? Or do we seek to reduce the gaps in some vital dimensions between the nonpoor and the poor?[47]

[46] Felicity Skidmore, "Welfare Reform: Some Policy Alternatives," *Tax Notes,* 3 (July 21, 1975): 22.
[47] S. M. Miller and Pamela A. Roby, *The Future of Inequality* (New York: Basic Books, Inc., Publishers, 1970), pp. 183–184.

As this passage implies, in America poverty has not been viewed as a form of structural inequality. Consequently, the solutions to poverty adopted have not been designed to reduce structural inequality. Those who see poverty as a form of structural inequality advocate solutions that would radically change the stratification structure. One of those solutions is income equality.

In theory, *income equality* involves the distribution of income equally among members of the population. It has been estimated, for example, that if the annual total personal income of all Americans were evenly divided, a family of four would receive more than $15,000 annually. Or, if only 10 per cent of the after-tax income of families with incomes above $15,000 were distributed to those families with annual incomes under $4,000, the income of the latter would increase by more than half.[48]

Certain changes will have to occur before specific proposals for income redistribution will be seriously considered by politicians. First, the disadvantaged will have to demand change and be successful in having their viewpoint accepted as legitimate by politicians and by the public. Second, those with high incomes (or at least their children) will have to begin to believe that they have a larger share of the economic resources than they rightfully should have.

Opposition to income equality is strong in America. It is unacceptable to the public, partly because it conflicts with some key aspects of American culture such as the work ethic, competition, self-help, and individualism. In his study, Feagin asked for a response to this statement about income equality: "Every family in this country should receive the same income, about $10,000 or so."[49] Eighty per cent of the respondents were opposed to income equality. People of all social classes, including those of low income, did not favor income equality. Those who opposed income equality gave such reasons as "people should work for a living," "it makes no allowance for differences in ability," "people should get what they work for," and "it would be communistic."

Although many Americans with low incomes oppose income equality, opposition to it is stronger among the powerful and rich because it conflicts with their interests. As Edward Herman states, "the high and relatively stable degree of inequality in the United States reflects the success of dominant, mainly business interest groups, in maintaining political and social power and in defining public and private priorities."[50] Or, as Pamela Roby puts it:

[48] Herbert J. Gans, "The New Egalitarianism," *Saturday Review* (May 6, 1972), p. 46.
[49] Feagin, *Subordinating the Poor,* op. cit., pp. 137–138.
[50] Edward S. Herman, "The Income 'Counter-Revolution'," *Commonweal,* 10 (January 1975): 296.

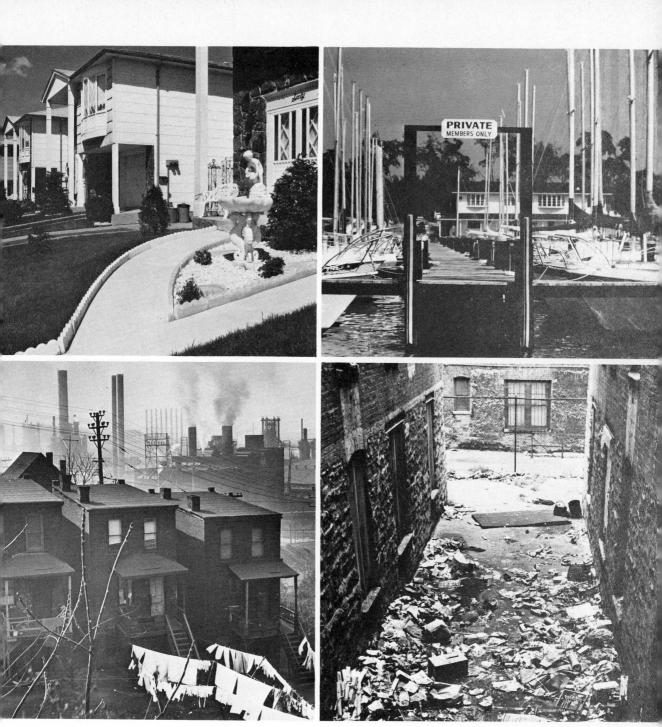

The poor are condemned in practice to inequality of opportunity and inequality in results. (Top left and right: Courtesy of E. P. A. Bottom left: Courtesy of A. Devaney, photo by David Corson. Bottom right: Courtesy of Joe Molnar.)

The preservation of a capitalistic political and economic system has been, to date, the primary goal of the establishment. Because the preservation of this system is the establishment's number one priority, the reduction of poverty is important only when poverty threatens the system; and the elimination of inequality is considered out of the realm of possibility, for inequality is intrinsic to the system.[51]

Because proposals for income equality conflict so strongly with contemporary American culture and vested interests, it is not surprising that there have been few American advocates of income redistribution as an approach to fighting poverty. Some prominent American proponents of extensive income redistribution include Upton Sinclair, Henry George, and Huey Long. One of the most recent supporters of income redistribution is Herbert Gans.[52] America, writes Gans, has a tradition of equality of opportunity. This, however, has not led to income equality because those at the bottom of the stratification structure do not have the resources (money, education, power, social contacts) to take advantage of the economic opportunity that allegedly exists. On the whole, the poor tend to remain poor from generation to generation; because of their disadvantages, they are condemned in practice to inequality of opportunity and inequality in results. Gans contends that the poor not only should have *opportunity* to achieve an adequate income, but should actually *receive* adequate economic resources. Equality in *result* rather than in *opportunity,* he asserts, is true equality.

A totally equalitarian society is so far from realization, contends Gans, that it does not belong in a serious discussion today. In his view, the central issue is not the achievement of *total* income equality but the institution of some changes that would promote *greater* equality than presently exists:

> Unemployment and underemployment have to be eliminated, and the poverty line raised so that the gaps between those at the bottom, middle, and top are reduced and no one earns less than 60 per cent of the median income and eventually no less than 70 per cent: $7,000 for a family of four by today's census figures and income definition. How high a ceiling on top incomes and how great a redistribution of wealth are economically necessary remains to be seen, although both are socially desirable, and even now there is considerable uproar over millionaires who pay no taxes.[53]

[51] Pamela Roby, ed., *The Poverty Establishment* (Englewood Cliffs, N.J.: Prentice-Hall, Inc., 1974), p. 16.

[52] Herbert J. Gans, *More Equality* (New York: Vintage Books, 1973).

[53] Ibid., p. 29.

CAN POVERTY REALLY BE ABOLISHED IN AMERICA?

Can poverty in the United States be abolished within the limits of the welfare state? Or does the present commitment to end the scandal of economic misery in the richest nation history has known require measures which will go beyond the present theories and practices of American society?

The answer is, I think, clear enough. The Johnson administration's War on Poverty is basically inadequate, a fact which can be demonstrated by the government's own figures. The liberal-labor proposals for social investments which would both generate jobs and destroy the very physical environment of poverty represent a considerable advance over the present program and deserve vigorous support. But even these measures have implications which are considerably more radical than liberal reform. Understanding that the poor need a planned allocation of resources in their favor is but a first step toward the knowledge that a revolutionary technology is subverting some of the most cherished myths and principles of the entire society and demands fundamental changes in our economic and social structure.

Michael Harrington, "The Politics of Poverty," in Jeremy Larner and Irving Howe, eds., *Poverty: Views from the Left* (New York: William Morrow & Co., Inc., 1968), p. 13.

Given the opposition to it, it is unlikely that greater income equality will occur in the near future. But if a significant improvement in the distribution of income is ever to take place, it will have to be promoted by the poor themselves, operating as an effective interest group. Political pressure must be applied if the barriers of cultural bias and vested interest are to be overcome.

The Poor as an Interest Group

If the nature of the American economy contributes heavily to the creation and maintenance of income inequality, its indispensable partner is the existence of political inequality. "If the nonpoor make the rules," states Bruno Stein, "anti-poverty efforts will only be made up to the point where the needs of the nonpoor are satisfied rather than the needs of the poor."[54] The poor are without power because they have not become an effective interest group in national politics and because they are a minority in a political system based on majority rule. The poor find it difficult to compete with a variety of more powerful interest groups that, despite their different special interests, can

[54] Bruno Stein, *On Relief* (New York: Basic Books, Inc., Publishers, 1971), p. 191.

agree that little should be done for the poor. Thus, although "out-voted minorities are not totally without political resources . . . generally speaking they obtain only the leftovers from the political dinner table. . . ."[55]

There have been some recent efforts, however, to organize the poor for political action. One attempt on the part of the poor to organize themselves is the Poor People's Campaign, an outgrowth of Martin Luther King's Southern Christian Leadership Conference. Its success has not been substantial, because it has spread itself too thin. It is difficult with limited resources to deal with problems as diverse as hunger in the South and the property rights of Indians in the West.[56]

A second effort to organize the poor—the National Welfare Rights Organization (NWRO)—has been more successful than the Poor People's Campaign. Founded in 1966 and composed mostly of black welfare recipients (primarily black mothers on AFDC), NWRO has a specific goal: to increase welfare benefits and improve the conditions of welfare assistance. Most of its daily activities involve efforts to handle complaints of welfare recipients regarding public relief. According to Gilbert Steiner, NWRO performs three functions for its members that cannot be handled by any other existing organization:

1. It provides mutual reinforcement for a depressed social and economic group whose members heretofore have waged lonely fights, if they fought at all, against policies and procedures of the public agency with which they dealt.
2. It provides for participant representation in policy discussion, independent of social workers or any other surrogate spokesman.
3. It provides an associational tie for AFDC clients that can be their equivalent of the League of Women Voters or Planned Parenthood.[57]

The relatively limited focus of NWRO is at once its main strength and weakness. It has survived and been effective in part because, unlike the Poor People's Campaign, it did not spread itself too thin by trying to achieve several broad goals beyond the welfare system. At the same time, NWRO has not had much influence on the national scene; most of its accomplishments have been on the local level. Still, NWRO provides organization and leadership for the poor where little had existed before. It seems to be an important beginning in the emergence of the poor as an interest group.

Although some progress against poverty has been made in recent years, continued improvement will require some basic reshaping of American values

---

[55] Herbert J. Gans, *More Equality,* op. cit., pp. 134–135.
[56] Gilbert Y. Steiner, *The State of Welfare* (Washington, D.C.: The Brookings Institution, 1971), p. 281.
[57] Ibid., p. 285.

VARIABLES INFLUENCING CAPACITY TO EXERT POLITICAL PRESSURE

	The Poor (bottom income fifth)	The Affluent (middle income fifth)	The Rich (portion of top income fifth)
(1) Size of Population	large	quite large	relatively small
(2) Distribution of Population	rural and urban large mass in cores	urban, large mass in suburbs of large cities	rural and urban, relatively high degree of dispersion
(3) Level of Organization	low, fragmented	high: unions, professional associations, corporations, and trade associations	high: corporations and trade associations
(4) Type of Organization	fragmented, decentralized, loosely coordinated national confederations	highly centralized, tightly coordinated national confederations	highly centralized, overt and covert confederations
(5) Financial Resources	meager	great	very great
(6) Supportive Ideas	value of humanitarianism and some tenets of a Welfare Ethic	Work and Welfare Ethic, national interest, trickle down	national interest, trickle down
(7) Nonsupporting Beliefs	series of unfavorable stereotypes	none	mild conflict with Work Ethic and values of activism, achievement and freedom
(8) Lobbying Tradition	short	long	long
(9) Established Influence Channels	few	many	many

Jonathan H. Turner and Charles E. Starns, *Inequality: Privilege and Poverty in America* (Pacific Palisades, Calif.: Goodyear Publishing Co., Inc., 1976), p. 83.

and social structures. Some drastic changes in the structure of opportunities will have to be made to ensure that the poor do, in fact, escape poverty. Otherwise, the prized cultural value of equal opportunity must be recognized as an empty slogan for a substantial part of the American people.

Additional Readings

Baetz, Reuben C. "A Guaranteed Annual Income: Pie in the Sky?" *Public Welfare,* 28 (July 1970): 256–264.

Boulding, Kenneth E., and Martin Pfaff, eds. *Redistribution to the Rich and the Poor: The Grants Economics of Income Distribution.* Belmont, Calif.: Wadsworth Publishing Co., Inc., 1972.

Caplovitz, David. *The Poor Pay More: Consumer Practices of Low-Income Families.* New York: The Free Press, 1967.

Cootz, Stephanie, et al. *Life in Capitalist America: Private Property and Social Decay.* New York: Pathfinder Press, Inc., 1975.

Ferman, Louis A., Joyce L. Kornbluh, and Alan Haber, eds. *Poverty in America.* Ann Arbor: The University of Michigan Press, 1965.

Fishman, Leo, ed. *Poverty Amid Affluence.* New Haven: Yale University Press, 1966.

Gottschalk, Shimon S. "The Community-Based Welfare System: An Alternative to Public Welfare," *The Journal of Applied Behavioral Science,* 9 (March–June 1973): 233–242.

Harrington, Michael. *Socialism.* New York: Saturday Review Press, 1972.

Heilbroner, Robert L. *Between Capitalism and Socialism.* New York: Vintage Books, 1970.

Jencks, Christopher, et al. *Inequality: A Reassessment of the Effect of Family and Schooling in America.* New York: Basic Books, Inc., Publishers, 1972.

Lampman, Robert J. *Ends and Means of Reducing Income Poverty.* Chicago: Markham Publishing Company, 1971.

Larner, Jeremy, and Irving Howe, eds. *Poverty: Views from the Left.* New York: William Morrow & Co., Inc., 1968.

Liebow, Elliot. *Tally's Corner: A Study of Negro Streetcorner Men.* Boston: Little, Brown and Company, 1967.

Marris, Peter, and Martin Rein. *Dilemmas of Social Reform: Poverty and Community Action in the United States.* Chicago: Aldine Publishing Company, 1973.

Moynihan, Daniel P. *Maximum Feasible Misunderstanding.* New York: The Free Press, 1969.

———, ed. *On Understanding Poverty: Perspectives from the Social Sciences.* New York: Basic Books, Inc., Publishers, 1969.

Parker, Richard. *The Myth of the Middle Class.* New York: Harper & Row, Publishers, 1974.

"Poverty Status of Families Under Alternative Definitions of Income," Congress of the United States, Congressional Budget Office, Background Paper No. 17, January 1977.

Rainwater, Lee. *What Money Buys: Inequality and the Social Meanings of Income*. New York: Basic Books, Inc., Publishers, 1974.

Schiller, Bradley R. "Moving from Welfare to Workfare?" *Public Policy,* 21 (Winter 1973): 125–133.

Seligman, Ben B., ed. *Aspects of Poverty*. New York: Thomas Y. Crowell Company, 1968.

Stern, Philip M. "How 381 Super-Rich Americans Managed Not to Pay a Cent in Taxes Last Year," *The New York Times Magazine* (April 13, 1969): 30–31, 157–164.

Tawney, Richard H. *Equality*. New York: Capricorn Books, 1931.

Theobald, Robert. *Free Men and Free Markets*. New York: Clarkson N. Potter, Inc., 1963.

Thurow, Lester C., and Robert E. B. Lucas. "The American Distribution of Income: A Structural Problem," A Study for the Joint Economic Committee, Congress of the United States. Washington, D.C.: U.S. Government Printing Office, 1972.

Wogaman, Philip. *Guaranteed Annual Income*. Nashville, Tenn.: Abingdon Press, 1968.

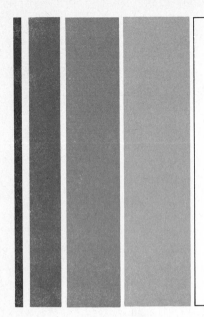

prejudice, discrimination, and inequality

Prejudice and discrimination are usually so firmly entrenched that people either are often unaware of their presence or rationalize away their existence. Many of the Founding Fathers could retain the slaves on which their wealth was based and still sign the Declaration of Independence which began with the idea that all people are created equal with the same "unalienable" rights. This contradiction was usually resolved through the belief that slaves were property rather than human beings. The ignorance and irrationality surrounding minority relations are two reasons why it is so difficult to combat these problems.

Racial resentment is real, deep, and sometimes explosive, but violence is only one consequence of prejudice and discrimination. Other consequences are physical and social segregation of minorities in such areas as employment, politics, and education. Such exclusion is experienced not only by black Americans. Ethnic minorities such as Italian-Americans, Irish-Americans, Spanish-speaking Americans, and Jews also have felt the sting of prejudice and unequal treatment in American society. More recently, attention has been called to other groups and categories of people who are subject to various negative consequences of prejudice and discrimination. These include women, the aged, the mentally and the physically handicapped, ex-convicts, drug addicts, and homosexuals.[1]

[1] Edward Saragin, ed., *The Other Minorities* (New York: John Wiley & Sons, Inc., 1971).

THE FOUNDING FATHERS ON SLAVERY

According to Professor Staughton Lynd: "Even the most liberal of the Founding Fathers were unable to imagine a society in which whites and Negroes would live together as fellow-citizens. Honor and intellectual consistency drove them to favor abolition; personal distaste, to fear it."

As Lynd points out, "Unable to summon the moral imagination required to transcend race prejudice, unwilling to contemplate social experiments which impinged on private property, the Fathers, unhappily, ambivalently, confusedly, passed by on the other side." The document which emerged as the Constitution would have nothing to say about eliminating the institution of slavery, accepted the notion of the Negro as property, and recognized no discrepancy between a democratic form of government and racial slavery; a document which created a government on the principle of checks and balances would provide no program for eventual freedom for slaves.

Reading the Declaration of Independence and the Constitution of the United States, one could never glean that there existed in America a total division between white and black barring the latter from participation in every aspect of societal activity. Although there was debate and argument over the problem of slavery in America, the outcome, as revealed by these two documents, is as if no debate had occurred at all.

The failure to nullify the institution of slavery, and to look for ways to encourage a unified American community was the decisive precedent for future developments in the evolution of the United States. By ignoring its greatest dilemma in favor of its most ignoble motives, America put off what would later extract its bloody toll in the Civil War, and maybe, again, today.

Barry N. Schwartz and Robert Disch, *White Racism* (New York: Dell Publishing Co., 1970), p. 23.

MINORITIES, PREJUDICE, AND DISCRIMINATION

What Is a Minority?

In everyday usage, *minority* refers to a relatively small number of people. Actually, a minority may not be numerically smaller than the majority. Blacks in South Africa and in parts of the Southern United States, for example, are considered to be minorities even though they outnumber whites.[2] There is obviously something more than size that distinguishes a minority. Louis Wirth notes some of these additional characteristics:

[2] George Eaton Simpson and J. Milton Yinger, *Racial and Cultural Minorities: An Analysis of Prejudice and Discrimination,* 4th ed. (New York: Harper & Row, Publishers, 1972), p. 11.

THE OTHER MINORITIES

Barbara was married right after graduating from college. Now five years and four kids later, she frequently becomes depressed and anxious. She believes she has everything a woman could ask for—a husband who makes a decent living, four healthy and active children, and a nice home. She thinks something must be very wrong with her. She is frightened because she cannot imagine what it could be.

Bill was just released from prison after serving a four-year term for armed robbery. Now 25 years old, he must start life outside prison all over again. Most of his old friends are gone, and those few he did locate shy away from associating with an "ex-con." He would like to hang around with the friends he made in prison, but if he gets caught at it he will be violating his parole and could get sent back.

Cosette is 75 years old. Her husband of almost 50 years died some time ago, as have all of her lifelong friends. She is increasingly lonely and lives for the infrequent visits from her son and his wife and their children. Considering her age, she is fairly healthy, but fears being a burden on others more than she fears death. Her Social Security benefits barely cover the expense of food and the rent on her small apartment.

Jack was bored with his life. At first drinking was something to do—it made his life a little more interesting. Now Jack has his first drink of the day right after he wakes up. By nightfall, he has already consumed almost a quart of whiskey.

Sandy is a bright 8-year-old. But he is causing increasing concern to his teacher and parents due to his "rebellious behavior." When he refused to do a disciplinary assignment of staying after school and writing a hundred times on the blackboard, "I will never talk to my neighbors during class again"—on the grounds that it was stupid and a waste of time—he was suspended. This and other similar incidents at home and at school are supporting the growing fears that Sandy's lack of respect for rules and authority indicates the presence of a potentially severe "behavior problem."

Laura is five feet, four inches tall and weighs almost 200 pounds. She has tried to diet many times, but has never been very successful at these attempts. She has a few close friends, but has become used to snickers or grunts of disgust from among the small crowds of students as she walks across the college campus. She has yet to be asked out on a date. When she becomes depressed over this situation, she always reacts the same way—she eats.

All of these people are *outsiders*. They are trapped in a system—socioeconomic, legal, or political—and stigmatized by societal attitudes.

Don Spiegel and Patricia Keith-Spiegel, *Outsiders, USA* (Corte Madera, Calif.: Rinehart Press, 1973), pp. xi, xii.

We may define a minority as a group of people who, because of their physical or cultural characteristics, are singled out from the others in the society in which they live for differential and unequal treatment, and who therefore regard themselves as objects of collective discrimination. The existence of a minority in a society implies the existence of a corresponding dominant group with higher social status and greater privileges. Minority status carries with it the exclusion from full participation in the life of the society.[3]

There are several key ideas in this definition of a minority. First, a minority must possess some distinctive physical or cultural characteristics that can be used to distinguish its members from the majority. Such characteristics are used both as a reminder to the majority that the minority is different and as a means for determining whether a given person is a member of a minority. This is more evident in the case of physical characteristics than it is for cultural ones. Culturally a person can "pass" as a member of the majority by a change in name, the shedding of an accent, or the adoption of the culture of the majority. Alterations in skin color and sex are more difficult to achieve.

A second element in Wirth's definition of a minority is that whatever its numerical size, the minority is dominated by the majority. This dominance is especially reflected in a society's stratification structure. In almost any society there are desired goods, services, and privileges. Because these "good things" are usually in limited supply, there is competition for them. The majority dominates largely because it has accumulated enough power to obtain an unequal share of the desired goods, services, and privileges. The dominant group can deny minority group members access to desirable resources by limiting opportunities to compete on an equal basis.

A final aspect of Wirth's definition is that members of a minority are denied equal treatment. The distinctive cultural or physical traits of a minority are usually judged by the majority to be inferior to their own. This presumed inferiority is then used as a justification for the unequal treatment given the minority.

The Nature of Prejudice and Discrimination

Prejudice refers to emotional attitudes that are based on limited personal experience. Prejudiced individuals are not open to new information that might

---

[3] Louis Wirth, "The Problem of Minority Groups," in Ralph Linton, ed., *The Science of Man in the World Crisis* (New York: Columbia University Press, 1945), p. 347.

Prejudice refers to attitudes. Discrimination is a prejudice attitude acted upon. (Top: courtesy of Joe Molnar; bottom: courtesy of Magnum.)

change such attitudes.[4] Prejudice involves an either/or type of logic: a group is either good or bad, and it is assumed that *each* member of the group possesses the characteristics attributed to the group. Prejudice involves overgeneralization based on biased or insufficient information. Such overgeneralizations are usually defended either by citing limited personal experiences with minority group members or by reciting stories told by others about their experiences. Because additional information is inadmissible, prejudiced attitudes are not altered either by new personal experiences or by accounts from others. When a person with a prejudiced attitude encounters contradictory evidence, the response is emotional.

Prejudice refers to attitudes. When a prejudiced attitude is acted upon, discrimination occurs. *Discrimination* refers to the unequal treatment of persons on the basis of their membership in some group. While prejudice does not always result in discrimination, it often does. Gordon Allport summarizes some of the major types of discrimination that may be the result of prejudice.

1. *Antilocution.* Most people who have prejudices talk about them. With like-minded friends, occasionally with strangers, they may express their antagonism freely. But many people never go beyond this. . . .
2. *Avoidance.* If the prejudice is more intense, it leads the individual to avoid members of the disliked group, even perhaps at the cost of considerable inconvenience. . . . The bearer of prejudice does not directly inflict harm upon the group he dislikes. He takes the burden of accommodation and withdrawal entirely upon himself.
3. *Discrimination.* Here the prejudiced person makes detrimental distinctions of an active sort. He undertakes to exclude all members of the group in question from certain types of employment, from residential housing, political rights, educational or recreational opportunities, churches, hospitals, or from some other social privileges.
4. *Segregation.* [This is] an institutionalized form of discrimination, enforced legally or by common custom.
5. *Physical attack.* Under conditions of heightened emotion, prejudice may lead to acts of violence or semiviolence. An unwanted Negro family may be forcibly ejected from a neighborhood, or so severely threatened [as to] leave in fear. Gravestones in Jewish cemeteries may be desecrated. The Northside's Italian gang may lie in wait for the Southside's Irish gang.
6. *Extermination.* Lynchings, pogroms, massacres, and the Hitlerian program of genocide mark the ultimate degree of violent expression of prejudice.[5]

---

[4] Simpson and Yinger, *Racial and Cultural Minorities,* op cit.; and Gordon W. Allport, *The Nature of Prejudice* (Garden City, N.Y.: Doubleday Anchor Books, 1958), pp. 3–16.

[5] Ibid.; pp. 14–15.

Prejudice is usually considered the cause of discrimination. However, discrimination may occur without prejudice. Some analysts go even further to contend that discrimination in some situations may be the cause of prejudice. For example, unskilled workers may believe that their jobs are in jeopardy because of the massive immigration of a new ethnic or racial group. This fear of economic threat may lead to the unequal treatment of members of that group. In order to justify this discrimination, threatened workers may attempt to show why the minority group deserves unequal treatment.[6] This occurs in part through the creation of stereotypes.

A *stereotype*—a set of ideas based on distortion, exaggeration, and over-simplification applied to all members of a group—msy be used as a justification for prejudiced attitudes and discrimination. An example is the colonists' treatment of the American Indians. Early relationships between the colonists and Indians were relatively peaceful and cooperative, but as the population of the colonies grew, conflicts became more frequent and intense. Population growth led to deeper and deeper penetration of whites into the wilderness. To rationalize this expansion, the colonists developed a stereotype of the Indians.

> It was easier to develop a picture of the lying, thieving, murdering savages, pagan in religion, racially stupid except for a kind of animal cunning. Such a person has no rights; the only good Indian is a dead Indian. . . . There were qualifications and exceptions and ambivalent feelings, of course. These were never strong enough, however, to prevent the continuing seizure of Indian lands with a minimum of compensation, the decimation of the Indian population to scarcely more than one-third its original size, and the development of a rationalizing prejudice that moved with the white man across the continent.[7]

CAUSES OF PREJUDICE AND DISCRIMINATION

Prejudice and discrimination against certain groups cannot be accounted for by any single factor; the causes are many, complex, and interrelated. Explanations for the existence of prejudice and discrimination can be classified into three broad categories: psychological explanations, the power differential explanation, and cultural explanations.

[6] Simpson and Yinger, *Racial and Cultural Minorities,* op. cit., p. 29.
[7] Ibid., pp. 111–12.

RACIAL STEREOTYPES

By the eighteenth century the physical and biological sciences had begun to develop rapidly. One of the most important developments was the effort to classify plants and animals systematically and in a uniform manner. Carolus von Linnaeus (1707–1778) devised a system with definite principles for defining genera and species and a uniform naming procedure. *Homo sapiens* was included as a major division of animal life.

For the subdivision *Homo sapiens,* Linnaeus chose skin color as the primary criterion but he also included temperament, customs, and habits. Of the six varieties that he described in his *A General System of Nature,* four correspond approximately to the populations of the major continents:

American   Copper-colored, choleric, erect
        Hair black, straight, thick; *nostrils* wide; *face* harsh; *beard*
        scanty; *obstinate,* content, free. *Paints* himself with fine red lines.
        Regulated by customs.
European   Fair, sanguine, brawny
        Hair yellow, brown, flowing; *eyes* blue; *gentle,* acute, inventive.
        Covered with close vestments. *Governed* by laws.
Asiatic   Sooty, melancholy, rigid
        Hair black; *eyes* dark; *severe,* haughty, covetous. *Covered* with
        loose garments. *Governed* by opinions.
African   Black phlegmatic, relaxed
        Hair black, frizzled; *skin* silky; *nose* flat; *lips* tumid; *crafty,* indolent, negligent. *Annoints* himself with grease. *Governed* by
        caprice. (1802, vol. 1, p. 9)

From B. Eugene Griessman, *Minorities* (New York: Holt, Rinehart and Winston, 1975), pp. 56–57.

Psychological Explanations

In psychological explanations of prejudice and discrimination, attention is focused on the prejudiced person's personality, how it developed, and how it functions in the present. The following questions may be asked about prejudiced persons: What was their relationship with their parents or with others significant to them? What are their values, attitudes, and beliefs? How high is their self-esteem? Two prominent psychological explanations of prejudice and discrimination are frustration-aggression and the authoritarian personality.

Frustration-Aggression. According to the frustration-aggression explanation, prejudice and discrimination may be the product of deep-seated hostility and aggression that stem from frustration.[8] This is most likely when hostility builds up that cannot be directed at the actual source of frustration. Pent-up hostility and frustration may be subsequently redirected toward some substitute object, which is less threatening than the one causing the frustration. These substitute objects, known as scapegoats, serve as convenient and less feared targets on which to place the blame for one's own troubles, frustrations, failures, or sense of guilt. John Dollard, the originator of the frustration-aggression explanation, contends that the frustrations experienced by the Germans after World War I help to account for their acceptance of anti-Semitism. Loss of the war, the disappearance of international prestige, forced acceptance of the Treaty of Versailles, and a ruined economy all contributed to tremendous frustration among the German people. Because direct aggression against the allies was not an alternative, they channelled their aggression on other targets, one of which was the Jews.[9] The best scapegoats are those who have already been singled out by the majority for unequal treatment and who, therefore, have the least chance to defend themselves.

The Authoritarian Personality. Another psychological explanation contends that there is a personality type—the authoritarian personality—that tends to be more prejudiced than other types. The authoritarian personality is said to be characterized by excessive conformity, submissiveness to authority figures, inflexibility, repression of impulses, desires, and ideas, fearfulness, and arrogance toward persons or groups thought to be inferior. T. W. Adorno and his colleagues, the originators of this theory, summarize it this way:

> The most crucial result of the . . . [study of the authoritarian personality] . . . is the demonstration of close correspondence in the type of approach and outlook a subject is likely to have in a great variety of areas, ranging from the most intimate features of family and sex adjustment through relationships to other people in general, to religion and to social and political philosophy. Thus a basically hierarchical, authoritarian, exploitative parent-child relationship is apt to carry over into a power-oriented, exploitatively dependent attitude toward one's sex partner and one's God and may well culminate in a political philosophy and social outlook which has no room for anything but a desperate

---

[8] John Dollard et al., *Frustration and Aggression* (New Haven, Conn.: Yale University Press, 1939).

[9] For another example, see Everett Cherrington Hughes, *French Canada in Transition* (Chicago: University of Chicago Press, 1943).

clinging to what appears to be strong and a disdainful rejection of whatever is relegated to the bottom.[10]

The Differential Power Explanation

Another theory—the differential power explanation—traces the existence of prejudice and discrimination to group interests rather than to personality needs. A majority may use prejudice and discrimination as weapons of power in the domination of a subordinate group. Such domination may be motivated by the majority's desire to gain or increase its control over scarce goods and services. Gerhard Lenski's theory of differential power contributes to our understanding of a majority's use of prejudice and discrimination as weapons of power in the domination of a minority.[11]

Two assumptions are crucial to Lenski's theory of differential power. First, it is assumed that when persons must make an important decision they will do so in a way favoring their own or their group's interests. Second, it is assumed that the demand for available desirable objects always exceeds supply. Humans, Lenski contends, will share the fruits of their labor, and will cooperate with others when that sharing and cooperating contributes to the survival of others whose productivity is necessary or helpful to them. If a group's survival or well-being depends upon others, then the competition with those others for desirable goods and services is muted. This was generally the case in preindustrial societies and is still true in hunting and gathering groups.

But what happens when there is a surplus of goods and services beyond the requirements for survival as is the case in modern industrial societies? Because important decisions are made on the basis of self or group interest, says Lenski, a surplus leads to conflict and competition. It is in this situation that power comes into play. According to Lenski, power determines who gets most of the desirable goods and services in societies with a sufficient surplus. The result of the competition for scarce goods and services is determined by the differential power held by various individuals and groups.

Lenski's ideas can be applied to minority relations. It can be argued that a majority uses prejudice and discrimination as weapons of power in the struggle for control over scarce goods and services. By dominating the subor-

[10] T. W. Adorno, Else Frenkel-Brunswik, Daniel J. Levinson, and R. Nevitt Sanford, *The Authoritarian Personality* (New York: Harper & Row, Publishers, 1950), p. 971.
[11] Gerhard Lenski, *Power and Privilege* (New York: McGraw-Hill Book Company, 1966).

dinate group through prejudice and discrimination, the majority can prevent a minority from being an effective competitor. Eliminating or neutralizing a minority group as a competitor is especially effective when the elites of a society are able to convince the nonelite members of the majority that a minority should be subjugated. In William Wilson's words:

> Of crucial importance . . . is the manner in which the ruling classes of the dominant racial group, particularly the segments controlling the government and the means of production, are able to get the masses to support and reinforce racial stratification even though the latter may not materially benefit from minority subjugation.[12]

The theory of differential power seems to fit the case of slavery in America. After the introduction of the cotton gin, the concept of the slave as a piece of property, devoid of human rights, became strengthened as political control over blacks was necessitated by the desire for profit. Out of political and economic need came an onslaught of prejudicial beliefs and attitudes about blacks:

> After 1830 an extensive literature to justify slavery appeared. It attempted to show that slavery was contrary neither to nature nor to religion, and that since the Negro was inferior and subhuman, it was even harmonious with democracy. Occasionally a writer would recognize the economic [and political] foundation of these beliefs.[13]

Prejudice and discrimination cannot be accounted for solely by psychological and differential power explanations. These explanations do not explain why particular groups are selected as targets for prejudice and discrimination. And they have nothing to say about why prejudice and discrimination are directed at some specific group even when no self-interest can be satisfied by doing so. Cultural explanations add to our understanding of the creation and persistence of prejudice and discrimination.

---

[12] William J. Wilson, *Power, Racism, and Privilege: Race Relations in Theoretical and Sociohistorical Perspectives* (New York: Macmillan Publishing Co., Inc., 1973), pp. 24–25. Also see Oliver C. Cox, *Caste, Class, and Race: A Study in Social Dynamics* (New York: Doubleday & Company, Inc., 1948); Carey McWilliams, *Brothers Under the Skin* (Boston: Little, Brown and Company, 1964); and Sidney M. Wilhelm, *Who Needs the Negro?* (Cambridge, Mass.: Schenkman, 1970).

[13] Simpson and Yinger, *Racial and Cultural Minorities*, op. cit., p. 114.

Cultural Explanations

Culture refers to humanly created patterns of thinking, feeling, and behaving. Culture is created by people and it must be learned by people. *Socialization* is the process through which culture is transmitted to new members of a society. Prejudice and discrimination, just like other aspects of culture, are learned through socialization. Members of a society or group tend to believe that their ways of thinking, feeling, and behaving are the best. This viewpoint, called *ethnocentrism,* usually leads people to judge as inferior those who think, feel, and behave differently from them. Such judgments are often expressed as prejudices and discrimination.

Socialization. Members of a group learn to be prejudiced in much the same way that they learn the countless other aspects of their culture. Gordon Allport describes two stages in the learning of prejudice.[14] In the first stage, the pregeneralized learning period, children have not yet learned to generalize as do adults. The idea that blacks, Jews, and Chicanos each form a distinct grouping is beyond their understanding. When a child hears a parent object to people of some specific group moving into the neighborhood, he is introduced to the second stage of learning prejudice, that of total rejection. By this stage, the child has learned the name of the group he is supposed to dislike and can identify those individuals who belong to it. When a child reaches the second stage, all members of the minority group are rejected, on all counts, in all situations. Robert Blake and Wayne Dennis graphically illustrate the total rejection stage in their study which included fourth- and fifth-graders in an all-white Southern school.[15] Faced with a list of questions about the virtues of blacks and whites (for example, "Who is more cheerful?" "Who is more cruel?" "Who is more emotional?") these children thought that nearly all virtues were the exclusive property of their own kind. They thought, for example, that blacks were less cheerful than whites, were less easy-going, and had less of a sense of humor.

Learning to be prejudiced or, in Allport's terms, to move from the pregeneralization to the total rejection stage is not always simple or automatic. Some children do not succumb to the teachings, threats, punishments, and

---

[14] Allport, *The Nature of Prejudice,* op. cit., pp. 292–95.

[15] Robert Blake and Wayne Dennis, "The Development of Stereotypes Concerning the Negro," *Journal of Abnormal and Social Psychology,* 38 (October 1943): 525–31.

Prejudice must be learned. (Courtesy of the United Nations, photo by J. Ralph.)

racial and ethnic jokes to which they are exposed. Others deliberately reject the prejudice that surrounds them. Still others become prejudiced only after long years of exposure. However, because children are so emotionally and physically dependent on their parents, and because they need to belong to some of the groups around them, they are often bent to the prejudiced will of their parents and peers.

Ethnocentrism.   Ethnocentrism is the judgment by members of one group that their ways of thinking, feeling, and behaving are superior to those of other groups. Ethnocentrism involves judging the characteristics of members of other groups by the cultural standards of one's own group. Ethnocentrism exists in virtually all groups and societies, largely because of successful socialization. Members of a group are taught the ''rightness'' of their culture from many sources, including their parents, church, and friends. The fact that members of a minority group may dress differently, eat different kinds of food, and worship God in a way different from the majority group may be used as an indication of the minority's inferiority.

Ethnocentrism usually involves considerable distortion of the nature of the outside group. Such distortions are perpetuated through the creation of stereotypes. Stereotypes, linked as they are to ethnocentrism, serve as a justification for prejudiced attitudes and discriminatory behavior.

PREJUDICE AND DISCRIMINATION IN AMERICA

The Melting Pot

Almost from the beginning, the United States was regarded as a gigantic "melting pot" in which a wide variety of ethnic and racial groups were to mix and produce a unified national culture shared by all Americans. A key ingredient of this mixture was equality for all, regardless of race, religion, or culture. Milton Gordon describes the historical origin of the melting pot concept in America:

> While Anglo-conformity, in various guises, has probably been the most prevalent ideology of assimilation in the American historical experience, a competing viewpoint with more generous and idealistic overtones has had its adherents and exponents from the eighteenth century onward. Conditions in the virgin continent were modifying the institutions which the English colonists brought with them from the mother country. Immigrants from non-English homelands, such as Germany, Sweden, and France, were similarly exposed to this fresh environment. Was it not possible, then, to think of the evolving American society not simply as a slightly modified England but rather as a totally new blend, culturally and biologically, in which the stocks and folkways of Europe were, figuratively speaking, indiscriminately mixed in the political pot of the emerging nation and melted together by the fires of the American influence and interaction into a distinctly new type?[16]

The melting pot survives as a myth, but a unified national culture shared by all did not emerge, and equality of social and economic opportunity was not granted to all ethnic and racial groups. Those immigrants most like

THE MELTING POT MISUNDERSTOOD

Archie Bunker: When I was a kid we didn't have no race problem—an' you know why? Nobody called themselves Chicanos. Or Mexican-Americans, or Afro-Americans. *We was all American* . . . Then after that if a guy was a Spic or a Jig it was *his* business. I mean it was his business, if he wanted to cling with his own kind. Which most of them did. That's how you get your Harlem and your Chinatown and your Little Italy.

The Wit and Wisdom of Archie Bunker, (New York: Popular Library, 1971), p. 183.

[16] Milton M. Gordon, *Assimilation in American Life: The Role of Race, Religion, and National Origins* (New York: Oxford University Press, Inc., 1964), p. 115.

THE MELTING POT REJECTED

"The ethnic problem within the United States at some point has to emerge simply because we were lied to, accepted the lie, and there is no greater danger to a man than when he fools himself. We expect the opposition to fool us; but when we fool ourselves we are in deep trouble. We consistently have fallen for the old melting pot concepts. But there *never* was a melting pot; there is not *now* a melting pot; there never will be a melting pot; and if there were, it would be such a tasteless soup that we would have to go back and start all over!"

Bayard Rustin (April, 1972)

From Michael Novak, "The New Ethnicity," *Humanist*, 33 (1973): 18.

Anglo-Saxons found it easier to become part of the mainstream of American society and to become socially and economically successful. Because various Scandinavian peoples, for example, shared in the cultural and racial characteristics of the Anglo-Saxons, they were able to overcome the barriers to assimilation. Other immigrant groups such as Puerto Ricans, blacks, Jews, and Eastern European peoples have found integration into American society much more difficult.

Racial and ethnic diversity is still very much a part of America. Despite efforts by the federal government and other organizations, prejudice and discrimination against minorities still operate to their disadvantage.

Consequences of Prejudice and Discrimination

The costs of prejudice and discrimination to their victims can be documented in the areas of housing, law, politics, employment, education, income, as well as in human, psychological terms. Prominent victims of prejudice and discrimination in America today are blacks, Indians, Spanish-speaking people, and women.

Blacks

Blacks are the largest of America's minorities, numbering about 24 million, or 11 per cent of the total population. They are also one of the oldest minorities; the first blacks were brought to the United States in 1619. Despite both

BLACKS AND INTERNAL COLONIALISM

There appear to be four basic components of the colonization complex. The first component is the mode of entry into the dominant society. Colonization begins with a forced, involuntary entry. Second, there is the impact on culture. The effects of colonization on the culture and social organization of the colonized people are more than the results of such "natural" processes as contact and acculturation. The colonizing power carries out a policy that constrains, transforms, or destroys indigenous values, orientations, and ways of life. Third is a special relationship to governmental bureaucracies or the legal order. The lives of the subordinate group are administered by representatives of the dominant power. The colonized have the experience of being managed and manipulated by outsiders who look down on them.

   The final component of colonization is racism. Racism is a principle of social domination by which a group seen as inferior or different in alleged biological characteristics is exploited, controlled, and oppressed socially and psychically by a superordinate group.

   . . . Many ethnic groups in America have lived in ghettos. What makes the black ghettos an expression of colonized status are three special features. First, the ethnic ghettos arose more through voluntary choice: the choice to immigrate to America and the choice to live among fellow ethnics. Second, the immigrant ghettos of the inner city were one- or two-generation phenomena—way stations along the road of acculturation and assimilation. When ethnic communities persist, they tend to reflect voluntary decisions to live among one's fellows and maintain group institutions, as in the case of the so-called "gilded ghettos" of the Jewish suburban middle class. The black ghettos . . . have been more permanent, though their boundaries expand and change and some individuals do escape them. But most relevant is the third point, that black communities are, to a great extent, controlled from the outside. For many Europeans—the Poles, Italians, and Jews, for example—there was only a brief period, often less than a generation, during which their residential buildings, commercial stores, and other enterprises were owned by outsiders. Afro-Americans are distinct in the extent to which their segregated communities have remained under outside control: economic, political, and administrative.

Robert Blauner, *Racial Oppression in America,* (New York: Harper & Row, Publishers, 1972), pp. 84, 86.

these facts, a disproportionate percentage of blacks remain near the bottom of the stratification structure.

   Why have blacks remained a target of prejudice and discrimination for so long? One reason is that blacks are physically identifiable. It has been much more difficult for them to be absorbed into the larger society than it has been for white minorities.

A second reason lies in the nature of slavery in America. According to Frank Tannenbaum, the attitudes and practices associated with *manumission*—the transition from slave to free person—are the most important aspects of any slave system:

> the case of manumission bespeaks, even if only implicitly, a friendly attitude toward the person whose freedom is thus made possible and encouraged, just as the systematic obstruction of manumission implies a complete, if unconscious, attitude of hostility to those whose freedom is opposed or denied.[17]

Under the law in the United States, slavery was generally a permanent condition. Manumission existed, but support for it was weak, and there were numerous barriers to it. Freed slaves constantly ran the risk of being returned to slavery. For instance, in Maryland in 1717, any freed slave who married a white person was returned to slavery for life. In Virginia, an emancipated slave could be sold into slavery again if still in the state after one year.[18] Those slaves who did manage to gain and keep their freedom were barred from most jobs and were denied such basic rights as owning property, holding public office, and voting.

As a consequence of the nature of the American form of slavery, slaves freed prior to the Civil War were denied upward social mobility. According to Richard Hofstadter:

> the Anglo-Americans of the North American mainland quickly became committed to sharp race separation, took a forbidding view of manumission, defined mulattoes simply as Negroes, and made outcasts of free Negroes. Hence there was as little upward mobility from slavery as possible, especially in the Southern colonies and states, and even where masters chose to manumit slaves.[19]

The denial of opportunity for upward mobility did not end with the Civil War. Although slavery was then legally abolished, the legacy of prejudice and discrimination produced by American slavery affects black Americans to this day. This is reflected in the gap between blacks and whites in education, income, and employment.

[17] Frank Tannenbaum, *Slave and Citizen: The Negro in the Americas* (New York: Alfred A. Knopf, Inc., 1947), p. 69.
[18] Ibid., pp. 67–68.
[19] Richard Hofstadter, *America at 1750: A Social Portrait* (New York: Vintage Books, 1973), p. 114.

SEGREGATION REMEMBERED

"Like most black Americans, my roots are in the South." So writes TIME *Atlanta Correspondent Jack White, 30, who reported on many of the stories in this issue before taking nine months' leave for a Nieman Fellowship at Harvard. Here is White's personal account of being brought up under segregation:*

My father's father was born a slave somewhere near Savannah, Ga. My mother's father was the son of a white undertaker and his mulatto concubine in a small town in North Carolina.

Like many other blacks, my parents migrated North to find education and better opportunities. My father went to Howard University medical school, and my mother went to Howard's nursing school. My parents wanted to shelter their children from segregation and all its belittling aspects, so they settled in Washington, which turned out to be as segregated a city as one could find.

In the 1950s, a clerk in a department store refused to let me sip from a water fountain, despite my mother's plea that "he's just a little boy." Later, when my family got its first television set, I was entranced by the ads for Glen Echo amusement park. My mother couldn't really explain why she couldn't take me there. The reason, of course, was that Glen Echo did not admit blacks. Nor did many restaurants, movie theaters and other public facilities.

My deepest realization of what the Old South was really like came in about 1962, when my father, brother, a friend and I drove South to my grandmother's house in Stuart, Fla. On the way we were denied a room in a Holiday Inn in Savannah, and wound up sleeping in a "rooming house" (read whorehouse) that hadn't had an overnight guest in years. In Stuart, my father went into a hardware store to buy a Thermos bottle. The white clerk asked my dad, a distinguished professor of surgery at least 20 years his senior, "What you want, boy?" My father struggled to maintain his dignity as he told the clerk what he wanted. I felt in my gut, for the first time, how hard it had been for black men to preserve their self-respect under a rigid system of white supremacy.

Time, September 27, 1976, p. 48.

Although the gap in education has gradually decreased since 1960, it is still true that a higher percentage of whites than blacks graduate from high school. As of the mid-1970s, the black rate of high school completion was 72 per cent compared to 85 per cent for whites.[20] On the college level, the difference between blacks and whites not only is wide, but is increasing

[20] "The State of Black America 1977," National Urban League, Inc., January 11, 1977, p. 15.

WHAT IT MEANS TO BE BLACK IN AMERICA TODAY

Being black in America means quite probably the inheritance of inequality in virtually every aspect of life that makes a difference. Much the same also can be said for Mexican, Puerto Rican, and American Indian people living in the U.S. . . . These are some of the hard facts of race and what it means to be black in the U.S. today:

- The chances are 1 in 3 that you will be poor, compared with 1 in 10 for white persons.
- There is almost twice the likelihood, as compared with whites, that you will be unemployed and an even greater likelihood that you will be underemployed.
- The chances are 1 in 10 of being a professional or a manager, compared with 3 in 10 among whites.
  The chances are 1 out of 5 that, if you are a black woman who is working, it will be as a domestic; if you are a man, it will be the same chance that you are working as an unskilled laborer.
- If you are between the ages of 14 and 19, there is about 1 chance in 6 that you are a high school dropout, compared with about 1 chance in 13 if you were white.
- If you are a black mother, yours could be one of the 23 out of every 1,000 infants that will die within the first month of life, compared with a rate of 14.7 per 1,000 for whites.
- For every 1,000 unmarried black women, there are 86.6 illegitimate births, compared with a much lower 13.2 for every 1,000 unmarried white women. The rate for black women, by the way, has fallen in the last decade while it has increased sharply for white women.
- For every 100,000 black women, 849 of them have been the victims of a violent crime, compared with 164 white women. For men, the respective rates are 523 and 394.

Leonard Reissman, *Inequality in American Society* (Pacific Palisades, Cal.: Goodyear Publishing Company, Inc., 1976), pp. 71–72.

slightly.[21] The percentage of white college graduates is two and a half times greater than the percentage of black college graduates.[22]

Blacks also lag behind whites in the area of employment. The employment situation can be summarized as follows:

[21] *The Social and Economic Status of the Black Population in the United States, 1973, Current Population Reports,* Special Studies Series P-23, No. 48, U.S. Department Of Commerce, Social and Economic Statistics Administration, Bureau of the Census (Washington, D.C.: U.S. Government Printing Office, 1974), p. 69.
[22] "The State of Black America 1977," op. cit., p. 17.

black men and women continued to be overrepresented in lower-paying, less-skilled jobs and underrepresented in better-paying, higher-skilled jobs. . . . [B]lack workers . . . represented about 6 per cent of the professional and technical workers, 3 per cent of the managers and administrators, and 6 per cent of the craft and kindred workers. In marked contrast, they made up about 20 per cent of the nonfarm laborers and a similar proportion of service workers.[23]

The disadvantage of blacks compared to whites can also be seen in unemployment. Black joblessness is about twice as high as that among whites. The unemployment rate among blacks stands at 13 per cent. However, when "hidden unemployment"—discouraged workers and persons with part-time jobs who prefer full-time jobs—is considered, the actual rate of black unemployment approaches the Depression figure of one out of every four workers.[24] It is among black teenagers that the greatest unemployment problem exists. According to the latest official statistics, two out of every five black teenagers are unemployed. Taking hidden unemployment into account, it is estimated that 60 per cent of all black teen-agers are unsuccessfully looking for full-time work.[25] Consequently, thousands of black youths are becoming adults without job experiences so vital to securing steady jobs in the future.

Black income is about 61 per cent that of whites. This means that in terms of averages, for every $100 a white family earns, a black family earns $61.[26] The discrepancy between black and white income is brought into sharper focus when educational and occupational levels are considered. Table 3.1 shows that while income tends to rise with educational level for both blacks and whites, it increases much less for black males (and women of both races) than for white males. At each level of schooling, black males earn less than their white peers. More startling is the fact that white male high school dropouts have higher incomes than black males with high school diplomas. White high school graduates, on the average, earn nearly as much each year as black males with 18 or more years of education. It should be noted that black women appear to improve their earning power through education to a greater extent than white women. This, however, is probably because a larger percentage of black women are employed full-time.

[23] *The Social and Economic Status of the Black Population in the United States, 1973,* op. cit., p. 51.
[24] "The State of Black America 1977," op. cit., p. 1.
[25] Ibid.
[26] "We the Black Americans," U.S. Department of Commerce, Social and Economic Statistics Administration, Bureau of the Census (Washington, D.C.: U.S. Government Printing Office, 1973), p. 7.

Table 3-1. Income Disparities by Sex, Race, and Education (Total Money Income includes full- and part-time workers, 25 and over, March 1975)

Mean Income	Total	Years of Schooling					
		7 or less	8	9–11	12	13–15	18 or more
White Males with Income	$11,902	$6,114	$ 7,816	$ 9,987	$12,010	$13,591	$17,499
Black Males with Income	$ 7,240	$4,595	$ 5,957	$ 7,146	$ 8,877	$ 9,631	$11,360
Mean Income, Full-Time Males	$14,119	$8,829	$10,334	$11,751	$13,299	$15,134	$20,582
White Females with Income	$ 4,692	$2,730	$ 3,150	$ 3,908	$ 4,760	$ 5,541	$ 7,546
Black Females with Income	$ 4,129	$2,277	$ 2,669	$ 3,748	$ 4,787	$ 5,909	$ 8,874
Mean Income, Full-Time Females	$ 7,794	NA	NA	$ 5,605	$ 7,070	$ 8,087	$ 9,757

Spanish-Speaking Americans

Spanish-speaking Americans, numbering just over 11 million, are a diverse group that includes Mexican Americans, Puerto Ricans, Cubans, and persons from Central or South America.[27] Because of this diversity, it is misleading to speak of Spanish-speaking Americans as a homogeneous group. For this reason, Mexican Americans, Puerto Ricans, and Cubans are sometimes distinguished in the following discussion.

Like blacks, Spanish-speaking Americans are far behind white Americans in formal education. The median educational level for the total American population is 12 years, or high school graduation, but for all Spanish-speaking Americans it is less than 10 years.[28]

Spanish-speaking American workers are concentrated in the lowest-level jobs offering the least chance for upward mobility. Over two thirds of all Spanish-speaking American male workers are in blue-collar and service jobs, and less than one fourth are in white-collar positions. Their joblessness is almost double that of whites.[29]

[27] For a demographic analysis of America's Spanish-speaking ethnic groups, see U.S. Bureau of the Census, *Current Population Reports,* P-20, No. 302, "Persons of Spanish Origin in the United States: March 1976" (Washington, D.C.: U.S. Government Printing Office, 1976).

[28] Paul M. Ryscavage and Earl F. Mellor, "The Economic Situation of Spanish-Americans," *Monthly Labor Review,* 96 (April 1973): p. 8.

[29] Roberta V. McKay, "Americans of Spanish Origin in the Labor Force: An Update," *Monthly Labor Review,* 99 (September 1976): 3.

Table 3-2. Median Earnings of Men and Women 16 Years Old and Over, by Occupation, for Whites and Persons of Spanish Heritage, Selected States, 1970

Sex and Occupation	Five Southwestern States			Three Middle Atlantic States			Florida		
	White	Spanish American[1]	Spanish as a Per Cent of White	White	Spanish American[2]	Spanish as a Per Cent of White	White	Spanish American[3]	Spanish as a Per Cent of White
Men:									
Total experienced labor force	$ 8,069	$5,963	74	$ 8,270	$5,474	66	$ 7,169	$5,621	78
Professional, managerial and kindred workers	11,482	9,195	80	11,874	7,441	63	10,010	8,425	84
Craftsmen, foremen, and kindred workers	8,471	7,125	84	8,569	6,274	73	7,378	6,226	84
Operatives	6,987	5,959	85	7,220	5,239	73	5,691	4,991	88
Laborers, except farm	4,513	4,523	100	5,799	5,005	86	3,411	3,965	116
Farmers and farm managers	5,373	4,663	87	5,344	4,468	84	5,595	8,022	143
Farm laborers except unpaid and farm foremen	3,333	3,123	94	2,987	2,807	94	3,495	2,706	77
Women:									
Total experienced labor force	$ 3,868	3,065	79	4,054	3,868	95	3,553	3,222	91
Clerical and kindred workers	4,411	3,847	81	4,577	4,478	98	3,964	3,761	95
Operatives	3,480	3,151	91	3,721	3,594	97	3,101	3,139	101

[1] Persons of Spanish language or surname, primarily Mexican Americans.
[2] Persons of Puerto Rican birth or parentage.
[3] Persons of Spanish language, primarily Cubans.
Reprinted from Paul M. Ryscavage and Earl F. Mellor, "The Economic Situation of Spanish Americans," *Monthly Labor Review*, 96 (April 1973): 6. Original source was U.S. Department of Labor, Manpower Administration, special tabulations from the 1970 Census.

The income of Spanish-speaking Americans is well below that of whites in general. Although only 10 per cent of the total population is below the poverty line, one fourth of Spanish-speaking families are poor.[30] Among males, Puerto Ricans earn about 66 per cent as much as whites, Mexican-Americans earn approximately 75 per cent as much as their white peers, and Cubans earn nearly 80 per cent as much as all employed whites (see Table 3-2). Moreover, the greatest disparity in earnings between whites and Spanish-speaking Americans occurred at the higher occupational levels. The general earnings gap between white women and Spanish-speaking women is not quite as large as it is for men. However, Spanish-speaking women are even more concentrated in lower-level jobs than are males.

American Indians

Indians, currently numbering almost 800,000, are America's most disadvantaged minority. Over the years the federal government has vacillated from a policy of complete paternalism to one of almost total neglect. Both alternatives have left American Indians outside the mainstream of social and economic opportunity.

Almost half of all American Indians live in cities. For several reasons, including lack of education and job skills, prejudice, and discrimination, Indians have not fared much better in the cities than on reservations. Jonathan Turner sums up both past and present Indian policy as follows:

> the legacy of economic exploitation, especially the great "land grabs" by whites in this century, has forced Indians into urban areas because they can no longer support themselves on their reservations. Yet the legacy of isolation on the reservation prevents many Indians from making the cultural and psychological transition to urban, industrial life. And the burden of change has been placed on the *individual Indian,* for white institutions—from factories to labor unions and welfare agencies—display little flexibility in adjusting to Indian patterns. The contemporary Indian is therefore faced with impoverishment no matter what course of action he chooses: to stay on the reservations results in poverty, but to leave the reservation and encounter the hostile white economic system in urban areas also results in poverty.[31]

[30] "Persons of Spanish Origin in the United States: March 1976," op. cit., p. 11.
[31] Jonathan H. Turner, *American Society: Problems of Structure* (New York: Harper & Row, Publishers, 1972), p. 112.

The truth of Turner's words is mirrored in a 1973 report on Indian affairs by the then secretary of the interior, Rogers Morton. His statement underscores the philosophy that, despite the barriers created by prejudice and discrimination, Indians must compete on the white world's terms:

> It seems to me this is a prayer [for the social and economic integration of Indians into American society] that can be answered—not only by the actions of a committed government and people, but more by the Indian himself climbing steadily rung by rung from a base of opportunity unmatched for any group in the society of the world.[32]

If the Indians are "climbing steadily rung by rung," they are on a very short ladder.[33] Although the level of education among Indians improved somewhat during the 1960s, the median number of school years completed for the total Indian population is still less than 10 years; only 33 per cent are high school graduates, and less than 4 per cent have college degrees. The unemployment rate of American Indians is twice as high as it is for the total civilian labor force.

Table 3-3 shows the major occupational categories in which American Indians were employed in 1960 and 1970. They have made only scant penetration into the upper levels of the occupational structure. Although some gains were made during the 1960s, only 16 per cent of all employed American Indian males and 13 per cent of all employed Indian females are in professional, technical, managerial, or administrative positions. At this time, about 60 per cent of the employed males are in blue-collar jobs (craftsmen, foremen, operatives, and nonfarm laborers). More than two thirds of Indian women are concentrated in clerical, operative, and service jobs.

As of 1970, 63 per cent of American Indian males earned less than $6,000 a year. Only 9 per cent earned $10,000 or more annually, the median

---

[32] "Secretary of the Interior Morton Reports on Indian Matters," U.S. Department of the Interior, Office of Communications, Washington, D.C., March, 1973.

[33] The following summary of education, employment, and income among American Indians is based on these sources: U.S. Bureau of the Census, *Census of Population: 1960,* Subject Reports, *Nonwhite Population by Race,* Final Report PC (2)-IC (Washington D.C.: U.S. Government Printing Office, 1963), pp. 12, 26, 104; U.S. Bureau of the Census, *Census of Population: 1970,* Subject Reports, *American Indians,* Final Report PC (2)-IF (Washington, D.C.: U.S. Government Printing Office, 1973), pp. 18, 27, 111, 120; "We, the First Americans," U.S. Department of Commerce, Social and Economic Statistics Administration, Bureau of the Census (Washington, D.C.: U.S. Government Printing Office, June 1973); and "American Indians in Transition," U.S. Department of Agriculture, Economic Research Service, Agricultural Economic Report No. 283, Washington, D.C., April 1975.

Table 3-3. Employment of American Indians in 1960 and 1970 by Major Occupational Categories

Major Occupational Categories	1960[1]		1970[2]	
	Males	Females	Males	Females
Professional, technical and kindred workers	4.2%	6.9%	9.7%	10.6%
Managers and administrators, except farm	2.4	1.5	6.0	2.7
Sales workers	1.3	2.7	2.3	2.6
Clerical and kindred workers	2.8	10.7	5.4	23.2
Craftsmen, foremen, and kindred workers	13.1	0.1	24.3	3.3
Operatives, including transport	18.6	11.5	24.4	17.7
Laborers, except farm	17.1	1.3	11.6	1.4
Farmers and farm managers	8.0	2.0	2.6	1.2
Farm laborers and foremen	11.9	5.9	4.5	1.8
Service workers, except private household	5.1	19.6	9.1	28.6
Private household workers	0.3	12.7	0.1	6.7
Occupation not reported	15.4	24.1	—	—

SOURCE: U.S. Bureau of the Census, 1960 and 1970.
[1] Figures refer to the major occupational categories for employed males and females.
[2] Figures refer to the major occupational category of employed male and female heads of households.

income level of the United States population at the time of the last census. Forty per cent of all Indians are below the federally established poverty line.

Women

Women numerically constitute a majority. Nevertheless, as noted at the beginning of this chapter, there is more to being a minority than numbers.[34] In 1944, the Swedish economist, Gunnar Myrdal, in *An American Dilemma*, drew a parallel between the social and economic situation of blacks and women.[35] He contended that American blacks and women are victims of a paternalistically dominated society and quotes from George Fitzhugh's *Sociology for the South* to illustrate his point:

> A beautiful example and illustration . . . is found in the instance of the Patriarch Abraham. His wives and his children, his men servants and his maid ser-

[34] The idea that women are a minority group is not a new idea generated by the women's liberation movement. For an early and excellent call for viewing women as a minority group, see Helen Mayer Hacker, "Women as a Minority Group," *Social Forces*, 30 (October 1951): 60–69.

[35] Gunnar Myrdal, *An American Dilemma* (New York: Harper & Row, Publishers, 1944), pp. 1073–78.

SEX ROLE STEREOTYPES

Characteristics	Masculine Traits	Feminine Traits
Physical	Virile, athletic, strong, sloppy, worry less about appearance and aging, brave	Weak, helpless, dainty, non-athletic, worry about appearance and aging, sensual, graceful
Functional	Breadwinner, provider	Domestic, maternal, church-going
Sexual	Sexually aggressive, experienced, single status acceptable, male "caught" by female	Virginal, inexperienced, double standard, must be married, female "catches" spouse, sexually passive, uninterested, responsible for birth control, seductive, flirtations
Emotional	unemotional, stoic, doesn't cry	Emotional, sentimental, romantic, can cry, expressive, compassionate, nervous, insecure, fearful
Intellectual	Logical, intellectual, rational, objective, scientific, practical, mechanical, public awareness, contributor to society, dogmatic	Scatterbrained, frivolous, shallow, inconsistent, intuitive, impractical, perceptive, sensitive, "arty," idealistic, humanistic
Interpersonal	Leader, dominating, disciplinarian, independent, free, individualistic, demanding	Petty, flirty, coy, gossipy, catty, sneaky, fickle, dependent, over-protected, responsive, status conscious, competitive, refined, adept at social graces, follower, subservient, submissive
Other Personal	Aggressive, success-oriented, ambitious, proud, egotistical, confident, moral, trustworthy, decisive, competitive, uninhibited, adventurous	Self-conscious, easily intimidated, modest, shy, sweet, patient, vain, affectionate, gentle, tender, soft, not aggressive, quiet, passive, tardy, innocent, non-competitive

SOURCE: Janet Saltzman Chafetz, *Masculine/Feminine or Human?* (Itasca, Ill.: F. E. Peacock Publishers, Inc., 1974), pp. 35–36. Reprinted by permission of the publisher.

vants, his camels and his cattle, were all equally his property. He could sacrifice Isaac or a ram, just as he pleased. He loved and protected all, and all shared, if not equally, at least fairly, in the products of their light labour. Who would not desire to have been a slave of that old Patriarch, stern and despotic as he was? . . . Pride, affection, self-interest moved Abraham to protect, love, and take care of his slaves. The same motives operate on all masters and secure comfort, competency, and protection to the slave. A man's wife and children are his slaves, and do they not enjoy, in common with himself, his property.[36]

This legacy still influences the social and economic conditions under which contemporary American women live.

Despite the dramatic increase in female participation in the labor market, women are still concentrated in lower-level jobs. More than 40 per cent of all employed women are in clerical and sales jobs, just over one fifth are service workers, and approximately 15 per cent are blue-collar workers (craftsmen, foremen, machine operators, laborers). Women are underrepresented in higher-status occupations; only about 15 per cent are in professional and technical occupations and only 5 per cent are managers or administrators. Moreover, most of those women in professional occupations are either noncollege teachers, nurses, or medical technicians.[37]

There is a wide discrepancy between the earnings of American men and women. On the average, women earn about half that earned by men.[38] The discrepancy between the income of males and females is increasing. In the mid-1950s, the average income for full-time women workers was 63 per cent of the median income of men. By 1973, the income of women had fallen to 57 per cent of that earned by men.[39] (See Table 3-4.) The earnings gap between women and men persists regardless of occupation and education. (See Table 3-5.)

[36] George Fitzhugh, *Sociology for the South* (Richmond, Va.: A. Morris, Publisher, 1854), p. 297.

[37] Detailed reviews of the occupational distribution of women are presented in Elizabeth Waldman and Beverly J. McEaddy, ''Where Women Work—An Analysis of Industry and Occupation,'' *Monthly Labor Review,* 97 (May 1974): 3–13; and *1975 Handbook on Women Workers,* U.S. Department of Labor, Employment Standards Administration, Women's Bureau, Bulletin 297, 1975.

[38] Dixie Sommers, ''Occupational Rankings for Men and Women by Earnings,'' *Monthly Labor Review,* 97 (August 1974): 34–51; and *1975 Handbook on Women Workers,* op. cit., p. 127.

[39] Ibid., 131. Also, see Fabian Linden, *Women: A Demographic, Social, and Economic Presentation* (New York: The Conference Board, 1973).

Table 3-4.   Earnings of Workers by Income Class and Sex
(Year-round, full-time workers, 1971)

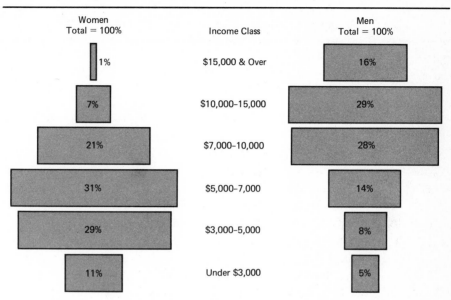

Women Total = 100%	Income Class	Men Total = 100%
1%	$15,000 & Over	16%
7%	$10,000–15,000	29%
21%	$7,000–10,000	28%
31%	$5,000–7,000	14%
29%	$3,000–5,000	8%
11%	Under $3,000	5%

SOURCE: Fabian Linden, *Women: A Demographic, Social and Economic Presentation* (New York: The Conference Board, 1973), p. 30.

Psychological Costs of Prejudice and Discrimination

Minorities are the victims of more than social and economic damage. Although less visible and harder to detect, prejudice and discrimination carry psychological costs, the most important of which are a damaged sense of self-worth, self-hatred, and hatred of one's own group. These negative attitudes are a result of the minority group's acceptance of their rejection by the majority. Minority members may become so well socialized that they may subscribe to the negative images of themselves perpetuated by the majority.

Studies have revealed that minority children identify with majority children whereas majority children prefer their own kind.[40] Many studies have

[40] For a brief review of these studies, see J. Kenneth Morland, ''Race Awareness among American and Hong Kong Chinese Children,'' *American Journal of Sociology,* 75 (November 1969): 360–374. The most famous of these studies is Kenneth B. Clark and Mamie P. Clark, ''Skin Color as a Factor in Racial Identifications of Negro Pre-School Children,'' *Journal of Social Psychology,* 11 (February 1940): 159–169.

Table 3-5. Median Income of Workers by Selected Characteristics (Year-round, full-time workers, 1971)

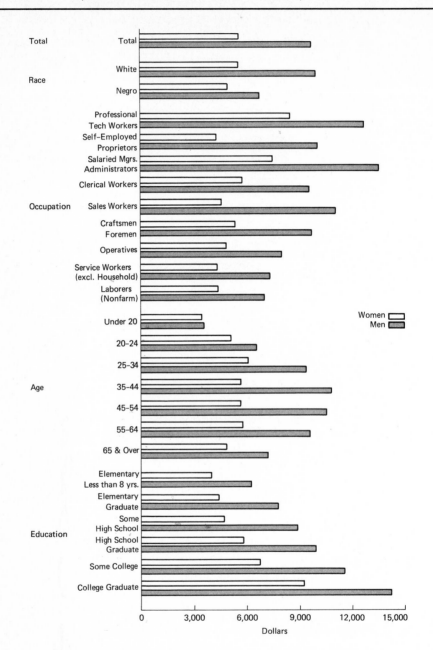

Women ☐
Men ▨

Dollars

SOURCE: Fabian Linden, *Women: A Demographic, Social, and Economic Presentation* (New York: The Conference Board, 1973), pp. 32–33.

100

shown that both sexes in America place a higher value on men than on women. To test the idea that women are prejudiced against themselves, Philip Goldberg asked a group of college females to read and evaluate a series of six articles.[41] Three of six articles in one of the booklets given to the participants were said to be authored by a female and three carried the name of a male author. The other booklet contained the same articles but with the female and male "authors" reversed. The female college students tended to rate articles as more valuable and their authors more competent when the apparent authors were male, even though the articles were exactly the same as those bearing female names. It may well be that "women have long suffered from an image of the self that paralyzes the will and short-circuits the brain, that makes them deny the evidence of their senses and internalize self-doubt to a fearful degree."[42]

The current emphasis on racial and ethnic pride may help to reduce these psychological costs. The trend toward ethnic pride has been well publicized in the case of blacks, American Indians, and Puerto Ricans. The interest of "white ethnics" in maintaining their cultural identity is less well known. Until recently, white ethnic groups such as the Poles, Italians, Greeks, and Slavs have placed great emphasis on becoming part of the larger American culture. Their goal was to become "Americanized." Now many members of these ethnic groups are becoming interested in their own roots—their culture, language, and history. Most advocates of this new accent on maintaining ethnic diversity are not seeking to reject the American way of life; they are interested in understanding and appreciating their own origins. This viewpoint has been expressed by Michael Novak, an outspoken supporter of this "new ethnicity":

> My interest is not . . . in defining myself over against the American people
> and the American way of life. . . . What I should like to do is to come to a

[41] Philip Goldberg, "Are Women Prejudiced Against Women?" *Trans-action,* 5 ((April 1968): 28–30. For studies showing that other minority groups also tend to evaluate the majority more highly than their own group, see J. A. Bayton, "The Racial Stereotypes of Negro College Students," *Journal of Abnormal and Social Psychology,* 36 (January 1941): 97–102; Ozzie G. Simmons, "The Mutual Images and Expectations of Anglo Americans and Mexican Americans," *Daedalus,* 90 (Spring 1961): 286–299; Anthony Gary Dworkin, "Stereotypes and Self-Images Held by Native-Born and Foreign-Born Mexican Americans, *Sociology and Social Research,* 49 (1965): 214–224; and Anthony Gary Dworkin, "National Origin and Ghetto Experience as Variables in Mexican American Stereotypy," in Nathaniel N. Wagner and Marsha J. Haug, eds., *Chicanos: Social and Psychological Perspectives* (St. Louis: The C. V. Mosby Company, 1971) pp. 80–84.

[42] Vivian Gornick and Barbara K. Moran, eds., *Women in Sexist Society: Studies in Power and Powerlessness* (New York: New American Library, 1974), p. xx.

LEARNING SELF-HATRED

One day I saw white children at a game of marbles. Innocent of any evil thought or expectations, I joined their game. As my misfortune would have it, I shot all their marbles out of the ring. A white boy, livid with rage, called me a "nigger." "Nigger?" I repeated, not understanding. "What does 'nigger' mean?" The boys burst out laughing and I laughed with them good-naturedly. But the incident hereupon went beyond name-calling.

"Do you want to know what 'nigger' means?" asked the white boy spitefully. "Let me show you."

Together with the other boys he began to pelt me with stones and I fled for dear life. After a while, tiring of their sport, they let me alone. With feelings smarting more than did the bruises on my body, I ran to my mother, weeping. Between my sobs, I managed to gasp the all-important question:

"Mother, what does 'nigger' mean?"

A look of pain and indignation came into her face. She wanted to know who had used that nasty word to me. When I had explained, she put on the sing-song voice that she always used whenever she read out the Scriptures. She intoned the following verse from the Song of Songs:

"Look not at me so because I am black for the sun hath burned me, the children of my father were angry with me and they made me watchman of their vineyard, but my own vineyard I have not kept."

She went on to explain to me that because we Negroes sinned against God, against His only begotten Son, and the Holy Ghost, therefore He has humbled us in our pride and vanity; He has made slaves of us for the white man to oppress and to mistreat, so that we might learn to be obedient and to walk in His way, and sin no more. . . . As I listened to her, a deep sense of guilt came over me. To be sure, I must be a sinner too, and the fact that the white boys called me "nigger" must have been the will of God. Already I felt as if by this act alone, by being humiliated in spirit and brusied in body, that I was expiating for the pride and the vanity which my mother charged against our race. . . .

Angelo Herndon, *Let Me Live,* in David Jay, ed. *Growing Up Black* (New York: Pocket Books, 1969), pp. 48, 49.

better and more profound knowledge of who I am, whence my community came, and whither my son and daughter, and their children's children, may wish to head in the future: I want to have a history.[43]

[43] Michael Novak, "White Ethnic," *Harpers,* 243 (September 1971): 50. Also see Michael Novak, *The Unmeltable Ethnics: Politics and Culture in the Seventies* (New York: Macmillan Publishing Co., Inc., 1973); and Michael Novak "The New Ethnicity," *The Humanist,* 33 (May–June 1973): 18–21.

The social changes related to minorities that occurred during the 1960s appear to have had a positive effect on the self-image and racial and ethnic identity of American minority members. This is not surprising because:

> Social movements generally tend to have a positive psychological impact upon minority-group members. Movements for civil rights, black liberation, the Chicanos, and women's liberation, each of which stresses system blame for social ills rather than personal blame, tend to aid minority-group members in dealing with majority stereotypes. The movements not only affect the images the majority hold of the minority but also provide minority-group members with a vocabulary of motives to shape new self-identities and to account for majority-held images.[44]

Earlier studies indicated that minority children tend to show a preference for white dolls over dolls of their own color. The rise of black consciousness in the 1960s may have turned this situation around for black children. Repeating an earlier study showing that black children had low self-esteem and a low sense of racial identity, Joseph Hraba and Geoffrey Grant reported in 1971 that a sample of black and white public school children *both* tended to prefer dolls of their own color.[45] If the results of this research accurately reflect an improvement in self-image and racial identity among blacks, it is reasonable to expect that similar changes are occurring among other traditional targets of prejudice and discrimination in America.[46]

WHAT CAN BE DONE?

Recent Progress

There are some signs of progress in recent years. Opinion polls showed that 30 per cent of white Americans in 1942 supported integrated schooling, com-

[44] Anthony Gary Dworkin and Rosalind J. Dworkin, eds., *The Minority Report: An Introduction to Racial, Ethnic, and Gender Relations* (New York: Praeger Publishers, Inc., 1976), p. 84.

[45] Joseph Hraba and Geoffrey Grant, "Black is Beautiful: A Reexamination of Racial Preferences and Identification," *Journal of Personality and Social Psychology*, 16 (November 1970): 398–402. Also see John D. McCarthy and William L. Yancey, "Uncle Tom and Mr. Charlie: Metaphysical Pathos in the Study of Racism and Personal Disorganization," *American Journal of Sociology*, 76 (January 1971): 648–672; and William C. Yancey, Leo Rigsby, and John D. McCarthy, "Social Position and Self-Evaluation: The Relative Importance of Race," *American Journal of Sociology*, 78 (September 1972): 338–359.

[46] For evidence supporting this point among Chicanos, see Dworkin and Dworkin, *The Minority Report*, op. cit., pp. 84–85.

THEM AND ME

Everyone is dissecting the race riots. The conservatives are blaming the liberals, the liberals are blaming the bigots, the bigots are smiling smugly. The insurance companies are worried about claims, the politicians about reelection. And the editorial writers are urging more respect for law and order. The sociologists are talking of "lack of economic opportunity," the psychiatrists of "frustrations." The civil rights workers are shaking their heads and saying the cause of equality under the law has suffered "a severe setback."

Yet all I can think of is they wanted to kill me. The uneasiness grew slowly. The first day it seemed just another riot. A shame. But these things will happen. Then came the next day. And the next. At first, I tried to imagine how the rioters felt, smashing and burning. I thought I could sense how a young Negro boy must feel as he heaved a rock through a plate glass window. The release. The rebellion without hope of success. The simple act of saying to hell with a world you could never conquer. It was an act, really, of complete defeat. How terribly sad that was.

Then, slowly, as story followed story, the thread of hatred broadened "Get Whitey! Kill him! Kill, kill, kill!" And picture followed picture. The sullen faces, the narrowed eyes. The hatred. Slowly I came to understand that they wanted to kill *me*. Quite literally, if they could only lay their hands on me, they would relish shooting me, stabbing me or beating me to death. Quite literally, paranoiac though it may sound, they wanted to kill me. They hated Me.

Suddenly it was no longer a deprived minority rebelling against the system that oppressed them. Suddenly the whole thing descended to a far more basic level—They and I, Them and Me. If They live in Los Angeles and Newark and Detroit hated me, what about They who live in our own ghettos? Those near my own house? What about the bootblack? We've always gotten along so well, kidding and joshing. Does he seem a little surly this morning? What of the cleaning lady I like so well? Is there a new touch of defiance in her tone? And what of the big longshoreman coming my way down the street? What is that look in his eyes? What are They really thinking? How much do They hate Me? How awful it is to be hated. How unfair. I keep wanting to say, Don't hate me. If you must hate, hate the Thurmonds, the Eastlands, the Wallaces. Hate those who won't rent you a room or serve you a meal or give you a job. But don't hate me. I don't want it to be Them and Me. We are all fellow human beings. We are all in the same boat. Don't hate me.

In the end, I told a long-time Negro friend (I think he is a friend) of my fear and anger. I told him how awful it was to be hated. How insecure it made you, never to be sure what They were thinking. How terribly, terribly unfair it was to be despised, not for anything you'd said, or done, or been. But simply because you were white.

"I know how it is," he said, nodding. "Simply because I'm black."

From *The Perfect Solution to Absolutely Everything* by Arthur Hoppe (Garden City, N.Y.: Doubleday & Company, Inc., 1968). Reprinted by permission of Doubleday & Company, Inc.

pared with 48 per cent in 1956 and 60 per cent in 1968. Similarly, in 1942, only 35 per cent of white Americans expressed a willingness to have a black of their same social class as a neighbor. The percentage who would accept such a neighbor had increased to 51 per cent by 1956 and to 65 per cent by 1968. A similar trend can be observed in the attitudes of whites toward equality of employment opportunity for minorities.[47]

Blacks provide the most dramatic illustration of improvement during the 1960s.[48] Although few blacks are in positions of national power, several large cities now have black mayors and there is now a substantially larger percentage of blacks in other elective offices. During the 1960s, the number of blacks in professional and technical occupations—doctors, engineers, lawyers, teachers, writers—increased by 128 percent. The number of blacks who are managers, officials, or self-employed was twice as high in 1971 as it was in 1960. It is estimated that slightly more than half of American black families are now members of at least the lower middle class. Finally, the annual family income for black families increased by 100 per cent during the 1960s.

During this period of progress, however, the percentage of blacks in welfare programs rose, and black families still have an annual family income 38 per cent below that of white families. Also, the high school dropout rate among black males is 50 per cent higher than that among white males; white males under 35 years of age graduate from college at a rate four times as high as their black peers; the unemployment rate among black teenagers is alarmingly high; and blacks are far from being proportionally represented politically.[49]

Obviously, the progress of blacks and other minorities has not canceled the need for further efforts to reduce the consequences of prejudice and discrimination. Even those who point to the recent social and economic progress of blacks are quick to say that improvements already realized, as well as the improvements that must come in the future, depend on continuing the struggle for the achievement of opportunity for minorities. Many approaches to this

[47] Jerome H. Skolnick, *The Politics of Protest* (New York: Ballantine Books, 1969), p. 181.

[48] Ben J. Wattenberg, *The Real America: A Surprising Examination of the State of the Union,* rev. ed. (New York: Capricorn Books, 1976), pp. 124–151. Wattenberg reports the disparity between black and white unemployment rates decreased, the per cent of blacks in craft and operative occupations rose, and blacks became better educated. Also, see "America's Rising Black Middle Class," *Time,* 103 (June 17, 1974): 19–28; Shirley H. Rhine, "The Economic Status of Black Americans," *The Conference Board Record,* 9 (August 1972): 27–36; and *"We the Black Americans,"* op. cit.

[49] Reynolds Farley and Albert Hermalin, "The 1960s: Decade of Progress for Blacks?" *Demography,* 9 (August 1972): 353–367; and Reynolds Farley, "Trends in Racial Inequalities: Have the Gains of the 1960s Disappeared in the 1970s?" *American Sociological Review,* 42 (April 1977): 189–208.

WHAT IS THE MIDDLE CLASS?

What does "middle class" mean? As used here it obviously does not refer exclusively to doctors, lawyers and businessmen with cabin cruisers and expense accounts. It refers instead to Americans who have safely put poverty behind them and are now looking ahead, not back. In the words of Thomas Sowell, a black sociologist with the Urban Institute, we are talking about "black men and women who go to work five days a week, pay their bills, try to find some happiness for themselves, and raise their children to be decent people with better prospects than they had. . . ."

To begin then at the bottom, "middle class" means that at the very least individuals have the basic necessities of life: enough to eat, healthy, if not necessarily expensive clothes to wear, housing that is at least safe and sanitary.

But that, of course, is only the very beginning. . . . Once the necessities of food, shelter and clothing are provided for, a vast flow of secondary criteria must also be met.

Middle-income parents want their children to go to good schools, to stay in high school and graduate, and then hopefully go on to college.

The young adults come out of college and they want jobs as programmers, not porters.

A middle-income family wants not only a housing structure that is safe and sanitary but a safe and sanitary housing structure in a safe and sanitary neighborhood.

Ben J. Wattenberg, *The Real America* (New York: Capricorn Books, 1976), pp. 126–127.

end have been advocated, including increased social contact between the majority and minorities, governmental actions, and the organization of minorities into interest groups with political power.

Increased Social Contact

Social contact may increase or decrease prejudice and discrimination, depending on the circumstances of the contact. Social interaction may heighten prejudice and discrimination if one group dominates the other or if contact occurs infrequently, involuntarily, or within a context of tension.[50] But under certain conditions, prejudice and discrimination may decline as the frequency of social contact increases.[51]

[50] Simpson and Yinger, *Racial and Cultural Minorities*, op. cit., p. 683.
[51] Robin M. Williams, Jr., *Strangers Next Door* (Englewood Cliffs, N.J.: Prentice-Hall, Inc., 1964), pp. 167–168.

There are several conditions thought to promote a reduction in prejudice and discrimination through increased social contact.[52] One such condition is that members of the majority and minority share important characteristics such as educational level, social class, and occupational status. Another is that minority and majority group members work together in activities that require mutual cooperation. Research during World War II revealed that as the exposure to blacks under combat conditions increased, the prejudices of white soldiers diminished.[53] Finally, if members of a minority are seen in social positions not normally associated with them, prejudice tends to decline. Stereotypes about American Indians, for example, are more easily retained if they are observed as poor, uneducated residents of reservations, than if they are observed as doctors, lawyers, executives, or skilled craftsmen. When majority members can picture minority members holding social positions equal to or higher than their own, they can more easily interact with them as individuals rather than as stereotypes.

If social contact does help to reduce prejudice and discrimination, then the most recent efforts of the federal government to promote equal opportunities for minorities should produce some favorable results. Given adequate implementation of recent laws, policies, and programs, minority members will increasingly be in positions equal to those held by members of the majority.

Governmental Intervention

It is considered a truism that morals cannot be forced on people. Although it may be correct that attitudes and beliefs resist legislative, judicial, and administrative order, this does not seem to be so for behavior. Even if the peoples' minds cannot be immediately changed by law, their actions can be. In the belief that the ways people behave can more easily be affected than how they think, the federal government has directed its efforts at discrimination rather than prejudice.

Government concern about educational equality for minorities in public schools dates from the Civil War period. But real progress dates from a historic Supreme Court decision in 1954. That decision rejected the traditional claim that educational facilities can be "separate but equal." The Civil Rights Act of 1964 went much further. The assignment of students to or

[52] Simpson and Yinger, *Racial and Cutlural Minorities,* op. cit., p. 683.
[53] Samuel A. Stouffer et al. *The American Soldier* (Princeton, N.J.: Princeton University Press, 1949), pp. 594–595.

within public schools on the basis of race, color, religion, or national origin was forbidden, and the attorney general of the United States was granted authority to initiate legal proceedings against violators of the act. Finally, a 1971 Supreme Court decision ended de facto school segregation with its ruling that segregated schools could not be maintained on the basis of the residential composition of the area served by the schools.

One of the most positive steps toward equal employment opportunity taken by the federal government was the Civil Rights Act of 1964. That legislation prohibited job discrimination based on race, color, religion, sex, or national origin. Another significant trend in the area of equal employment opportunity is the federal government's policy of affirmative action. This policy states that employers must be more aggressive and more positive in their recruitment and training of minority members. Affirmative action means that private and public employers are actively to seek out minority members who are already employable with their present skills and to create special training programs for those who could be qualified were it not for their lack of education and training.

Solutions to the problems of prejudice, discrimination, and inequality discussed to this point lie outside the efforts of minority groups themselves. A recent trend is the formation of minority interest groups that seek to influence both public opinion and governmental policies and programs. This trend began with blacks in the 1960s and has since been adopted by other minorities.

Minorities as Interest Groups

Blacks. Action by blacks for equality can be divided into three phases: non-violence (1955–1964), militancy (1964–1969), and political participation (1969 to present).[54] The nonviolent phase began in 1955 when Rosa Parks' refusal to give up her bus seat to a white person sparked the Montgomery, Alabama bus boycott, led by Martin Luther King, Jr. After that initial success, the Reverend King spearheaded direct action against segregation and discrimination on many fronts throughout the South. During that phase, the goal of the black movement was integration into the mainstream of American society. It was assumed that existing institutions such as the federal government and

[54] See Joseph S. Himes, *Racial and Ethnic Relations* (Dubuque, Iowa: Wm. C. Brown Company, Publishers, 1974), pp. 38–39.

BLACK POWER

The concept of Black Power rests on a fundamental premise: *Before a group can enter the open society, it must first close ranks.* By this we mean that group solidarity is necessary before a group can operate effectively from a bargaining position of strength in a pluralistic society. Traditionally, each new ethnic group in this society has found the route to social and political viability through the organization of its own institutions with which to represent its needs within the larger society. Studies in voting behavior specifically, and political behavior generally, have made it clear that politically the American pot has not melted. Italians vote for Rubino over O'Brien; Irish for Murphy over Goldberg, etc. This phenomenon may seem distasteful to some, but it has been and remains today a central fact of the American political system. . . .

The point is obvious: black people must lead and run their own organizations. Only black people can convey the revolutionary idea—and it is a revolutionary idea—that black people are able to do things themselves. Only they can help create in the community an aroused and continuing black consciousness that will provide the basis for political strength. In the past, white allies have often furthered white supremacy without the whites involved realizing it, or even wanting to do so. Black people must come together and do things for themselves. They must achieve self-identity and self-determination in order to have their daily needs met.

Black Power means, for example, that in Lowndes County, Alabama, a black sheriff can end police brutality. A black tax assessor and tax collector and county board of revenue can lay, collect, and channel tax monies for the building of better roads and schools serving black people. In such areas as Lowndes, where black people have a majority, they will attempt to use power to exercise control. This is what they seek: control. When black people lack a majority, Black Power means proper representation and sharing of control. It means the creation of power bases, of strength, from which black people can press to change local or nation-wide patterns of oppression—instead of from weakness.

Stokely Carmichael and Charles V. Hamilton, *Black Power* (New York: Random House, Inc., 1968), pp. 54–56.

the judicial system could be counted on to aid in the fight against racism and discrimination. Nonviolence and mass-participation were the cornerstones of that phase, which relied on such techniques as boycotts, sit-in demonstrations, marches, and freedom rides.

The nonviolent phase was overshadowed in the mid-1960s by militancy and the cry of "black power." Behind that slogan lay a fundamental redirection of the black movement, a move away from integration into American society and toward cultural independence and black pride. Challenges to Martin Luther King, Jr., and his nonviolent philosophy came from such civil rights leaders as Stokely Carmichael, H. "Rap" Brown, Floyd McKissick, and Bobby Seale. They believed that only power generated by blacks could combat white majority power. Members of the white majority could not be counted on for help, they argued, because the very sources of their troubles were built into white society. Racism and discrimination were viewed as problems of structure that could not be solved without radical change. Force, violence, and self-defense were held by many to be the only appropriate tools for needed changes.

At the close of the 1960s, the third phase of the black response—political participation—began. The broad concept of black power became more specifically black *political* power. One manifestation of that shift was when Bobby Seale, the Black Panther party leader, ran a rather conventional political campaign for the office of Mayor in Oakland, California in 1973. Like many other blacks, Seale saw a potentially strong political base in central cities, which, because of heavy white migration to the suburbs, were becoming overwhelmingly black.

Seizing on this potential political power base, black leaders began to conduct voter registration drives and to run for public office in greater numbers. They were successful on both counts. The number of black voters in the

Table 3-6. Black Elected Officials in the United States, 1969–1973

Year	Total	Difference from Previous Year	Percentage Increase	
			Previous Year	1969
1969	1,185	0	0	0
1970	1,469	284	19%	19%
1971	1,860	391	26%	56%
1972	2,264	404	22%	91%
1973	2,621	357	15%	121%

SOURCE: Prepared by Office of Research, Joint Center for Political Studies, 1426 H Street, N.W., Washington, D.C. Taken from James E. Blackwell, *The Black Community: Diversity and Unity* (New York: Dodd, Mead & Company, 1975), p. 211.

South increased from just over 1 million in 1952 to nearly 6 million in 1966 following the Voting Rights Act of 1965. It has climbed steadily every year since 1966. Now more than 60 per cent of all voting age blacks are registered to vote, compared with the 70 or so per cent of whites who are registered to vote.[55] Blacks can now be found in elected positions in city halls, state legislatures, and the Congress of the United States. In 1965, there were less than 100 elected black officials in the eleven states of the old Confederacy; today that number has reached approximately 1,500. In 1975 blacks held 72 seats in the House of Representatives, and mayoralities in six cities with population exceeding 250,000.

Spanish-Speaking Americans. Among Spanish-speaking Americans, the Mexican-Americans, or Chicanos, have been the most active in the formation of interest groups.[56] The best-known Chicano interest group is Cesar Chavez's National Farm Workers' Association, which, starting with the 1965 grape strike in California, gave the Chicano movement a more militant tone.

Largely because of Chavez's efforts, the ''brown power'' movement has since resulted in the creation of even more militant groups such as the Alianza Federal de Mercedes (Federal Alliance of Land Grants) and the Brown Berets. Founded in 1963, the Alianza attempted to reclaim lands earlier taken from the Spanish-speaking people by the Anglos. Frustrated in their efforts to improve the hostile relations between police and Mexican-Americans in Los Angeles, the leaders of the Young Citizens for Community Action formed the Brown Berets, which subsequently became a further symbol of militancy for the Chicano movement.

Similar to the black experience, as the militancy among Mexican-Americans has waned, their interest in more conventional politics has increased. Although Mexican-Americans have been recognized politically on the national level, their greatest political advances have been on the state and local levels. Largely as a result of their participation in the federal antipoverty programs and Model Cities programs of the early 1960s, Mexican-Americans

---

[55] James E. Blackwell, *The Black Community: Diversity and Unity* (New York: Dodd, Mead & Company, 1975), pp. 208–211.

[56] Armando Rendon, ''La Raza—Today Not Mañana,'' in John H. Burma, ed., *Mexican-Americans in the United States* (New York: Schenkman Publishing Company, 1970), pp. 307–324; John Howard, ed., *Awakening Minorities* (Chicago: Aldine Publishing Company, 1970), pp. 89–122; Livie Isauro Duron and H. Russell Bernard, eds., *Introduction to Chicano Studies: A Reader* (New York: Macmillan Publishing Co., Inc., 1973); and Manuel P. Servin, ed., *An Awakened Minority: The Mexican-Americans,* 2nd ed. (Beverly Hills: Glencoe Press, 1974).

A DECLARATION OF INDEPENDENCE

THE SPIRITUAL PLAN OF AZTLÁN

In the spirit of a new people that is conscious not only of its proud heritage, but also of the brutal "gringo" invasion of our territories, *we,* The Chicano, inhabitants and civilizers of the northern land of Aztlán, from whence came our forefathers, reclaiming the land of their birth and consecrating the determination of our people of the sun, *declare* that the call of our blood is our power, our responsibility, and our inevitable destiny.

We are free and sovereign to determine those tasks which are justly called for by our house, our land, the sweat of our brows, and by our hearts. Aztlán belongs to those that plant the seeds, water the fields, and gather the crops, and not to the foreign Europeans. We do not recognize capricious frontiers on the Bronze Continent.

Brotherhood unites us, love for our brothers makes us a people whose time has come and who struggles against the foreigner "gabacho" who exploits our riches and destroys our culture. With our heart in our hand and our hands in the soil, we declare the independence of our mestizo Nation. We are a bronze people with a bronze culture. Before the world, before all of North America, before all our brothers in the Bronze Continent, we are a Nation. We are a union of free pueblos. We are *Aztlán.*

To hell with the nothing race.

All power for our people.
March 31, 1969

Crusade for Justice Youth Conference, Denver, Colorado. Taken from Armando B. Rendon, *Chicago Manifesto* (New York: Macmillan Publishing Co., Inc., 1971), pp. 336–337.

of all social classes have become involved in the inner workings of party politics.[57]

American Indians. "Red power," the slogan symbolizing the most recent American Indian challenge to the federal government, represents a new militancy.[58] This militancy began in 1961 at the American Indian Chicago Conference when some 420 Indians representing 67 tribes formulated and adopted a "Declaration of Indian Purpose," a declaration of their independence from

[57] See Joan N. Moore and Harry Pachon, *Mexican Americans,* 2nd ed. (Englewood Cliffs, N.J.: Prentice-Hall, Inc., 1976), pp. 150–158.

[58] See Vine Deloria, Jr., *God Is Red* (New York: Dell Publishing Co., Inc., 1973), especially pp. 3–22; Raymond Friday Locke, ed., *The American Indian* (Los Angeles: Mankind Publishing Company, 1970), especially pp. 7–14; and Council on Interracial Books for Children, *Chronicles of American Indian Protest* (Greenwich, Conn.: Fawcett Publications, Inc., 1971).

(Above left) Cesar Chavez—president of the United Farm Workers Organizing Committee; (lower left) Jesse Jackson—founder and director of Operation Push (People United to Save Humanity) (Both courtesy of the Environmental Protection Agency). (Right) Dennis Banks—leader of AIM (American Indian Movement) (Kevin McKiernan, distributed by Magnum Photos, Inc.).

white domination. In 1969 several incidents, including the occupation of Alcatraz Island, further sparked the militant efforts of the American Indians. A major confrontation between American Indians and the federal government occurred in 1972, when the Trail of Broken Treaties protesters took over the Bureau of Indian Affairs headquarters in Washington, D.C. The American Indian Movement (AIM), the most militant new civil rights group, has since taken further dramatic action (including the occupation of the town of Wounded Knee in South Dakota) to publicize its goals.

Despite the new militancy, there is not complete agreement among American Indians. The more militant Indians reject the idea of being assimilated into American society. They prefer the restoration of some of their own land, illegally taken by the violation of hundreds of treaties, the right of self-determination, and the freedom to preserve their own culture. Other, less militant, are in favor of seeking higher income, equal education and occupational opportunity, and a larger share of existing resources. If these are to be achieved, Indians cannot remain on reservations. These two philosophies are contradictory and internal conflict must be resolved if American Indians are to become a unified and effective interest group.

Women. "Women's liberation" is a diverse movement. Its activities range from consciousness-raising sessions in local neighborhoods to more structured efforts to fight sexual inequality such as the National Organization of Women (NOW), Catalyst, National Women's Political Caucus, Women United, and Women's Lobby, Inc.[59] Part of the Women's liberation movement is concerned primarily with equal employment opportunities, equal compensation for the sexes, equal educational opportunities in professional schools, and equal legal treatment.

Other feminists look beyond such specifics to the negative consequences of assigned sex roles. They believe that the very existence of sex roles ensures the perpetuation of sexual inequality. These feminists argue for the eradication of the ideologies of sexism and male supremacy. Liberation from sex roles, say these feminists, must precede true sexual equality. Kate Millett, for example, describes the relationship between men and women as "sexual politics."[60] Female-male relationships, she argues, are political because in almost all civilizations males have ruled females. The sex role, Millet contends, "assigns domestic service and attendance upon infants to the

---

[59] See Susan Deller Ross, *The Rights of Women: The Basic ACLU Guide to a Woman's Rights* (New York: Avon Books, 1973), pp. 376–380.
[60] Kate Millett, *Sexual Politics* (New York: Doubleday & Company, Inc., 1970).

WHAT THE ERA WILL DO FOR WOMEN

The amendment will restrict only governmental action, and will not apply to purely private action. What constitutes state action will be the same under the Fourteenth Amendment, and as developed in Fourteenth Amendment litigation on other subjects.

Under the ERA, special restrictions on the property rights of married women would be unconstitutional. A married woman could engage in business as freely as a member of the male sex. Inheritance rights of widows would be the same as for widowers. This means, for example, that married women in Alabama, Florida, Indiana, North Carolina, and Texas will be able to sell their property without their husbands' permission. Wives will be allowed to start an independent business without the approval of the court or their husbands in California, Florida, Nevada, Pennsylvania, and Texas.

Dower rights will not be nullified. They will simply be extended to men in those few states where men do not have a right in their wives' estates.

Married women will be able to manage their separate property, such as inheritances and earnings.

. . . The major, most important effect of the ERA will be on the *employment* of women.

Restrictive work laws for women will be unconstitutional. There will be no more maximum hours laws, night work laws, or weight-lifting restrictions on women. It is for this reason that the ERA is of vital importance to the women of the country, and it is for this reason that the most formidable opponent to the ERA has been organized labor. It is no secret that there is a shortage of jobs; the white male workers are fighting (in decreasing numbers, fortunately) to keep women out of the good jobs. It has long been a practice in many states to forbid women to take particular jobs—bartender, for example; to enter particular industries—coal mining, for example; to work overtime; to work throughout a day without a specified "break"; to work at night; and to lift objects weighing more than a certain amount.

Karen DeCrow, *Sexist Justice* (New York: Random House, Inc., 1974), pp. 297–99.

female, the rest of human achievement, interest, and ambition to the male."[61] Feminists such as Millet contend that sexual equality is a matter of power:

To *recognize* the political nature of woman's condition, to see that it constitutes one half of a binding relation of power to powerlessness, to see further that the

[61] Ibid., p. 26.

power conceives of itself as predicated on the continuing life of the powerless, is vital to any understanding of women's liberation and of the women's liberation movement.[62]

For these feminists, reform of the legal system and equal opportunity are insufficient. Women must unite so as to become powerful enough to challenge male control of social institutions successfully.

The Equal Rights Amendment (ERA), passed by Congress in 1972, is an important test for the women's movement as an interest group. The ERA amendment reads simply: "Equality of rights under the law shall not be denied or abridged by the United States or by any state on account of sex." This sounds like a straightforward guarantee of rights due any American citizen. Yet there are many opponents to ERA, both male and female. Critics range from women who fear that passage of the ERA would undermine a man's legal obligation to support his family to men who wish to protect women from military combat duty.[63]

Minorities have increasingly become more aware of the negative consequences of the prejudice and discrimination that are built into America's social structures. They have moved from a concern with their individual problems resulting from structured inequality to an emphasis on their collective disadvantage. The 1960's and 1970's brought some improvements for minority groups. Inequalities, however, are still great and prejudice and discrimination remain. We do not yet know if the recent social and economic advances experienced by minorities are merely temporary gains or an indication of a long-term trend toward achieving racial, ethnic, and sexual equality. We do know that this progress began to slow down in the mid-1970's. A continued lack of social, political, economic, and educational progress is not likely to be accepted passively by organized and socially aware minorities. They have learned to press their demands actively and will probably become more militant if progress does not continue in the future.

Additional Readings

Bahr, Howard M., Bruce A. Chadwick, and Robert C. Day. *Native Americans Today: Sociological Perspectives*. New York: Harper & Row, Publishers, 1972.

[62] Gornick and Moran, *Woman in Sexist Society,* op. cit., p. xvii.

[63] For a discussion of the pros and cons of the ERA, see Karen DeCrow, *Sexist Justice* (New York: Vintage Books, 1975), pp. 293–324.

Baxter, Paul, and Basil Sanson. *Race and Social Difference*. Baltimore: Penguin Books, 1972.

Bernard, Jessie. *Women and the Public Interest: An Essay on Policy and Protest*. Chicago: Aldine Publishing Company, 1971.

Blauner, Robert. *Racial Oppression in America*. New York: Harper & Row, Publishers, 1972.

Dixon, Vernon J., and Badi Foster, eds. *Beyond Black or White: An Alternate America*. Boston: Little, Brown and Company, 1971.

Fey, Harold E., and D'Arcy McNickle, *Indians and Other Americans: Two Ways of Life Meet*. New York: Harper & Row, Publishers, 1970.

Fitzpatrick, Joseph P. *Puerto Rican Americans: The Meaning of Migration to the Mainland*. Englewood Cliffs, N.J.: Prentice-Hall, Inc., 1971.

Gerard, Harold B., and Norman Miller. *School Desegregation: A Long-Term Study*. New York: Plenum Publishing Corporation, 1975.

Glazer-Malbin, Nona, and Helen Youngelson Waehrer. *Woman in a Man-Made World: A Socioeconomic Handbook*. Skokie, Ill.: Rand McNally & Company, 1972.

Grebler, Leo, Jean W. Moore, and Ralph C. Guzman. *The Mexican American People: The Nation's Second Largest Minority*. New York: The Free Press, 1970.

Huber, Joan, ed. "Changing Women in a Changing Society." *American Journal of Sociology,* 78 (January 1973): 763–1054 (entire issue).

Janeway, Elizabeth. *Man's World, Woman's Place: A Study in Social Mythology*. New York: Dell Publishing Company, 1971.

Josephy, Alvin M., Jr., ed. *Red Power: The American Indians' Fight for Freedom*. New York: American Heritage Press, 1971.

Levitan, Sar, William Johnston, and Robert Taggart. *Still A Dream: The Changing Status of Blacks from 1960 to 1973*. Cambridge, Mass.: Harvard University Press, 1974.

Masters, Stanley H. *Black-White Income Differentials: Empirical Studies and Policy Implications*. New York: Academic Press, Inc. 1975.

Meier, Matt S., and Feliciano Rivera. *The Chicanos: A History of Mexican Americans*. New York: Hill and Wong, 1972.

Pinkney, Alphonso. *Black Americans*. 2nd ed. Englewood Cliffs, N.J.: Prentice-Hall, Inc., 1975.

Silberman, Charles E. *Crisis in Black and White*. New York: Random House, Inc., 1964.

Smith, Arthur L. *Rhetoric of Black Revolution*. Boston: Allyn & Bacon, Inc., 1970.

Stoddard, Ellwyn R. *Mexican Americans*. New York: Random House, Inc., 1973.

Wax, Murray L. *Indian Americans: Unity and Diversity*. Englewood Cliffs, N.J.: Prentice-Hall, Inc., 1971.

Yetman, Norman R., and C. Hoy Steele. *Majority and Minority: The Dynamics of Racial and Ethnic Relations*. 2nd ed. Boston: Allyn & Bacon, Inc., 1975.

the political institution

The true crime of Richard Nixon was simple: he destroyed the myth that binds America together, and for this he was driven from power.

The myth he broke was critical—that somewhere in American life there is at least one man who stands for law—the President. That faith surmounts all daily cynicism, all evidence or suspicion of wrongdoing by lesser leaders, all corruptions, all vulgarities, all the ugly compromises of daily striving and ambition. That faith holds that all men are equal before the law and protected by it; and that no matter how the faith may be betrayed elsewhere, at one particular point—the Presidency—justice will be done beyond prejudice, beyond rancor, beyond the possibility of a fix. It was that faith that Richard Nixon broke, betraying those who voted for him even more than those who voted against him.

Theodore H. White, *Breach of Faith: The Fall of Richard Nixon* (New York: Dell Publishing Co., Inc., 1976), p. 409.

The word *Watergate,* overused and tired, still symbolizes much of what is thought to be wrong with the political institution in the United States. Seymour Martin Lipset and Earl Raab contend that Watergate was the culmination of events that had been building for decades: "The Watergate affair, standing as it does for the whole bag of White House horrors, was not just the creation of evil men; it was the symptomatic rumbling of a deep strain in American society, of which Richard Nixon has come to seem the almost perfect embodiment.''[1] From this perspective, the bugging, deception, corruption, surveillance, lying, and obstruction of justice of the Nixon administration are best seen as a reflection of some long-standing problems within the American political institution. Before we discuss these problems, however, it is necessary to understand what a political institution is.

NATURE OF A POLITICAL INSTITUTION

A *political institution* is concerned with the acquisition and exercise of power in the coordination and administration of a society. A primary function of a political institution is the maintenance of order within the society. The need for public order arises from the conflicts created by individuals and groups attempting to fulfill their own desires and needs. The basic reason for such conflicts is competition for scarce resources. Conflict arises over competition for material things such as land, food, and natural resources as well as for nonmaterial valuables such as power, honor, and freedom.[2] Even if there were enough resources to meet the desires and needs of everyone, the means of acquiring them would still be a source of conflict. Socially accepted procedures and rules for settling disputes are thus essential. It is also necessary that appropriate punishments be given to those who violate those procedures and rules. A second major function of a political institution is the protection of citizens from dangers outside the society. To provide this kind of protection, the state maintains military forces and spends money for weapons and military supplies.

As societies become more complex, their governments tend to assume more functions. For example since the 1930s, the American government has become involved in the provision of economic welfare for all citizens. Other added governmental functions pertain to energy conservation, environmental protection, and the reduction of educational, social, and economic inequality. Many of the strains in the American political institution come from government's assumption of responsibility in these areas. Bernard Baruch summarized the concern about the contemporary strains on government:

> The role of government and its relationship to the individual has been changing so radically that today government is involved in almost every aspect of our lives.

[1] Seymour Martin Lipset and Earl Raab, ''An Appointment with Watergate,'' *Commentary,* 56 (September 1973): 35.
[2] Gerhard Lenski, *Power and Privilege: A Theory of Stratification* (New York: McGraw-Hill Book Company, 1966).

Political, economic and racial forces have developed which we have not yet learned to understand or control. If we are ever to master these forces, make certain that government will belong to the people, not the people to the government, and provide for the future better than the past, we must somehow learn from the experiences of the past.[3]

The nature of the problems now confronting the American political institution has not changed since the founding of this country as an independent nation.[4] The American Revolution was waged against an abuse of power by the English government, against the lack of colonial representation in the English government, and against the implementation of illegitimate policies such as the Stamp Act and the Townshend Acts. After two hundred years, the problems of concentration of power, inadequate governmental representation, and the illegitimacy of certain government actions still exist. This is because these three problems are fundamental to any democratic political institution.

CONCENTRATION OF POWER

Who Has the Power in American Society?

Who has the power to determine the course of events in the United States? The theory known as *pluralism* depicts decision-making on the national level as the outcome of competition, bargaining, and compromise among diverse special interest groups; in this view, power is widely distributed throughout society. On the other hand, according to the theory of *elitism*, American society is controlled from the top by a unified and enduring few; power is said to be concentrated in the hands of an elite group with common interests and backgrounds.

Pluralism. America is popularly depicted as a society in which power is distributed widely among a variety of interest groups, so that control is not continually in the hands of any one group. Robert Dahl summarizes the theory of pluralism:

---

[3] Quoted in *The New York Times,* May 11, 1964.
[4] See Samuel Eliot Morison, *The Oxford History of the American People,* vol. 1 (New York: New American Library, 1972), pp. 354–355.

The theory and practice of American pluralism tends to assume . . . that the existence of multiple centers of power, none of which is wholly sovereign, will help (may indeed be necessary) to tame power, to secure the consent of all, and to settle conflicts peacefully:

- Because one center of power is set against another, power itself will be tamed, civilized, controlled, and limited to decent human purposes, while coercion, the most evil form of power, will be reduced to a minimum.
- Because even minorities are provided with opportunities to veto solutions they strongly object to, the consent of all will be won in the long run.
- Because constant negotiations among different centers of power are necessary to make decisions, citizens and leaders will perfect the precious art of dealing peacefully with their conflicts, and not merely to the benefit of one partisan but to the mutual benefit of all the parties to the conflict.[5]

Gary Wasserman illustrates the bargaining and compromise process that the theory of pluralism contends dominates American politics:

When Ralph Nader, the consumer advocate, proposes that automobile makers be required to install more safety devices in their cars, numerous interests get involved in the process of turning that proposal into law. The car manufacturers worry about the increased costs resulting in less sales and less profits, and they may try to limit the safety proposals. Labor unions may want to make sure that the higher costs do not result in lower wages. Insurance companies may be interested in how greater safety will affect the claims they have to pay out. Oil companies may worry about the effect on gasoline consumption. Citizens' groups, like Common Cause, may try to influence the legislation so that it provides the greatest protection for the consumer. The appropriate committees of the House and Senate, and the relevant parts of the bureaucracy, will weigh the competing arguments and pressures as they consider bills covering automobile safety. The resulting legislation will reflect the relative power of the competing groups as well as the compromises they have reached.[6]

In all of this, national political leaders are depicted as referees, as those charged with the responsibility of balancing the public welfare with the self-centered desires of special interest groups.

Robert Dahl's study of New Haven, Connecticut offers a confirmation of pluralism.[7] Dahl studied political power in that community by focusing on

---

[5] Robert A. Dahl, *Pluralist Democracy in the United States: Conflict and Consent* (Skokie, Ill.: Rand McNally & Company, 1967).

[6] Gary Wasserman, *The Basics of American Politics* (Boston: Little, Brown and Company, 1976), pp. 187–188.

[7] Robert Dahl, *Who Governs? Democracy and Power in an American City* (New Haven, Conn.: Yale University Press, 1961).

specific issues such as community welfare, city government, and public education. Finding that the group wielding the most power varied with the issue involved, he concluded that a number of quite different groups controlled various political decisions. The groups trying to influence political decisions on public education were not the same groups competing, bargaining, and compromising on the issue of highway construction. Power in New Haven was not concentrated in the hands of one group of elite citizens.

Critics of pluralism contend that studies such as Dahl's focus on specific issues and do not get the total picture of where the power lies. They argue that there are many issues that powerful elites do not allow to become public. The decision to construct a highway system or to invest in a new military weapons system, for example, may be made by a small group of elites before others even become aware of it. The actual political decision may be merely a formality.[8]

Elitism. As a theory of power distribution, elitism holds that an integrated elite dominates society and seeks to satisfy its own interests. It does this, in part, by preventing other groups from threatening its interests, and, in part, by manipulating the rest of society to suit its needs.

A well-developed formulation of this is C. Wright Mills' theory of the "power elite."[9] According to Mills, America no longer has *separate* economic, political, and military spheres of power. Rather, the leaders in military, economic, and political positions have coalesced to form a power elite. The common interests and needs they share are the basis for the exercise of power within that elite. According to Mills, "the men of the higher circles are not representative men. They are not men held in responsible check by a plurality of voluntary associations which connect debating publics with the pinnacles of decision."[10]

Stanley Eitzen has found some inconsistencies between Mills' theory of the power elite and the realities of modern political and economic life.[11] First, although the corporate elite are said to have a slight edge in power, Mills depicts the business, political, and military elite as equals. This does not square with the apparent domination of the military by the executive

---

[8] In a study supporting the theory of elitism on the local community level, Floyd Hunter found that Atlanta, Georgia was controlled by a ruling elite of approximately 100 businessmen. See Floyd Hunter, *Community Power Structure* (Chapel Hill, N.C.: University of North Carolina Press, 1953).

[9] C. Wright Mills, *The Power Elite* (New York: Oxford University Press, Inc., 1956).

[10] Ibid., p. 361.

[11] D. Stanley Eitzen, *Social Structure and Social Problems in America* (Boston: Allyn & Bacon, Inc., 1974), p. 132.

ELITISM AND PLURALISM

		Elitism	Pluralism
1. Levels		a. Unified power elite	a. No dominant power elite
		b. Diversified and balanced plurality of interest blocs	b. Diversified and balanced plurality of interest blocs
		c. Mass of unorganized people who have practically no power over elite	c. Mass of unorganized people who have some power over interest blocs
2. Operation		a. One group determines all major policies	a. Who determines policy shifts with the issue
		b. Manipulation of people at the bottom by bloc at the top	b. Monopolistic competition among organized blocs
3. Bases		a. Coincidence of interests among major institutions (economic, military, governmental)	a. Diversity of interests among major organized blocs
			b. Sense of weakness and dependence among those in higher as well as lower status
4. Changes		a. Increasing concentration of power	a. Increasing dispersion of power

SOURCE: Adapted from William Kornhauser, " 'Power Elite' or 'Veto Groups'?" in S. M. Lipset and Leo Lowenthal, eds., *Culture and Social Character* (New York: The Free Press, 1961), p. 261.

branch of the federal government and by corporate leaders. Second, Mills believed that corporate, governmental, and military elites constitute a close group with common goals. This is contradicted by the fierce in-fighting that often takes place among the leaders of these three segments of political and economic life.

Others criticize Mills for underestimating the extent to which power in America is concentrated in the hands of a few. Some believe that Mills' "power elite" is simply a puppet of the rich ruling class. One advocate of this viewpoint is David Horowitz: "The locus of power and interest [of the ruling upper class] is the giant corporations and financial institutions which dominate the American economy, and moreover, the economy of the entire

Western world.''[12] According to Ferdinand Lundberg, the elites in Mills' theory are at best subordinate advisers and technicians, and at worst, ''office boys,'' ''fat boys,'' court jesters, and errand boys for the rich and super-rich.[13] Most political, military, and economic leaders are said to be only the representatives of the ruling class. Their power is derived from those at the top who actually hold the power. In the view of William Domhoff, the upper class or ''corporate rich'' governs America by virtue of its control of major institutions including the executive branch of the federal government, the major corporations, large foundations, elite universities, key regulatory agencies, the military, the Central Intelligence Agency (CIA), the Federal Bureau of Investigation (FBI), and the federal judicial system.[14] Mills' power elite, says Domhoff, is simply an operating arm of the upper class.

According to Arnold Rose, the theories of elitism and pluralism are both partially correct. Pluralism, he contends, appears to be more accurate in describing the running of the internal affairs of the nation. Foreign affairs, on the other hand, tend to be dominated by a small, influential group that bears a similarity to Mills' power elite.[15] While Rose's distinction has some merit, it ignores the existence of the military-industrial complex in America, which is a prime illustration of how national elites cooperate to pursue common ends. Economic and social costs of this corporate-government alliance have been substantial.

The Military-Industrial Complex

While serving as chief of staff of the United States Army in 1946, Dwight Eisenhower expressed concern about the development of a close relationship among the military, industry, government, and universities.[16] By January

---

[12] David Horowitz, ed. *Corporations and the Cold War* (New York: Monthly Reader, 1970), p. 11.

[13] Ferdinand Lundberg, *The Rich and the Super-Rich* (New York: Bantam Books, Inc., 1969), pp. 543–552.

[14] Domhoff's ideas have been presented in a series of books. See G. William Domhoff, *Who Rules America?* (Englewood Cliffs, N.J.: Prentice-Hall, Inc., 1967); G. William Domhoff and Hoyt B. Ballard, eds. *C. Wright Mills and the Power Elite* (Boston: Beacon Press, 1968); and G. William Domhoff, *The Higher Circles: The Governing Class in America* (New York: Random House, Inc., 1970).

[15] Arnold Rose, *The Power Structure: Political Process in American Society* (New York: Oxford University Press, Inc., 1967).

[16] For the text of a memorandum expressing this view, see ''Appendix A: General Eisenhower as Founder of the 'Military-Industrial Complex' in 1946,'' in Seymour Melman, *Pentagon Capitalism: The Political Economy of War* (New York: McGraw-Hill Book Company, 1970), pp. 231–234.

1961, when he made his presidential farewell address to the nation, he indicated that his earlier fears were being realized. Using the term *military-industrial complex* for the first time, President Eisenhower warned against the undue exercise of power by a combination of military, political, and business leaders:

> Our military organization today bears little relation to that known by any of my predecessors in peacetime, or indeed by the fighting men of World War II and Korea.
>
> Until the latest of our world conflicts, the United States had no armaments industry. American makers of plowshares could, with time and as required, make swords as well. But now we can no longer risk emergency improvisation of national defense; we have been compelled to create a permanent armaments industry of vast proportions. Added to this, 3½ million men and women are directly engaged in the Defense Establishment. We annually spend on military security more than the net income of all United States corporations.
>
> This conjunction of an immense Military Establishment and a large arms industry is new in the American experience. The total influence—economic, political, even spiritual—is felt in every city, every statehouse, every office of the Federal Government. We recognize the imperative need for this development. Yet we must not fail to comprehend its grave implications. Our toil, resources, and livelihood are all involved; so is the very structure of our society.
>
> In the councils of government we must guard against the acquisition of unwarranted influence, whether sought or unsought, by the military-industrial complex. The potential for the disastrous rise of misplaced power exists and will persist.[17]

Events since this warning have confirmed President Eisenhower's fears. Both corporations and the military have grown dramatically.

The Growth of the Corporation. At the beginning of the twentieth century, only a few industries—railroading, shipping, steel, oil, mining—were organized as corporations. Today, corporations provide everything from diaper pins to rest homes for the elderly. America's largest 500 corporations account for two thirds of all industrial sales in America.[18] More than half of all America's manufacturing assets are controlled by the largest 100 corpora-

[17] Ibid., p. 237. A complete text of Eisenhower's farewell address appears on pp. 235–239.

[18] John Kenneth Galbraith, *The New Industrial State*, 2nd ed., rev. (Boston: Houghton Mifflin Company, 1971), p. 1.

tions; over 75 per cent of these assets are controlled by the largest 500 corporations.

The size of large corporations in America is enormous and growing. In 1965, General Motors, the world's largest corporation, had annual sales of almost $21 billion; by the mid-1970's, its annual sales figure was over $36 billion. Standard Oil of New Jersey, the second largest corporation in the world, has increased its annual sales from just over $10 billion in the mid-1960's to over $25 billion today. To place this in proper perspective, GM's annual budget is larger than any existing economic entity except for the governments of the United States and the Union of Soviet Socialist Republics.

The Rise of the Military.   For most of its history, the military in the United States was kept under civilian control and wars were waged by a small federal army. This changed during World War II when Americans first began to associate war with economic prosperity.[19] For ten years prior to the start of World War II, Americans had suffered through unprecedented unemployment and economic decline. President Franklin Roosevelt's New Deal did not end the Great Depression; rather, World War II brought full employment and economic prosperity. This experience laid the groundwork for the development of a large, permanent military bureaucracy.

Events following World War II—the Russian atomic bomb test in 1949, the Korean War (1950–1953), and the Cold War based on fear of a worldwide communist conspiracy—further promoted an atmosphere that made a huge military establishment acceptable to the American public. During the 1950's, national security became a leading preoccupation of the government and the American people. The power of the Pentagon increased dramatically during this period.

Another factor contributing to the current size and power of the Pentagon was Robert McNamara's reorganization of the Department of Defense under President Kennedy in the 1960s. Although the reorganization established tighter civilian control of the military, it also brought closer together the economic, political, and military elites:

> The Pentagon was converted from a loose military complex of informal allegiances and alliances among military, business, and congressional leaders into a highly centralized military establishment with the elites of the Pentagon possessing increased control of defense contractors. . . . A giant and highly

[19] Seymour Melman, *The Permanent War Economy: American Capitalism in Decline* (New York: Simon & Schuster, Inc., 1974), p. 15.

WHAT THE PENTAGON PAPERS TELL US ABOUT POWER

The guarded world of the government insider and the public world are like two intersecting circles. Only a small portion of the government circle is perceived from the public domain. Vigorous internal policy debates are only dimly heard and high-level intelligence analyses that contradict policy are not read outside. But, as the Pentagon papers demonstrate, knowledge of these policy debates and the dissents from the intelligence agencies might have given Congress and the public a different attitude toward the publicly announced decisions of the successive administrations.

The segments of the public world—Congress, the news media, the citizenry, even international opinion as a whole—are regarded from within the world of the government insider as elements to be influenced. The policy memorandums repeatedly discuss ways to move these outside "audiences" in the desired direction, through such techniques as the controlled release of information and appeals to patriotic stereotypes. The Pentagon papers are replete with examples of the power the Executive Branch has acquired to make its influence felt in the public domain.

The papers also make clear the deep-felt need of the government insider for secrecy in order to keep the machinery of state functioning smoothly and to maintain a maximum ability to affect the public world. And even within the inner world, only a small number of men at the top know what is really happening. During the five-day bombing pause in May, 1965, for instance, Secretary McNamara, in order to guard against leaks, sent a top-secret but misleading order through the entire military command structure stating that the purpose was to permit reconnaissance aircraft to conduct "a thorough study of [North Vietnamese] lines of communication."

The real purpose of the pause, the history says, was to provide an opportunity to secretly deliver what amounted to "a 'cease and desist' order" to Hanoi to call off the insurgency in the South. When this "demand for their surrender" was rejected, the history continues, the seemingly peaceful gesture of the pause would provide political credit for an escalation of the air war against North Vietnam afterwards. As President Johnson explained in a personal cable directly to General Maxwell D. Taylor, then the American Ambassador in Saigon, he wanted a pause "which I could use to good effect with world opinion."

"You should understand that my purpose in this plan is to begin to clear a path either toward restoration of peace or toward increased military action, depending upon the reaction of the Communists," the President said. "We have amply demonstrated our determination and our commitment in the last two months, and I now wish to gain some flexibility."

Such sharp and fresh detail in the Pentagon papers on the hitherto gray workings of the Executive Branch poses broad questions, for all spectrums of American political opinion, about the process of governing.

The principal actors in this history, the leading decision-makers, emerge as confident men—confident of place, of education and of accomplishment. They are problem-solvers, who seem rarely to doubt their ability to prevail. In a memorandum to President Johnson on Feb. 7, 1965, recommending a full-scale bombing campaign against North Vietnam, McGeorge Bundy, the former Harvard dean who was now the special presidential assistant for national security affairs, remarked in self-assured tones that "measured against the costs of defeat in Vietnam, this program seems cheap. And even if it fails to turn the tide—as it may—the value of the effort seems to us to exceed its cost." In the same memorandum, Mr. Bundy assured the President that General Taylor and the other senior members of the United States Mission in Saigon were "outstanding men, and United States policy within Vietnam is mainly right and well directed."

"None of the special solutions or criticisms put forward with zeal by individual reformers in Government or in the press is of major importance, and many of them are flatly wrong," Mr. Bundy told the President. "No man is perfect, and not every tactical step of recent months has been perfectly chosen, but when you described the Americans in Vietnam as your first team, you were right."

Of the generals, like William C. Westmoreland, the military commander in Vietnam, and Earle G. Wheeler, the Chairman of the Joint Chiefs of Staff, the history remarks that they were "men accustomed to winning."

The Pentagon Papers (New York: Bantam Books, Inc., 1971), pp. xiii–xiv.

centralized governmental corporation . . . was thus created under the Kennedy administration. The distinction among economic, political, and military elites is now less sharp, for they are all converging into one centralized establishment with an affinity of interests in a powerful military profile in America.[20]

Sources of the Military's Power. One important source of the military's power is its size. As of 1975, the Department of Defense employed more than 3 million persons. Of these, almost 1 million are civilians.[21]

A second source of the military's power is its vast financial resources. In 1950, the Department of Defense budget was just over $13 million. In 1976, its budget had grown to $115 billion, and by 1978, it is expected to reach almost $130 billion.[22] During the Great Depression, the military received about

[20] Jonathan H. Turner, *American Society: Problems of Structure,* 2nd ed. (New York: Harper & Row, Publishers, 1976), p. 51.
[21] *The U.S. Fact Book, The Statistical Abstract of the U.S.* (New York: Grossett & Dunlap, Inc., 1977), Table 530, p. 334.
[22] Ibid., Table 515, p. 327. The 1978 figure is based on preliminary budget figures submitted by the Pentagon in November 1976.

WHY DOES THE MILITARY ESTABLISHMENT ACT THAT WAY?

The Follow-on Imperative

A large and established aerospace production line is a national resource—or so it seems to many high officers in the armed services. The corporation's managers, shareholders, bankers, engineers, and workers, of course, will enthusiastically agree, as will the area's congressmen and senators. The Defense Department would find it risky and even reckless to allow one of only eight or less large production lines to wither and die for lack of a large production contract. This is especially so because, for each of the aircraft production sectors (strategic bombers, fighters, and military transports), there are actually only four or five potential production lines. . . . Strategic bombers are likely to be competed for and produced only by General Dynamics, North American Rockwell, Boeing, and perhaps Lockheed-Georgia; air defense and tactical fighters only by General Dynamics, North American Rockwell, Boeing, McDonnell division, and Grumman; and military transports only by Boeing, Lockheed-Georgia, Douglas division, and, for small transports, Grumman. Thus, there is at least latent pressure upon the Defense Department from many sources to award a new, major contract to a production line when an old major contract is phasing out. Furthermore, the disruption of the production line will be least and the efficiency of the product would seem highest if the new contract is structurally similar to the old, in the same functional category or production sector—i.e., is a follow-on contract.

This latent constraint, or rather compulsion, imposed on weapons procurement by industrial structure might be called the follow-on imperative and contrasted with the official imperative. The *official imperative* for weapons procurement might be phrased as follows: If a military service needs a new weapon system, it will solicit bids from several competing companies; ordinarily, the service will award the contract to the company with the most cost-effective design. The *follow-on imperative* is rather different: If one of the eight production lines is opening up, it will receive a new major contract from a military service (or from NASA); ordinarily, the new contract will be structurally similar to the old—i.e., a follow-on contract. Relatedly, the design competition among production lines is only a peripheral factor in the award.

The Bail-Out Imperative

. . . We can chart the major military aerospace systems according to the corporation to which the U.S. government awarded the contract and according to the years in which it did so. . . . [These awards often coincide with] years in which the corporation suffered either (1) a drop in sales of almost 10 percent or more from the previous year, (2) a deficit in income, or (3) a drop in employment of almost 10 percent or more from the previous year.

> There have been many occasions when an aerospace corporation has experienced one or more of these three difficulties. In twelve cases the U.S. government within the next year has awarded the corporation a new, major, military contract. . . . These observations suggest that the government comes to the aid of corporations in deep financial trouble, that there is what might be called a bail-out imperative.
>
> James R. Kurth, "Aerospace Production Lines and American Defense Spending," in Richard G. Head and Ervin J. Rokke, *American Defense Policy* (Baltimore: The Johns Hopkins University Press, 1973), pp. 629, 631, 632.

10 per cent of the total federal budget. As of the mid-1970s, between a third and a half of the total budget of the federal government (depending on what is included under "military expenditures") is controlled by the military establishment.[23] Only eight countries in the world—the United States, Russia, Japan, West Germany, France, the United Kingdom, China, Italy—have a gross national product in excess of the American military budget in 1974.[24]

It is not money itself but the uses to which large amounts of money can be put that creates power. A third source of the military's power lies in the successful utilization of these vast financial resources.[25] Some legislators vote for military projects in the hope that part of the allocations will be spent in their home states and, thereby, generate jobs and votes. Areas in which a significant part of local or state economies are based on defense-related industries become dependent on the Pentagon. Congressmen and senators from such states are likely to be promilitary. Every state as well as the District of Columbia, in fact, receives defense money. The smallest amount in 1977 was in Idaho ($79 million); the largest amount that same year went to California ($11,830,000). The total amount of defense money in 1975, including both contract awards and payrolls, was $69,975,000, an average of $1,372,000 per state.[26]

A fourth source of the military's power is its own and others' lobbying activities. Although the Pentagon budget for propaganda and lobbying has been limited to $30 million by the Congress, the amount spent annually for

[23] *The American Almanac for 1974, The Statistical Abstract of the U.S.* (New York: Grosset & Dunlap, Inc., 1974), Figure 27, p. 388.
[24] Melman, *The Permanent War Economy,* op. cit., p. 23.
[25] See Turner, *American Society,* op. cit., p. 54.
[26] *The U.S. Fact Book,* op. cit., Table 527, p. 333.

THE ECONOMIC BENEFITS OF MILITARY SPENDING AT THE STATE AND LOCAL LEVELS

The example of Lockheed-Georgia illustrates the pervasive economic influence of a defense industry on a city, region, and state. Located at Marietta, Georgia, Lockheed does more than two billion dollars of defense business a year. It pays about two hundred million dollars a year in wages to twenty-six thousand workers who come from about one-third of the state's one hundred and fifty-nine counties. According to Jack Raymond in the *Harvard Business Review,* "Lockheed buys everything from soft drinks to metal parts from Georgia suppliers. Last year, the company spent one hundred and thirteen million dollars with about 1,730 suppliers, many of them small businesses."

Donald McDonald, "Militarism in America," *The Center Magazine,* 3 (January-February 1970): 25, 27.

these purposes is probably twice that amount.[27] This budget allows the Pentagon to keep over 300 lobbyists in Washington, the largest professional group of lobbyists in the capital. Those large corporations who do much of their business with the Pentagon naturally find it in their best interests to attempt to exert promilitary influence in Washington. Labor unions also lobby for the military in order to protect the ever-growing number of jobs in defense-related industries.

President Eisenhower warned Americans of the dangers of the alliance he saw developing between the government, the military, and big business. Critics have since pointed out some of the economic and social costs of this concentration of power.

National Costs of the Military-Industrial Complex.   The most significant cost of the military-industrial complex is the damage it is doing to competition within America's economic system. How is this happening?

Economic competition is undermined by the relative lack of competitive bidding on defense contracts. The Armed Services Procurement Act, passed after World War II, contains 17 exceptions to the requirement that competitive bidding must exist on defense contracts. These exceptions are quite general and give the military considerable freedom to negotiate with the company rather than to require formal bids from several companies. In 1974, approxi-

[27] Dennis Farney, "War of Words: Pentagon's Promotion of its Own Activities Upsets Many Cities," *The Wall Street Journal* (November 13, 1970), p. 1.

THE MILITARIZED ECONOMY

The American economy is increasingly becoming militarized. A list of Pentagon contractors and contractors for the allied Atomic Energy Commission and NASA reads like a "who's who" of large American corporations. Since these corporations control smaller companies, the amount of direct and indirect control of the economy by the military establishment can be far-reaching. Some major corporations, such as General Motors, Ford, and Standard Oil of New Jersey, have only a small proportion of their production geared toward the military. Many corporations, however, such as General Dynamics, Lockheed, Boeing, North American Rockwell, Ling-Temco-Vought, may soon become little more than divisions of "Military, Inc." Although these companies are not owned by the military establishment, they are under its influence because a clear majority of their total sales are to the government. Other major corporations, including General Electric, General Tire, Sperry-Rand, Westinghouse, RCA, Bendix, IBM, Kaiser Industries, General Telephone, Litton Industries, and Pan American, sell a large proportion—but not a majority—of their products to the military. In many cases, were these corporations to lose their defense contracts, they would suffer financially—thus giving the Pentagon tremendous manipulative power. If the trends of the last 20 years continue into the next decades, the Pentagon may have direct and indirect control of a major part of the economy, with the result that it will be increasingly difficult to convert economic enterprise toward nonmilitary goals.

Jonathan H. Turner, *American Society: Problems of Structure* (New York: Harper & Row, Publishers, 1972), p. 171.

mately 90 per cent of the Pentagon's contracts and 98 per cent of NASA (National Aeronautics and Space Administration) contracts were negotiated under the exception rules. In 1975, 91 per cent of the Department of Defense military procurement contracts were negotiated rather than advertised; this increased to 92 per cent in 1976. The lowest percentage of negotiated contracts for military procurement since 1960 is 82 per cent.[28]

Also, competition in the American economy is undermined by the dependency relationship that develops between the government and defense contractors. As military procurement has increased in recent years, an increasing number of companies have based a greater proportion of their total business on military-related contracts.[29] At the same time that large corporations are becoming more dependent on government contracts, the government

[28] Richard F. Kaufman, "The Military-Industrial Complex," *The New York Times Magazine* (June 22, 1969), p. 68; and the *U.S. Fact Book,* op. cit., Table 525, p. 332.
[29] Ibid., pp. 11, 68–69.

becomes dependent upon contractors. Once a contractor has done ground-breaking work on a project (for example, a new weapons system), that firm gains an advantage over potential competitors in the future. Because only certain companies are capable of supplying the military with complicated hardware (based on the knowledge and capabilities gained from previous contracts), the government often has to protect these companies from economic failure. A case in point is the Lockheed Aircraft Corporation to which the federal government in 1971 loaned a vast sum of money to prevent its bankruptcy. Many critics share this harsh assessment of the government's support of large suppliers of military hardware:

> In . . . recent decades, billions have been poured into the rescue of weapons firms in difficulty. . . . Lockheed Corporation is the champion applicant for bailout assistance, however, having got one arbitrary price increase of $1 billion on two aircraft orders and then a loan of another billion that came by legislation. The truth is that the American taxpayer has bought a number of these companies, but has no deed to prove it.[30]

The military-industrial complex also weakens the economy because the government's dependence on large corporations tends to squeeze out smaller firms. Big corporations seem to be rewarded despite their failures. Smaller companies, on the other hand, tend to be closely held to their contractual commitments by the Pentagon. A study by the Office of Management and Budget revealed that contractors with the poorest performance on their military contractual commitments consistently have profits above average on their military business.[31]

Another criticism of the military-industrial complex is leveled at the tendency of defense contractors to hire ex-Pentagon personnel and of ex-defense contractors to gain employment in the Department of Defense. Senator William Proxmire found that at the end of the 1960s the 100 largest defense contractors employed over 2,000 retired military officers holding the ranks of Army Colonel, Navy Captain, or higher. Retired military officers working for defense industry companies can use their friendships with those still in the Pentagon to negotiate contracts. In addition, contends Senator Proxmire, "there is the subtle or unconscious temptation to the officer still on active duty. After all, he can see that over 2,000 of his fellow officers work for the

---

[30] Duane Lockard, *The Perverted Priorities of American Politics,* 2nd ed. (New York: Macmillan Publishing Co., Inc., 1976), p. 319.
[31] Ernest Fitzgerald, "The Pentagon as the Enemy of Capitalism," *World,* 2 (February 27, 1973): 18–21.

ONE GENERAL'S VIEW OF THE MILITARY ESTABLISHMENT

Our militaristic culture was born of the necessities of World War II, nurtured by the Korean War, and became an accepted aspect of American life during the years of cold war emergencies and real or imagined threats from the Communist bloc. Both the philosophy and the institutions of militarism grew during these years because of the momentum of their own dynamism, the vigor of their ideas, their large size and scope, and because of the dedicated concentration of the emergent military leaders upon their doctrinal objectives. The dynamism of the defense establishment and its culture is also inspired and stimulated by vast amounts of money, by the new creations of military research and matériel development, and by the concepts of the Defense Department-supported "think factories." These latter are extravagantly funded civilian organizations of scientists, analysts, and retired military strategists who feed new militaristic philosophies into the Defense Department to help broaden the views of the single service doctrinaries, to create fresh policies and new requirements for ever larger, more expensive defense forces.

Somewhat like a religion, the basic appeals of anti-Communism, national defense, and patriotism provide the foundation for a powerful creed upon which the defense establishment can build, grow, and justify its cost. More so than many large bureaucratic organizations, the defense establishment now devotes a large share of its efforts to self-perpetuation, to justifying its organizations, to preaching its doctrines, and to self-maintenance and management. Warfare becomes an extension of war games and field tests. War justifies the existence of the establishment, provides experience for the military novice and challenges for the senior officer. Wars and emergencies put the military and their leaders on the front pages and give status and prestige to the professionals. Wars add to the military traditions, the self-nourishment of heroic deeds, and provide a new crop of military leaders who become the rededicated disciples of the code of service and military action. Being recognized public figures in a nation always seeking folk heroes, the military leaders have been largely exempt from the criticism experienced by the more plebeian politician. Flag officers are considered "experts," and their views are often accepted by press and Congress as the gospel. In turn, the distinguished military leader feels obliged not only to perpetuate loyally the doctrine of his service but to comply with the stereotyped military characteristics by being tough, aggressive, and firm in his resistance to Communist aggression and his belief in the military solutions to world problems. Standing closely behind these leaders, encouraging and prompting them, are the rich and powerful defense industries. Standing in front, adorned with service caps, ribbons, and lapel emblems, is a nation of veterans—patriotic, belligerent, romantic, and well intentioned, finding a certain sublimation and excitement in their country's latest military venture. Militarism in America is in full bloom and promises a future of vigorous self-pollination—unless the blight of Vietnam reveals that militarism is more a poisonous weed than a glorious blossom.

General David M. Shoup, "The New American Militarism," *The Atlantic Monthly,* 223 (April 1969): 56.

big companies. How hard a bargain does he drive with them when he is one or two years away from retirement?''[32]

There are negative consequences of the military-industrial complex beyond the reduction of economic competition. The diversion of too much of our economic resources into the military sphere, it is charged, has resulted in the erosion of our economic strength and vitality. Below are some examples of how the emphasis on military production has contributed to the deterioration of America's industrial-technological base:

1. By 1968, United States industry operated the world's oldest stock of metal-working machinery; 64 percent was 10 years old and over.
2. No United States railroad has anything in motion that compares with the Japanese and French fast trains.
3. The United States merchant fleet ranks 23rd in age of vessels. In 1966, world average-age of vessels was 17 years, United States 21, Japan 9.
4. While the United States uses the largest number of research scientists and engineers in the world, key United States industries, such as steel and machine tools, are in trouble in domestic markets: in 1967, for the first time, the United States imported more machine tools than it exported.[33]

Depletion is also reflected on a human scale. Inflation and high unemployment have been attributed to the prominence of the military-industrial complex in America's economic life. Diversion of money into military production has caused us to shortchange problems associated with education, health, cities, crime, poverty, energy, and the environment.

The military-industrial complex has been discussed as an illustration of how corporate and governmental elites cooperate for their mutual benefit. It is the rest of the society that has to bear the economic, social, and military costs of this concerted use and abuse of power.

INADEQUATE GOVERNMENTAL REPRESENTATION

Representative democracy is a form of government in which elected representatives are expected to make political decisions that coincide with the desires and needs of those who elected them. It is assumed that, once elected, the

---

[32] Kaufman, ''The Military-Industrial Complex,'' op cit., p. 70.
[33] Melman, *Pentagon Capitalism,* op. cit., p. 3.

representatives will accurately reflect the wishes of their constituents and work for their welfare. Policies embraced by candidates during their political campaigns are expected to be adhered to following election to office. When an elected official has the right to appoint people to governmental positions, he or she is expected to appoint individuals who will work for the betterment

AMERICA: A DEPLETED SOCIETY?

Once upon a time the United States was the standout performer, world-wide, as a vigorous, productive society, exceptionally strong in basic industries and in mass-producing consumer goods. American design and production methods set world standards in many fields. . . .

But the United States now is the scene of a drama different from that implicit in her confident ideology. A process of technical, industrial, and human deterioration has been set in motion within American society. The competence of the industrial system is being eroded at its base. Entire industries are falling into technical disrepair, and there is massive loss of productive employment because of inability to hold even domestic markets against foreign competition. Such depletion in economic life produces wide-ranging human deterioration at home. The wealthiest nation on earth has been unable to rally the resources necessary to raise one fifth of its own people from poverty. The same basic depletion operates as an unseen hand restricting America's relations with the rest of the world, limiting foreign-policy moves primarily to military-based initiatives.

This deterioration is the result of an unprecedented concentration of America's technical talent and fresh capital on military production. While United States research programs for civilian purposes are grossly understaffed, and many industries do virtually no research at all, more than two thirds of America's technical researchers now work for the military. We have constructed the most awesome military organizations in human history, with the actual power to destroy what we call civilization on this earth, a power which rational men dare not use. Military extravagance has been undermining the world value of the dollar and with it the world-banking position of the United States.

The price of building colossal military power, and endlessly adding to it, has been the depletion of American society, a process now well advanced in industry, civilian technology, management, education, medical care, and the quality of life. The prospect of "no future" has become a permanent part of government security policies that depend mainly on the threat of using nuclear weapons. Never before were men made to feel so powerless, so incapable of having a voice over their own fate.

Seymour Melman, *Our Depleted Society* (New York: Holt, Rinehart and Winston, 1965), pp. 3–4.

of the society rather than for selfish ends. The essence of this form of government is that its policies are continually subject to criticism and revision by the citizens, who, if they are displeased, may demand changes.[34] The actions of both elected representatives and appointed officials are assumed to be open to public scrutiny at all times, with the possible exception of issues related to national security or national defense. Those who are elected to office in a democratic system remain responsible to their constituents and hold office only for a specified period of time.[35]

There are a number of reasons why representative democracy does not operate as it is supposed to in theory. The most important of these reasons are the selective support of basic political principles by citizens, the disproportionate power of special interest groups, and the fact that representation is not always ensured through voting.

Selective Support of Basic Political Principles

Research has consistently found that Americans selectively support the basic political principles of their form of government.[36] Herbert McCloskey found that 75 per cent of the voting-age citizens he studied supported democratic beliefs when they were stated in general terms, such as, "regardless of a person's political ideology and belief system, he or she must be afforded the same legal rights and protections as any other citizen."[37] At the same time, 50 per cent of those same people agreed with the statement that only those books that "do not contain wrong political views should be published." Philip Converse and his associates found that more than 50 per cent of those they questioned disapproved of protest meetings to oppose a political issue—in spite of the fact that the right to peaceful assembly is a basic political right in a democratic society.[38]

[34] Robin M. Williams, Jr., *American Society: A Sociological Interpretation,* 3rd ed. (New York: Alfred A. Knopf, Inc., 1970), pp. 253–257.

[35] Gresham M. Sykes, *Social Problems in America* (Glenview, Ill.: Scott, Foresman and Company, 1971), pp. 241–243.

[36] Raymond W. Mack and John Pease, *Sociology and Social Life* (New York: D. Van Nostrand Company, 1973), pp. 380–385.

[37] Herbert McCloskey, "Consensus and Ideology in American Politics," *American Political Science Review,* 58 (June 1964): 361–382.

[38] Philip E. Converse, Warren E. Miller, Jerrold G. Rusk, and Arthur C. Wolfe, "Continuities and Change in American Politics: Parties and Issues in the 1968 Elections," *American Political Science Review,* 63 (December 1969): 1083–1105.

In another study, college students were asked whether they agreed or disagreed with some statements without the knowledge that these statements were based on the Bill of Rights in the United States Constitution.[39] As shown in Table 4-1, on none of the constitutional rights did 100 per cent of the students agree. In fact, over 50 per cent of them disagreed with three of the provisions set forth in the amendments to the Constitutions: the Fifth Amendment, which protects the individual from being tried twice for the same crime; the Sixth Amendment, which guarantees the right to confront one's accuser; and the Ninth and Tenth Amendments, which reserve for the people any powers not specifically designated as powers of the federal government.

Table 4-1. Extent of Agreement with the Bill of Rights (N = 560)

Amendment	Provision	Per Cent Indicating:		
		Agree	Disagree	No Opinion
I	Freedom of speech, press	82.5	14.3	3.2
I	Freedom of religion	77.1	13.6	9.3
I	Peaceable assembly	56.8	35.7	7.5
II, III	Bear arms, quartering of troops	63.6	20.3	16.1
IV	Search and seizure	81.8	14.6	3.6
V	Self-incrimination	56.1	33.2	10.7
V	Due process	70.0	25.7	4.3
V	Double jeopardy	23.6	71.8	4.6
VI	Public trial	54.3	34.3	11.4
VI	Confront accuser	23.9	67.5	8.6
VI	Informed of accusation	94.8	2.3	2.9
VI, VII	Trial by jury	89.6	9.3	1.1
VIII	Excessive bail and punishment	61.4	32.2	6.4
IX, X	Reserved rights of people	44.3	51.1	4.6

SOURCE: Raymond W. Mack, "Do We Really Believe in the Bill of Rights?" *Social Problems,* 3 (April 1956): 267.

Disproportionate Power of Interest Groups

The Nature of Interest Groups. An *interest group* is a coalition of persons with some shared attitudes and interests who seek to gain some particular ad-

---

[39] Raymond W. Mack, "Do We Really Believe in the Bill of Rights?" *Social Problems,* 3 (April 1956): 264–269.

vantage through influencing political decisions. Persons who belong to an interest group do not have to share a great number of attitudes and interests. They need share only those on which they are basing their claim for governmental action on their behalf.[40]

Americans are particularly prone to forming and joining organizations for the purpose of pursuing some specific objectives.[41] In 1975, there were 12,866 nonprofit national organizations in the United States, representing everything from trade associations to Greek letter societies.[42] The combined number of national and local organizations is large enough that almost no American is denied the opportunity to be represented by some group.

The existence of a large number of interest groups does not mean, however, that every American is equally represented. Those interest groups with the most power, financial resources, and capable leaders are the most likely to be effective.

The most powerful interest groups are those representing *business*. There are two types of business groups—those that speak for the business sector in general, such as the National Association of Manufacturers, and those that are concerned only with a particular segment of business, such as the American Petroleum Institute.[43] *Labor,* represented by the AFL-CIO, is the second most powerful interest group in America. Unlike European labor, which often forms its own political party, American labor unions have for the most part chosen to influence the political process from the outside. The same route has been chosen by a third powerful category of interest groups, those representing *agriculture*. Although comparatively small in membership, *professional* groups such as the American Medical Association and the American Bar Association are able to exert extensive influence in politics because of their high status, wealth, and access to special knowledge not readily available to the general public. A number of other organizations represent the interests of various religious denominations, ethnic and minority groups, and specialized reform movements. These include the NAACP, CORE, the League of Women Voters, the American Civil Liberties Union, and Common Cause. Consumer advocate, environmental protection, and conservation groups have emerged in recent years.

[40] Raymond E. Wolfinger, Martin Shapiro, and Fred I. Greenstein, *Dynamics of American Politics* (Englewood Cliffs, N.J.: Prentice-Hall, Inc., 1976), p. 215.

[41] Alexis de Tocqueville, *Democracy in America,* trans. George Lawrence (New York: Harper & Row, Publishers, 1966), p. 485.

[42] *The U.S. Fact Book,* op. cit., Table No. 67, p. 48.

[43] See Austin Ranney, *The Governing of Men,* 3rd ed. (New York: Holt, Rinehart and Winston, 1971), pp. 352–360.

Interest groups use a variety of activities to influence political decisions, the most important of which is *lobbying,* the attempt to persuade members of Congress to introduce, pass, alter, or oppose legislation. Some lobbyists have at times offered bribes to legislators and applied unethical tactics, but most lobbyists use more subtle tactics. More effective methods include providing legislators with campaign funds, allowing them to capitalize on business deals, sending their law firms large annual retainer fees, and paying them large honoraria for making speeches at industrial or commercial conventions. According to one lobbyist, his main strategy is to make friends with the legislators he wishes to influence:

> Psychological pressures are far sounder than financial or political pressures. I spend by far the largest part of my time on personal attention. Say for example that I'm talking to a senator . . . and I notice that he's coming down with a cold. Well, after I leave I stop off at the nearest drugstore and send a messenger with a bottle of cold tablets to him. Who could accuse me of trying to buy anyone with a dollar's worth of cold tablets? But it's remembered. It's thoughtful. Or say one of his staffers is leaving to take another job back home. I hear about it, and the next time I see the senator I mention what a good egg this fellow is and that I'd like to give him a nice sendoff. How about if I bring a pile of steaks and a case of Scotch to the senator's house and we all have a cookout? After all, the man is leaving, so how could this be considered pressure? But it's another thoughtful act.[44]

The major problem with lobbying is that some lobbyists have more prestige, power, and money than others. Since lobbyists are not equal in resources, their ability to influence legislators is not equal. Powerful lobbies such as those representing large labor unions, home builders, and the oil industry usually succeed regardless of the public interest. Consequently, all citizens do not receive equal representation within the interest group system.

How Interest Groups Prevent Representation.   The issue of gun control illustrates how a powerful interest group can thwart a majority public opinion. The first Gallup Poll to ask for citizen's opinions on gun control, taken in 1938, found that 84 per cent of the American people believed that "all owners of pistols and revolvers should be required to register with the Government."[45] Subsequent polls have consistently shown that a majority of the

---

[44] This quote appears in Richard Harris, *A Sacred Trust* (New York: New American Library, 1966), pp. 91–92.

[45] Rodney Stark, *Social Problems* (New York: Random House, Inc., 1975), p. 227.

GUN CONTROL: SHOT DEAD

In Massachusetts, a pioneering effort to ban all handguns fell to a crushing defeat. The referendum proposal was aimed at the nation's most common murder weapon, the cheap Saturday Night Specials; it would have limited possession of handguns to the police, the military and such organizations as museums and historical societies. The proposal was put on the ballot by a volunteer citizens' organization called People Versus Handguns led by popular Middlesex County Sheriff John Buckley. It was also supported by much of the state's press, like the influential Boston *Globe*, which in one editorial published the roster of 73 people, including two children (ages two and 14), who had been killed by handguns since Jan. 1, 1975. But Massachusetts was blanketed by pro-gun propaganda put out by the National Rifle Association and Smith & Wesson, the nation's largest manufacturer of Saturday Night Specials, which happens to be located in Springfield, Mass.

Time, November 15, 1976, p. 57.

population favors federal gun control legislation. In spite of favorable public attitudes toward gun regulation, there is still no effective gun control law.

The lack of effective gun control legislation is largely due to the lobbying efforts of the National Rifle Association (NRA), a powerful interest group which has maintained a strong and consistent campaign against gun control.[46] The lobbying activities of the NRA seems to be in direct conflict with the best interests of the public. Whereas the NRA argues that "if guns are outlawed, only outlaws will have guns," statistics reveal that most people who are killed by handguns are shot by an acquaintance (often someone in their own family) rather than by an "outlaw." In the heat of an argument, a handgun often turns a minor dispute into a tragedy.

Another example of how interest groups interfere with representation is the struggle between the citizens of Santa Barbara, California and the combined forces of the oil industry and the government after a large oil spill in 1969.[47] The residents of that community suffered damage to their beaches, wildlife, air, and economic base (tourism), and they lost their struggle with those in power.

Because the citizens of Santa Barbara were largely members of the upper and upper-middle class, they had the time, money, and connections to protest

---

[46] Michael J. Harrington, "The Politics of Gun Control," *Nation,* 218 (January 12, 1974): 41–45.
[47] Harvey Molotch, "Oil in Santa Barbara and Power in America," *Sociological Inquiry,* 40 (Winter 1970): 131–144.

the oil spill. A local organization of citizens, called GOO (Getting Oil Out), was formed in an attempt to influence both the state and the federal government to prevent further drilling in the area. Its activities included petitions, demonstrations, rallies, legal suits, and legislative lobbying. Under the leadership of a former state senator and a local corporate executive, GOO took a militant stance, arguing that the government had granted permission for the oil company to drill in the Santa Barbara Channel even though it was known the area was geologically unstable and the danger of a leak developing was high. The group sent President Nixon a petition asking the state of California and the federal government to stop offshore oil operations, to issue no further leases in the Santa Barbara Channel, and to have the oil platforms and rigs removed from the Channel.

The results were disillusioning. The group's efforts met no success with the California state government, the federal executive branch, federal regulatory agencies, or Congress. Harvey Molotch concludes that governmental ordering of priorities favored private industry's right to exploit natural resources for a profit over protection of the natural environment and the desires of local citizens:

> American democracy came to be seen [by the residents of Santa Barbara] as a much more complicated affair than a system in which governmental officials actuate the desires of the "people who elected them" once those desires came to be known. Instead, increasing recognition came to be given to the "all-powerful oil lobby," to legislators "in the pockets of Oil," to the academicians "bought" by Oil, and to regulatory agencies which lobby for those they are supposed to regulate.[48]

As these examples indicate, powerful interest groups are often able to influence government to achieve their own narrow interests, interests that are sometimes harmful to the rest of society.

Representation Not Ensured Through Voting

Voting is often cited as the major means for ensuring governmental representation. The ballot box, however, is not always effective in promoting representation. The most important reasons for this are the high cost of political

---

[48] Ibid., p. 132.

campaigning, the congressional seniority system, and lack of political participation.

High Cost of Campaigning.   In 1960, candidates for national offices spent almost $32 million. By 1968, that had more than doubled to nearly $70 million, and by 1972, it had climbed to over $225 million.[49] Although part of the large increase in 1972 was caused by changes in the regulations regarding the reporting of campaign expenditures, there is little question that campaigning becomes increasingly expensive each year. The high cost of campaigning limits the chances of a candidate without personal wealth winning an election unless adequate financial backing can be gained from others.

If a political candidate receives financial backing from special interest groups, representation is diminished because "strings" are often attached to such money. Much controversy was aroused when it was revealed that three dairymen's associations had made substantial contributions to President Nixon's campaign fund in 1972, after which the dairymen were allowed to raise the price of milk.[50]

Congressional Seniority System.   The seniority system in Congress is another major obstacle to adequate representation in government.[51] In spite of recent reforms, the chairmanships of full congressional committees are still generally assigned to members of the majority party with the longest continuous service on those committees.

The seniority system violates the principle of representation in two ways. First, chairmanships are disproportionally controlled by older senators and representatives. The average age of the Senate's committee chairmen is just over 60 years; in the House of Representatives, the average age of committee chairmen is over 65 years. Second, because congressmen from rural areas are more likely to be re-elected repeatedly, many of the most senior members of Congress are from Southern rural areas. As a consequence, Congress is dominated in many respects by legislators who have strong rural, agricultural interests, and who are more conservative than the congressional membership as a whole. Such rural domination is not truly representative of a nation where three fourths of the population live in urban areas.

The seniority system affects representation because of the power of com-

---

[49] *The U.S. Fact Book,* op. cit., Tables No. 755 and 756, pp. 471–472.
[50] See "The Land of Milk and Money," *Time* (December 3, 1973), p. 22; and "Money in Politics: Spilled Milk," *Newsweek* (February 7, 1972), p. 28.
[51] See Wolfinger, Shapiro, and Greenstein, *Dynamics of American Politics,* op. cit., pp. 328–332.

THE WASHINGTON PAY-OFF

George Meany of the AFL-CIO is fawned over in Washington . . . , but not entirely for his intellectual brilliance. And not because he can deliver labor's votes. He can't. What he can deliver and does deliver is political money.

The present U.S. Ambassador to Great Britain was not appointed for his contributions to creative foreign policy and diplomacy . . . but for his contributions of political money.

This is not new. Back in the fifties, the President appointed one of his big contributors—ambassador to a country—when it was found he didn't even know where the country was.

So, jobs like that, and Washington influence, are in effect for sale. All it takes is money, . . . political contributions in election years. If you give enough, Washington's favors can be yours—influence, flattery, social success, invitations to swell affairs . . . and even ambassadorships to countries with nice climates and cheap servants. Perhaps more important—influence on domestic policy, such as taxes, affecting your own business and income.

Running for office has become incredibly expensive, and candidates have to get money somewhere. The Democrats get a lot of it from the unions, and the Republicans a lot of it from rich individuals and corporations.

No doubt there are some rich unions and people of charitable soul who will give money expecting nothing in return, but they are scarce. A big political contribution usually is seen as an investment. It's a scandal everyone admits. . . . But it's worse now because running for office costs more.

Public cynicism about politics and politicians already runs high. If this is not cleaned up, the political system will come apart . . . with influence, dominance, and even control put up for sale to the highest bidder.

David Brinkley
NBC Nightly News

November 16, 1971

Quoted from Robert N. Winter-Berger, *The Washington Pay-Off* (New York: Dell Publishing Co., Inc., 1972), pp. 9–10.

mittee chairmen. Only the party leaders in the House of Representatives and in the Senate have more power than committee chairmen. Legislation reaches the floor of Congress only after passing through a committee. Chairmen can effectively kill a bill by blocking its passage out of committee, or they can push the passage of a bill by giving it high priority. Decisions regarding the nation's laws are often heavily influenced by senior members of Congress who represent the values, attitudes, and interests of only a fourth of the population.

Lack of Political Participation.   Americans with the lowest level of political participation are the young, the uneducated, the poor, and most minorities. The factor that most affects political participation is education:

> The richer someone is, or the better job one has, the more likely that person is to vote. . . . whites are somewhat more likely than blacks to vote, and both groups have a vastly higher turnout level than Spanish-heritage citizens. But none of these differences is so great as (that) between better and less educated people. In fact, the other factors largely reflect differences in education, for the rich are better educated than the poor, whites better educated than blacks, and so on.[52]

The better educated are more active in politics, including voting, because they are more interested, feel that their participation can affect events, and are more comfortable about political activities. Those with the lowest degree of political participation share a common characteristic besides a low level of education and income—their interests have traditionally been the least represented by government. Those groups with the highest levels of political participation are better able to achieve their political ends than those who avoid politics.

'I DON'T VOTE'

Linda Jones (a pseudonym) lives in a Harlem housing project with her mother, who is on welfare, and her daughter. She dropped out of high school five years ago because of pregnancy. With limited skills, she hasn't been able to find a job. She entered a community college, but couldn't continue because of a lack of funds. More recently, she entered a city training program that may be forced to close for lack of money.

●

When I was young, I was more or less my aunt's daughter. That's why I guess I had it so good, because my aunt used to give me a lot of things and used to talk to me more than my mother did. She told me almost everything I can really think of, and then what I learned in the street. Other than that, it's kind of shaky.

Today, if people don't watch their children, they're going to be selling drugs as soon as they get old enough. They hit eleven, or twelve, or ten, they'll

[52] Ibid., p. 130.

be selling it out there. Because a lot of kids don't go to school as much as they used to. They drop out of school; they get bored with school. "Why should I get a diploma when I can get out here and sell dope and make much more money?" So, they're dropping out of school. . . .

When I was growing up in Harlem, it seemed much better and looked like an easier life to handle. You didn't see many bums on the street, or people selling drugs and all. They were doing it, but you just didn't see it out in the open. You didn't see somebody 15 or 16 with a car, and it just seemed like life was just a little bit better then. . . .

There's really no jobs out here for nobody. You've got to have this experience or that experience or you're skipping from one job to another or you just landed in programs you weren't qualified for. It was just so many hang-ups trying to get a job, so a lot of people just turned to selling drugs in the street. I can't really say they're wrong for selling it and I can't say they're right for selling it, but this is their way of getting up, selling drugs. . . .

Me, being around a bunch of women that haven't seen the street in a long time? Oh, God, I think I'll fall out for dead! Shucks, they might try to rape you and all that. I be thinking so much about jail that I'm scared to go out there. If I wasn't thinking about that, I'd probably be right out there with the rest of them and I think I might be just as good as the rest of them because I know a lot of people out there who's shooting drugs. But, that's a hard life. You've got to be ducking and dodging and looking who you're talking to and you never know who's going to run up to you and shoot you.

I don't vote for the simple reason that I don't believe most of the things the candidates are telling people, and my vote might count but then yet I think: I'm just one person, you know. That's the attitude of a lot of people and I guess that's why they can't really change or get the President who they want.

So, I don't know . . . I wish these politicians would do something, they need to do something. What are they going to do, run for [President] and help 49 states and leave one just hanging? You know, New York's just hanging in the breeze.

You can't eat cereal every day. These young kids who are growing up, if they cut the welfare out and their mother can't really provide for them like she should, you know, they might see all this as they're growing up and as they get older the welfare can't help them at all or offer them anything. They might think that everybody's against them and all this sort of mess and they might go in the street and start doing their little number in the street trying to make money, or trying to help Momma eat a little better.

ILLEGITIMATE ACTIONS OF GOVERNMENT

The list of illegitimate offenses committed by governmental leaders in recent years is astounding—Watergate and related matters, the handling of the Vietnam War, sex scandals in Congress, governmental misuse of the FBI and Internal Revenue Service (IRS), bribery, FBI files on private citizens, illegal surveillance. The list goes on.[53] It is understandable that the public's confidence in the political institution has diminished. A national survey in 1976 revealed that a majority of Americans do not have a "great deal of confidence" in various aspects of the political institution: the White House (11 per cent); U.S. Supreme Court (22 per cent); and Congress (9 per cent); state government (16 per cent); local government (18 per cent).

Many areas of illegitimate governmental activity have been made public recently. Two of these areas are invasion of privacy and secrecy and deception.

Invasion of Privacy

Americans have always been concerned about the government's invasion of their privacy. And many believe that the government knows much more about the private lives of its citizens than it should. It is feared that computer technology is providing government an unpredecented means for gathering, storing, and dispensing private information about citizens.

In 1967, Congress proposed to consolidate all of the information files on citizens into a national data bank. Intense opposition caused that proposal to be abandoned. Yet a national data bank is being created informally at the present time because the computer systems of various government agencies can pass information to each other. This interfacing of computer systems allows a person operating a terminal thousands of miles away to find out how much money you owe, how many times you've moved, how many children you have, and whether or not you've ever been arrested.

According to a Senate subcommittee, investigators for the federal government now have access to 100 million credit dossiers, almost 300 million psychiatric reports, 264 million police records, and over 300 million medical files.[54] Government agencies collecting, storing, and dispensing information

---

[53] For many detailed accounts of crime and deception in government, see Jethro K. Lieberman, *How the Government Breaks the Law* (Briarcliff Manor, N.Y.: Stein & Day Publishers, 1972).

[54] Michael Sorkin, "The FBI's Big Brother Computer," *The Washington Monthly,* 4 (September 1972): 30.

on citizens include the Secret Service; the U.S. Civil Service Commission; the Justice Department; the Armed Forces; the Defense Department; the Department of Housing and Urban Development; the Department of Health, Education and Welfare; the CIA; and the FBI. According to a Senate Judiciary

IS YOUR NAME IN A FEDERAL COMPUTER?

More than 50 federal agencies, according to a survey by a Senate Judiciary Subcommittee on Constitutional Rights, have 858 separate data banks, containing more than a billion records on individuals. In these data banks, available at the touch of a button, are diverse bits of information on just about every American. Some examples—

DEPARTMENT OF HEALTH, EDUCATION AND WELFARE: 61 data banks, with 402 million records—including information on recipients of Social Security, medicare and welfare payments, among others.

DEPARTMENT OF COMMERCE: 8 data banks, with 204 million records—including those on businessmen, recipients of loans.

TREASURY DEPARTMENT: 46 data banks, containing 156 million records— dealing with taxpayers, individuals under scrutiny by the U.S. Secret Service, people with access to the White House, among others.

JUSTICE DEPARTMENT: 19 data banks, with 139 million records—including fingerprint cards on file, details on individuals arrested on criminal charges, on people in "sensitive" Goverment jobs.

VETERANS ADMINISTRATION: 29 data banks, with 73 million records—including files on veterans and dependents now getting benefits or those who received them in the past.

PENTAGON: 497 banks, with 61 million records on service personnel, other persons investigated for employment, security or criminal reasons.

DEPARTMENT OF LABOR: 4 data banks, with 24 million records—many involving people in federally financed work and training programs.

CIVIL SERVICE COMMISSION: 13 data banks, with 19 million records—including data on people at work in the Government or who have applied for jobs.

DEPARTMENT OF HOUSING AND URBAN DEVELOPMENT: 27 banks, with 10 million records—including information on people who have bought homes with loans guaranteed by the Federal Housing Administration.

DEPARTMENT OF TRANSPORTATION: 18 data banks, with 6 million records— including files on Americans who have been denied drivers' licenses and those whose permits have been suspended or revoked.

U.S. News & World Report, 77 (July, 1974): 41.

Subcommittee on Constitutional Rights, 850 separate data banks, containing more than a billion records on citizens, exist among 50 federal agencies.

The facts surrounding these records are disturbing. Only 10 per cent of the federal data banks are legally authorized. More than 40 per cent do not tell individuals that records are being maintained on them. Finally, the keepers of about 50 per cent of the data banks will not allow individuals to view or correct the files kept on them.[55]

Even though legislation to create a consolidated national data bank in 1967 failed, the FBI has bypassed Congress and has created its own national computer system. Michael Sorkin describes the FBI's national data bank system:

> Under the FBI's system, every time an individual has any contact with the law, his name and the details of the incident will be placed into the computer. Literally millions of Americans will have criminal files even though they have never been arrested or convicted of a crime. There is no requirement that the computer show whether a person has been indicted or tried, or if he was, whether he was found guilty or innocent. . . .
>
> The network will function through separate computer centers set up by each state, where all criminal records will be stored and also transmitted to the FBI for a filing in the National Crime Information Center (NCIC). All 50 states will be able to "talk" to each other through the FBI master computer. In addition, every major municipal police department in the country will be hooked into the network, either with its own computer or a less expensive teletype operation. There are already 135 local and state police agencies that are using or will soon be using the memory links to the FBI. Before long, 75 percent of the nation's police agencies will be plugged in; and by 1975 the figure should rise to 95 percent.[56]

As of 1975, the FBI had 58 million index cards containing information on Americans; over 1 million new cards are filed each year, and only 400,000 are eliminated. The FBI receives over 7 million sets of fingerprints each year from state and local police. In all, FBI records are kept on about 80 million American citizens.[57] Obviously, some of these files reflect the legitimate investigatory powers of the FBI, but it is doubtful that a fourth of the citizens of the United States can be regarded as potentially dangerous to society.

[55] *U.S. News & World Report* (July 1, 1974), p. 41.
[56] Sorkin, "The FBI's Big Brother Computer," op. cit., p. 24.
[57] TRB, "House of File Cards," *The New Republic,* 172 (March 15, 1975): 2.

AN INVASION OF PRIVACY

In May, 1970, Dr. David T. Lykken, a clinical psychologist and professor at the University of Minnesota, held a meeting in his home to raise funds for a group that wanted to halt construction of a missile base in Nakoma, North Dakota. An announcement of the meeting had been posted on the University Bulletin Board; the flyer indicated a "donation and cash bar."

The day before the Saturday-night meeting police officers who had obtained a copy of the flyer consulted with Edward Vavreck, an Assistant City Attorney of Minneapolis. He told them that the evidence was insufficient to permit a search warrant to be issued. Police decided, therefore, to catch Dr. Lykken in the act.

At 10:00 on Saturday night, two police officers in plain clothes came to the Lykken home, engaged in conversation with one of the guests, and "purchased or acquired several bottles of beer." After observing baskets for donations, three women drinking beer or liquor, and most of the guests watching the late news on television, the two officers regrouped outside, where they met other policemen who were waiting to participate in the planned raid. At 11:30, with seventeen guests left in the house (at its peak, the party consisted of no more than thirty people), nineteen policemen entered the house without a search warrant and proceeded to look through every cranny (and toilet bowl) of its three stories. Outside a number of squad cars and two paddy wagons waited. . . . Dr. Lykken (but not his wife) and the remaining seventeen guests were taken off to police headquarters, where Dr. Lykken was charged with "operating a disorderly house" and with "selling liquor without a license." Mrs. Lykken and the seventeen guests were charged with "participating in a disorderly house." Eleven days later the various books, papers, letters, and other items unrelated to the charges were placed in a sealed box. Vavreck, the Assistant City Attorney, told Hennepin County Municipal Court Judge David R. Leslie that the defendants' complaint about the seizure was meaningless because the materials were to be returned within a week to ten days. (Dr. Lykken privately asked Vavreck whether he could burglarize the City Attorney's home so long as the stolen items were later returned. Vavreck thought the analogy neither amusing nor relevant.)

Jethro Lieberman, *How the Government Breaks the Law* (Briarcliff Manor, N.Y.: Stein & Day Publishers, 1972), pp. 79–80.

The CIA, specifically empowered only to collect and analyze information pertaining to foreign affairs, has admitted maintaining secret files on thousands of United States citizens and their activities within this country, including some members of Congress. The CIA has also admitted to domestic break-ins, wiretaps, physical surveillance, and illegal inspection of mail.[58] These practices are in direct violation of federal legislation and represent a frightening picture of deliberate and illegal government surveillance and invasion of privacy.

The federal government, acting through agencies such as the FBI and CIA, has also been actively involved in the surveillance and harassment of individuals and groups whose values are believed to be undesirable. FBI documents, for example, indicate that the Bureau has waged a ten-year campaign to disrupt the Socialist Workers Party in America.[59] This campaign involved the secret interference by the FBI in political campaigns, the promotion of racial unrest, and anonymous mailings of abusive letters. Similar activities were directed toward the Ku Klux Klan and the National States' Rights Party.[60] On the conviction that college dissenters and black student groups were a threat to America's wellbeing, the FBI, in conjunction with the state and local intelligence agencies, engaged in a wide variety of illegal surveillance practices during the 1960s and 1970s.[61]

Of course, much of the information on citizens is collected in order to serve the public. Some government agencies, such as the Department of Health, Education and Welfare and the Civil Service Commission, could not operate without certain information on citizens. Still, the dangers of a persistent pattern of governmental invasion of privacy and misuse of collected data remain.

Secrecy and Deception

If the government sometimes knows too much about the private lives of its citizens, there is much it does not want citizens to know about its operations. Secrecy and deception on the part of government officials is neither new nor restricted to any particular part of the government.

Probably the most blatant practices of government secrecy, distortion, lying, and falsification were those associated with the Vietnam War.[62] The

[58] Leslie H. Gelb, "The CIA and the Press," *The New Republic,* 172 (March 22, 1975): 13–16.

[59] Margaret Gentry, "FBI Harassed Socialist Workers Party," *The Beacon Journal* (Akron, Ohio), March 19, 1975, p. 9A.

[60] Associated Press, "FBI Papers Show Attempts to Disrupt 'White Hate Groups,' " The Courier-Journal (Louisville, Kentucky), August 16, 1975, p. A2.

[61] Frank Donner, "The Theory and Practice of American Political Intelligence," *The New York Review of Books,* 16 (April 22, 1971): 27–39.

[62] David Halberstam, *The Best and the Brightest* (Greenwich, Conn.: Fawcett Publications, Inc., 1973).

THE NATURE OF THE FBI FILES

The files are a repository for the black deeds of criminals—murderers, rapists, arsonists, thieves, blackmailers, panderers and the like. The files are also heavy with the names of Americans who have committed no crime other than to take stands that are contrary to the attitudes Hoover imposed on the FBI. There are actors and writers, teachers and students, athletes and physicians, preachers and atheists, whites and blacks (an incredible number of blacks). The political files do not match the criminal files in either number or volume, but their mass is substantial, and their existence is irrefutable proof that the FBI is, indeed, a political police force, deeply involved in thought control.

All the files are sacred property, supposedly hidden from the eyes of all save the FBI, although choice tidbits are sometimes officially bootlegged to influential politicians. We have had access to these forbidden files.

Even the thickest folders contain little wisdom and no wit. They provide typical police blotter information—name, height, weight, address; identification of parents, mates, and children; previous arrests, even for the most trivial offenses and even if the charges were later dropped or dismissed. The FBI folders serve also as repositories of rumors, chitchat, and vicious slander. Little of this information is generated by the FBI itself. Instead, a network of informers feeds the FBI's agents, and the whispers become the basis of turgid prose forwarded to Washington.

Newspaper and magazine articles are also dutifully clipped, pasted on special forms, and sent on to become part of the massive mountain of catalogued minutiae. Occasionally the Central Intelligence Agency, the Secret Service and the National Security Agency contribute items. Frequently the FBI violates the law by obtaining information from banks and telephone companies without subpoenas. This data, too, is shoveled into the files.

Read singly, the political files seem merely another dreary example of bureaucratic excess. Examined in larger lots, they provide an intriguing case-by-case study of just how far the government has intruded into the lives of Americans.

When actress Jane Fonda told a friend she wanted to overthrow "the establishment," an FBI informant was listening. She opposed the war.

When Dr. Benjamin Spock, whose book on child care has helped millions of Americans raise their children, planned a visit to Australia, the FBI had his itinerary. He advocated peace.

When Roy Innis called for a separate school board for Harlem, the FBI made another entry in his folder. He is a black leader.

When an obviously phony diatribe against Jews was circulated under the misspelled name of Muhammad Ali, it was included in the boxer's dossier, which the FBI labeled "Cassius Clay." He is a Black Muslim.

When the *Washington Post* reported that David Eaton was named senior minister for All Souls Unitarian Church, the news made its way into the FBI records. Eaton, too, is black.

Jack Anderson, *The Anderson Papers* (New York: Random House, Inc., 1974), pp. 245–247. Reprinted by permission of Random House, Inc.

Pentagon Papers dramatically reveal that the truth and what the government tells us are not always the same. That deception began when the Defense Department created false intelligence reports on the Gulf of Tonkin incident to convince the Senate that President Johnson's desire to conduct a war against North Vietnam was justified. Deception continued throughout the war as bombing records and death counts were deliberately falsified by military personnel to support the government's optimistic portrayal of how the war was going.

Another example of governmental secrecy and deception is found in the cooperation of the CIA, the executive branch, and the International Telephone and Telegraph Company (ITT) in an attempt to stop the election of Chile's Marxist president, Salvador Allende, in 1970. Because Allende did not win a majority of votes in the presidential election of September 1970, the president had to be selected by the Chilean Congress. During the seven-week period between the election and the Congressional decision, ITT marshalled its influence and financial resources against Allende. At stake was ITT's multimillion-dollar interest (estimated at $153 million) in the Chilean telephone system, which Allende threatened to nationalize if elected.

For its own economic benefit, ITT was willing to throw the Chilean economy into chaos in the hope that a military coup would occur. It was assumed that a military coup would strengthen their candidate in the congressional selection of a president.[63] In 1974, CIA Director William Colby gave secret testimony to Congress that the CIA had been authorized by the United States government to use $8 million for the overthrow of Allende's government. The governmental unit alleged to have given this authorization was the "40 Committee," composed of President Nixon's assistant for national security, the deputy secretary of defense, the undersecretary of state for political affairs, the director of the CIA, and the chairman of the joint chiefs of staff.[64] There also is evidence that the Chilean ambassador from the United States, Edward Korry, was given permission by the State Department to "move in the name of President Nixon." The message gave him maximum authority to to "do all possible—short of a Dominican Republic-type action—to keep Allende from taking power."[65]

[63] Jack Anderson, *The Anderson Papers* (New York: Ballantine Books, Random House, Inc., 1974), p. 151.

[64] David Wise, "Cloak and Dagger Operations: An Overview," in Jerome H. Skolnick and Elliott Currie, eds., *Crisis in American Institutions,* 3rd ed. (Boston: Little, Brown and Company, 1976), pp. 94–95.

[65] Anderson, *The Anderson Papers,* op. cit., p. 153.

THE CIA'S CLANDESTINE MENTALITY

Deeply embedded within the cladestine mentality [of the CIA] is the belief that human ethics and social laws have no bearing on covert operations or their practitioners. The intelligence profession, because of its lofty "national security" goals, is free from all moral restrictions. There is no need to wrestle with technical legalisms or judgments as to whether something is right or wrong. The determining factors in secret operations are purely pragmatic: Does the job need to be done? Can it be done? And can secrecy (or plausible denial) be maintained?

One of the lessons learned from the Watergate experience is the scope of this amorality and its influence on the clandestine mentality. E. Howard Hunt claimed that his participation in the Watergate break-in and the other operations of the plumbers group was in "what I believed to be the . . . the best interest of my country." In this instance, at least, we can accept Hunt as speaking sincerely. He was merely reflecting an attitude that is shared by most CIA operators when carrying out the orders of their superiors.

Hunt expanded on this point when interrogated before a federal grand jury in April 1973 by Assistant U.S. Attorney Earl Silbert.

SILBERT: Now while you worked at the White House, were you ever a participant or did you ever have knowledge of any other so-called "bag job" or entry operations?

HUNT: No, sir.

SILBERT: Were you aware of or did you participate in any other what might commonly be referred to as illegal activities?

HUNT: Illegal?

SILBERT: Yes, sir.

HUNT: I have no recollection of any, no, sir.

SILBERT: What about clandestine activities?

HUNT: Yes, sir.

SILBERT: All right. What about that?

HUNT: I'm not quibbling, but there's quite a difference between something that's illegal and something that's clandestine.

SILBERT: Well, in your terminology, would the entry into Mr. Fielding's [Daniel Ellsberg's psychiatrist] office have been clandestine, illegal, neither or both?

HUNT: I would simply call it an entry operation conducted under the auspices of competent authority.

Within the CIA, similar activities are undertaken with the consent of "competent authority." The Watergate conspirators, assured that "national security" was at stake, did not question the legality or the morality of their methods; nor do most CIA operators. Hundreds if not thousands of CIA men have participated in similar operations, usually—but not always—in foreign countries; all such operations are executed in the name of "national security." The clandestine mentality not only allows it; it veritably *wills* it.

Victor Marchetti and John D. Marks, *The CIA and the Cult of Intelligence* (New York: Alfred A. Knopf, Inc., 1974), pp. 249–250.

WHAT CAN BE DONE?

Controlling the Corporate-Government Alliance

The starting point for any significant degree of political reform is the realization that not all governing is done by those in formal government positions. Much of what passes for the actions of government is actually the result of cooperative efforts between political and corporate elites. If the governing from nonofficial sources is to be subject to the public's control, then it must be exposed and combatted. The corporate-government alliance is formidable, yet there are some means available for reducing its power.

Changing Public Opinion. Strong public opinion against the abuses of the corporate-government alliance is a potentially powerful weapon. If values, attitudes, and beliefs change such that those abuses are greeted with public protest rather than with indifference, then even large, unresponsive bureaucracies must react.

The greatest hope for the future rests with America's youth. According to a recent survey, today's young people are aware of the power and abuses of the corporate-government alliance, and a large proportion of them believe that fundamental reform is needed.[66] Although today's college and noncollege youth differ somewhat politically, the two groups share many values, attitudes, and beliefs. A majority of both groups believes that America is democratic in name only and is actually controlled by special interests. Whereas college youth see the giant corporations as controlling the country, noncollege youth believe that the real power is more evenly balanced between big business and Congress. Over 90 per cent of both groups believe that business is too concerned with profits and not concerned enough about public responsibility. Sixty per cent of noncollege youth and 50 per cent of college youth believe that "the Establishment unfairly controls every aspect of our lives." On the matter of change, both groups overwhelmingly contend that the defense budget should be reduced in favor of domestic needs, and a substantial percentage of each group favors fundamental reform of big business, the military, and the Congress.

Some specific mechanisms for coping with the corporate-government alliance already exist, but they must be strengthened. These include the Gen-

---

[66] This comparison of college and noncollege youth is based on Daniel Yankelovich, *The New Morality: A Profile of American Youth in the 1970s* (New York: McGraw-Hill Book Company, 1974), pp. 115–128.

eral Accounting Office (GAO), regulatory agencies in government, public interest groups, and political campaign reform.

GAO. Although the GAO is not technically a regulatory agency, it acts as a major watchdog for Congress of all bookkeeping in the executive branch of government. Its staff tries to determine if governmental units are getting their money's worth and if they are spending their money legally. It has a budget of almost $1.5 million to scrutinize how appropriated funds are spent and to report the results to Congress. In recent years, the GAO has moved beyond strictly auditing books to examining management practices in general. It now has a special staff that can launch investigations at the request of congressional committees or, in some instances, individual members of Congress. The subpoena power recently given the GAO in this regard has added substantially to its effectiveness.

The GAO cannot uncover all misuses of appropriated money, but it has retained its independence of other government agencies and has been one of the few forces able to circumvent the Department of Defense's barriers to secure information on such abuses as cost overruns on defense contracts, costly failures of defense contractors to meet deadlines, and questionable contract negotiations. The GAO's ability to make an accurate and independent assessment of the technical, economic, and political aspects of national defense has been a great help to Congress. In the early 1970s, the GAO successfully disputed the claim by the director of defense research and engineering in the Pentagon that a wide gap in military research and development was emerging between the United States and the Soviet Union.[67] As a consequence of that report, skepticism within the Congress led to a refusal to increase funds in the area of research and development of military weapons.

Government Regulatory Agencies. There are now more than 100 government regulatory agencies. Some, such as the Federal Power Commission, the Federal Trade Commission, and the Interstate Commerce Commission, are independent of the executive branch. Others, including the Food and Drug Administration, the Federal Highway Administration, and the Federal Aviation Administration, are within departments in the executive branch of the federal government. Both types of regulatory agencies include such activities as setting rates industries can charge, determining which products and ser-

[67] Ernest J. Yanarella, *The Missile Defense Controversy: Strategy, Technology, and Politics, 1955–1972* (Lexington, Ky.: University Press of Kentucky, 1977), pp. 201, 220.

vices can be offered by whom, ruling on mergers, and granting transportation routes to airlines.

Regulatory agencies and commissions were created to protect the public from abusive and illegal business practices, such as monopoly, price gouging, and fraud, unhampered by political pressures. In order to reduce political pressures, commission members are appointed by the president for staggered terms of service so that the same people will not be serving together for extended periods of time. Neither presidential appointment nor staggered terms, however, have worked as well as was expected.

Ironically, the broadest charge against regulatory agencies is that they operate to serve and protect those whom they are supposed to regulate, rather than the public welfare.[68] The Federal Communications Commission (FCC) is accused of serving the television industry, the Food and Drug Administration (FDA) is charged with failing to ban harmful drugs or fight artificially high drug prices, and the Securities and Exchange Commission (SEC) is said to look the other way concerning questionable stock market practices. This situation exists partly because presidents tend to appoint to a regulatory agency persons with a vested interest in the area of business that the agency is supposed to regulate. Television executives are appointed to the FCC, drug manufacturing executives sit on the FDA, and stockbrokers serve on the SEC. These commission members usually return to private business. While on a commission, therefore, they tend to make friends rather than enemies in the industries to which they will return.

A regulatory commission's actions are usually enmeshed in cross pressures from politicans, public interest groups, experts with conflicting points of view, and industry representatives. Any important decision made by a regulatory agency is the result of considerable compromise by the parties involved. Often, the final decision is not made by the commission. An illustration is offered by Newton Minow from his experience on the Federal Communications Commission:

> A good example which I know something about is the creation of policy . . . concerning international communication satellites. Here, we succeeded in getting Comsat launched and thus preserved American leadership in the world.

---

[68] For a source contending that regulatory agencies, on the whole, have served the public well in many respects, see Henry J. Friendly, *The Federal Administrative Agencies: The Need for Better Definition of Standards* (Cambridge, Mass.: Harvard University Press, 1962).

But we succeeded only because the FCC was willing to compromise with various competing economic interests . . . , governmental and private agencies, and because we turned to the President and the Congress for the final word. This required an understanding of the political process; the essence of that process will almost always require compromise.[69]

The Federal Trade Commission also learned it was necessary to deal with many other groups when it offered to Congress its proposals regarding the placement of health warnings in cigarette advertising and on cigarette packages.[70]

What must be done to make regulatory agencies more effective buffers between big business and the public? It would help if presidents would stop appointing to commissions persons with vested interests in areas they are to police. Also, Congress must more closely scrutinize the activities and decisions of regulatory agencies. Finally, it is sometimes necessary to set up agencies to regulate the regulatory agencies. An example is the legislation proposed in 1977 to create a Federal Consumer Protection Agency to protect the consumer by dealing with other regulatory agencies. Public interest groups such as Common Cause and Ralph Nader's various consumer organizations are strong forces in the current push to control the abuses of the business-government alliance and to increase governmental representation of the public.

Increasing Governmental Representation

Control of Lobbyists.   The Federal Regulation of Lobbying Act of 1946 requires lobbyists to register and to file official reports of their expenses.[71] As presently interpreted, there are some major loopholes in the law. It does not apply to organizations in which lobbying is not the principal purpose. Because lobbying is incidental to the main purpose of most organizations that lobby, they are not subject to the law. The law defines lobbying as direct con-

---

[69] Erwin G. Krasnow and Lawrence D. Longley, *The Politics of Broadcast Regulation* (New York: St. Martin's Press, Inc., 1973), Preface.

[70] A. Lee Fritschler, *Smoking and Politics: Policymaking and the Federal Bureaucracy,* 2nd ed. (Englewood Cliffs, N.J.: Prentice-Hall, Inc., 1975).

[71] This discussion of controlling lobbyists is drawn from Wolfinger, Shapiro, and Greenstein, *American Politics,* op. cit., pp. 243–244.

tact with congressmen for the purpose of discussing federal legislation, which exempts indirect means of influencing members of Congress such as letter-writing campaigns among their constitutents. Indirect lobbying is one of the main techniques of lobbyists. This loophole allowed the National Association of Manufacturers to spend $2.5 million for indirect lobbying during one period without reporting it.[72] The effect of these two loopholes is that most organizations underreport the money spent on lobbying. This explains why Common Cause, a "people's lobby" that reports all of its expenditures, reported spending eight times as much on lobbying as the American Petroleum Institute in 1973.[73]

Numerous legislative proposals to close these loopholes have been introduced in Congress in the wake of the Watergate revelations. Various bills seek to accomplish the following:

1. Expand the definition of lobbying to include [such] grassroots efforts [as] stimulating letter writing campaigns.
2. Relax the "principal purpose" criterion so as to apply the law to all organizations that seek to influence legislation.
3. Require lobbyists to keep records of all officials whom they see and the specific measures they are trying to influence.
4. Expand the law to cover lobbying the executive branch as well as lobbying Congress, a form of group representation that many political scientists consider more important than attempts to influence legislation . . .
5. Require members of the executive branch to keep logs of all contacts with private citizens. The idea here is to discourage "secret meetings" with people looking for favors.[74]

Some government agencies have voluntarily adopted such practices as recording visits by private citizens and announcing such visits in advance, but none of the proposals listed are currently part of the law. If public representation is to be increased, lobbyists will have to be more tightly controlled. In order to accomplish this, some changes in the law such as the ones listed above will have to be made.

Public Interest Groups. Groups pressing for special interests have been around for a long time. A more recent development is the emergence of groups whose purpose is to protect the "public interest." They do this

[72] *Weekly Report,* July 27, 1974, p. 1949.
[73] Congressional Quarterly Service, *The Washington Lobby* (Washington, D.C.: Congressional Quarterly, Inc., 1974), 2nd ed., p. 38.
[74] Wolfinger, Shapiro, and Greenstein, *Dynamics of American Politics,* op. cit., p. 244.

through publicity, gathering and publishing information, and through lawsuits. The National Citizens Committee for Broadcasting, for example, along with other groups, pressured advertisers to withdraw sponsor support of excessively violent television shows. Although some companies have denied any connection between that effort and their actions, corporations such as Sears, Roebuck and Company, Schlitz Brewing Company, Union Oil Company, and General Motors announced in 1977 their intentions to stop buying advertising time for the more violent prime-time television shows. Many environmental organizations have taken legal actions against companies that violate pollution laws, and have forced some government regulatory agencies to investigate illegal environmental practices, often ignored in the past.

The best-known public interest groups are Common Cause and Ralph Nader's consumer advocate units such as Nader's Raiders and the Center for the Study of Responsive Law. Ralph Nader has increased the political representation of consumers more than any single person. His 1965 book *Unsafe at Any Speed* is credited with beginning the consumer movement. The book attacked General Motors' Corvair, a compact car that Nader contended was deadly even at low driving speeds. General Motors hired a private investigator to gather information to discredit Nader. An attempt was made to set him up in a sexual escapade. Nader's suit against General Motors for invasion of privacy gained him $280,000 in damages and a base of public and financial support for his consumer protection campaign.

Nader's efforts have aided in the passage of the National Traffic and Motor Vehicle Safety Act, the Highway Safety Act, the Wholesome Meat Act, the Coal Mine Health and Safety Act, the Comprehensive Occupational Safety and Health Act, the Gas Pipeline Safety Act, and the Radiation Control for Health and Safety Act. His various organizations also have attacked the use of cyclamates, challenged the genuineness of the oil crisis in the mid-1970s, and exposed abuses in nursing homes.

Common Cause was founded in 1970 by John Gardner, who had served as secretary of Health, Education and Welfare in the Johnson administration. Political corruption and wasteful spending in government have been its primary targets. Common Cause has focused on such problems as the registration of lobbyists, campaign financing, reformation of the congressional seniority system, and tax reform. Common Cause has a membership of about 350,000 and about $7 million in annual financial backing.

Campaign Reform. Campaign reform traditionally has not been initiated because those in power benefited from the status quo. In 1971, Common

Cause sued the Republican and Democratic parties for violating the Federal Corrupt Practices Act of 1925. When the court denied both political parties' motions for dismissal, members of Congress realized that citizen litigation could compel United States attorneys general to enforce campaign-financing statutes. That motivated Congress to enact the Federal Election Campaign Act of 1971.

Maurice Stans and Herbert Kalmbach, who headed the finance committee of the Committee to Re-elect the President (CREEP), and many candidates applied pressure to obtain as much money as possible before the law went into effect in 1972. Common Cause took CREEP to court for violating the 1925 statute and forced the disclosure of CREEP's secret list of contributors. Those disclosures, along with the Watergate affair, led Congress to pass the Campaign Finance Reform Act of 1974.[75] This legislation placed limits on the contributions of individuals and organizations, the amount candidates for the Senate, House, and presidency can spend, and the outlays of national parties. It also provided for the reporting and disclosure of contributions and expenditures. Public funding was made available for presidential elections. Presidential candidates could not use private contributions if they accepted money from public funding. A committee to report all campaign contributions and expenditures had to be formed for each presidential or congressional candidate.[76]

The United States Supreme Court in 1976 ruled that placing limits on the amount of personal or family money a candidate can spend in an election violates the First Amendment right of free speech. Spending limits, the Court ruled, could be imposed only if a candidate chooses public financing, but any candidate who raises all money privately can spend without restriction. This leaves the door open for wealthy individuals to buy their way into public office. This decision also states that persons unconnected with a campaign who have not been approached by a candidate or his campaign officials can spend unlimited amounts. The Court did, however, uphold provisions about disclosure, public financing, and limits on individual contributions. This leaves intact very important reforms which will, if enforced, alter some of the longstanding abuses in campaign financing.

Citizen Political Activism.   According to a longstanding belief in American political life, if the government fails to protect its citizenry, the people have

---

[75] Herbert E. Alexander, ed. *Campaign Money: Reform and Reality in the United States* (New York: The Free Press, 1976), pp. vii–viii.
[76] For a full description of this law, see *Congressional Quarterly Weekly Report,* October 12, 1974, pp. 2865–2870.

the right to put pressure on it to serve the public welfare. Consistent with this belief, Americans have created many organizations to influence the government's conception of what constitutes the public interest. These organizations range from the Anti-Saloon League of the early nineteenth century to today's public interest groups such as John Gardner's Common Cause and Ralph Nader's Center for the Study of Responsive Law. Political activism among citizens involves more than single organizations such as these. Broader-based efforts to influence the government's definition of the public interest, sometimes called public interest "movements," have also been part of citizen political activism in America. The black civil rights movement, the women's liberation movement, the environmental movement, and the antiwar movement of the 1960s are all examples of broad-based public interest movements.[77]

The potential for a public interest movement's success is demonstrated in the increasing political participation of blacks since the 1950s. In 1940, 5 per cent of all Southern blacks were registered to vote. That figure reached 27 per cent by 1962. It was with the Voting Rights Act of 1965 that black registration really began to accelerate. As a result of progress since 1965, blacks in the South now register and vote at rates close to those of whites.[78] For the country as a whole, "blacks participate *more* than whites at equivalent levels of income. That is, well-off blacks are more active than well-off whites, middle-class blacks more active than middle-class whites, and poor blacks more active than poor whites."[79]

Reducing Illegitimate Actions of Government

Protection of Privacy. The protection of privacy from government is becoming a concern of American citizens. According to a 1974 Harris Poll, 23 per cent of the public felt "threatened" by having personal information in government files; 32 per cent felt that way by 1977. In the 1977 Harris Poll, 75 per cent favored the enactment of legislation to protect the public from the misuse of information collected and stored by the government. Leg-

[77] These points are made in John Guinther, *Moralists and Managers: Public Interest Movements in America* (Garden City, N.Y.: Anchor Books, 1976), pp. xv–xvi.

[78] See Neal R. Pierce, *The Deep South States of America* (New York: W. W. Norton & Company, Inc., 1974).

[79] Sidney Verba and Norman H. Nie, *Participation in America: Political Democracy and Social Equality* (New York: Harper & Row, Publishers, Inc., 1972), p. 152.

islation is one possible answer. Other possibilities are a comprehensive ruling by the Supreme Court and the creation of a regulatory agency.

Since the 1950s, the Supreme Court has made a number of rulings sympathetic to the protection of the privacy of individuals. Although the Court has not been able to cite a specific constitutional provision guaranteeing the right of privacy, it has used different parts of the Constitution to support its defense of privacy as the nature of specific cases has varied. While the Court's decisions supporting the right of privacy have been generally supportive, they are a patchwork. A comprehensive legal position that places governmental intrusion of privacy under the legal requirements of due process should be developed.[80]

There also is a need for legislative action. Alan Westin has suggested some general guidelines for legislation dealing with privacy and the use of surveillance technology.[81] First, rules are needed to control who can engage in surveillance. For example, surveillance should be limited to the FBI and military agencies on the federal level and to district attorneys' offices and state attorney generals' offices on the state level. Second, detailed regulations are needed to specify the scope of surveillance, how long an instance of surveillance may last, and the ways in which the surveillance may be carried out.

A flood of bills on this issue has been submitted in Congress over the last few years, but none have been passed. This, contends Arthur Miller, is because most members of Congress understand neither the new information technologies nor their social implications.[82] Unless this situation changes there is little hope for comprehensive legislation.

Despite the considerable deficiencies of regulatory agencies noted previously, a watchdog agency within the federal government has some potential advantages that should not be overlooked. First, a regulatory agency would be staffed by persons knowledgeable about information technologies. Administrative rules and regulations are flexible enough to permit experimentation, and they can be revised more quickly and easily than laws.

It would be possible to place regulatory authority regarding the protection of privacy in the hands of existing agencies such as the Federal Communications Commission or the Federal Trade Commission. However, it

---

[80] W. H. Ferry, "Must We Rewrite the Constitution to Control Technology?" *Saturday Review,* 51 (March 2, 1968), 50–54.

[81] Westin, *Privacy and Freedom,* op. cit., p. 376.

[82] Arthur R. Miller, *The Assault on Privacy: Computers, Data Banks, and Dossiers* (Ann Arbor: The University of Michigan Press, 1971), pp. 227–228.

would probably be wiser to create a new, independent agency. The semiautonomous General Accounting Office would appear to be the best model for the creation of such an agency. A truly independent regulatory agency could be quite effective in protecting the privacy of American citizens against information technology.[83]

Safeguards Against Secrecy and Deception. Secrecy and deception in government are so widespread that they must be controlled by a variety of means, such as improving and enforcing existing legislation, making government officials responsible for their actions, creating a watchdog agency, and establishing the principle of "open government."

Actually, legislation already exists which was intended to protect the public's "right to know" by making governmental records more accessible to the public. However, this law, the Freedom of Information Act, enacted by Congress in 1966, has failed to live up to its promise because it has consistently been circumvented by government officials.[84] This is unfortunate because it is a reasonably balanced law. On the government side, it specifies eight categories of information considered too sensitive for public disclosure. These exemptions included national defense or foreign policy information. On the public's side, anyone denied information can sue the agency in federal court, with the burden of proof placed on the agency. If the court rules against the agency, it can require that the information be made available and can cite the officials for contempt of court if they refuse to comply.[85]

How can this law be made to work? Compliance should be forced through the formation of public interest groups to collect and make public information about the inner workings of the government. This seems a natural avenue now that public interest groups are using lawsuits as one of their major weapons. Congress should also be more insistent in demanding that it be provided information to which it is now entitled. Finally, loopholes in the law should be plugged to make information pertaining to the national security available to the public after a reasonable period of time.

It is traditional for government officials to blame the "bureaucracy" rather than assume personal responsibility for the consequences of their actions. There have been at least two suggestions for changing this pattern. One solution is the development of what Edward Weisband and Thomas Franck

---

[83] Ibid., pp. 229, 233.
[84] Lieberman, *How the Government Breaks the Law,* op. cit., p. 258.
[85] Westin, *Privacy and Freedom,* op. cit., pp. 386–387.

call "ethical autonomy" among government officials.[86] When officials disagree with some policies or actions in government, they should make public the grounds for their dissent and should "resign in protest." A second solution is to make officials legally responsible for their actions. Using the Vietnam war as a case study, Ralph Stavins, Richard Barnet, and Marcus Raskin contend that government policies are made through the individual decisions of identifiable persons, not by the faceless "system."[87]

Although aware of the limitations of watchdog agencies, Jethro Lieberman has suggested the creation of an "ombudsman" who would be empowered to investigate citizen complaints about government without being directly supervised by other public officials.[88] The sole function of an ombudsman would be to investigate and make public all illegal or oppressive actions on the part of government.

The principle of "open government" should be accepted in both the executive and legislative branches of the federal government. In 1974, a Senate subcommittee reported that over a ten-year period executive branch agencies had refused information requested by Congress in 225 instances.[89] As late as 1971, over one third of all congressional committee meetings were held in secret.[90] In 1973, the House Democratic caucus did vote to open all committee meetings to the public *unless* a majority of the members voted not to do so. But it subsequently agreed to publish votes taken in caucus *only if* a majority of the members voted for disclosure. House Republicans and both parties in the Senate have taken neither step. Congress is in a weak position to demand information from the executive branch until it does more to establish the principle of open government for itself.[91]

Each of the possible solutions is important, but the wide range of problems within the political institution will not be adequately combatted until the public feels strongly enough about them to demand and expect reform. That means prevailing values, attitudes, and beliefs must change to the point that the current problems within the political institution are widely viewed as in-

[86] Edward Weisband and Thomas M. Frank, *Resignation in Protest* (New York: Grossman Publishers, 1975).

[87] Ralph Stavins, Richard J. Barnet, and Marcus G. Raskin, *Washington Plans an Aggressive War: A Documented Account of the United States Adventure in Indochina* (New York: Vintage Books, 1971).

[88] Lieberman, *How the Government Breaks the Law,* op. cit., p. 271.

[89] *National Journal Reports,* 6 (September 7, 1974): 1344.

[90] Dennis C. Pirages and Paul P. Ehrlich, *Ark II: Social Responses to Environmental Imperatives* (New York: The Viking Press, 1974), p. 180.

[91] Theodore C. Sorensen, *Watchmen in the Night: Presidential Accountability After Watergate* (Cambridge, Mass.: The MIT Press, 1975), p. 103.

tolerable. Revelations about the inner workings of government during the 1960s and 1970s may have well started such a change. Public interest groups are becoming more numerous and more influential, Congress has formulated a new code of ethics for itself, and citizens are becoming more aware of how the government daily invades their private lives.

Additional Readings

Agee, Philip. *Inside the Company: CIA Diary.* New York: Bantam Books, Inc., 1976.

Bone, Hugh A., and Austin Ranney. *Politics and Voters,* 3rd ed. New York: McGraw-Hill, Inc., 1971.

Buenker, John D. *Urban Liberalism and Progressive Reform.* New York: Charles Scribner's Sons, 1973.

Deakin, James. *The Lobbyists.* Washington, D.C.: Public Affairs Press, 1966.

Flanigan, William H. *Political Behavior of the American Electorate.* Boston: Allyn and Bacon, Inc., 1968.

Goldwin, Robert A. *How Democratic is America?: Responses to the New Left Challenge.* Chicago: Rand McNally & Company, 1971.

Hayes, Edward C. *Power Structure and Urban Policy: Who Rules in Oakland?* New York: McGraw-Hill Book Company, 1972.

Holtzman, Abraham. *Interest Groups and Lobbying.* New York: Macmillan Publishing Co., Inc., 1966.

Key, V.O., Jr. *The Responsible Electorate.* Cambridge, Mass.: The Belknap Press of Harvard University Press, 1966.

Lane, Robert E. *Political Ideology: Why the American Common Man Believes What He Does.* New York: The Free Press, 1962.

Lapp, Ralph E. *The Weapons Culture.* New York: W. W. Norton & Company, Inc., 1968.

Lipset, Seymour Martin, and Earl Raab. *The Politics of Unreason: Right-Wing Extremism in America, 1790–1970.* New York: Harper & Row, Publishers, 1970.

Nader, Ralph, and Mark J. Green. *Corporate Power in America.* New York: Grossman Publishers, 1973.

Novak, Michael. *Politics: Realism and Imagination.* New York: Herder and Herder, 1971.

O'Brien, David J. *Neighborhood Organization and Interest-Group Process*. Princeton, New Jersey: Princeton University Press, 1975.

Pilisuk, Marc, and Thomas Hayden. ''Is There a Military-Industrial Complex Which Prevents Peace?: Consensus and Countervailing Power in Pluralistic Systems,'' in Robert Perucci and Marc Pilisuk, eds. *The Triple Revolution: Social Problems in Depth*. Boston: Little, Brown and Company, 1968, pp. 73–94.

Sampson, Anthony. *The Sovereign State of ITT*. Greenwich, Conn.: Fawcett Publications, Inc., 1974.

Yarmolinsky, Adam. *The Military Establishment: Its Impacts on American Society*. New York: Harper & Row, Publishers, 1971.

Zisk, Betty H., ed. *American Political Interest Groups: Readings in Theory and Research*. Belmont, Calif.: Wadsworth Publishing Company, 1969.

education

When the history of our times is written, it may designate the two decades following World War II as the golden age of American education. Never before was education more highly valued. Never before was so much of it so readily available to so many. Never before had it been supported so generously. Never before was so much expected of it.

But in [the present] decade of the twentieth century public education in this country appears to be in trouble. Taxpayers are revolting against the skyrocketing costs of education. Schools are being denied the funds they say they need for quality education. Teachers are uniting to press demands for higher pay and easier working conditions.

College and high school students have rebelled against what they call "the Establishment," resisting and overturning regulations, demanding pupil-directed rather than teacher-directed education, and turning in some cases to drink, drugs, and delinquency. Minorities are demanding equal treatment, which is surely their right. But when integration makes social differences more visible, and when equality of opportunity is not followed quickly by equality of achievement, frustration turns to anger, which sometimes leads to violence.

Robert L. Ebel, "What Are Schools For?" *Phi Delta Kappan,* 54 (September 1972): 3.

Education is an important institution in modern society, and as the opening passage indicates, it is in trouble. Two important questions about the functions of education have emerged in recent years: Are children taught con-

COLONIAL EDUCATION

Elementary education—the "three R's"—became a parental responsibility by act of the Bay Colony in 1642; and five years later, settlements with fifty or more families were required to appoint a schoolmaster "to teach all such children as shall resort to him to write and read." The same act of 1647 (shortly copied by Connecticut and New Haven) required towns of 100 families or more to set up a grammar school on the English model. These grammar schools took in boys at six or eight years of age and kept them for six years, during which they studied Latin and Greek grammar and literature, and arithmetic.

. . . The dynamic motive in colonial education, and in American higher education generally, until the rise of the public high school and the state university, was religious as well as humane. Boys had to learn to read in order to read the Bible, to write and speak "pieces" in order to communicate; to "cipher" in order to do business.

Samuel Eliot Morison, *The Oxford History of the American People*, vol. 1 (New York: The New American Library, Inc., 1972), pp. 113–114.

formity at the expense of creativity and individuality in order that they will better fill bureaucratic niches? Are individuals who fail to succeed flawed in some way or do schools serve to prevent the academic, social, and economic success of minority and lower-class children? Critics who object to the school's emphasis on obedience, conformity, and control are calling for child-centered rather than adult-centered schools. Because children are individuals with different interests, abilities, and personalities, it is argued, schools must provide enough freedom for these differences to develop. Those at the bottom of the stratification structure—blacks, American Indians, Spanish Americans—are demanding that education lead them to economic and occupational *results* on a par with the majority.[1]

WHAT ARE SCHOOLS FOR?

The Importance of Education in Modern Society

There is a relationship between education and socialization in all societies because young people must be taught the things they need to know to function successfully as adults. In preindustrial society, education took place either

[1] Martin Carnoy, ed., *Schooling in a Corporate Society: The Political Economy of Education in America,* 2nd ed. (New York: David McKay Co., Inc., 1975), pp. 12–19.

at home or at a nearby work site. Because family members could gain needed occupational knowledge in or near the home, there was no need for formal schooling. But when employment began moving from households to factories in the early nineteenth century, the family could no longer serve effectively as an economic training ground for its children. This created the need for formal schools in which children could learn basic skills needed for later employment.[2]

As a society becomes more industrialized, opportunities for undereducated persons to obtain higher-level jobs diminish. The self-made person who succeeds without an education becomes a rarity as economic development proceeds. This is so because industrialization brings about a shift from unskilled and semiskilled jobs toward professional and technical occupations. In 1960, 43 per cent of the American labor force were in white-collar occupations; by 1985 this is expected to reach 53 per cent (see Table 5-1). During this same period, the labor force in blue-collar jobs is expected to decrease from 36 per cent to 32 per cent.

Table 5-1. Percentage Distribution of Employment by Major Occupational Group, 1960 and 1972, and Projected 1980 and 1985

Occupational Group	1960	1972	1980	1985
Total	100.0%	100.0%	100.0%	100.0%
White-collar workers	43.1	47.8	51.5	52.9
Professional and technical	11.0	14.0	15.7	16.8
Managers and administrators	11.2	9.8	10.5	10.3
Sales workers	6.4	6.6	6.6	6.4
Clerical workers	14.5	17.4	18.7	19.4
Blue-collar workers	36.3	35.0	33.1	32.3
Craftsmen and kindred workers	13.3	13.2	12.8	12.8
Operatives	17.3	16.6	15.6	15.1
Nonfarm laborers	5.7	5.2	4.7	4.4
Service workers	12.7	13.4	13.3	13.2
Private household workers	3.0	1.8	1.3	1.1
Other service workers	9.7	11.6	12.0	12.9
Farm workers	7.9	3.8	2.1	1.6

SOURCE: Neal H. Rosenthal, "The United States Economy in 1985: Projected Changes in Occupations," *Monthly Labor Review*, 96 (December 1973): 19.

[2] The development of formal schooling was also promoted by a desire for a literate voting public in America and by the scientific revolution in both Europe and America. See Ralph L. Pounds and James R. Bryner, *The School in American Society,* 3rd ed. (New York: Macmillan Publishing Co., Inc., 1973), pp. 57–66.

Advanced industrialization has made education the ticket to better jobs and higher incomes. Shown in Table 5-2 are figures on the relationship between educational level and occupational status for American males. The proportion of workers in upper-level occupations is greater at each successively higher level of education. As Table 5-3 reveals, incomes and education are also positively related.

Table 5-2. Level of School Completed by Employed Males 25 to 64 Years Old, by Occupational Level, 1971

		High School Graduate		
Occupational Group	Not High School Graduate	No Years of College	1–3 Years of College	4 Years of College or More
Professional, technical, and kindred workers	1.5%	6.7%	20.1%	55.7%
Managers and administrators, except farm	7.5	14.6	23.6	24.5
Clerical and kindred workers	4.0	8.8	9.6	4.0
Sales workers	2.2	6.3	11.6	9.3
Craftsmen and kindred workers	28.6	29.2	15.6	2.5
Operatives, including transport workers	29.4	18.9	9.1	1.0
Service workers	9.3	7.7	5.9	1.7
Farm laborers and foremen	2.4	0.4	0.2	0.2
Laborers, except farm	10.5	4.1	2.2	0.5

SOURCE: U.S. Bureau of the Census, *Current Population Reports,* Series P-20, No. 243, "Educational Attainment: March 1972" (Washington, D.C.: U.S. Government Printing Office, 1972), p. 5.

Table 5-3. Level of School Completed by Employed Males 25 to 64 Years Old, by Income, 1971

		High School Graduate		
Income	Not High School Graduate	No Years of College	1–3 Years of College	4 Years of College or More
Under $6,000	30.0%	15.8%	12.8%	9.4%
$6,000 to $9,999	39.8	37.9	29.2	18.3
$10,000 to $14,999	21.6	33.9	36.5	29.0
$15,000 and over	5.6	12.5	21.4	43.3

SOURCE: United States Bureau of the Census, *Current Population Reports,* Series P-20, No. 243, "Educational Attainment: March 1972" (Washington, D.C.: U.S. Government Printing Office, 1972), p. 6.

However, an underlying assumption of many critics of the schools is that, although the preparation of students for future occupational life is important, it should not be the only goal of the schools. The quality of their lives while in school should also be a paramount concern.

The Factory Model of Schooling

Our schools are, in a sense, factories in which the raw products (children) are to be shaped and fashioned into products to meet the various demands of life. The specifications for manufacturing come from the demands of the twentieth-century civilization, and it is the business of the school to build its pupils to the specifications laid down. This demands good tools, specialized machinery, continuous measurement of production to see if it is according to specifications, the elimination of waste in manufacture, and a large variety in output.[3]

Children are not pots and pans to be shaped by patterns sent down from a central office. Teachers are not drudges to be ordered about by a master mechanic. Education is an artistic form of industry; its normal product leads to imperfect output. The teacher is a skilled workman, or more accurately, an artist. Methods must vary with teachers; crowded classrooms, systematic and numerous reports bound up in red tape, clock-like precision and central office management convert the school into a factory.[4]

Although both of these were written at the turn of the present century, they reflect very different views of the nature of education. Behind the so-called factory model of education is the desire to mold children to fit into society after their schooling is over. There is a "hidden curriculum" that goes far beyond the learning of grammar, mathematics, reading, and other academic skills.[5] The "hidden curriculum" teaches children such things as discipline, order, cooperativeness, and conformity, skills thought to be needed to be successful in modern bureaucratic society, whether one becomes a doctor, college president, salesman, or assembly line worker.

A variety of means are used in the schools to prepare people for "twentieth century civilization." Life in schools is, like the "real world," run by

[3] Ellwood P. Cubberley, *Public School Administration* (Boston: Houghton Mifflin Company, 1916), p. 338. Cited in Philip Wexler, *The Sociology of Education: Beyond Equality* (Indianapolis, Ind.: The Bobbs-Merrill Co. Inc., 1976), pp. 29–30.

[4] Frank Tracy Carlton, *Education and Industrial Evolution* (New York: Macmillan Publishing Co., Inc., 1908), pp. 309–310. Cited in Wexler, *The Sociology of Education,* op. cit., p. 38.

[5] Philip W. Jackson, *Life in Classrooms* (New York: Holt, Rinehart and Winston, 1968).

Education provides the skills thought to be needed in modern bureaucratic society. (Courtesy of Gordon Alexander.)

the clock. Whether or not a student really understands something he has been working on, and whether or not the child is psychologically ready to switch to a completely different subject, a bell signals that *all* children must move to the next scheduled event. Getting through a predetermined set of activities within a given time period often becomes more important than whether or not any learning is occurring. There are rules and regulations to cover almost all activities—how to dress, how to wear one's hair, which side of the hall to walk on, when to speak in class, when to go to the bathroom. Teachers reward children with praise and acceptance when they recite the "right" answers, behave "properly," or exhibit the "desirable" attitudes. Children may be embarrassed or ignored when they fail in the teacher's eyes.[6]

Socialization for order, obedience, conformity, and cooperativeness begins early. Harry Gracey has described kindergarten as an academic "boot camp" in which children are taught to follow rules and routines without questioning them, even when the rules make no sense whatever to

[6] John Holt, *How Children Fail* (New York: Dell Publishing Company, Inc., 1967).

SCHOOL AS PRISON

What is Milgrim High like? It is a big, expensive building, on spacious but barren grounds. Every door is at the end of a corridor; there is no reception area, no public space in which one can adjust to the transition from the outside world. Between class periods the corridors are tumultuously crowded; during them they are empty; but they are always guarded with teachers and students on patrol duty. Patrol duty does not consist primarily in the policing of congested throngs of moving students, though it includes this, or the guarding of property from damage. Its principal function is the checking of corridor passes. Between classes, no student may walk down the corridor without a form, signed by a teacher, telling where he is coming from, where he is going, and the time, to the minute, at which the pass is valid. A student caught in the corridor without such a pass is taken to the office where a detention slip is made out against him, and he is required to remain at school for two or three hours after the close of the school day. He may do his homework during this time, but he may not leave his seat or talk.

. . . Milgrim High's most memorable arrangements are its corridor passes and its johns; they dominate social interaction. "Good morning, Mr. Smith," an attractive girl will say pleasantly to one of her teachers in the corridor. "Linda, do you have a pass to be in your locker after the bell rings?" is his greeting in reply. There are more different kinds of washrooms than there must have been in the Confederate Navy. The common sort, marked just "Boys" and "Girls," are generally locked. Then, there are some marked "Teachers, Men" and "Teachers, Women," unlocked. Near the auditorium are two others marked simply "Men" and "Women," intended primarily for the public when the auditorium is being used for some function. During the school day a cardboard sign saying "Adults only" is added to the legend on these washrooms; this is removed at the close of the school day. Girding up my maturity, I used this men's room during my stay at Milgrim. Usually it was empty; but once, as soon as the door clicked behind me, a teacher who had been concealed in the cubicle began jumping up and down to peer over his partition and verify my adulthood.

Edgar A. Friedenberg, *Coming of Age in America* (New York: Vintage Books, 1965), pp. 28–30.

them.[7] Gracey contends this training will ultimately make the transition from school to employment in a bureaucratic society relatively easy:

Once out of the school system, young adults will more than likely find themselves working in large-scale bureaucratic organizations, perhaps on the assem-

[7] Harry L. Gracey, "Learning the Student Role: Kindergarten as Academic Boot Camp," in Peter I. Rose, ed., *The Study of Society: An Integrated Anthology,* 3rd ed. (New York: Random House, Inc., 1973), pp. 481–491. Also see Jackson, *Life in Classrooms,* op. cit., p. 33.

bly line in the factory, perhaps in the paper routines of the white-collar occupations, where they will be required to submit to rigid routines imposed by "the company" which may make little sense to them. Those who can operate well in this situation will be successful bureaucratic functionaries. Kindergarten, therefore, can be seen as preparing children not only for participation in the bureaucratic organization of large modern school systems, but also for the large-scale occupational bureaucracies of modern society.[8]

In elementary and secondary schools, as well as in college, the goal of "getting through" often overrides student interest in learning. Schools are saturated with competitiveness; students are constantly being evaluated. This pressure leads to self-protection. Charles Silberman has outlined several strategies students use in their struggle for survival.[9] Students learn to falsify their behavior. They also learn to deny their own feelings, emotions, wishes, and interests in favor of those imposed on them by their teachers. Some students protect themselves by adopting an "I don't care how I do in school" frame of mind. Some assume this attitude in rebellion rather than out of apathy. A rebellious response creates further entanglements with school authorities. Finally, students may use docility and conformity as aids to getting through school. Students quickly discover that those who meet the teachers' expectations get the greatest rewards. They learn that teachers often value conformity to school rules and classroom procedures more than academic excellence.

A host of critics have attacked the way schools are run.[10] They agree that the big losers in the process of education are children. What they lose is their individuality and creativity. John Holt represents this line of argument:

> In a great many other ways he learns [in school] that he is worthless, untrustworthy, fit only to take other people's orders, a blank sheet for other people to write on. Oh, we make a lot of nice noises in school about respect for the child and individual differences and the like. But our acts, as opposed to our talk, say to the child, "Your experience, your concerns, your curiosities, your needs, what you know, what you want, what you wonder about, what you hope for, what you fear, what you like and dislike, what you are good at or not so

[8] Gracey, "Learning the Student Role . . . ," op. cit., pp. 490–491.

[9] Charles E. Silberman, *Crisis in the Classroom: The Remaking of American Education* (New York: Vintage Books, 1971), pp. 151–155; and Jackson, *Life in Classrooms,* op. cit., pp. 26–27.

[10] Jackson, ibid.; Edgar Z. Friedenberg, *Coming of Age in America: Growth and Acquiescence* (New York: Vintage Books, 1965); Herbert Kohl, *36 Children* (New York: New American Library, 1967); Jonathan Kozol, *Death at an Early Age* (Boston: Houghton Mifflin Company, 1967); George B. Leonard, *Education and Ecstasy* (New York: Dell Publishing Co., Inc., 1968); Neil Postman and Charles Weingartner, *Teaching as a Subversive Activity* (New York: Delacorte Press, 1969); Silberman, *Crisis in the Classroom,* op. cit.

IT'S NOT *WHAT* YOU'RE TAUGHT THAT DOES THE HARM BUT *HOW* YOU'RE TAUGHT

In fact, for most of your school life, it doesn't make that much difference what subject you're taught. The real lesson is the method. The medium in school truly is the message. And the medium is, above all, coercive. You're forced to attend. The subjects are required. You *have* to do homework. You *must* observe school rules. And throughout, you're bullied into docility and submissiveness. Even modern liberal refinements don't really help. So you're called an underachiever instead of a dummy. So they send you to a counselor instead of beating you. It's still not your choice to be there. They may pad the handcuffs—but the handcuffs stay on.

. . . It's how you're taught that does the harm. You may only study geometry for a semester—or French for two years. But *doing what you're told,* whether or not it makes sense, is a lesson you get every blessed school day for twelve years or more. You know how malleable we humans are. And you know what good learners we are—how little time it takes us to learn to drive a car or a plane or to play passable guitar. So imagine what the effect must be upon our apt and impressionable minds of a twelve-year course in servility. Think about it. Twelve years of tardy bells and hall passes; of graded homework, graded tests, graded conduct; of report cards, GPA's, honors lists, citizenship ratings; of dress codes, straight lines and silence. *What is it that they're teaching you?* Twelve years pitted against your classmates in a daily Roman circus. The game is Doing What You're Told. The winners get gold stars, affection, envy; they get A's and E's, honors, awards and college scholarships. The losers get humiliation and degradation. The fear of losing the game is a great fear: it's the fear of swats, of the principal's office, and above all the fear of failing. What if you fail and have to watch your friends move past you to glory? And, of course, the worst could happen: you could be expelled. Not that very many kids get swats or fail or are expelled. But it doesn't take many for the message to get across. These few heavy losers are like severed heads displayed at the city gates to keep the populace in line.

And, to make it worse, all of this pressure is augmented by those countless parents who are ego freaks and competition heads and who forcibly pass their addiction on to their kids. The pressure at school isn't enough; they *pay* the kids for A's and punish them for D's and F's.

Jerry Farber, *The Student as Nigger* (New York: Pocket Books, 1969), pp. 19–21.

good at—all this is of not the slightest importance, it counts for nothing. What counts here, and the only thing that counts, is what we know, what we think is important, what we want you to do, think, and be.'' The child soon learns not to ask questions: the teacher isn't there to satisfy his curiosity. Having learned to hide his curiosity, he later learns to be ashamed of it. Given no chance to find out who he is, and to develop that person, whoever it is, he soon comes to accept the adults' evaluation of him. Like some highly advantaged eighth graders I once talked with in a high-powered private school, he thinks of himself, ''I am nothing, or if something, something bad; I have no interests or concerns except trivial ones, nothing that I like is any good, for me or anyone else; any choices or decisions I make will be stupid; my only hope of surviving in this world is to cling to some authority and do what he says.''[11]

Why Are Schools That Way?

The structure of schools depends largely on those who teach, those who administer, and, not least, those who pay the bills. Many critics of the schools' emphasis on order, obedience, discipline, and conformity trace this condition to the social background of teachers and administrators. Various studies indicate that teachers and administrators are increasingly coming from lower middle- and upper working-class homes. Over half of America's teachers have fathers who were farmers or blue-collar workers; 6 per cent have fathers in clerical or sales positions.[12] Because teaching is a middle-class occupation, a large proportion of teachers has experienced upward mobility. They have risen in the world through education. Education has proved a valued means of becoming successful. Teachers and administrations pass the value that industrial society places on conformity and cooperativeness along to their students. Children must be prepared to fit into the occupational mold awaiting them so that they too can be successful in life.

But, if the social class background of teachers influences the way schools are, it is also true that the structure of schools has an impact on teachers. Teachers are not only expected by school administrators to maintain order, their competency is evaluated in large part on their ability to maintain order. Teachers who cannot control a class are in constant jeopardy of criticism from their superiors and colleagues. Rigid control of students contri-

---

[11] John Holt, *The Underachieving School* (Belmont, Calif.: Pitman Publishing Corporation, 1969), pp. 25–26.
[12] Robert J. Havighurst and Bernice Neugarten, *Society and Education,* 4th ed. (Boston: Allyn & Bacon, Inc., 1975), pp. 403–404.

butes to job security. Teachers also do their jobs within the factorylike atmosphere of the schools. Their workday is geared to the clock because certain subjects are to be covered during specified time periods. They have little time to help individual students whose capacity to grasp a topic does not coincide with the arbitrary time limits set by school administrators. Teachers often have no voice in the nature of the curriculum or in the selection of class materials. If they are part of the curriculum and textbook decision-making process, it is as part of a group; individual desires must often be subordinated to the larger school picture. Finally, teachers are subject to something like an inspection when, at the end of the year, students are given national achievement tests to see how they compare to the national average. Teachers are

---

NO TALKING PLEASE!

. . . There was one heady moment when I was able to excite the class by an idea: I had put on the blackboard Browning's "A man's reach should exceed his grasp, or what's a heaven for?" and we got involved in a spirited discussion of aspiration vs. reality. Is it wise, I asked, to aim higher than one's capacity? Does it not doom one to failure? No, no, some said, that's ambition and progress! No, no, others cried, that's frustration and defeat! What about hope? What about despair?—You've got to be practical!—You've got to have a dream! They said this in their own words, you understand, startled into discovery. To the young, clichés seem freshly minted. Hitch your wagon to a star! Shoemaker, stick to your last! And when the dismissal bell rang, they paid me the highest compliment: they groaned! They crowded in the doorway, chirping like agitated sparrows, pecking at the seeds I had strewn—when who should appear but [the administrative assistant to the principal].

"What is the meaning of this noise?"

"It's the sound of thinking, Mr. McHabe," I said.

In my letter box that afternoon was a note from him, with copies to my principal and chairman (and—who knows?—perhaps a sealed indictment dispatched to the Board?) which read:

"I have observed that in your class the class entering your room is held up because the pupils exiting from your room are exiting in a disorganized fashion, blocking the doorway unnecessarily and *talking*. An orderly flow of traffic is the responsibility of the teacher whose class is exiting from the room."

The cardinal sin, strange as it may seem in an institution of learning, is talking.

Bel Kaufman, *Up the Down Staircase* (Englewood Cliffs, N.J.: Prentice-Hall, Inc., 1964), pp. 55–56.

forced to press children to learn those things that will help them score higher on these examinations because their own performance is based partly on how well their students do.

There is evidence that schools may be the way they are partly because that's what parents want. Opinion polls indicate that the majority of American parents are more interested in the social and economic benefits of education for their children than in its intellectual benefits. A 1972 Gallup Poll found that about 40 per cent of the parents think that the purpose of education is "to get better jobs," "to get along better with people at all levels of society," and "to make more money." Only 15 per cent of the parents think that the purpose of education is to stimulate the minds of their children. Given these attitudes, it is not surprising that this same Gallup Poll found that parents rank "teaching students to respect law and authority" at the top of their list of matters to which schools should give more attention. They also cite discipline as the paramount problem in public schools today. Forty-one per cent believe that students are given an excess of rights and privileges.

Other Gallup Polls suggest that a majority of American parents do not approve of what they perceive as low standards and permissiveness in the public schools. One recent poll asked this question of a national sample:

> In some cities, parents of school children are being given the choice of sending their children to a special public school that has strict discipline, including a dress code, and puts emphasis on the three *R*s. If you lived in one of these cities and had children of school age, would you send them to such a school or not?

Fifty-seven per cent indicated they would send their children to such a school, 10 per cent were either undecided or did not answer the question, and 33 per cent said they would not send their children to such a school. In that same poll, a similar percentage of parents (of both elementary and high school students) believed that school children were not given enough work to do; only a small per cent of the parents thought school children were required to work too hard.

Many defenders of traditional education contend that schools should not be used for such ends as keeping problem children "off the streets" or "entertaining children."[13] Schools must place an accent on order and conformity if they are to control the behavior of large numbers of young people who are

---

[13] Robert L. Ebel, "What Are Schools For?" *Phi Delta Kappan,* 54 (September 1972): 3–7.

WHAT SCHOOLS ARE *NOT* FOR

—Schools are not custodial institutions responsible for coping with emotionally disturbed or incorrigible young people, for keeping nonstudents off the streets or out of the job market.

—Schools are not adjustment centers, responsible for helping young people develop favorable self-concepts, solve personal problems, and come to terms with life.

—Schools are not recreational facilities designed to entertain and amuse, to cultivate the enjoyment of freedom, to help young people find strength through joy.

—Schools are not social research agencies, to which a society can properly delegate responsibility for the discovery of solutions to the problems that are currently troubling the society.

I do not deny that society needs to be concerned about some of the things just mentioned. What I do deny is that schools were built and are maintained primarily to solve such problems. I deny that schools are good places in which to seek solutions, or that they have demonstrated much success in finding them. Schools have a very important special mission. If they accept responsibility for solving many of the other problems that trouble some young people, they are likely to fail in their primary mission, without having much success in solving the rest of our social problems.

Robert L. Ebel, "What Are Schools For?" *Phi Delta Kappan*, 54 (September 1972): 3.

---

concentrated in one place for long periods of time. Without rules and disciplinary measures, it is reasoned, the inevitable disruptions and disorder would make it impossible for schools to accomplish anything resembling education:

> If everyone who so desired tried to speak at once, or struggled for possession of the big scissors, or offered a helping hand in threading the movie projector, classroom life would be much more hectic than it commonly is. If students were allowed to stick with a subject until they grew tired of it on their own, our present curriculum would have to be modified drastically. Obviously, some kinds of controls are necessary if the school's goals are to be reached and social chaos avoided.[14]

[14] Jackson, *Life in Classrooms,* op. cit., p. 13.

The desires of parents cannot be ignored. Nor should the points made by defenders of the more traditional school model be dismissed. It may well be that the so-called factory model of education can be abandoned, or at least greatly modified, while at the same time taking into account the more traditional viewpoints.

Because occupational and economic success are related to one's level of education, educational equality is intolerable to those hurt by it. The negative consequences of educational inequality promise to become even worse because of the predicted oversupply of college graduates into the 1980s:

> the projected available supply of college graduates (including those with the doctorate) will exceed the demand by 750,000, and this oversupply will simply exacerbate the problem of college graduates holding jobs previously performed by those less qualified. . . . [And] the problem of the college graduate is at the same time the problem of the less-educated worker, for . . . those without college will find jobs for which they *could* qualify taken by the graduates who will opt for the best available positions to be had. Moreover, those without college will have less chance for advancement as employers cling to the notion that regardless of the skills that may be required in a work task, the greater the education the better the person's job performance.[15]

EDUCATIONAL INEQUALITY

The Meaning of Educational Inequality

> No novelty in the United States struck me more vividly during my stay there than the equality of conditions. It was easy to see the immense influence of this basic fact on the whole course of society. It gives a particular turn to public opinion and a particular twist to the laws, new maxims to those who govern and particular habits to the governed.
>
> I soon realized that the influence of this fact extends far beyond political mores and laws, exercising dominion over civil society as much as over the government; it creates opinions, gives birth to feelings, suggests customs, and modifies whatever it does not create.[16]

---

[15] Lee Baude, *Work and Workers: A Sociological Analysis* (New York: Praeger Publishers, Inc., 1975), pp. 49–50.

[16] Alexis de Tocqueville, *Democracy in America* (New York: Harper & Row, Publishers, 1966), p. 3. (Originally published in 1835.)

Alexis de Tocqueville, that astute Frenchman who wrote of democracy in America, was right: the idea, if not the practice, of democracy in the United States does extend beyond government to all aspects of social life. Education is no exception. From the beginning of public education in America, stress was placed on equality of educational opportunity. That meant all children must be provided a free public education: all children, regardless of their social and economic backgrounds, must be exposed to the same curriculum; regardless of background, all children within a given locality must attend the same school; and all schools within a locality should be equally financed by local tax dollars.[17]

Despite this rhetoric, *all* children have not been thought deserving of a formal education. Indians and blacks were specifically excluded. In the 1850s it was believed that slaves could not and should not be educated. It was not until slavery was abolished and ex-slaves began to assume industrial jobs that they eventually were included among those Americans thought to be educable. Still, blacks were not given equal educational treatment. In the *Plessy v. Ferguson* case of 1896, the Supreme Court made "separate but equal" part of America's legal framework. This doctrine held that equal treatment was being given when blacks and whites had substantially equal facilities, even when these facilities were separate.[18]

It was not until 1954 that the separate but equal doctrine was seriously challenged by the judicial system. In the *Brown v. Board of Education of Topeka* decision in 1954, Chief Justice Earl Warren wrote, as part of the Court's opinion: "Does segregation of children in public schools solely on the basis of race, even though the physical facilities and other 'tangible' factors may be equal, deprive the children of the minority group of equal educational opportunities? We believe that it does."[19] Warren went on to say that the separate but equal doctrine had no place in America's public educational structure and that separate educational facilities are inherently unequal. Still, it took the civil rights movement of the 1950s and 1960s to elevate the long-existing inequality in educational opportunity for blacks and other minorities to the status of a social problem of national importance. One result was the

[17] For a fuller discussion of the history of equal educational opportunity, see Edmund W. Gordon, "Toward Defining Equality of Educational Opportunity," in Frederick Mosteller and Daniel P. Moynihan, eds., *On Equality of Educational Opportunity* (New York: Vintage Books, 1972), pp. 423–426; and James S. Coleman, "The Concept of Equality of Educational Opportunity," in *Equal Educational Opportunity* (Cambridge, Mass.: Harvard University Press, 1969), pp. 9–24.

[18] See Albert P. Blaustein and Clarence Clyde Ferguson, Jr., *Desegregation and the Law: The Meaning and Effect of the School Segregation Cases,* 2nd ed. rev. (New York: Vintage Books, 1962), pp. 297–312.

[19] Ibid., p. 301.

Civil Rights Act of 1964, which prohibits discrimination on the grounds of race, color, religion, or national origin in any educational program or activity receiving financial support from the federal government.

The most recent concept of educational equality involves equality in the *effects* of schooling. Schools are equal if the students in them have the same general levels of academic performance. If black and white students attend schools with equal resources but either race performs academically below the other, then educational inequality exists. The most significant shift, then, has been from equal educational *opportunity* to equality in *results*. This shift can be traced to a nationwide study conducted by James Coleman in the mid-1960s.[20]

From Resources to Results

In 1964, James Coleman was commissioned by Congress to conduct a survey of the impact of discrimination on educational inequality. From information on approximately 600,000 students and 60,000 teachers in some 4,000 schools, Coleman found some consistent differences in black and white schools. On the average, black students had fewer school facilities—laboratories for physics, chemistry, and languages were less plentiful; textbooks were in shorter supply; and fewer books per pupil were available in their school libraries. Coleman reported that minorities also suffer in relation to the majority when it comes to curricular and extracurricular matters. Blacks in secondary schools are less likely to be in accredited schools, college-preparatory and accelerated curriculums are less accessible to minorities, and whites generally enjoy better access to such academically related extracurricular activities as debating teams and student newspapers. An important source of these differences was the inequality of school financing. Using the survey data collected by Coleman, Christopher Jencks reported that about 15 to 20 per cent more funds were spent for the average white school child per year than for the average black student.[21]

It perhaps was not surprising that Coleman found some differences in resources allocated to majority and minority schools. It was surprising, however, that the differences in resources accounted for only a small part of the

[20] James S. Coleman et al., *Equality of Educational Opportunity* (Washington, D.C.: Government Printing Office, 1966).

[21] Christopher Jencks et al., *Inequality: A Reassessment of the Effect of Family and Schooling in America* (New York: Basic Books, Inc., Publishers, 1972), p. 28.

differences in majority and minority student performance on standardized achievement tests.[22] Most other researchers have not been able to substantiate convincingly the idea that school resources make a difference in student outcomes. In a review of 18 studies, Harvey Averch and his colleagues conclude that "there is very little evidence that school resources in general have a powerful impact upon student outcomes."[23]

What are the major factors accounting for variation in educational achievement? The prevailing answer among social scientists lies in the impact of a child's social environment:

> Taking all these results together, one implication stands out above all: . . . schools bring little influence to bear on a child's achievement that is independent of his background and general social context; and . . . this very lack of an independent effect means that the inequalities imposed on children by their home, neighborhood, and peer environment are carried along to become the inequalities with which they confront adult life at the end of school.[24]

According to Coleman, then, school quality affects student performance through student background outside of school. If educational equality is to exist, schools must overcome educational inadequacies children bring with them from home. It is not enough, therefore, to provide minority children with equal school resources; educational equality exists only if the school performance of minority children is equal to that of nonminority students. Results rather than resources are the test of educational equality.

An Alternative Explanation: Biology Over Environment?

Despite considerable agreement among social scientists on the importance of social environment for learning and school performance, some contend that differences in educational achievement among races are attributable to biological rather than environmental differences.[25]

It is true that the average IQ score of black American children is about

---

[22] Coleman, *Equality of Educational Opportunity*, op. cit., p. 22.

[23] Harvey A. Averch et al., "How Effective Is Schooling? A Critical Review and Synthesis of Research Findings," U.S. Department of Health, Education and Welfare, Office of Education, Educational Resources Information Center, Washington, D.C., 1971, p. 48.

[24] Coleman, *Equality of Educational Opportunity*, op. cit., p. 325.

[25] Arthur Jensen, "How Much Can We Boost IQ and Scholastic Achievement?," *Harvard Educational Review*, 39 (Winter 1969): 1–123.

15 per cent below the average for white children.[26] This does not mean that every black child scores lower on IQ tests than every white child. In fact, many black children have higher IQs than many white children. It means that blacks have an *average* score below that of whites. In general, social scientists believe that this discrepancy in IQ scores is more the result of variations in social and educational environment than of genetic differences.[27] Arthur Jensen, however, believes that some evidence contradicts this belief. He uses some of Coleman's results to bolster his case. Coleman examined several environmental characteristics considered to be primary causes of individual and group differences in academic performance, including preschool attendance, reading materials in the home, parents' educational desires for their children, and parents' interest in their children's schoolwork. Among blacks, those who had preschool experience, had reading materials at home, and whose parents were interested in their schooling tended to do better in school. However, says Jensen, when blacks are compared to American Indians, the relationship between home atmosphere and school performance does not hold. In fact, he says, American Indians as a group have higher IQ and school achievement scores than blacks, despite the fact that their home atmosphere is less favorable than it is for blacks.[28] Jensen argues that we should admit the existence of intelligence differences among racial groups and that educational goals, techniques, and facilities should be geared to these differences:

> the ideal of equality of educational opportunity should not be interpreted as uniformity of facilities, instructional techniques, and educational aims for all children. Diversity rather than uniformity of approaches and aims would seem to be the key to making education rewarding for children of different patterns of ability.[29]

Some of Jensen's critics question his assumption that IQ tests really measure intelligence. They argue that intelligence tests are designed for

---

[26] Ralph M. Dreger and Kant S. Miller, "Comparative Psychological Studies of Negroes and Whites in the United States: 1959–1965," *Psychological Bulletin, Monograph Supplement* 70 (September 1968): 1–58; and Audrey M. Shuey, *The Testing of Negro Intelligence,* 2nd ed. (New York: Social Science Press, 1966).

[27] Otto Klineberg, "Race Differences: The Present Position of the Problem," *International Social Science Bulletin,* 2 (1950): 460–466. For a later statement from social scientists supporting Klineberg, see "Statement on Race and Intelligence," *Journal of Social Issues,* 25 (Summer 1969): 1–3.

[28] Jensen, "How Much Can We Boost IQ and Scholastic Achievement?," op. cit., pp. 85–86.

[29] Ibid., p. 117.

middle-class children and are so culturally biased that the results measure learning and environment rather than intellectual ability.[30] That is, items in intelligence tests reflect the experiences of upper middle-class children more than lower-class children. Consider this IQ test item:[31]

A symphony is to a composer as a book is to what?

( ) paper   ( ) sculptor   ( ) author
( ) musician   ( ) man

Higher-status children will find this question easier to answer correctly than lower-status children because they are more likely to have been exposed to information about classical music. Others have criticized Jensen for failing to consider adequately the impact of the social, psychological, and economic climate experienced by children of various racial and ethnic minorities. For example, research has consistently shown that middle-class black children score about as high on IQ tests as middle-class white children. Even a recent study by Jensen himself lends some support to the environmental argument.[32] Jensen compared changes in IQ among black and white siblings in a small rural town in southeastern Georgia. Among the blacks, who were very poor, a decline of about one IQ point each year occurred between the ages of five and 18. No significant decline with age occurred among whites, who were mostly from more affluent homes than the blacks in the study. Moreover, in an earlier study, Jensen found considerable stability in IQ between the ages of five and 12 among relatively affluent young blacks in California. If the decline in IQ among blacks were genetically caused, then it would have appeared in both the poor Georgia and affluent California blacks. Instead, only the Georgia blacks, who suffered infinitely greater environmental disadvantages than those in California, experienced a decline in measured intelligence. While denying that these findings weaken the genetic theory, Jensen concedes that black children apparently do experience some environmental damage.

What can one conclude from the environment versus biology debate? Relatively little is known about the relationship between genes and intelligence among individuals and even less is known about the link between biology and intelligence among races. Most social scientists would probably agree with the conclusion of Havighurst and Neugarten:

---

[30] See Robert L. Williams, "Scientific Racism and IQ—The Silent Mugging of the Black Community," *Psychology Today,* 7 (May 1974): 32–41, 101; and a series of articles in *Psychology Today,* 6 (September 1972): 39–50.

[31] Havighurst and Neugarten, *Society and Education,* op. cit. p. 69.

[32] Arthur R. Jensen, "Cumulative Deficit in IQ of Blacks in the Rural South," *Developmental Psychology,* 13 (May 1977): 184–191.

TRY THE S.O.B. TEST

Robert Williams developed the Black Intelligence Test of Cultural Homogeneity because he felt that there should be a test that was as fair to the majority of blacks as the Wechsler Intelligence Scale for Children was to the majority of whites. While the Wechsler measured blacks' knowledge of the white experience, the BITCH measured whites' knowledge of the black experience. The S.O.B. test, son of the original BITCH test, continues the tradition. Here are some words, terms and expressions taken from the black culture. Circle the letter of their correct meaning as *black* people use them. The answers follow.

1 *the bump*
   a) a condition caused by a forceful blow
   b) a suit
   c) a car
   d) a dance
2 *running a game*
   a) writing a bad check
   b) looking at something
   c) directing a contest
   d) getting what one wants from another person or thing
3 *to get down*
   a) to dominate
   b) to travel
   c) to lower a position
   d) to have sexual intercourse
4 *cop an attitude*
   a) leave
   b) become angry
   c) sit down
   d) protect a neighborhood
5 *leg*
   a) a sexual meaning
   b) a lower limb
   c) a white
   d) food

ANSWERS:
1-d
2-d
3-d
4-b
5-a

Psychology Today, 7 (May 1974): 101. Reprinted by permission of Robert Williams.

the theory of innate group differences of intelligence cannot be accepted as a basis for operating schools in a democracy. . . . Whatever future scientific research may reveal regarding innate group differences, the school system in a democracy must pursue a policy that aims to enhance each child's abilities.[33]

One of the important functions of schools is the identification and development of talent. There are factors interfering with the school's ability to perform this function besides racial inequality. One of the most important of these factors is social class.

EDUCATION AND STRATIFICATION

An important factor bearing on educational level is social class: the higher the social class, the greater the chance of attending college. In 1970, almost 90 per cent of upper and upper middle-class males and females entered college, compared to only 20 per cent of lower working-class males and 10 per cent of lower working-class females (see Table 5-4). This cannot, however, be attributed to differences in ability among social classes. Havighurst and Neugarten point out:

Table 5-4. Social-Class Origins of College Entrants

Social Class	1920	1940	1950	1960	1970 Males	Females
Upper and upper-middle	40	70	75	80	90	86
Lower-middle	8	20	38	45	70	57
Upper-working	2	5	12	25	48	32
Lower-working	0	0	2	6	20	10
Percent of total age group entering college	6	16	22	33	53*	41*

SOURCE: Robert J. Havighurst and Bernice L. Neugarten, *Society and Education,* 4th ed. (Boston: Allyn & Bacon, Inc., 1975), p. 93. Reprinted by permission.
*When 1970 figures for males and females are averaged, the percent of the total age group who enter college is approximately 47.

[33] Havighurst and Neugarten, *Society and Education,* op. cit., p. 71.

Although ability alone is a major factor in determining level of education, the picture is greatly modified when we consider the additional factor of social status. Youth from upper middle-class families are likely to go to college even though they have only average ability, while youth from lower-status families have less chance of entering college even when they have high ability.[34]

Havighurst and Neugarten examined the educational attainment of students of all social classes who were in the top quarter of their school class on IQ tests. Even though these youth were equal in ability, 90 per cent of the upper and upper middle-class students entered college and 80 per cent graduated, but only 66 per cent of the working-class students enrolled in college and only 29 per cent finished college. Summarizing ten years of his own research on the relationship between social class and achievement, William Sewell concludes:

> we estimate that a high SES [socioeconomic status] student has almost 2.5 times as much chance as a low SES student of continuing in some kind of post-high school education. He has an almost 4 to 1 advantage in access to college, a 6 to 1 advantage in college graduation, and a 9 to 1 advantage in graduate or professional education. . . . Even when we control for academic ability by dividing our sample into youths according to the students' scores on standardized tests, we find that higher SES students have substantially greater post-high school educational attainment than lower SES students.[35]

Part of the difference in the educational levels of persons in the upper and lower social classes is attributable to differences in economic resources. But the effect of social class on educational attainment is more complex than money alone because college is increasingly accessible to the members of all social classes. Some of the differential impact of social class on educational attainment is due to "tracking" and its consequences.

The Concept of Tracking

Tracking is the term for ability-grouping—placing children of similar ability and background in the same school group. This practice is intended to help both teachers and students. Teachers with a homogeneous group can more

[34] Ibid., p. 66.
[35] William H. Sewell, "Inequality of Opportunity for Higher Education," *American Sociological Review,* 36 (October 1971): 795.

easily keep the class at the same pace and better understand the needs of each student. Students of below average and average ability are not discouraged from exposure to "faster" students, and the progress of more advanced students is not hindered by "slower" ones.

Tracking in Practice

Ideally, the selection of students for certain tracks is based on present ability and potential. In practice, tracking in both primary and secondary schools tends to perpetuate the stratification system. In primary schools, the weaker desire for achievement and the feeling of educational inferiority that already burden lower-class and minority children are reinforced by the biased expectations of teachers.[36] This is illustrated in a study by Robert Rosenthal and Leonore Jacobson, who found that among students of equal ability, those thought by their teachers to be brighter performed better academically.[37] They also found that teachers responded negatively toward children who started to improve academically when they were not expected to do so. This "pygmalion effect" was supported by Eleanor Leacock in a study of second- and fifth-graders in black and white low- and middle-income schools.[38]

High schools have a different type of tracking system, one based on the type of curriculum or the course of study. Most high schools have a series of curricula: college preparatory, commercial, vocational, and general for those who are undecided about their occupational future. As in the lower grades, social class and race are associated with placement. Walter Schafer, Carol Olexa, and Kenneth Polk found that social class and race heavily affect the tracks taken by high school students, regardless of their past academic achievement or IQ.[39] This study also revealed that subsequent levels of academic performance by these students were influenced more by their track than by their intelligence or past scholastic performance. Regardless of earlier school performance or IQ, the subsequent academic performance of those bound for college increased, whereas the performance of those on a non-

[36] For a discussion of achievement values and social class, see Wexler, *The Sociology of Education,* op. cit., pp. 14–17.

[37] Robert Rosenthal and Leonore Jacobson, *Pygmalion in the Classroom* (New York: Holt, Rinehart and Winston, 1968).

[38] Eleanor Burke Leacock, *Teaching and Learning in City Schools* (New York: Basic Books, Inc., Publishers, 1969).

[39] Walter E. Schafer, Carol Olexa, and Kenneth Polk, "Programmed for Social Class: Tracking in High School," *Trans-action,* 7 (October 1970): 39–46.

college track decreased. The effects of tracking extended beyond academic matters. Placement on a noncollege track produced lower self-esteem, encouraged dropping out of school, lessened involvement in extracurricular school activities, and heightened the likelihood of behavior problems in and out of school.

Partly because of tracking in primary and secondary schools, the talents and abilities existing among youth from the lower class are frequently not developed, and they find themselves in occupations on the lower end of the stratification structure. The educational system serves to perpetuate the stratification structure by channeling upper- and middle-class children into high-level occupations while guiding lower-class children into jobs with lower prestige and limited financial rewards. The observable link between educational achievement and "life chances" is one of the most important reasons for coping with the problem of educational inequality. In a complex and changing economy, the achievement of educational equality is a crucially important goal.

WHAT CAN BE DONE?

Changing the Nature of Schools

As noted earlier, radical critics of schools reject the ways in which children are being educated. Children enter school, they contend, with a desire to learn new things but gradually learn to suppress their natural curiosity in order to fit the mold provided by their teachers. This, say the critics, is out of step with modern society. Society is now changing so rapidly that people are required to adjust to change, learn new jobs, and make choices from an almost bewildering number of alternatives.

Several alternatives to the traditional design of schools have been suggested. These range from the radical (deschooling) to the moderate (open education) plans for reform.

Deschooling Society.   Ivan Illich has attempted to wage a major assault on schools. According to Illich, all schools are based on the following assumptions: preparation for adulthood must come through schooling; what is not taught in schools is of slight value; everyone must spend nearly the same number of years in school; social progress depends upon better and better

EDUCATION—PAST AND FUTURE

Mass education was the ingenious machine constructed by industrialism to produce the kind of adults it needed. The problem was inordinately complex. How to pre-adapt children for a new world—a world of repetitive indoor toil, smoke, noise, machines, crowded living conditions, collective discipline, a world in which time was to be regulated not by the cycle of sun and moon, but by the factory whistle and the clock.

The solution was an educational system that, in its very structure, simulated this new world. . . .

The most criticized features of education today—the regimentation, lack of individualization, the rigid systems of seating, grouping, grading and marking, the authoritarian role of the teacher—are precisely those that made mass public education so effective an instrument of adaptation for its place and time.

Young people passing through this educational machine emerged into an adult society whose structure of jobs, roles and institutions resembled that of the school itself. The schoolchild did not simply learn facts that he could use later on; he lived, as well as learned, a way of life modeled after the one he would lead in the future. . . .

For education [in the future] the lesson is clear: its prime objective must be to increase the individual's "cope-ability"—the speed and economy with which he can adapt to continual change. And the faster the rate of change, the more attention must be devoted to discerning the pattern of future events.

It is no longer sufficient for Johnny to understand the past. It is not even enough for him to understand the present, for the here-and-now environment will soon vanish. Johnny must learn to anticipate the directions and rate of change. He must, to put it technically, learn to make repeated, probabilistic, increasingly long-range assumptions about the future. And so must Johnny's teachers.

Alvin Toffler, *Future Shock* (New York: Bantam Books, 1970), pp. 400, 401, 403.

schooling; and knowledge carries a market value.[40] Under these assumptions, Illich argues, learning becomes a marketable commodity monopolized by the schools. The more years one spends in school, the greater one's right to enjoy special privileges, to have high income, and to exercise power.

Illich's solution is to deschool society; to abolish formal learning. By deschooling society Illich means that self-motivated learning should replace the present system, which he believes attempts to promote learning through bribery and coercion. According to Illich, an educational system should at-

---

[40] Ivan Illich, "The Alternative to Schooling," *Saturday Review*, 54 (June 19, 1971): 44–48, 59–60.

tempt to accomplish three goals: make resources available for anyone who wants to learn, regardless of age; facilitate communication among those who want to learn about a topic and those who want to share their knowledge about it; and provide an outlet for those who want to express themselves to the public on a social issue. Learners should not be forced to follow a pre-determined curriculum, and employment should be based on a person's qualifications to do a job rather than on formal educational credentials.

He proposes that learning resources be organized not on the basis of educators' objectives but, rather, in such a way that individuals can use them to define and reach their own goals. Illich outlines four avenues by which this could be accomplished:

1. Reference Services to Educational Objects—which facilitate access to things or processes used for formal learning. Some of these things can be reserved for this purpose, stored in libraries, rental agencies, laboratories, and showrooms like museums and theaters; others can be in daily use in factories, airports, or on farms, but made available to students as apprentices or on off-hours.
2. Skill Exchanges—which permit persons to list their skills, the conditions under which they are willing to serve as models for others who want to learn these skills, and the addresses at which they can be reached.
3. Peer-Matching—a communications network which permits persons to describe the learning activity in which they wish to engage, in the hope of finding a partner for the inquiry.
4. Reference Services to Educators-at-Large—who can be listed in a directory giving the addresses and self-descriptions of professionals, para-professionals, and free-lancers, along with conditions of access to their services. Such educators . . . could be chosen by polling or consulting their former clients.[41]

Some of Illich's critics contend that education cannot be left strictly to individual preference if the quality of education is to be high. Arthur Pearl states this objection to deschooling:

To learn what one likes is to learn prejudice. If there is one thing we know about human beings, it is that they don't want to know what they don't want to know. . . . The important truths of today are painful truths. People will do everything they can to avoid them. Important truths will require enormous changes in attitudes and life-style. Education self-selected will be no educa-

[41] Ivan Illich, *Deschooling Society* (Harper & Row, Publishers, 1971), pp. 112–113.

SOME PROBLEMS WITH DESCHOOLING

The flaws in [Ivan Illich's *Deschooling Society*] . . . can be traced to a number of assumptions . . . widely held by other romantic critics of the school system who draw back from his extremist remedies. He assumes that because children learn to speak their own language casually without going to school and without explicit instruction, they learn most other things in the same way. . . . all human history testifies that they do not learn to read and write as effortlessly. Before compulsory schooling was introduced the vast majority of mankind remained illiterate. Illich . . . assumes that literacy can be more readily acquired by abolishing schools and relying upon the casual operation of his networks to effect mastery of elementary skills. To claim that we will all learn from and teach one another as need and interest manifest themselves is to invoke pious hope that flies in the face of overwhelming evidence. Not everyone who knows something, even when he knows it well, can teach it, not to mention teach it effectively. Not everyone who is able to teach is willing or in a position to do so. Even speech depends upon the models imitated and can be immensely improved by proper schooling.

Further, some skills are best learned in youth, like writing and arithmetical computation, as well as certain habits of work, and of thoughtfulness for others.

Sidney Hook, "Illich's Deschooled Utopia," *Encounter*, 38 (January 1972): 55.

tion—we have such education currently available to us (it comes to us on a half a dozen simultaneous channels on television), and there we find a Gresham's law of culture: bad drives out good, and the frivolous outdraws the serious.[42]

It seems safe to conclude that deschooling is too radical for adoption in most societies. But Illich's extreme line of argument calls attention in a forceful way to the need for educational reform.[43]

Open Education.   Open education comes under a variety of labels: the open school, the free school, informal education, the free day. The diversity of labels indicates the diversity of specific programs and practices in different schools. As Charles Silberman states, open education "is less an approach or method than a set of shared attitudes and convictions about the nature of childhood, learning, and schooling."[44] Although there is no precise defini-

[42] Arthur Pearl, "The Case for Schooling America," *Social Policy*, 2 (March–April 1972): 52.

[43] James B. McKee, *Introduction to Sociology*, 2nd ed. (New York: Holt, Rinehart and Winston, 1974), p. 318.

[44] Silberman, *Crisis in the Classroom*, op. cit., p. 208.

tion of open education, there are some guiding principles on which most of its advocates can agree:

> children are naturally curious and motivated to learn by their own interests and desires. The most important condition for nurturing this natural interest is freedom, supported by adults who enrich the environment and offer help. In contrast, coercion and regimention only inhibit emotional and intellectual development. [45]

PORTRAIT OF AN OPEN CLASSROOM

The sight of a small boy sliding down a bannister greets the two visitors to P.S. 84, situated at 92d Street between Columbus Avenue and Central Park West. The sliding boy and a companion, who is taking the more conventional route down a short flight of stairs from a first floor landing, are conversing animatedly.

Walking up a half dozen steps, we come upon a first floor corridor that is the connecting passage between four primary classrooms that open off it. At 10 A.M. in the corridor, four kindergarten girls, seated crosslegged on some cushions with a pile of magazines, a paste pot and a very large sheet of brown paper, are cutting and pasting. Nearby, a third grader is reading a story to a younger child; both are giggling at the antics of "Curious George." Two girls sitting side by side on the corridor floor are each absorbed in a book, as is a boy leaning against the opposite wall. Several youngsters are writing in notebooks or on loose sheets of paper. A large, bright yellow wooden tub on wheels, with two children and an oversized stuffed dog crowded into it, is being pushed along the corridor by a highly energetic boy.

The children who are working do not look up as the cart rolls by. No adult is present in the corridor aside from the visitors. From time to time, a child gets up and goes into one of the classrooms to ask some available adult a question; occasionally, a child turns to us for help. One asks, "How do you spell Morison?," the name of the school's principal to whom she is writing a letter. Presently, a teacher comes out of a classroom and offers the four kindergarten girls a few more illustrated magazines. The girls speak English to their teacher, and converse quietly in Spanish together.

The institutional tile walls of the corridor are covered with a variety of art work and posters. Any child who wants to can tape up his work. It is not long past Halloween and a group of highly individualistic jack-o'-lanterns leer down. A poster, one of many, provides the following information: "We guessed how much our pumpkin would weigh. Risa thought it weighed 21 pounds. She weighed it and it weighed 20 pounds. After we took out the seeds and pulp, it weighed 16 pounds." In the corridor we are nearly surrounded by words, words

---

[45] Allen Graubard, "The Free School Movement," *Harvard Educational Review*, 42 (August 1972): 352.

of songs, poems, stories, announcements, news items—all placed at a convenient height for children to read.

A third-grade classroom opens off the corridor. At first our eyes are assailed by the apparent chaos of the scene—a profusion of movement, sounds, colors, shapes. Gradually, however, the organization of the class reveals itself. The room is perhaps a little smaller than is standard and has a class register of 30 children, a few of whom are in the corridor or visiting other classes. What is most striking is that there are no desks for pupils or teachers. Instead, the room is arranged as a workshop.

Carelessly draped over the seat, arm and back of a big old easy chair are three children, each reading to himself. Several other children nearby sprawl comfortably on a covered mattress on the floor, rehearsing a song they have written and copied neatly into a song folio.

One grouping of tables is a science area with equipment ranging from magnets, mirrors, a prism, magnifying glasses, a microscope, a kaleidoscope, batteries, wires, an electric bell, to various natural objects (shells, seeds, feathers, bones and a bird's nest). Also on nearby shelves are a cage with gerbils, a turtle tank and plants grown by the children. Several other tables placed together and surrounded by chairs hold a great variety of math materials such as shaped blocks known as "geo blocks," combination locks and Cuisenaire rods, rulers and graph paper. A separate balance table contains four scales.

The teacher sits down at a small, round table for a few minutes with two boys, and they work together on vocabulary with word cards; her paraprofessional assistant is at the blackboard with several children who are writing. A student teacher (available in the mornings only) praises a drawing a girl has brought over to show her; other children display their work to the visitors with obvious pride.

Children move in and out of the classroom constantly. The teacher seems alert to the nuances of all the activity. To a boy trying to explain to a classmate how to construct a rather complex paper fan, she suggests, "As a game, see if you can describe it to her with your hands behind your back." To a child who has produced a collection of ink-blot pictures, she casually introduces the idea of "symmetry." She keeps a record book handy in which she jots notations on each of the children. Seeing a child filling and emptying different sized plastic containers at the sink, she stops for a moment and talks about pints and quarts. Weighing, measuring and graph-making appear to be favorite activities.

In spite of all that is happening—the constant conversation, the singing— the noise level is quite subdued. The children look engaged, brighteyed, happy. A little boy breaks into an impromptu rock 'n' roll dance; nobody takes any particular notice. Apparently satisfied, he returns to the math area.

Charles E. Silberman, *The Open Classroom Reader* (New York: Random House, Inc., 1973), pp. 40–41. Reprinted by permission of Random House, Inc.

Despite some differences in programs and practices among schools in the open education movement, these guiding principles produce schools *without* the following: large classes, sharp authority line between teachers and students, predetermined curriculum for all children of a given age, emphasis on discipline and obedience, constant comparison of the performance of students, use of competition as a motivator, and tracking of children according to ability. Open schools attempt to avoid most of those features of public schools, yet the open education movement stops far short of Illich's more radical deschooling.

Most schools based on open education principles are attempting to reproduce what has existed in English "informal" schools for several years. Until the late 1960s, almost all of these schools were consciously based on the model provided by A. S. Neill.[46] By 1972 there were about 600 schools in the United States founded on the concept of freedom for children to learn and develop in an enriched environment, according to their own unfolding interests, inclinations, and abilities.

The Evidence on Open Education.   There is no research evidence on the practicality or consequences of the type of educational system envisioned by Illich because his radical vision has never been put into action. Research, however, has been done on free schools. The supporters of open education are convinced of its superiority over the traditional form of schooling, but the evidence does not completely support them. Jonathan Kozol, one of the leaders of the free school movement, points out that the average life span of a free school in the United States is nine months.[47] The major cause of failure in free schools, he states, is the unwillingness to teach hard skills. One of the reasons that parents withdraw their children from free schools is the children's failure to advance in reading performance. Free schools fail, according to Kozol, because of the underlying assumption that nothing can be successfully taught a child who doesn't want to know it. If free schools are to survive, he argues, they must recognize that some basic skills, particularly reading, can and must be taught.

However, defenders of open education emphasize that research in England shows informal schools do as good a job in traditional areas of learning,

[46] A. S. Neill, *Summerhill: A Radical Approach to Child Rearing* (New York: Hart Publishing Company, 1960).

[47] Jonathan Kozol, "Free Schools Fail Because They Don't TEACH," *Psychology Today,* 5 (April 1972): 30 ff.

WHAT'S WRONG WITH FREE SCHOOLS?

In the face of many intelligent and respected statements on the subject of "spontaneous" and "ecstatic" education, the simple truth is that you do not learn calculus, biochemistry, physics, Latin grammar, mathematical logic, Constitutional law, brain surgery, or hydraulic engineering in the same organic fashion that you learn to walk and talk and breathe and make love. Months and years of long, involved, and—let us be quite honest—sometimes nonutopian labor in the acquisition of a single unit of complex and intricate knowledge go into the expertise that makes for power in this nation. The poor and black cannot survive the technological nightmare of the next ten years if they do not have this expertise.

Jonathan Kozol, "Free Schools: A Time for Candor," *Saturday Review,* 55 (March 4, 1972): 52.

including reading, as formal schools.[48] Moreover, they contend that research demonstrates the superiority of informal schools in such areas as spoken and written English, art, ingenuity, nonschool interests, critical thinking, initiative, and desire to learn and work. Charles Silberman emphasizes the non-cognitive gains in informal schools such as self-confidence, spontaneity, and openness to new experience:

> the consequences of different modes of schooling [formal and informal] should be sought less in academic attainment than in their impact on how children feel about themselves, about school, and about learning. For three hundred years or more, schools have been denounced for their capacity to destroy children's spontaneity, curiosity, and love of learning, and for their tendency to mutilate childhood itself. To create and operate schools that cultivate and nurture all these qualities without reducing children's academic attainment—that is a magnificent achievement.[49]

Alternative Schools. Alternative schools are based on the idea that each school system should provide a number of alternatives rather than a monolithic program. Students, parents, and teachers are allowed to participate in the selection of program options. Mario Fantini, a former radical critic of traditional education, now favors alternative schools:

[48] See Silberman, *Crisis in the Classroom,* op. cit., pp. 256–262 for further development of this viewpoint.
[49] Ibid., p. 262. For a critique of this position, see Mary Jo Bane, "Essay Review: Open Education," *Harvard Educational Review,* 42 (May 1972): 277.

At one time during the Sixties I considered myself a change agent. That is, I had a certain concept of reform—say like team teaching or educational technology, and I would go into a school system and try and manipulate the situation so it would come out my way. Now I feel this is a wrong strategy to use. . . . The idea of providing alternative learning options is based on an entirely different conception of change. For rather than pushing people around, you provide options that attract people to them. They choose. They make decisions. . . . In an area as important as education, I want a situation where every parent, every student and every teacher is making decisions for themselves.[50]

The most ambitious experiment in alternative schools was begun in 1971 in Berkeley, California.[51] The public school system in Berkeley is racially mixed—45 per cent black, 44 per cent white, and 11 per cent Chicano and Asian—and was voluntarily desegregated via busing in 1968.

With $7 million from the U.S. Office of Education and more than a half million dollars from the Ford Foundation, the Berkeley school system set up 24 alternative schools involving 4,000 elementary and secondary school children, or approximately one fourth of the city's student population. Some of the new alternative schools are set up at regular school sites; others are located in former homes, factories, churches, and store fronts. Some of these alternative schools are limited to 50 students; others accommodate more students than do the traditional schools. Parental participation is extensive in some schools but not in others. Despite great diversity each of the 24 experimental schools strives to accomplish two goals: eliminate racism and ensure that all students receive basic academic skills.

The early results of this experiment have been mixed. Whatever the final result of Berkeley's innovative experiment, the successes and failures will be helpful to other school systems interested in creating alternative schools. Other schools could also benefit from a study of Berkeley's voluntary desegregation accomplished through busing in 1968.

Reducing Educational Inequality

Does Desegregation Work? The Coleman Report has been widely used to support the idea that desegregation will improve the school achievement of

---

[50] Mario Fantini, "Learning Options," in *Changing Schools: An Occasional Newsletter on Alternative Schools,* No. 002, p. 3. Quoted in Havighurst and Neugarten, *Society and Education,* op. cit., p. 279.
[51] Diane Divoky, "Berkeley's Experimental Schools," *Saturday Review,* 55 (September 16, 1972): 44–50.

minority children. Specifically, Coleman reported that black children in classrooms that are more than one-half white scored higher on achievement tests.[52] The finding that minority children perform better academically when placed in desegregated, middle-class schools has been verified by several other studies.[53] In a broad review of school desegregation research, Meyer Weinberg concluded that black children consistently experience higher academic achievement in desegregated schools. Also, he states, research among blacks indicates that desegregation tends to enhance their aspirations, self-esteem, and self-acceptance.[54]

Several studies have shown that racially balanced classrooms can have either positive or negative effects on the academic achievement of minority group children. Mere physical desegregation may have a detrimental impact on black children. In contrast, desegregated classrooms in which an atmosphere of respect and acceptance prevails promote improved academic performance among black children.[55]

Robert Crain and Carol Weisman report some postschooling benefits of desegregation for blacks: Blacks who had attended desegregated public schools secured higher occupational positions and earned higher incomes than blacks in segregated schools.[56] They did not attribute this solely to differences in educational attainment; the increased social contacts with middle-class whites also contribute to better employment opportunities and more information about the availability of jobs. A report by the United States Commission on Civil Rights notes that over 71 per cent of the northern public

[52] Coleman, *Equality of Educational Opportunity,* op. cit., p. 332.

[53] Some of these studies are reviewed in Thomas F. Pettigrew, "Race and Equal Educational Opportunity," in *Equal Educational Opportunity,* op. cit., pp. 70–73. See also A. B. Wilson, "Residential Segregation of Social Classes and Aspirations of High School Boys," *American Sociological Review,* 24 (December 1959): 836–845; Stuart Cleveland, "A Tardy Look at Stouffer's Findings in the Harvard Mobility Project," *Public Opinion Quarterly,* 26 (Fall 1962): 453–454; John A. Michael, "High School Climates and Plans for Entering College," *Public Opinion Quarterly,* 25 (Winter 1961): 585–595; and U.S. Commission on Civil Rights, *Racial Isolation in the Public Schools,* Vol. II (Washington, D.C.: U.S. Government Printing Office, 1967), pp. 165–206.

[54] Meyer Weinberg, *Desegregation Research: An Appraisal,* 2nd ed. (Bloomington, Ind.: Phi Delta Kappan, 1970), p. 378.

[55] See Irwin Katz, "Desegregation or Integration in Public Schools? The Policy Implications of Research," *Integrated Education,* 5 (December 1967–January 1968): 15–28; and U.S. Commission on Civil Rights, *Racial Isolation in the Public Schools,* Vol. 1, op. cit.

[56] Robert L. Crain, "School Integration and Occupational Achievement of Negroes," *American Journal of Sociology,* 75 (January 1970), Part II, pp. 593–606; and Robert L. Crain and Carol S. Weisman, *Discrimination, Personality and Achievements: A Survey of Northern Blacks* (New York: Seminar Press, 1972).

SCHOOL DESEGREGATION WORKS

At the end of what has been an exciting experience for the members of the [United States] Commission [on Civil Rights], there is one conclusion that stands out above all others: Desegregation works. It is working in Hillsborough County, Florida; Tacoma, Washington; Stamford, Connecticut; Williamsburg County, South Carolina; Minneapolis; Denver; and many other school districts where citizens feel that compliance with the law is in the best interests of their children and their communities. It is even working in the vast majority of schools in Boston and Louisville in spite of the determination of some citizens and their leaders to thwart its progress. The efforts of law-abiding citizens in these and other desegregating districts are not well known, although they are more representative of the total desegregation experience than the more publicized resistance of opponents. . . .

School officials throughout the country have noted that institutional renewal frequently accompanies the desegregation process. The educational program is reviewed and revamped to include new instructional techniques and materials, to provide for the needs of language-minority students, to develop programs to assist gifted children and those achieving below their potential, and to promote racial and ethnic harmony among faculty and students. In addition, community race relations and the level of parental participation in school activities usually improve during the course of desegregation. School districts which have experienced desegregation for several years generally report that minority student achievement rises and that these students often exhibit greater motivation that ultimately leads to pursuit of higher education. Majority group students hold their own academically and they commonly report that experiences with minority students have dispelled long-held stereotypes.

United States Commission on Civil Rights, *Fulfilling the Letter and Spirit of the Law: Desegregation of the Nation's Public Schools,* Washington, D.C. 1976, pp. 293–294.

schools have minority enrollments that exceed half the total school enrollment, in comparison with 54 per cent in the South.[57]

Desegregation and Busing. Opposition to busing as a means of achieving racial balance in the schools has increased in recent years. Factors that point to future resistance to busing include parental opposition to busing, lack of enforcement of busing-related legislation by government agencies, and recent legislative actions and judicial decisions on busing.

[57] *The Federal Civil Rights Enforcement Effort—1974, Volume III, To Ensure Equal Educational Opportunity,* a report of the U.S. Commission on Civil Rights (January 1975), pp. 50–51.

Parents object to the time their children spend on a bus going to and from school. They also argue that if schools are located miles from children's neighborhoods, parents will lose input in their activities, policies, and programs. Many are convinced that the money spent on busing could better be used to improve the quality of education. Others fear that attempts to improve minority academic achievement through busing can only hurt their own children's performance. Finally, busing violates the traditional practice of children attending their neighborhood school.

Some blacks also raise objections of their own to busing. They are concerned that white teachers will not treat their children fairly and that their children's needs will not be met. Other blacks see school desegregation as a threat to the maintenance of black culture.[58]

What is the evidence on the impact of busing? David Armor has concluded that busing does not improve the academic performance of black students. According to Armor, busing "heightens racial identity and consciousness, enhances ideologies that promote racial segregation, and reduces opportunities for actual contact between the races."[59] Similarly, in another study, Coleman concludes that school desegregation in the largest cities has generally resulted in a wider breach between blacks and whites.[60] This, he contends, is because desegregation, implemented via court-ordered busing, has caused many white middle-class parents either to move to the suburbs or to send their children to private schools. This "white fight," argues Coleman, has actually increased racial isolation in the nation's 20 largest cities, although it continues to be a successful tool in cities with a population of less than 1 million.[61]

The response to both Armor and Coleman has been critical. Thomas Pettigrew makes the following statement regarding Armor's study:

> In a real sense, Armor's article does not concern itself with "busing" at all, save for its title and conclusions. It does not provide us with direct evidence on

---

[58] David K. Cohen, "Public Schools: The Next Decade," *Dissent,* 18 (April 1971): 162; and Robert Staples, *Introduction to Black Sociology* (New York: McGraw-Hill Book Company, 1976), pp. 35–36.

[59] David J. Armor, "The Evidence on Busing," *The Public Interest,* 28 (Summer 1972): 90–126.

[60] Coleman's study included approximately 12,000 school districts, ranging from the largest to the smallest. See James S. Coleman, Sara Kelly, and John A. Moore, *Trends in School Segregation, 1968–73* (Washington, D.C.: The Urban Institute, 1975).

[61] Coleman still stands by the conclusion of his 1966 study that blacks in integrated schools with a majority of white middle-class students will have higher achievement than blacks in totally black schools. It is, then, not desegregation that Coleman feels has failed but court-ordered busing as a means of achieving desegregation in the largest metropolitan areas.

the "busing" of school children for racial desegregation, for it never treats "busing" as an independent variable. Rather, his article is an attack upon the racial desegregation of public schools that often, but not always, involves "busing." [62]

Reynolds Farley, who studied 125 of the country's largest cities in both the North and the South between 1967 and 1972, disagrees with Coleman about the relationship between busing and white flight.[63] According to Farley, in neither the North nor the South is there a significant relationship between school desegregation and the white exodus from the cities. He does not believe that an immediate halt to court-ordered busing and school desegregation would end white flight. With or without court-ordered busing, city schools will soon be predominantly black.

The U.S. Commission on Civil Rights, in evaluating federal agencies that have the responsibility for ensuring equal educational opportunity, charges that efforts to secure compliance with desegregation laws have not been forceful enough.[64] It contends that the Department of Health, Education and Welfare (HEW)—the agency responsible for monitoring the use of federal monies in schools to ensure adherence to civil rights laws—has failed to act swiftly when noncompliance is found. Instead, HEW is accused of permitting negotiations to stretch over a period of several years. HEW is also cited for failing to press vigorously for metropolitan school desegregation; that is, HEW has not actively encouraged desegregation of minority inner city school districts through the use of busing to white suburban school districts.

If HEW has been reluctant to press for busing as a way of achieving desegregation, it is partly because of recent restrictive legislation. In 1972, legislation banned the use of federal funds for busing unless such funds are requested in writing by school officials. A 1974 bill providing federal aid to elementary and secondary schools contains a prohibition against the courts ordering the busing of children beyond the school next closest to their home.[65] Finally, in 1976 an HEW appropriations bill wrote the neighborhood school concept into law, prohibiting the use of federal funds to force any child to attend any school except the one nearest his home.

[62] Thomas F. Pettigrew, Elizabeth L. Useem, Clarence Normand, and Marshall S. Smith, "Busing: A Review of the Evidence," *The Public Interest,* Number 30 (Winter 1973): 112. For a rebuttal to Pettigrew and his colleagues, see David J. Armor, "The Double Double Standard: A Reply," *The Public Interest,* Number 30 (Winter 1973): 119–131.

[63] Farley, Reynolds, "Racial Integration in the Public Schools, 1967 to 1972: Assessing the Effects of Governmental Policies," *Sociological Focus,* 8 (January 1975): 3–26.

[64] *The Federal Civil Rights Enforcement Effort—1974,* op. cit.

[65] Ibid., p. 52.

DIFFERENT FAMILIES, DIFFERENT WORRIES

On the night before school began in Louisville, Elmer Woods, a brewing company sales supervisor, took his sons, Byron, 13, and Kenneth, 12, aside. "Keep cool and watch yourselves," he told them. "No matter what they yell at you, just ignore it."

Next morning, the boys got up at 5:45 a.m. to have breakfast before their father drove them ten blocks to catch a school bus at 6:50 a.m. Then they rode for 40 minutes to cover 16 miles to their new school, Stuart High, in suburban Jefferson County. The bus was pelted with rocks; passing motorists honked horns as a sign of antibusing protest and hurled racial insults. But there was no serious trouble at school, and the Woodses, a black middle-class family with an income of $20,000, felt the ordeal was well worthwhile.

That does not mean they enjoy busing. "I'm really not for it," says Woods. "I'd much rather have the boys closer to home." Last year Ken walked to Martin Luther King School, only two blocks from his trim red brick home in the city's predominantly black West End. Byron attended Shawnee Junior High School, ten blocks away. Says the boys' mother, Mary, a medical lab technician at Jewish Hospital: "If there was a better way of bringing about racial equality in the schools, we'd go for it, but there doesn't seem to be."

Mrs. Woods frets, too, about the boys being so far from home. Both may want to stay after school for sports. To accommodate them, Woods says he is ready to drive out late every afternoon to pick them up.

But neither the parents nor the boys consider those disadvantages as too much. They have found the Stuart curriculum much broader than anything in the West End schools. Byron, who has been weak in math, is pleased that he can take an extra math course to catch up. "I know that I'm going to have to work harder," he says, "but I can do it. The teachers are closer to you here. They explain things more." Ken is taking an elective in chess. Neither had any problems with white classmates on opening day. Said Byron of one white boy: "I sat down in class; then he did. I moved closer, and pretty soon we were friends."

For the parents, the most important factor is the educational opportunities now offered to their boys. Says Woods about the busing plan: "It's the best thing that has happened since the Supreme Court ruling of 1954. We're 20 years late, but it is going to better my kids." Noting that white students will be bused out of their neighborhoods for only two years, while the arrangement is long-term for blacks, he wonders, "Can't they stand something for two years? We have suffered much more than they have."

Mrs. Woods notes that she had not been closely exposed to whites until college. "Why must someone wait half his life for that?" she asks. "If busing is going to mean a long struggle, then so be it." Nevertheless, Mrs. Woods is worried. "What," she asks, "is going to happen after all the police leave?"

On the day of school opening in Louisville, the three children of Al and

Mildred McCauley—David, 15, Danny, 14, and Debbie, 10—remained in their brick home in Highview, a white middle-class suburb in Jefferson County. Debbie, who was not scheduled for busing and could have attended her old school a few blocks away, asked, "Mommy, when can I go? If I don't pretty soon, I'm going to be far behind." Mrs. McCauley shook her head and looked away.

McCauley, a dry-wall finisher from the Kentucky hill country, and his wife, an articulate spokeswoman for Save Our Community Schools, are keeping their children home to protest the busing plan. Their two boys would have had to get up at 6:35 a.m. and ride a bus for 50 minutes to reach Parkland Junior High, a black ghetto school 22 miles away in Louisville. "They won't go there—ever," vows Mrs. McCauley.

The parents object primarily to what they consider the inferior education and disorderly conditions at Parkland. Mrs. McCauley visited it last year and claims that "it hadn't been painted in eight years. There was no maintenance." Moreover, they have heard rumors of stabbings, rapes and other crimes in the Parkland neighborhood.

Fern Creek, the school the boys attended last year, has a minor drug problem, but its neighborhood is bucolic by comparison. David, who is already one year behind in school, feels he would slip further at Parkland: "It won't help me. I don't see why I should have to go." Agrees Danny: "I like Fern Creek; I don't like Parkland."

The McCauleys understand blacks who want to go to better schools. "But," asks McCauley, "why don't they just upgrade their schools? I just can't see sending my children in there to get a lower education so that *they* can get a better one."

More broadly, the McCauleys feel put upon by Government. "We've been shoved," says Mrs. McCauley. "Unemployment is running wild; inflation is killing us. Now the Federal Government steps in and orders this busing. We're fighting for our freedom as Americans." Sadly she adds, "I get up some mornings and feel like I want to secede."

They are even wondering about whether to stay in Highview. But they figure their house is worth $38,000 and so many homes in the outlying country are for sale that they doubt they can get what they want for it.

So the boys sit idle, watching TV and helping their parents with various chores. Police had sealed off the nearby schools; thus Danny for a time could not play tennis there as he did this summer. Debbie plays with neighborhood youngsters but appears confused. "Busing—yech. It stinks," she says.

As the boycott seems to lose momentum, the McCauleys worry that truancy charges may be brought against the children. "We feel like there's a gun in our back," protests Mrs. McCauley. They say they would never resort to violence to block busing. But, predicts McCauley, "after the Guard leaves, all hell is going to break loose."

In 1974, the Supreme Court ruled against a plan to desegregate Detroit's primarily black school system that would unite it with the white school systems in several suburban counties. Contrary to earlier lower court decisions in the late 1960s and in the early 1970s, which ruled that entire metropolitan areas had to be considered in planning school desegregation via busing, in this decision the Supreme Court ruled that busing across community-wide school districts was not an appropriate solution to the problem of school segregation. The reality remains that in large cities some busing will probably be necessary to desegregate the schools:

> Whether busing is the only way cities can be desegregated is still an open question, but most of the techniques that do not involve busing have unquestionably failed. The segregated housing patterns that prevail in cities which have seriously attempted to desegregate either voluntarily or under court order almost always necessitate additional transportation.[66]

Still, busing is only one way to achieve school desegregation. Given the current opposition to busing, it may well be that other means for desegregating schools will augment it in the next few years.

Alternatives to Busing. Busing is now often referred to as "court-ordered" or "forced," both of which imply coercion. Two voluntary methods that have been proposed to achieve school desegregation are residential desegregation and the voucher method.

Impediments to residential desegregation include white opposition and discrimination in the real estate business. However, a change may be occurring. A 1972 National Opinion Research Center survey found that over 80 per cent of a national sample of whites indicated that it would not matter if a black family with comparable income and education moved onto the same street. This is encouraging because the present pattern of residential segregation cannot be attributed solely to economic differences between blacks and whites.[67] Also, a majority of blacks prefer to live in racially mixed neighborhoods rather than in totally black neighborhoods.[68]

[66] Gordon Foster, "Desegregating Urban Schools: A Review of Techniques," *Harvard Educational Review,* 43 (February 1973): 31.

[67] Albert I. Hermalin and Reynolds Farley, "The Potential for Residential Integration in Cities and Suburbs: Implications for the Busing Controversy," *American Sociological Review,* 38 (October 1973): 595–610; Karl E. Taeuber, "Demographic Perspectives on Housing and School Segregation," *Wayne Law Review,* 21 (March 1975): 833–849; and Karl E. Taeuber and Alma F. Taeuber, *Negroes in Cities* (Chicago: Aldine Publishing Company, 1965).

[68] Thomas F. Pettigrew, "Attitudes on Race and Housing: A Social-Psychological View," in Amos H. Hawley and Vincent P. Rock, eds., *Segregation in Residential Areas* (Washington, D.C.: National Academy of Sciences, 1973).

According to the voucher method, each school-age child in every family would be eligible for a voucher worth approximately the amount of money spent annually on each student in the public school system.[69] This voucher would be redeemable at any private or public school of the parent's choice; state and/or federal money would be paid to the school at which the voucher was assigned. Public schools would have to support themselves from the vouchers they attract. This would mean that public schools in one neighborhood would have to compete with other public and private schools for funds.

Blacks living in predominantly black neighborhoods could send their children to more racially balanced schools. Unregulated use of the voucher method, however, could increase school segregation. If schools were free to accept or reject vouchers on any grounds (such as IQ, ethnicity, or race), then desegregation could be prevented. Desegregation could be slowed by schools charging tuition in excess of the amount covered by the voucher, thus excluding children from low-income families.

Several suggestions have been made for regulating voucher systems in order to promote school desegregation.[70] Financial incentives for accepting lower class and minority student vouchers should be part of the package. Another proposal is to make the vouchers of poorer children of higher value than those given children from affluent families. A further suggestion is that schools accept vouchers of minority children in proportion to their numbers who have applied. Finally, school desegregation via the voucher method would be increased if a large proportion of the student body in a school (as high as one half) were chosen by lottery in cases where there are more applicants than can be accepted.

Desegregation (whether achieved through busing or other means) is still the most prominently suggested solution to educational inequality. However, compensatory education and increased community control of schools are now being proposed as alternatives to desegretation as means for achieving educational equality.

Compensatory Education.   Central to compensatory education is the idea that special preschool programs can benefit deprived children and overcome an inferior intellectual environment. The best-known attempt at compensatory education is Head Start, a federally supported program for preschoolers from

[69] For a fuller discussion of the voucher method, see Havighurst and Neugarten, *Society and Education,* op. cit., pp. 275–277.
[70] See Cohen, "Public Schools: The Next Decade," op. cit., pp. 168–169.

disadvantaged homes that was originated as part of the Office of Economic Opportunity in 1965. Head Start was conceived in part to prepare disadvantaged preschoolers for entrance into the public school system. Its goal was to provide disadvantaged children with equal opportunity to develop their potential.

A majority of studies indicate that the children's scores on IQ tests, general ability tests, and learning readiness significantly improve after exposure to Head Start programs. Many studies report that in full-year programs, the scores of Head Start participants, who normally enter the program at a distinct disadvantage, eventually reach the national average on tests of general ability and learning readiness.[71] Attitudinal, motivational, and social progress has also been observed among children after some time in Head Start programs. However, one study concludes that although Head Start participants are ahead of comparable non-Head Start children when both groups enter the first year of formal schooling, the gap had either been reduced or eliminated by the end of the year.[72]

But the study also conceded some worthwhile results. Head Start programs were judged to be more effective among blacks, within central cities programs, and in the southeastern portion of the United States. It can be argued that these are the areas having the greatest need for Head Start. Also, the parents of Head Start children were pleased with the program's impact on their children and with their own extensive involvement in it. Finally, Head Start participants were superior to non-Head Start children on certain tests of cognitive development in the area of learning readiness.

Community Control.   Traditionally, the legal authority to finance and administer elementary and high schools lies with the states rather than with the federal government. The states in turn delegate most of this authority to local school systems. Ultimately, then, power over schools rests with school administrators who carry out policies established by the local school boards. The local school board was thought to represent the interests of the community residents, and it was assumed that administrators represented the professional needs of the teachers and the educational needs of the students.

These assumptions have recently been challenged. It has been argued that the current school governance arrangement has become so centralized

[71]*A Report on Evaluation Studies of Project Head Start,* Project Head Start, Office of Child Development, U.S. Department of Health, Education and Welfare, 1970, pp. 11–12.
[72]*The Impact of Head Start: An Evaluation of the Effects of Head Start on Children's Cognitive and Affective Development,* Westinghouse Learning Corporation, Ohio University, July 12, 1969.

WHY BLACKS WANT COMMUNITY CONTROLLED SCHOOLS

The debate is no longer over the pace of desegregation, but whether it should occur at all. Outside the South, the most articulate opponents of school integration are blacks who argue that desegregation amounts to little more than brutal assimilation; that black children need education responsive to their special backgrounds; that the only way to attain this is by setting up black community-controlled schools within the public system.

Though many of the arguments for community control or decentralization are historical—stressing the slowness of Southern school desegregation and its virtual absence in the North—these really distract from the main point: the path to social integration for American minority groups is now seen to lie in group solidarity—cultural unity, community economic development, and political control of community institutions. In this view, the public schools should help develop managerial and political competence in the adult community, serve to create and transmit an authentic black culture, and instill a sense of group identity and pride in black students.

David K. Cohen, "Public Schools: The Next Decade," *Dissent*, 18 (April 1971): 162.

and bureaucratic that accountability to parents and others in the local neighborhood is rare.[73] Political decentralization in urban areas, which would place direct control of each school in the hands of neighborhood residents, is desirable, it is argued, because the present remote, bureaucratic structure fails to meet the needs of children, needs that vary from one neighborhood to another. This is held to be a particular disadvantage by minorities who charge that schools are oriented to white students' needs and are not responsive to the problems of minority students. Black Congresswoman Shirley Chisholm sums up this viewpoint:

> Community control is a way of providing that much needed link between the school and the area's residents which it serves. By involving parents in this type of endeavor, it forces the curriculum to become relevant . . . in terms of reflecting the cultures of the Black and Puerto Rican communities [and] . . . in terms of no longer being influenced by those who refuse to reach out to the community. . . . Community control seems to hold out a promise to bring education that needed step closer . . . to creating an environment that is truly democratic and rife with equal opportunity.[74]

[73] Noel A. Day, "The Case for All-Black Schools" *Equal Educational Opportunity*, op. cit., p. 209.
[74] Shirley Chisholm, "The New Thrust in Education Today," a speech at the University of Illinois Chicago Circle, November 18, 1972.

Although many school administrators have agreed to share major decisions with parents, it remains to be seen if they are willing to share their power with parents. There is also the question of whether neighborhood schools can raise enough money to ensure quality education. Finally, there is the possibility that community control will increase school segregation.

Critics claim that the educational institution is, by its nature, conservative. That is, it functions to pass on dominant values and to prepare children for living in society as it exists. There are, however, some signs that the critics may not be completely right. Schools seem to be showing considerably more concern with their internal problems and a greater desire to handle these problems with innovative approaches. One thing seems clear: if the problems associated with the educational institution are to be properly handled, schools must be a positive force for change rather than a guardian of tradition and the status quo.

Additional Readings

Bolnar, James, and Robert Shanley. *Busing: The Political and Judicial Process*. New York: Praeger, 1974.

Crain, Robert L. *The Politics of Desegregation*. Chicago: Aldine Publishing Company, 1968.

———. "Discussion: How Much Can We Boost IQ and Scholastic Achievement?" *Harvard Educational Review*, 39 (Spring 1969): 273–356.

Davis, Allison. *Social-Class Influences Upon Learning*. Cambridge, Mass.: Harvard University Press, 1965.

Glazer, Nathan. "Is Busing Necessary?" *Commentary*, 53 (March 1972): 39–52.

Greeley, Andrew, and Paul Sheatsley. "Attitudes Toward Racial Integration." *Scientific American*, 225 (December 1971):13–19.

Hart, Harold H. *Summerhill: For and Against*. New York: Hart Publishing Company, 1970.

Hassett, Joseph D., and Arline Weisberg. *Open Education: Alternatives Within Our Tradition*. Englewood Cliffs, N.J.: Prentice-Hall, Inc., 1972.

Holt, John. *Freedom and Beyond*. New York: Dell Publishing Co., Inc., 1972.

Jencks, Christopher, and Marsha Brown. "The Effects of Desegregation on Student Achievement: Some New Evidence from the Equality of Educational Opportunity Survey," *Sociology of Education,* 48 (Winter 1975):126–140.

Kozol, Jonathan. *Free Schools.* Boston: Houghton Mifflin Company, 1972.

Levin, Henry M. "Schooling and Inequality: The Social Science Objectivity Gap," *Saturday Review—Education,* 55 (December 1972):49–51.

Mills, Nicholaus, ed. *The Great School Bus Controversy.* New York: Teachers College Press, 1973.

Nyquist, Ewald B., and Gene R. Hawes, eds. *Open Education: A Sourcebook for Parents and Teachers.* New York: Bantam Books, 1972.

Passow, A. Harry, ed. *Reactions to Silberman's "Crisis in the Classroom."* Worthington, Ohio: Charles A. Jones Publishing Company, 1971.

Peddiwell, J. Abner. *The Saber-Tooth Curriculum.* New York: McGraw-Hill Book Company, 1939.

Repo, Satu, ed. *This Book Is About Schools.* New York: Pantheon Books, Inc., 1970.

Richardson, Ken, and David Spears, eds. *Race, Culture, and Intelligence.* Baltimore: Penguin Books, Inc., 1972.

St. John, Nancy. *School Desegregation: Outcomes for Children.* New York: John Wiley & Sons, Inc., 1975.

Stinchcombe, Arthur L. "Environment: The Cumulation of Events," *Harvard Educational Review,* 39 (Summer 1969):511–522.

Taylor, William L. "Busing: Realities and Evasions," *Dissent,* 19 (Fall 1972):586–594.

United States Commission on Civil Rights. *The Diminishing Barrier: A Report on School Desegregation in Nine Communities.* Washington, D.C.: U.S. Government Printing Office, 1972.

part

problems of structure: changing values

the family

The truth as I see it is that contemporary marriage is a wretched institution. It spells the end of voluntary affection, of love freely given and joyously received. Beautiful romances are transmuted into dull marriages, and eventually the relationship becomes constricting, corrosive, grinding, and destructive. The beautiful love affair becomes a bitter contract.[1]

Why are writers such as Mervyn Cadwallader expressing such negative feelings about marriage and, by implication, about the most basic of all human institutions—the family? Why are these views being expressed now, not only in the works of popular writers but in social science literature as well?

The family in Western society has undergone many changes in its long history; yet, critics say these changes have not kept pace with alterations in other parts of the society. Changes in the family institution do not come easily, for family life is heavily laden with emotion; family structure is deeply intertwined with feelings of identity and adequacy. Suggested changes in the structure and functioning of the family are often perceived as personally threatening, and many people prefer to ignore rather than to acknowledge problems with the American family. This chapter will explore these problems within the context of the functions performed by the modern family.

[1] Mervyn Cadwallader, "Marriage as a Wretched Institution," in J. Gipson Wells, ed., *Current Issues in Marriage and the Family* (New York: Macmillan Publishing Co., Inc., 1975), pp. 26–31.

To speak about *the* American family, of course, is to speak about something that does not really exist. There are many different types of families in the United States. What does exist—and what most modern criticisms are leveled against—is a set of ideals describing what marriage and the family *should* be like. Many writers argue that these ideals were developed in response to social conditions that have long since ceased to exist.

THE FAMILY AND SOCIAL CHANGE

The family of colonial and frontier America was relatively self-sufficient in that it produced most of the goods and services members needed. Further, the extended family, in which three or more generations were included in the household, was typical.[2] The physical strength necessary to perform much of the work in a primarily agricultural society helped to assure a rather clear-cut division of labor along sex lines, with the male the dominant figure, although the tasks typically performed by women also required no small amount of physical stamina.[3] A woman needed a husband to perform such dangerous tasks as producing or hunting food and providing protection. A man needed a wife to preserve and prepare food, make clothing, and help provide him with other necessities of life. Children and unmarried relatives were welcomed as extra hands to help with all of these chores. Life was hard and often short; marriage and family living were centered around producing the things the family needed to stay alive. In essence, the family was a unit oriented toward a continuous struggle against the elements, hunger, disease, and outside enemies.[4] Affection and emotional support, although undoubtedly important, were much less so than they are today.[5] As Frank Scarpitti has noted, "In preindustrial days, a number of basic social and economic functions served, in effect, to solder the union between husband and wife. Enlightened self-interest, if nothing else, dictated the expedience of staying together under almost any circumstances."[6]

[2] For a history of the American family, see Arthur W. Calhoun, *A Social History of the American Family* (New York: Barnes & Noble Books, 1945); see also Willystine Goodsell, *A History of the Family as a Social and Educational Institution* (New York: Macmillan Publishing Co., Inc., 1919).

[3] For example, see William Forrest Sprague, *Women and the West: A Short Social History* (New York: Arno Press Reprints, 1940).

[4] Some scholars have questioned the extent to which this picture accurately portrays the early American family. For example, see William J. Goode, *World Revolution and Family Patterns* (New York: The Free Press, 1963), pp. 6–7.

[5] Hugo G. Beigel, "Romantic Love," *American Sociological Review*, 16 (1951): 326–334.

[6] Frank R. Scarpitti, *Social Problems* (New York: Holt, Rinehart and Winston, 1974), p. 75.

The cumulative effects of industrialization and modernization have changed the Western family from a large, extended, relatively self-sufficient patriarchal structure to a smaller nuclear unit that is far from self-sufficient. (Top: Photo by René Burri; bottom: photo by Leonard Freed. Both: courtesy of Magnum.)

With the advent and spread of the industrial way of life, the extended family of the past has declined and the relatively isolated nuclear family—composed of husband, wife, and their children—has increased.[7] The decline of the extended family has been accompanied by a loss of the stability and solidarity offered by a system that included several generations under one roof

[7] See Ernest W. Burgess, Harvey J. Locke, and Mary M. Thomes, *The Family: From Tradition to Companionship*, 4th ed. (New York: Van Nostrand Reinhold Company, 1971); William F. Ogburn and Meyer F. Nimkoff, *Technology and the Changing Family* (Boston: Houghton Mifflin Company, 1955).

and that placed great emphasis upon tradition and respect for the authority of elders. A number of changes were brought about or accelerated by the industrial revolution.

An important change was that of the father's place of work. No longer did he work at home, but rather, in a factory or office. The physical removal of the father from the home for a significant portion of each day contributed to the undermining of patriarchal authority in the family.

Another change accompanying industrialization was a greater emphasis on individualism. The view of the individual as the most important entity in the society tended to reduce the cohesiveness of the family unit. An accompanying trend was a growing emphasis upon equality. In preindustrial times, one's social position was usually rigidly fixed by custom and by birth. Marked degrees of inequality separated the different social classes; the hierarchical nature of this form of class system was reflected in the patriarchal nature of the family.

The industrial revolution helped to break down a sex-based division of labor, for it created new kinds of jobs for which no previous traditions had been established. That freed women from total dependency on men and helped move them toward equality within the family. Industrialization also encouraged the family to become a mobile group, both geographically and socially, because it became necessary for people to move to wherever jobs were located.

The cumulative effects of industrialization and modernization have changed the Western family from a large, extended, relatively self-sufficient patriarchal structure to a much smaller nuclear unit that is far from self-sufficient. Many of the functions previously performed by the family have been transferred to other social institutions. It has been suggested that the family of today really performs only two tasks: providing for the emotional stability of adults and carrying out the socialization of children.[8] Industrialization and modernization have also contributed to changes in the values and norms that guide family life.

FAMILY FUNCTIONS AND FAMILY PROBLEMS

There is general agreement among social scientists that some essential activities, necessary for the survival of a society, are carried out by the family in

[8] Talcott Parsons, "The American Family: Its Relations to Personality and to the Social Structure," in Talcott Parsons and Robert F. Bales, *Family, Socialization and Interaction Process* (New York: The Free Press, 1955).

all societies. They are referred to as the universal functions of the family. There is little agreement as to how many universal functions the family has, but most lists include these: regulation of sexual behavior, reproduction, child-rearing, provision of affection, status assignment, protection, and economic production and consumption.[9]

Sexual Regulation

All societies have placed great emphasis upon the regulation of sexual behavior. Although the nature of this regulation varies widely from one society to another, no society leaves the expression of sexual drives entirely to the discretion of individuals. Why should societies place restrictions on this basic human activity?

Kingsley Davis has offered a possible answer.[10] He notes that within any society the family system carries out many activities that are necessary for the society's survival. Even in primitive societies the bearing and rearing of children is a demanding task that is difficult for a single individual to handle alone. A woman is relatively defenseless in the later stages of pregnancy and is severely restricted by the needs of the baby for some time after birth; survival chances for both mother and child are much higher if another adult helps protect them and provide them with food. The woman therefore grants an adult male regular and exclusive sexual favors in return for his efforts to protect and provide for her and their child. The man and woman teach the child the skills and attitudes necessary for survival, thus accomplishing the socialization of the child. Davis suggests that the exclusive sexual bond is an important factor in maintaining the lasting male-female relationship required for successful reproduction and socialization of children and, thus, for the continuation of the society. If sexual satisfaction were freely available anywhere, anytime, and with anyone, there would be less incentive for men and women to remain together long enough to socialize children properly and to teach them the skills they need to cope effectively with their physical and social environment.

Davis perhaps places too much emphasis upon the importance of an exclusive sexual bond as the factor that holds couples together and thereby preserves social stability. Gerald Leslie notes that perhaps as few as 5 per

[9] Paul B. Horton and Chester L. Hunt, *Sociology,* 2nd ed. (New York: McGraw-Hill Book Company, 1968), pp. 220–223.

[10] Kingsley Davis, "Sexual Behavior," in Robert K. Merton and Robert A. Nisbet, eds., *Contemporary Social Problems,* 3rd ed. (New York: Harcourt Brace Jovanovich, Inc., 1971), p. 319.

cent of the world's societies limit acceptable sexual intercourse to marital partners only.[11] In all societies, however, norms regulating sexual behavior are directed primarily toward assuring that children will be born into a stable, long-lasting social group that will be responsible for their upbringing. The norms in American society stipulate that *all* sexual behavior should be confined to marital relationships. If Davis and others are correct, this strict regulation exists because it increases the society's chances for survival. From this perspective, the widespread breaking of sex-related norms is a social problem because it will lead to a weakening of a society's survival potential. If sex norms are widely ignored, children will be born without assurance that any social group will take responsibility for their protection and socialization.

If it is true that norms regulating sexual behavior exist to assure the continuation of the society, the degree to which actual behavior deviates from these norms constitutes an important social problem. The available evidence strongly suggests that the actual behavior of Americans often violates sex-related norms. Several factors contribute to this situation.

For one thing, there is much encouragement of heterosexual activities among the young. Unmarried Americans are actively encouraged to seek the company of the opposite sex at an early age. Dating often begins in junior high school or earlier.[12] Most young Americans are actively involved in dating by the time they reach their mid-teen years and may, in fact, be regarded as social failures if they are not. At the time of puberty, when physiological changes bring questions about sexual identity and functioning to the fore of young persons' consciousness, they are encouraged to associate with members of the opposite sex, usually without adult supervision.

Second, although Americans are expected to confine sexual activity to marriage alone, they are continually bombarded with sexual stimulation from a variety of sources.[13] The advertising industry has capitalized on sex as an effective means of selling all manner of products. In addition to the thinly camouflaged sexual messages of the advertising world, rather vivid portrayals of sexuality are readily available in art theaters, paperback bookstores, and supermarket magazine racks, not to mention television and Hollywood movies in neighborhood theaters.

[11] Gerald R. Leslie, *The Family in Social Context,* 2nd ed. (New York: Oxford University Press, 1973), p. 375.

[12] Robert R. Bell and Jay B. Chaskes, "Premarital Sexual Experience Among Coeds, 1958 and 1968," *Journal of Marriage and the Family,* 32 (February 1970): 81–84. See also Carlfred B. Broderick and Stanley Fowler, "New Patterns of Relationships Between the Sexes Among Preadolescents," *Marriage and Family Living,* 23 (February 1961): 27–30.

[13] See Vance Packard, *The Sexual Wilderness* (New York: David McKay Co., Inc., 1968), pp. 54–67; Charles A. Reich, *The Greening of America* (New York: Random House, Inc., 1970), pp. 171–193.

Third, Americans are encouraged to place personal satisfactions above all else. This emphasis has consequences in the sexual realm. After all, the argument goes, if we are encouraged to develop our potential in all other areas of life, why should we not develop our sexual potential as well?

Another feature of American society that has contributed to deviation from traditional sex-related norms is the movement toward equality for women. In the past, sexual norms in America reflected a double standard. As women have moved toward equality in all areas of life, however, they have become increasingly unwilling to accept this view of sex. Recent studies indicate that women are becoming less restricted and less inhibited in their sexual behavior.[14]

With such cultural factors acting to undermine them, American sex-related norms have been less than completely successful in confining sexual expression to married couples. Although the increasing rates of premarital and extramarital coitus provide some measure of the ineffectiveness of these norms, another kind of measure is provided by the degree of guilt experienced by those who break these norms. If individuals accept the traditional norms as appropriate guidelines for behavior, then they should experience strong feelings of guilt when they deviate from them. Numerous studies have indicated that this is not the case. In the Kinsey studies, 77 per cent of the married women and 69 per cent of the unmarried women who had had premarital intercourse reported no guilt feelings; an additional 12 per cent of the married and 13 per cent of the unmarried women expressed only minor guilt.[15] In a later study, Ernest Burgess and Paul Wallin found that 84 per cent of the women and 96 per cent of the men they studied, who had experienced premarital coitus, expressed no guilt feelings about it.[16] Other studies have shown that feelings of guilt are not usually strong inhibitors of premarital sexual activity.[17]

It seems undeniable that American sexual behavior is becoming more liberal and that the traditional sex-related norms are often broken, usually without creating strong feelings of guilt. Illegitimacy is one consequence of this increased premarital sexual activity that demands investigation as a social problem.

[14] For example, see Bell and Chaskes, op. cit.

[15] Alfred C. Kinsey, Wardell B. Pomeroy, Clyde E. Martin, and Paul H. Gebhard, *Sexual Behavior in the Human Female* (Philadelphia: W. B. Saunders Co., 1953), p. 316.

[16] Ernest W. Burgess and Paul Wallin, *Engagement and Marriage* (Philadelphia: J. B. Lippincott Company, 1953).

[17] Ira Reiss, "How and Why America's Sex Standards Are Changing," *Trans-action*, 5 (March 1968): 26–32.

Illegitimacy.   It is estimated that some 340,000 children are now born out of wedlock each year in the United States.[18] There is evidence that increasingly permissive premarital sexual behavior has resulted in an increase in illegitimacy. There were seven births per 1,000 unmarried women (ages 15–44) in 1940; by 1967, illegitimate births had more than tripled, to 24 per 1,000 unmarried women.[19]

Although illegitimacy is not limited to any one social category, rates are higher in some groups than in others. Studies have found that illegitimacy is approximately four times as likely to occur among women of the lower class than among those from the middle class.[20] This fact is significant because illegitimacy often acts to perpetuate the cycle of poverty. If the lower-class woman chooses to keep and rear her child, her financial situation often becomes critical. The federal government's Aid to Families with Dependent Children program provides only minimal support. The kinds of jobs available to untrained persons in American society provide only a limited income. Babysitting expenses may exceed these wages, and low-cost day-care facilities for women with limited incomes are generally not available. The woman and her child therefore find it difficult to escape poverty.

Reproduction

The idea that all married couples should have children is a basic family value that extends far back into the history of Western culture. In Biblical times and in the classical ages of Greece and Rome, barrenness was sufficient grounds for a man to divorce his wife. In colonial America, single men were regarded with suspicion and were penalized through special taxes for not doing their part to help increase the population. High rates of infant and child mortality meant that couples had to produce several children to be reasonably certain that at least a few of them would live to provide for their parents' old age.

In spite of this strong emphasis on the desirability of children, the long-term trend in the fertility rate in the United States has been generally downward, as Table 6-1 indicates. There are several factors that help to explain

---

[18] Robert H. Neuhaus and Ruby H. Neuhaus, *Family Crises* (Columbus, Ohio: Charles E. Merrill Publishing Company, 1974), pp. 62–65.
[19] Leslie A. Westoff and Charles F. Westoff, *From Now to Zero* (Boston: Little, Brown and Company, 1971), p. 279.
[20] Ibid., pp. 299–300.

Table 6-1. Crude Birth Rate, 1910–1974

Year	Births per 1,000 Population	Year	Births per 1,000 Population
1910	30.1	1954	25.3
1920	23.7	1955	24.6
1930	18.9	1956	24.9
1935	16.9	1957	25.0
1936	16.7	1958	24.6
1937	17.1	1959	24.3
1938	17.6	1960	23.7
1939	17.3	1961	23.3
1940	17.9	1962	22.4
1941	18.8	1963	21.7
1942	20.8	1964	21.1
1943	21.5	1965	19.5
1944	20.2	1966	18.4
1945	19.5	1967	17.9
1946	23.3	1968	17.4
1947	25.8	1969	17.7
1948	24.2	1970	18.2
1949	23.9	1971	17.3
1950	23.6	1972	15.6
1951	24.9	1973	14.9
1952	25.0	1974	14.9
1953	25.1		

SOURCE: National Center for Health Statistics, various publications.

this trend. For example, whereas children may be an economic asset in a predominantly rural economy, they are a financial liability in a modern industrialized society. The estimated cost of rearing a child from birth to maturity ranges from $30,000 to $100,000, depending on the parents' social class and whether or not the child goes to college. For the average family, rearing two, three, or more children represents a financial outlay that may be beyond their means.

A further explanation for the decline of the fertility rate results from the widening options for females. As long as the major responsibility of child-rearing falls upon women, the presence of children places limits upon the extent to which women can develop interests or careers outside the home. Although some women may successfully manage a home, a career, and a house full of children, the percentage of individuals who can simultaneously do an adequate job of all three is probably quite small. Some spokespersons for the Women's Liberation Movement strongly reject the idea that mother-hood is essential for a woman's fulfillment. Betty Rollin states: "Motherhood is in trouble, and it ought to be. A rude question is long overdue: Who needs it? The answer used to be (1) society and (2) women. But now, with the impending horrors of overpopulation, society *doesn't* need it. And women don't either."[21]

Rollin and others have contended that American cultural norms that en-courage *all* women to marry and produce children restrict the options open to women.[22] Children are still highly valued, but these writers argue that the time has come for motherhood to become a consciously chosen option, one among many options, rather than an automatic, unthinking act. Judith Blake has found some support for this claim.[23] Although she discovered that the no-child or the one-child family is not seen as desirable by the vast majority of Americans, she also found that from 1961 to 1971 the percentage of college-age respondents who stated that couples should be able to choose such op-tions if they so desired increased from 3 to 10 per cent.

Even when children are desired, child-rearing may place a strain on the husband-wife relationship. After surveying a number of studies of the effects of children on marital satisfaction, Mary Hicks and Marilyn Platt conclude that "children tend to detract from, rather than contribute to, marital happin-ess."[24] In another survey, Gerald Leslie concludes that some studies have found that the arrival of children increases the couple's marital satisfaction; many studies, however, have found that couples without children report con-siderably higher levels of marital happiness.[25]

A decision not to have a child is sometimes made after conception has taken place. Then abortion becomes an important issue.

Abortion. In the past, couples were expected to accept as many children "as providence sends," but many couples now express openly the wish to limit their family size. According to Leslie and Charles Westoff,

[21] Betty Rollin, "Motherhood: Who Needs It?" *Look,* 34 (September 22, 1970): 15.

[22] See Ellen Peck, *The Baby Trap* (New York: Bernard Geis Associates, 1971); Anna Silverman and Ar-nold Silverman, *The Case Against Having Children* (New York: David McKay Co., Inc., 1971); Shirley L. Radl, *Mother's Day Is Over* (New York: Charterhouse, 1973).

[23] Judith Blake, "Can We Believe Recent Data on Birth Expectations in the United States?" *Demography,* 11 (February 1974): 25–44.

[24] Mary Hicks and Marilyn Platt, "Marital Happiness and Stability: A Review of the Research in the Six-ties," in Carlfred Broderick, ed., *A Decade of Family Research and Action, 1960–1969* (Minneapolis: Na-tional Council on Family Relations, 1971), p. 75.

[25] Leslie, op. cit., pp. 508–510.

'I HAVE 7 CHILDREN,' SHE SAID TO WILD APPLAUSE
By Ellen Peck

Susan, on "As the World Turns," has just had a baby. She is not the only one. Turning the daytime dial, we see that Chris, on "Where the Heart Is," has just had a baby, too. Within the past year, babies have also been born to Janet on "Search for Tomorrow," Meredith on "One Life to Live," Edie on "All My Children," Angel on "Love is a Many-Splendored Thing," Diana on "General Hospital," Linda on "Days of Our Lives," Mary on "Where the Heart Is," Carolee on "The Doctors" . . . and "Another World's" Pat Randolph has twins.

Actually, the birth rate on daytime TV seems to rival that of Latin America!

If the pregnancies per se are demographically questionable, the way in which they are presented is often psychologically alarming: pregnancy is shown as woman's way to become the center of attention, retreat from unresolved conflicts, or compete for men.

A classic natalist competition took place recently on "As the World Turns." Susan is married to Dan, who is in love with Liz (and is, in fact, the father of Liz's child). Sensing her husband's attraction to Liz, Susan became pregnant, hoping thus to win Dan's permanent affection.

That pregnancy was planned—at least by Susan—and such planning is rare on the daytime dramas. Most pregnancies are accidental. . . .

Actually, were all pronatalist, glory-of-motherhood-and-reproductive-function comments to be combined and presented to the F.C.C. Fairness Doctrine Committee, daytime TV would owe Planned Parenthood, Zero Population Growth and the National Organization for Non-Parents approximately 18,200 minutes of "equal time" *for the past year's shows alone*. . . .

Strong impressions are conveyed here: pregnancy will save your marriage; motherhood will fulfill you; bearing a man's child will make you supremely important to that man. Such messages are misleading (the "baby holds man" myth is dispelled by a simple glance at the divorce statistics); nevertheless, 12 of the 16 daytime dramas carry strong reproductive themes.

Daytime quiz and talk shows offer scant relief. Recently on "The Dating Game" a contest question was, "How many children do you want?" (Responses were "three," "three," and "five.") That same week, Garry Moore asked a "To Tell the Truth" contestant, "And what do you do?" She replied, "I'm a housewife and mother of seven children," and the audience applauded mightily. . . .

An episode of last season's "Dick Van Dyke" series also deserves examination. It was called "Off and Running"; I call it "I Didn't Mean Us."

Situation: Dick hosts his own talk show. After interviewing an author and commending a book, "Overpopulation Begins at Home," Dick returns to his own home to learn that another child is on the way. He and Jenny already have a 16-year-old son and a 9-year-old daughter. Sample dialogue:

JENNY: You've always been so outspoken about the dangers of over-population and how responsible couples should replace only their own number . . .

DICK: Honey . . .

JENNY: Didn't you mean what you were saying?

DICK: Yes, but . . . I didn't mean us. . . .

© 1972 by The New York Times Co. Reprinted by permission.

Between 1960 and 1965, in this country, it is estimated that some 4.7 million births occurred that were probably unwanted. This is an average estimate between the 5.3 million unwanted by at least one parent and the 4 million reported to have been unwanted by both parents. . . . These 4.7 million births—about three quarters of a million a year—constituted nearly 20 per cent of all children born during that period.[26]

The same authors point out that the percentage of unwanted births increases as the number of children increases; for example, 44 per cent of all fifth-born children and more than 50 per cent of all sixth or later births were reported as unwanted.

It is difficult to determine what proportion of unwanted pregnancies are ended by abortions. All indications are that the demand for abortions is extensive. Before 1973, when the Supreme Court ruled that states could not without good reason forbid a woman to have an abortion, it is estimated that there were approximately 300 abortions for every 1,000 live births.[27] Prior to the Supreme Court decision, most states had restrictive laws that allowed abortion only if the woman's life would be endangered by continuation of the pregnancy. Under such restrictions, approximately 20,000 legal, therapeutic abortions were performed in 1969. By 1970, however, after several states had passed more liberal abortion laws, 200,000 legal abortions were performed.[28] In 1971, there were 500,000 legal abortions reported.[29]

The issue of abortion has been controversial throughout human history. The debate focuses upon two related questions: At what point does human

[26] Westoff and Westoff, op. cit., pp. 293–294.
[27] John H. Knowles, "Public Policy on Abortion," *Society*, 11 (July-August 1974): 15.
[28] Ibid.
[29] Ibid.

life begin, and what are the legal rights of the unborn fetus? Those who argue against abortion propose that human life begins at the moment of conception and that abortion should therefore be regarded as murder. The Catholic church has taken this position since 1869, when Pope Pius IX rejected the then-existing less rigid stance.[30] A more liberal position is that although the fetus possesses life, humanness begins only at the moment of birth.[31] Destruction of the fetus therefore, although not to be taken lightly, is not murder.

An alternative answer to the question of when a fetus becomes a human being requires that some development must have taken place. This approach has a long history. Aristotle, for example, proposed that "the fetus develops steadily and is endowed successively with three types of soul: At conception, a vegetative soul inhabits the embryo; soon thereafter an animal soul takes over; on the fortieth day of gestation a human soul moves in."[32] (It is interesting to note that this was the case only for a male fetus; the female fetus, he believed, did not receive its human soul until the eightieth day of gestation.)

Closely related to the question of when a fetus should be regarded as a human being are questions regarding the legal rights of the fetus. Some believe that because a fetus should be regarded as a human being from the moment of conception, it is entitled to the same protection under the law as any other human being. Others have argued that because the fetus cannot sustain itself outside of the womb, it should be regarded as prehuman and should not be protected by law. There was no federal policy on this matter until 1973, when the Supreme Court took a position that lies between the two extremes. Two cases were decided in that year, *Roe* v. *Wade* and *Doe* v. *Bolton,* in which the Court's stance was that abortion decisions were to be made entirely by the woman and her physician during the first trimester (three months) of pregnancy.[33] After the first trimester, however, the state may regulate abortion in ways that are reasonably related to maternal health. After the fetus has reached viability (is able to live outside the womb), abortion may be regulated and even proscribed unless expert medical opinion indicates severe danger to the woman's life or health.

The Supreme Court decision by no means ended the controversy surrounding the legal aspects of abortion. Various groups have proposed a con-

---

[30] Westoff and Westoff, op. cit., pp. 127–128.

[31] David M. Feldman, *Birth Control in Jewish Law* (New York: New York University Press, 1968), especially chapter 15.

[32] Paul W. Rahmeier, "Abortion and the Reverence for Life," *The Christian Century,* 88 (May 5, 1971): 556–560.

[33] See "The 'Abortion' Cases," *Supreme Court Reporter,* 93 (February 15, 1973): 705–763.

stitutional amendment to prohibit abortion and are actively lobbying to promote its passage. Legal harassment has been used to intimidate doctors and to discourage them from performing legal abortions.[34]

Abortion law has a direct bearing upon family problems in at least three ways. First, when legal abortions are not available, many women turn to illegal means. Although legal abortion performed in a hospital or clinical setting by a competent physician is a relatively safe operation, illegal operations carried out by semiskilled or unskilled persons are often dangerous. The possibilities of puncturing the uterus and of incurring infection are high. Christopher Tietze, a leading expert on abortion, indicates that mortality rates for women who have illegal abortions may be as much as 30 times higher than for those who have legal abortions.[35]

A second kind of burden may be placed upon families when restrictive abortion laws prevent aborting a fetus that is likely to be defective. If a woman develops certain diseases such as German measles during the early stage of pregnancy, there is increased risk that the fetus will fail to develop properly. Certain drugs also increase this risk.

A third type of impact that restrictive abortion laws may have upon families is illustrated by a study conducted by Hans Forssman and Inga Thuwe.[36] These researchers carried out a 25-year follow-up of 120 children born to Swedish women whose requests for abortions had been denied. The children, all born between 1939 and 1941, were compared with a control group of children of the same age and social background who had been wanted by their parents. Differences between the two groups at the age of 21 were marked.

> More of the unwanted children had received psychiatric care: 28 percent compared with 15 percent among the control group. More had records of delinquency: 18 compared with 8 percent. More had received public assistance between the ages of sixteen and twenty-one: 14 to 3 percent. More had been declared unfit for military service: 15 to 7 percent. Fewer of the unwanted children (14 percent) had attended university than those in the control group (33 percent). And by age twenty-one, more of the unwanted children had married and started raising families.[37]

[34] Nathan Lewin, "Abortion and Dr. Edelin," *The New Republic*, 172 (March 1, 1975): 16–19.
[35] Christopher Tietze, "Mortality with Contraception and Induced Abortion," *Studies in Family Planning*, 45 (September 1969): 6–8.
[36] Hans Forssman and Inga Thuwe, "One Hundred and Twenty Children Born After Application for Therapeutic Abortion Refused," *Acta Psychiat. Scand.*, 42 (1966): 71–78.
[37] Westoff and Westoff, op. cit., p. 297.

A denied abortion may thus lead to an unwanted child who grows up in a hostile home environment. The psychic costs to the child and to the family and the social costs to the society may be great.

Public acceptance of the idea that a woman should have the right to an abortion on demand has made sizable gains over the past decade. Westoff and Westoff summarize a number of public opinion polls conducted since 1965.[38] In 1965, 5 per cent of women respondents accepted the idea of abortion on demand. By 1967, the figure had risen to 21 per cent; by 1969, 40 per cent. By 1971, two polls of college students found approximately one half and two thirds, respectively, accepting the idea of abortion on demand.

Child-Rearing

According to Robert Thamm, the parent-child relationship has developed several negative characteristics as the American family has changed from the extended form composed of many individuals to the nuclear form with few individuals.[39] While the extended family of yesteryear provided grandparents, aunts, uncles, and cousins with whom the child could interact and use as role models, the nuclear family system has removed all of these persons from the family's inner circle. Thus, in the nuclear family, parents are able to impose their personal biases and idiosyncrasies upon their children without other adults serving as corrective forces.

A second child-rearing problem associated with the nuclear family is that a child is exposed only to individuals within a narrow age range:

> Parents are usually between 20 and 35 years of age during the child-raising period. When children are in their formative years, they tend to get little exposure to teen-aged, middle-aged, and elderly people. Older siblings and grandparents may serve temporarily in this capacity but they are becoming less available with the increased fragmentation and mobility of the modern family.[40]

The result of this limited age range is that the child grows up with little experience in relating to people in different age categories.

[38] Ibid., pp. 149–150.

[39] Robert Thamm, *Beyond Marriage and the Nuclear Family* (San Francisco: Canfield Press, 1975), pp. 35–39.

[40] Ibid., p. 37.

Another problem is that there are often no satisfactory substitutes available for child care when both parents are out of the home. Because of desire for a career or out of economic necessity, increasing numbers of mothers now work outside the home.[41] Often there are no satisfactory day-care services for those who work but do not want to leave their children unsupervised. Such problems of child care rarely existed in the extended family, for there were usually many individuals available to care for children when the parents were absent.

A final problem identified by Thamm involves the effects of intensive child-rearing upon the mother. In the extended family, the constant pressures exerted by small children could be shared with other adults. In the nuclear family of today, the mother usually has no other adults available to her for temporary relief. Thamm suggests that this may contribute to such things as nervous breakdowns, mental illness, alcoholism, and child abuse.[42]

Whereas Thamm argues that child-rearing problems arise from the fact that the nuclear family cannot handle the many demands made upon it, Urie Bronfenbrenner contends that modern society has transferred too many of the socialization functions previously handled by the family to other institutions such as the school, the church, and the juvenile court.[43] The result is that parents have less control over their children than is desirable.

The majority of Americans now live in either urban or suburban areas. The husband and father may commute many miles to work; if so, he leaves early in the morning, perhaps before his small children are awake, and returns late in the evening, at times after the children are asleep. The wife travels to shop, to attend social events, to work, or to engage in volunteer activity. Because many parents spend much of their time away from home, children now spend more time with their peers than they do with their parents once they reach the upper levels of grade school. Bronfenbrenner notes that peer groups serve to fill the vacuum created in the life of a child who receives an insufficient amount of attention from the parents. He also points to a number of studies that indicate peer-oriented children engage in more antisocial behavior than do adult-oriented children.[44]

Nor is the time that the child spends at home necessarily a constructive

[41] Ibid., pp. 37–38.
[42] For example, see Jessie Bernard, *The Future of Marriage* (Cleveland: William Collins & World Publishing Co., Inc., 1972).
[43] Urie Bronfenbrenner, *Two Worlds of Childhood* (New York: The Russell Sage Foundation, 1970), chap. 4.
[44] Ibid., pp. 103–109.

period. The average American child between the ages of 6 and 16 spends approximately 22 hours per week watching television. Bronfenbrenner cites research findings that watching aggressive behavior, whether in real life, on the movie screen, or on television, significantly increases the expression of aggressive impulses in both children and adults.

Some observers suggest that not only have parents lost control over their children, but often children have gained control over parents. James Coleman has observed that the highly segmented, mobile nature of American society gives adolescents a kind of power over their parents that was unknown in earlier times. [45] In a real sense, the suburban development may be simply a bedroom rather than a real community for adults. Adolescents, however, spend most of their time in the area. Communication networks develop among the children of a suburb, but not among the adults. When a child says, "Why can't I do this? All the other kids get to do it!" many adults do not know what other parents permit their children to do; they may not even know the other parents.

Provision of Affection

In preindustrial society, the family was primarily a unit of survival. The individual was expected to receive psychological and emotional support primarily from the extended family and the small, closely knit community. Now, the nuclear family stands more or less on its own. Husband, wife, and children are expected to obtain almost all of their emotional support and satisfaction from one another. One of the norms associated with monogamous marriage is the expectation that an individual will love only one person, his or her spouse. Close emotional attachments between adult men and women who are not married to each other are often regarded with suspicion in American society. The assumption is that such attachments will lead to adulterous relationships. This, in essence, means that each husband is expected to be all things to his wife, and vice versa.

Divorce.   It has been argued that the divorce rate provides one measure of the degree to which the nuclear family is failing to provide for the emotional needs of spouses. The divorce rate in the United States has been seen recently

[45] James S. Coleman, "Community Disorganization and Conflict," in Robert K. Merton and Robert A. Nisbet, eds., *Contemporary Social Problems*, 3rd ed. (New York: Harcourt Brace Jovanovich, Inc., 1971), pp. 690–691.

as a cause for alarm. Paul Glick compared the divorce rate in the United States with those of other countries:

> In 1972, the most recent date for which many international figures are available, the divorce rate was highest in the U.S.A., with a rate of 3.72 per 1,000 population. Other countries with high 1972 levels of divorce were the U.S.S.R. with a rate of 2.64 and Hungary with a rate of 2.32. More recently, the U.S. divorce rate climbed on up to 4.4 per 1,000 population in 1973 and to 4.5 per 1,000 during the 12 months ending in August, 1974.[46]

The divorce rate continues to rise. By the mid-1970s the American divorce rate had increased to almost 5 divorces per 1,000 population.

As can be seen in Table 6-2, the probability of divorce is inversely related to the age of women. The highest rates of divorce are found in the

Table 6-2. Age-Specific Divorce Rates for Selected States

State	Age of Women										
	14–19	20–24	25–29	30–34	35–39	40–44	45–49	50–54	55–59	60–64	65 & Over
Hawaii	21.17	28.58	24.77	19.50	16.47	12.77	10.20	7.46	3.75	3.28	2.15
Illinois	23.83	34.50	25.55	19.24	15.34	11.73	8.25	5.58	3.49	2.10	1.07
Iowa	38.94	32.13	20.21	13.57	10.66	8.19	5.24	3.44	2.25	1.43	0.65
Kansas	34.53	42.53	30.51	20.14	16.46	11.76	8.87	6.25	3.69	2.32	1.42
Maryland	9.21	19.77	18.06	13.25	10.93	8.40	6.33	4.69	2.65	2.10	0.88
Montana	43.80	52.31	32.37	22.25	19.64	16.13	9.86	5.94	5.03	4.67	1.49
Nebraska	29.64	30.52	18.34	13.54	10.18	8.81	6.52	3.51	1.94	1.33	0.82
Oregon	49.89	46.67	31.57	25.26	21.44	16.49	10.22	7.64	5.41	3.19	1.58
Rhode Island	10.22	19.26	16.52	11.55	9.92	7.10	5.05	2.63	2.26	1.43	0.58
South Carolina	20.75	20.25	16.47	12.47	9.77	7.38	5.45	3.62	1.77	1.77	0.07
Tennessee	46.54	42.15	29.53	21.10	17.07	12.65	9.87	7.37	4.01	3.18	1.62
Texas	54.96	43.47	30.75	22.05	19.36	14.73	11.64	7.90	5.26	3.82	2.21
Utah	31.83	32.81	27.07	17.75	15.78	10.52	8.17	6.82	3.85	1.94	1.32
Vermont	10.47	24.58	19.57	15.70	11.58	8.26	8.11	3.68	2.79	1.36	0.71
Virginia	14.38	22.13	18.37	14.11	10.90	8.91	6.47	4.96	3.14	2.23	1.16
West Virginia	9.32	28.13	27.05	16.75	13.74	12.13	9.77	8.46	5.93	5.50	2.84
Total	33.7	33.1	24.2	17.6	14.5	11.2	8.2	5.7	3.7	3.7	3.1

SOURCE: J. Lynn England and Phillip R. Kunz, "The Application of Age-Specific Rates to Divorce," *Journal of Marriage and the Family,* 37 (February 1975): 44.
Note: Divorces by age category per 1,000 married women.

[46] Paul C. Glick, "A Demographer Looks at American Families," *Journal of Marriage and the Family,* 37 (February 1975): 22.

younger age categories. Although marriages involving young women are more likely to result in divorce, divorce rates for the teen years are not substantially higher than rates for women in their twenties.

Divorce rates tell relatively little about the dynamics of divorce and its effects upon those who experience it. A divorce can cost more than $3,000 in legal fees plus alimony and child support payments.[47] In addition to the financial burden, divorce involves emotional costs. Joseph Epstein argues that, whatever else a divorce accomplishes, it always means that both partners experience a deep sense of personal failure.[48] In addition, a divorced person faces a number of disadvantages. Married persons often see the divorced as a threat to their own marriages because the formerly married provide living proof that marriages do fail. Also the divorced person may be seen as being "on the prowl," seeking either sexual adventure or a second marriage, possibly to one's own spouse. Another disadvantage of divorce is that American social life for adults is geared almost entirely around couples, which leaves the single adult feeling like an outsider.

The nature of American divorce laws also adds to the burdens of the divorcing individuals. Divorce laws are left to the discretion of the individual states because there is no federal divorce law. Traditionally, most states follow the adversary procedure in divorce proceedings based on the assumption that there is both a guilty and an innocent party. The innocent party must prove that the guilty one has committed acts that fall within the legally organized grounds for divorce in that state. The adversary procedure helps to make the divorce court a potential battleground.

The answer to unrealistic divorce laws has been a movement toward some form of "no-fault" divorce, in which a couple simply declares to the court that their marriage is no longer workable. As of 1975, 28 states had enacted some form of no-fault divorce. (The current status of divorce laws is summarized in Table 6-3.) It should be noted, however, that most of the current no-fault statutes have simply been added to existing adversary laws. In a contested divorce (one in which one of the spouses takes legal steps to prevent the divorce being granted), the adversary procedure still holds.

The effects of divorce upon children are a major concern. The majority of American divorces involve couples with children under the age of 18.[49] The separated spouses and their children can find the period following di-

---

[47] "The High Cost of Divorce in Money and Emotions," *Business Week,* February 10, 1975, pp. 83–90.
[48] Joseph Epstein, *Divorced in America* (New York: Penguin Books, 1974).
[49] Robert R. Bell, *Marriage and Family Interaction,* 4th ed. (Homewood, Ill.: The Dorsey Press, 1975), p. 553.

Table 6-3   What the Divorce Laws Say Coast to Coast, 1975

	Grounds for Divorce					Division of Property			Alimony		
	Breakdown of Marriage	Standard Fault Grounds	Incompatability	Separation	Alcoholism or Drug Use	Court Cannot Make a Distribution	Court Empowered to Distribute	Community Property —Joint Ownership	To Either Spouse	To Wife Only	No Alimony
Alabama	●	●		●	●	●				●	
Alaska		●	●		●		●		●		
Arizona	●							●	●		
Arkansas		●		●	●		●			●	
California	●							●	●		
Colorado	●						●		●		
Connecticut	●	●		●	●		●		●		
Delaware	●						●		●		
Dist. of Columbia		●		●			●			●	
Florida	●					●			●		
Georgia	●	●			●	●				●	
Hawaii	●	●				●			●		
Idaho	●	●	●					●		●	
Illinois		●			●		●			●	
Indiana	●	●					●		●		
Iowa	●						●		●		
Kansas		●	●		●		●		●		
Kentucky	●						●		●		
Louisiana		●		●	●			●			●*
Maine	●	●					●		●		
Maryland		●		●		●				●	
Massachusetts		●			●	●			●		
Michigan	●						●		●		
Minnesota	●						●		●		
Mississippi		●			●	●				●	
Missouri	●						●		●		
Montana	●	●					●		●		
Nebraska	●						●		●		

Table 6-3 (Continued)

	Grounds for Divorce					Division of Property			Alimony		
	Breakdown of Marriage	Standard Fault Grounds	Incompatability	Separation	Alcoholism or Drug Use	Court Cannot Make a Distribution	Court Empowered to Distribute	Community Property—Joint Ownership	To Either Spouse	To Wife Only	No Alimony
Nevada		●	●		●			●		●	
New Hampshire	●	●		●	●		●		●**		
New Jersey	●			●			●		●		
New Mexico		●	●					●		●	
New York		●		●		●				●	
North Carolina		●		●		●					●***
North Dakota		●	●		●		●		●		
Ohio		●		●	●	●			●		
Oklahoma		●	●		●		●		●		
Oregon	●						●		●		
Pennsylvania		●				●					●
Rhode Island		●		●	●	●				●	
South Carolina		●		●	●	●				●	
South Dakota		●		●			●			●	
Tennessee		●		●	●		●			●	
Texas		●		●				●			●
Utah		●		●	●		●		●		
Vermont		●		●			●		●		
Virginia		●		●		●				●	
Washington	●							●	●		
West Virginia		●		●	●		●		●		
Wisconsin		●		●	●		●			●	
Wyoming		●		●	●		●			●	

Reprinted from the February 10, 1975 issue of *Business Week* by special permission. © 1975 by McGraw-Hill, Inc.

Notes: Standard fault grounds include adultery, cruelty, desertion. Separation means living apart with normal financial support provided. In division of property, when court cannot make a distribution, property goes to husband or wife, depending on who has legal title.

*Louisiana limits alimony to ⅓ of the husband's income

**New Hampshire limits alimony to a term of three years (subject to renewal)

***North Carolina provides for alimony only if the spouse is unable to work

vorce difficult. Yet it is not known which may be more damaging to a child, a divorce or a home filled with tension and hostility between parents who stay together "for the sake of the children."

Opinion on the meaning of the American divorce rate is divided. Some critics see the high divorce rate as signaling the decline of the nuclear family and the coming fall of the entire social order.[50] Others feel that a high divorce rate is a normal and even necessary consequence of mate choice based upon romantic attraction and definition of marital satisfaction in terms of personal happiness.[51]

Status Assignment

Status assignment refers to the placing of individuals within the stratification structure of a society. In all societies, the family plays a major role in the placement process. In earlier times, a person's social class was largely determined by the social class position of the family into which he or she was born. In modern American society, the individual is supposedly able to attain whatever social position his or her innate intelligence and learned skills will allow.

Two problems related to the family's impact on status assignment have attracted attention. First, males are relatively free to achieve whatever social position their capabilities will allow, whereas women are almost inevitably assigned the social position of their husbands. This means that a man is able to determine his own position in the social hierarchy (ideally, at least), whereas a woman—no matter how bright or capable she may be—has her social position determined for her by someone else.

A second problem is the fact that, because families at different levels in the stratification structure teach their children different kinds of attitudes, values, and skills, it is difficult for children in the lower classes to acquire the aspirations and abilities needed to move up the hierarchy.[52] Schools may provide some of the values and skills required for social mobility, but the children who are most in need of assistance are likely to attend substandard inner-city schools where the quality of education is lowest. James Coleman, in his nationwide study of factors affecting the performance of children in

---

[50] Carle C. Zimmerman, "The Atomistic Family—Fact or Fiction?" *Journal of Comparative Family Studies*, 1 (Autumn 1970): 5–16.

[51] Parsons, op. cit.

[52] Alan C. Kerckhoff, *Socialization and Social Class* (Englewood Cliffs, N.J.: Prentice-Hall, Inc., 1972).

SEX ROLE DISCRIMINATION IN CHILDREN'S LITERATURE

What Boys Can Be

a fireman who squirts water on the flames, and
a baseball player who wins lots of games.
a bus driver who helps people travel far, or
a policemen with a siren in his car.
a cowboy who goes on cattle drives, and
a doctor who helps to save people's lives.
a sailor on a ship that takes you everywhere, and
a pilot who goes flying through the air.
a clown with silly tricks to do, and
a pet tiger owner who runs the zoo.
a farmer who drives a big red tractor, and
on TV shows, if I become an actor.
an astronaut who lives in a space station, and
someday grow up to be President of the nation

What Girls Can Be

a nurse, with white uniforms to wear, or
a stewardess, who flies everywhere.
a ballerina, who dances and twirls around, or
a candy shop owner, the best in town.
a model, who wears lots of pretty clothes,
a big star in the movies and on special TV shows.
a secretary who'll type without mistakes, or
an artist, painting trees and clouds and lakes.
a teacher in a nursery school some day, or
a singer and make records people play.
a designer of dresses in the very latest style, or
a bride, who comes walking down the aisle.
a housewife, someday when I am grown, and
a mother, with some children of my own

Quoted in Lenore J. Weitzman et al., "Sex-Role Socialization in Picture Books for Preschool Children," *American Journal of Sociology,* 77 (May 1972): 1144.

public schools, concludes that the most important of these factors is the child's family and socioeconomic background.[53] The bright child in a lower-class family may be socialized by that family in a manner that discourages his or her movement up the social ladder.

[53] James S. Coleman, "Equal Schools or Equal Students?" *The Public Interest,* 4 (Summer 1966): 70–75.

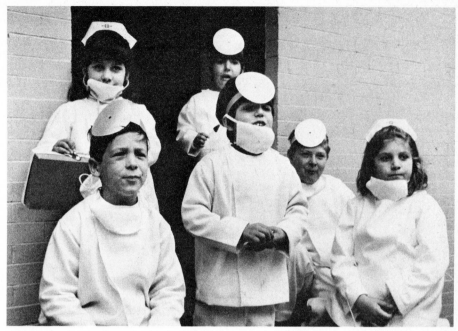

A boy can be "a doctor who helps to save people's lives." A girl can be "a nurse, with white uniforms to wear." (Courtesy of Magnum; photo by Abigail Heyman.)

Protection

In preindustrial societies, the extended family unit provided protection from physical harm, care in times of illness and in old age, and protection from starvation in times of crop failure or famine. In modern societies most of the protective functions have been delegated to other social institutions. The police and the courts are meant to protect us from our fellow citizens, the military protects us from foreign enemies, Social Security helps to care for the aged, Medicare and Medicaid assist in providing for the ill, and unemployment insurance and workmen's compensation provide some security against the loss of jobs. Critics argue that the modern family performs poorly even those few protective functions that it retains.

The Aged. The condition of the elderly in America represents a problem of major magnitude. In 1970, approximately 10 per cent of the American population was 65 years of age or older.[54] This will increase dramatically in the

---

[54] D. Stanley Eitzen, *Social Structure and Social Problems in America* (Boston: Allyn & Bacon, Inc., 1974), p. 265.

future as baby-boom children age. People in the "65 or older" category face numerous difficulties.

Earning power is one area in which older people are at a distinct disadvantage. Many workers are forced to retire at age 65 in spite of the fact that they still enjoy good health and are willing and able to continue working. This promotes a feeling of uselessness among the aged. Even when the elderly person receives a pension, the amount of the pension is usually inadequate to maintain a satisfactory standard of living. Because pensions seldom are adjusted to compensate for inflation, each increase in the cost of living affects the elderly directly. Whereas in previous times most needs of the elderly would have been provided by the extended family, today basic necessities such as shelter, food, and transportation must be purchased by the aged. Often, even with aid from grown children, the income of many of the elderly is too limited to provide an adequate diet or decent housing.

Elderly persons are likely to live alone; less than one third of the elderly live with their adult children. A number of studies have shown that adult Americans keep in contact with their parents, but there is some question as to the nature of these contacts. Paul and Lois Glasser found that intergenerational relations tend to be characterized by a strong theme of noninterference, meaning that adult offsprings and elderly parents do not become involved in potentially controversial issues with each other.[55] Bert Adams, in his study of kinship relations, found that people visited their elderly parents partly for enjoyment and partly out of a sense of obligation.[56] Children feel less obligation to visit elderly parents when both parents are living, as shown in Table 6-4. Such studies suggest that even though adult children maintain contact with their aged parents, the level of emotional support offered to the parents may be somewhat superficial.

Protection Against Unemployment. The extended family had many workers; the loss of employment by one of them was not likely to have a severe effect upon the family's stability. In contrast, many nuclear families depend upon the husband alone to provide the major portion of the family's income; consequently, the ability of the husband to obtain and keep a satisfactory job becomes crucial to the family's survival. If he is laid off during a recession, as happened to many families in the 1970s, the financial situation of the family may become critical. Similarly, if the husband becomes ill or is in-

[55] Paul H. Glasser and Lois N. Glasser, "Role Reversal and Conflict Between Aged Parents and Their Children," *Marriage and Family Living,* 24 (February 1962): 46–51.
[56] Bert N. Adams, *Kinship in an Urban Setting* (Chicago: Markham Publishing Company, 1968), chap. 3.

Table 6-4. Importance of Sense of Obligation and of Sense of Enjoyment as Reasons for Keeping in Touch with Elderly Parents

Sex of the Young Adults	Which Parent(s) Living	Number of Respondents	Important Reasons for Keeping in Touch, in Per Cent	
			Obligation	Enjoyment
Males	Both	(187)	51%	76%
	Widow	(75)	63	57
Females	Both	(257)	44	83
	Widow	(109)	50	72

SOURCE: Adapted from Bert N. Adams, *Kinship in an Urban Setting* (Chicago: Markham Publishing Company, 1968), p. 87. Reprinted by permission of the author.

jured so that he cannot work, the entire family is likely to suffer economically. About 40 per cent of married women work outside the home, but they tend to be concentrated in low-status, low-paying jobs and would not be able to maintain the family's standard of living for long.

Violence and the Family. Recently, it has become increasingly apparent that many persons need protection from members of their own families. A large percentage of all calls to the police are requests for help in breaking up family fights.[57]

Suzanne Steinmetz and Murray Strauss have explored a number of aspects of family violence.[58] They point out that although violence tends to be somewhat more prevalent in the lower social classes, it is by no means limited to that section of society. Violence between spouses and the battering of children also occurs in the middle and upper classes with some regularity.

Regardless of class level, several factors are thought to contribute to violence between spouses. Steinmetz and Strauss claim that American society defines violence or aggression as a "normal" response to frustration.[59] Since

[57] Albert J. Reiss, Jr., *The Police and the Public* (New Haven, Conn.: Yale University Press, 1971).
[58] Suzanne K. Steinmetz and Murray A. Strauss, eds., *Violence in the Family* (New York: Dodd, Mead & Company, 1974).
[59] Ibid., pp. 17–21.

the intimate environment of the nuclear family affords ample opportunities for frustrations to appear, it is not surprising that violence often occurs. According to another theory, sexual aggression is a logical outcome of any social order that encourages a rigid division between male and female roles.[60] In essence, this theory suggests that rigid sex roles set in motion a destructive circle of events. Child care is defined as an exclusively feminine duty; women therefore rear the children, both male and female. This leads male children to have severe problems of sexual identity, and they overreact against women in order to bolster their feelings of masculinity. The males avoid roles regarded as feminine (such as child-rearing) and thereby guarantee that the next generation will experience the same problems. The result is a high level of hostility—and often violence—between husbands and wives.

The Battered Child. Family violence does not occur only between spouses. Some estimates of the number of children physically battered by their parents range between 10,000 and 75,000 per year.[61] Other estimates run as high as 250,000 to 4 million per year.[62] Exact assessments are impossible because of problems involved in proving that a child's bruises, burns, or broken bones are *deliberately* inflicted by its parents. Even the minimum estimates, however, suggest that physical abuse of children has been rather extensive. The consensus among those who have studied the issue is that child-battering has increased significantly in recent years.

Economic Production and Consumption

The extended family often functioned in preindustrial times as a unit of production. The family produced most of the goods and services needed for its own survival. Family members often built their own house, made clothes, and grew and preserved food. The modern family functions as a basic unit of consumption. Frank Scarpitti points out this emphasis:

> To the producers of American television commercials, it is obvious what the family's function in America is: to consume. With few exceptions, commer-

[60] Ibid., pp. 12–13.

[61] Jerome E. Leavitt, ed., *The Battered Child: Selected Readings* (Morristown, N.J.: General Learning Press, 1974), p. 3.

[62] David Gil, "Incidence of Child Abuse and Demographic Characteristics of People Involved," pp. 19–40 in R. Helfer and C. H. Kempe, eds., *The Battered Child* (Chicago: University of Chicago Press, 1968), p. 25.

cials depict a mother and father and two children, one boy, one girl, enjoying either their home or their car. They are companionable, mobile, and happy. The commercials are true, to a certain extent; the "average" American family these days does have two children, they are mobile and they do consume products and services at a very high rate.[63]

Jules Henry, a noted American anthropologist, suggests that advertising and the accompanying high rate of consumption has become a "philosophical system" in America.[64] Buying and consuming has been defined as a positive good, regardless of what it does to the family as a unit or to the person as an individual. An example might be the nationwide campaign by the automobile industry during the "lean times" of late 1974 and early 1975. Americans were told, in effect, that it was their patriotic duty to buy a new car. "Rebates" of $300 to $500 were offered to anyone who would buy a new automobile, which would ordinarily cost the family between $3,000 and $5,000. It seems unlikely that a 10 percent reduction in the cost of the car actually helped most families' budgets significantly; it may, however, have helped induce many families to go into debt for an item they did not really need, and at a time when there was a possibility that the principle breadwinner might lose his job. As financial difficulties are often mentioned as a cause of divorce, emphasizing the family's role as a unit of economic consumption may contain elements which are destructive to the family.

Finally, some writers have argued that the modern family may be seen as an emotional refueling station for individuals who find the work world to be cold, impersonal, and demanding.[65] If tensions develop in the office or the factory, it is expected that the individual will find release and rejuvenation within the family setting so that he or she can return to work the following day with a renewed store of energy. However, when home and work are as distinctly separate as they are in the United States, spouses may not be able to offer each other the kind of sympathetic support each needs. The man who is under pressure at the office to develop a complex technological innovation for a highly specialized research project may be unable to communicate to his wife just what it is that he is doing; the wife who does not work outside the home may be unable to convey to her husband the degree of frustration she feels after an exasperating day with their child. In addition, women increasingly hold jobs of their own outside the home. The wife may therefore come

[63] Scarpitti, op. cit., p. 67.
[64] Jules Henry, *Culture Against Man* (New York: Vintage Books, 1963), chap. 3.
[65] Parsons, op. cit.

home from work filled with work-related tensions of her own. The idea that the family provides a haven in which to recuperate from the tensions of the work world may have had greater applicability in an earlier era than it has today.

WHAT CAN BE DONE?

Just as the institution of the family has had no shortage of problems, it also has not suffered from a lack of suggested remedies. Most of these remedies propose some type of change in family relationships.

Counseling

Herbert Otto suggests that Americans take better care of their cars than they do of their marriages.[66] Otto feels that a considerable amount of marital discord could be avoided if a nationwide system of federally funded marriage counseling clinics could be established. Couples would be encouraged to visit these clinics at periodic intervals. Their marriage and family life would be evaluated by trained experts who could presumably detect impending problems before they occurred.

This solution is based on the assumption that the current structure of American family life is essentially sound and that only minor periodic adjustments are required. Many would agree with this idea. However, it must be noted that counseling programs aimed at solving other social problems, such as drug addiction or alcoholism, have not been notably successful. There is, then, some question whether this approach would be any more successful in solving current family problems.

Voluntary Childlessness

As many have pointed out, the presence of children in the family brings not only joys but tensions and frustrations as well. Critics such as Betty Rollin encourage married couples to consider carefully the positive *and* the negative features of child-rearing before they undertake parenthood.[67]

[66] Herbert A. Otto, "Has Monogamy Failed?" *Saturday Review,* 53 (April 25, 1970): 23–25.
[67] Rollin, op. cit.

To refrain voluntarily from having children violates deeply held beliefs regarding the desirability of children in American society. At the present, such a choice is being made by a small minority of couples. One study estimated that approximately 10 per cent of the American population will remain childless throughout life.[68] It is not known what proportion of couples who remain childless do so voluntarily and what proportion have no children because of sterility. Present estimates suggest that perhaps 1 to 3 per cent of the population is childless by choice.

In a 1973 survey, Judith Blake found that 85 per cent of the respondents felt that a marriage with children is happier than one without children.[69] As shown in Table 6-5, she also found, however, that although college-educated women "are not willing to affirm the virtues of childlessness, . . . they are not as ready as other women to extol the advantages of having children."[70]

In a study of voluntarily childless married couples, Ellen Nason found that husbands were often neutral on the question of having children.[71] The decision not to have children was definitely a mutual decision, involving both husband and wife, but the wife more often had strong views regarding childlessness. Among the reasons wives gave for choosing to remain childless

Table 6-5. Female Responses to "Is a Marriage Happier with Children or Without Children?" by Education

	Response		
Educational Level	Happier with Children	Happier without Children	Don't Know
No college	88%	6%	6%
College	79	5	16

SOURCE: Constructed from data in Judith Blake, "Can We Believe Recent Data on Birth Expectations in the United States?" *Demography,* 11 (February 1974): 36–37.

[68] Ronald Freedman, Pascal K. Whelpton, and Arthur A. Campbell, *Family Planning, Sterility, and Population Growth* (New York: McGraw-Hill Book Company, 1959), p. 26.

[69] Blake, op. cit., p. 36.

[70] Ibid., p. 37.

[71] Ellen M. Nason, "Voluntarily Childless Couples: An Exploration of a Variant Family Form," Master's Thesis, Department of Sociology, The University of Akron, August 1974.

were the desire to enjoy the companionship of one's spouse more completely, opportunities to develop occupational interests outside the home, and freedom to pursue one's own interests. These childless marriages seem to reflect the advantages claimed by Rollin and others. For a small proportion of the population, the child-free marriage may provide an alternative to many of the tensions and responsibilities inherent in the nuclear family.

Contract Marriage

Anthropologist Margaret Mead created a public sensation in 1966 when she suggested that marriage should take place in two steps: individual marriage and parental marriage.[72] Individual marriage would allow a couple to marry and legitimately live together, but it would be understood that no children would be conceived and that the marriage could be dissolved at any point. In this way, couples would have a chance to develop a meaningful relationship and work out their differences within a socially approved context before making a permanent commitment to each other. If differences proved to be irreconcilable, the couple would be able to dissolve the marriage with a minimum of pain to themselves—and no pain to children, as there would be none. If the individual marriage proved satisfactory, the couple could then apply for a parental marriage. In the parental marriage, the couple would be allowed to have children and it would be understood that they would stay together until the children were grown. A parental marriage would not be granted to any couple that had not first had a successful individual marriage.

Somewhat similar to Mead's proposal is the idea of marriage as a contract for a specified time period. At the end of the period, the marriage is officially over, and couples must decide whether or not they wish to renew their contract. The seriousness with which such proposals are being regarded is reflected in a bill introduced into the Maryland state legislature in 1972.[73] This bill proposed to make marriage a three-year contract, with an option to either renew or discontinue the contract at the end of every three-year period. While the bill was not passed, its supporters intend to reintroduce it.

Proposals to limit marriage to specified terms assume that people and their interests change over time and that it therefore makes little sense to require a man and woman to remain together for an entire lifetime. Marriage

---

[72] Margaret Mead, "Marriage in Two Steps," *Redbook Magazine,* 127 (July 1966): 48ff.
[73] House Bill No. 42, State of Maryland, January 12, 1972.

for a lifetime may have been appropriate in 1790, when the life span was shorter and people were quite often "old" by the age of 40; now, however, a couple marrying at age 20 can reasonably expect to live another 50 years. To assume that the same person will continue to meet one's needs at age 40, 50, 60, or 70 is seen by some as unrealistic. These critics argue that trauma stems from the process of divorce. Therefore, they would eliminate the concept of divorce and rely instead on the concept of contract renewal. They also suggest that marriage for a specified time period would force couples to reassess continually their relationships and would prevent marriages from becoming routinized and stale. Because the contract proposals seldom include any mention of changing the structure of the monogamous nuclear family, however, it is questionable whether they would solve many of the problems associated with the contemporary American family.

Cohabitation

In a study of cohabitation among unmarried college students at an eastern university, Eleanor Macklin discovered that the kind of "trial marriage" proposed by Margaret Mead is already taking place. When she asked unmarried junior and senior college women who were living with males to explain why such relationships develop, they gave the following reasons:

> They mention youth's search for meaningful relations with others and the consequent rejection of the superficial "dating game"; the loneliness of a large university and the emotional satisfaction that comes from having someone to sleep with who cares about you; the widespread questioning of the institution of marriage and the desire to try out a relationship before there is any, if ever, consideration of permanency; the desire on the part of many to postpone commitment until there is some certainty that individual growth will be compatible with growth of the relationship; the fact that young people mature earlier and yet must wait so long until marriage is feasible; and the fact that the university community provides both sanction and feasibility for such a relationship to develop.[74]

Of the women in this study, 60 per cent felt that a strong, affectionate relationship should be developed or a period of "going steady" experienced

[74] Eleanor D. Macklin, "Heterosexual Cohabitation Among Unmarried College Students," in Marvin B. Sussman, ed., *Non-Traditional Family Forms in the 1970s* (Minneapolis: National Council on Family Relations, 1972), p. 98.

before a couple begins to live together. An additional 8 per cent of the women in the study said the couple should be engaged, at least tentatively. These women clearly regarded cohabitation as a form of trial marriage.

Most studies of cohabitation have been based upon small samples of college students. While these investigations can reveal much about the dynamics of cohabitation, they do not reveal how widespread the practice might be. Evidence on this question is provided by Richard Clayton and Harwin Voss, who surveyed a carefully chosen nationwide sample that was representative of all men born in the United States between the years of 1944 and 1954.[75] They found that 18 per cent of these men, at some point in their lives, had lived for a period of six months or more with a woman to whom they were not married. At the time the survey was conducted, however, in late 1974 and early 1975, only 5 per cent of the respondents were cohabiting. Approximately one third of the men who had cohabited had married, suggesting that they may have viewed cohabitation as a trial marriage.

Open Marriage

Nena and George O'Neill offer another approach to family structure. Their proposal, which they term *open marriage,* focuses on how the marital relationship can help each partner develop his or her potential. The O'Neills explain: "The expectations of closed [traditional] marriage—the major one being that the partner will be able to fulfill all of the other's needs (emotional, social, sexual, economic, intellectual, and otherwise)—present obstacles to growth and attitudes that foster conflict between partners.[76]

Open marriage is presented as a possible solution to this problem. Its basic features and assumptions are as follows:

1. Living for the present, rather than for the past or the future. Future goals are too often materialistic and interfere with the development of a meaningful relationship.

2. Granting privacy to one's partner. Privacy is essential for self-examination and regeneration of psychic energy.

3. Role flexibility, which avoids labeling certain things as "his" tasks and others as "hers." When people interact *primarily* on the basis of rigid

---

[75] Richard R. Clayton and Harwin L. Voss, "Shacking Up: Cohabitation in the 1970s," *Journal of Marriage and the Family,* 39 (May 1977): 273–283.

[76] Nena O'Neill and George O'Neill, "Open Marriage: A Synergic Model," in Sussman, op. cit., p. 38.

roles, they fail to develop as individuals. Exchanging roles helps the partners to better understand each other's feelings and frustrations.

4. Open and honest communication is essential to eliminate barriers that prevent true understanding of one's partner and of one's self. This communication includes relating to others, including members of the opposite sex, outside of the marriage relationship.

5. Equality of partners is essential for an open marriage. The partners must relate to each other as peers, rather than as "leader" and "follower."

6. Each partner must establish his or her own identity through interacting with the marital partner and others, and through developing his or her own potential.

7. Trust in each other must be built through utilizing the first six characteristics of open marriage.

Another feature of open marriage is the use of *synergy*. According to the O'Neills, "synergy means that two partners in marriage can accomplish more personal and interpersonal growth together than they could separately without the loss of their individual identities."[77] Synergy is the mutual reinforcement that flows out of the efforts of two people trying to help each other develop themselves as much as possible. This mutual support may take many non-traditional forms, such as accepting deep friendships and sexual relationships outside of marriage. The O'Neills suggest that only a limited proportion of the population may be able to develop completely open marriages, but they propose that the family structure would be strengthened if couples would utilize those aspects of open marriage that they find acceptable.

Group Marriage and Communal Families

Another alternative to traditional marriage received considerable attention with the publication of Robert Rimmer's *The Harrad Experiment*.[78] This novel extolled the virtues of group marriage in which several members of each sex combine to form a single marital unit. Within this type of family, Rimmer's characters are portrayed as being able to rise above jealousy and learn that they can truly love more than one person at a time and thus develop into more complete, mature human beings.

[77] Ibid., p. 39.
[78] Robert Rimmer, *The Harrad Experiment* (New York: Bantam Books, 1966).

In a communal family structure, children would have many adults of both sexes and varying ages around them at all times and would have many role models to follow. (Courtesy of Magnum; photo by Dennis Stock.)

Robert Thamm develops Rimmer's basic idea into a rather extensive plan for the family structure of the future.[79] Thamm and others hold that a group marriage and communal family structure would solve many of the problems associated with the nuclear family. As people would have numerous spouses, no individual would have to depend entirely upon only one person for emotional support, sexual gratification, or other needs.

In a communal family structure, children would have many adults of both sexes and varying ages around them at all times and would have many role models to follow. This would make it less likely that any one incompetent parent could damage a child. Because there would be many adults present at any given time, women would no longer be forced to devote their lives to child care and would gain a new freedom to develop their abilities in other roles. Although individual family members might come and go, the communal unit would remain stationary. This would restore some of the geographic stability of the family of the past. The communal family would be more economically stable than the present nuclear family; at any given time a

[79] Thamm, op. cit.

number of adults would be contributing financial support. The loss of a job by one person would no longer plunge the family into economic hardship. Because the communal family would be large and there would be many different kinds of tasks to do, a place within the family would also be provided for the elderly.

Many of these suggestions may appear to be strictly modern innovations, but at least one American experiment in restructuring the family had already put most of these ideas into practice more than a century ago. The Oneida Community existed in New York state from 1848 to approximately 1879 under the leadership of John Humphrey Noyes.[80] It was a religious movement whose members practiced *complex marriage,* in which all adult males were regarded as married to all adult females. Children were reared communally and were encouraged to identify with all adults in the community, rather than exclusively with their biological parents. Attempts to replace the nuclear family with a communal family structure have met with varying degrees of success. The most notable current example is the *kibbutz* system of Israel.[81] This family structure practices communal ownership of property, communal rearing of children, and the equality of the sexes; in general, it meets many of the criteria that Thamm sets forth for the communal family of the future. Many of the so-called hippie communes that began in the United States during the 1960s provide further examples.[82] Whether such communal structures can meet the needs of a significant proportion of any nation's population on a long-term basic remains to be seen.

It seems unlikely that drastic changes in the American family structure will take place in the near future. Changes that occur are likely to be those that are consistent with the dominant cultural values, attitudes, and beliefs of the society. In general, it seems probable that two current trends affecting American family life will continue. One of these is the increasing movement toward equality of the sexes. As more opportunities are opened to women in all fields of endeavor, women can be expected to invest a larger proportion of their time and talents outside of the family setting. It is too early to predict accurately what effect this will have upon family structure. The second major trend involves increased freedom to choose one's life style from among a

[80] Constance Noyes Robertson, *Oneida Community: An Autobiography,* 1851–1876 (Syracuse, N.Y.: Syracuse University Press, 1970).

[81] William F. Kenkel, *The Family in Perspective,* 4th ed. (Santa Monica, California: Goodyear Publishing Company, Inc., 1977), chap. 6.

[82] Rosabeth Moss Kanter, *Communes: Creating and Managing the Collective Life* (New York: Harper & Row, Publishers, 1973).

growing number of alternatives. It may well be that more and more people will choose life styles other than the one represented by the nuclear family, such as cohabitation and voluntary childlessness.

Additional Readings

Albrecht, Ruth E., and E. Wilber Bock, eds. *Encounter: Love, Marriage, and Family.* Boston: Holbrook Press, Inc., 1975.

Bell, Robert R. *Premarital Sex in a Changing Society.* Englewood Cliffs, N.J.: Prentice-Hall, Inc., 1966.

Benson, Leonard. *Fatherhood: A Sociological Perspective.* New York: Random House, 1968.

Blood, Robert O., Jr., and Donald M. Wolfe. *Husbands and Wives.* Glencoe, Ill.: The Free Press, 1960.

Carter, Hugh, and Paul C. Glick. *Marriage and Divorce: A Social and Economic Study.* Cambridge, Mass.: Harvard University Press, 1970.

Cavan, Ruth Shonle, ed. *Marriage and Family in the Modern World: A Book of Readings.* New York: Thomas Y. Crowell Company, 1969.

Chafetz, Janet Saltzman. *Masculine/Feminine or Human?* Itasca, Ill.: Peacock Publishers, Inc., 1974.

Christensen, Harold T., ed. *Handbook of Marriage and the Family.* Chicago: Rand McNally & Company, 1964.

Coser, Rose Laub. *The Family: Its Structure and Functions.* New York: St. Martin's Press, 1964.

de Beauvoir, Simone. *The Coming of Age.* Great Britain: Cox and Wyman, Ltd., 1973.

Goode, William J. *After Divorce.* Glencoe, Ill.: The Free Press of Glencoe, 1956.

Hardin, Garrett. *Stalking the Wild Taboo.* Los Altos, Calif.: Wm. Kaufmann, 1973.

Hill, Reuben. *Families Under Stress.* New York: Harper & Row Publishers, 1949.

Hill, Robert B. *The Strengths of Black Families.* New York: Emerson Hall Publishers, Inc., 1972.

Holmstrom, Lynda Lytle. *The Two-Career Family.* Cambridge, Mass.: Schenkman Publishing Company, 1973.

Hunt, Morton. *The World of the Formerly Married*. New York: McGraw-Hill Book Company, 1966.

Komarovsky, Mirra. *Blue-Collar Marriage*. New York: Random House, Inc., 1962.

Lopata, Helena Znaniecki. *Widowhood in an American City*. Cambridge, Mass.: Schenkman Publishing Company, 1973.

McKinley, Donald G. *Social Class and Family Life*. Glencoe, Ill.: The Free Press, 1963.

Petras, John W., ed. *Sex: Male. Gender: Masculine*. Port Washington, N.Y.: Alfred Publishing Company, 1975.

Rheinstein, Max. *Marriage Stability, Divorce and the Law*. Chicago: University of Chicago Press, 1972.

Reiss, Ira L. *The Social Context of Premarital Sexual Permissiveness*. New York: Holt, Rinehart and Winston, 1967.

Safilios-Rothschild, Constantina, ed. *Toward a Sociology of Women*. New York: John Wiley & Sons, Inc., 1972.

Seidenberg, Robert. *Marriage Between Equals: Studies from Life and Literature*. Garden City, N.Y.: Doubleday & Company, Inc., 1973.

Stephens, William, ed. *Reflections on Marriage*. New York: Thomas Y. Crowell, 1968.

Sussman, Marvin B., ed. *Sourcebook in Marriage and the Family*. 4th ed. Boston: Houghton Mifflin Company, 1974.

Townsend, Claire. *Old Age: The Last Segregation*. New York: Grossman Publishers, 1971.

Vincent, Clark. *Unmarried Mothers*. Glencoe, Ill.: The Free Press, 1961.

Willie, Charles V., ed. *The Family Life of Black People*. Columbus, Ohio: Charles E. Merrill Publishing Company, 1970.

Winch, Robert F. *Mate Selection*. New York: Harper & Row, Publishers, 1958.

Yorburg, Betty. *The Changing Family*. New York: Columbia University Press, 1973.

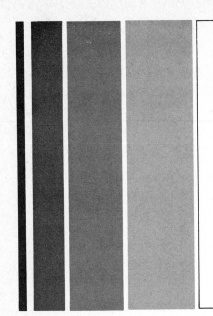

work and work dissatisfaction

Female Office Worker

I've felt more productive in the last few weeks doing what I've wanted to do than I have in the last year doing what I was officially supposed to be doing. . . .

Since I've been doing what I want to do, my day goes much faster. When I was assistant to the regional director, an awful lot of my time was taken up with endless meetings. I spent easily twenty or more hours a week in meetings. Very, very nonproductive. . . .

I've been work oriented all my life. I can't go on drawing a paycheck doing what I want to do—that's my conditioning. My dad worked in a factory. I was taught work is something you *have* to do. You do that to get money. It's not your life, but you must do it. Now I believe—I'm getting around to it (laughs)—you should get paid for doing what you want to do. I know it's happening to me. But I still have this conditioning: it's too good to be true. . . .

The reasons people get paid now are wrong. I think the reward system should be different. I think we should have a basic security—a decent place to live, decent food, decent clothing, and all that. So people in a work situation wouldn't be so frightened. People are intimidated and the system works to emphasize that. They get what they want out of people by threatening them economically. It makes people apple polishers and ass kissers. I used to hear people say, "Work needs to be redefined." I thought they were crazy. Now I know they're not.[1]

Male Factory Worker

"Is it true," an auto worker asked wistfully, "that you get to do fifteen different jobs on a Cadillac?" "I heard," said another, "that with Volvos you follow one car all the way down the line."

Such are the yearnings of young auto workers at the Vega plant in Lordstown, Ohio. Their average age is twenty-four, and they work on the fastest auto assembly line in the world. Their jobs are so subdivided that few workers can feel they are making a car.

The assembly line carries 101 cars past each worker every hour. Most GM lines run under sixty. At 101 cars an hour, a worker has thirty-six seconds to perform his assigned snaps, knocks, twists, or squirts on each car. The line was running at this speed in October when a new management group, General Motors Assembly Division (GMAD or Gee-Mad), took over the plant. Within four months they fired 500 to 800 workers. Their jobs were divided among the remaining workers, adding a few more snaps, knocks, twists, or squirts to each man's task. The job had been boring and unbearable before. . . .

Hanging around the parking lot between shifts, I learned immediately that to these young workers, "It's not the money."

"It pays good," said one, "but it's driving me crazy."

"I don't want more money," said another. "None of us do."

"I do," said his friend. "So I can quit quicker."[2]

In most cultures an individual's status in the community as well as his own feelings of self-worth have been closely linked with work. Nowhere has this been more true than in America. One of the first questions one American asks another is "what do you do?" Americans identity themselves to others by referring to their work.

Recently, however, this traditional devotion to work has come under attack. "Workaholic" has become an epithet. Some critics have depicted modern work as meaningless and empty and have predicted the coming of a generation that will follow a new set of values contradicting the traditional work ethic. The quotes from the office and factory worker at the beginning of this chapter reflect a growing discontent among American workers, particularly the young, who increasingly seem to be saying that there should be more to

[1] Studs Terkel, *Working: People Talk About What they Do All Day and How They Feel About What They Do* (New York: Pantheon Books, 1974), pp. 346–347.

[2] Barbara Garson, "Luddites in Lordstown," *Harper's Magazine*, 244 (June 1972): 68.

work than money, status, fringe benefits, and job security. There appears to be a desire among American workers for more challenge, autonomy, and self-fulfillment from their jobs. An understanding of what work means today will be enhanced by a look at the views of work held in earlier historical periods.[3]

THE CHANGING MEANINGS OF WORK

Meanings of Work Before the Protestant Reformation

Work to the Greeks was a curse, an evil to be endured only for the sake of surviving, for maintaining freedom from the rich and powerful, and for pursuing the Greek ideals of cultural, intellectual, and personal development. Romans shared the Greek disdain for work. Both Greeks and Romans believed that the accumulation of wealth was justified only if it promoted the achievement of esthetic ideals. Cicero expressed the view of work held by most Romans:

> there are but two occupations worthy of a free man; first, agriculture; next, big business, especially if it leads to an honorable retirement into rural peace as a country gentleman. All other pursuits are vulgar and dishonoring, handcraft not less than petty trade, the hiring out of one's arms not less than usury. They chain the soul to the desires of other men, to the thirst for gain.[4]

Departing somewhat from the Greek and Roman view, early Hebrews gave some meaning and dignity to work by linking it with religion. Humans had to work in order to atone for the original sin committed by Adam and Eve in the Garden of Eden. The positive value of work lay in repaying God and recovering one's own spiritual integrity. Still, the ancient Hebrews looked upon work as a drudgery. Early Christians adopted the Hebrew belief that work was God's punishment on a sinful people. But they added a more positive note: one should work not only for self-support but to be able to share with the less fortunate. Tying work to charity removed the traditional stigma attached to the amassing of wealth.

---

[3] This review of the meanings of work prior to today is based primarily on Adriano Tilgher, *Homo Faber: Work Through the Ages* (Chicago: Henry Regnery Company, 1958).
[4] Quoted from Cicero's *De Officiis* in ibid., p. 8.

Work and the Protestant Reformation

The foundation for the modern view of work was laid during the Protestant Reformation. Martin Luther argued that the ideal way to serve God was to do one's work as competently as possible. Work was given spiritual dignity in Luther's teachings. John Calvin's seventeenth-century doctrines included the idea that every person, even the rich, must work because it is God's will that they do so. Work had dignity if it contributed to the establishment of the Kingdom of God on earth.

The term *Protestant Ethic* was originated by Max Weber, the German sociologist who wrote on the connection between Protestantism and modern capitalism.[5] According to Weber, the theological doctrines of Luther and Calvin encouraged the early development of capitalism by promoting frugality, dedication to hard work, earning of profits, and reinvestment of profits.

The Meaning of Work in Modern Society

The Protestant Ethic has been a durable creation. While work has lost its association with religion since the Protestant Reformation, work as an important activity in itself has grown in strength. As noted at the beginning of this chapter, work in modern society is thought to stand at the center of one's place in the community and one's self-esteem.[6] Two national studies of attitudes toward work—one of blue- and white-collar workers, the other of only blue-collar workers—indicate that about 80 per cent of American workers would continue working even if they inherited enough money to live comfortably without doing so.[7]

Many think that until recent years American workers viewed work primarily as a means to an end—the enjoyment of time off the job. Writing in the late 1920s, Adriano Tilgher depicted a "faltering of the religion of work" in favor of an emphasis on consumption and leisure. His words have a distinctly modern sound even though they were written fifty years ago:

[5] Max Weber, *The Protestant Ethic and the Spirit of Capitalism,* trans. Talcott Parsons (New York: Charles Scribner's Sons, 1958).

[6] Everett C. Hughes, *Men and Their Work* (New York: The Free Press, 1958), pp. 42–43.

[7] Nancy C. Morse and Robert S. Weiss, "The Function and Meaning of Work and the Job," *American Sociological Review,* 20 (April 1955): 191–198; and Curt Tausky, "Meanings of Work Among Blue Collar Men," *Pacific Sociological Review,* 12 (Spring 1969): 49–55.

> Industry needs to create the demand which merchandise is to satisfy, to create
> conditions favorable for the consumption of the ever greater supply of goods
> which it is continually producing. This causes installment buying, high wages,
> short working days, all kinds of incitements to spend and especially to waste.
> These are all indispensable conditions if industry is to work full time at the
> highest rate of production. Thus in the very homeland of the religion of work, a
> still later religion is growing up, the religion of large buying and of amuse-
> ments, a religion of comfort, of well-being, of convenience, of cleanliness, a
> religion of the body.[8]

Curt Tausky found that three out of four of the blue-collar workers in his national sample either related work to their interests as a consumer without any
qualifications or were committed to work as a means of satisfying their
consumer desires if the job were socially acceptable.[9]

To find a link between work and consumption is not surprising in an advanced industrial society. The economies of such societies are based on the
principle of ever-increasing consumption. Yet there are several attractions of
work beyond its contribution to consumption. These include keeping oneself
occupied, receiving the approval of others for earning one's own living, feeling useful to society, and experiencing enjoyment from the intrinsic nature of
one's job. There is some indication that the intrinsic nature of work may be
becoming more important, especially among the young and women.

A special task force report to the Secretary of Health, Education and
Welfare in 1972, entitled *Work in America,* addresses the problems now
known as the blue-collar blues and the white-collar woes. According to this
report, young Americans are not abandoning the work ethic, they are simply
rejecting dull, repetitive jobs performed under strict supervision:

> significant numbers of American workers are dissatisfied with the quality of
> their working lives. Dull, repetitive, seemingly meaningless tasks, offering
> little challenge or autonomy, are causing discontent among workers at all oc-
> cupational levels. This is not because work itself has greatly changed; indeed,
> one of the main problems is that work has not changed fast enough to keep up
> with the rapid and widescale changes in worker attitudes, aspirations, and val-
> ues. A general increase in their educational and economic status has placed
> many American workers in a position where having an interesting job is now as
> important as having a job that pays well. . . .
>
> Many workers at all occupational levels feel locked-in, their mobility

[8] Tilgher, op. cit., pp. 141–142.
[9] Tausky, op. cit., p. 51.

THE AMERICAN WORK ETHIC

A study on basic American life values . . . in the mid 1960s showed that a majority of the adult population at that time associated four cultural themes with work. These themes link work with peoples' life values and form essential parts of what we mean by the American work ethic:

The *"Good Provider" Theme*—The breadwinner—the man who provides for his family—is the real man.

Here is the link between making a living and the society's definition of masculinity. Masculinity has little to do with sexual prowess or physical strength or aggressiveness or a virile appearance. For almost 80 percent of the adult population to be a man in our society has meant being a good provider for the family. The concept of masculinity here at issue also conveys overtones of adulthood, responsibility, intensity of loving care for others.

The *Independence Theme*—To make a living by working is to "stand on one's own two feet" and avoid dependence on others. Work equals autonomy. To work and be paid for it means one has gained—and earned—freedom and independence.

The *Success Theme*—"Hard work always pays off." Hard work leads to success, its form dependent on one's abilities, background, and level of education. For the majority, the "payoff" comes in the form of a home of one's own, an ever rising standard of living, and a solid position in the community.

The *Self-respect Theme*—Hard work of any type has dignity whether it be menial or exalted. A man's inherent worth is reflected in the act of working. To work hard at something and to do it well: a person can feel good about himself if he keeps faith with this precept.

Daniel Yankelovich, "The Meaning of Work," in Jerome M. Rosow, ed., *The Worker and the Job: Coping with Change* (Englewood Cliffs, N.J.: Prentice-Hall, Inc., 1974), p. 22.

blocked, the opportunity to grow lacking in their jobs, challenge missing from their tasks. Young workers appear to be as committed to the institution of work as their elders have been, but many are rebelling against the anachronistic authoritarianism of the workplace.[10]

The evidence of a change in the work ethic is particularly strong among younger workers and women of all ages, although such a change may also be beginning to occur among older workers: "White males in the middle

[10] *Work in America: Report of a Special Task Force to the Secretary of Health, Education and Welfare* (Cambridge, Mass.: MIT Press, 1973), p. xvi.

years—30 to 50—and in the middle-income range, are beginning to feel the faint stirring of new ideas about the quality of working life." [11]

College Youth.   People under the age of 30 now comprise over 25 per cent of the American labor force (about 23 of 85 million workers). It is often said of this affluent and well-educated generation that it has rejected the traditional values of work, achievement, and materialism. The evidence does not support this assessment. Surveying college students from 1968 to 1971, Daniel Yankelovich found that almost 80 per cent believed that a meaningful career is a very important aspect of life and that 75 per cent think it is dishonest for those able to work to collect welfare money. Only 30 per cent indicated they would prefer less accent on hard work. [12]

While college youth are not rejecting work, the expectation for meaningful and self-fulfilling work seems to be an important part of an emerging work ethic among them. In a 1973 national survey, Yankelovich asked a sample of college students to rank the importance of several factors influencing their choice of a job or career. As Table 7-1 reveals, these students gave high rank to "challenge of the job," "opportunity to make a contribution," and "self-expression on the job." Money, job security, advancement, and occupational prestige are important to them but they are less important than job features related to self-fulfillment in work. A young woman expresses the frustrations of a college graduate whose job expectations have not been met.

> I didn't go to school for four years to type. I'm bored; continuously humiliated. They sent me to Xerox school for three hours. . . . I realize that I sound cocky, but after you've been in the academic world, and after you've had your own class (as a student teacher) and made your own plans, and someone tries to teach you to push a button—you get pretty mad. They even gave me a gold-plated plaque to show I've learned how to use the machine. [13]

Noncollege Youth.   According to Yankelovich, noncollege youth are more ambivalent and confused on the matter of self-fulfillment in work than those who have completed college. Meaningful and challenging work is desired by high school graduates, but, he asserts, they do not expect to get those kinds

---

[11] Daniel Yankelovich, "The Meaning of Work," in Jerome M. Rosow, ed., *The Worker and the Job: Coping with Change* (Englewood Cliffs, N.J.: Prentice-Hall, Inc., 1974), p. 36.

[12] Daniel Yankelovich, *The Changing Values on Campus: Political and Personal Attitudes on Campus* (New York: Washington Square Press, 1972).

[13] Quoted in *Work in America,* op. cit., p. 44.

Table 7-1. Major Influences on Choice of Job or Career

	Total Students (%) 1973
Challenge of the job	77%
Able to make meaningful contribution	72
Free time for outside interests	69
Ability to express yourself	68
Money you can earn	61
Security of the job	58
Chance to get ahead	51
Prestige/status of job	28
Lack of pressure/not too demanding	22
Other	1

Reprinted by permission of the author and publisher from Daniel Yankelovich, "The Meaning of Work," in American Assembly, Columbia University, *The Worker and the Job: Coping with Change,* © 1974, p. 39. Reprinted by permission of Prentice-Hall, Inc., Englewood Cliffs, New Jersey.

of jobs. Consequently, they tend to look outside the job for their self-fulfillment. But isn't this the same work ethic held by their fathers? Yankelovich thinks not:

> Today's young people are less fearful of economic insecurity than in the past. They want interesting and challenging work, but they assume that their employers cannot—or will not—provide it. By their own say-so, they are inclined to take 'less crap' than older workers. They are not as automatically loyal to the organization as their fathers, and they are far more cognizant of their own needs and rights. Nor are they as awed by organizational and hierarchical authority. Being less fearful of 'discipline' and the threat of losing their jobs, they feel free to express their discontent. . . . They are better educated than their parents, even without a college degree. They want more freedom and will bargain hard to keep their options open. A bitter fight over the right to refuse mandatory overtime, for example, does not mean that young workers will not work overtime. It does mean that the freedom to say 'no' assumes symbolic significance as an expression of freedom and autonomy. Moreover, if the work itself is not meaningful to them, they will opt for 'thirty and out' forms of retirement, shorter work weeks, frequent absenteeism, more leisure, and other methods for cutting back and cutting down on their job commitment.[14]

[14] Yankelovich, op. cit., p. 42.

The idea that a new work ethic is emerging among the young (college educated or not) is increasingly being accepted by employers and union leaders. The personnel director of a large bank says, "We've been forced to look at individual needs. And the young people are greatly responsible for this. Today they look at a job and if it isn't worth doing, they simply won't do it." A United Automobile Workers Union official makes a similar observation: "The younger workers are saying they are not going to accept the authoritarianism . . . that their fathers accepted in the plant; they are intelligent human beings, and they want to be part of the decision-making process." A recent publication of the Ford Motor Company makes this statement: "The traditional concept that hard work is a virtue and a duty, which older workers adhered to, is not applicable to younger workers, and the concepts of the younger work force must be taken into account."[15]

An illustration of the changing work ethic among young blue-collar workers is the strike in 1972 at a General Motors Vega plant at Lordstown, Ohio, where the average age of the workers was 24. In a reaction to the lack of opportunity to contribute significantly to the product they were turning out, 97 per cent of those who voted favored the strike and 85 per cent of the workers went to the union hall to vote.[16] According to one labor consultant with General Motors at that time, "Lordstown workers rebelled at the way they were treated because rotten jobs are being rejected wherever they may be, whether workers are young or old, in the city or in the country."[17]

Women. The stereotypical views of working men and women in American society are as follows:

> The American man works to support his family, to contribute to society, to find his place under the sun. He wants a job that challenges him intellectually. Above all in our achievement-oriented society, he wants to get ahead. The American woman works for pin money. She does that only when she has to. She is indifferent to intellectual challenge, not interested in finding work that contributes to her identity. What concerns her are friendly co-workers and whether or not she gets home in time to fix dinner.[18]

---

[15] *Ford Facts*, 32 (February 14, 1972): 1.

[16] Garson, "Luddites in Lordstown," op. cit., pp. 68–73.

[17] Quoted in Nancy Creedman and Michael Creedman, "Angst, The Curse of the Working Class," *Human Behavior*, 6 (November–December 1972): 10.

[18] Joan E. Crowley, Teresa E. Levitin, and Robert P. Quinn, "Seven Deadly Half-Truths About Women," *Psychology Today*, 6 (March 1973): 94.

MONEY IS NO LONGER ENOUGH

The average age of workers in auto plants has been declining, and often on the less desirable night shifts it is close to 20. The young workers are of the same generation as the students who have turned the universities into battlegrounds. Like college students, they are feisty, ebullient and unwilling to put up with things as they are. As union members, they are an unsettling force, pushing labor leaders to heighten their demands for fear of being voted out of their own jobs. In many instances, young unionists have ousted the old leadership. This year rank-and-file members have rejected a record one out of twelve contracts negotiated by their embarrassed and harassed leaders. In San Francisco last month, the ironworkers won a 30% increase in a one-year contract, a raise of $2.01 an hour. Even so, says their leader Jewel Drake, 56, "the younger leadership is not satisfied. I don't understand what they really want, what it would take to satisfy them."

Money alone will not do it. The young workers are revolting against the job itself, or at least the way it is organized. They reject the principle enunciated in 1922 by Henry Ford I: "The average worker wants a job in which he does not have to put much physical effort. Above all, he wants a job in which he does not have to think." The job that has no meaning must often be performed in factories that seem bereft of human feeling. Auto plants are often old, dirty and so noisy that conversation is impossible. "That's why so many young people just go from shop to shop," says Eugene Brook, director of labor education at Detroit's Wayne State University. . . . "Then he sees it's all the same. The young guy asks: 'Is this all there is to America?' They're not buying the myth any more."

Time, November 9, 1970, p. 71.

Joan Crowley, Teresa Levitin, and Robert Quinn refuted these stereotypical views in a nationwide study.[19] They found that women are similar to men in their desire to have interesting work, to develop their special abilities, and to do the things they do best.

A growing number of women are taking jobs for nonfinancial reasons. A 1973 Yankelovich survey indicated that three out of ten working women place self-fulfillment ahead of economic need. In earlier studies only a negligible percentage felt this way. Increasingly, work outside the home is becoming a source of identity for women. More and more women are viewing a

[19] Ibid.

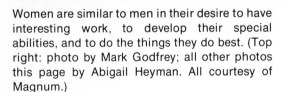

Women are similar to men in their desire to have interesting work, to develop their special abilities, and to do the things they do best. (Top right: photo by Mark Godfrey; all other photos this page by Abigail Heyman. All courtesy of Magnum.)

career as an avenue for personal growth, meaning, and self-fulfillment. Many working women would now agree with this statement:

> I had no confidence in myself, except at my job. I kept on feeling, if only I could find some missing element, I could enjoy cleaning house. But the whole thing is structured so that a woman loses her identity, so that she puts herself aside for another person. Men don't benefit either, but they don't lose so much. It was no problem for my husband. He didn't need to get his identity from our marriage. He got it from his job.[20]

While women want the same intrinsic rewards on the job as men, they are less likely to have jobs that provide such rewards. Many women are going to work expecting to find some degree of self-fulfillment, and they are dissatisfied when they find themselves trapped in uninteresting, low-paying, low-prestige jobs. This contributes to the higher rate of job dissatisfaction among women than men.

The educational level of women also affects their work attitudes. College-educated women are happier in outside employment than at home on a full-time basis. Noncollege women are not necessarily more unhappy when they are not employed.[21] This is partly because more highly educated women tend to have better jobs and higher career motivation than less educated women.

Why Is the Work Ethic Changing?

The reasons for the change in the work ethic are the increased levels of education, security, and affluence of the American worker. Today, most young people finish high school and almost 60 per cent enter college. The desire for work-related responsibility, autonomy, challenge, and the like increases with education. As the educational level of the American worker has increased, the work attitudes and expectations traditionally held by only a small proportion of the labor force have become more widespread.

American workers now make more money, have a higher standard of living, work under safer conditions, receive better fringe benefits, and enjoy

---

[20] Aileen Jacobson, ''Marriage Rethought: The Very Private Impact of the Women's Movement,'' *Washington Post: Potomac Magazine,* June 4, 1972.
[21] Angus Campbell, Philip E. Converse, and Willard L. Rodgers, *The Quality of American Life: Perceptions, Evaluations, and Satisfactions* (New York: Russell Sage Foundation, 1976), pp. 425–426.

THE IMPORTANCE OF WORK

"You know that boy came in last night? That Black Moozlem? That's what I ought to be doing. I ought to be in his place."

"What do you mean?"

"Dressed nice, going to [night] school, got a good job."

"He's no better off than you, Tally. You make more than he does."

"It's not the money. [Pause] It's position, I guess. He's got position. When he finish school he gonna be a supervisor. People respect him. . . . Thinking about people with position and education gives me a feeling right here [pressing his fingers into the pit of his stomach]."

"You're educated, too. You have a skill, a trade. You're a cement finisher. You can make a building, pour a sidewalk.". . .

"Anybody can do what I'm doing and that's what gives me this feeling. [Long pause] Suppose I like this girl. I go over to her house and I meet her father. He starts talking about what he done today. He talks about operating on somebody and sewing them up and about surgery. I know he's a doctor 'cause of the way he talks. Then she starts talking about what she did. Maybe she's a boss or a supervisor. Maybe she's a lawyer and her father says to me, 'And what do you do, Mr. Jackson?' [Pause] You remember at the courthouse, Lonny's trial? You and the lawyer was talking in the hall? You remember? I just stood there listening. I didn't say a word. You know why? Cause I didn't even know what you was talking about. That's happened to me a lot."

"Hell, you're nothing special. That happens to everybody. Nobody knows everything. One man is a doctor, so he talks about surgery. Another man is a teacher, so he talks about books. But doctors and teachers don't know anything about concrete. You're a cement finisher and that's your specialty."

"Maybe so, but when was the last time you saw anybody standing around talking about concrete?"

Elliot Liebow, *Tally's Corner* (Boston: Little, Brown and Company, 1967), pp. 61–62.

greater job security than any workers in history. Consequently, the concern of workers has shifted from economic security and job security (which are part of what is called the "extrinsic" side of work) to "intrinsic" aspects of work, such as how interesting and challenging a job is. Abraham Maslow's theory of a hierarchy of human needs helps to explain how this shift from extrinsic to intrinsic aspects of work has contributed to a change in the work ethic. Maslow categorized the basic needs of humans as follows:

1. *Physiological:* basic physical and biological needs.
2. *Safety:* physical and psychological security.
3. *Social:* love, affection, and social intercourse.
4. *Esteem:* self-respect, independence, and prestige.
5. *Self-realization:* self-fulfillment, accomplishment, and personal identity.[22]

According to Maslow, these needs have different priorities and certain needs become dominant only after other needs have been fulfilled. The first priority needs are physiological—food, sleep, and shelter. These are followed by the other needs, in the order listed. For example, as physiological needs are satisfied, the need for physical safety and psychological security becomes the dominant concern of the individual. As that second-order priority need is met, the dominant concern moves to the next level (social needs). Because the lower-level needs are generally being satisfactorily met among American workers, higher-level needs are becoming their dominant concern. They want jobs that will provide self-esteem and self-realization.

If the work ethic is now beginning to encompass the desire for interesting and challenging work, then work dissatisfaction should be rising. Why? Because more and more Americans are employed in large, bureaucratic organizations which are built on principles of work that conflict with the workers' desire for freedom, interest, and challenge on the job.

WORK DISSATISFACTION IN MODERN SOCIETY

Employment in Bureaucratic Organizations

Most economies contain agricultural, manufacturing, and service sectors, but the balance of these sectors varies in different societies. Preindustrial society was built on an agricultural base. With the coming of industrial society, manufacturing employed most of the labor force in producing goods. Postindustrial society now employs most of the labor force in service occupations, including government, research, education, health, transportation, trade, and finance. That the United States is in the postindustrial stage is reflected in the composition of its labor force. Since World War I, the fastest growing occupations have been white-collar. In 1956, white-collar workers for the first

[22] Abraham Maslow, "A Theory of Human Motivation," *Psychological Review,* 50 (July 1943): 370–396.

time accounted for a larger proportion of the labor force than did blue-collar workers. By 1980, it is projected that white-collar workers will comprise 51 per cent of the labor force, compared to 33 per cent blue-collar and 3 per cent farmers.[23]

In the postindustrial era, workers increasingly are employed in large, bureaucratic organizations. The decline in self-employment reflects this trend. In the middle of the nineteenth century, less than half of the labor force worked for someone else. By 1940, only about 22 per cent of the labor force was self-employed. This percentage had dropped to less than 9 per cent by the mid-1970s.[24] The site of employment has moved from the home and small, self-owned firms to large, bureaucratic organizations. This shift in the type of workplace has created some special types of social-psychological problems for the modern worker, one of which is an increase in work dissatisfaction.

Is Working in a Bureaucracy Unhealthy?

There is, psychologists tell us, a human personality need, variously labeled the need for ego and self-fulfillment, self-realization, or psychological growth.[25] This personality need, it is argued, is usually thwarted at work because it clashes with the nature of bureaucracy. Bureaucracies require job specialization, a strict chain of command, behavior that is determined by rules and regulations, close supervision, and impersonality. Work in a bureaucratic organization permits little worker control over job activities, provides minimal outlet for use of creative abilities, and tends to make workers passive, dependent, and submissive.

In *The Human Side of Enterprise*, Douglas McGregor contends that bureaucratic organizations are grounded in certain assumptions that managers make about human nature. These assumptions he called Theory X:

---

[23] Daniel Bell, "Labor in Post-Industrial Society," *Dissent*, 19 (Winter 1972): 170.

[24] *Statistical Abstract of the United States: 1973*. 94th ed. (Washington, D.C.: U.S. Bureau of the Census, 1973), p. 233.

[25] See Chris Argyris, *Personality and Organization: Conflict Between the System and the Individual* (New York: Harper & Row, Publishers, 1957); Chris Argyris, *Integrating the Individual into the Organization* (New York: McGraw-Hill Book Company, 1964); Chris Argyris, *The Applicability of Organizational Sociology* (Cambridge, England: Cambridge University Press, 1972); Rensis Likert, *New Patterns of Management* (New York: McGraw-Hill Book Company, 1961); Rensis Likert, *The Human Organization: Its Management and Value* (New York: McGraw-Hill Book Company, 1967); Douglas McGregor, *The Human Side of Enterprise* (New York: McGraw-Hill Book Company, 1960); and Douglas McGregor *The Professional Manager* (New York: McGraw-Hill Book Company, 1967).

MANAGERIAL AUTHORITY HAS A LONG HISTORY*

1. Office employes will daily sweep the floors, dust the furniture, shelves and showcases.
2. Each clerk will bring in a bucket of water and a scuttle of coal for the day's business.
3. Clerks will each day fill lamps, clean chimneys, trim wicks. Wash the windows once a week.
4. Make your pens carefully. You may whittle nibs to your individual taste.
5. This office will open at 7 a.m. and close at 8 p.m. daily, except on the Sabbath, on which day it will remain closed.
6. Men employees will be given an evening off each week for courting purposes, or two evenings a week, if they go regularly to church.
7. Every employe should lay aside from each pay a goodly sum of his earnings for his benefits during his declining years, so that he will not become a burden upon the charity of his betters.
8. Any employe who smokes Spanish cigars, uses liquor in any form, gets shaved at a barber shop, or frequents pool or public halls, will give me good reason to suspect his worth, intention, integrity, and honesty.
9. The employe who has performed his labors faithfully and without fault for a period of 5 years in my service, who has been thrifty and attentive to his religious duties, and is looked upon by his fellowmen as a substantial and law-abiding citizen, will be given an increase of 5 cents per day in his pay, providing a just return in profits from the business permits it.

*Posted in 1872 by the owner of a carriage and wagon works.

1. The average human being has an inherent dislike of work and will avoid it if he can.
2. Because of this dislike of work, most people must be coerced, controlled, directed, and threatened with punishment in order to get them to put forth adequate effort toward the advancement of organizational objectives.
3. The average human being prefers to be directed, wishes to avoid responsibility, has relatively little ambition, and wants security above all.[26]

The assumptions of Theory X have not been supported by scientific research, and some modern managers operate on the basis of quite opposite assumptions. McGregor labeled this alternative set of assumptions Theory Y:

[26] McGregor, *The Human Side of Enterprise,* op. cit., pp. 33–34.

1. The expenditure of physical and mental effort in work is as natural as play or rest. The average human being does not inherently dislike work.

2. External control and the threat of punishment are not the only means for bringing about effort toward organizational objectives. Human beings will exercise self-direction and self-control in the service of objectives to which they are committed.

3. Commitment to objectives is a function of the rewards associated with their achievement. The most significant of such rewards, the satisfaction of ego and self-realization needs, can be the products of effort directed toward organizational objectives.

4. The average human being learns, under proper conditions, not only to accept but to seek responsibility. Avoidance of responsibility, lack of ambition, and emphasis on security are generally consequences of experience, not inherent human characteristics.

5. The capacity to exercise a relatively high degree of imagination, ingenuity, and creativity in the solution of organizational problems is widely, not narrowly, distributed in the population.

6. Under the conditions of modern industrial life, the intellectual potentialities of the average human being are only partially utilized.[27]

Is work in bureaucratic organizations detrimental to the needs of human beings? Considerable research on work satisfaction suggests a clash between the modern demands of work and worker desires and expectations. One consequence is work dissatisfaction among both blue- collar and white-collar workers.

Blue-Collar Blues.   Many researchers believe that the level of job satisfaction reported in public opinion polls and other scientific surveys is overestimated (the percentage of satisfied workers has ranged between 85 to 90 per cent over the last decade) because the norms in American society discourage the expression of negative attitudes toward work. One reflection of the possible existence of lower job satisfaction than the polls indicate can be found in the reasons people have for working. Morse and Weiss asked blue-collar workers why they would continue to work if they no longer needed the money.[28] Thirty per cent gave as their reason "to keep occupied." Negative

[27] Ibid., pp. 47–48.
[28] Morse and Weiss, op. cit.

THE LOSS OF MEANING IN WORK

What sort of work do you do?

No trade. Laborer. Strictly muscle work. . . . Pick it up, put it down, pick it up, put it down. We take things off the hook. We handle manually, I'd say, between 40,000 and 50,000 pounds of steel a day. There's nothing automated about it, you just pick it up, put it down. (Laughs) I know this is hard to believe—from 400 pounds down to three- and four-pound pieces. The work I do is part of a dying kind. Manual labor.

You can't take pride anymore. You remember when a guy could point to a house he built, tell how many logs he stacked. He did something physical. He built it and he was proud of it. I don't really think I could be proud if a contractor built a home for me. . . . It's hard to take pride when you work for a large steel company. It's hard to take pride in a bridge you're never gonna cross, in a door you're never gonna open. You're mass-producing things and you never see the end result of it. Whereas, (muses) . . . I worked for a trucker one time. And I got this tiny satisfaction when I loaded a truck. At least, I could see the truck depart loaded. That's small, that's very tiny. In a steel mill, forget it. You don't see where nothing goes.

Studs Terkel, "A Steelworker Speaks," *Dissent,* 19 (Winter 1972): 9.

responses such as "would feel lost," "bored," "go crazy," and "habit" comprised another third of the sample. Only 9 per cent said that they would continue working with the financial incentive removed because they enjoyed the kind of work they were doing.

A study by Arthur Kornhauser also reveals the overestimation of job satisfaction among American blue-collar workers.[29] He asked a sample of factory workers to indicate their goals in life. From their answers it was obvious that goals such as greater financial security, health and happiness of self and family, and job security were dominant. A quite different picture emerged, however, when these same workers were asked to respond to a checklist of goals, one of which related to to the job itself. When the enjoyment of work was called to their attention as a possible goal in work, Kornhauser found that it ranked third among their life goals. Kornhauser suggests that desires for personal growth, self-expression, and independence on the job exist in workers but are suppressed because they have been thwarted for so long. It may be

[29] Arthur Kornhauser, *Mental Health of the Industrial Worker: A Detroit Study* (New York: John Wiley & Sons, Inc., 1965), pp. 242–252.

that workers do not spontaneously think about enjoying intrinsic aspects of work, but when offered such an alternative, they recognize its importance. Kornhauser concludes that workers have the capability and want to make contributions on the job but are asked to do so little that their capabilities and desires are not evident, even to themselves.

Another way to gain a more accurate picture of work satisfaction among blue-collar workers is to compare their attitudes with those of people in other occupations. Table 7-2 shows that workers in higher-level occupations are more satisfied with their jobs than those in lower-status occupations. Professionals consistently represent the highest percentage who would choose the same type of work again. Those who would choose similar work again range from 93 per cent among urban university professors to 75 per cent among lawyers working alone. Professionals are followed by white-collar (43 per cent) and blue-collar workers (24 per cent). Among blue-collar workers, the percentage choosing the same type of work again is highest among skilled printers (52 per cent) and lowest among the unskilled steel and auto workers (21 and 16 per cent).

There are differences in the degree of work satisfaction even among

Table 7-2. Percentages in Occupational Groups Who Would Choose Similar Work Again

Professional and Lower White-Collar Occupations	%	Working-Class Occupations	%
Urban university professors	93	Skilled printers	52
Mathematicians	91	Paper workers	42
Physicists	89	Skilled autoworkers	41
Biologists	89	Skilled steelworkers	41
Chemists	86	Textile workers	31
Firm lawyers	85	*Blue-collar workers, cross section*	*24*
Lawyers	83	Unskilled steelworkers	21
Journalists (Washington correspondents)	82	Unskilled autoworkers	16
Church university professors	77		
Solo lawyers	75		
White-collar workers, cross section	*43*		

Reprinted by permission of the publisher from *Work in America* (Cambridge, Mass.: The MIT Press, 1973), p. 16.

On the line. (Courtesy of A. Devaney, Inc., New York.)

workers at the same occupational level, as illustrated in Charles Walker and Robert Guest's study of automobile assembly line workers.[30] They found that utility and repair workers were more satisfied with their jobs than workers with specified jobs on the assembly line. Because utility workers substitute for employees all along the assembly line (some have as many as 30 different jobs), they experience more control and variety on the jobs than do assembly line workers who are tied to the line all day. The same is true for repair workers who are not as strictly tied to the assembly line as most workers. In one worker's words:

[30] Charles R. Walker and Robert H. Guest, *The Man on the Assembly Line* (Cambridge, Mass.: Harvard University Press, 1952).

I prefer a job off the line. Mine is pretty good because I don't have to keep up with the line. When I was on the line, I thought I was back in the Army. Just regimentation. You're like a big army, and the foremen are master sergeants.[31]

White-Collar Woes. Increasing work dissatisfaction is not confined to blue-collar workers. White-collar workers (clerks, key-punch operators, stenographers, typists, secretaries, sales clerks, and so forth) are also showing signs of rising dissatisfaction.[32] This is partly because many characteristics of factory work now apply to office work. Ida Hoos reports that many office machine operators found their jobs prior to computerization more interesting because they had performed a wider variety of tasks, such as filing, checking, posting, and typing.[33] Their new jobs are more simplified, but require both accuracy and speed. Deprived of freedom of movement about the office and interaction with other employees or customers, many office machine operators feel they are chained to their machines. Like factory work, many office jobs involve extreme job specialization, strict production deadlines, monotonous shift work, and machine noise.

Dissatisfaction in the office is also rising because the organizations in which white-collar employees work are becoming larger and larger. As organizational size increases, office workers are increasingly exposed to the impersonality of the factory setting. Recognition of the individual worker in the office is decreasing with expanding organizational growth:

> The organization acknowledges the presence of the worker only when he makes a mistake or fails to follow a rule, whether in factory or bureaucracy, whether under public or private control.[34]

The changing educational background of today's white-collar employees contributes to job dissatisfaction. In the past, lower-level white-collar workers

---

[31] Ibid., p. 56. For more recent research on the relationship between job characteristics and work satisfaction, see Robert Blauner, "Work Satisfaction and Industrial Trends in Modern Society," in Walter Galenson and Seymour Martin Lipset, eds., *Labor and Trade Unionism: An Interdisciplinary Reader* (New York: John Wiley & Sons, Inc., 1960), pp. 334–343; Robert Blanner, *Alienation and Freedom: The Factory Worker and His Industry* (Chicago: University of Chicago Press, 1964); and Jon M. Shepard, *Automation and Alienation: A Study of Office and Factory Workers* (Cambridge, Mass.: MIT Press, 1971).

[32] Judson Gooding, "The Fraying White Collar Worker," *Fortune,* 84 (December 1971): 78 ff.

[33] Ida Hoos, "When the Computer Takes Over the Office," *Harvard Business Review,* 38 (July–August 1961): 102–114. Also see Shepard, *Automation and Alienation,* op. cit.; and Barbara A. Kirsch and Joseph J. Lengermann, "An Empirical Test of Robert Blauner's Ideas on Alienation in Work as Applied to Different Type Jobs in a White-Collar Setting," *Sociology and Social Research,* 56 (October 1971): 180–194.

[34] *Work in America,* op. cit., pp. 38–39.

were mostly high school graduates. These jobs are now increasingly being taken by young people with at least some college education. Despite the increase in educational requirements for office jobs, the prestige, pay, and nature of the work has not been upgraded. A large percentage of workers now report that they have more education than their jobs require. This is particularly true among workers with some college education but without college degrees.[35] It is predictable that well-educated workers in low-paying, routine, and specialized jobs will be dissatisfied.[36]

Consequences of Work Dissatisfaction

Mental and Physical Health. Numerous studies have demonstrated a connection between work and mental health. Research conducted by the University of Michigan's Institute for Social Research over the last 20 years has shown that job dissatisfaction is related to such aspects of mental health as low self-esteem, anger, anxiety, tension, psychosomatic symptoms, worry, and difficulty in getting along with people.[37] A study by Arthur Kornhauser linked mental health and the type of work people do. Kornhauser concluded that better mental health is associated with higher-level jobs:

> The outstanding finding is that mental health varies consistently with the level of jobs the men hold. When we compare factory workers by occupational categories, the higher the occupation (in respect to skill and associated attributes of variety, responsibility, and pay), the better the average mental health. Those in skilled jobs have highest mental-health scores, followed by the upper semiskilled, the ordinary semiskilled, and lowest of all, the men in routine, repetitive types of work. Data from comparable groups of small-town factory workers, Detroit blue-collar workers in non-factory employment, and white-collar workers support the conclusion that mental health is least satisfactory among men in low-level production jobs.[38]

From information on a sample of 3,101 men, representing all males employed in civilian occupations in the United States, Melvin Kohn and

---

[35] Robert P. Quinn, Graham L. Staines, and Margaret R. McCullough, "Job Satisfaction: Is There A Trend?" Manpower Research Monograph No. 30, U.S. Department of Labor, Manpower Administration, Washington, D.C., 1974, p. 13.

[36] Ibid., p. 39.

[37] *Work in America,* op. cit., p. 82.

[38] Kornhauser, op. cit., p. 261.

THE INTELLECTUAL TAXICAB COMPANY

My friend Danny hung his Boston University diploma below the hack license in his cab.

After seventeen years of education in the finest schools in America, Danny, at 22, couldn't fix his stopped sink, repair a burnt connection in his fuse box, replace a pane of glass in his kitchen or locate the carburetor in his car.

Danny is an educated man. He is a master of writing research papers, taking tests, talking and filling out forms. He can rattle off his social-security number as easily as he can his name because it was also his student identification number. He can analyze Freud from a Marxian viewpoint and he can analyze Marx from a Freudian viewpoint.

In short, Danny is an unskilled worker and he has a sociology degree to prove it. He is of very little use to American industry.

Broken Cycle

This is nothing new. Colleges have been turning out unskilled workers for decades. Until five years ago, most of these unskilled workers took their degrees in sociology, philosophy, political science or history and marched right into the American middle class. Some filled executive positions in business and government but many, if not most, went into education, which is the only thing they knew anything about. Once there, they taught another generation the skills necessary to take tests and write papers.

But that cycle broke down. Teachers are overabundant these days, college applications are down, plumbers are making $12 an hour and liberal-arts graduates are faced with a choice—graduate school or the taxicab.

Danny chose the taxicab because driving was about the only marketable skill he possessed. Danny refers to his job as "Real World 101." He has been shot at, punched, sideswiped and propositioned. But he has also acquired some practical skills—he can get his tickets fixed; he knows how to cheat the company out of a few extra dollars a week; he found his carburetor and he can fix it.

Soon, I will be in the same position. I'll graduate from Boston University with a B.S. in journalism. Whatever skills that degree symbolizes are not currently in demand. I suppose I could go to graduate school but, Christ, I've been doing the same thing for seventeen years and I'm getting a little tired of it. Besides, there are a lot of grad-school graduates who are driving cabs, too.

And that brings me to the Intellectual Taxicab Company.

Danny and I were discussing the hack business recently and we came up with the idea. It is the simple answer to a simple question: why should all that college education go to waste reading road signs when masses of people are looking for knowledge and riding in cabs?

What America needs is a system to bring together all the knowledgeable cabbies and the undereducated rest of the country. The system we propose is the Intellectual Taxicab Company.

The Intellectual Taxicab Company would consist of a dispatcher and a fleet of cabs driven by recent college graduates. When you need a ride, you call the company and say something like: "I'd like to go from Wall Street over to East 83rd and I'd like to discuss the world monetary situation."

"All right, sir, we'll have an NYU economics graduate over in five minutes."

Or: "Hello, I'm in Central Square and I'd like to go to Brookline and discuss whether or not there is a God."

"You're in luck, madame, we have a Harvard philosophy graduate who minored in Comparative Religions right in the neighborhood."

The educational possibilities of this plan are staggering. English and Drama graduates could take the after-theater run, explaining the literary ramifications of the shows. Political Science graduates could hack around Capitol Hill or City Hall. Regular bus runs could be set up to conduct seminars on popular topics.

Elevating the Cabbie

The Intellectual Taxicab Company would bring adult education to the streets. It would also give all those alienated college graduates a feeling that they didn't waste four years and all that tuition money. And it would elevate the snotty cabdriver to an art form: cabbies would quote Voltaire while they rant about how bad the mayor is.

Surely there must be some foundation money or unimpounded Federal funds available to begin such a noble experiment in education. If there is, Danny and I are ready to start immediately. In fact, Danny is licking his lips in anticipation. "Just think how much my tips will go up," he said.

Peter Carlson, "The Intellectual Taxicab Company," *Newsweek*, June 3, 1974, pp. 133–134. Copyright 1974 by Newsweek, Inc. All rights reserved. Reprinted by permission.

Carmi Schooler conclude that American workers seem to thrive under challenging job conditions.[39] They contend that the most important element in good psychological functioning is the opportunity for workers to direct their own occupational activities and to exercise initiative, thought, and independent judgment.

Work also affects physical health. Job dissatisfaction and occupational stress have been found to be highly related to such illnesses as migraine,

[39] Melvin L. Kohn and Carmi Schooler, "Occupational Experience and Psychological Functioning: An Assessment of Reciprocal Effects," *American Sociological Review*, 38 (February 1973): 97–118.

heart disease, peptic ulcers, and arthritis. Even the length of life has been found to be associated with work. One study, conducted over a 15-year period, revealed that work satisfaction was the strongest predictor of longevity.[40]

Nonwork Aspects of Life.   There is evidence that dissatisfaction with work also affects some aspects of nonwork life. Martin Meissner offers an illustration:

> When work is socially isolating, workers reduce their exposure to situations in which they have to talk, and also spend less time in organized . . . activities. They make up for it and spend a lot more time fishing on the weekend, and pushing the shopping cart through the supermarket on workdays. Lack of opportunity to talk on the job is associated with dramatically reduced rates of participation in associations, that is, in activity commonly believed to help integrate individuals into the community.[41]

According to Arthur Kornhauser, the nonwork activities of most factory workers are routine, narrow, unrelated to larger social purposes, and make little or no contribution to self-development and self-expression.[42] In their comparison of satisfied and dissatisfied blue-collar and white-collar workers, Harold Sheppard and Neal Herrick report that those dissatisfied with their work have less trust in others, are pessimistic about a future in general, believe that the government is not concerned with their welfare, think that the condition of mankind is deteriorating, and feel powerless to affect political processes.[43]

If the nature of work denies self-fulfillment, what can be done? Two possible solutions to the problem of work dissatisfaction are job enrichment and organizational democracy.

---

[40] Erdman B. Palmore, "Predicting Longevity: A Follow-up Controlling for Age," *The Gerontologist,* 9 (Winter 1969): 247–250.

[41] Martin Meissner, "The Long Arm of the Job: A Study of Work and Leisure," *Industrial Relations,* 10 (October 1971): 260.

[42] Kornhauser, op. cit., pp. 266–267.

[43] *Work in America,* op. cit.; Kohn and Schooler, op. cit.; and Harold L. Sheppard and Neal Q. Herrick, *Where Have All the Robots Gone?: Worker Dissatisfaction in the 70s* (New York: The Free Press, 1972).

WHAT CAN BE DONE?

Job Enrichment

All job enrichment programs share characteristics that tend toward increased worker self-fulfillment. According to Frederick Herzberg, the principles of job enrichment include removing some controls over employees while increasing their personal accountability, assigning each employee a complete, natural unit of work, increasing job freedom, giving work-related feedback to each employee, periodically introducing employees to new and more complex tasks, and allowing employees to become experts in a designated area. These major principles of job enrichment, along with the personality needs to which each principle is related, are presented in Table 7-3.

Table 7-3. Principles of Job Enrichment and Mature Personality Needs That They Meet

Job Enrichment Principle	Mature Personality Needs
1. Removing some controls while retaining accountability	Responsibility and personal achievement
2. Increasing the accountability of individuals for own work	Responsibility and recognition
3. Giving a person a complete, natural unit of work (module, division, area, and so on)	Responsibility, achievement, and recognition
4. Granting additional authority to an employee in his activity; job freedom	Responsibility, achievement, and recognition
5. Making periodic reports directly available to the worker himself rather than to the supervisor	Internal recognition
6. Introducing new and more difficult tasks not previously handled	Growth and learning
7. Assigning individuals specific tasks, enabling them to become experts	Responsibility, growth, and advancement

Adapted by permission from Frederick Herzberg, "One More Time: How Do You Motivate Employees?" *Harvard Business Review,* 46 (January–February 1968): 57.

Numerous studies have shown that job enrichment programs produce positive results for both employees and companies.[44] Several of these studies are summarized in Table 7-4. Positive results of job enrichment programs have been observed among both white-collar and blue-collar employees.

Job Enrichment in the Office. Office workers in one company performed work tasks thought by management to be both complex and challenging.[45] Yet, nearly all indicators of performance and measures of work satisfaction were low, and as employees left the company they reported that their jobs were actually not challenging at all. To combat this problem, an experimental job enrichment program was begun. This job enrichment experiment included four work groups: an experimental group in which jobs were enriched according to the principles contained in Table 7-3, a control group that continued with work as usual, and two groups in which employees were examined to see if their job attitudes and performances increased merely because they thought management was paying special attention to them. In these latter two groups, no changes in the job were made. After a six-month period, members of the experimental group were significantly more satisfied with their jobs and were more productive than those in the other three groups. The experimental group also had a lower absenteeism rate and, ultimately, a higher promotion rate.

Job Enrichment in the Factory. A job enrichment program was begun at a General Foods manufacturing plant because of serious employee problems.[46] These problems were reflected in sabotage, violence, frequent plant shutdowns because of worker apathy and inattention, resistance to changes that would have improved the use of manpower, reduced loafing, and increased productivity. Utilizing the advice of both workers and management consultants, these new features were installed:

1. *Autonomous work groups.* Groups of workers became self-management teams, responsible for an entire section of the production process. It was up to members of each team (eight to twelve workers) to decide who

---

[44] See *Work in America,* op. cit.; *Job Design for Motivation* (New York: The Conference Board, Inc., 1971); Robert N. Ford, *Motivation Through the Work Itself* (New York: American Management Associations, Inc., 1969); and Fred Faulkes, *Creating More Meaningful Work* (New York: American Management Association, 1969).

[45] Frederick Herzberg, "One More Time: How Do You Motivate Employees?" *Harvard Business Review,* 46 (January–February 1968): 53–62.

[46] See *Work in America,* op. cit., pp. 96–99; and Richard E. Walton, "How to Counter Alienation in the Plant," *Harvard Business Review,* 50 (November–December 1972): 70–81.

would do which jobs. Much decision making and coordination relevant to their part of the production process was left to group members.

2. *Integrated support functions.* A group's responsibilities went beyond turning out a product. Functions normally handled by supporting work units—maintenance, personnel, quality control, custodial—were made a part of each work group's responsibilities. Each group not only had to produce something, but they were also responsible for its quality.

3. *Challenging job assignments.* Dull, boring, and repetitive jobs were eliminated wherever possible, in favor of creating more stimulating, responsible, and mentally demanding ones. Nonchallenging tasks such as custodial functions were performed by all workers instead of by only certain workers on a continuing basis.

4. *Financial rewards for learning.* Workers were financially rewarded for learning more about the total production process. Pay increases were tied to the learning of new jobs. The more jobs workers knew (first in their own work group and then elsewhere in the plant), the higher their pay.

5. *Elimination of supervision.* A team leader replaced the supervisor. Whereas the functions of the supervisor was to plan, direct, and control the activities of workers, the team leader within each work group facilitated team decision-making.

6. *Self-government.* No plant rules were formulated by management in advance. Rather, rules were adopted as they seemed necessary from the experience of workers and management.

7. *Minimization of status symbols.* Differential status symbols such as separate parking lots for office and factory workers and different entrances to the plant for blue- and white-collar employees were eliminated.

The results of this job enrichment experiment were positive for both General Foods and the employees. After 18 months, the fixed overhead of the plant was 33 percent of what it had been before the job enrichment program. The plant saves $600,000 a year because of such improvements as 92 per cent fewer quality rejects and an absenteeism rate 9 per cent below the industry average. The plant's safety record is one of General Foods' best and its turnover rate is far below average. Workers, team leaders, and managers have all become more involved in their work and their job dissatisfaction has declined. The program has also improved the nonwork life of workers and plant managers, who have become more active in civic affairs than the employees of other companies in their community.

Table 7-4. Illustrations of the Positive Effects of Job Enrichment Programs

	General Foods (Blue-Collar)	AT&T (Blue-Collar)	AT&T (White-Collar)	Bell System (Blue- and White-Collar)	Polaroid Corp. (Blue-Collar)
1. Establishment(s) or Employee Groups	Pet Food Plant Topeka, Kans. All plant employees.	Long Lines Plant, N.Y. Private Line Telephone District. Framemen.	Shareholder Correspondents, Treasury Department.	17 groups of workers in diverse occupations, including toll operators, installers, clerks, equipment engineers.	Production line employees.
2. Year Initiated	1971	1966	1965	1967	1959
3. No. Employees Affected	70	35–40	95–120	about 1,200	2,000+
4. Problem	In designing this new plant management sought to solve problems of frequent shut downs, costly recycling and low morale that plagued an existing plant making the same product.	There was low productivity, high errors, schedule slippage and no worker's pride.	High turnover, absenteeism, low morale, low productivity.	Are the methods and results of the AT&T Shareholder Correspondents Study transferable to other employee groups?	Top management wanted to increase the meaningfulness of work.

5. Technique Used	Workers were organized into relatively autonomous work groups with each group responsible for a production process. Pay is based on the total number of jobs an employee can do.	The framemen's work was expanded to include taking full responsibility for the job and negotiating with the "customer."	Workers were given less supervision and more job freedom. The authors of letters to complainants were allowed to sign without review by supervisors.	Same as AT&T Shareholder Corespondents Study.	Factory operators were rotated between their factory jobs and more desirable nonfactory jobs.
6. Human Results	Job attitudes a few months after the plant opened indicated "positive assessments" by both team members and leaders. Increased democracy in the plant may have led to more civic activity.	Grievances were practically eliminated (from rate of one per week). Morale was higher in the year's experiment.	There was more pride in group achievement. Higher job satisfaction was measured.	After a year's experience, where measured, attitudes improved and grievances dropped.	For some there was challenge and reward while learning, then frustration until they were permanently transferred.
7. Economic Results	The plant is operated by 70 workers, rather than the 110 originally estimated by industrial engineers. Also, there were "improved yields, minimized waste and avoidance of shut downs."	There was no significant change in absenteeism or tardiness. However, at the end there was a slight increase in productivity with fewer workers and less overtime.	After a year's trial, absenteeism decreased from 2% to 1.4%. Turnover practically eliminated.	Turnover decreased by 9.3% in the experimental group and increased 13.1% in the control group. Overtime hours decreased about 50%.	Turnover and absenteeism decreased. Recruitment was easier for factory jobs, since they were no longer deadend.

Reprinted by permission from *Work in America* (Cambridge, Mass.: MIT Press, 1973), pp. 188–189.

WORKER REACTIONS TO JOB ENRICHMENT

I'm doing a better job. I just like this place so much, I just think it's wonderful. I've never worked in a place where we've had so much closeness with supervisors.

> —Ruth Moulton, assembler, Corning Glass Works,
> Medfield, Massachusetts

We work as teams, decide on our own goals—we're really involved in making the decisions. If everyone doesn't work, we can't make it, so we have a meeting and talk it over.

> —John Meyer, shape cutter, Donnelly Mirrors, Inc.,
> Holland, Michigan

Now all the inspection is not left to the inspector—we all watch out for each other's defects. If one girl has machine trouble other girls jump up and help her. It's wonderful to help each other.

> —Mae Darby, machine operator,
> R. G. Barry Corp., Columbus, Ohio

You don't have anyone hovering over you. We can make decisions. Now there's more responsibility on the individual.

> —Shirley McCullough, wax assembler,
> Precision Castparts Corp., Portland, Oregon

It's a terrific place to work, you have freedom, you're on your own, you make it or not. Other places I've worked were controlled, 'you don't leave that chair.' Here, things are wide open for advancement.

> —Ronald Weinberg, assembler promoted to draftsman,
> Non-Linear Systems, Inc., Del Mar, California

It's a heck of a company—you're treated as a human being, you're made to feel a part of everything. Polaroid doesn't dog you. The responsibility they give you is just great. There are big opportunities to move up.

—Martin Deeran, machine operator promoted to personnel department, Polaroid Corp., Cambridge, Massachusetts

Judson Gooding, "It Pays to Wake Up the Blue-Collar Worker," *Fortune*, 82 (September 1970): 134.

Organizational Democracy

Karl Marx's solution to the problems of worker dissatisfaction, alienation, and exploitation was a worker's revolution—the proletariat was to overthrow the capitalist class and take control of the means of production. Contemporary radical critics of the capitalist economic system have been forced to search for other, less extreme, solutions. A major strategy in recent years is worker control, or industrial democracy.[47] Since this strategy has also been adopted by many nonradicals and applied to the office as well as to the factory, the term *organizational democracy* best describes this solution.

Organizational democracy exists when employees influence work-related decisions, as David Jenkins explains:

> [Organizational democracy] is a radical change from the traditional, rigid, pyra-midal, authoritarian management structures that are virtually universally ac-cepted. At the very least, democracy means a firm check on . . . dictatorial management. . . . It means an end to the assumption that 'managers' and 'em-ployees' are somehow fundamentally different, the former endowed with vastly superior thinking powers, the latter totally incapable of formulating decisions of their own, able only to follow instructions, and at that only under threat of punishment. It means that the intelligence and knowledge of employees . . . can be put into action to the benefit of both employees and organization. Mindless jobs . . . can be remolded into reasonable occupations worthy of the attention of dignified human beings.[48]

Employee participation in United States' firms is generally limited to job-related matters, such as employment conditions, work load, the organiza-tion of work tasks, and the pace of work. Occasionally, as in one Proctor and Gamble plant, workers control decision-making on such matters as hiring and firing and pay scales.[49] In some companies in Israel, Yugoslavia, West Ger-many, Norway, Sweden, and France, employee representatives serve as members of their company's board of directors.[50] In these companies, work-ers and management *together* determine what will be produced, the quantities in which it will be produced, where it will be produced, and how much it will cost.

The application of organizational democracy in some of the kibbutz in Israel has provided outstanding illustrations of carefully planned, carefully implemented, and comprehensive programs. The results of a study comparing

[47] Bertram Silverman and Murray Yanowitch, eds., *The Worker in "Post-Industrial" Capitalism: Liberal and Radical Responses* (New York: The Free Press, 1974), p. 18.

[48] David Jenkins, *Job Power: Blue and White Collar Democracy* (Baltimore: Penguin Books, Inc., 1974), pp. 1–2.

[49] David Jenkins, "Democracy in the Workplace: The Human Factories," *The Nation*, 218 (January 12, 1974): 47.

[50] For example, see Milton Derber, "Worker Participation in Israeli Management," *Industrial Relations*, 3 (October 1963): 51.

12 Israeli firms, six at kibbutzim operated democratically, and six privately owned and conventionally run, show the following:

> On every count, the kibbutzim outperformed the privately owned companies—in productivity of labor (22 percent higher in the Kibbutz companies), productivity of capital (40 percent when stated as profit on investment and 38 percent when stated as sales per unit of fixed assets), and net profit per production worker (38 percent higher). And administrative costs were on the average, 8 percent lower on the kibbutzim.[51]

ULTIMATE ORGANIZATIONAL DEMOCRACY: WORKER OWNERSHIP

WELCOME TO SOUTH BEND LATHE, AMERICA'S LARGEST 100 PERCENT EMPLOYEE OWNED COMPANY.

So reads the proud sign in front of a sprawling red brick factory in South Bend, Ind. Little more than a year ago, the 70-year-old machine-tool maker faced liquidation because its performance was not up to the expectations of its owners, Amsted Industries Inc., a Chicago-based conglomerate. But South Bend was a solid company with good years ahead of it, thought some of its top executives. They went shopping for a way to buy the company and pump in enough working capital to keep it going until times got better. Today South Bend is doing well and is totally independent, with most of its stock already deposited in a trust in which each of the company's 440 employees share, according to salary and seniority. SBL's turn-around probably owes much to the U.S. economic recovery, which has sharply driven up orders for machine-tool producers. But the company might not exist at all were it not for a financial device called ESOP, or Employee Stock Ownership Plan. . . .

According to the Internal Revenue Service, more than 250 firms now operate some form of ESOP program, including such corporate successes as Hallmark Cards of Kansas City, Mo.; Gamble-Skogmo, a Minneapolis-based retailer with 18,000 employees; E-Systems, Inc., a Dallas defense contractor; and Houston's Zapata Corp.

---

[51] Jenkins, op. cit., p. 82. For a review of the results of other programs of organizational democracy in countries throughout the industrialized world, see ibid.; and Carole Patemen, *Participation and Democratic Theory* (Cambridge, England: Cambridge University Press, 1970). For criticisms, see William Gomberg, "The Trouble with Democratic Management," *Trans-action,* 3 (July–August 1966): 30–35; George Strauss and Eliezer Rosenstein, "Worker Participation: A Critical View," *Industrial Relations,* 9 (February 1970): 197–214; and Samuel C. Florman, "The Job Enrichment Mistake," *Harper's,* 252 (May 1976): 18–22.

Tax Break

The main attraction is that an ESOP gives a company a huge tax break. The mechanism: an employee trust is set up, borrows money and uses it to buy newly issued stock from the company. Then the company makes contributions to the trust that are used to repay the loan; they are contributions to an employee benefit plan and are tax deductible. Had the company borrowed the money directly, it would be able to deduct only the interest as a business expense. When the money goes through ESOP, the company can in effect deduct principal repayments too, thus cutting borrowing costs by as much as half.

Even that is not all. In recent years Russell B. Long, the conservative but populist chairman of the Senate Finance Committee, has . . . pushed through legislation increasing the 10% investment-tax credit that a company gets for purchases of new equipment to 11%—provided that the extra 1% is used to pay for company stock distributed to employees through an ESOP. This year Long pushed further; that 1% special credit (which is directly subtracted from the tax a company owes) has increased to 1½%. . . . The extra half-point, however, is available only if employees dig into their own pockets and invest a matching amount in the company's stock. American Telephone and Telegraph Co., which has more than 770,000 employees, is now considering setting up a limited ESOP. Such a plan could have saved Ma Bell $80 million in 1975 taxes alone.

Critics of the tax breaks argue that they amount to a gift from the Government that will mainly benefit high-salaried workers in such capital-intensive industries as oil drilling and machine tools. They are the industries that use the investment-tax credit most heavily. . . .

But the ESOP idea has strong support from Congress's Joint Economic Committee, and the Economic Development Administration of the Department of Commerce is actually requiring that some companies to which it gives loans establish ESOPs. . . .

ESOP, says Long in a burst of lyricism, "is better than Geritol. It will increase productivity, improve labor relations, promote economic justice. It will save this economic system."

Measuring Up.

Labor leaders have been ambivalent about ESOP, but at South Bend Lathe, United Steelworkers Union members are enthusiastic, and two local representatives sit on the company's board of directors. Union Organizer June Molnar, 26, a tool and cutting grinder, reports that workers check out new recruits to be sure they measure up. Slacking off is not tolerated. Says Molnar, who expects to get about $2,000 deposited in her ESOP account this year: "It's 'Hey, you've got your hand in my pocket if you don't do your job.'" Molnar's boss, SBL President Richard Boulis, 53, is just as ebullient. Contemplating a 20% rise in productivity in the past year and close to 10% more pretax profits during the first year of independent operation, he exults, "Worker-owned companies are the way to go."

Time (October 4, 1976): 80.

The Decline of Bureaucracy?

If work in a bureaucratic organization tends to promote job dissatisfaction, then problems should decrease if a more suitable organizational structure were to replace bureaucracy. Some social scientists are predicting such an occurrence. According to Warren Bennis, more work organizations in the future will focus on the solving of specific problems by work teams assembled for a limited period of time.[52] A number of persons with diverse knowledge, training, and skills will be assembled to work on a project that may last for a few days, a few weeks, a few months, or a few years. Once the problem has been solved, the work group will be dissolved and its members will move on to other similar "temporary" work structures. Some examples of such temporary work structures already exist. These include task groups in advertising agencies, a group of state, local, and federal law enforcement officers assembled to capture a criminal, scientists and doctors assembled to work on a cancer research project, a national committee to reelect a president.

It seems unlikely that bureaucratic organizations will entirely disappear in the future. Certain economic activities, especially in manufacturing industries, may take a long time to change. In fact, Bennis projects that about 20 per cent of the labor force will probably always be employed in bureaucratic organizations. Still, should Bennis' forecast be even partially correct, the proportion of the labor force in jobs that permit autonomy, freedom, meaning, responsibility, and self-fulfillment will increase. Should the traditional bureaucratic form of organizing work become less dominant in the future, then the extent of work dissatisfaction should decline.

The American work ethic is changing. Although leisure time remains important to American workers, they are beginning to want more from work than money to buy enjoyment off the job. More and more workers, particularly the young, are rejecting the authoritarian work place, dull and repetitive tasks, and jobs with little challenge or autonomy. Managerial recognition of this growing conflict between traditional work arrangements and the expectations of modern workers is reflected in the rise of organizational democracy and job enrichment, two currently popular solutions to the blue-collar blues and white-collar woes. American management has not universally accepted these solutions. There is, however, a growing recognition that these solu-

---

[52] Warren G. Bennis, *Changing Organizations* (New York: McGraw-Hill Book Company, 1966), pp. 3–15. Also see Eugene Litwak, "Models of Bureaucracy Which Permit Conflict," *American Journal of Sociology,* 67 (September 1961): 177–184.

tions, when appropriate and properly implemented, are both workable and beneficial. Managers are becoming aware of those companies that have solved many of their employee morale problems through organizational democracy and job enrichment. If the worth ethnic continues to develop in its present direction, and there is reason to believe that it will, management will be compelled to adopt these and other solutions to soften the organizational consequences of rising worker dissatisfaction.

Additional Readings

Banks, J. A. *Industrial Participation.* Liverpool, England: Liverpool University Press, 1963.

Bell, Daniel. *The End of Ideology.* New York: Collier Books, 1961.

Best, Fred. *The Future of Work.* Englewood Cliffs, N.J.: Prentice-Hall, Inc., 1973.

Blumberg, P. *Industrial Democracy: The Sociology of Participation.* London: Constable & Company Ltd., 1968.

Coates, K., ed. *Can the Workers Run Industry?* London: Sphere Books, 1968.

Davis, Louis E., and Albert B. Cherns, eds. *The Quality of Working Life. Vol. One: Problems, Prospects, and the State of the Art.* New York: The Free Press, 1975.

Emery, Fred, and Einar Thorsrud. *Democracy at Work: The Report of the Norwegian Industrial Democracy Program.* Leiden, The Netherlands: Martinus Nijoff, 1976.

Faunce, William A. *Problems of an Industrial Society.* New York: McGraw-Hill Book Company, 1968.

Ford, Robert N. "Job Enrichment Lessons from AT&T," *Harvard Business Review,* 51 (January–February 1973).

Goldthrope, John H., David Lockwood, Frank Bechhofer, and Jennifer Platt. *The Affluent Worker: Industrial Attitudes and Behavior.* Cambridge, England: Cambridge University Press, 1968.

Herbst, Ph.G. *Alternatives to Hierarchies.* Leiden, The Netherlands: Martinus Nijoff, 1976.

Sennett, Richard, and Jonathan Cobb. *The Hidden Injuries of Class.* New York: Vintage Books, 1973.

Shepard, Jon M., ed. *Organizational Issues in Industrial Society*. Englewood Cliffs, N.J.: Prentice-Hall, Inc., 1972.

Tannenbaum, Arnold S. *Social Psychology of the Work Organization*. Belmont, Calif.: Wadsworth Publishing Co., Inc., 1966.

Toffler, Alvin. *Future Shock*. New York: Random House, Inc., 1970.

Vanek, Jaroslav, ed. *Self-management: Economic Liberation of Man*. New York: Penguin Books, 1975.

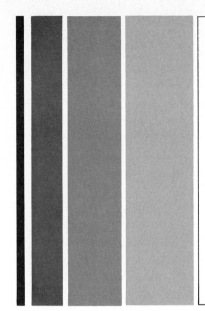

population and urbanization

Four-fifths of the one billion additional earthlings expected in the next 15 years will live—subsist is a better word—in the underdeveloped areas of the globe where hunger is a way of life. And just as there has been and continues to be a polarizing of rich and poor nations, so, too, a parallel process is taking place within nations as well. The world's burgeoning collection of slums, shanty towns, barrios, and the like is ample evidence of this. Not only is there not enough land for everyone to farm, what land remains is increasingly denuded for other purposes such as lumber, forage, and fuel. The rich get richer and the poor poorer all over the underdeveloped world.[1]

Rapid population growth is one of the most serious problems facing mankind. Currently, population growth adds the equivalent of a Peoria, Illinois, or approximately 200,000 people, to the world's population every day; a new Moscow, or 6 million people, every month; and a new Brazil, or nearly 70 million people, every year.[2] To place the problem of such rapid population growth in perspective, consider what it means for a country's population to double in size in 20 years:

[1] Judith Randal, as quoted in Herman Kahn and A. J. Wiener, ''Overpopulation and Undernourishment'' in Paul B. Weisz, ed., *The Contemporary Scene* (New York: McGraw-Hill Book Company, 1970), p. 311.
[2] Ibid., p. 309.

There would be nearly twice as many families in 20 years. . . . In order to maintain present living standards, such a country must, in two decades, duplicate every amenity for the support of human beings. Where there is one home today there must be two (or their equivalent). Where there is one schoolroom there must be two. Where there is one hospital, garage, judge, doctor, or mechanic, there must be two. Agricultural production must be doubled. Imports and exports must be doubled. The capacity of roads, water systems, electric generating plants, and so on, must be doubled.[3]

It is highly unlikely that even a developed nation such as the United States, with its rich natural resources and vast industrial base, could double its facilities in 20 years. Yet, in many poorer nations, the population is growing so rapidly that it will indeed double within that time.

The prophecy of "doom and gloom" as a result of population growth is by no means new. In 1798, Thomas Malthus suggested that pressure of population on the food supply was inevitable.[4] He argued that, without restrictions on population growth, human populations tend to increase in a geometric ratio, that is, by multiplication (for example, 2, 4, 8, 16 . . .). On the other hand, he believed that food supplies could, at best, increase in an arithmetic progression (for example, 1, 2, 3, 4 . . .). The result, he predicted, would be hunger and starvation, epidemics of disease, and war.

Thus far, Malthus' gloomy prediction has not been fulfilled in industrialized nations because agricultural production has almost kept up with population growth, and the practice of birth control, which Malthus considered immoral, has limited population growth. The green revolution or the introduction of high-yield wheats and rices to underdeveloped areas has alleviated somewhat the pressure on the food supply. Nevertheless, in 1973 food had to be airlifted into several African nations to prevent mass starvation, and India and Bangladesh had critical food shortages.

The population has grown so rapidly in many of the poorer nations of the world that the food supply is already too limited to provide adequate nutrition. Approximately 1 billion persons in the world today suffer from nutritional deficiencies, and experts attribute millions of deaths annually to inadequate diets.[5] In the more affluent nations, such as the United States,

[3] Paul R. Ehrlich and Anne H. Ehrlich, *Population, Resources, Environment: Issues in Human Ecology,* 2nd ed. (San Francisco: W. H. Freeman and Company, Publishers, 1972), pp. 2–3.
[4] Thomas Malthus, "A Summary View of the Principle of Population," in Thomas Malthus, Julian Huxley, and Frederick Osborn, *Three Essays on Population* (orig. pub., 1830) (New York: New American Library, 1960), pp. 13–59.
[5] René Dumont and Bernard Rosier, *The Hungry Future* (trans., Rosamund Linell and R. B. Sutcliffe) (New York: Frederick A. Praeger, 1969), p. 35.

population growth, in part because it has been less rapid, has not led to food shortages. But population growth has played a part in the environmental crisis, producing problems as diverse as water shortages, air pollution, water pollution, and solid waste disposal, all of which are examined in Chapter 9.

Changes in the distribution of population have also created problems. Throughout the world, the cities are overcrowded. In the affluent countries, the growth of suburbs has led to urban sprawl as well as decay of the inner cities. In the poorer countries, shantytowns have been built outside cities to house the millions of recent migrants, but they lack such essential services as water, sewers, and schools.

COMPONENTS OF POPULATION CHANGE

The study of the size, composition, and distribution of human populations is known as *demography*. A population can change in three ways: people are born; people die; and people move. These are the components of population change. The way some basic demographic rates are calculated is shown in Figure 8-1. In 1974, the birth rate in the United States was 15.0 per 1000, and the death rate was 9.1 per 1000; hence, the rate of natural increase was 5.9 per 1000. In 1974, the excess of legal immigrants over emigrants amounted to 395,000, or a rate of approximately 1.8 per 1000. In contrast with the other rates, growth rates are calculated per 100 rather than per 1000 people. The growth rate in the United States in 1974 was 0.8 per cent. That may seem to be a small figure, but if that rate continues the population of 1974 will double in 90 years; that is, in the year 2064 there would be approximately 420 million people in this country.[6]

CAUSES OF POPULATION GROWTH AND DISTRIBUTION

While the contemporary population explosion is unprecedented in terms of its magnitude and potential impact, it is well to recognize that there have been other population explosions. Throughout history, technological changes have influenced the growth and distribution of the population. Some 10,000 years ago, when human beings were nomadic and supported themselves by hunting and gathering fruits, berries, and plants, there were only about 5 million peo-

[6] Leon F. Bouvier, "U.S. Population in 2000—Zero Growth or Not?" *Population Bulletin*, 30, no. 5 (1975): 5.

$$\text{Birth Rate} = \frac{\text{Number of Births per Year}}{\text{Population}} \times 1{,}000$$

$$\text{Death Rate} = \frac{\text{Number of Deaths per Year}}{\text{Population}} \times 1{,}000$$

Rate of Natural Increase = Birth Rate − Death Rate

Net Migration = Immigration − Emigration

$$\text{Growth Rate} = \frac{\text{Birth Rate} - \text{Death Rate} + \dfrac{\text{Net Migration}}{\text{Population}}}{10} \times 1{,}000$$

Annual Growth Rate (Percentages)	Doubling Time (Years)
0.05	1,400
0.20	350
0.50	140
1.00	70
1.50	47
2.00	35
2.50	28
3.00	23

FIGURE 8-1. Demographic Rates. [Source: *Options: A Study Guide to Population and the American Future* (Washington, D.C.: Population Reference Bureau, Inc., 1973), p. 31.]

ple on the earth. With the invention of agriculture (cultivation of crops by means of the hoe) and the domestication of animals around 8000 B.C., people settled near their fields, and population density increased.[7] Agriculture altered the restraints on population growth that had been imposed by the scarcity of food. It is estimated that by 4000 B.C. the population of the world had increased to 87 million, at which time another population explosion occurred. Technological changes, including invention of the plow and use of systematic irrigation, produced agricultural surpluses. This spurred population growth and altered the distribution of the population. Some people were freed from the task of food production and settled in urban areas because agricultural workers could produce sufficient food for city dwellers as well as themselves. The scope of this expansion is reflected in the fact that at the beginning of the

[7] V. Gordon Childe, *Man Makes Himself* (New York: New American Library, 1951).

Christian era, the total human population numbered 200 to 300 million and by 1650 had reached 500 million.

The current population explosion is largely a result of the industrial revolution and the accompanying developments in medicine and sanitation. A fundamental element in the industrial revolution was the use of inanimate sources of energy such as coal and oil. By introducing power-driven machinery, the industrial revolution led to the rise of the factory system:

> The Industrial Revolution is characterized by the replacement of hand production centered in a craftsman's home or small shop by machine production centered in factories, by the production of standardized goods with interchangeable parts, by the rise of a class of factory workers who work for wages and do not own the means of production or the goods they produce, by a great increase in the proportion of the population engaged in nonagricultural occupations, and by the growth of numerous large cities.[8]

The invention of the steam engine in the eighteenth century signaled the beginning of man's reliance on fossil fuels (coal, oil, and natural gas) as energy sources, rather than exclusive reliance on the labor of human beings and work animals such as the horse and ox. The industrial revolution began in England and then spread to other European countries, to the United States, and subsequently, although to a lesser extent, to other parts of the world.

Machinery was used in the fields as well as in the factories, and developments in agriculture resulted not only in increased agricultural production but also in an excess of workers in rural areas. These people were displaced through technological developments, which served as a "push" factor increasing migration to the city, and the possibility of employment in the emerging factories constituted a "pull" factor. Thus, the industrial revolution had and continues to have a tremendous impact on the distribution of the population.

Industrialization initially relied on steam for power, and this led to the concentration or centralization of the population in cities. Steam can be produced cheaply only in large quantities and must be used close to where it is produced; this led to a compact city.[9] Lacking transportation facilities other than the horse-drawn streetcar, many of the early industrial workers walked to the factories or rode short distances on horse-drawn streetcars; therefore, they had to live near the factories. The use of electricity and, later, the inter-

---

[8] George A. Theodorson and Achilles G. Theodorson, *A Modern Dictionary of Sociology* (New York: Thomas Y. Crowell Company, 1969), p. 201.

[9] J. John Palen, *The Urban World* (New York: McGraw-Hill Book Company, 1975), p. 53.

nal combustion engine in transportation had the opposite effect. The introduction of the electric-powered streetcar in 1888 meant that workers could commute several miles to their jobs.

The industrial revolution produced rapid population growth. As previously noted, there were some 500 million people in 1650. Two hundred years later, this number had doubled, reaching approximately 1 billion. In 1900, the world population was about 1.5 billion; by 1930, it had reached 2 billion, and by 1950, some 2.5 billion. In 1977, the world population stood at 4 billion.

TWO PATTERNS OF POPULATION GROWTH

Demographers and other social scientists have found it useful to distingusih between the developed countries and the underdeveloped countries. These terms refer to economic conditions, not cultural development. The real distinction is between the "haves" and "have nots"; the term *underdeveloped country* is a euphemism, a polite way of saying poor country. In relative terms, the developed countries are affluent and industrialized, whereas the underdeveloped countries are poor and largely agricultural.

Population growth in the developed and underdeveloped countries has taken two different paths. The differences are important for an understanding of the potential for population growth in the different regions of the world. One path followed the industrial revolution and involved population growth over a period of more than a century in the developed countries. The other followed the introduction of chemicals and drugs from the developed countries and occurred in the post-World War II period in the underdeveloped nations of Asia, Africa, and Latin America.

Developed Countries

A distinctive pattern of changes in the birth and death rates has been observed in the developed nations.[10] The initial stage, prior to industrialization, is one in which there were high birth and death rates and little or no population growth. Experiencing the effects of the industrial revolution in the form of better nutrition, medical care, and improved sanitation, they entered a second

---

[10] David M. Heer, *Society and Population* (Englewood Cliffs, N.J.: Prentice-Hall, Inc., 1968), p. 10.

stage. The death rate declined, but in conjunction with a continued high birth rate, the result was rapid population growth.

In the third stage, prior to World War II, the birth rate declined and population growth slowed. Apparently, the decline in the birth rate resulted from the changing status of children. In an agricultural setting, children are potential workers and, therefore, an economic asset. In an industrial city, children are consumers to be fed, clothed, and educated. To maintain or improve their economic status, couples presumably limited the number of children they had. The depression of the 1930s also influenced the birth rate.

The fourth stage, following World War II, was again one of rapid population growth as developed countries experienced a baby boom. The postponement of births because of the war and changes in age at marriage and childbearing contributed to the dramatic rise in the birth rate. As Leslie and Charles Westoff observe, "Women were marrying at younger ages and having their children sooner and closer together."[11] Although these factors were important, the primary reason for the baby boom was an increase in the average size of families among those who married after World War II. As a result of the post-war baby boom, demographers now recognize that the declines in the birth and death rates over the past two centuries in the developed countries were not the inevitable result of industrialization, economic development, and urbanization. Consequently, they emphasize that the changes in the developed countries do not offer a blueprint for future population change in underdeveloped countries.

Underdeveloped Countries

The history of demographic changes in underdeveloped countries has only two stages. The first, characterized by high birth and death rates, lasted until the end of World War II. This stage is comparable to the initial one in developed countries. However, the demographic changes that have taken place in the underdeveloped regions of the world since World War II have a radically different source than the changes in the economy and style of life in developed countries following the industrial revolution.

Since 1945, there has been a rapid decline in the death rate in underdeveloped countries. The death rate has dropped because the products of the de-

[11] Leslie A. Westoff and Charles F. Westoff, *From Now to Zero: Fertility, Contraception and Abortion in America* (Boston: Little, Brown and Company, 1971), p. 213; Heer, op. cit., p. 11.

veloped nations—antibiotics and other drugs and public health measures—have been introduced in these countries. By means of pesticides, medical technology, and public health measures, malaria, yellow fever, smallpox, and other infectious diseases have been controlled or eliminated in much of the underdeveloped portion of the world. The effect has been a sizable reduction in the death rate among children and young adults.

It is important to recognize that in the developed countries the death rate declined gradually over a period of years, not abruptly through changes introduced from the outside, as in the underdeveloped regions. The causes underlying the transition from a high birth rate to a low birth rate in developed countries are not fully known, but may be attributed to changes in the way of life or outlook of people living in industrial nations. Comparable changes have not occurred in many of the underdeveloped regions, and the combination of high birth rates and low death rates has produced rapid population growth.

WORLD POPULATION PROJECTIONS

A team of experts has calculated that if current fertility and mortality rates continue, in 1,000 years there would be a billion billion people on earth, or 1,700 persons per square yard of the earth's land and water surface.[12] Estimates of the world's population in this century are of more immediate concern. Projections of the population in various regions of the world are prepared regularly by the United Nations. The most recent projections were prepared in 1977. The United Nations projected that the world population would increase by 73 per cent between 1970 and 2000, from 3.6 billion to 6.3 billion. As may be seen in Table 8-1, sizable increases in population are anticipated in Africa, Latin America, and South Asia; most of the increase in population will take place in the underdeveloped regions of the world. An increase in population of 25 per cent is projected for the developed regions; in contrast, the projected growth in population from 2.5 to 4.9 billion in the underdeveloped regions constitutes an increase of 94 per cent.

In *The Future of Population Growth,* Tomas Frejka has taken a different approach.[13] He projected what the size of the world's population would be if

---

[12] Paul R. Ehrlich, Anne H. Ehrlich, and John P. Holdren, *Human Ecology: Problems and Solutions* (San Francisco: W. H. Freeman and Company, 1973), p. 46.

[13] The assumptions underlying Frejka's projections are that death rates will decline at the current rate for 10 to 15 years and then more gradually and that life expectancy for females will stabilize at 75 years. See Tomas Frejka, *The Future of Population Growth: Alternative Paths to Equilibrium* (New York: John Wiley & Sons, Inc., 1973), pp. 41–43.

Table 8-1. Estimates of Population, 1970–2000 (in millions)

Region	1970 Population	Projections					
		1975	1980	1985	1990	1995	2000
World total	3,610	3,968	4,374	4,817	5,280	5,763	6,254
Developed regions	1,084	1,132	1,181	1,231	1,277	1,320	1,360
Underdeveloped regions	2,526	2,836	3,193	3,586	4,003	4,443	4,894
Africa	352	401	461	532	614	708	814
Latin America	283	324	372	426	486	551	620
Northern America	226	237	249	262	275	286	296
East Asia	927	1,006	1,088	1,165	1,233	1,302	1,370
South Asia	1,101	1,250	1,427	1,625	1,836	2,054	2,267
Europe	459	473	487	500	514	527	540
Oceania	19	21	23	26	28	30	33
USSR	243	255	268	282	294	305	315

SOURCE: United Nations, Department of Economic and Social Affairs, *Population Bulletin of the United Nations, no. 8—1976* (New York: United Nations, 1977), p. 98.

the net reproduction rate declined to 1.0 in different periods of time. A net reproduction rate of 1.0 reflects the replacement level of reproduction—on the average, each woman would have one daughter who could be expected to live to bear children. Frejka used demographic data for the years 1965–1970 in making his projections. Three of his projections or paths are shown in Figure 8-2. He refers to them as the immediate path, the rapid path, and the slow path.

The immediate path would lead to zero growth by the end of the next century. For the world's population, the net reproduction rate was 1.9 in 1965–1970. According to Frejka, this figure would have had to be cut by one half by 1975 for population growth to follow the immediate path. The term *rapid path* may be somewhat misleading in that achievement of replacement-level fertility by 2000 to 2005 would be rapid only for the underdeveloped regions, not for the developed regions of the world. If replacement-level fertility were achieved shortly after the turn of the century, then the world's population would reach nearly 6 billion in 2000 and ultimately would total some 8 billion in 2100. The slow path allows 70 years to reduce the net reproduction rate to 1.0. If this proves to be the course that population growth takes, nearly 7 billion people would be on the earth in 2000. The world's population would continue to grow until the twenty-second century, when it would total 15 billion, or some four times the present world population.

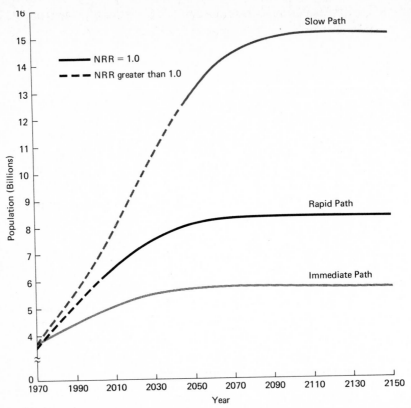

FIGURE 8-2. Growth potential of the world population, selected paths, 1970–2150. [Source: Tomas Frejka, *The Future of Population Growth: Alternative Paths to Equilibrium* (New York: John Wiley, 1973), p. 54. Reproduced by permission.]

There is a striking difference in the age distribution of the developed and underdeveloped countries of the world. In the developed countries, 26 per cent of the population are under 15 years of age, whereas in the developing nations almost 42 per cent are below the age of 15. The rate of population growth in the developed and underdeveloped countries also differs. Both the birth and death rates are low—18 and 10 per 1000, respectively—in the developed countries; consequently, the growth rate is approximately 1 per cent. In the underdeveloped countries, taken together, the birth and death rates are 41 and 15 per 1000, respectively; the rate of growth is 2.6 per cent. The differences in the birth rate, age distribution, and rate of population growth mean that the underdeveloped countries have a greater potential for population growth than the developed countries.

POPULATION GROWTH IN THE UNITED STATES

The first census of the population of the United States was conducted in 1790, at which time there were 4 million people in this country. A comparable enumeration of the population has been made every succeeding ten years; in the most recent tabulation in 1970, the United States population had reached 205 million.[14] Thus, in a span of 180 years, the population increased some 200 million.

Immigration

With the exception of the native American Indians, we are all descendants of relatively recent immigrants to this country. Natural increase played a part in the growth of the population, but millions of immigrants to the United States played a vital role in the country's population growth. It has been estimated that between 30 and 45 million immigrants have come to the United States since 1820; this constitutes the largest mass migration that has occurred in the world.[15] The "old migration" took place in the early part of the nineteenth century; it reached a peak in 1854 when 428,000 immigrants arrived. They were predominantly Irish and German. The Irish left their home country largely as a result of a potato famine, whereas many of the Germans were political refugees. The "new migration" occurred toward the end of the nineteenth century; the peak year was 1907, when 1.3 million immigrants entered the country. They were largely from Eastern and Southern European countries such as Poland and Italy.

After World War I, concern was expressed about the flood of immigrants for such reasons as communism, crime, and job competition. The result was the passage of the Immigration Act of 1924, which set a quota of 150,000 immigrants per year. That legislation assigned 85 per cent of the quota to residents of Northern and Western Europe, particularly England,

---

[14] Beginning in 1985, the census will be conducted every five years in the United States.
[15] Palen, op. cit., p. 208.

Germany, and Ireland so that the number of new arrivals would be proportional to the national origins of those already here.

The immigration laws were revised in 1965, with emphasis shifted from concern regarding national origins to considerations of reunifying families, providing asylum for refugees, and obtaining needed skills and professions. Because preference was given to skilled persons, such as physicians, the effect has been a "brain drain" on other countries. Currently, as many as 395,000 persons may immigrate to the United States in a year. Immigration accounted for 40 per cent of the population growth between 1900 and 1910, but in the decade of the 1960s, only 16 per cent of the nation's growth was attributable to net migration.

Table 8-2. Leading Sources of Immigration, 1975

1.	Mexico	62,205
2.	Philippines	31,751
3.	Korea	28,362
4.	Cuba	25,955
5.	China (Taiwan)	18,536
6.	India	15,773
7.	Dominican Republic	14,066
8.	Portugal	11,845
9.	Italy	11,552
10.	Jamaica	11,076
11.	United Kingdom	10,807
12.	Greece	9,984
13.	Canada	7,308
14.	Colombia	6,434
15.	Trinidad and Tobago	5,982

SOURCE: U.S. Immigration and Naturalization Service.

Other Demographic Changes

In addition to changes in migration, significant changes in the other components of population growth have occurred. The data in Table 8-3 show the demographic changes that have occurred in the twentieth century. In only 70 years, the population of the United States increased by 129 million people, but the rate of growth declined from 2.3 per cent in 1900 to 1.1 per cent in 1970. The death rate declined from 17 to 9 per 1000 between 1900 and 1970.

Table 8-3. Demographic Perspective of 20th-Century United States

	Around 1900	Around 1970
Population	76 million	205 million
Life expectancy	47 years	70 years
Median age	23 years	28 years
Births per 1000 population	32	18
Deaths per 1000 population	17	9
Immigrants per 1000 population	8	2
Annual growth	1¾ million	2½ million
Growth rate	2.3 per cent	1.1 per cent

SOURCE: Commission on Population Growth and the American Future, *Population and the American Future* (Washington, D.C.: U.S. Government Printing Office, 1972), p. 17.

In 1970, life expectancy at birth was 70 years, or 23 years more than it was in 1900.

The difference between the birth and death rates was 15 per 1000 in 1900; natural increase accounted for approximately two thirds of the growth in population, with immigration producing the remainder. The birth rate declined to approximately 18 per 1000 during the depression years of the 1930s; as Philip Hauser observed, the bottom dropped out of the baby market as well as out of the stock market.[16] After World War II, the birth rate moved upward to a peak of 27 per 1000 and remained relatively high for nearly two decades.

Effects of the Baby Boom

The baby boom following World War II has had far-reaching effects on American society. In the mid-1950s, there were severe shortages of classrooms and teachers in elementary schools. Later, colleges and universities experienced growing enrollments as the boom generation reached college age. The Commission on Population Growth and the American Future attributed 50 per cent of the increase in the number of arrests for serious crimes

[16] Philip M. Hauser, "On Population and Environmental Policy and Problems," in Noël Hinrichs, ed., *Population, Environment and People* (New York: McGraw-Hill Book Company, 1971), p. 25.

between 1960 and 1970 to demographic shifts in the population, particularly the increasing proportion of young people in the population.[17]

The Commission also noted that between 1945 and 1965, 48 million Americans reached the age of 20. Between 1965 and 1985, more than 78 million persons will reach that age.[18] This is already producing increased demands for housing and employment. When the boom generation reaches retirement age, pressure on the federal Social Security System can be expected.

At the present time, the children born during the baby boom are in their childbearing years. If immigration ceased and the net reproduction rate dropped to the replacement level—couples having two children on the average—the population would continue to grow for at least 70 years because of the large proportion of young people in our population.

Population Projections for the United States

The Commission on Population Growth and the American Future has based its projections of the future population on the assumptions that the current level of immigration will continue and that couples will have an average of two or three children. These projections are shown in Figure 8-3. Based on the two-child average, the population of the United States in the year 2000 is projected to be 271 million. If each family has an average of three children, then the population would number 322 million in the year 2000. The Commission noted that the difference between families averaging two or three children will have substantial impact on the economy, resources, environment, and social conditions.

Various paths that would result in a stationary population were considered by the Commission. One of these would lead to an end to population growth in about 50 years, at which time the population would total 278 million, exclusive of net migration. To achieve this, the net reproduction rate would have to decline to the replacement level in 20 years:

> This would result if: (1) the proportion of women becoming mothers declined from 88 to 80 percent; (2) the proportion of parents with three or more children declined from 50 to 41 percent; and (3) the proportion of parents with one or

---

[17] The Commission on Population Growth (CPG) and the American Future, *Population and the American Future* (Washington, D.C.: U.S. Government Printing Office, 1972), p. 22.
[18] Ibid.

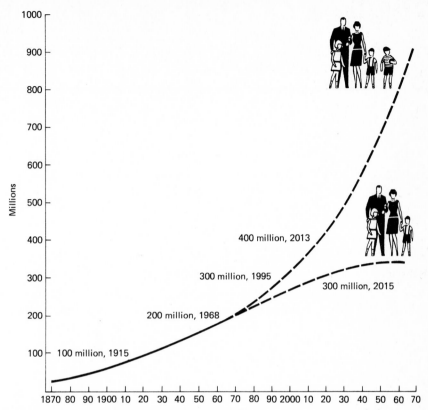

FIGURE 8-3. Projected U.S. population with two- and three-children families. [Source: Commission on Population Growth and the American Future, *Population and the American Future* (Washington, D.C.: U.S. Government Printing Office, 1972), p. 23.]

two children rose from 50 to 59 percent. Also in this illustration, the average age of mothers when their first child is born would rise by two years, and the average interval between births would rise by less than six months.[19]

A number of factors suggest that this path to a nongrowing population, or a variant of it, may take place. The average family size has declined, and couples now indicate that they wish to have fewer children than did the previous generation.

[19] Ibid., p. 111.

THE WORLD-WIDE TREND TOWARD URBANIZATION

Along with the growth of the world's population in recent decades, there has been a population shift from rural to urban areas. The significance of this world-wide trend lies in the problems that are characteristic of many cities. In cities in the United States, property crimes and violent crimes are important problems, as are problems of crowding, littered streets, polluted air, and inadequate garbage collection. In addition to crowding and disease, sizable parts of the urban population in many underdeveloped countries do not have access to services such as schools, sewers, and safe drinking water.

Extent of Urbanization

A demographer, Kingsley Davis, has described the world-wide trend toward urbanization in terms of the number of persons residing in large cities, those with populations of 100,000 or more.[20] The population in such cities has increased rapidly. In 1970, some 860 million people lived in large cities, more than double the number 20 years earlier. For the year 2000, Davis projects that 39.5 per cent of the world's population, or some 2.5 billion people, will reside in cities of 100,000 or more.

The underdeveloped or developing countries are predominantly rural, but they have also experienced urbanization. In 1950, these countries had only 8.6 per cent of their population living in large cities, whereas 32.5 per cent of the people in developed countries resided in cities of 100,000 or more. In 1970, residents of large cities comprised 13.7 per cent of the population of the underdeveloped countries and 44.0 per cent of the total population of developed countries.[21]

In the underdeveloped nations, large cities have experienced spectacular growth. Between 1950 and 1970 the number of residents of large cities increased by 260 million in these countries; this represents an amazing growth rate of 67 per cent per decade and a doubling time of 13.5 years. There are now more city inhabitants in these countries than there were in the entire world in 1950.

Another notable difference is in population growth in rural areas. Be-

[20] Kingsley Davis, "Introduction," in Kingsley Davis, comp., *Cities: Their Origin, Growth and Human Impact* (San Francisco: W. H. Freeman and Company, Publishers, 1973), pp. 1–4.
[21] Kingsley Davis, "Burgeoning Cities and Rural Countries," in Davis, op. cit., pp. 219–220. One third of the world's cities and inhabitants of large cities are located in underdeveloped countries.

tween 1950 and 1970, the rural population in underdeveloped countries increased 16 per cent, which translates into a doubling time of 47 years; in contrast, the rural population in developed countries declined 8 per cent in the same 20-year span. According to Davis, population growth in the underdeveloped countries is double-barreled—both the rural and urban populations are growing through natural increase.[22]

Problems of Urbanization in Underdeveloped Countries

The pattern of urban growth in the underdeveloped countries is not comparable with that of the developed countries. When industrialization occurred in the developed countries, agricultural advances led to a surplus of agricultural workers who were attracted to the city by the availability of jobs. This is not the case in the developing nations. As John Palen observes: "Workers flood into the cities, not because of the availability of jobs, but because the situation in the rural areas and small villages is even worse. People are being pushed to the cities by rural overpopulation rather than being drawn there by urban economic expansion."[23]

This pattern of migration has led to major problems. Construction of adequate housing has not kept pace with population growth, and this has led to the erection of shantytowns of squatters on the outskirts of major cities in underdeveloped countries. Shanties constructed of packing crates and other scraps constitute the housing for millions of recent migrants to the city.[24] Electric power lines may be strung from shack to shack, but these settlements generally lack water, schools, and health facilities. Another major problem in cities in developing nations is unemployment. In many cities one fourth of the labor force is unemployed, and many of those who have jobs are underemployed in that they are not utilizing the skills they possess.[25]

In addition to causing problems of inadequate housing and unemployment, rapid population growth and the resulting high proportion of young dependents impedes economic development. As previously noted, 42 per cent of the population in underdeveloped countries is under the age of 15, in comparison with 26 per cent in the developed nations. A high proportion of dependent children means that funds must be diverted for housing, education,

[22] Ibid., pp. 221–222.
[23] Palen, op. cit., p. 324.
[24] Ibid.; see William Mangin, "Squatter Settlements," in Davis, op. cit., pp. 233–240.
[25] Palen, op. cit.

food, and clothing that otherwise might be invested in economic development. Between 1960 and 1970, the per capita output of the developed countries increased 43 per cent, in contrast with a 27 per cent increase in the underdeveloped countries.[26] This suggests that the underdeveloped status of many nations may become relatively permanent unless they have valuable resources such as oil.

While the economic outlook is bleak, expectations in the underdeveloped countries have been rising. The "revolution of rising expectations" is one of outlook or perspective. Through the mass media of communication, residents of these countries, particularly those living in cities, have been exposed to the existence of higher standards of living in other parts of the world. Awareness that poverty is not characteristic of life everywhere may lead to recognition that poverty is not inevitable or the natural condition of mankind. The result may be explosive. Distribution of food to keep people barely alive may prove to be inadequate to prevent rioting and other kinds of political disturbances.

URBANIZATION IN THE UNITED STATES

Congestion, overcrowding, and pollution are major problems in Tokyo, London, Paris, New York, and other large cities. In most metropolitan areas in the developed world, urban sprawl and urban blight are also found. Since many of the problems resulting from urbanization in developed countries are similar, the United States may be used as a typical example.

As in other developed countries, the process of urbanization has influenced the distribution of the population in this country. When the first census was conducted in 1790, the United States was a predominantly rural nation. An area was defined as urban if it had 2500 or more inhabitants. In 1790, 5 per cent of the nation's population lived in urban areas. As may be seen in Table 8-4, the percentage of the population residing in urban areas increased greatly in subsequent decades. In 1970, 74 per cent of all Americans lived in urban places, making the United States one of the most urbanized nations in the world.

Metropolitan Areas

Because both small towns and cities are classified as urban, the concept of a metropolitan area is more useful to describe the extent of urbanization in the

[26] Ibid., p. 323.

Congestion, overcrowding, and pollution are major problems in all large cities. (Courtesy of Magnum; photo by Matthew Klein.)

United States. A metropolitan area consists of a city (or two contiguous cities) with 50,000 or more inhabitants and the surrounding area that is socially and economically integrated with the city. In 1970, there were 243 metropolitan areas in the United States, and although they occupied less than 1 per cent of the land area, 58 per cent of the population resided in metropolitan areas. In contrast, the rural population comprised only 5.5 per cent of the population, but occupied 50 per cent of the land.

In most of these metropolitan areas, particularly the larger ones, the process of building the central cities was essentially completed prior to the outbreak of World War I. Between 1880 and 1920, there was a sustained building boom in the central cities:

> Much of what was built then still stands. The fact that New York, Chicago, Philadelphia, and St. Louis, to name only a few, are essentially cities of before the twentieth century and before the automobile is a problem we have to cope with today. Any attempt to deal with present-day transportation or pollution problems has to take into account the fact that these American cities were

Table 8-4. Urban Population of the United States: 1790–1970

	Per Cent of Total Population
Current urban definition [a]	
1970	73.5
1960	69.9
1950	64.0
Previous urban definition	
1960	63.0
1950	59.6
1940	56.5
1930	56.1
1920	51.2
1910	45.6
1900	39.6
1890	35.1
1880	28.2
1870	25.7
1860	19.8
1850	15.3
1840	10.8
1830	8.8
1820	7.2
1810	7.3
1800	6.1
1790	5.1

SOURCE: *U.S. Census of Population, 1970. Number of Inhabitants. United States Summary.* Final Report PC(1)—A1, p. 42.

[a]The change in the definition involved inclusion in the urban category of densely settled, but unincorporated sections outside the city. According to the previous definition, these areas were classified as rural.

planned and built in the nineteenth century. We still live largely in cities designed for the age of steam and the horse-drawn streetcar.[27]

The advent of the depression in the 1930s and World War II in the early 1940s resulted in little new construction. As a result, it was not until the postwar years that urban sprawl, or the dispersion of the population throughout metropolitan regions, occurred.

[27] Ibid., p. 52.

QUALITY OF LIFE IN MAJOR METROPOLITAN AREAS

How do you measure something as elusive as "the quality of life" in a city? What things do you take into consideration if you want to compare one city with others as a good place to live? As city problems mount, urban research agencies and "think tanks" around the country have been spending a lot of time on such questions.

One of them, the Urban Institute of Washington, DC, rated 18 major metropolitan areas as shown on the chart accompanying (1 is best; 18 is worst).

Here, for example, are some of the questions the Urban Institute raised in the ranking process:

• HEALTH—How many people are hospitalized? What's the ratio of hospital beds/doctors to the population? What's the infant mortality?

• POVERTY—How many people in the city are at or near the federally defined poverty level? What kind of help is available to these people?

Metropolitan Area	Unemployment	Poverty	Income level	Housing	Health	Public order	Racial equality	Community concern	Educational attainment	Citizen participation	Transportation	Air quality
New York	9	9	4	17	9	18	1	18	14	9	1	10
Los Angeles/Long Beach	18	15	3	10	2	11	3	17	11	3	7	8
Chicago	2	5	5	13	18	14	6	15	2	7	13	16
Philadelphia	7	9	14	9	17	6	9	10	8	13	2	15
Detroit	17	3	1	5	12	17	8	7	5	13	8	14
San Francisco/Oakland	16	17	2	14	2	13	2	13	7	2	16	1
Washington	1	2	8	11	5	15	7	16	18	1	10	3
Boston	4	1	17	18	6	3	N.A.	12	2	6	15	5
Pittsburgh	14	12	13	3	11	5	5	2	2	13	3	17
St. Louis	10	13	12	8	10	9	11	6	11	17	14	18
Baltimore	5	11	16	4	15	16	4	14	14	18	9	11
Cleveland	12	7	9	15	8	10	12	1	9	9	6	13
Houston	5	17	11	1	16	12	10	11	16	9	17	5
Minneapolis/St. Paul	14	4	6	6	1	7	N.A.	5	1	3	11	2
Dallas	3	16	7	2	14	8	N.A.	9	18	3	4	3
Milwaukee	10	5	15	16	4	1	N.A.	8	5	7	4	11
Cincinnati	7	14	10	7	7	2	N.A.	3	11	13	12	9
Buffalo	12	8	18	12	13	4	N.A.	4	10	9	18	5

N.A. Not Available

Reprinted by permission from "A Study in Comparative Urban Indicators: Conditions in 18 Large Metropolitan Areas," Michael J. Flax, The Urban Institute, Washington, D.C., 1972.

The Growth of Suburbs

Since World War II, the distribution of the population has shifted as a result of suburban development. This process has occurred rapidly. Some 26 million Americans, or 20 per cent of the population, resided in suburbs in 1940. The percentage of the population residing in suburbs increased to 24 per cent in 1950, 33 per cent in 1960, and 37 per cent in 1970. According to the Census Bureau, virtually all population growth in metropolitan areas in the decade of the 1960s took place in suburbs.[28]

In 1970, the population residing in suburbs exceeded the population of the central cities for the first time. The population distribution was as follows: suburban areas, 76 million; central cities, 64 million; and nonmetropolitan areas, 63 million.

Americans' adoption of the automobile as the primary means of transportation permitted the decentralization of the population throughout metropolitan regions. Yet it was not simply the existence of the car that led to suburban growth. An important reason for suburban growth was that the space within the central cities had been developed earlier. New housing, of necessity, was constructed in other parts of the metropolitan area. Agricultural land was converted to residential use in the form of housing developments. Following World War II, federal programs to guarantee mortgages, such as FHA and GI loans, required smaller down payments for the purchase of a new home than for an existing dwelling in the city. Another economic reason for suburban development was that the tax rates were lower than in the central city. The postwar baby boom also contributed to suburban growth; a two-bedroom house in the city was scarcely adequate for a family that had or intended to have three or four children.

The image of the suburb as a purely residential area offering no other services is essentially incorrect. Not only were schools and churches built, but entertainment facilities and suburban shopping centers also were developed. Industries were attracted to suburban industrial parks as the development of the interstate highway system meant that trucks, rather than railroads, could transport raw materials and manufactured goods. A further attraction was the availability of inexpensive land, at least in comparison with its cost in the central city:

[28] Bureau of the Census, ''Trends in Social and Economic Conditions in Metropolitan and Nonmetropolitan Areas,'' *Current Population Reports,* series P-23 (No. 33) (Washington, D.C.: U.S. Government Printing Office, 1970), p. 8.

Business is moving out for a variety of reasons. The explanation immediately after World War II was the attraction of cheap land in the suburbs, permitting single-story factories that were convenient for truck loading. In recent years, the motive is more push than pull. Executives complain about the abominable phone service in many cities, horrendous commuting conditions, rapidly rising crime. Even bomb threats are mentioned; when GT&E actually had a bomb go off in the buiding, the bosses lost no time in making the final decision to get the hell out. Then there are problems with the work force. Many young women seem to be avoiding the big cities, while young execs no longer consider a move to the New York office a promotion; indeed, they demand differential pay to cover the increased cost of living. There is also the desire to get away from it all, which was one of the big reasons why Xerox moved its top men from Rochester to pastoral Connecticut: the company president felt that they would get a better perspective of the whole company from the new, more isolated locale. . . . But the biggest appeal of the suburbs, of course, is that much of the population, housing and development is there, or headed there.[29]

Problems of Metropolitan Growth

Financial Woes of Cities. The flight to the suburbs has taken the more affluent part of the population away from the inner city. The loss of industries has also reduced the central city's tax base. Not only have central cities lost jobs; they have also lost population. Of the 21 cities which had populations of 500,000 or more in 1960, 15 lost population by 1970. In addition, more than 40 per cent of the 3098 counties in the United States lost population in the decade of the 1960s. The central or inner cities and the depopulating rural areas share some common features. In the rural areas, it is the young and the better educated who move out; left behind are the elderly and others most in need of social services. As the counties lose population, they lose the tax base needed to provide social services. Similarly, affluent taxpayers have left the central city for residence in the suburbs. Left behind are the elderly, the poor, and members of minority groups. With a shrinking tax base, the central city faces difficulty in meeting the social and financial needs of its residents.

Today's urban blight, the deterioration of buildings in the central city, is in part a reflection of the flight to the suburbs. If the more affluent citizens had remained in the central cities, they undoubtedly would have expended money to renovate or to replace these structures. Urban blight is, of course,

---

[29] Robert Cassidy, "Moving to the Suburbs," *New Republic*, 166 (January 22, 1972): 21.

also a reflection of the aging of the stores, residences, and factories that were built many years ago. Inner-city residents either do not own these buildings or cannot afford extensive repairs. Nor does the local government have an adequate tax base to finance a rebuilding program.

Regional shifts in the population have also contributed to the financial woes of cities such as New York. The bicentennial year of 1976 marked the first time that the population of the South and West exceeded that of the North Central and Northeast regions. The same factors—personal preferences, energy needs, new modes of technology and transportation, and labor force availability—that led to population movement from the central city to the suburb have contributed to the regional shift in population. These same factors also influence the location of industry and of jobs.

Little concern was expressed in the East when the textile industry moved to the South because the over-all level of industrial output was maintained through growth in such industries as electronics.[30] Yet, loss of the textile industry contributed to unemployment in the Northeast region, and much of the garment district in New York City stands empty. Along with such things as a heavy burden of welfare clients and high wages for city employees in view of the cost of living, the loss of industry in New York City contributed to its financial distress in the 1970s.[31] Between 1969 and 1974 the city lost an average of 43,000 manufacturing jobs each year—12,000 in the apparel industry alone—and, hence, lost tax revenues.[32] The loss of 20,000 jobs each year in that five-year period in wholesale and retail trade and in the printing industry also led to shrinkage in the tax base. As plants in the North and East become obsolete, industries are likely to relocate, and other cities may face fiscal crises similar to that experienced by New York City.

Racial and Economic Separation. The growth of suburbs and regional migration have altered the racial composition of the population in metropolitan areas. A long-term pattern of migration has been the movement of blacks from the South to the North. However, among whites there has been a net migration in the opposite direction, from the North to the South. In this exchange of population, the migrating whites have settled in the suburbs, whereas the mobile blacks have taken up residence in central cities.

[30] William H. Miernyk, "Decline of the Northern Perimeter," *Society,* 13 (May–June 1976): 24.
[31] See Susan S. Fainstein and Norman I. Fainstein, "The Federally Inspired Fiscal Crisis," *Society,* 13 (May–June 1976): 27–32.
[32] George Sternlieb and James W. Hughes, "New York: Future Without a Future?" *Society,* 13 (May–June 1976): 21.

TAXES AND URBAN BLIGHT

In a study conducted for the Senate Subcommittee on Intergovernmental Relations in 1972, the Arthur D. Little Company found for properties in ten major cities (Atlanta, Baltimore, Chicago, Detroit, Nashville, Oklahoma City, Philadelphia, Portland (Me.), Providence, and San Francisco) the following impact of property taxes on urban blight:

1. Poor quality housing in blighted neighborhoods occupied by low income tenants is taxed at a substantially higher rate than property in other neighborhoods.

2. A great number of respondents reported that they feared property improvements would result in reassessment.

3. Inequality of tax levels among neighborhoods in the same city may contribute significantly to urban blight.

4. Reassessment as a result of rehabilitation of property *in blighted neighborhoods* is the exception rather than the rule.

5. In many cities the high level of property taxes resulting from inequitable assessment practices lessens the opportunity for transfer to more activist owner-managers who would improve property in the blighted neighborhood.

6. In downward transitional neighborhoods, the failure to reassess property downward in line with depreciating capital values undermines the ability of the owner-occupant to retain ownership.

7. Most cities avoid any reassessment of building improvements in *upward transitional neighborhoods* (except in Philadelphia), with the result that poorer neighborhoods are forced to subsidize, through their tax payments, the tax concessions granted to the improving area.

8. In stable neighborhoods the property tax does not contribute to a suburban exodus. In less affluent areas, where the rising level of the tax threatens buildings maintained out of pride of ownership and neighborhood cohesiveness, the tax can serve as an undermining influence.

William G. Colman, *Cities, Suburbs and States* (New York: The Free Press, 1975), pp. 39–40.

As shown in Table 8-5, although there was little difference in the percentage of blacks and whites in metropolitan areas in 1970, a much larger percentage of blacks than whites lived in central cities. Less than 5 per cent of the 76 million suburban residents in 1970 were blacks. In terms of racial composition, the suburbs are essentially white. However, in 1970, blacks comprised more than one half of the population in six central cities.

Table 8-5. Population Distribution and Change, Inside and Outside Metropolitan Areas, 1970

	Black		White	
	Population (in millions)	Percentage	Population (in millions)	Percentage
United States	22.7		177.6	
Metropolitan Areas	16.8	74	121.3	68
Central cities	13.1	78*	49.5	41*
Outside central cities	3.7	22*	71.8	59*
Outside Metropolitan Areas	5.8	26	56.4	32

Change, 1960–1970

	Black		White	
	Number Change (in millions)	Percentage Change	Number Change (in millions)	Percentage Change
United States	3.8	20	18.8	12
Metropolitan areas	4.1	32	14.9	14
Central cities	3.2	33	.6	−1
Outside central cities	.8	29	15.5	28
Outside metropolitan areas	−.3	−4	3.9	7

SOURCE: U.S. Bureau of the Census, "The Social and Economic Status of Negroes in the United States, 1970," *Current Population Reports,* series P-23, no. 38 (Washington, D.C.: U.S. Government Printing Office), p. 12.

*These percentages were calculated on the basis of the population residing in metropolitan areas.

The distribution of the population that has resulted from urbanization, the growth of suburbs in metropolitan areas, and regional migration has produced racial and economic separation and unequal opportunity for employment. The poor and disadvantaged are concentrated in our central cities; the more affluent and whites have moved to the suburbs. With many industries shifting to suburban locations, residents of central cities are at a distinct disadvantage in terms of job opportunities.

WHAT CAN BE DONE?

Choices About Future Growth

It is apparent that the world's population cannot continue to grow indefinitely. If it were to do so, humans would literally find themselves facing a situation in which there was "Standing Room Only." The only choices available with respect to future world population growth involve changes in the number of births and deaths.

Various goals may be sought: (1) reduction in the growth rate (not necessarily to zero); (2) stabilization of population, or zero population growth; and (3) achievement of a negative growth rate to reduce the total number of people. There currently is greater acceptance of the first goal than of the other two.[33] Recognizing that population growth interferes with economic development in underdeveloped countries, many demographers and economists accept the first goal, at least for the developing countries. Proponents of the second and third goals emphasize that the world's food supply is already too limited to meet demands. Another argument for these goals is that the world's population has reached or exceeded its optimum size. The optimum population has been defined "as the population size below which welfare per person is increased by further growth and above which welfare per person is decreased by further growth."[34] The concept of welfare may be equated with the equally elusive notion of "quality of life." Yet, at a minimum, both concepts involve provision of the physical necessities, food, clothing, shelter, clean air and water, and opportunities for employment and recreation.

The term *compulsory population control* means the regulation of population growth by society. In India, a proposal to require sterilization of males with three or more children was abandoned because of opposition on moral grounds and because the needed medical personnel were not available. Thus far, no nation has instituted coercive measures to control population growth. In the belief that additional population is essential for development, some underdeveloped countries are still encouraging population growth.

In 1970, Congress established the Commission on Population Growth and the American Future to study trends in U.S. population growth and internal migration in the next 30 years and to assess their impact. The Commis-

---

[33] Ehrlich, Ehrlich, and Holdren, op. cit., p. 225.
[34] Ibid., p. 227.

sion found "no convincing argument for continued national population growth." Further, the Commission reported, "Neither the health of our economy nor the welfare of individual businesses depend on continued population growth. In fact, the average person will be markedly better off in terms of traditional economic values if population growth slows down than if it resumes the pace of growth experienced in the recent past."[35] According to the Commission, pursuit of the goal of reduced population growth would permit the use of resources to deal with the problems of the poor, the elderly, and minorities.

Family Planning

In its first specific reference to family planning in 1966, the United Nations stated that the size of the family should be the free choice of each individual family; a few years later, this idea was extended in the declaration of the International Conference on Human Rights that couples have a right to decide freely and responsibly the number and spacing of their children.[36] Whether in poor or affluent nations, the purpose of family planning is to provide couples the opportunity to achieve the family size they desire.

Family planning is useful, but it is not a panacea. It should not be confused with compulsory population control because it permits free choice. It is not designed to achieve stabilization of population size or to reach some optimum population size. The basic assumption underlying family planning programs appears to be that the only obstacle to translating desired family size into actual family size is the availability of an effective contraceptive. This assumption is naive, because such factors as family structure, early marriage, high infant mortality rates, and the desire for a male heir promote high birth rates in underdeveloped countries. Few would disagree with the argument that no nation's growth should result from ignorance, misinformation, or lack of access to effective means to control fertility. As a result of family planning programs, contraceptive techniques are being used more extensively than before, and their use has reduced the rate of population growth in many nations.

---

[35] CPG, op. cit., p. 75.
[36] Population Reference Bureau, *World Population Growth and Response, 1965–1975* (Washington, D.C.: Population Reference Bureau, Inc., 1976), p. 21.

Birth Control

To limit the growth rate or to achieve an optimum population size, a program to control births is essential. Among sexually active women who use no contraceptive technique, 80 per cent become pregnant in a one-year period.[37] A variety of birth control methods have been used throughout history. Abortion, or termination of pregnancy, has been a common response to unwanted pregnancies in many nations. In this country, it is a controversial topic. According to a 1973 ruling of the Supreme Court, a woman has a right to a legal abortion, but strenuous opposition to abortion has been voiced. Regardless of the moral issues, legal abortions are much safer than illegal ones performed in unsanitary places by persons who lack medical skills.

From the standpoint of health, an abortion performed in a medical setting by a qualified physician is a safe procedure during the first 12 weeks of a pregnancy; in fact, it is safer than a completed pregnancy. Performed later, the risk of death or complications is considerably higher. On the basis of a survey of 208 countries, it was estimated that 55 million women terminated pregnancies in 1971 through legal or illegal abortions, a total of four abortions for every 10 babies born.[38]

For couples who have the number of children they desire, sterilization offers an effective means to avoid an unwanted pregnancy. Either partner can be sterilized, but the procedure is simpler for males than for females. Sterilization does not interfere with sexual activity. According to a national survey in 1970, 3 million men and women in this country, almost equally divided by sex, and under the age of 45, had opted for sterilization.[39]

Other than abortion or sterilization, the oral contraceptive known as the pill is the most effective means of birth control available. In studies of women using the pill, the pregnancy rate for a one-year period ranges from 0 to 3 per cent. If taken as directed, the pill is essentially 100 per cent effective. It has the additional advantage of not involving any mechanical devices. However, a woman may forget to take it every day; there also may be undesirable side effects such as the formation of blood clots.

The intrauterine device (IUD) is a plastic or metal object that is placed in the uterus. These devices are inexpensive and quite effective, with only 2 per cent of their users becoming pregnant in a one-year period. However, approx-

[37] Ehrlich, Ehrlich, and Holdren, op. cit., p. 233.
[38] Population Reference Bureau, op. cit., p. 24.
[39] CPG, op. cit., p. 100.

imately 10 per cent of all women spontaneously expel the device, at times without their knowledge.[40] Other disadvantages include such adverse side effects as pain, bleeding, and pelvic inflammation.

Studies of the effectiveness of other methods of birth control show varied results because failure of the technique and carelessness in its use are not distinguished. In terms of the percentage of women who become pregnant in a one-year period, the most effective alternatives to the pill or IUD are rhythm, 0 to 38 per cent; jelly or cream, 4 to 38 per cent; suppositories, 4 to 42 per cent; diaphragm and jelly, 4 to 35 per cent; and condoms, 7 to 28 per cent.[41] The low figures indicate these methods are quite successful, but the high figures suggest that great care must be taken if they are to be effective. With the exception of rhythm, which involves abstinence during the few days each month a woman can conceive, these are artificial approaches.

Although some states have recently changed their laws to permit minors over 15 years of age to obtain medical services in such areas as drugs, venereal disease, and birth control without parental consent, there are legal obstacles in many states that block not only young but older persons from obtaining contraceptive information and services. According to the Population Commission, all Americans, regardless of age, marital status, or income, should be helped to avoid unwanted births; only children that are wanted should be brought into the world. To implement this policy, the Commission recommended the elimination of legal restrictions on access to contraceptive information and services and the development by the states of affirmative legislation to permit all persons, including minors, to receive such information and services.[42] The importance of removing barriers to contraceptive information and services is apparent in the figures on unplanned pregnancies. Americans are reluctant to admit that young, unmarried people engage in sexual activity. Yet, in a national study it was found that 27 per cent of 15- to 19-year-old girls had had sexual relations, often without using any form of birth control.[43] In 1968, women under 20 years of age gave birth to 600,000 infants (17 per cent of all births in the United States); 27 per cent of these babies were born out of wedlock.[44]

[40] Ehrlich, Ehrlich, and Holdren, op. cit., p. 232.
[41] Ibid.
[42] CPG, op. cit., p. 99.
[43] Melvin Zelnik and John F. Kantner, "Sexuality, Contraception and Pregnancy Among Young Unwed Females in the United States," in Charles F. Westoff and Robert Parke, Jr., eds., Commission on Population Growth and the American Future, Research Reports, vol. I, *Demographic and Social Aspects of Population Growth* (Washington, D.C.: U.S. Government Printing Office, 1972), pp. 355–374.
[44] CPG, op. cit., p. 88.

There are also many unplanned pregnancies and unwanted births among married couples. According to a national fertility study, 44 per cent of all births to married women between 1966 and 1970 were unplanned, and the parents reported that 15 per cent of the births were not wanted.[45] Rarely (1 percent) were first children not wanted, whereas two thirds of the sixth or later children were unwanted. It was also discovered that unwanted births occurred most frequently among women with limited education and income.

Factors Affecting the Birth Rate

Interest in establishing family planning programs in the underdeveloped countries in the 1960s led to a number of surveys on the subjects of fertility, birth control, and desired family size. Approximately one half of the surveys showed desired family size was less than four; the others revealed the ideal family size was between four and six.[46] Most of those who preferred smaller-size families lived in large urban centers. Comparable surveys in developed countries show that people want small (two or three children) families. Some demographers argue that family planning alone will not lower the birth rate substantially or lead to stabilization of the population in underdeveloped countries.[47]

The birth rate is not simply a reflection of preferences for small or large families. Because death rates, particularly among young children, are relatively high in many underdeveloped countries, use of birth control involves a risk of childlessness. Many of these countries are patrilineal, and it is considered a tragedy not to have a son to carry on the family name. According to the death rates in 1960, it was estimated that a couple in India had to have 6.3 children to be relatively certain one son would survive to adulthood.[48]

Reductions in death rates in underdeveloped countries have been achieved as a result of Western medical techniques and public health measures, such as DDT spraying, antibiotics, and vaccinations. These measures are imported and put into effect by local governments, but they have not al-

[45] Ibid., p. 97; see Norman B. Ryder and Charles F. Westoff, *Reproduction in the United States: 1965* (Princeton, N.J.: Princeton University Press, 1971).

[46] Bernard Berelson, "KAP Studies on Fertility," in Bernard Berelson et al., *Family Planning and Population Programs* (Chicago: University of Chicago Press, 1966), pp. 655–668; Valerie K. Oppenheimer, *Population* (New York: Foreign Policy Association, Inc., 1971), pp. 44–45. (KAP refers to knowledge, attitudes, and practices.)

[47] Oppenheimer, op. cit., p. 46.

[48] Ibid., p. 42.

tered the people's way of life. The populations have grown rapidly, but there has not been a general improvement in the economic and physical well-being of the people.

Valerie Oppenheimer observes that family patterns encouraging early marriage lead to large families because women are exposed to the risk of pregnancy for a maximum number of years.[49] The lack of socially approved roles for women other than motherhood in many underdeveloped countries means that nearly all women contribute to the birth rate.

Preference for a particular family size and access to birth control techniques are important factors influencing the birth rate, but so also are educational levels of the population, the degree of urbanization, opportunities for employment of women outside the home, age at marriage, and motivation to use contraceptive methods.

Whether a reduced growth rate or stabilization of the population at a particular size is the goal selected, the key to its attainment lies in people's attitudes. Not even compulsory population control measures would succeed unless the importance of limiting human numbers was accepted. Both educational programs and economic incentives have been proposed to change attitudes toward family size and to motivate people to use birth control methods. For example, tax incentives could be provided for delaying marriage until the age of 25 or for having a small family.[50]

Metropolitan Growth

Metropolitan Government. Most metropolitan areas in the United States are governed by a multiplicity of political units. The legal boundaries of most central cities have not been altered since the turn of the century; suburban residents, desiring local autonomy, have opposed annexation by the city. This has an important implication because decisions regarding such matters as the location of highways, housing, and industry have an impact on all of the residents of a metropolitan area. When jurisdiction over the functional or real city is divided among numerous units of local government, as it is today, the individual units cannot cope with problems that extend beyond their jurisdictions. Urban sprawl, the haphazard development of metropolitan areas, has

[49] Ibid., p. 48.
[50] Kingsley Davis, "Population Policy: Will Current Programs Succeed?" *Science*, 158 (November 10, 1967): 730–739.

occurred in part because planning for metropolitan development has been impeded by the diversity of governmental units in such areas.

More attention must be devoted to the problems arising from concentration of the population in metropolitan areas. One solution to fragmented political structures involves the merger of local governmental units into a metropolitan government. This approach would reduce inequities in the distribution of public services and provide a more adequate tax base to meet the needs of inner city residents. Metropolitan governments have been established in Miami, Florida; Lexington, Kentucky; Nashville, Tennessee; and Toronto, Canada. Even though these mergers have been quite successful, there has been no great movement toward this concept. Whites residing in suburbs fear loss of control over the schools as well as the prospect of higher taxes, and blacks fear the loss of political power that they have recently gained in central cities.

An alternative approach that might overcome such fears would be to create two levels of government. The metropolitan level would be responsible for services required throughout the area: waste disposal, water and sewer systems, hospitals, museums, streets, fire department, and control of air and water pollution. At the second level, the metropolitan area would be divided into smaller units, and local concerns—education, housing codes, and recreational facilities—would be controlled by the local community. The police force might well be under the control of the local level of government, but a metropolitan communications system would be needed. Dissatisfaction with the present system of fragmented governmental units has not as yet reached a sufficiently high level to create pressure for change.

Planning. Effective and comprehensive planning is also needed. Planning to guide urban growth should be done at the metropolitan level because the different aspects of a metropolitan area are interdependent. "The transportation system influences land-use patterns, which in turn influence housing patterns, which in turn influence transportation patterns, and so forth. The system of financing public services influences the quality of education which influences where people seek to live."[51]

One of the goals of metropolitan planning would be to prevent further urban sprawl. With metropolitan planning and strict zoning laws, development of an area for residential purposes would not be permitted unless it was accompanied by plans for the financing and construction of other services,

[51] CPG, op. cit., p. 121.

SUCCESS IN TORONTO

People the world over visit Toronto, Ontario, to see and learn about the Metro Plan. During the same period that U.S. cities divided into almost ungovernable central cities and not-too-happy suburbs, the city of Toronto took an opposite direction. Combining with the five surrounding boroughs, it created the 240-square-mile Metropolitan Toronto.

The example of Toronto could not be more timely. At present 67 percent of all Americans live in metropolitan counties; by the year 2000, it is estimated that this will increase to 75 percent. Yet even this is not the whole picture. Some urbanologists believe that the history of the United States will be written largely by six mega-metropolitan areas: Boston, New York, Washington, Chicago, Los Angeles and San Francisco.

The central purpose and achievement of the Toronto Metropolitan Plan is to combine opportunity for individuality in local communities with the economy and efficiency of federation.

The Municipality of Metropolitan Canada has major accomplishments to its credit: Reduction of automobile need by efficient public transportation; solution of water and sewage problems; a centralized and more effective police force; a saving of $50 million in interest and reduction of sprawl by better control of land use.

Toronto achievements represent no less than a major breakthrough in governmental structure. Modified to suit the needs of individual areas and taking into consideration different lifestyles, personal tastes, as well as economic and geographical constraints, the Toronto Metro experience is proving highly beneficial as a guide to metropolitan reform in the United States.

Leon Sager, "UNIGOV—Piercing Together City Government," *Current* (November 1970), p. 20.

including sewage treatment, schools, recreational facilities, and other essential community services.

New Towns. The establishment of entirely new towns or cities on previously unoccupied land is another alternative. Some planned communities have been built in the Scandinavian countries, and in the early 1970s, the United States Department of Housing and Urban Development provided funds to help develop 14 new towns, which, when completed in 10 to 30 years, would have some 240,000 dwelling units and a projected population of approximately 800,000 persons. However, it is unlikely that such planned communities will house more than a fraction of the population in the near future.

Urban Renewal and Housing Dispersal. In many cities, slums have been cleared in urban renewal projects, but often the area has been used to provide for expansion of hospitals and universities and to construct apartment houses and office buildings. Apartments and office buildings were emphasized because they expanded the tax base of the city. Less attention has been devoted to construction of low-cost housing in the central city. Consequently, the effect of urban renewal has often been the creation of new slums, as people displaced by clearance projects crowd into other sections of the city.

Housing dispersal has been proposed as one solution to the problem of residential segregation. This involves placement of a limited number of units of moderate- and low-income housing throughout a metropolitan area, including the surrounding suburbs. Federal funds have been used to implement this approach, and some single-family dwelling units were constructed on vacant lots in cities and suburbs in the past decade. However, in 1977, the Supreme Court ruled that a suburban community did not have to alter its zoning laws to provide housing for low-income families. This ruling limits the effectiveness of housing dispersal.

Revitalizing Cities. Another way to cope with urban blight and the shortage of adequate housing is through revitalizing existing structures. Until recently, FHA regulations encouraged purchasers to invest in new homes. This policy was altered in the late 1960s, but thus far relatively few FHA loans have been made for rehabilitation of older inner-city dwellings. The federal government needs to take steps to translate into reality its housing policy, formulated in 1949. The aims of that policy are as follows:

1. Eliminate substandard and other inadequate housing through clearance of slums and blighted areas.
2. Stimulate housing production and community development sufficient to remedy the housing shortage.
3. Realize the goal of a decent home and a suitable living environment for every American family.[52]

Mass Transit Systems. In addition to revitalizing our cities, the imbalance between transportation by automobiles and by mass transit systems must be

[52] Martin Anderson, *The Federal Bulldozer* (Cambridge, Mass.: MIT Press, 1964), p. 4, as cited in Palen, op. cit., p. 241.

corrected. Suburban commuters clog the expressways and narrow city streets originally designed for streetcars, not automobiles and trucks. Fewer city dwellers than suburban residents own cars. Many of them find that mass transportation to suburbs, where jobs may be available in industrial parks, is nonexistent. The transportation problem reflects an imbalance between reliance on cars and mass transportation systems. At present, we have too many cars and not enough public transportation. Since 1950 the federal government has spent billions of dollars on interstate highway construction. The federal government paid 90 per cent of the construction costs, in effect, subsidizing users of autos and the trucking industry. Development of highways encouraged use of the auto and discouraged use of public transportation. The number of public transit systems in operation and the number of passengers using public transportation have declined sharply in recent decades.

Because higher costs for highway usage can substantially reduce demand, a simple economic approach to discourage reliance on the auto for transportation, particularly during peak periods, would involve toll charges. Additional taxes on gasoline would also discourage automobile use. Car pools and ''Park and Ride'' bus systems, in which commuters drive to a suburban location and take an express bus to the city, are other possibilities that would help to relieve highway congestion.

However, the only long-term solution to the problem of urban transportation involves expansion of public transportation systems. The Mass Transportation Act of 1968 has encouraged the development of such systems. The bill authorized the expenditure of $10 billion in grants between 1971 and 1982. The grants would cover two thirds of the cost of development and construction. Unfortunately, Congress did not provide automatic funding for the bill. Nevertheless, mass transit systems are under development in a number of cities.

The effects of the contemporary population explosion and the prospects for future growth have led many observers to adopt pessimistic views. The conclusion is inescapable that population growth cannot continue without difficult, if not catastrophic results. At best, the planet will become overcrowded, but mass starvation is also likely. The proposed solutions to the problems resulting from population growth and changes in the distribution of population require that citizens make a number of difficult decisions. Fortunately, human beings possess the ability to choose the course of action they wish to pursue. Rapid population growth contributes to the environmental crisis involving depletion of natural resources, pollution, hunger, and starvation. Thus, the problem of population growth is intertwined with the environmental crisis, and unless population growth is restricted, efforts to preserve the environment for future generations will be of little or no avail.

Additional Readings

Kenneth J. Arrow, James G. March, James S. Coleman, and Anthony Downs. *Urban Processes as Viewed by the Social Sciences*. Washington, D.C.: The Urban Institute, 1973.

Birnbaum, Max, and John Mogey. *Social Change in Urban America*. New York: Harper & Row, Publishers, 1972.

Bogue, Donald J. *Principles of Demography*. New York: John Wiley & Sons, Inc., 1969.

Borgstrom, Georg. *Too Many: A Study of Earth's Biological Limitations*. London: Macmillan & Company Ltd., 1969.

Borrie, W. D. *Population, Environment, and Society*. Auckland, New Zealand: Auckland University Press, 1973.

Elias, C. E., Jr., James Gillies, and Svend Riemer. *Metropolis: Values in Conflict*. Belmont, Calif.: Wadsworth Publishing Co., Inc., 1964.

Foreign Policy Association. *How Many People?* New York: Foreign Policy Association, Inc., 1973.

Freedman, Ronald, ed. *Population: The Vital Revolution*. Garden City, N.Y.: Doubleday & Company, Inc., 1964.

Hadden, Jeffrey K., Louis H. Masotti, and Calvin J. Larson, eds. *Metropolis in Crisis: Social and Political Perspectives*. Itasca, Ill.: F. E. Peacock Publishers, Inc., 1967.

Hardin, Garrett, ed. *Population, Evolution, and Birth Control: A Collage of Controversial Ideas*. 2nd ed. San Francisco: W. H. Freeman and Company, Publishers, 1969.

Hodge, Patricia L., and Philip M. Hauser. *The Challenge of America's Metropolitan Population Outlook, 1960 to 1985*. New York: Praeger Publishers, Inc., 1968.

Kahn, E. J., Jr. *The American People: The Findings of the 1970 Census*. New York: Weybright and Talley, 1974.

Loewenstein, Louis K., ed. *Urban Studies: An Introductory Reader*. 2nd ed. New York: The Free Press, 1977.

Milgram, Stanley. "The Experience of Living in Cities." *Science,* 167 (March 13, 1970).

Rodwin, Lloyd. *Nations and Cities: A Comparison of Strategies for Urban Growth*. Boston: Houghton Mifflin Company, 1970.

Stein, Maurice R. *The Eclipse of Community: An Interpretation of American Studies*. Princeton, N.J.: Princeton University Press, 1960.

Walton, John, and Donald E. Carns. *Cities in Change: Studies on the Urban Condition*. Boston: Allyn & Bacon, Inc., 1973.

Westoff, Charles F., and Norman B. Ryder. *The Contraceptive Revolution*. Princeton, N.J.: Princeton University Press, 1977.

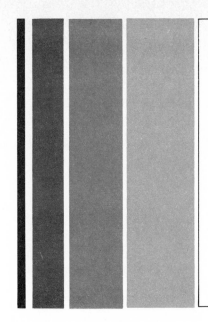

the environmental crisis

The natural environment of America—the woods and waters and wildlife, the clear air and blue sky, the fertile soil and the scenic landscape—is threatened with destruction. Our growing population and expanding industries, the explosion of scientific knowledge, the vast increase in income levels, leisure time, and mobility—all of these powerful trends are exerting such pressure on our natural resources that many of them could be effectively ruined over the next ten or fifteen years.

Our overcrowded parks are becoming slums. Our birds and wildlife are being driven away or killed outright. Scenic rural areas are blighted by junkyards and billboards, and neon blight soils the outskirts of most cities. In our orgy of expansion, we are bulldozing away the natural landscape and building a cold new world of concrete and aluminum. Strip miners' shovels are tearing away whole mountains and spreading ugly wastes for miles around. America the affluent is well on the way to destroying America the beautiful.[1]

Gaylord Nelson, a Senator from Wisconsin, identifies a number of dimensions of the environmental crisis and some of the trends that have produced environmental problems. Ecologists, who study man's relation to the environment, have voiced the opinion that environmental deterioration in the form of pollution and depletion of natural resources cannot continue indefinitely with-

[1] Gaylord Nelson, "The National Pollution Scandal," *The Progressive*, 31, no. 2 (February 1967): 12.

out disastrous results, such as the "death" of the oceans, energy shortages, mass starvation, epidemics, or political unrest. Yet, for most people, growth and development reflect progress; a major goal of most nations is economic development. The conventional indicator of such development is the Gross National Product (GNP), or the total revenues obtained from the sale of goods and services. However, it is important to understand what the GNP is not:

> It is not a measure of the degree of freedom or health of a nation's people, nor of the equity of its distribution of goods and resources. It is not a measure of the state of depletion of natural resources nor of the stability of the environmental systems upon which life depends. It is not a measure of security from the threat of war. It is not, in sum, a comprehensive measure of the quality of life, although it is often misused as such a measure.[2]

Kenneth Boulding characterizes the economic system in the United States as a *cowboy economy* to reflect our reckless, exploitative approach to the environment.[3] Such an economy is based on the premises that resources are abundant and that the atmosphere and waterways have an unlimited capacity to absorb wastes.

High levels of production and consumption are the definitive characteristics of affluent, developed countries. The application of technology to agriculture and particularly to industry to produce such high levels of affluence has created such problems as air and water pollution and the need to dispose of large quantities of garbage. That we are using—but not reusing or recycling—the earth's mineral resources is reflected in our garbage cans. In 1920, the average urban resident produced 2.75 pounds of refuse a day; in 1974, this figure had increased to 5.3 pounds.[4] If this trend continues, by 1980 each person will produce some 7.5 to 8 pounds of garbage a day and as much as 10 pounds per day in the year 2000.

Whereas hunger and dietary deficiencies are critical problems for many residents of poor nations, the environmental crisis is, in part, a consequence

---

[2] Paul R. Ehrlich, Anne H. Ehrlich, and John P. Holdren, *Human Ecology: Problems and Solutions* (San Francisco: W. H. Freeman and Company, Publishers, 1973), p. 260.

[3] Kenneth E. Boulding, "The Economics of the Coming Spaceship Earth," in Henry Jarrett, ed., *Environmental Quality in a Growing Economy* (Baltimore: The Johns Hopkins University Press, 1966), pp. 3–14.

[4] Grahame J. C. Smith, Henry J. Steck, and Gerald Surette, *Our Ecological Crisis: Its Biological, Economic, & Political Dimensions* (New York: Macmillan Publishing Co., Inc., 1974), p. 39; Joseph Spengler, *Population Change, Modernization, and Welfare* (Englewood Cliffs, N.J.: Prentice-Hall, Inc., 1974), p. 87.

A GROWING GARBAGE PILE

Americans now generate some 150 million tons of household garbage each year—and it's increasing at an alarming rate.

With the banning of open-burning dumps, most municipal wastes end up on the land. There are presently some 18,500 known land disposal sites in the U.S., but fewer than 6,000 of them meet even minimal state standards for disposal of garbage on the land.

"Almost half of our cities estimate that they will run out of known and available municipal waste disposal sites within a few years," points out Thomas F. Williams of the EPA's Office of Solid Waste. . . .

Obviously, both waste recycling and waste reduction efforts must be intensified. "Even if we double our present projections of resource recovery plants by 1985," adds EPA's Williams, "we would still have over 70 percent—or 145 million tons annually—of the municipal solid waste stream unrecovered."

Source: National Wildlife's Annual Environmental Quality Index, *National Wildlife* (Feb./March 1977): 31.

of the high levels of consumption of food, mineral resources, and energy in the affluent countries. In terms of the amount of energy consumed by appliances and machines, each American "owns" the equivalent of 400 slaves, who do what slaves traditionally did—cook food, transport people, produce clothes and other objects, play music, and remove garbage.[5]

Until recently, most Americans had only a limited awareness of their dependence on the natural environment. To a considerable extent this was due to the fact that we were no longer a nation of farmers; instead, we purchased our food in grocery stores or restaurants and had electric power and water readily available in our houses or apartments. Residences in this country were heated—and cooled—by means of electricity, oil, or natural gas. To many citizens, then, the "war against nature" apparently had been fought and won. There has been widespread failure to recognize that regardless of their size, the level of their technology, or the complexity of their social organization, all societies are ultimately dependent upon other animals and plant species, as well as upon air, water, and proper temperature. It was not until the 1973 oil embargo, gasoline shortages, and increased prices that many Americans became aware of our dependence on energy. The closing of

[5] Barbara Ward and René Dubos, *Only One Earth: The Care and Maintenance of a Small Planet* (New York: W. W. Norton & Company, Inc., 1972), p. 10.

businesses, industries, and schools in much of the country as a result of fuel shortages during the winter of 1977 proved that natural resources were not inexhaustible.

Other environmental problems have been brought to the attention of the American people. In *Silent Spring,* Rachel Carson informed the public of the adverse effects of widespread use of the chlorinated hydrocarbon pesticides, such as DDT.[6] The mass media have publicized accounts of the pollution of rivers and lakes, resulting in death of marine life, and warnings have been issued regarding the dangers to the health of humans stemming from radiation and from industrial chemicals. Accounts of specific incidents, such as the death of wildlife following an oil spill in California and the dangerously high levels of mercury discovered in tuna, have been widely circulated.

Such reports have not, as yet, dispelled the view that science and technology will ultimately solve such environmental problems. It is perhaps not surprising that many citizens of a country whose science and technology succeeded in sending men to the moon have confidence that a "technological fix" is possible. Those who are optimistic about technological solutions speak of further increases in agricultural production, of a larger water supply produced by removing salt from sea water, or of an abundance of inexpensive energy derived from nuclear power plants. Yet, it is essential to recognize that the environmental crisis is real. It cannot be attributed to any single cause; rather, it is the result of mankind's far-reaching impact on the earth.

BASIC ECOLOGICAL CONCEPTS

In the words of the President's Council on Environmental Quality, ecology is "the science of the intricate web of relationships between living organisms and their living and nonliving surroundings."[7] The word *ecology* is derived from the Greek *oikos,* meaning house, home, or place to live in. The development of the field of ecology may be traced to the writings of Charles Darwin, particularly his *Origin of Species* and *Descent of Man.*[8] Describing his general conception metaphorically as the "web of life," Darwin per-

[6] Rachel Carson, *Silent Spring* (Boston: Houghton Mifflin Company, 1962).

[7] Council on Environmental Quality (CEQ), *Environmental Quality* (Washington, D.C.: U.S. Government Printing Office, 1970), p. 6.

[8] Charles Darwin, *On the Origin of Species by Means of Natural Selection* (London: John Murray, 1859); Charles Darwin, *The Descent of Man, and Selection in Relation to Sex* (New York: D. Appleton & Co., 1871).

ceived all life as a dynamic system of highly complex relations in which not only the physical environment but also every organism and species were involved.

Population, Community, Ecosystem, and Ecosphere

Ecologists have continued to study the "web of life," but they have introduced four new terms: population, community, ecosystem, and ecosphere. The term *population* refers to all members of the same species of organism in a specified area. The various plant and animal species found in a given area make up a *community*. A community, along with the physical environment, is known as an ecological system, or an *ecosystem*. The ecosystems of the different parts of the world are linked together by the movement of air and water into a global ecosystem, or *ecosphere*.

Interdependence

What all these terms suggest is that mutual dependence is a fundamental characteristic of an ecosystem. The first law of ecology is that everything is related to everything else.[9] The second law of ecology is that nature knows best. The changes human beings make in ecological systems may be beneficial in some ways but may have other unanticipated and undesirable effects. Such is the case because the parts of an ecosystem are linked together in complex patterns that are not always apparent. The third law of ecology is that everything must go somewhere; there is no waste in an ecosystem that is untouched by human activity. Plants and animals are dependent on each other's activities. In nature, there are no wastes comparable to human garbage; one organism's waste products are another's food. The fourth and final law of ecology is that there is no such thing as a free lunch. According to Barry Commoner, we may in the short run obtain an advantage or a gain, but in the process a debt is incurred: "Because the global ecosystem is a connected whole, in which nothing can be gained or lost and which is not subject to over-all improvement, anything extracted from it by human effort must be replaced. Payment of this price cannot be avoided; it can only be delayed."[10]

[9] This and the following laws of ecology were formulated in Barry Commoner, *The Closing Circle: Nature, Man, and Technology* (New York: Alfred A. Knopf, Inc., 1971), pp. 33–46.
[10] Ibid., p. 46.

Balance of Nature

There is a continual turnover of individuals within an ecosystem, but deaths are balanced by births, and over time the system reaches a steady state or equilibrium. A number of mechanisms operate to keep the system in balance; that is, an increase in one component results in compensation by another component to restore the balance. For example, if conditions changed somewhat so that the population of plants increased, the population of herbivores, or plant consumers, would increase. This would lead to a decline in the plant population and eventually to a decline in the number of herbivores. Similarly, if an insect attacked soft or delicate tree leaves, the process of natural selection would favor the survival of trees having thicker leaves or those containing a chemical that served as an insect repellant.

Limits

There are limits to the range of environmental conditions that a particular species can tolerate. In general, plants require certain inorganic nutrients, including water and carbon dioxide, and the energy of sunlight to carry out the process of photosynthesis. However, plant species differ in their tolerance for variations in temperature, in sunlight, in water, and in various nutrients in the soil. Whereas some species have a narrow tolerance for one or more of these aspects of the environment, others can survive under a wide range of conditions. There are also limits to the quantities of resources available in a particular ecosystem or in the ecosphere. Mankind has recognized for many years that there is only so much land available on earth. Yet, recognition of the limited mineral resources, particularly in the form of fossil fuels (oil, natural gas, and coal) in the earth has been relatively recent.

Carrying Capacity

Closely related to the idea of limits on the earth's resources is the idea of the carrying capacity of the environment. Ecologists use the term *carrying capacity* "to describe the population size of a particular species that can be permanently maintained in an area. A population of this size would not deplete the resources available to the next generation."[11] In addition to the activities of a

[11] Smith, Steck, and Surette, op. cit., p. 36.

Rapid human population growth threatens to exceed the limits and the carrying capacity of the environment. (Courtesy of E.P.A.)

species' natural enemies, the availability of food serves to limit population size. It is not, however, the sole factor in population control. Also important are the availability of suitable breeding sites and territoriality. Among many kinds of animals—fishes, birds, lizards, and mammals—it has been found that a pair or a social group inhabiting a particular area will defend it against the intrusion of other members of the same species. Thus, territoriality serves to space the members of a particular species with the effect that the population size remains below the limit imposed by the availability of food supplies.[12]

Pollution

In efforts to increase agricultural and industrial production, human beings have introduced a wide variety of substances into the natural environment.

[12] Robert Ardrey, "Control of Population," in Michael E. Adelstein and Jean G. Pival, eds., *Ecocide and Population* (New York: St. Martin's Press, Inc., 1972), pp. 13–26.

John Holdren classifies these substances as *qualitative* pollutants, or the synthetic substances produced and released only by mankind, and *quantitative* pollutants, or substances that are present in nature but are released into the environment in significantly greater amounts by human activities.[13]

Among the better known qualitative pollutants are the pesticides such as DDT, the industrial chemicals called PCBs, and some herbicides. An important characteristic of these substances is that they are not biodegradable; that is, the bacteria and fungi that decompose dead plant and animal matter cannot break them up and thereby release the minerals they contain for reuse. Carbon dioxide is an example of a quantitative pollutant; the amount of carbon dioxide in the atmosphere has been increased by the burning of fossil fuels, as in the combustion of gasoline in car engines.

Pollution is a difficult concept because often a substance that is a pollutant in one situation may constitute a useful resource in another setting. Animal biological waste becomes a useful resource when applied as a fertilizer, but its accumulation in a body of water in the form of sewage constitutes a form of pollution. A pollutant, then, may be described as "a resource that is out of place in a particular environment in that it destroys some aspect of an otherwise stable ecosystem."[14] The accumulation of pollutants in an ecosystem may alter conditions sufficiently that the tolerance limits of some species are exceeded, and they will be unable to survive. Nature has the capacity to absorb limited amounts of quantitative pollutants but cannot handle an unlimited quantity, nor can it dispose of qualitative pollutants that are not biodegradable.

To understand pollution, two of the laws of ecology deserve repetition: (1) there is no waste in an ecosystem untouched by human activity, and (2) the global environment is a connected whole in which nothing can be gained or lost. The latter point has been expressed as follows:

> Gross National Production equals Gross National Pollution. Economists and ecologists argue that for every pound of resources going into the GNP, a pound must come out in some form of waste, either as junk metal such as tin cans and cars, waste paper from packaging, chemical pollutants such as those that abound in our air and water, or human waste.[15]

[13] John P. Holdren, "Man as a Global Ecological Force," in Harrison Brown, John P. Holdren, Alan Sweezy, and Barbara West, eds., *Population: Perspective 1973* (San Francisco: Freeman, Cooper & Co., 1973), p. 28.

[14] Smith, Steck, and Surette, op. cit., p. 33.

[15] J. Holton Wilson and Cathy R. Wilson, *Economics in American Society: An Introduction to Economic Issues* (Beverly Hills, Calif.: Glencoe Press, 1977), p. 162.

In the broadest sense, pollution is a matter of waste products resulting from human activity.

Because of the interdependence of ecosystems and of the ecosphere, pollutants that initially enter either the air, the water, or the soil are likely to reappear in the other two. For example, pesticides and fertilizers are applied to the soil, but with water runoff, they enter lakes and rivers, and eventually the ocean. Similarly, the radioactive particles released by the explosion of a nuclear device in the atmosphere reach the land and oceans in rain or snow.

The popular assumption that the land, air, and water have a tremendous capacity to absorb pollutants has often been stated in the expression, "The solution to pollution is dilution." It is true that, with complete mixing, in a laboratory, the addition of two gallons of a toxic substance to one million gallons of water produces a concentration of only two parts per million (ppm), but in nature such complete mixing or dilution rarely occurs. Rather, food chains act as amplifiers and lead to increasing concentrations of toxic substances—DDT, copper, mercury, and radioactive material—as one moves up a food chain. Such substances as DDT are not readily metabolized or converted into energy. With consumption of large quantities of organisms lower in a food chain, the nonmetabolized substances present in the lower organisms become concentrated in the fat cells of the higher-level consumers. Relatively little of the nonmetabolized substance is lost at each step along a food chain; the result is increasing concentration of this substance at each successive level. For example, oysters obtain food by filtering the water in which they live; this happens to be in the shallow water along the shore where the water is most likely to be polluted. Oysters have been found with concentrations of chlorinated hydrocarbons, or the residue of DDT, 70,000 times higher than in their environment.[16] The storage of a toxic substance may not interfere with the existence of an organism at a lower level in a food chain, but when these organisms are ingested by higher-level consumers and concentration is again increased, the result may be harmful or even fatal. Given mankind's position at the top of several food chains, the process of concentration is important.

THE NATURE OF THE ENVIRONMENTAL CRISIS

Scientists had been commenting for years about the depletion of supplies of fossil fuels and other mineral resources, but not until November 9, 1965,

[16] Ehrlich, Ehrlich, and Holdren, op. cit., p. 166; see Paul R. Ehrlich, John P. Holdren, and Richard W. Holm, eds., *Man and the Ecosphere* (San Francisco: W. H. Freeman and Company, Publishers, 1971).

were their warnings dramatized for many Americans.[17] On that date the northeastern part of the United States experienced a blackout as a result of a massive electric power shortage. In other parts of the country, similar but less dramatic experiences were to occur in the summer months, as electricity shortages led to so-called brownouts. These shortages of electricity reflect the inadequate expansion of power plants to meet the needs of a growing population. One dimension, then, of the current environmental crisis involves energy. This problem is a double-barreled one. First, it involves the supply of fossil fuels and the depletion of the limited stores of mineral resources in the world. Second, it involves the rising cost of this type of energy.

Population growth has produced another aspect of the environmental crisis: continuing increases in demands for food. Although the oceans provide a part of the food supply for mankind, land suitable for conventional agriculture is the primary resource for producing food. A suitable climate, appropriate soil composition, and an adequate supply of water, either through rainfall or irrigation, are required to grow crops. The land area of the earth covers approximately 60 million square miles, but less than one third of this land is arable or potentially suited for agriculture. The carrying capacity of the world, in terms of its ability to produce food, is limited by the supply of arable land. To determine the absolute carrying capacity of the earth, or the number of people it can support, one must first decide whether to calculate the number that can be kept alive at subsistence levels or the number that can receive adequate diets. According to the latter criterion, food production is currently insufficient for the world's population. Greater use of mechanical equipment, fertilizer, and pesticides following World War II and the so-called green revolution have increased food production. These developments helped the food supply to keep pace with population growth, and increased agricultural production resulting from the green revolution may meet minimal needs in the underdeveloped countries in the next 15 to 20 years. However, it is questionable whether continued increases in the food supply can be achieved to meet the needs of a growing world population to avert famine and starvation.

The other major dimension of the environmental crisis does not involve shortages, but rather an abundant supply of substances in places where they are not wanted. This, of course, is the problem of pollution. Population growth and rising levels of affluence, reflected in the doubling of the GNP in

[17] Richard Saltonstall, Jr., and James K. Page, Jr., *Brown-Out & Slow-Down* (New York: Walker and Co., 1972).

the 25 years after the end of World War II played their part. Suburban growth contributed to the increased number of miles automobiles were driven and, hence, to the amount of air pollution. Many experts attribute much of the problem of pollution to changes in technological processes. Commoner notes that while developments in physics led to atomic power and advances in chemistry produced pesticides such as DDT, modern technology ignored the biology of the environment.[18]

Technological developments have, of course, increased the range of material goods enjoyed in this affluent country, but they have also drastically changed the kinds of goods produced. More attention has been devoted to the convenience of consumer goods than to their durability, and many of the new products, such as synthetic fibers, plastics, and pesticides, are not biodegradable. The idea that mineral resources are abundant has produced a throwaway mentality, and the result is an accumulation of vast quantities of waste products that threaten the natural environment.

DEPLETION OF RESOURCES

The use of fossil fuels as energy sources played a key role in the industrial revolution. Since that time, industrial development, and the accompanying rise in the material prosperity of the developed nations, has been based on the use of such energy.

Demand and Supply

World-wide energy consumption has more than doubled since the end of World War II. If current trends continue, energy consumption will be three times higher in the year 2000 than it is now. Since World War II the number of cars, buses, and trucks in use in the United States has tripled. We have also built bigger houses, and stores have increased both in number and average size. As part of our economic expansion, industrial use of energy has also increased. In 1972, demand for energy in the United States was distributed as follows: industrial users, 28.5 per cent; transportation, 25.4 per cent;

---

[18] Commoner, op. cit., p. 133; see Asa Briggs, "Technology and Economic Development," in Gene I. Rochlin, comp., *Scientific Technology and Social Change* (San Francisco: W. H. Freeman and Company, Publishers, 1974), pp. 90–99.

residential and commercial users, 20.4 per cent; and electricity generating utilities, 25.7 per cent.[19]

Today, reliance is placed almost exclusively on the combustion of fossil fuels for energy. Figures for 1975 show that fossil fuels produced 92 per cent of the energy consumed in the United States; hydroelectric and nuclear sources produced the other 8 per cent.[20] Petroleum supplied almost 44 per cent of the energy, and around one third of the petroleum supply was imported. Natural gas supplied about one third of the energy, with coal accounting for the remainder.

Energy Reserves and Resources

While the existing supplies of fossil fuels are extensive, a considerable portion are of low quality or are so inaccessible that their extraction is not economically feasible on the basis of current technology. In technical terms, our energy *reserves,* or the supplies recoverable with existing technology and at current prices, are limited. However, our *resources,* the quantities available but not recoverable because of high costs or limited technology, are much more extensive.

High-quality fossil fuels are in short supply. Coal reserves are estimated at 5 trillion tons. M. King Hubbert of the United States Geological Survey has calculated that this supply would last three centuries at the present rate of consumption, but if coal becomes the major source of energy, it will last only 150 years.[21] Usable reserves of high-quality petroleum, including the deposits recently discovered in Alaska, total some 2,500 billion barrels. If present levels of oil consumption continue, this seemingly large supply will be substantially depleted within this century. New supplies may be discovered, or a means of processing low-grade oil that is both technologically and economically feasible may be developed, but the basic point remains: Sources of energy are finite.

[19] Wilson and Wilson, op. cit., p. 171; see Earl Cook, ''The Flow of Energy in an Industrial Society,'' in Rochlin, op. cit., pp. 273–282; Joel Darmstadter, ''Energy,'' in Ronald G. Ridker, ed., Commission on Population Growth and the American Future, Research Reports, vol. III, *Population, Resources, and Environment* (Washington, D.C.: U.S. Government Printing Office, 1972), pp. 103–150.

[20] Wilson and Wilson, op. cit.; see Philip H. Abelson and Allan L. Hammond, eds., *Materials: Renewable and Nonrenewable Resources* (Washington, D.C.: American Association for the Advancement of Science, 1976).

[21] M. King Hubbert, ''Energy Resources,'' in Preston Cloud, ed., *Resources and Man* (San Francisco: W. H. Freeman and Company, Publishers, 1969), pp. 201–205.

Costs

The energy crisis is not simply a matter of limited reserves; another important aspect involves the rising cost of energy. Three factors will lead to continuing increases in energy prices worldwide—higher extraction costs, environmental concerns, and the demands of the oil-producing nations. As supplies of high-quality fossil fuels are exhausted, reliance must be placed on fuels of lower quality or on resources that are relatively inaccessible. Their extraction will entail higher costs, which will result in higher prices. The installation of pollution control devices at petroleum processing plants and electricity generating stations, as well as requirements that strip mined land be reclaimed, will also increase prices. Finally, the role of the Middle East in escalating energy costs cannot be overlooked. The oil-producing nations in the Middle East recently initiated a series of price increases for crude petroleum that were artificial in that they were not solely a consequence of increased production costs.

World oil prices increased from $2.59 to $11.65 per barrel from January 1, 1973, to January 1, 1974, and the effect was disruption of the economies of nations throughout the world. In this country rising energy prices led to unemployment, particularly in the auto industry, when consumers avoided large cars. "The effects of high oil prices rippled through the economy, eventually producing price rises in the coal industry, electric utilities, natural gas, raw materials, plastics, and synthetics. All of these contributed to inflation in the economy."[22] In the less developed countries, increased oil prices interfered with economic development, since these countries, like the developed countries, depended on cheap energy for expansion of their industrial output.[23]

Other Mineral Resources

Considerable attention has been devoted to shortages of fossil fuels and rising energy prices, but we face similar shortages of other mineral resources. According to the Council on Environmental Quality:

[22] Wilson and Wilson, op. cit., pp. 177–178.
[23] Ronald G. Ridker, ed., *Changing Resource Problems of the Fourth World* (Washington, D.C.: Resources for the Future, 1976); United Nations, Department of Economic and Social Affairs, *1974 Report on the World Social Situation* (New York: United Nations, 1975).

Even taking into account such economic factors as increased prices with decreasing availability, it would appear at present that the quantities of platinum, gold, zinc, and lead are not sufficient to meet demands. . . . Silver, tin, and uranium may be in short supply even at higher prices by the turn of the century. By the year 2050, several more minerals may be exhausted if the current rate of consumption continues. . . . Despite spectacular recent discoveries, there are only a limited number of places left to search for most minerals. Geologists disagree about the prospects for finding large, new, rich ore deposits. Reliance on such discoveries would seem unwise in the long term.[24]

To estimate the supplies of mineral resources that will be available in the future, the usual approach has been to assess the number of years known reserves will last given present consumption levels. This approach produces a static reserve index, as shown in Table 9-1. The static approach does not consider the possibility that higher levels of consumption may characterize future years. Nor does it take into account the fact that there is little incentive to search for additional supplies of a mineral when enough has been discovered to meet demands in the immediate future.

Another approach involves calculation of an exponential reserve index. This method takes into account the current trend in consumption of each mineral resource and is based on the assumption that the actual amount of a mineral in the ecosphere is as much as five times greater than the known reserves. The length of time this amount will meet needs, if current trends in consumption continue and new mineral deposits are discovered, is also shown in Table 9-1.

Inequalities in Consumption

There are fundamental inequalities in the distribution and consumption of fossil fuels and mineral resources in different parts of the world. To some extent the inequalities in consumption reflect differences in the distribution of these resources. In addition to using their own resources, the developed countries are also dependent on the resources of the poorer nations, such as the raw materials produced by rubber plantations in Laos, bauxite mines in Jamaica, copper mines in Zambia, and oil from countries in the Middle East.

The affluence of the developed countries is, of course, based on heavy consumption of these resources. In a recent year, the United States, Canada,

[24] CEQ, op. cit., p. 158.

Table 9-1. World Resource Depletion

Resource	Static Index [a] (years)	Exponential Index [b] (years)	U.S. Consumption as Percentage of World Total
Aluminum	100	55	42
Chromium	420	154	19
Coal	2,300	150	44
Cobalt	110	148	32
Copper	36	48	33
Gold	11	29	26
Iron	240	173	28
Lead	26	64	25
Manganese	97	94	14
Mercury	13	41	24
Natural Gas	38	49	63
Nickel	150	96	38
Petroleum	31	50	33
Platinum	130	85	31
Silver	16	42	26
Tin	17	61	24
Tungsten	40	72	22
Zinc	23	50	26

SOURCE: Donella H. Meadows, Dennis L. Meadows, Jørgen Randers, and William W. Behrens, III, *The Limits to Growth* (New York: Universe Books, 1972), pp. 56–60.
[a]The number of years global reserves will last at current consumption levels.
[b]The number of years that five times known global reserves will last with consumption growing at the average annual rate of growth.

Europe, the U.S.S.R., Japan, and Australia consumed nearly 90 per cent of the energy and steel produced in the world.[25] The United States alone, with only 6 per cent of the world's population, accounted for 35 per cent of the consumption of energy and mineral resources.

FOOD AND HUNGER

According to the President's Science Advisory Committee, the quantity of food available in 1965 was barely adequate to feed the world's population.[26]

[25] Ehrlich, Ehrlich, and Holdren, op. cit., p. 65.
[26] President's Science Advisory Committee, Panel on the World Food Supply, *The World Food Problem*, vol. II (Washington, D.C.: U.S. Government Printing Office, 1967), p. 49.

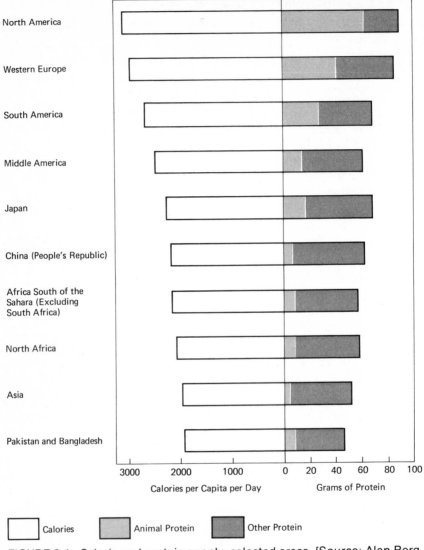

FIGURE 9-1. Calorie and protein supply, selected areas. [Source: Alan Berg, "Nutrition, Development, and Population Growth," *Population Reference Bureau,* 29 (1973):19.]

Further, inequalities exist in food consumption, as may be seen in Figure 9-1, and in most regions of the world, daily nutritional requirements are not being met.

The Committee concludes that 20 per cent of the people in underdeveloped countries are undernourished—that is, they do not obtain a sufficient supply of calories each day—and 60 per cent are malnourished in that their diets do not include adequate amounts of essential ingredients, particularly protein. Since two thirds of the world's population reside in such countries, this means that at least one third of the world's population—at least 1 billion persons—suffer from dietary deficiencies.

It may also be noted in Figure 9-1 that the amount of protein obtained from animal sources differs by region. This is an important difference because the quality of protein in meat is higher than that in other sources. In many underdeveloped areas one half or more of the calories and protein are obtained from cereal grains, which provide protein of lower quality. Rice alone is the staple food for 2 billion of the world's people. In the underdeveloped countries nearly all of the cereal grain is consumed directly, whereas in the developed countries, 80 per cent of it is used to feed animals to provide a rich source of protein. The result is a crucial difference between the developed and underdeveloped countries in the adequacy of nutrition; in the underdeveloped countries dietary deficiencies—or hunger—constitute a major problem.

The importance of nutrition cannot be stressed too strongly. Malnutrition affects physical development, intellectual development, and productivity. It has been shown that a diet of 1,800 calories results in the loss of 30 per cent of a person's muscle strength and a 15 per cent loss of precision of movement. Further, some experts attribute as many as 10 to 20 million deaths each year to malnutrition and starvation; many of these deaths are officially attributed to infectious and parasitic diseases, but it is argued that with proper nutrition, these individuals would have survived the illnesses.[27]

ENVIRONMENTAL DETERIORATION

Land Degradation

To meet the growing demands for food and to utilize the energy of draft animals, livestock herds have been increased. Through overgrazing, these herds are stripping the land of its natural cover. The forests are also being cut

[27] Alan Berg, "Nutrition, Development, and Population Growth," *Population Bulletin,* 29, No. 1 (1973), p. 7; René Dumont and Bernard Rosier, *The Hungry Future* (trans., Rosamund Linell and R. B. Sutcliffe) (New York: Frederick A. Praeger, 1969), p. 35; see Michael C. Latham, "Nutrition and Infection in National Development," in Philip H. Abelson, ed., *Food: Politics, Economics, Nutrition, and Research* (Washington, D.C.: American Association for the Advancement of Science, 1975), pp. 69–73.

down to provide additional agricultural lands and to obtain fuel. When the earth's surface is stripped of its grass and trees, the topsoil is vulnerable to erosion by wind and rain, resulting in the loss of valuable agricultural land. Land degradation is occurring in many parts of the world, particularly in North Africa, the Middle East, and India.

Much of what is now the Sahara Desert was once productive land. As a result of overgrazing, faulty irrigation, and deforestation, as well as gradual climatic changes over the centuries, the Sahara Desert, which is now advancing southward at a rate of several miles per year, is partly man-made.[28] A lesser known example is that of the Thar Desert in western India; at one time the center of the desert was a jungle.

The processes of extracting, transporting, and burning fossil fuels have also played a part in the deterioration or degradation of the environment. Of the techniques for extraction, strip mining is the most drastic in its ravaging of the landscape. In the United States, some 3 million acres have been strip mined, and in only one third of this land have efforts toward reclamation been made. Both underground and strip mining produce large quantities of waste products, and acids running off from these slag heaps contribute to water pollution.

Water Pollution

One of the paradoxes of human history is that mankind has always been dependent on water and yet has disposed of wastes in the lakes and rivers from which much of the drinking water is obtained. Humans have been using waterways as sewers to transport wastes for centuries, but in recent decades the growth of industry, changes in agricultural techniques, and population growth have greatly increased the pollution of most waterways. Substances found in our waterways "range from raw sewage to chemical fertilizers and animal dung, from acids and poisons generated by industry to silts and salts drained from strip mines, city streets and farmlands, from crankcase oils and detergents to disease carrying bacteria, from herbicides and pesticides to radioactive contaminants from mines and atomic plants."[29] Some of the substances being discharged into the water are nonbiodegradable materials that bacteria cannot decompose, and others are toxic to aquatic life.

---

[28] Ehrlich, Ehrlich, and Holdren, op. cit., pp. 159–160.
[29] Joseph L. Myler, "The Dirty Animal—Man," in Cecil E. Johnson, ed., *Eco-Crisis* (New York: John Wiley & Sons, Inc., 1970), p. 118.

Mankind has always been dependent on water and yet has disposed of wastes in the lakes and rivers from which the water is obtained. (Courtesy of E.P.A.)

Sewage contains not only human wastes but also such household products as laundry detergents containing phosphates, which are an important source of water pollution. The phosphates in sewage lead to a virtual population explosion in certain species, especially algae, fungi, and bacteria. This rapid growth of algae results in a lowered oxygen content in the water; the tolerance limits of fish and other organisms may be exceeded, resulting in their death. The population of algae may become so great that light cannot penetrate the water. This will kill plants living on the bottom because they will be unable to carry out the process of photosynthesis.

Recognition of the impact of phosphates on bodies of fresh water led to substitution of NTA (nitrilo-triacetic acid) in detergents. However, when NTA breaks down in water, it releases nitrogen which is the element that limits plant growth in ocean water.[30] The oceans are vast, and contribute 15 per cent of the world's protein supply, but the plants on which fish feed grow primarily in shallow coastal areas where light penetrates and where pollution is most extensive.

[30] John H. Ryther and William M. Dunstan, "Nitrogen, Phosphorus, and Eutrophication in the Coastal Marine Environment," *Science*, 171 (March 12, 1971): 1008–1013.

The major sources of water pollution are industrial discharges, municipal wastes, agricultural fertilizers and animal wastes, and soil erosion. According to the Council on Environmental Quality, water-using factories in this country discharge three to four times more wastes into the water than all of the municipal sewers.[31] The volume of wastes that various industries produce is shown in Table 9-2. It is apparent that more than one half of the water pollution is produced by the paper, chemical, petroleum, and steel industries. Industrial wastes are discharged in large quantities in the Northeast, Ohio River basin, Great Lakes states, and Gulf Coast states, and, to a lesser extent, in parts of the Southeast and the Pacific Coast states.

Another industrial waste, thermal pollution, results from the use of water as a coolant in electric generating plants and other industrial processes and occurs when heated water is discharged into lakes, rivers, and oceans.[32] The heated water accelerates biological processes, thereby harming aquatic life. The electric power industry currently accounts for 81 per cent of thermal pollution.

Municipal waste treatment plants process sewage from residences, businesses, and industry. Homes and businesses account for 55 per cent of the wastes treated in such plants; the remainder consists of industrial wastes. The Council on Environmental Quality indicates the inadequacy of present facilities:

> Less than one-third of the Nation's population is served by a system of sewers and an adequate treatment plant. About one-third is not served by a sewer system at all. About 5 percent is served by sewers which discharge their wastes without any treatment. And the remaining 32 percent have sewers but inadequate treatment plants. . . . The greatest municipal waste problems exist in the areas with the heaviest concentrations of population, particularly the Northeast.[33]

Two new agricultural practices have also contributed to the problem of water pollution. To restore essential plant nutrients, chemical fertilizers have been used in place of the older practices of rotating crops and spreading manure. Chemical fertilizers, containing nitrogen and phosphates, add to the pollution of streams and rivers. Two thirds of the beef cattle produced in the

---

[31] CEQ, op. cit., p. 32.

[32] John R. Clark, "Thermal Pollution and Aquatic Life," in Rochlin, op. cit., pp. 361–370.

[33] CEQ, op. cit., p. 35. Many communities are served by a single sewer system; following a storm the treatment system may become overloaded, and raw sewage is discharged into streams.

Table 9-2. Estimated Volume of Industrial Wastes Before Treatment, 1964[1]

Industry	Waste Water Volume (billion gallons)	Process Water Intake (billion gallons)	BOD (million pounds)	Suspended Solids (million pounds)
Food and kindred products	690	260	4,300	6,600
Meat products	99	52	640	640
Dairy products	58	13	400	230
Canned and frozen food	87	51	1,200	600
Sugar refining	220	110	1,400	5,000
All other	220	43	670	110
Textile mill products	140	110	890	N.E.
Paper and allied products	1,900	1,300	5,900	3,000
Chemical and allied products	3,700	560	9,700	1,900
Petroleum and coal	1,300	88	500	460
Rubber and plastics	160	19	40	50
Primary metals	4,300	1,000	480	4,700
Blast furnaces and steel mills	3,600	870	160	4,300
All other	740	130	320	430
Machinery	150	23	60	50
Electrical machinery	91	28	70	20
Transportation equipment	240	58	120	N.E.
All other manufacturing	450	190	390	930
All manufacturing	13,100	3,700	22,000	18,000
For comparison: Sewered population of United States	[2]5,300		[3]7,300	[4]8,800

SOURCE: Council on Environmental Quality, *Environmental Quality* (Washington, D.C.: U.S. Government Printing Office, 1970), p. 32.
[1] Columns may not add, due to rounding.
[2] 120,000,000 persons times 120 gallons times 365 days.
[3] 120,000,000 persons times 1/6 pound times 365 days.
[4] 120,000,000 persons times 0.2 pound times 365 days.

United States are no longer fed in pastures but are fattened for market in confined feedlot areas. Some of the animal wastes from feedlots reach and pollute waterways. It has been estimated that the waste products of beef and dairy cattle, horses, hogs, sheep, and chickens in the United States equal the wastes of 2 billion people.[34]

The primary source of wastes in surface waters is soil erosion. According to the Council on Environmental Quality, the volume of sediments or suspended solids in waterways in the United States as a result of erosion is at least 700 times greater than the amount attributable to sewage discharge.

[34] Ibid., p. 36.

Croplands, unprotected forest soils, overgrazed pastures, strip mines, and construction sites produce soil erosion and contribute sediments to waterways.

The discharge of oil from various sources also contributes to water pollution. Dr. Edward Goldberg of the Scripps Institute of Oceanography estimates that leaks and spills from oil tankers and other ships produce one million tons of pollution a year. Service stations also dispose of 350 million gallons of used oil annually and much of it finds its way to our waters. The often overlooked discharges of the 110,000 commercial fishing vessels and 8 million recreational boats in the United States also contribute to the pollution of our waterways.

Air Pollution

Air pollution has become such a public concern that many television stations provide a report on the day's level of air pollution. According to the official tabulations, the major pollutants are carbon monoxide, sulfur oxides, hydrocarbons, nitrogen oxides, soot, smoke, and a miscellaneous category including lead (from auto fuel), fluorides, beryllium, arsenic, asbestos, and many other chemicals as well as a variety of pesticides, herbicides, and fungicides.[35] Air pollution is a by-product of urban and industrial society in which our daily lives are heavily dependent on the process of combustion and at the same time are endangered by the quality of air we inhale.

Most of the pollutants in the air are produced by burning. Natural gas, oil, and coal are burned to provide energy in industrial plants and to heat residences. In many cities, garbage is burned in the backyard or at the city dump. Automobiles are mobile burners while in use and become a part of the nation's solid waste problem when discarded.

As a result of the concentration of population and industry, air pollution is a problem in almost every city of the world. Dr. John T. Middleton, then Director of the National Air Pollution Control Administration, cited the hazard to humans' health:

> On any busy thoroughfare you'll certainly breathe in lead . . . nitrogen oxide . . . carbon monoxide and organic matter such as the polynuclear hydrocarbons, . . . sulfur oxides, a variety of particulates and oxides of iron, aluminum

---

[35] Myler, op. cit., p. 126.

As a result of the concentration of population and industry, air pollution is a problem in almost every city of the world. (Courtesy of E.P.A.)

and other metals. . . . Both [the gases and particulates] can be harmful by themselves. But what greatly disturbs us is the fact that a mixture of them is often even more harmful. It's not just an additive effect—it's an enhancing one.[36]

Ranked in order of importance, the major sources of air pollution are transportation, electricity generation and space heating, industrial plants, and municipal waste disposal installations (Table 9-3). Automobile and truck emissions outweigh all other sources of air pollution, accounting for 42 per cent of the air pollution in the United States and perhaps 60 to 70 per cent of the air pollution in metropolitan areas. According to the research director of the Los Angeles Air Pollution Control District, the daily operation of 1,000 autos in an urban area burdens the air with 3.2 tons of carbon monoxide, 400

[36] John T. Middleton, "The Air We Breathe," *Population Bulletin*, 24 (December 1968): 118.

Table 9-3. U.S. Air Pollution Emissions in 1968 (In Millions of Tons)

Source	Carbon Monoxide	Particulates	Nitrogen Oxides	Sulfur Oxides	Hydrocarbons	Total
Fuel burned for transportation	63.8	1.2	8.1	0.8	16.6	90.5
Fuel burned in stationary sources[a]	1.9	8.9	10.0	24.4	0.7	45.9
Other Industrial processes[b]	9.7	7.5	0.2	7.3	4.6	29.3
Solid waste burning	7.8	1.1	0.6	0.1	1.6	11.2
Miscellaneous[c]	16.9	9.6	1.7	0.6	8.5	37.3
Total	100.1	28.3	20.6	33.2	32.0	214.2

SOURCE: Council on Environmental Quality, *Environmental Quality* (Washington, D.C.: U.S. Government Printing Office, 1970), p. 63.
[a] Primarily electricity generation, industrial processes, and space heating for residences, businesses, and industries.
[b] Primarily pulp mills, smelters, refineries, and cement plants.
[c] Primarily forest fires, agricultural burning, and coal waste fires.

to 800 pounds of hydrocarbons, and 100 to 300 pounds of nitrous oxides, as well as smaller amounts of sulfur and other chemicals.[37]

The movement of masses of air over the North American continent brings fresh air to most cities in the United States. Ordinarily, the air is warmer at the ground than at higher altitudes; the upward movement of warm air creates updrafts that carry away pollutants. At times these natural processes of ventilation fail. One way in which air movement may be stopped is through a thermal inversion. Such a phenomenon occurs when a layer of warm air forms at a higher altitude and traps cold air beneath it. This creates a lid that prevents normal air circulation. The concentration of pollutants in the air near the ground increases, creating a serious health hazard, particularly for persons with respiratory ailments. Thermal inversions have been linked to human deaths in 1948 in Donora, Pennsylvania, and in 1952 in London.

In addition to health problems among humans, livestock and the crops of farms near large cities, home furnishings, clothes, exterior paint, and automobiles are damaged by air pollution. It is estimated that the damage to vegetation, buildings, and other material possessions from air pollution totals several billion dollars a year in this country.

[37] Walsh McDermott, "Air Pollution and Public Health," in Kingsley Davis, comp., *Cities: Their Origin, Growth and Human Impact* (San Francisco: W. H. Freeman and Company, Publishers, 1973), p. 134.

Solid Wastes

Each year Americans produce more than 250 million tons of solid wastes, or more than one ton for every man, woman, and child. Approximately 190 million tons of waste are collected and disposed of at a cost of $3.5 billion a year. The trend toward packaging products in disposable containers has increased the volume of paper, plastics, glass, and metals in refuse. Many of these are qualitative pollutants and resist natural decomposition processes. Included in the solid waste collected in a recent year were 30 million tons of paper and paper products; 4 million tons of plastics; 100 million tires; 30 billion bottles; 60 billion cans; and millions of tons of grass, food wastes, and other products.[38] Shown in Table 9-4 is a breakdown of household wastes, according to the proportion, by weight, of various types of products. Paper and paper products account for nearly four times the volume of garbage, or food wastes.

Most communities have inadequate facilities for disposal of solid wastes. The two most common approaches are incineration and dumps or landfills. According to the Council on Environmental Quality, only 13 per cent of the solid waste in this country is disposed of in sanitary landfills that are operated properly; 77 per cent of the solid waste is deposited in dumps scattered around the country; 8 per cent of the solid waste is burned; the remainder is salvaged, composted, or dumped at sea. Most waste disposal operations are far below the standards essential to avoid the additional problems of dust, odors, fires from flammable gases, and pollution of underground water. They are havens for disease-bearing rats, flies, and other pests. Each year, millions

Table 9-4. Composition of Household Wastes in the United States

Waste	Weight per cent	Waste	Weight per cent
Cardboard	7	Leather, rubber,	
Newspaper	14	molded plastic	2
Misc. paper	25	Garbage	12
Plastic film	2	Grass clippings,	
Wood	7	dirt	10
Glass, ceramics,		Textiles	3
stone	10	Metal	8

SOURCE: Richard H. Wagner, *Environment and Man,* 2nd Ed. (New York: W. W. Norton & Company, Inc., 1974), p. 454.

[38] CEQ, op. cit., p. 108.

Each year Americans produce more than 250 million tons of solid wastes. (Courtesy of E.P.A.)

of tons of waste are dumped into the ocean, and additional pollutants eventually are deposited in them from inland waterways.

In addition to scarring the landscape and polluting our water, we currently waste valuable resources by our means of disposing of solid wastes. Although more paper was recycled than any other material, in 1973, only 16 per cent of the waste paper was reused. Only a small proportion of waste metal is recycled—1 per cent of steel, 4 per cent of aluminum, and, with the exceptions of lead and copper, negligible amounts of other metals.[39] More lead is obtained from scrap than from mineral ores, and almost one half of the current copper supply comes from scrap.[40] Nevertheless, millions of tons of valuable metals that are discarded each year could be recycled.

Solid wastes not only represent the loss of valuable resources but also destroy the beauty of the landscape. Such scenic blight takes a number of forms—refuse in the streets and vacant lots, litter along highways, in parks, and on beaches, and abandoned cars on city streets and throughout the countryside.

[39] CEQ, *Environmental Quality: The Sixth Annual Report* (Washington, D.C.: U.S. Government Printing Office, 1975), p. 92.
[40] CEQ, op. cit., p. 190; see Philip H. Abelson, ed., *Energy: Use, Conservation and Supply* (Washington, D.C.: American Association for the Advancement of Science, 1974).

Pesticides

Although pesticides have been of great benefit to mankind in the production of food, they have also had serious consequences for the environment. The chlorinated hydrocarbons—DDT, dieldrin, and endrin—are long lived. DDT may remain toxic for 20 years. Its use to control house and garden pests, shade tree pests, tobacco pests, and pests in aquatic areas was prohibited in the United States in 1969, but it remains the most widely used pesticide in the world.

DDT became commercially available in 1946 for the control of insects harmful to crops. It has killed not only those insects but also their natural predators. Once again, the principle of natural selection comes into operation:

> The side effects of DDT on crop pests were . . . threefold: it produced insects that were resistant to it, it removed insect predators, and it created new species of pest insects.[41]

Through the process of concentration, DDT is reducing the populations of many predatory birds; consequently, some species of owls, hawks, and eagles may soon become extinct. The accumulation of DDT upsets the metabolism of calcium in these creatures; as a result, the shells of their eggs are thin and easily broken.

The effects of pesticides on human health are virtually unknown, but the possibility of pesticide poisoning as the result of the accumulation of DDT in human fat tissue cannot be overlooked. In one study in which data were obtained through autopsies, a statistical correlation, but not necessarily a causal relation, was found between the level of pesticides in fat tissue and cause of death.[42] The concentrations of DDT and the pesticide dieldrin were found to be significantly higher in the fat of persons who died of cerebral hemorrhage, hypertension, and various forms of cancer than among those who died of infectious diseases.

Radiation

Human beings have always lived in a virtual sea of radiation deriving from the sun's rays and other radioactive substances in the earth's surface and the

[41] Smith, Steck, and Surette, op. cit., p. 49.
[42] Ehrlich, Ehrlich, and Holdren, op. cit., p. 134.

atmosphere. That does not mean that human additions to the natural level of radiation can be regarded as harmless. The atomic bombs dropped on Hiroshima and Nagasaki devastated those Japanese cities in World War II. However, recognition of the possibility of widespread harmful effects of radiation did not occur until the testing of a nuclear device in Project Bravo in 1954. It was anticipated that a small area of the Pacific Ocean would be affected and that the radioactive particles would be diluted to harmless and undetectable levels. However, research showed that high concentrations developed in ocean food chains in which the radioactive particles were consumed by small plants that subsequently were consumed by small fish which, in turn, were eaten by larger ones.[43] Through the process of concentration, radioactive levels increased at each successive level in the food chain. Humans, as consumers of large fish, are at the end of the food chain.

In addition to food contamination, nuclear fallout presents danger for human beings in the form of radioactive iodine. This is one of the substances contained in the particles that reach the earth in rain or snow. Falling on the grass, it is consumed by cows whose radioactive milk is consumed by humans. The danger of radioactive iodine is that it is concentrated in the thyroid gland, which controls the rate of metabolism. Also, genetic mutations may be caused by relatively low doses of radiation, and it may be passed on to subsequent generations. As a result of the 1963 treaty by the United States, the United Kingdom, and the Soviet Union to ban surface testing of nuclear devices, the hazards of atmospheric radiation from that source have been reduced. Today, most of the radiation that poses a threat to health stems from the use of X-rays by physicians and dentists for diagnostic purposes. According to the Council on Environmental Quality, 68 per cent of the radiation to which the population is exposed comes from natural sources. However, 85 per cent of the man-made sources involve diagnostic X-rays, and another 8 per cent involve therapeutic X-rays.[44]

Another potentially dangerous source of radioactive contamination is the use of nuclear reactors in the production of electricity. In 1976, the 61 nuclear plants in operation produced 8 per cent of the nation's electricity, and it is estimated that 22 per cent of our electricity will be produced by nuclear energy in 1980. Nuclear reactors are viewed as part of the answer to the problem of declining supplies of fossil fuels. However, the dangers associated with the operation of such plants and the storage of radioactive

---

[43] Smith, Steck, and Surette, op. cit., p. 44.
[44] Ehrlich, Ehrlich, and Holdren, op. cit., p. 140; CEQ, op. cit., p. 142.

wastes must be considered in relation to the benefits of increased energy production. Thus far, the record of the commercial nuclear power industry has been good. In a 17-month period in the mid-1970s, some 850 minor accidents were reported but no deaths or radiation injuries occurred. To date, leakage from storage tanks which led to some land and water contamination has been the major problem.

Noise

Like other forms of pollution, noise involves something that is out of place. Noise may be defined as unwanted sound. According to federal regulations, the limit for industrial noise is 90 decibels for prolonged exposure (8 hours a day). Many of the everyday noises in urban areas exceed this limit.

Those who live or work in cities are exposed to high levels of noise much of the time. (Courtesy of E.P.A.)

Those who live or work in cities are exposed to high levels of noise much of the time. Traffic noise alone may measure 90 decibels. Trucks, buses, motorcycles, and railroad systems are the worst offenders, but airplanes contribute substantially to a noisy world. At 200 feet a four-engine jet aircraft generates 120 decibels of sound. Industrial machinery, as well as compressors, jackhammers, and other construction tools, add to the city's noise. Nor are the suburbs free of noise. The friction of tires on the nearby freeway, garbage trucks, lawn mowers, air conditioners, and kitchen appliances all create noise.

Excessive noise can have physiological effects, the most common of which is temporary or permanent hearing loss. It is generally agreed that regular exposure to approximately 90 decibels of sound can cause permanent hearing loss. A federal agency estimates that 1 million workers suffer some degree of hearing loss as a result of industrial noise, and about 6 to 16 million are exposed to noise levels that may produce hearing loss.[45]

WHAT CAN BE DONE?

Reckless exploitation of natural resources and pollution of the environment have produced serious problems. Although the magnitude of the problems may make the situation appear hopeless, various steps can be taken to cope with the environmental crisis.

Energy Conservation

Addressing the Congress on the topic of energy in April, 1977, President Carter proposed that steps be taken to achieve the following goals by 1985: Reduce the annual growth rate in energy demand to less than 2 per cent; reduce gasoline consumption by 10 per cent; cut imports of foreign oil to 6 million barrels a day; establish a strategic petroleum reserve of one billion barrels, about 10 months' supply; increase coal production by more than two thirds, to over one billion tons a year; insulate 90 per cent of American homes and all new buildings; and use solar energy in more than 2.5 million homes.[46] To achieve these goals, the President asked Congress to curb

[45] Myler, op. cit., p. 131.
[46] *The Courier-Journal*, Louisville, Ky., April 21, 1977, p. 7.

America's enormous appetite for energy by making gasoline, heating oil, natural gas, and large cars more expensive. President Carter emphasized specific steps that can be taken to conserve energy. A key idea underlying the President's proposals is that both energy consumption and production are sensitive to price changes. Whatever steps Congress enacts, energy prices will continue to rise.

The development of mass transportation systems would help to reduce energy use. Individual citizens can contribute to energy conservation by supporting and using mass transit, walking to nearby stores, insulating their homes, and turning down their thermostats. Such efforts will not solve the energy crisis, but they will help until new energy sources are developed.

New Sources of Energy

The federal government has already expended large sums of money to support the development of alternative energy sources, and continued support may produce a shift away from fossil fuels to more abundant nuclear and solar energy sources in the next 10 to 15 years. In the short run, greater reliance on coal is essential to reduce consumption of natural gas and oil.

Because the existing supplies of natural gas and petroleum are limited in comparison with coal reserves, energy needs in the immediate future may be met by converting coal to gas and oil. The processes involved are known as gasification and liquefaction, respectively. A number of plants designed to carry out these processes are currently either in the planning stage or under construction. It is anticipated that before the decade of the 1970s ends, they will be in commercial use.

Shale oil, a crude oil obtained from shale (rock), is a fossil fuel that may provide additional energy.[47] The amount of oil available in shale is more than double the known reserves of petroleum, and 75 per cent of it is in the United States. A major question is whether it will be economically feasible to extract and process shale oil. To extract oil, shale must be crushed and heated, and disposal of the solid residue will pose another problem. Greater reliance on electricity may be mandatory in the future, and nuclear energy constitutes a new source of electricity.[48] According to the Atomic Energy Commission, 22

---

[47] Bert Bolin, "The Carbon Cycle," in Gerald Piel and Dennis Flanagan, comp., *The Biosphere* (San Francisco: W. H. Freeman and Company, Publishers, 1970), pp. 49–56.
[48] John F. Hogerton, "The Arrival of Nuclear Power," in Rochlin, op. cit., pp. 283–293.

per cent of the electricity in the United States will be produced in nuclear plants by 1980, and this figure is likely to increase to 50 or 60 per cent by the year 2000. Another possibility, which is under study, is controlled nuclear fusion as a source of electricity. In comparison with nuclear fission, fusion produces relatively little radioactivity and there is less risk of accidents.

The technology has not yet developed to permit large-scale use of energy from the sun. To provide electricity for a city of 1 million, a collection device covering at least 20 square miles would be needed. However, with rising electricity costs, devices mounted on roofs of houses to collect the sun's energy are now economically competitive with conventional sources. The cost of the unit can be recovered in the form of lower utility bills. Use of solar energy is a distinct possibility in many parts of the United States.

Another potential source of energy in some areas is the superheated underground water that was trapped in rock formations as a result of volcanic activity. When wells are drilled into such steam reservoirs, the steam that is released can be used by conventional steam electric plants. Plants for the conversion of this energy have been built in a number of countries; in the United States, they are in operation in California. Although negligible amounts of geothermal energy are available in the eastern part of the country, some experts believe that by the end of the century, more electricity will be derived from this source than is currently produced by all of the electric power plants in the country today.[49]

Late in 1976, it was announced that the first plant in the United States to convert solid wastes (garbage) into steam that would be sold to industries would be built in Louisville, Kentucky. Besides providing additional energy, this approach can help to solve the problem of solid waste disposal.

Increased Food Production

There are two ways of increasing the amount of food produced by conventional agriculture: the amount of land under cultivation can be expanded or the output of cultivated areas can be increased. Until the middle of the present century, the primary means of increasing the food supply was through expansion of the amount of land under cultivation. Since that time, however, such efforts have become less successful and more expensive. More successful have been the attempts to increase yields through plant genetics and the

---

[49] Oliver S. Owen, *Natural Resource Conservation: An Ecological Approach,* 2nd ed. (New York: Macmillan Publishing Co., Inc., 1975), p. 578; see Abelson, *Energy,* op. cit.

application of agricultural chemicals. *The green revolution* is the term used to describe the spread of high-yield wheats and rices since 1965 to the underdeveloped areas of the world.[50] The effect of planting hybrid grains and applying chemicals to fertilize the soil and to control pests has been an increase in the amount of food produced on an acre of land. More widespread use of these agricultural techniques holds the promise of further increases in the food supply. Scientists are optimistic that the spread of the green revolution will increase food production to meet the world's needs for the next 15 to 20 years, and research is underway to develop grain varieties that are richer in protein than those currently available.

Nearly one half of the eight billion arable acres of land on earth is currently under cultivation, and it would be costly to clear, irrigate, and fertilize the remaining land for food production. In recent years, the average cost of opening land in unsettled areas for agricultural production has been $460 per acre.[51] According to the United Nations' Food and Agriculture Organization (FAO), it is not economically feasible to open more land to cultivation in most parts of Asia, Africa, and Latin America, where additional food is sorely needed; in fact, the FAO suggests that in the drier areas of these regions, the marginal and submarginal lands should be returned to permanent pasture.[52]

Whether or not it proves to be economically feasible to open more land to cultivation, there is reason to believe that the key to further increases in the food supply lies in the use of desalinated water. Desalination, or the removal of salt from ocean water, may not only provide a solution to the problem of water shortages in some parts of this country, but may also contribute to the solution of the problem of hunger. Desalinated water may permit irrigation and cultivation of land that is currently too arid to permit agricultural production. Even if this is not possible, desalinated water could be used to irrigate land currently under cultivation to increase crop yields. Two techniques of desalination have already been developed: electrodialysis and flash distillation.

[50] Lester R. Brown, *Seeds of Change: The Green Revolution and Development in the 1970's* (New York: Praeger Publishers, 1970).

[51] President's Science Advisory Committee, op. cit., p. 460; see Thomas T. Poleman, "World Food: A Perspective," in Abelson, *Food: Politics, Economics, Nutrition, and Research,* op. cit., pp. 8–16; see also United Nations, *Report of the World Food Conference: Rome, 5–16 November 1974* (New York: United Nations, 1975).

[52] Food and Agriculture Organization of the United Nations, *Provisional Indicative World Plan for Agricultural Development,* vol. I (Rome: Food and Agriculture Organization of the United Nations, 1970), p. 41; see Sterling B. Hendricks, "Food from the Land," in Cloud, op. cit., pp. 65–85.

Electrodialysis.   Electrodialysis is a desalination process in which electrical charges remove sodium from salt water. The first city in the United States to provide its fresh water supply by this means was Coalinga, California. In this community the desalination process reduces the salt content of the well water from 2,200 to approximately 300 parts per million and yields 25,000 gallons each day. This process is suitable primarily for small communities because only a limited amount of water can be processed daily, but it could be used in at least 1,000 communities in this country.[53]

Flash Distillation.   A flash distillation plant is in operation in Freeport, Texas. Salt water from the gulf is superheated to 250° F, vaporized, condensed in cool coils, and transported to storage tanks. The plant has the capacity to desalinate 1 million gallons of water a day; in fact, its product has such a flat taste that salt must be added to it. The feasibility of such a process is illustrated by an incident in the early 1960s. A flash distillation plant that was constructed in San Diego, California, was dismantled and shipped to Cuba when Castro threatened to cut off the water supply to the Guantanamo Naval Base in Cuba. With a capacity of 1 million gallons a day, the plant assured a continuous supply of fresh water for the military base. Plants with a capacity of 500 million gallons a day may be in operation in areas with water shortages by the mid-1980s.[54]

Combatting Pollution

Assessing Costs.   In the present economic system, the price of a commodity does not reflect the pollution that results from its production. Economists refer to the environmental pollution associated with production as external social costs. A mechanism is needed to include these costs in the price of commodities:

> If there were a way to make the price structure shoulder these external costs— taxing the firm for the amount of discharge, for instance—then the price for the goods and services produced would reflect these costs. . . . A price structure that took environmental degradation into account would cause a shift in prices, hence a shift in consumer preferences and, to some extent, would discourage buying pollution-producing products.[55]

[53] Owen, op. cit., p. 178.
[54] Ibid.
[55] CEQ, op. cit., p. 12; see Ronald G. Ridker, "The Economy, Resource Requirements, and Pollution Levels," in Ridker, *Population, Resources, and Environment,* op. cit., pp. 35–64.

What is needed is an environmental impact inventory for each area of production, comparable to the Environmental Impact Statement required by a 1970 federal law before a new federal project, such as a dam, can be constructed. Environmentalists have used these statements to halt projects considered to be potentially harmful. Of course, this approach could be extended to environmental costs other than those caused by air and water pollution. For example, the cost of land restoration could be included in the price of a ton of coal obtained by strip mining.

Water Pollution. To meet minimum water quality standards, new sewage treatment plants need to be built and existing facilities require expansion. In the years 1972 through 1977, the federal government authorized grants totaling $18 billion to finance construction of municipal waste water collection and treatment systems. In 1972, the Federal Water Pollution Control Act was amended so that all industrial sources of water pollution would be regulated by a national permit system. Any industry that discharges wastes into a waterway must obtain a permit which restricts the amount of pollution that may be discharged. The goal is the elimination of all discharge of pollutants into waterways by 1985.

In addition to the increasingly stringent requirements placed on industries to control water pollution, the electric power industry has been prodded by federal and state environmental protection agencies into reducing thermal pollution. One device used to reduce thermal pollution is a cooling tower, a structure some 400 feet tall. Heated water is piped to a high level in the tower and then sent downward over a series of baffle plates. The cooled water is then either discharged into a lagoon for further cooling or into the stream from which it was originally drawn.

Air Pollution. The amount of air pollution resulting from stationary sources—electricity generation, industrial production, and waste disposal—can be reduced by use of nonpolluting fuels or by pollution control devices. A number of technological processes to remove sulfur from coal and oil prior to combustion or from gases produced by burning fuel have been developed. Large amounts of sulfur oxides and other pollutants can be intercepted in smokestacks by various combinations of baffles, scrubbers, and electrostatic precipitators.

Actually, the quality of air in the United States is better today than it was in 1970. The installation of pollution control devices on autos has had some beneficial effects. Between 1970 and 1974, particulate emissions dropped some 29 per cent and sulfur dioxide declined 8 per cent.[56] In the same period of time, emissions of carbon monoxide declined 12 per cent, and hydrocarbon emissions dropped about 5 per cent, even though many older cars with no control devices were still in use.

Limited success has been achieved, but not all the pollution problems associated with automobiles have been solved. Technological advances are possible, but it may be necessary for Americans to abandon the auto as the primary means of transportation and shift to mass transit systems. At a minimum a shift to small cars appears to be essential. In addition to the fact that they produce less air pollution, small cars require less space on highways and in parking lots. Some experts suggest that "immediate relief from a major portion of our air-pollution problems and substantial reduction in demand for steel, lead, glass, rubber, and other materials would result from the replacement of our present automobiles with small, low-horsepower, long-lasting cars designed for recycling."[57]

Reducing Solid Wastes

There are a number of ways in which the volume of solid waste can be reduced and natural resources conserved by recycling. Innovative approaches will require research and development. Economic incentives, in the form of direct payments for ecologically sound actions or tax incentives for businesses, may be necessary.

Some imaginative uses of landfills have been accomplished. In the Chicago area, clay was dug out of a section known as the Badlands and used as an impermeable cover for compacted garbage.[58] The result was a new recreational area with a landscaped hill used as a ski slope, appropriately named Mount Trashmore.

Waste products can also be used to restore land that has been strip mined. Chicago's sewage plants generate 1,000 tons of sludge each day, and when disposal sites became scarce, an ingenious approach to the disposal problem was suggested. It was proposed that the sludge be treated to remove odors and eliminate any health hazard and then be piped to strip mined land to the southwest of Chicago.[59] This approach, which helps to restore

---

[56] CEQ, Sixth Annual Report, op. cit., p. 305.
[57] Ehrlich, Ehrlich, and Holdren, op. cit., p. 263.
[58] Ward and Dubos, op. cit., p. 83.
[59] Owen, op. cit., p. 167.

unproductive land, costs only one third as much as the use of conventional landfills for disposal of sludge. Transportation of sludge, either by pipeline or railroad tank car, may be economically feasible in other parts of the country.

As has been noted, little effort has been made to link the cost of disposing of waste products to the price of consumer goods. There are an estimated 2.5 to 4.5 million abandoned cars on city streets, in back alleys, and along rural roads. To promote prompt scrapping of automobiles, it may be necessary to impose a special tax or fee on owners of automobiles. The Council on Environmental Quality, however, favors an alternative approach involving improvement in state title laws and stiff financial penalties for abandonment of autos.[60]

Each year more than 40 billion glass bottles and metal cans containing beer or soft drinks are produced, and legislation banning or taxing nonreturnable beverage containers has been introduced in all 50 state legislatures. In 1975, three states, Oregon, Vermont, and South Dakota, had laws restricting beer and soft drink containers, and Minnesota had laws that restricted all types of packaging wastes. Since 1972, Oregon has required a minimum two-cent refund for beer and soft drink containers that are reusable and a five-cent refund for all other beverage containers. In addition, the law prohibits the sale of fliptop or pulltab beverage containers. A study of the effects of the Oregon law in 1975 showed that sales of beer and soft drinks had not declined, but litter in the form of beverage containers had been reduced by two thirds.[61]

Pesticides

Pest control is essential to protect people from disease and to produce a sufficient food supply. A wide variety of nonpersistent pesticides can be substituted for the more persistent types. Another possibility is natural biological control. This involves introduction of a pest's natural enemies. When scale insects, accidentally introduced from Australia, threatened the California citrus industry, its natural enemy, the bedalia beetle, led to control of this pest. The use of attractants and sterilization constitute other forms of biological control. Attractants have been employed to lure pests into traps where they may be killed or sterilized. Use of pest-resistant species developed by selective breeding and the planting of diverse crops have also proven to be highly

---

[60] CEQ, op. cit., p. 116.
[61] CEQ, Sixth Annual Report, op. cit., pp. 96–97; see Harrison Brown, ''Human Materials Production as a Process in the Biosphere,'' in Piel and Flanagan, op. cit., pp. 117–124.

effective. An increase in crop diversity is not only sound ecologically but may be economically profitable. In California, strips of alfalfa are now cultivated in cotton fields. A pest of cotton, the lygus bug, prefers alfalfa to cotton and also serves to keep in check the populations of other insect pests that feed on cotton.

Noise Control

In some instances, a simple but satisfactory solution to noise pollution is to locate the source of noise away from the population. Airports and highways may be located some distance from residential areas. The establishment of a green belt between residential areas and sources of noise can also be effective if zoning laws are enforced to block encroachment on the green belt. Where vegetation cannot be used as a sound barrier, the use of insulation is often quite effective. For individuals who must work in a noisy environment, protective equipment can be provided to reduce the noise level. Richard Wagner notes how one offender in urban areas, subway noise, can be reduced:

> Subway noises have been sharply reduced by rubber-tired cars in some of the newer subway systems of the world. But even existing obsolete systems, such as those in Boston, New York, and Philadelphia, could be greatly improved with welded rails, aluminum-centered steel wheels, polyurethane foam between the ties, insulation pads under the tracks, and sound-deadening materials on car underbodies and station walls.[62]

There will be no significant change until a noise control code is enacted and vigorously enforced. Standards need to be established regarding the maximum amount of noise emitted by all sources. Adequate fines for violation of the permissible noise level would lead to a rapid replacement of noisy air compressors and lawn mowers with quieter equipment.

In 1972, Congress passed the Noise Control Act, which represents a major step toward control of noise on a nationwide basis. All of the major sources of noise are included within the act's provisions, and the law authorized the expenditure of $21 million over a three-year period for efforts directed at noise control. The inclusion of penalties in the legislation should provide incentive for compliance with the law.

[62] Richard H. Wagner, *Environment and Man,* 2nd ed. (New York: W. W. Norton & Company, Inc., 1974), p. 177; see also Leo L. Beranek, "Noise," in Davis, op. cit., pp. 158–167.

Solutions to the problems of the environment require commitment on the part of government as well as the citizenry. Some of the suggestions for coping with the environmental crisis require the expenditure of large sums of money. Hopefully, as citizens become aware of the various dimensions of the crisis, they will support programs designed to cope with environmental problems. It is imperative that action be initiated now. Perhaps the warnings about the harmful effects of many of our practices have come in time so that we will not destroy the intricate web of life, in which we are so integrally involved.

Additional Readings

Berechman, Joseph. "The Land Use Planning Problem of New Towns." *Journal of Environmental Systems*, 4 (Fall 1974): 241–250.

Cole, H. S. D., Christopher Freeman, Marie Jahoda, and K. L. R. Pavitt, eds. *Thinking About the Future: A Critique of The Limits to Growth*. London: Chatto & Windus, 1973.

Commoner, Barry. *Science and Survival*. New York: The Viking Press, Inc., 1967.

Curtis, Richard, and Elizabeth Hogan. *Perils of the Peaceful Atom: The Myth of Safe Nuclear Power Plants*. Garden City, N.Y.: Doubleday & Company, Inc., 1969.

Ehrlich, Paul R., and Anne H. Ehrlich. *Population, Resources, Environment: Issues in Human Ecology*. 2nd ed. San Francisco: W. H. Freeman and Company, Publishers, 1972.

Hall, Edward T. *The Hidden Dimension*. Garden City, N.Y.: Doubleday & Company, Inc., 1966.

Hardin, Garrett. *Exploring New Ethics for Survival: The Voyage of the Spaceship Beagle*. New York: The Viking Press, Inc., 1972.

Hinckley, Alden D. *Applied Ecology: A Nontechnical Approach*. New York: Macmillan Publishing Co., Inc., 1976.

Holdren, John P., and Paul R. Ehrlich, eds. *Global Ecology: Readings Toward a Rational Strategy for Man*. New York: Harcourt Brace Jovanovich, Inc., 1971.

Kamen, Charles S., and Peretz Darr Dalinsky. "Attitudes Toward Payment for Resource Use: The Case of Domestic Water Consumption." *Journal of Environmental Systems*, 4 (Spring 1974), 1–21.

Kneese, Allen V., and Blair T. Bower, eds. *Environmental Quality Analysis: Theory and Method in the Social Sciences*. Baltimore: The Johns Hopkins University Press, 1972.

Landau, Norman J., and Paul D. Rheingold. *The Environmental Law Handbook*. New York: Ballantine Books, 1971.

Lave, Lester B., and Eugene P. Seskin. "Air Pollution and Human Health." *Science*, 169 (August 21, 1970): 723–733.

Love, Glen A., and Rhoda M. Love, eds. *Ecological Crisis: Readings for Survival*. New York: Harcourt Brace Jovanovich, Inc., 1970.

Matthews, William H., Frederick E. Smith, and Edward D. Goldberg, eds. *Man's Impact on Terrestrial and Ocean Ecosystems*. Cambridge, Mass.: Massachusetts Institute of Technology Press, 1971.

Meadows, Dennis L., and Donella H. Meadows, eds. *Toward Global Equilibrium: Collected Papers*. Cambridge, Mass.: Wright-Allen Press, Inc., 1973.

Shepard, Paul, and Daniel McKinley, eds. *The Subversive Science*. Boston: Houghton Mifflin Company, 1969.

Study of Critical Environmental Problems. *Man's Impact on the Global Environment*. Cambridge, Mass.: Massachusetts Institute of Technology Press, 1970.

Swift, Jeremy. *The Other Eden: A New Approach to Man, Nature and Society*. London: J. M. Dent & Sons Ltd., 1974.

Taylor, Theodore B., and Charles C. Humpstone. *The Restoration of the Earth*. New York: Harper & Row, Publishers, 1973.

part

problems of
deviance

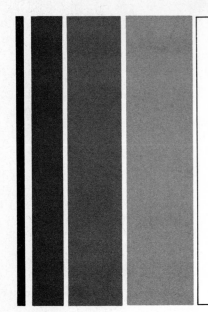

crime and juvenile delinquency

Crime is not just a tough teenager snatching a lady's purse. It is a professional thief stealing cars "on order." It is a well-heeled loan shark taking over a previously legitimate business for organized crime. It is a polite young man who suddenly and inexplicably murders his family. It is a corporation executive conspiring with competitors to keep prices high. . . .

A skid-row drunk lying in a gutter is crime. So is the killing of an unfaithful wife. A Costa Nostra conspiracy to bribe public officials is crime. So is a strong-arm robbery by a 15-year-old boy. The embezzlement of a corporation's funds by an executive is crime. So is the possession of marihuana cigarettes by a student.[1]

Crime and delinquency are among the nation's most important social problems because "the existence of crime, the talk about crime, the reports of crime, and the fear of crime have eroded the basic quality of life of many Americans."[2] There were more than 11 million serious crimes reported to the police in 1975, and surveys indicate that many crimes are not reported. It is no wonder that one third of all Americans believe that it is unsafe to walk alone at night in their neighborhoods and keep guns in their homes for protection against criminals.[3]

[1] The President's Commission on Law Enforcement and Administration of Justice, *The Challenge of Crime in a Free Society* (Washington, D.C.: U.S. Government Printing Office, 1967), pp. v, 3.
[2] Ibid., p. v.
[3] Ibid.

The existence of crime, the talk about crime, the reports of crime, and the fear of crime have eroded the basic quality of life of many Americans. (Courtesy of Magnum.)

THE NATURE OF CRIME

Criminals are deviants, but crime and deviance are not identical concepts. *Deviance* includes all violations of a group's norms, whereas *crime* refers only to acts that are in violation of the criminal law.[4] Four characteristics of an ideal, rational system of criminal law help to distinguish it from other sets of rules: politicality, specificity, uniformity, and penal sanction.

The rules defining behavior as crime are enacted by the legislative branch of government, and only violations of the rules made by such a duly constituted political authority are crimes. In the application of the law, court decisions become a part of the body of rules. The law, then, not only consists of the rules enacted by legislatures, but also includes the "law in action" or case law. Many criminologists also treat the administrative regulations of governmental agencies as part of the criminal law because these rules ultimately have the force of the criminal law behind them.

Richard Quinney claims that acts defined as crimes represent behavior that conflicts with the interests of the segments of society that possess the power to shape the law.[5] This is essentially correct for regulations of personal morality, but not for crimes such as burglary, murder, and rape. These offenses are condemned by almost everyone. Further, powerful groups may, in fact, violate the law to promote their own interests. In view of the Watergate burglary and other activities associated with the 1972 presidential election, including the dirty tricks used to discredit opponents in the primaries, Quinney's idea that crime involves behavior that conflicts with the interests of powerful groups is only partially correct.

The criminal law usually provides technical definitions of specific acts that are prohibited. In the event there is a question as to whether a person's behavior fits the definition, a finding in favor of the defendant is to be expected. Uniformity is included as a characteristic of the criminal law because in the United States and other democratic societies justice is ideally to be dispensed equally and without consideration of a person's social position. Because rigid adherence to the ideal of uniformity often would result in injustice, the police and courts do exercise discretion, taking into account the circumstances in which the offense occurred and characteristics of the offender, such as the person's age and whether the person is a first offender or a re-

[4] Daniel Glaser, *Social Deviance* (Chicago: Markham Publishing Co., 1971), p. 4.
[5] Richard Quinney, *The Social Reality of Crime* (Boston: Little, Brown and Company, 1970), pp. 16–18.

peater. Ignorance of the law is not an adequate defense against a criminal charge, but a first offender may be treated more leniently than a repeater, particularly if there is reason to believe that he or she did not fully recognize the illegal nature of an act.

The ideal of uniformity is violated at times in cases involving powerful, wealthy, or prominent individuals. Although his forced resignation as vice-president was a form of punishment, Spiro Agnew was allowed to plead no contest to charges of income tax evasion and was not sentenced to prison. Richard Nixon was forced to resign as president because information on the tape recordings showed that, contrary to his public statements, he played a part in the Watergate cover-up. His successor, Gerald Ford, granted Nixon a pardon, giving the former president immunity from prosecution. Many of the Watergate conspirators were released from prison after serving only a few months. The only federal judge ever sentenced to prison, Otto Kerner, was convicted on charges of accepting bribes and entered prison in 1974. He was released after serving seven months when it was discovered that he had cancer. Yet, for other convicts, serious illness does not result in their release. In view of the long prison terms served by ordinary citizens convicted of other criminal charges, the treatment of these prominent individuals does not reflect uniform application of the law.

The final characteristic of a rational system of criminal law is penal sanction. The idea that violators will be punished or at least threatened with punishment is encompassed in the concept of penal sanction; a law that provides no penalty for violators cannot be enforced. The imposition of punishment is reserved for the state. Neither the victim nor the victim's family or friends have the right to punish the offender.

TYPES OF CRIME

Many Americans think of crime as including a narrow range of behavior, but there are more than 2,800 acts that are considered crimes by federal law and many more that violate state and local statutes. To understand causes, to make preventive efforts, and to institute effective treatment approaches, it is essential to distinguish different types of crime. In addition, juvenile delinquency and adult criminality must be differentiated.

Juvenile Delinquency

The concept of juvenile delinquency is based on the idea that individuals must be of a certain age, usually 18, before they are to be held fully responsible for their actions. If offenders have not yet reached the legal age of accountability, parents are assigned responsibility for the misdeeds of their offspring. If they cannot control their child's behavior, the juvenile court can use the concept of *parens patriae,* or the state as parent, to declare the child a ward of the state. The objectives underlying establishment of specialized juvenile courts have been separation of juveniles from hardened adult offenders and substitution of individualized justice for the prevailing concept in the criminal court that the punishment should fit the crime. The goal of the juvenile court is rehabilitation, not punishment, and juveniles are handled in a separate correctional system.

Statutory definitions of delinquency not only include violations of the criminal law but also a number of *juvenile status offenses,* a vaguely defined collection of acts and conditions proscribed only for juveniles. These prohibitions permit the juvenile court to deal with youths who have not committed a criminal act but have behavior problems, including habitual truancy, incorrigibility, "knowingly associating with thieves, vicious or immoral persons," running away from home, immoral or indecent conduct, or "habitually using vile, obscene, or vulgar language in public places." These offenses are so vaguely defined that almost any youthful behavior regarded as undesirable by local authorities may lead to court referral. While young persons are often charged with juvenile status offenses, they also commit acts that are violations of the criminal law. Juveniles commit many property crimes. They also commit sizable numbers of two kinds of violent crime, forcible rape and robbery.

Violent Crime

Violent crimes are those in which physical injury is inflicted on a victim or an attempt is made to harm a person. Included in this category are criminal homicide or "murder," aggravated assault, forcible rape, armed robbery, and kidnapping. Murder and aggravated assault are similar in that an attempt is made to injure a person. They differ in outcome in part because of rapid access to medical treatment. Forcible rape, the act of sexual intercourse with a woman by force and without her consent, is distinguished from statutory rape, or intercourse with a female who has not attained a specific age, usually sixteen, necessary to give consent. Armed robbery involves the use of force or threat of violence to obtain money or valuables from a person. These are, of course, the kinds of offenses that produce fear in citizens.

The victim often plays a part in violent crime. In a study of police records in Philadelphia, Marvin Wolfgang found that in 26 per cent of the cases of criminal homicide the victim was the first to use physical force or violence in an argument or dispute. In a comparable study in Chicago, 38 per cent of the homicides involved victim precipitation.[6]

Rates of violent offenses differ not only from culture to culture but also from area to area within a given culture. In an effort to explain these variations, it has been suggested that there is a subculture of violence in which the use of violence or force is an acceptable means of settling disputes.[7]

Professional Crime

Criminologists distinguish between amateurs and professional criminals who steal for a living. The term *professional* is used when offenders are highly skilled and are accorded high status among criminals. They usually avoid apprehension; if they are detected, professional criminals are fairly successful in avoiding prison terms by offering restitution to their victims or by attempting to "fix" their case through bribery. In contrast with organized crime, which relies on force or the threat of force, professional criminals are generally nonviolent property offenders. Their activities have included pickpocketing, shoplifting, burglary of places of business, passing bad checks, extorting money from persons engaged in illegal sexual activities, and operating a variety of confidence games.

Other Property Crime

Professional criminals exhibit considerable skill in their criminal activities and work full time as criminals; in contrast, other property offenders are less

---

[6] Marvin E. Wolfgang, *Patterns in Criminal Homicide* (New York: John Wiley & Sons, Inc., 1958); Harwin L. Voss and John R. Hepburn, "Patterns in Criminal Homicide in Chicago," *Journal of Criminal Law, Criminology and Police Science,* 59 (December 1968): 499–508.

[7] Marvin E. Wolfgang and Franco Ferracuti, *The Subculture of Violence: Towards an Integrated Theory in Criminology* (London: Tavistock Publications, Ltd., 1967).

THE COST OF CRIME

The economic cost of crime is estimated in various ways at various times. Various estimates have ranged from $10 to $50 billion annually. For example, the Bureau of Domestic Commerce has estimated the distribution of direct costs of crimes against business (e.g., robbery, theft, vandalism) at $4.8 billion for retailing, $2.7 for services, $1.8 for manufacturing, $1.5 for transportation, and $1.4 for wholesaling. In addition, businesses are spending an increasing amount of money in services, equipment, and other crime prevention measures.

More comprehensive estimates have placed the total cost of crime to the national economy over $50 billion, made up of the following categories: organized crime—$20 billion (gambling, narcotics, hijacked goods, loan sharking, prostitution); crimes against property and business—$13 billion (kickbacks, business thefts, robbery, embezzlement, vandalism, shoplifting); other crimes—$4 billion (loss of earnings and medical costs from homicides and assaults and from accidents resulting from drunken driving); private crime-fighting costs—$5–6 billion (services and equipment); law enforcement costs—$9 billion (police, court system, and corrections).

By any estimate the drain on the national economy from criminal activity is great and growing; the strain upon the nation's social fabric is incalculable.

From William S. Colman, *Cities, Suburbs and States* (New York: The Free Press, 1975), p. 125.

skilled and commit offenses occasionally or on a part-time basis. Both youth and adults who have limited skills run a high risk of apprehension, conviction, and incarceration. Consequently, many of the persons in prisons in the United States are relatively unskilled property offenders.

Organized Crime

Organized crime refers to syndicates that participate in illegal activities offering maximum profit at minimum risk of interference from law-enforcement agencies. Through political contributions, delivery of votes (either legitimate or fraudulent), and direct bribes, organized crime may corrupt the police, courts, and other governmental agencies so its members are relatively immune from criminal prosecution. Among the activities in which organized crime figures prominently are gambling, loan-sharking or the lending of money above the legal limit, narcotics, racketeering or extortion of money from firms as "protection" against violence, prostitution, and pornography.

According to the President's Commission, organized crime consists of 24 families allied in a loose confederation.[8] Each group is called a family, and membership ranges from 20 to 700 men. There is only one family in most cities, but New York has five. The family may be known as the outfit, mob, syndicate, Mafia, or Cosa Nostra.

Each family has definite levels of authority and is headed by a boss who has absolute authority in matters pertaining to his family. Beneath each family head is an underboss or deputy director. At the same level, but not a part of the chain of command, there is a *consigliere* who is a counselor or advisor. Below the underboss are the *caporegime,* or lieutenants, who serve as buffers between the higher levels of the family and the lower-echelon personnel. Commands and information travel through these trusted lieutenants; to avoid legal problems, the leaders of a family do not communicate directly with workers. There is also "one or more fixed positions for 'enforcers,' whose duty it is to maintain organizational integrity by arranging for the maiming and killing of recalcitrant members. And there is a position for a 'corrupter,' whose function is to establish relationships with those public officials and other influential persons whose assistance is necessary to achieve the organization's goals."[9] At the lowest level of membership in the family are the *soldati,* or soldiers. A soldier operates an illicit enterprise on a commission basis or pays a portion of his profits to the organization. Beneath the soldiers are many employees who do most of the actual work: taking bets, selling narcotics, and operating lotteries.

Occupational and Corporate Crime

According to Edwin Sutherland, *white-collar crime* is "a crime committed by a person of respectability and high social status in the course of his occupation."[10] In the field of medicine, for example, a specialist may enter into illegal fee splitting with general practitioners in payment for referral of patients, or a physician may file a fraudulent insurance claim. Similarly, a lawyer may misappropriate funds or seek false testimony from a witness. Recognition that middle- and upper-class persons may commit crimes in the course of their occupations led criminologists to consider offenses that may occur in any legitimate occupation, not simply white-collar ones. Actually, nearly all

[8] *The Challenge of Crime in a Free Society,* op. cit., p. 192.
[9] Ibid., p. 193.
[10] Edwin H. Sutherland, *White Collar Crime* (New York: Holt, Rinehart and Winston, 1949), p. 9.

legitimate occupations offer possibilities for criminal violations. Even the small farmer is not immune; he can add water to the milk that he sells to a dairy.

Criminologists divide white-collar crime into two types, occupational crime and corporate crime, on the basis of whether the individual or the company benefits from a violation. *Occupational crime* includes the offenses of employees against their employers, as in the case of embezzlement, and the offenses committed by individuals in the course of their occupations for their own benefit. *Corporate crime* "consists of the offenses committed by corporate officials for their corporation and the offenses of the corporation itself."[11] Included in this category are misrepresentation in advertising, illegal restraint of trade, patent or copyright infringement, unfair labor practices, illegal rebates, price-fixing, manufacture of adulterated foods and drugs, illegal campaign contributions, and environmental pollution. The drug industry offers an excellent example of price-fixing. Between 1953 and 1961, 100 tablets of the antibiotic tetracycline cost as little as $1.52 to manufacture, but the retail price was about $51.00. After indictments for criminal conspiracy were issued, a decade later the retail price of the same quantity of the drug was approximately $5.00.[12]

Occupational and corporate crimes are generally handled by governmental agencies, and compliance with the law is sought by such means as injunctions (cease and desist orders) and fines. In the 1960s, General Electric, Westinghouse, and other companies were convicted of price-fixing in the sales of several billion dollars worth of electrical equipment. In view of corporate earnings, the $437,000 fine assessed against General Electric was comparable to a $3 parking ticket for a man with an income of $15,000.[13]

THE EXTENT AND DISTRIBUTION OF CRIME AND DELINQUENCY

Uniform Crime Reports

If a society is to prevent and control crime and delinquency, something must be known about the extent and dimensions of these phenomena. The major

---

[11] Marshall B. Clinard and Richard Quinney, *Criminal Behavior Systems: A Typology,* 2nd ed. (New York: Holt, Rinehart and Winston, 1973), p. 188.

[12] Ralph Nader and Mark Green, "Crime in the Suites," *The New Republic,* 166 (April 29, 1972): 17.

[13] Ibid., pp. 18–20; see Gilbert Geis, "The Heavy Electrical Equipment Antitrust Cases of 1961," in Gilbert Geis, ed., *White-Collar Criminal: The Offender in Business and the Professions* (New York: Atherton Press, 1968), pp. 103–118.

source of statistics on crime is the FBI's *Uniform Crime Reports* (UCR) in which offenses such as robbery and burglary are broadly defined.[14] These official statistics are gathered by the FBI from police departments across the country. There are approximately 40,000 independent law-enforcement organizations in the United States, and the FBI serves as the national clearinghouse for crime reports. In 1975, reports were submitted voluntarily by law-enforcement agencies serving 95 per cent of the nation's population.

Data on arrests are gathered for 29 crime categories, and information on "crimes known to the police" are collected from seven *index crimes:* murder, forcible rape, robbery, aggravated assault, burglary, larceny-theft, and motor vehicle theft. In 1975, the number of index crimes known to the police totaled 11,256,600. Violent crime—murder, forcible rape, aggravated assault, and robbery—comprises about 10 per cent of the known crimes, and property crime—burglary, larceny-theft, and motor vehicle theft—accounts for 90 per cent of the known index offenses, as shown in Table 10-1.

Table 10-1. Estimated Number and Rate of Crimes Reported to the Police in the United States, 1975

	Estimated Crime	
Crime Index Offenses	Number	Rate Per 100,000 Inhabitants
Total	11,256,600	5,282
Violent crimes	1,026,280	482
Property crimes	10,230,300	4,800
Murder	20,510	10
Forcible rape	56,090	26
Robbery	464,970	218
Aggravated assault	484,710	227
Burglary	3,252,100	1,526
Larceny-theft	5,977,700	2,805
Motor vehicle theft	1,000,500	469

SOURCE: Federal Bureau of Investigation, *Uniform Crime Reports: Crime in the United States, 1975* (Washington, D.C.: U.S. Government Printing Office, 1976), p. 11. The number of crimes in areas not covered by police reports is estimated on the basis of the information received from similar areas. These estimates are added to the number of crimes reported to the police.

[14] Federal Bureau of Investigation, *Uniform Crime Reports: Crime in the United States, 1975* (Washington, D.C.: U.S. Government Printing Office, 1976), pp. 6–7.

In 1975, the police made approximately 9 million arrests, as shown in Table 10-2. However, only 21 per cent of the index crimes known to the police were cleared in 1975. A crime is cleared when the police identify the offender, obtain sufficient evidence to file charges, and take the person into custody. A conviction is not required for a case to be cleared. Higher percentages of crimes against persons than against property are cleared because of the availability of witnesses and more intensive police investigation.

Sex.   There are significant patterns with regard to sex, age, and race in the arrest statistics. In 1975, arrests of males for index offenses outnumbered those of females by five to one. According to arrest statistics, males committed 94 per cent of all robberies, burglaries, and auto thefts. They also accounted for 90 per cent of all violent crime. They committed all forcible rapes, but 132 women were arrested because they assisted males in the rape of other females. The index crimes for which women were arrested in sizable numbers were murder, with 15 per cent female offenders; aggravated assault, 13 per cent; and larceny, in which 31 per cent of the arrests involved women.

Since 1960, arrests of females have increased more rapidly than have arrests of males. The greatest increase has been in property crimes, particularly burglary. Except for murder and aggravated assault, from 1960 to 1975 females registered higher percentage increases in arrests than males for each of the index crimes.

Age.   Persons under 25 years of age comprised three fourths of those arrested for index crimes in 1975. Juveniles under 15 accounted for one fifth of the arrests for burglary and larceny. One third of the arrests for robbery and one half of the arrests for burglary, larceny, and auto theft involved juveniles under the age of 18. Persons under 25 accounted for one half of the arrests for murder, manslaughter, and aggravated assault. The percentages of all arrested persons who were under 25 for the other index crimes were forcible rape, 58 per cent; robbery, 77 per cent; burglary, 85 per cent; larceny-theft, 75 per cent; and motor vehicle theft, 85 per cent. Young persons accounted for most of the property crime, insofar as may be determined from arrest statistics.

Race.   In crimes of violence, racial differences in arrest are pronounced. Blacks comprise 11 per cent of the population of the United States, but 54 per cent of the persons arrested for murder in 1975 were black. Of those arrested for robbery, 59 per cent were black, as were 45 per cent of those charged

Table 10-2. Estimated Number of Arrests in the United States, 1975

Total	9,273,600
Criminal homicide:	
Murder and nonnegligent manslaughter	20,180
Manslaughter by negligence	3,720
Forcible rape	26,670
Robbery	158,870
Aggravated assault	245,600
Burglary—breaking or entering	553,900
Larceny—theft	1,139,100
Motor vehicle theft	150,800
Violent crime	451,310
Property crime	1,843,800
Subtotal for above offenses	2,298,900
Other assaults	422,700
Arson	18,600
Forgery and counterfeiting	67,100
Fraud	171,300
Embezzlement	12,200
Stolen property; buying, receiving, possessing	122,000
Vandalism	230,700
Weapons; carrying, possessing, etc.	166,400
Prostitution and commercialized vice	68,200
Sex offenses (except forcible rape and prostitution)	64,400
Narcotic drug laws	601,400
Opium or cocaine and their derivatives	78,800
Marijuana	416,100
Synthetic or manufactured narcotics	28,300
Other—dangerous narcotic drugs	78,200
Gambling	62,200
Bookmaking	5,500
Numbers and lottery	10,400
All other gambling	46,800
Offenses against family and children	68,900
Driving under the influence	947,100
Liquor laws	340,100
Drunkenness	1,217,000
Disorderly conduct	748,400
Vagrancy	40,000
All other offenses (except traffic)	1,209,200
Suspicion (not included in total)	36,200
Curfew and loitering law violations	146,400
Runaways	250,100

SOURCE: Federal Bureau of Investigation, *Uniform Crime Reports: Crime in the United States, 1975* (Washington, D.C.: U.S. Government Printing Office, 1976), p. 179.

with forcible rape. Blacks accounted for approximately 30 per cent of the arrests for burglary, larceny, and motor vehicle theft. Part of the explanation for the high rates of arrest of blacks may lie in the fact that in some cities ghetto or slum areas are patrolled more heavily by the police. It is generally thought that for the same offense blacks are more likely than whites to be arrested.[15] Blacks are also concentrated in the lower socioeconomic level, and regardless of race, poor persons have high arrest rates. Although it is important to recognize these factors, the higher arrest rates for blacks also indicate that blacks commit more crime than whites.

Limitations. Although UCR provides considerable information about crime and delinquency, these official statistics have some limitations. Not all offenses are known to the police, and reporting varies by type of offense. For example, thefts of inexpensive items and assaults that do not result in serious injury are not as likely to be reported to the police as are murders and auto thefts. Prostitutes and intoxicated persons are subject to arrest in public places but are relatively safe in private settings where the police cannot enter without a warrant. In addition, few violations committed by government officials, corporate executives, and other occupational offenders are included in official crime statistics. In areas such as unfair advertising and job discrimination, the laws are enforced through special administrative boards; the criminal process is rarely used. Recognition of these limitations has led to use of two alternative approaches, victim surveys and self-report studies.

NORC Victim Survey

To obtain more accurate information about the amount and kinds of crime than is available in UCR, the President's Commission asked the National Opinion Research Center (NORC) to make the first national study of crime victimization. NORC conducted a survey of 10,000 households to determine the extent to which citizens are the victims of crime.[16] Approximately 20 per cent of the households surveyed had been victimized in the preceding year. However, a sizable portion of these victimizations involved minor crimes—

[15] Robert M. Terry, "Discrimination in the Handling of Juvenile Offenders by Social-Control Agencies," *Journal of Research in Crime and Delinquency,* 4 (July 1967): 218–230.

[16] President's Commission on Law Enforcement and Administration of Justice, *Crime and Its Impact—An Assessment* (Washington, D.C.: U.S. Government Printing Office, 1967), p. 17; see Phillip H. Ennis, "Crime, Victims, and the Police," *Trans-action,* 4 (June 1967): 36–44.

simple assault, petty larceny, malicious mischief, and consumer fraud. The incidence of such minor offenses was more than double the number of serious or index crimes, a category which includes murder, forcible rape, robbery, aggravated assault, burglary, larceny, and motor vehicle theft.

According to the NORC survey, the amount of crime in the United States is considerably higher than is indicated by the data gathered by the FBI. In fact, the incidence of index crimes was twice the amount reported in UCR. For burglary and forcible rape, the NORC rate is three or more times the reported rate. It is only in the categories of homicide and auto theft that the NORC and UCR rates are similar, as may be seen in Table 10-3.

In approximately one half of the incidents uncovered in the survey, the offense was not reported to the police. Most of the aggravated assaults, grand larcenies, and auto thefts were reported, but relatively few of the petty thefts and simple assaults were. Four reasons were given for victims not notifying the police. Of the victims who did not report the incident, 55 per cent believed that the police could not do anything about it, would not apprehend the offender, or would not want to be bothered. Some 34 per cent did not believe

Table 10-3. Comparison of NORC Survey and UCR Rates (Per 100,000 population)

Index Crimes	NORC Survey 1965–66	UCR Rate for Individuals 1965*	UCR Rate for Individuals and Organizations 1965*
Willful homicide	3.0	5.1	5.1
Forcible rape	42.5	11.6	11.6
Robbery	94.0	61.4	61.4
Aggravated assault	218.3	106.6	106.6
Burglary	949.1	299.6	605.3
Larceny ($50 and over)	606.5	267.4	393.3
Motor vehicle theft	206.2	226.0	251.0
Total violence	357.8	184.7	184.7
Total property	1,761.8	793.0	1,249.6

SOURCE: President's Commission on Law Enforcement and Administration of Justice, *Task Force Report: Crime and Its Impact—An Assessment* (Washington, D.C.: U.S. Government Printing Office, 1967), p. 17.

*"Uniform Crime Reports," 1965, p. 51. The UCR national totals do not distinguish crimes committed against individuals or households from those committed against businesses or other organizations. The UCR rate for individuals is the published national rate adjusted to eliminate burglaries, larcenies, and vehicle thefts not committed against individuals or households. No adjustment was made for robbery.

the incident was a police matter; they considered it to be a private affair, rather than a criminal one. Another 9 per cent did not want to take the time or trouble to call the police, and 2 per cent feared reprisal, either physically from the offender's friends or economically through cancellation or an increase in insurance rates.

National Crime Panel Surveys

In 1972, the Law Enforcement Assistance Administration (LEAA) in the Department of Justice initiated a series of surveys to assess the extent to which persons age 12 and over, households, and commercial establishments are victimized by crime. In these National Crime Panel surveys, attention is focused on certain types of crime: for commercial establishments, burglary and robbery; for households, burglary, larceny, and motor vehicle theft; and for individuals, rape, robbery, assault, and personal larceny. Personal larceny is defined as "the theft or attempted theft of property or cash with or without contact between victim and offender, but without force or the threat of force."[17]

Crime in the Nation's Five Largest Cities.   The first LEAA-sponsored survey dealt with crime in the nation's five largest cities—New York, Los Angeles, Chicago, Philadelphia, and Detroit—and provided information on the extent of crime in the year 1972.[18] In each city, about 10,000 households (including approximately 22,000 persons) and 3,500 businesses were surveyed by the Bureau of the Census.

Detroit had the highest rate for violent crimes, and Los Angeles ranked

[17] *Criminal Victimization in the United States, January–June 1973,* Vol. I, A National Crime Panel Survey Report, National Criminal Justice Information and Statistics Service (Washington, D.C.: U.S. Government Printing Office, 1974), p. 1.

[18] *Criminal Victimization Surveys in the Nation's Five Largest Cities,* National Crime Panel Surveys of Chicago, Detroit, Los Angeles, New York, and Philadelphia, National Criminal Justice Information and Statistics Service (Washington, D.C.: U.S. Government Printing Office, 1975). Comparable surveys were carried out in eight other cities in the latter part of 1972 and in 13 additional cities early in 1974; these studies produced similar findings. See *Crime in Eight American Cities,* National Crime Panel Surveys of Atlanta, Baltimore, Cleveland, Dallas, Denver, Newark, Portland, and St. Louis, Advance Report, National Criminal Justice Information and Statistics Service (Washington, D.C.: U.S. Government Printing Office, 1974); *Criminal Victimization Surveys in 13 American Cities,* National Crime Panel Surveys in Boston, Buffalo, Cincinnati, Houston, Miami, Milwaukee, Minneapolis, New Orleans, Oakland, Pittsburgh, San Diego, San Francisco, and Washington, D.C., National Criminal Justice Information and Statistics Service (Washington, D.C.: U.S. Government Printing Office, 1975).

first for thefts. For offenses involving households, Detroit had the highest and New York, the lowest victimization rate. Commercial victimization rates were highest in Detroit.

Nationwide Crime Panel Survey.   The results of a nationwide survey are also available. This report of the National Crime Panel covers the first six months of 1973 and is based on a representative sample of 60,000 households and 15,000 businesses.[19] Comprising 41 per cent of the victimizations, personal larceny was the single most prevalent type of crime. Crimes of violence—rape, robbery of persons, and assault—accounted for 15 per cent of the victimizations, but the bulk of these offenses involved simple assault. The survey indicates that 90,000 rapes occurred in the first half of 1973. Whereas 51,000 rapes were reported to the police in all of 1973, the actual number of rapes was found, as in the NORC survey, to be approximately 3.5 times higher than the number reported to the police.

Like the earlier NORC study, the panel survey shows that there are striking differences in the risk of victimization by race, sex, age, and income level. Blacks are more likely than whites to be victims of crimes against the person. Males are victimized more frequently than females. For crimes against the person, the highest rate of victimization is found among persons 12 to 19 years of age, and the rates decline progressively with increases in age.

Income is also related to victimization, but the patterns differ for property and personal crimes. Members of families with incomes under $3,000 are more likely to be victims of personal crimes of violence, whereas those with family incomes of at least $15,000 are more often the victims of larceny. Just as victimization studies reveal more crime than is officially recorded, so do self-reports.

Self-reports

Instead of inquiring whether a person has been the victim of crime, some investigators have asked juveniles and adults directly about the nature and extent of their involvement in illegal acts. Numerous studies of self-reported delinquency, conducted in various parts of the country, consistently reveal that (1) almost everyone has violated some criminal law or committed a juve-

[19] *Criminal Victimization in the United States,* op. cit.

nile status offense, such as truancy; (2) juveniles vary considerably in the extent to which they are involved in delinquency; (3) there is an enormous volume of hidden delinquency; and (4) the chances of a police contact as a result of a delinquent act are affected by one's social position.[20] While nearly all juveniles admit violations of the law, most of them have committed only a few infractions. Further, the persistent offenders are more likely to be the ones who commit serious crimes.

The findings in a study of high school students in California are typical.[21] Although the differences were not as great as would be expected on the basis of official statistics, the investigators found support for the inference from official sources that males are more likely to be involved in delinquent acts than are females. The males reported more delinquent acts than the females, and the differences were greatest for serious offenses. The males did most of the gang fighting, auto thefts, and robberies. On the other hand, the findings did not support the idea of differences in rates of delinquency by race. It was discovered that in the junior high school years, lower-class youth committed more delinquent acts, as well as more serious violations, than did adolescents in other social classes. However, in the high school years there appeared to be no association between social class and delinquency. One of the reasons why the findings of self-report studies seem to conflict with the official statistics may be that investigators have focused on juvenile status offenses and less serious violations of the law, rather than on such acts as robbery and burglary.

In the California study, another explanation for the apparent discrepancy emerged. For each 100 self-reported offenses, only five resulted in contact with the police. Thus, 95 per cent of the offenses that were admitted were not known to law-enforcement authorities. However, males, members of minority groups (particularly blacks), and lower-class offenders encountered a greater risk of police contact for each delinquent act they committed. For every 100 serious delinquent acts reported, boys had five police contacts and girls had only one. Similarly, 13 per cent of the serious violations reported by blacks, in comparison with 4 per cent among whites, resulted in police contact. The comparable figures for juveniles in the highest and lowest classes

---

[20] Summaries of the numerous self-report studies may be found in LaMar T. Empey, "Delinquency Theory and Recent Research," *Journal of Research in Crime and Delinquency,* 4 (January 1967): 28–42; Gwynn Nettler, *Explaining Crime* (New York: McGraw-Hill Book Company, 1974), pp. 73–97; Delbert S. Elliott and Harwin L. Voss, *Delinquency and Dropout* (Lexington, Mass.: Lexington Books, 1974), pp. 63–80.

[21] Elliott and Voss, op. cit.

were 1 and 9 per cent, respectively. As these rates take into account the frequency of violations, it is apparent that social position is related to one's chance of police contact.

In a recent nationwide study of drug use, self-report data were obtained in personal interviews with 2,510 men who were 20 to 30 years of age; in this investigation, a random sample was selected from the lists of Selective Service registrants across the United States.[22] The men were asked if they had ever committed each of thirteen illegal acts, including buying, selling, and stealing drugs. The percentages who admitted these criminal acts are shown in Table 10-4.

Table 10-4.   Percentage of Men 20 to 30 Years of Age Who Admitted Illegal Activities: 1974

Act	Percentage	Age	Percentage
Public intoxication	70	Illegal gambling	3
Driving while intoxicated	60	Check forgery	3
Auto theft	6	Prescription forgery	1
Burglary	13	Purchase of illicit drugs	41
Armed robbery	1	Selling of illicit drugs	19
Shoplifting	44	Stealing drugs	3
Robbery	3		

SOURCE: John A. O'Donnell, Harwin L. Voss, Richard R. Clayton, Gerald T. Slatin, and Robin G. W. Room, *Young Men and Drugs: A Nationwide Survey* (Rockville, Md.: National Institute on Drug Abuse, 1976), p. 82.

EXPLAINING CRIME AND DELINQUENCY

The Theory of Differential Association

To explain the differences in rates of crime and delinquency in terms of sex, age, and race, Sutherland suggests that in a complex society there are opposing definitions of what is expected and desirable in reference to the law. Some groups subscribe to criminal norms and thus support patterns of behavior that are defined as criminal in the society. A person may associate with in-

[22] John A. O'Donnell, Harwin L. Voss, Richard R. Clayton, Gerald T. Slatin, and Robin G. W. Room, *Young Men and Drugs: A Nationwide Survey* (Rockville, Md.: National Institute on Drug Abuse, 1976).

dividuals and groups who uphold the legal code, but may also interact with people who do not. An essential idea in differential association theory is that the learning of criminal behavior involves *differential exposure* to favorable and unfavorable definitions of the legal norms.

Differential association refers to the balance within a person of opposing definitions of laws. The effect of exposure to differing views of the law varies with their frequency and duration. An individual's relationship with the person presenting a procriminal or anticriminal view is also important. The definitions provided by one's close friends generally are more significant than those of teachers, policemen, and other representatives of society.

Sutherland proposes that criminal behavior is learned through interaction with other persons, and this learning occurs principally in primary groups. According to the theory of differential association, the process by which one becomes delinquent or criminal—the acquiring of attitudes favorable to delinquency or crime and the learning of the appropriate behavioral patterns—is the same as the process by which one becomes a Boy Scout. The difference in outcome is due to *what* is learned rather than *how* it is learned.[23]

People have misinterpreted the term *differential association* to mean that one becomes a criminal through association with criminals. However, an ex-convict might convince his or other children to obey the law by arguing that the risk of a long period of confinement outweighs the benefits of crime. In contrast, an otherwise saintly father may offer to his children rationalizations to justify violation of traffic laws, particularly speed limits.

Sutherland speaks of definitions favorable or unfavorable to crime, but in actual practice the theory of differential association must be translated into specific statements about kinds or types of criminal behavior. In other words, an excess of definitions favorable to income tax evasion would lead us to predict that kind of criminal act rather than auto theft. Persons with extensive exposure to definitions that justify breaking particular laws have a greater likelihood of committing such offenses than those who do not.

Sutherland's theory is based on the assumption that "a criminal act occurs when a situation appropriate for it, as defined by the person, is present."[24] Situations are important because they may or may not offer an

---

[23] Burgess and Akers have used behavioral learning theory, as proposed by B. F. Skinner, to restate Sutherland's theory. Robert L. Burgess and Ronald L. Akers, "A Differential Association-Reinforcement Theory of Criminal Behavior," *Social Problems*, 14 (Fall 1966): 146.

[24] Edwin H. Sutherland and Donald R. Cressey, *Criminology*, 9th ed. (Philadelphia: J. B. Lippincott Company, 1974), p. 75.

opportunity for a criminal act. For gang delinquents, a drunk alone in a dark alley offers an opportunity to "roll" him to get his money; if a policeman is also visible in the alley, the boys' view of the situation is considerably altered.

Sutherland's theory of differential association has been very influential. Like any influential theory, it has been modified and elaborated. Important variations on the basic theory lie in the concepts of techniques of neutralization, self-concept, and delinquent subcultures.

Techniques of Neutralization. Gresham Sykes and David Matza suggest that delinquents have accepted the norms and values of the society but have at their disposal a number of rationalizations or justifications that neutralize demands for conformity.[25] These justifications which protect them from feelings of guilt or self-condemnation are called techniques of neutralization. A delinquent can deny personal responsibility for his acts or can claim that no real harm was caused by his pranks. Another technique of neutralization is to shift attention to the behavior of those who disapprove of his violations—teachers may be condemned for showing favoritism by a student who is disruptive in school. Thefts from a store may be justified on the grounds that the owner had charged excessively high prices or sold inferior merchandise.

Self-concept. In the theory of differential association, the process of transmission of attitudes and patterns of behavior is emphasized so strongly that it gives the impression there is no possibility of choice on the part of the individual. The implication that violation of the law occurs automatically among those with extensive exposure to definitions favorable to criminality may be overcome by inclusion of the self-concept. In this vein, Walter Reckless and his coworkers attempted to determine why nondelinquent boys who live in areas with high delinquency rates remain nondelinquent. To account for these "good" boys, they suggest that a socially appropriate self-concept is the prime factor in influencing a youth away from delinquency.[26] "Particular kinds of self-concepts may serve the function of forestalling offenses, because the actor does not define himself as the kind of person who can roll a drunk, rob a service station, or take a pickup to a hotel room."[27]

[25] Gresham M. Sykes and David Matza, "Techniques of Neutralization: A Theory of Delinquency," *American Sociological Review,* 22 (December 1957): 664–670.

[26] Walter C. Reckless, Simon Dinitz, and Barbara Kay, "The Self Component in Potential Delinquency and Potential Non-Delinquency," *American Sociological Review,* 22 (October 1957): 566–570.

[27] Harwin L. Voss, "Differential Association and Containment Theory: A Theoretical Convergence," *Social Forces,* 47 (June 1969): 390.

Delinquent Subcultures.   A person's self-concept reflects the importance of group processes. It has been recognized for some time that clique or group formation is common during adolescence. Delinquent acts provide children with fun and excitement, but if they come into conflict with society, these loosely organized groups may become integrated gangs.[28] Albert Cohen proposes that many delinquent acts reflect participation in such gangs or delinquent subcultures that support beliefs, values, and norms unfavorable to the law.[29] Thefts are encouraged, intimidation of others is enjoyed, and truancy and disruptive behavior are honored.

Richard Cloward and Lloyd Ohlin distinguish three types of delinquent subcultures that are found among lower-class adolescent males in metropolitan areas: criminal, conflict, and retreatist.[30] The nature of the neighborhood affects the type of subculture that emerges among these youth. In some slum neighborhoods, there is sufficient residential stability that adolescents can develop relationships with adult criminals. In such "age-integrated" slums, youngsters can associate with sophisticated offenders, and adult criminals can serve as models and sources of criminal values and skills. In such a setting, the *criminal* subculture, which offers an "apprenticeship" for a position in organized crime, appears. In "unintegrated" areas, characterized by extensive mobility and transiency—perhaps epitomized by massive housing projects—criminal models, including the racketeer and the "fence" who deals in stolen merchandise, are not present. In such areas, the opportunity to learn how to perform successfully in criminal activities is not available, and *conflict* subcultures emerge in which the manipulation of violence serves as a route to status or reputation. These are the warrior gangs that attract the attention of the press and the public. Finally, the *retreatist* subculture emphasizes drug use. Participants in these drug subcultures presumably are alienated from conventional roles. Withdrawn from the life style and usual preoccupations of conventional persons, they live in pursuit of the "kick," or a search for ecstatic experiences.

The Labeling Perspective

The theory of differential association and the related ideas of techniques of neutralization, self-concept, and delinquent subcultures are useful in efforts to

[28] Frederic M. Thrasher, *The Gang: A Study of 1,313 Gangs in Chicago* (Chicago: University of Chicago Press, 1927).
[29] Albert K. Cohen, *Delinquent Boys: The Culture of the Gang* (New York: The Free Press, 1955), p. 59.
[30] Richard A. Cloward and Lloyd E. Ohlin, *Delinquency and Opportunity: A Theory of Delinquent Gangs* (New York: The Free Press, 1960).

explain crime, but in recent years criminologists have developed the labeling perspective to emphasize the importance of the process of making and applying rules. The central proposition in the labeling perspective is that deviance always involves social definition. Howard Becker suggests: "Social groups create deviance by making the rules whose infraction constitutes deviance, and by applying these rules to particular people and labeling them as outsiders. From this point of view, deviance is *not* a quality of the act the person commits, but rather a consequence of the application by others of rules and sanctions to an 'offender.' The deviant is one to whom that label has successfully been applied; deviant behavior is behavior that people so label."[31]

This statement has two unfortunate implications. It suggests that labeling is all that is required for an act to be deviant. However, deviance cannot be defined without some reference to norms or rules. In other words, it cannot be defined solely in terms of the reactions of others. If an act is not deviant unless it is labeled, there can be no such thing as secret or undetected deviance, nor can we describe as deviant most of the violations we conveniently classify under the headings of occupational crime and organized crime. Becker's statement also implies that the reactors are the culprits. In the enactment of laws, the legislature defines acts as criminal, but this does not mean that the legislature *causes* criminal acts by establishing laws. It is inappropriate to imply that a policeman who arrests a person who has violated the law is, somehow, at fault. If the criminal law were abolished, acts that result in injuries would not disappear: "A mugging by any other name hurts just as much."[32]

Although deviance cannot be defined without some reference to norms, this does not mean that labeling processes are unimportant. Future behavior may be affected by the way in which others respond to an individual's deviant acts. In this sense, labeling *produces* deviants. To assign a person the label of delinquent, criminal, drug addict, or prostitute is a form of social penalty that may lead to rejection and exclusion from conventional groups, and as a consequence may evoke further deviant acts.

The impact of labeling may be clarified by considering Edwin Lemert's distinction between primary and secondary deviation. *Primary* or initial acts of deviance do not affect a person's self-concept or interfere with functioning in socially acceptable roles. For example, juveniles may commit a few delinquent acts without becoming committed to a delinquent career or being

[31] Howard S. Becker, *Outsiders: Studies in the Sociology of Deviance* (New York: The Free Press, 1963), p. 9.
[32] Nettler, op. cit., p. 210.

regarded by themselves or others as delinquents. If the deviant acts are repeated and result in reactions from one's family, friends, and especially authorities, a person may become a *secondary* deviant, or "a person whose life and identify are organized around the facts of deviance."[33] The deviant role may engulf the person so that he develops a deviant identity and organizes his behavior largely in terms of his deviant role. The disapproval and isolation experienced by the person may be more important in explaining his subsequent behavior than the original causes of his deviant acts. The labeling perspective is best viewed as complementary to other theoretical positions, such as differential association, for it does not attempt to explain why individuals initially violate norms. Yet, recognition of the potentially harmful effects of official processing of deviants has led to development of ways to divert primary deviants from the criminal justice system.

WHAT CAN BE DONE?

In view of citizen concern about crime, it is important to recognize that many "solutions" that would effectively reduce the crime rate are not acceptable in a democratic society. As previously noted, the crime rate of young males is considerably higher than the rate among females or older persons. However, the suggestion that all young men be confined until they reach the age of 30, or extensive preventive detention, is clearly impractical. After all, there are 19 million men between the ages of 20 and 30. It also implies a willingness to violate the rights of a large class of our citizenry to achieve the goal of a reduced crime rate.

Less drastic solutions that nevertheless depart from our cultural heritage involve new legislation to permit the police to use electronic devices to obtain information and to control possession of guns. Use of electronic bugs would be highly effective, but would involve an infringement on our right to privacy. Their use would be inconsistent with recent judicial decisions that have expanded the scope of the *exclusionary rule,* which means that evidence obtained by illegal means (for example, without a search warrant or a coerced confession) is not admissible in court. Strict gun control laws are needed to reduce the rate of violent crime. Yet registration of firearms and total prohibition of handguns involve limitation on the freedom of citizens. What choice shall be made?

Like rejection of preventive detention, the acceptance of legal restraints on police investigations is essential to protect citizens' rights. This points to a

[33] Edwin M. Lemert, *Human Deviance, Social Problems, and Social Control* (Englewood Cliffs, N.J.: Prentice-Hall, Inc., 1967), p. 41.

fundamental conflict in democratic societies. It is not possible for citizens to have unlimited freedom and, at the same time, to make their lives and property secure against attack. Most Americans do not recognize this conflict. Where efforts to combat crime have been intensified, they have essentially involved additions to what we already had. More police, better communications equipment for the police, more judges and courts, more assistants for them and for prosecutors are prime examples. The problem of crime deserves rethinking. It may be necessary for citizens to surrender some of the rights they now enjoy, such as the right to own handguns, in order to reduce the crime rate. Thus far, we have attempted to provide maximum freedom for citizens, and our high crime rate reflects the extent of that freedom.

To combat crime and delinquency a variety of agencies and institutions have been created. The police, courts, and correctional system together comprise the criminal justice system. America's system of criminal justice operates on the premise that ''a person may be punished by the Government if, and only if, it has been proved by an impartial and deliberate process that he has violated a specific law.''[34] However, the system is not a unified or even a consistent one, in part because it was not designed at one time. Some parts of the system were carefully constructed and inspired by principle, while others were improvised and prompted by expediency. The system is both old and new: magistrates' courts, trials by jury, and bail have a long history, whereas professional policemen, probation, parole, and juvenile courts are relatively recent developments. The criminal justice system is essentially an adaptation of English common law and procedure to America's unique form of government, in which local communities have the authority to construct agencies to fit their special needs. The result is that every town, city, and state has its own criminal justice system, as does the federal government.

The police, courts, and corrections each have distinctive tasks; however, they comprise a system in that their activities are not independent. The courts deal primarily with those whom the police arrest, and the correctional branch handles persons convicted by the courts. If correctional efforts do not change violators into law-abiding citizens, they may again become the business of the police and courts.

The Police

The first step in the criminal justice process is investigation and arrest by the police. In the NORC survey of crime victims, persons who reported an of-

[34] *The Challenge of Crime in a Free Society*, op. cit., p. 7.

The first step in the criminal justice process. (Courtesy of Magnum, photo by M. Dain.)

fense to the police were asked how the police responded and how far the case proceeded through the criminal justice system. The police were notified in 1,024 of the 2,077 incidents, or about one half of them. They came to the scene or acknowledged the event in 787 of the reported cases. The police viewed 593 of the incidents as crimes, and they made an arrest in 120 of these cases. There was a plea of guilty or a trial in 50 of the cases. The outcome was proper punishment, as defined by the victim, in 26 cases; in the remainder, the defendant was freed or punished too leniently, according to the respondent.[35] Thus, there is extensive attrition from victimization to trial and sentencing.

[35] Ennis, op. cit., pp. 40–41.

POLICE SPECIALISTS STALK PIMPS

Detective Joe Haggerty, bearded and dressed in a leisure suit, and his partner, Thom Grace, clean-shaven and prematurely gray, settle comfortably in their unmarked police cruiser, turn onto 14th Street NW and casually scan the dark streets for the familiar faces. Haggerty and Grace are police specialists. They stalk pimps.

The world in which they work is filled with shadowy people—robbers and junkies, pickpockets and prostitutes, burglars and panhandlers who, like bats out of a cave, flock to 14th Street to prowl. They use stealth, weapons, and the con to whip their prey. . . .

Unlike other policemen, Haggerty and Grace see their quarry every night. They know many pimps by name and ask some how they're feeling. That very closeness, though, breeds frustration; pimps are among the most elusive criminals to jail.

"In most cases you have the crime and look for the crook," says Grace. "Here we have the crooks and we gotta find the crime. Basically we have to wait until a pimp [assaults a girl] and she comes to us. Without a complaint, we don't have anything." . . .

On one corner stands a man in a chartreuse jumpsuit with a leather cumberbund studded with rhinestones, and a wide-brimmed hat. On another corner is a young man in white mink. It might well be Easter on Fifth Avenue. Except the parade is on the sidewalks and the spectators are driving down the street. . . .

There are about 500 pimps in Washington and most are black men in their 20s, the detectives say. They have names like "Mr. Angel," "Delicious," "Gizmo," "Baby Ruth," and "Cornbread." . . .

Haggerty and Grace have spent much of their police careers chasing pimps. They have index cards with pictures of the pimps, and files full of long-time pimps and new ones. Most of them have not been caught. Women seldom turn their men in and when they do, judges turn them back out.

Police have arrested about 1,000 prostitutes this year, and about 20 pimps. They have sent the men to court for pandering (causing a woman to work as a prostitute) and procuring (setting up dates and receiving money) and related offenses, but none has received anything more than probation.

Why, then, the hunt that has consumed so many of Haggerty and Grace's nights, yet yielded so few arrests? Haggerty answers the question with a tape recording. It is an interview with Angela, a prostitute who had gone to the police for help.

Angela: ". . . He jumped on me today, but the last time he really beat on me was last week . . ."

Q. "What's he beaten you with?"

A. "Clothes hangers, jumper cables, sticks, pipes, anything he picks up. . . ."

Q. "Have you ever had any medical treatment for the beatings? . . ."

A. "Well, the day that I cut my wrist, he was beating me when I cut it 'cause like that was the only way I could get him up off me was to cut my wrist, and you know, for him to see this and leave me alone. . . ."

Q. "How long did you live there with him?"

A. "Going on two, two-and-a-half years. . . ."

Angela said she joined her pimp because he supplied her with drugs, she stayed with him because she was afraid to go, and because "before he was on narcotics he was a different person."

That's why they go after them, Haggerty and Grace, say, turning off the recorder. Pimps abuse women and coerce young girls into prostitution.

"They'll buy a girl a tube top and a bikini and make 'em sleep maybe two or three to a bed, and he'll take all the money, because he needs a new wardrobe, because he needs a new car," Haggerty says.

Why do the women put up with it? Some of them are attracted to the charisma, the domination of the man, he says. Others yield to drugs or fear. Or a lie.

The pimp says, "Oh, baby, we just gotta get ahead, get a bank account, then someday you and me'll get a place in the country," Grace says. "He says he loves her, but to a pimp love means money."

At 3 in the morning, a prostitute beckons the detectives at 14th and Corcoran. "Ask me for some ID so it looks like you're checking me out," she whispers, leaning into the cruiser. She has information. A pimp has an arrest record and has stashed a pistol in his room, a possible felony. She asks them to put in a good word for her with the U.S. Attorney's office. "We'll mention you helped," Grace says and the detectives head to the rooming house.

The man seems stunned when the detectives walk in. His woman sits up in bed, clutching a mongrel. She appears to be about 20. The man, wiry, graying, sits passively beside her as the officers begin rummaging his room. The wallpaper is peeling and the soiled curtains are falling off the rods. Clothes are piled, not hung, in the closet.

"Anywhere you want, look anywhere you want," the man says quietly.

Under the bed the detectives find half-eaten tins of sardines, mounds of dog excrement and dozens of used syringes.

The detectives find a rifle and take it with them.

"Anything you want," the man says.

After they leave the officers want to wash their hands.

From *The Washington Post,* October 11, 1977, pp. 1, A-6.

A major deterrent to needed changes, such as an increase in the size of the police force, has been the unwillingness of the public to support increased expenditures. More importantly, the police are called upon to handle many tasks having little to do with crime—issuing dog and bicycle licenses, escorting funeral processions and parades, transporting sick and elderly persons to medical facilities, and directing traffic. These activities are time-consuming and leave relatively few man-hours for criminal investigation.

The Courts

The process of criminal justice is depicted in Figure 10-1. It is important to note that there are many decision points along its course; a simple model of arrest-conviction-imprisonment inadequately portrays the operation of the system. The paths in Figure 10-1 reflect the differences in the handling of felonies, misdemeanors, petty offenses such as traffic violations, and juvenile cases. *Felonies* are usually defined as offenses in which the minimum penalty is a year and a day in prison. *Misdemeanors* are offenses for which the maximum penalty is one year in jail.

Booking—the administrative record of arrest. (Courtesy of Magnum.)

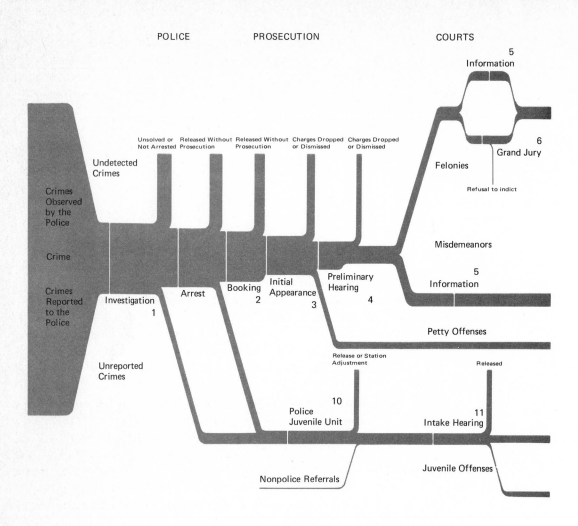

FIGURE 10-1. A general view of the criminal justice system.

POLICE　　　　　PROSECUTION　　　　　COURTS

Information　5

Undetected
Crimes

Unsolved or
Not Arrested

Released Without
Prosecution

Released Without
Prosecution

Charges Dropped
or Dismissed

Charges Dropped
or Dismissed

6
Grand Jury

Felonies

Refusal to indict

Crimes
Observed
by the
Police

Crime

Crimes
Reported
to the
Police

Investigation
1

Arrest

Booking
2

Initial
Appearance
3

Preliminary
Hearing
4

Misdemeanors

5
Information

Petty Offenses

Unreported
Crimes

Release or Station
Adjustment

Released

Police
Juvenile Unit
10

Intake Hearing
11

Nonpolice Referrals

Juvenile Offenses

1　May continue until trial.

2　Administrative record of arrest. First step at which temporary release on bail may be available.

3　Before magistrate, commissioner, or justice of peace. Formal notice of charge, advice of rights. Bail set. Summary trials for petty offenses usually conducted here without further processing.

4　Preliminary testing of evidence against defendant. Charge may be reduced. No separate preliminary hearing for misdemeanors in some systems.

5　Charge filed by prosecutor on basis of information submitted by police or citizens. Alternative to grand jury indictment; often used in felonies, almost always in misdemeanors.

6　Reviews whether Government evidence sufficient to justify trial. Some States have no grand jury system; others seldom use it.

CORRECTIONS

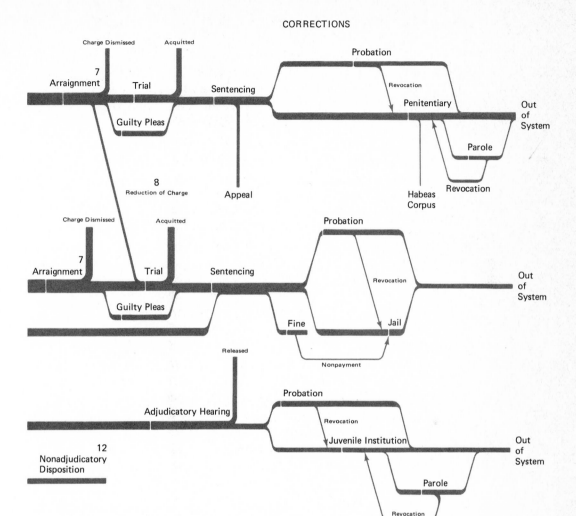

7 Appearance for plea; defendant elects trial by judge or jury (if available); counsel for indigent usually appointed here in felonies. Often not at all in other cases.

8 Charge may be reduced at any time prior to trial in return for plea of guilty or for other reasons.

9 Challenge on constitutional grounds to legality of detention. May be sought at any point in process.

10 Police often hold informal hearings, dismiss or adjust many cases without further processing.

11 Probation officer decides desirability of further court action.

12 Welfare agency, social services, counseling, medical care, etc., for cases where adjudicatory handling not needed.

Although the district attorney and grand jury have investigatory powers, the machinery of justice is usually set in motion by the arrest of an individual by the police. After an individual is apprehended, he or she is to be taken before a magistrate promptly or within twenty-four hours.[36] In the case of misdemeanors, a complaint or *charge* is filed against the person. Often the individual pleads guilty, and the case is disposed of swiftly. If the charge is a felony, the initial appearance before the magistrate is for the purpose of setting *bail*[37] and arranging for a *preliminary hearing*. This hearing also involves the magistrate, who determines whether there is sufficient evidence to warrant holding the accused for prosecution. According to Supreme Court decisions of the 1960s, the accused has a right to legal counsel in this initial court appearance. In about one half of the states, a grand jury, consisting of citizens selected from lists of property owners, car owners, or voters, hears the evidence in secret. They can dismiss the charge or produce an *indictment* or formal accusation. In other states, the prosecutor formulates the accusation, which is called an *information*.

At this point the prosecutor and defense attorney often engage in plea bargaining in which a deal is arranged. If the defendant agrees to plead guilty, some of the charges against him or her may be dropped or reduced. For the prosecutor, this offers the advantage of clearing a crowded court calendar, whereas the accused person does not risk a long prison sentence. There are also disadvantages in plea bargaining. Recent Supreme Court decisions require appointment of legal counsel for defendants who cannot afford a private attorney. Although this is laudable in terms of providing representation for the poor, public defenders are generally overworked and may advise an innocent person to plead guilty to a lesser charge. A private attorney, working for a fee, can take sufficient time and spend money for a thorough investigation and preparation of a case. For indigent defendants, some legal advice is probably better than none, but cases are often inadequately prepared, with the public defender seeing the accused only briefly; particularly when the accused is a juvenile, the first meeting between defendant and attorney may take place in court.

The next step after indictment is *arraignment*. The accused is read the indictment or information and enters a plea to the charge. In at least 80 per cent of the cases, a guilty plea is entered, and the accused is sentenced by the

---

[36] If a person is held without being taken to court, a *writ of habeas corpus* can be given to any judge in the area to obtain a hearing.

[37] Bail is a sum of money or title to an equivalent amount of property that is posted to obtain release; it may be forfeited if the accused does not appear in court at the appointed time.

judge. This occurs, in part, because the bulk of the business of the criminal justice system consists of less serious offenses, such as petty thefts, public drunkenness, domestic altercations, barroom disputes, and similar interpersonal difficulties. These cases are usually terminated in the early stages of the criminal justice process.

If the defendant pleads not guilty, a trial is held before a judge or trial jury. The cases that proceed all the way through the criminal justice system generally involve serious acts of violence or thefts of substantial amounts of property, although not all serious or major crimes follow this course. In 75 to 80 per cent of the trial cases, the defendant is found guilty. The convicted offender may be fined, placed on probation, or sentenced to prison.

Recently, the functioning of the court system has come under scrutiny. Problem areas include crowded court calendars, long delays between arraignment and trial, and failure of witnesses to appear because of numerous delays. These difficulties can be attributed largely to the inadequate number of courts. Expansion of court facilities, additional judges, and court clerks would alleviate these problems, but such change depends on the willingness of citizens to bear the financial burden.

The Correctional System

The American correctional system consists of diverse programs and facilities. Because it is administered by federal, state, municipal, and county governments, it does not really constitute a "system." Yet the scope of American corrections is reflected in operating budgets of over a billion dollars a year. On any given day, correctional institutions deal with some 1.3 million offenders and over the course of a year handle 2.5 million admissions.

National statistics on probation are not gathered regularly, but a survey of correctional operations in the mid-1960s revealed that on an average day 857,000 offenders were under the supervision of probation and parole agencies.[38] In 1973, there were 204,000 persons imprisoned in state or federal correctional institutions; another 142,000 were confined in local jails; 35,000 juveniles were held in training schools or other juvenile institutions; and 11,000 juveniles were in detention homes.[39]

---

[38] *The Challenge of Crime in a Free Society,* op. cit., p. 161.

[39] *Prisoners in State and Federal Institutions on December 31, 1971, 1972, and 1973,* National Prisoner Statistics Bulletin, National Criminal Justice Information and Statistics Service (Washington, D.C.: U.S. Government Printing Office, 1975), p. 1; *Children in Custody,* Advance Report on the Juvenile Detention

The most common forms of punishment for convicted offenders are fines and probation. A *fine* is a monetary penalty. The major difficulty with fines is that they do not affect the rich and poor equally. *Probation* involves the suspension of sentence on the condition that the offender maintains "good behavior" while at liberty in the community. To fine an offender or to place the offender on probation implies that the person is not dangerous to society. These alternatives are used primarily for less serious offenders.

Jails.   The jail was originally designed to detain persons awaiting trial, but soon became a place of punishment for persons convicted of misdemeanors. Many of the 3,921 jails in the United States resemble fortresses or dungeons and provide physically degrading and dehumanizing conditions. Few jails offer rehabilitation services, such as vocational training, counseling, and remedial education programs, or even adequate facilities for exercise and recreation, largely because of overcrowding and inadequate staffing. A national jail survey showed a total population of 141,600 of whom 42 per cent were serving sentences, 36 per cent were awaiting trial, and the remainder were in other stages of the criminal justice process.[40]

One obvious way of correcting some of the deficiencies of the jails would be to construct new facilities. This, of course, might lead to more incarceration and subsequent overcrowding. Another and perhaps more realistic approach, which has gained widespread acceptance in the field of corrections, is to reduce the jail population through the release of defendants on their own recognizance as opposed to reliance on the bail system.

The posting of bail, a sum of money or title to property, poses a heavy financial burden on poor persons or may be impossible to obtain even from a bondsman who charges a fee. If the accused does not make bail, he or she must spend the time between the preliminary hearing and trial in jail, a period of weeks or even months. Under the recognizance system, the accused, who must meet certain requirements regarding residence and other links to the community, promises to appear in court at the appointed time, without being required to post bond. A pilot program was initiated in New York City in 1961, and only 3 of 275 defendants failed to appear in court. In a similar

and Correctional Facility Census of 1972–73, National Criminal Justice Information and Statistics Service (Washington, D.C.: U.S. Government Printing Office, 1975), p. 1; *Survey of Inmates of Local Jails, 1972,* Advance Report, National Criminal Justice Information and Statistics Service (Washington, D.C.: U.S. Government Printing Office, 1974), p. 1.
[40] *Survey of Inmates of Local Jails, 1972,* op. cit., p. 3.

project in Michigan all but 12 of 12,400 defendants appeared in court as scheduled.[41]

Although correctional authorities believe that children and youth should not be held in jail, 9 per cent of the inmate population in 1972 were juveniles.[42] Ideally, juveniles would be held in a detention home, a secure, non-jail facility. However, most detention homes in this country are makeshift facilities that bear a strong resemblance to jails. It is generally conceded that releasing juveniles to their parents is preferable to detaining them in jail, particularly if the youth does not pose a threat to society. In some jurisdictions, however, juveniles apprehended for status offenses are jailed as a form of punishment because the police recognize that the court will not incarcerate such offenders.

Prisons. The prison, as we know it today, was developed in the United States. Believing that meditation in prison would lead to reformation, the Quakers erected the first prison in 1790 in Philadelphia. Today, there is considerable disagreement about the purpose of imprisonment. Prisons are said to serve four divergent purposes: retribution, deterrence, incapacitation, and rehabilitation. The idea of *retribution* is based on the ancient principle of "an eye for an eye and a tooth for a tooth." Today, commitment to prison is viewed as punishment; restriction on the prisoner's freedom is itself a severe form of punishment. Another purpose of incarceration is *deterrence.* The existence of prisons and the fact that some offenders are incarcerated is thought to deter other citizens from committing crimes. Imprisonment does *incapacitate* the offender, at least temporarily. Yet, according to Marshall Clinard, only 5 to 20 per cent of the people sent to prison pose a serious threat to society. Further, 95 per cent of all prison inmates are released, usually within one to five years.[43]

Although it is inconsistent with the idea of punishment, another purpose of the prison is *rehabilitation,* or treatment. The essential purpose of treatment is to change criminals into noncriminals. Because of the inherent conflict between punishment and treatment, any nonpunitive program—vocational training, library privileges, group therapy, psychotherapy, counse-

---

[41] Herbert Sturz, "An Alternative to the Bail System," *Federal Probation,* 26 (December 1962): 49–53; Talbot Smith, "A New Approach to the Bail Practice," *Federal Probation,* 29 (March 1965): 3–6.

[42] *Survey of Inmates of Local Jails, 1972,* op. cit., p. 3.

[43] Marshall B. Clinard, *Sociology of Deviant Behavior,* 4th ed.; (New York: Holt, Rinehart and Winston, Inc., 1974), p. 361.

ling—is considered to be treatment. These innovations as well as other prison reforms such as elimination of the lock-step, rules of silence, physical punishment or solitary confinement for rule violations, and limited visiting privileges are better viewed as efforts directed toward humane handling of prisoners, rather than as treatment.[44]

Many Americans continue to believe that the only appropriate way to deal with law violators is to imprison them. There are approximately 230 state and federal prisons for adult offenders and 190 correctional institutions for juveniles in the United States, many of which are old and overcrowded. To place all convicted offenders in prison would require a massive building program. Clearly, the cost of institutionalization of more than a fraction of all criminals and delinquents would be prohibitive.

There is a growing feeling that prisons may not be the best or the only solution to the problem of crime. Some citizens are aware that prisons are "schools for crime" in the sense that offenders emerge from prison as more hardened criminals than when they entered the institution. Social scientists recognize that it is difficult to change attitudes and behavior in an isolated, artificial prison setting, in which the prison subculture may operate to block rehabilitative efforts. Although prison guards and officials hold power over inmates, the informal rules of the prison subculture have a great effect on the prisoner's behavior. Conformity with "the code," which stresses loyalty among inmates and opposition to correctional authorities, is encouraged verbally and physically.

In the prison subculture, social positions are assigned to inmates in terms of compliance with the prison code. An inmate who betrays a fellow prisoner is a "rat" or squealer. Aggressive prisoners who quarrel and fight for little or no reason are called "toughs," whereas a "gorilla" deliberately uses violence to achieve his ends. The "merchant" or "peddler" exploits others by manipulation and trickery, not force. Inmates who express the values of conformity and side with prison officials are "Square Johns." In contrast, the inmate who fulfills the norms of the inmate code is a "right guy."[45] The inmate subculture presents a formidable barrier to therapeutic efforts and thus tends to negate the hope that imprisonment will lead to rehabilitation.

The stigma attached to the ex-convict also interferes with rehabilitation.

---

[44] Don C. Gibbons, *Society, Crime, and Criminal Careers: An Introduction to Criminology,* 2nd ed. (Englewood Cliffs, N.J.: Prentice-Hall, Inc., 1973), pp. 502–504.

[45] Gresham M. Sykes and Sheldon L. Messinger, "The Inmate Social System" in Richard A. Cloward et al., *Theoretical Studies in Social Organization of the Prison* (New York: Social Science Research Council, 1960), pp. 9–10.

There is a growing feeling that prisons may not be the best solution to the problem of crime. (Courtesy of Magnum.)

THE INMATE CODE

The chief tenets of the inmate code fall into five categories. First, "Don't interfere with inmate interests." The inmate should serve the least possible time, while enjoying the greatest possible number of pleasures and privileges. Specifically, he should be loyal to his fellow convicts and never serve as a "rat" or informer. Second, the inmate should avoid quarrels and arguments with other inmates: "Play it cool and do your own time." Third, prisoners should not take advantage of other inmates by means of force or fraud: "Don't exploit inmates." A fourth set of maxims concerns personal integrity: "Don't weaken. . . . Don't whine." Positively this means: "Be tough; be a man." Finally, prisoners should refuse to give respect to their captors: "Don't be a sucker. . . . In any situation of conflict between officials and prisoners, the former are automatically to be considered in the wrong. Furthermore, inmates should not allow themselves to become committed to the values of hard work and submission to duly constituted authority."

Source: Adapted from Gresham M. Sykes and Sheldon L. Messinger, "The Inmate Social System," in Richard A. Cloward et al., *Theoretical Studies in Social Organization of the Prison* (New York: Social Science Research Council, 1960), pp. 6–8.

Prisons may provide technical training, but it is difficult for persons released from prison to secure jobs because employers are hesitant to hire ex-convicts.[46]

Parole. Few of the persons committed to prison spend the remainder of their lives there. Many offenders are released outright upon completion of their sentences, but more than 60 per cent of the adults released from prison in the United States are paroled.[47] *Parole* is release from prison prior to the expiration of the maximum term of a sentence on the condition that the parolee submit to supervision and certain restrictions on his or her behavior. If the parolee violates the conditions of parole, he or she may be returned to prison.

The federal prison system is considered one of the best in the world. Of

[46] Richard D. Schwartz and Jerome H. Skolnick, "Two Studies of Legal Stigma," in Howard S. Becker, ed., *The Other Side: Perspectives on Deviance* (New York: The Free Press, 1964), pp. 103–117.

[47] Parole for juveniles is often referred to as "aftercare." Administration of programs for juveniles is so fragmented that it is impossible to determine the extent of its use. The figure of 60 per cent for adults is an average; the range is from 10 per cent in South Carolina to 100 per cent in New Hampshire and Washington.

the inmates released from federal prisons in 1970, over 67 per cent were successes (no new sentences of 60 days or more and no parole revocation) in the following two years. In an earlier study, Daniel Glaser found that 65 per cent of the 1,015 men released in 1956 were successes. Only 16 per cent of those convicted for income tax fraud or embezzlement returned to prison, but 47 per cent of the men sentenced for auto theft were failures.[48] This suggests that certain types of offenders are more likely to commit additional offenses than are others.

Probation. As previously noted, *probation* involves the suspension of sentence on the condition that the offender maintain good behavior while at liberty in the community. Like parole, the terms of probation generally include observance of all laws, payment of restitution or fines, regular employment, no use of alcohol or drugs, no association with criminals, and periodic reports to a specified probation officer. Other conditions may be imposed; often, the probationer cannot marry or obtain a divorce, change jobs or residence, or travel without the probation officer's permission.

Although parole involves offenders who have served time in prison, both parole and probation deal with the offender in the community. One difference is that the decision to grant parole is made by an administrative board. In 39 states, the parole board members are appointed by the governor. On the other hand, the granting of probation involves a judicial decision. A convicted felon may be sentenced to an institution or placed on probation. Legally, probation is an extension of the long-standing right of the court to suspend sentence.

Today, probation is available to juveniles and adult felons in every state, but one fourth of the counties in the United States have no probation department, and in some rural areas, probation officers serve on a part-time basis. In most states, statutory restrictions do not permit probation for offenders convicted of the most serious crimes, particularly crimes of violence. These restrictions reflect the continuing conflict between the punitive and the therapeutic or treatment reactions to crime.

Imprisonment is considerably more expensive than probation. Currently, it costs $10,000 to $15,000 to keep a juvenile in a state training school for a year, whereas probation costs one tenth that amount. For adults, it costs an

---

[48] U.S. Bureau of Prisons, "Success and Failure of Federal Offenders Released in 1970" (1974), p. 1; Daniel Glaser, *The Effectiveness of a Prison and Parole System* (Indianapolis: Bobbs-Merrill Co., Inc., 1964), p. 43.

average of $8,000 to keep a person in prison for a year, whereas probation costs about $1,000.[49]

Another approach to handling offenders involves the combination of prison and probation. In the 1960s, the states of Ohio, Maine, California, and Wisconsin and the federal government passed legislation permitting a mixed or split sentence in an approach known as "shock probation." To "shock" the individual into recognition of the realities of prison life, the offender serves part of his sentence in an institution. The remainder of the sentence is then suspended, and the felon is placed on probation.

National statistics on probation are not collected in this country, but reports of probation departments suggest that 75 per cent of all probationers succeed or have no further violations. An intensive study in California revealed "that the highest rates of violation of probation are found among the probationers who had previous criminal records, previous records of irregular work, low economic status, low occupational level, previous institutional placement, residence in deteriorated or commercial areas, families with records of crime or vice, immoral associates, great mobility in residences, and few or irregular contacts with schools or churches."[50] Yet, the fact that 75 per cent succeed suggests that programs located in the community may be successful in further reducing the violation rate.

Community-based Treatment.   Emphasizing assimilation of conventional norms, community-based programs may be able to overcome adherence to the prison code that presents a barrier to rehabilitation. A variety of innovative programs have been instituted in the last decade.

Because 70 per cent of the youth committed to institutions reappeared in the judicial and penal system after release, the state of Massachusetts recognized that the primary function of institutions is custodial and that such incarceration does not effectively rehabilitate offenders. Therefore, the state closed its training schools early in the 1970s. According to Yitzhak Bakal, no more than 5 per cent of the youth committed to the Department of Corrections require secure surroundings. With the exception of one facility for 35 to 40 youth, Massachusetts now relies on community-based correctional facilities such as group homes, foster homes, halfway houses, private board-

---

[49] Robert L. Polakow and Ronald M. Doctor, "A Behavioral Modification Program for Adult Drug Offenders," *Journal of Research in Crime and Delinquency,* 11 (January 1974):68.

[50] Sutherland and Cressey, op. cit., p. 478.

ing schools, and day care programs, which may provide an educational program, job training, or individual or family counseling and support.[51]

In the day treatment programs, the offenders live in their own homes; some may attend schools or have jobs but are required to attend daily counseling sessions in the center. A program of this type was developed in Provo, Utah, and the recidivism or return rate of the participants was lower than among comparable boys committed to training schools.[52]

In programs in other areas, some institutions permit selected inmates (both juveniles and adults) to work or study in the community during the day and return to the facility in the evening. Other programs provide minimum-security facilities or halfway houses to permit gradual release of offenders rather than direct discharge from institutions to society. In Mississippi, conjugal visits are permitted; elsewhere, limitations on visiting privileges have been relaxed. Some institutions now permit short home visits or furloughs.

The greatest change in the area of corrections, however, lies in the development of programs in which the resources of the community are mobilized. The prototype for many of these programs was initiated in New Jersey. In the Highfields project, 15 to 20 boys lived in the former Lindbergh residence. During the day, they could work for pay at a nearby state hospital; in the evenings, they participated in group therapy sessions. The boys remained in the program for only three or four months. The program was developed on the premise that delinquent boys differ from nondelinquents only in their anti-social attitudes and delinquent self-concepts. Studies showed a higher rate of success in the community, particularly among blacks, than for comparable juveniles committed to a state institution.[53]

Whether increased use of probation, community-based treatment, or other programs will be successful in combating the crime rate remains to be seen. Most of the programs are relatively recent and have not yet received adequate evaluation. One of the major determinants of the continued or expanded use of these innovative programs will be the attitude of the majority

---

[51] Yitzhak Bakal, ''The Massachusetts Experience,'' *Delinquency Prevention Reporter,* Youth Development and Delinquency Prevention Administration (Washington, D.C.: U.S. Government Printing Office, 1973), pp. 1–6; see Yitzhak Bakal, ed., *Closing Correctional Institutions: New Strategies for Youth Services* (Lexington, Mass.: Lexington Books, 1973).

[52] LaMar T. Empey and Maynard L. Erickson, *The Provo Experiment: Evaluating Community Control of Delinquency* (Lexington, Mass.: Lexington Books, 1972).

[53] H. Ashley Weeks, *Youthful Offenders at Highfields* (Ann Arbor: University of Michigan Press, 1958); see Lloyd W. McCorkle, Albert Elias, and F. Lovell Bixby, *The Highfields Story: An Experimental Treatment Project for Youthful Offenders* (New York: Holt, Rinehart and Winston, 1958).

of citizens toward the primary function of the criminal justice system—whether it is to be geared toward retribution or rehabilitation. It should also be recognized that, as a social problem, crime is related to other social problems. Efforts to combat crime may be successful only to the extent that they are part of an overall program, including attacks on unemployment, poverty, racial prejudice, and discrimination.

Additional Readings

Allen, Francis A. *The Crimes of Politics: Political Dimensions of Criminal Justice.* Cambridge, Mass.: Harvard University Press, 1974.

Cameron, Mary O. *The Booster and the Snitch: Department Store Shoplifting.* New York: The Free Press, 1964.

Chambliss, William J., and Milton Mankoff, eds. *Whose Law? Whose Order? A Conflict Approach to Criminology.* New York: John Wiley & Sons, Inc., 1976.

Chandler, Edna W. *Women in Prison.* Indianapolis: The Bobbs-Merrill Co., Inc., 1973.

Conklin, John E. *The Impact of Crime.* New York: Macmillan Publishing Co., Inc., 1975.

Garofalo, James. *Local Victim Surveys: A Review of the Issues.* National Criminal Justice Information and Statistics Service. Washington, D.C.: U.S. Government Printing Office, 1977.

Glaser, Daniel. *Strategic Criminal Justice Planning.* Center for Studies of Crime and Delinquency. Washington, D.C.: U.S. Government Printing Office, 1975.

Gove, Walter R., ed. *The Labelling of Deviance: Evaluating a Perspective.* New York: Sage Publications, Inc., 1975.

A Handbook on White Collar Crime. Washington, D.C.: Chamber of Commerce of the United States, 1974.

Homer, Frederic D. *Guns and Garlic: Myths and Realities of Organized Crime.* West Lafayette, Ind.: Purdue University Studies, 1974.

Inciardi, James A. *Careers in Crime.* Chicago: Rand McNally College Publishing Co., 1975.

Kassebaum, Gene. *Delinquency and Social Policy.* Englewood Cliffs, N.J.: Prentice-Hall, Inc., 1974.

Long, Elton, James Long, Wilmer Leon, and Paul B. Weston. *American Minorities: The Justice Issue*. Englewood Cliffs, N.J.: Prentice-Hall, Inc., 1975.

Pace, Denny F., and Jimmie C. Styles. *Organized Crime: Concepts and Control*. Englewood Cliffs, N.J.: Prentice-Hall, Inc., 1975.

Petersen, David M., and Charles W. Thomas, eds. *Corrections: Problems and Prospects*. Englewood Cliffs, N.J.: Prentice-Hall, Inc., 1975.

Platt, Anthony M. *The Child Savers: The Invention of Delinquency*. Chicago: University of Chicago Press, 1969.

Sagarin, Edward. *Deviants and Deviance: An Introduction to the Study of Disvalued People and Behavior*. New York: Praeger Publishers, Inc., 1975.

Schafer, Stephen. *The Victim and His Criminal: A Study in Functional Responsibility*. New York: Random House, Inc., 1968.

Schur, Edwin M. *Radical Non-Intervention: Rethinking the Delinquency Problem*. Englewood Cliffs, N.J.: Prentice-Hall, Inc., 1973.

Smith, Alexander B., and Harriet Pollack. *Some Sins Are Not Crimes: A Plea for Reform of the Criminal Law*. New York: New Viewpoints, 1975.

Thomas, Charles W., and David M. Petersen. *Prison Organization and Inmate Subcultures*. Indianapolis: Bobbs-Merrill Co., Inc., 1977.

Voss, Harwin L., ed. *Society, Delinquency, and Delinquent Behavior*. Boston: Little, Brown and Company, 1970.

Voss, Harwin L., and David M. Petersen, eds. *Ecology, Crime and Delinquency*. New York: Appleton-Century-Crofts, 1971.

alcohol and other drugs

Like Alice on the other side of the looking glass, our two year examination of drug use, misuse, and "abuse" has given us a constantly reinforced perception that all is not as it seems and that beliefs and realities are not always equal. All too often, familiar guideposts and landmarks, which we assumed could give us direction and purpose, faded, changed shape, or simply disappeared when carefully scrutinized. . . . Because of the scope of the drug issue, we realized that the old definitions, the old way of looking at these signs and symptoms of social dysfunction required a new set of working terms and a new perspective.[1]

The National Commission on Marihuana and Drug Abuse emphasizes that in American society considerable mythology surrounds the use of drugs—their effects are viewed as mystical and supernatural. This mythology includes the image of the drug user as a dope fiend, the belief that the user of marihuana inevitably proceeds to the use of heroin, and the idea that a person who uses heroin once will become addicted. Linked with the convenient fiction that tobacco and alcohol are not drugs, another myth has been that the United States is a relatively drug-free society.

However, the facts about drug use lead to the conclusion that ours is a drug-using society. In 1970, 5 billion doses of tranquilizers, 3 billion doses

---

[1] National Commission on Marihuana and Drug Abuse, *Drug Use in America: Problem in Perspective* (Washington, D.C.: U.S. Government Printing Office, 1973), p. 1.

of amphetamines, and 5 billion doses of barbiturates were manufactured in the United States. In 1971, physicians wrote 230 million prescriptions for psychoactive drugs; their retail sales totaled an estimated $972 million.[2] At the same time, Americans spent $24.2 billion for alcoholic beverages. The average consumption for all persons 15 years of age and over was 30.6 gallons, including 26 gallons of beer, 2 gallons of wine, and 2.6 gallons of distilled spirits. The average drinker annually consumes 3.93 gallons of absolute alcohol, which works out to about 44 fifths of whiskey, or 98 bottles of fortified wine, or 157 bottles of table wine, or 928 bottles of beer.[3] Further proof that we are a nation of drug users came in the mid-1960s, when LSD tripped out of the laboratory, the amphetamines and barbiturates escaped from the pharmacies and medicine cabinets to the streets, marihuana spread from the ghettos to the affluent suburbs, and use of heroin reached an epidemic level. The result was a highly emotional response by the public and many officials. However, contemporary attitudes toward drug use are inconsistent, even hypocritical. Use of amphetamines or tranquilizers by a business person is considered a matter of personal judgment, but the use of the same drug by a student preparing for examinations or a young person who wishes to experience their effects produces great concern.

DRUGS: WHAT ARE THEY?

In much of what is written on the topic, the term *drug* is used indiscriminately. Until recently, the general public viewed drugs as the equivalent of medicine for the treatment of illness or disease. Many of the drugs used illicitly have medical value, but at times the word *drug* refers to substances such as marihuana and heroin that have no recognized medical uses and are not sold in pharmacies.[4]

---

[2] See Arnold Bernstein and Henry L. Lennard, "Drugs, Doctors and Junkies," *Society,* 10 (May–June 1973): 14; *Drug Use in America: Problem in Perspective,* op. cit., p. 43.

[3] The average is a little more than three ounces of absolute alcohol per day. *Alcohol and Health,* First Special Report to the U.S. Congress from the Secretary of Health, Education, and Welfare, National Institute on Alcohol Abuse and Alcoholism (Washington, D.C.: U.S. Government Printing Office, 1971), pp. 10–12.

[4] Medicinal preparations sold without prescription are often referred to as over-the-counter (OTC) drugs; in an earlier era, they were called patent medicines. Technically, these substances are *proprietary drugs,* and the product's name, composition, and the manufacturing process are protected against competition. Heroin cannot be used in medical treatment in the United States, but in Great Britain doctors prescribe and pharmacies dispense heroin legally.

Legally, illicit drugs have been arbitrarily classified as *narcotics* and *dangerous drugs,* and people who "abuse" them are called *addicts* and *users*.

From the standpoint of pharmacology, "any substance that by its chemical nature alters structure or function in the living organism is a drug."[5] Although this may be useful for medical research, we need a definition more limited than one that includes all foods and spices, hormones, vitamins, pesticides, air pollutants, and synthetic chemicals. Therefore, we restrict the term to a class of substances with certain kinds of effects. A *psychoactive drug* is a chemical substance that alters mood, perception, or consciousness. In everyday language, socially approved substances are not called drugs. Alcohol is widely accepted for general use and is viewed as a beverage, rather than as a drug. Most drinkers do not consider themselves as drug users. However, alcohol is a drug, and we will treat it as such.

Drug Addiction and Drug Abuse

The World Health Organization defined *drug addiction* as "a state of periodic or chronic intoxication produced by the repeated consumption of a drug (natural or synthetic). Its characteristics include: (1) an overpowering desire or need (compulsion) to continue taking the drug and to obtain it by any means; (2) a tendency to increase the dose; (3) a psychic (psychological) and generally a physical dependence on the effects of the drug; (4) detrimental effect on the individual and on society."[6]

Drug abuse is the term the federal government currently employs. In this terminology, alcohol is ignored, and any use of drugs, other than for legitimate medical purposes, is equated with abuse. The distinction between use and abuse reflects societal approval or disapproval; drug abuse is a code word for unacceptable drug use. This terminology has at least two unfortunate consequences. First, two psychoactive drugs, tobacco and alcohol, are not generally regarded as drugs. Second, there is a tendency to exaggerate the dangers of illicit or street drugs and to minimize or overlook the risks of socially approved drugs. We will use the term *addiction* in reference to drugs that produce tolerance and physical dependence. For others, we will speak simply

[5] Walter Modell, "Mass Drug Catastrophes and the Roles of Science and Technology," *Science,* 156 (April 21, 1967): 346.

[6] Nathan B. Eddy, H. Halbach, Harris Isbell, and Maurice H. Seevers, "Drug Dependence: Its Significance and Characteristics," *Bulletin of the World Health Organization,* 32 (1965): 722.

of drug use. Some distinctive terms such as alcoholism and problem drinking have been developed for persons who experience problems with alcohol.

The three effects of repeated use of psychoactive drugs of greatest interest are tolerance, physical dependence, and psychological dependence. *Tolerance* refers to the fact that with repeated use of some drugs larger amounts are required to obtain the same effects. *Physical dependence* refers to the alteration of the individual's physiological system so that the drug must be present for continued functioning in a manner similar to the way it functioned prior to the first introduction of the drug. Withdrawal symptoms appear when the drug is abruptly discontinued; these symptoms indicate the development of physical dependence and their severity reflects the degree of dependence. For heroin and other opiates, withdrawal symptoms include chills, nausea, generalized body aches, stomach and muscle cramps, diarrhea, and dehydration. The opiates, alcohol, and the barbiturates produce tolerance and physical dependence, but marihuana and cocaine do not. The amphetamines and inhalants produce tolerance, but not physical dependence, and there is some evidence that this is also true for the hallucinogens. *Psychological dependence* involves a desire or craving for the drug and occurs when an individual relies on the drug for certain effects, such as feelings of well-being or elation (a ''high'' or ''kick''). The possibility of psychological dependence extends across the various classes of psychoactive drugs.

Alcoholism and Problem Drinking

When alcohol is consumed in limited or moderate quantities on social occasions, it is considered social drinking. Drinking of larger amounts that produces intoxication or drunkenness has long been regarded as immoral or sinful, and public drunkenness has been defined as a misdemeanor.

Elvin Jellinek, an authority in the field of alcohol studies, argued that alcoholism is a disease, and one of his associates offered this definition: ''Alcoholism is a chronic disease manifested by repeated implicative drinking so as to cause injury to the drinker's health or to his social or economic functioning.''[7] The ''disease'' definition shifts alcohol-related problems from the category of sin or crime to the category of sickness.

[7] Mark Keller, ''The Definition of Alcoholism and the Estimation of Its Prevalence,'' in David J. Pittman and Charles R. Snyder, eds., *Society, Culture, and Drinking Patterns* (New York: John Wiley & Sons, Inc., 1962), p. 316; see Elvin M. Jellinek, *The Disease Concept of Alcoholism* (New Brunswick, N.J.: Hillhouse Press, 1960).

Nevertheless, some experts are uneasy about this definition because one either has a disease or one does not, and physicians use tests for accurate diagnoses. However, there is no such test for alcoholism. The definition of alcoholism as a disease also supports the stereotype of the alcoholic as a skid row derelict. Consequently, many persons who regularly drink to excess and find their hangovers interfering with their jobs fail to recognize their drinking problem and do not seek treatment because they do not fit the stereotype.

Problems with alcohol are by no means confined to skid row derelicts, and to describe persons who experience problems as a result of their consumption of alcohol, the term *problem drinking* has been introduced. A useful definition of problem drinking is "a repetitive use of beverage alcohol causing physical, psychological, or social harm to the drinker or to others."[8] A problem drinker may be identified as anyone who drinks to cope with life, frequently becomes intoxicated, goes to work intoxicated, is physically injured as a result of intoxication, or does things the person claims he or she would never do without alcohol. Warning signs that a person is in the early stages of problem drinking are the need to drink before facing certain situations, frequent drinking sprees, a steady increase in intake, solitary drinking, early morning drinking, and blackouts or lapses of memory.

TYPES OF PSYCHOACTIVE DRUGS

Any drug classification tends to be misleading because no psychoactive drug, if taken in a dosage that does not produce stupor, coma, or death, has a single or uniform effect. A general classification describes *probable* outcomes, but factors other than the drug itself are also influential, including a person's mood, motives, and expectations about the drug and the social setting in which the drug is used.[9] With this in mind, we will consider in this section seven types of psychoactive drugs—alcohol, marihuana, stimulants, sedatives, opiates, hallucinogens, and inhalants.

Alcohol

Alcoholic beverages are so accepted in American life that it is difficult to recognize alcohol (technically, ethyl alcohol) as a psychoactive drug. Alcohol

[8] Thomas F. A. Plaut, *Alcohol Problems: A Report to the Nation by the Cooperative Commission on the Study of Alcoholism* (London: Oxford University Press, 1967), pp. 37–38.
[9] Richard H. Blum, "Mind-Altering Drugs and Dangerous Behavior: Dangerous Drugs," in President's Commission on Law Enforcement and Administration of Justice, *Narcotics and Drug Abuse* (Washington, D.C.: U.S. Government Printing Office, 1967), p. 22.

Alcoholic beverages are so accepted in American life that it is difficult to recognize alcohol as a psychoactive drug. (Courtesy of Magnum.)

acts as a depressant on the central nervous system. It is a source of calories (but not vitamins); unlike most foods, it does not have to be digested, but passes directly through the walls of the stomach and small intestine into the blood stream. In moderate amounts, alcohol produces a feeling of relaxation or tranquility. Further drinking produces a lack of coordination, confusion, and disorientation, and still larger amounts can lead to stupor, coma, or death. Although the cause is poorly understood, delerium tremens ("the DTs") is a serious, sometimes fatal condition in which chronic drinkers (particularly when they attempt to stop drinking) experience confusion, trembling or "the shakes," convulsions, and hallucinations.

The effect of alcohol is determined by the rate at which it is absorbed into the blood, and this varies with the kind of alcoholic beverage, how rapidly it is consumed, the amount and type of food in the stomach, and body weight. The blood-alcohol levels and effects of various amounts of alcohol on a 150-pound individual are shown in Table 11-1.

Table 11-1. The Effect of Alcoholic Beverages

Amount of Beverage Consumed*	Concentration of Alcohol Attained in Blood	Effect	Time Required for All Alcohol to Leave the Body
1 highball (1½ oz. whisky) or 1 cocktail (1½ oz. whisky) or 3½ oz. fortified wine or 5½ oz. ordinary wine or 2 bottles beer (24 oz.)	0.03%	No noticeable effects on behavior	2 hrs.
2 highballs or 2 cocktails or 7 oz. fortified wine or 11 oz. ordinary wine or 4 bottles beer	0.06%	Feeling of warmth—mental relaxation—slight decrease of fine skills—less concern with minor irritations and restraints	4 hrs.
3 highballs or 3 cocktails or 10½ oz. fortified wine or 16½ oz. (1 pt.) ordinary wine or 6 bottles beer	0.09%	Increasing effects with variation among individuals and in the same individuals at different times	Buoyancy—exaggerated emotion and behavior—talkative, noisy or morose	6 hrs.
4 highballs or 4 cocktails or 14 oz. fortified wine or 22 oz. ordinary wine or 8 bottles (3 qts.) beer	0.12%	Impairment of fine coordination—clumsiness—slight to moderate unsteadiness in standing or walking	8 hrs.
5 highballs or 5 cocktails or (½ pt. whisky)	0.15%	Intoxication—unmistakable abnormality of gross bodily functions and mental faculties	10 hrs.

SOURCE: Leon A. Greenberg, "Intoxication and Alcoholism: Physiological Factors," *The Annals,* 315 (January, 1958), p. 28.

*For those weighing considerably more or less than 150 pounds the amounts of beverage indicated above will be correspondingly greater or less. The effects indicated at each stage will diminish as the concentration of alcohol in the blood diminishes.

Marihuana

Marihuana is known by various slang names, such as weed, reefer, maryjane, pot, and grass. *Marihuana* is derived from the Indian hemp plant, *Cannabis sativa*. The male plant, a source of rope fibers, contains a lower concentration of the active ingredient than the female plant; the flowering tops, stems, and leaves of the female plant are preferred. The product is usually smoked in the form of a cigarette or in a pipe. From the standpoint of hallucinogenic effects, the marihuana available in the United States not only varies greatly, but also is generally about one tenth as potent as hashish, or "hash." *Hashish,* the concentrated gumlike substance in the hemp plant, is usually smoked in a pipe. Tetrahydrocannabinol, or THC, is the chemical in the hemp plant that produces a "high."

Stimulants

The stimulants include psychic-energizers, antidepressants, the synthetic (man-made) substances known as the amphetamines, and cocaine. The first two types are used to relieve the feelings of hopelessness and despair that may occur among elderly persons and patients with terminal illnesses, such as cancer.

Amphetamines.　Of the stimulants, the most widely used are the amphetamines that keep a person awake, elevate mood, increase confidence, and produce feelings of well-being and elation. In addition to their medical uses for relief of pain and in the treatment of some mental disorders, amphetamines such as Benzedrine and Dexedrine are used for weight reduction ("diet pills"). Some athletes use amphetamines in the hope of improving their performance, and they are also used by truck drivers on long-distance hauls. On the street, they are called bennies, uppers, or pep pills.

Cocaine.　Also known as coke, C, or snow, cocaine is derived from the leaves of the coca plant cultivated in South America.[10] It is a powerful stimulant that produces a euphoric effect when sniffed or injected. The euphoria lasts only a short time, so repeated use is necessary to maintain the effect. Users describe the effects of cocaine as highly pleasurable. However, repeated heavy use of cocaine may produce delusions, hallucinations, and paranoia. Today, cocaine is not used medically, although procaine, a cocaine derivative, is marked under the trade name of Novocaine and is widely used by dentists.

[10] Coca is not the same as cacao; cacao seeds are the source of chocolate.

METCALF'S COCA WINE

From Fresh Coca Leaves.

A Pleasant Tonic and Invigorator.

Coca Leaves have been in use by the native Indians in South America from the earliest times as a remedy for every malady, from a simple cut to neuralgia and headache ; and while chewing it, they pass whole days in traveling or working without food, eating heartily in the evening, without inconvenience, and passing the night in refreshing sleep.

Coca Leaves have been recommended by Ringer as valuable in **Febrile Disorders,** by restraining tissue metamorphosis, and for the same reason in Phthisis.

With decided anodyne and antispasmodic qualities, they have been employed in Typhus, **Scorbutus,** Gastralgia, Anæmia, Enteralgia, and to assist digestion.

Public Speakers, Singers, and Actors have found Wine of Coca (METCALF'S) to be a valuable tonic to the vocal cords, and also a sedative, allaying nervous fright without perceptible after effect.

It is agreeable to the taste and can be prescribed for children or convalescents. Athletes, Pedestrians and Base Ball Players have found by practical experience that a steady course of Coca taken both before and after any trial of strength or endurance will impart energy to every movement, and prevent fatigue and waste from the system. Elderly people have found it a reliable aphrodisiac, superior to any other drug.

Dr. Willard H. Morse says of Coca: "Its greatest worth is as an antidote for alcoholismus and the opium habit," and for this treatment he recommends Fluid Extract of Coca in tablespoonful doses.

Dr. W. S. Searle, A.M., M.D , says of Coca : "In relation to a New Form of Nervous Disease " : "It certainly is not homœopathic, but it is still, however it may act, one of the most reliable remedies for the palliation and, perhaps, cure of this malady."

Wine of Coca is probably the most valuable **Tonic** in the Materia Medica. With stimulating and anodyne properties combined, it acts without debilitating.

☞ Metcalf's Fluid Extract of Coca should be prescribed for alcoholismus or the cure of the opium habit, in tablespoonful doses.

Dose of Wine of Coca.—One-half to one wineglassful three times daily.

BAYER PHARMACEUTICAL PRODUCTS.

Send for samples and Literature to

ASPIRIN
The substitute for the salicylates

ARISTOL
The antiseptic and cicatrisant

PROTARGOL
The anti-gonorrhœicum

EUROPHEN
The odorless substitute iodoform

CREOSOTE CARB
The antitubercular antiseptic

QUINALGEN
The anti-malaricum

PIPERAZINE
The antiarthritic

GUAIACOL CARB
The odorless diffusible alterative

HEROIN-HYDROCHL.
The sedative for coughs

HEROIN
The sedative for coughs

LYCETOL
The uric acid solvent

FERRO-SOMATOSE
The ferruginous nutrient

SULFONAL
The reliable hypnotic

SOMATOSE
The most assimilable nutrient

PHENACETIN
The safest antipyretic

HEMICRANIN
The specific for headaches

IODOTHYRINE
The active principle of the thyroid gland

SYCOSE
The substitute for cane sugar

TRIONAL
The safest hypnotic

SALOPHEN
The antirheumatic and antineuralgic

FARBENFABRIKEN OF ELBERFELD CO.

40 STONE STREET, NEW YORK.

Left, the active ingredient of Metcalf's Coca Wine—shown in an 1889 ad in a medical journal—is cocaine, which could either be isolated from coca leaves, or after 1884, commercially synthesized. Cocaine was initially seized upon as the first satisfactory antidepressant available to the medical profession and the public. In its vogue it could be purchased in at least a dozen forms, such as coca cordial and coca cheroots.

Below left, this advertisement from a 1900 magazine juxtaposes two pharmaceuticals which have since achieved distinct images in the public mind: heroin and aspirin. Bayer introduced heroin in 1898 as a cough-suppressant that did not have the harmful effects of other opiates. Heroin is an acetylated product of morphine, just as aspirin is an acetylated product of salicyclic acid. Aspirin was produced in the same Bayer laboratories and released to the public a year later.

Opposite page: This 1903 advertisement for Glyco-Heroin promotes the physiological qualities ascribed to heroin at its introduction. Because heroin was produced by alteration of the morphine molecule, some writers quickly and hopefully suggested that it was also a cure for morphine addiction. Cocaine had also been used as a treatment for opiate addiction in the 1880's, but its ultimate value to medicine was as a local anesthetic. Manufacture of heroin in this country was prohibited in the mid-1920's.

Source: *Yale Alumni Magazine,* 35 (January 1972), pp. 18–19.

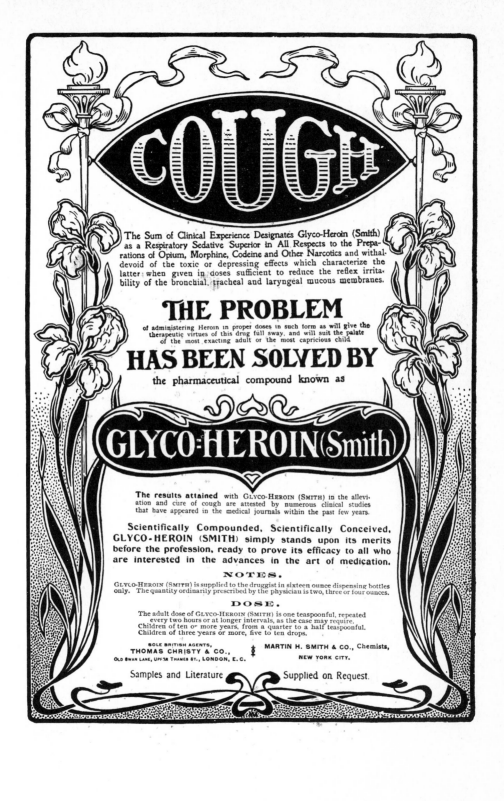

Sedatives

The most commonly used sedatives, also known as depressants, are the *barbiturates*. They are prescribed to induce sleep and to relieve anxiety and tension. On the street, they are known as downers, goof-balls, nimbies, or seccy. The barbiturates depress a variety of physiological functions, and in moderate doses they have the effect of mild sedation.[11] Heavy doses of barbiturates produce euphoria and release of anxiety and may result in impaired judgment, loss of emotional control, staggering, slurred speech, and tremor. Upon withdrawal, a person who is physically dependent on barbiturates may have convulsions or a delerium resembling alcoholic delerium tremens. There are other sedative and tranquilizing drugs, such as Valium, that are chemically unrelated to the barbiturates but that produce similar effects.

Opiates

Opiates are a class of drugs that includes opium; opium alkaloids, such as morphine and codeine; derivatives of the opiates, such as heroin and dilaudid; and synthetic equivalents such as meperidine and methadone that have different chemical properties but have effects similar to the opiates.

Derived from the seed pods of the poppy plant (*Papaver somniferum*), *opium* has been used for a variety of medical conditions throughout recorded history. In the nineteenth century many patent medicines contained opiates. As the old advertisements show, at the beginning of this century, pharmaceutical companies believed that heroin and cocaine had remarkable therapeutic qualities. Until quite recently, opiates were used for a variety of ailments, especially diarrhea and gynecological disorders. In current medical practice in this country, morphine, used for the relief of pain, and codeine, used in cough remedies, are the most commonly used opiates.

With the introduction of the hypodermic syringe, morphine was so widely administered to sick or wounded soldiers in the Civil War that for a time morphine addiction was known as the army disease. Heroin, isolated in 1898, was initially thought to be nonaddicting and was used as a "cure" for morphine addiction.[12] In the late 1960s, methadone, which also produces

---

[11] If the dosage of a sedative is sufficient to induce sleep shortly after administration, it is called a hypnotic.

[12] The founder of psychoanalysis, Sigmund Freud, used cocaine in an effort to cure a friend's morphine-dependence. Freud succeeded in stopping his morphine-dependence, but the friend became psychologically dependent on cocaine. See *Drugs: Who, What, Why?* (New York: Narcotic Addiction Control Commission, n.d.), pp. 12–13.

physical dependence, came into widespread use in the treatment of heroin addiction. In the 1970s, methadone, diverted from clinics, became available as a street drug. Morphine and other opiates stolen from pharmacies are also used on the street, but heroin is the favorite opiate of most street addicts.

Heroin.   Known by various names, such as H and junk, heroin is a morphine derivative, but its effects are more powerful and rapid than morphine. Heroin is a depressant that relieves anxiety and tension and diminishes the sex drive and appetite. The initial euphoria produced by heroin is followed by drowsiness and lethargy. American users prefer to adminster the drug by intravenous injection. As a result of commonly shared and unsanitary equipment, abscesses, hepatitis, and other infections often occur. Other detrimental effects include malnutrition and personal neglect.

Heroin is a depressant that produces an initial euphoria followed by drowsiness and lethargy. (Courtesy of Magnum.)

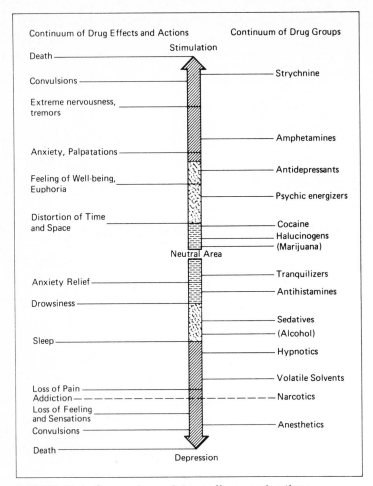

FIGURE 11-1. Comparison of drug effects and actions.

Hallucinogens

The hallucinogenic or psychedelic drugs include substances that have long been known, such as peyote and mescaline, and also newer synthetic drugs, including LSD, STP, and DMT. Peyote is derived from the button-shaped parts of the peyote (cactus) plant that grows wild in Mexico. Mescaline, a natural alkaloid found in the peyote plant, is the ingredient that produces hallucinations.[13] Another psychedelic, psilocybin, is found in certain mushrooms. The synthetic hallucinogens are more potent than peyote and mescaline, but all of these drugs can produce altered states of consciousness or "mind-bending."

For a number of years, investigators experimented with LSD (lysergic acid diethylamid) in the treatment of alcoholism and mental disorders. In the 1960s, LSD, or "acid," was used as a street drug. LSD produces a "trip" in which: "All senses appear sharpened and brightened; vivid, panoramic visual hallucinations of fantastic brightness and depth are experienced as well as hyperacusis [abnormal acuteness of hearing]. Senses blend and become diffused so that sounds are felt, colors tasted; and fixed objects pulsate and breathe. Depersonalization also occurs frequently so that the individual loses ego identity."[14] One of the hazards of LSD is a "bad trip" or state of panic. Also, without further use, flashbacks or new trips may occur. It is not known why flashbacks occur, nor are the long-term effects of psychedelics known. In the late 1960s, it was suggested that the use of LSD causes damage to the brain and the chromosomes and, thereby, birth defects in users' offspring, but the evidence for these claims is limited.

Inhalants

Inhalation of model airplane glue, lighter or cleaning fluids, industrial glues or solvents, gasoline, and paint thinner is called "sniffing." Glue is usually squeezed into a paper or plastic bag, and the fumes are inhaled. The initial effect is a feeling of euphoria, followed by changes in perception, dizziness, loss of coordination, slurred speech, and, at times, hallucinations. Sniffing may also produce delusions. At this stage, the user resembles a person intoxicated from alcohol. After 30 to 45 minutes, the user lapses into a state of drowsiness or stupor that lasts for up to an hour, and later the person is unable to remember what happened.

Initially, a few whiffs produce the desired effects, but habitual users may need the contents of as many as five tubes of glue. Such amounts can

[13] Members of the Native American Church of North America may legally use peyote in their religious services. This church claims a membership of 250,000 North American Indians from various tribes in the United States and Canada. Edward M. Brecher and the editors of Consumer Reports, *Licit and Illicit Drugs* (Boston: Little, Brown and Company, 1972), p. 339.

[14] Medical Society of the County of New York, *New York Medicine* (May 5, 1966), p. 5, as cited in *Narcotics and Drug Abuse,* op. cit., p. 5. See Harold A. Abramson, ed., *The Use of LSD in Psychotherapy and Alcoholism* (Indianapolis: The Bobbs-Merrill Co., Inc., 1967).

produce kidney damage or death. Cleaning fluids are "more dangerous than glue because the fumes can damage more organs, including the liver, brain, and lungs, as well as bone marrow."[15]

DRUG USE: EXTENT AND DISTRIBUTION

Alcohol

Surveys of alcohol use consistently find that 65 to 70 per cent of the adults (age 21 and over) in this country drink at least occasionally.[16] One national survey found that 68 per cent of the adult population—77 per cent of the men and 60 per cent of the women—drink at least once a year.[17] Types of social drinkers are defined in Figure 11-2; 5 per cent of the women and 21 per cent of the men are classified as heavy drinkers. Studies of high school students reveal that many teenagers drink. "Estimates based on an aggregation of such surveys show that, in recent years, about 57 percent of boys and 43 percent of girls aged 15 through 20 years are drinkers."[18]

Statistics on institutionalized alcoholic persons, the skid row population, and a complicated formula based on deaths from cirrhosis of the liver have been used to estimate the number of alcoholics in this country. The resulting estimates range from 4 to 18 million. Such estimates are unreliable, and a more useful approach involves measurement of the extent of alcohol-related problems. It is estimated that 7 per cent of the adult population—about 9 million persons—in the United States have alcohol-related problems.[19]

In a study of problem drinkers, Don Cahalan examined various types of problems.[20] Psychological dependence, the most common problem, was defined as drinking to escape everyday problems or to combat nervousness or depression. Frequent intoxication was the most serious problem for men,

[15] Barbara Milbauer, *Drug Abuse and Addiction* (New York: New American Library, Inc., 1970), p. 27.

[16] John W. Riley, Jr. and Charles F. Marden, "The Social Pattern of Alcoholic Drinking," *Quarterly Journal of Studies on Alcohol,* 8 (September 1947): 265–273; Robert Straus and Selden D. Bacon, *Drinking in College* (New Haven: Yale University Press, 1953). In the college study, 74 per cent of the students reported some use of alcohol.

[17] See Don Cahalan, Ira H. Cisin, and Helen M. Crossley, *American Drinking Practices: A National Study of Drinking Behavior and Attitudes* (New Brunswick, N.J.: Rutgers Center of Alcohol Studies, 1969).

[18] *Alcohol and Health,* op. cit., p. 9.

[19] Ibid., p. viii. The ratio of males to females is about 3 or 4 to 1.

[20] Don Cahalan, *Problem Drinkers* (San Francisco: Jossey-Bass, Inc., 1970) See Don Cahalan and Robin Room, *Problem Drinkers Among American Men* (New Haven: College and University Press, 1974).

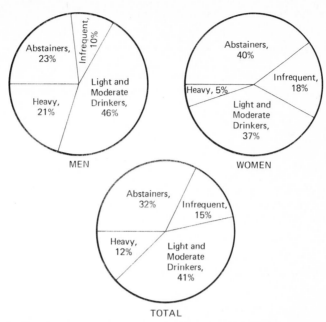

FIGURE 11-2. Percentage of abstainers and types of drinkers among adults. (age 21 and over) in the United States, 1964–1965. (Degree of drinking was classified according to a rather complex combination of the quantity of alcohol consumed per occasion and the frequency of drinking: *Heavy drinking*—drink nearly every day with five or more per occasion at least once in a while, or about once weekly with usually five or more per occasion; *moderate drinking*—drink at least once a month, typically several times, but usually with no more than three or four drinks per occasion; *light drinking*—drink at least once a month, but typically only one or two drinks on a single occasion; *infrequent drinking*—drink at least once a year, but less than once a month; *abstainers*—drink less than once a year or not at all. [Source: *Alcohol and Health,* First Special Report to the U.S. Congress from the Secretary of Health, Education, and Welfare, National Institute on Alcohol Abuse and Alcoholism (Washington, D.C.: U.S. Government Printing Office, 1971), p. 22.]

whereas the most serious problem for women involved their health. Frequent intoxication was often accompanied by psychological dependence, difficulty in stopping drinking, sneaking drinks, and blackouts.

The study also revealed that problem drinkers are not randomly distributed throughout the population. According to Cahalan, 15 per cent of the men and 4 per cent of the women had serious problems connected with drinking. Problems were most prevalent among men in their twenties. For women, alcohol-related problems appeared most frequently when they were in their thirties and forties.

Illicit Drugs

Although illicit drugs have aroused great public concern, national surveys of youth and adults suggest that, with the exception of marihuana, use of these substances is not extensive. Because street users of cocaine and heroin are underrepresented in a survey of households, the figures for these drugs for youth and adults in Table 11-2 are underestimates. The survey of men who registered with Selective Service reflects more widespread use of illicit drugs. Nevertheless, the "problem" of illicit drugs is largely a marihuana problem.

Marihuana. The first national survey on drug use, conducted in 1971 for the Marihuana Commission, revealed that 24 million Americans—15 per cent of the adults and 14 per cent of the 12- to 17-year-olds—had tried marihuana at least once, and 8.3 million were current users. Classified as heavy users (using more than once a day) were 2 per cent of the adults and 4 per cent of the youth. A similar survey conducted in 1975 by the Response Analysis Corporation showed an upward shift in the use of marihuana; otherwise, the two surveys produced similar results. In the survey of 20- to 30-year-old men, 55 per cent reported use of marihuana, and 38 per cent were current users.[21]

Clearly, experience with marihuana is related to age. Few persons under 13 have tried it, but 40 per cent of those 16 and 17 years old have. In the Response Analysis survey, 53 per cent of those between 18 and 25 years of age had used marihuana. The survey of 20- to 30-year-old men produced a similar percentage. Use is relatively uncommon among those over 35, as only 6 per cent had tried marihuana.

For adults, experience with marihuana is more extensive among men, persons with at least some college education, individuals with incomes of $15,000 or more, and those who have never married or are divorced or sepa-

[21] National Commission on Marihuana and Drug Abuse, *Marihuana: A Signal of Misunderstanding* (New York: New American Library, Inc., 1972), pp. 7, 38–42; Herbert I. Abelson and Patricia M. Fishburne, *Nonmedical Use of Psychoactive Substances* (Princeton, N.J.: Response Analysis Corporation, 1976), pp. 28–31; John A. O'Donnell, Harwin L. Voss, Richard R. Clayton, Gerald T. Slatin, and Robin G. W. Room, *Young Men and Drugs: A Nationwide Survey* (Rockville, Md.: National Institute on Drug Abuse, 1976), p. vii.

Table 11-2. Experience with Illicit Drugs Reported by Americans in 1975

Drug	Youth 12–17, Percentage	Adults 18 & over, Percentage	Young Men 20–30, Percentage
Marihuana	22.4	21.3	55.1
LSD or other hallucinogens	5.1	4.9	21.9
Glue or other inhalants	8.1	3.4	15.9
Cocaine	3.4	4.1	14.0
Heroin	0.5	1.2	5.9
Other opiates	6.3	5.3	19.6

SOURCE: The information shown in the first two columns was obtained in interviews with 986 youth and 2,590 adults. Herbert I. Abelson and Patricia M. Fishburne, *Nonmedical Use of Psychoactive Substances* (Princeton, N.J.: Response Analysis Corporation, 1976), pp. 11–12. The information on young men was obtained in interviews with 2,510 Selective Service registrants. John A. O'Donnell, Harwin L. Voss, Richard R. Clayton, Gerald T. Slatin, and Robin G. W. Room, *Young Men and Drugs: A Nationwide Survey* (Rockville, Md.: National Institute on Drug Abuse, 1976), pp. 29, 49, 140.

rated. Use of marihuana is more common among students than in any other occupational category. Among youth there is little difference between males and females in experience with marihuana. In a national survey of approximately 8,000 students in 48 representative colleges, it was found that 31 per cent had used marihuana and 14 per cent were regular users (used at least every week or two during the academic year).[22] Marihuana experience is higher in metropolitan than in rural areas, and the percentages of youth and adults who have ever used marihuana are highest in the West and lowest in the South. Other surveys of junior and senior high schools generally show the highest percentages of users in West Coast schools. In the 1975 national survey, more nonwhite adults than whites (25 per cent and 21 per cent, respectively) reported use of marihuana, but the percentage of white and nonwhite youth reporting some use of marihuana was identical (22 per cent).

[22] Peter H. Rossi, W. Eugene Groves, and David Grafstein, *Life Styles and Campus Communities: A Report of a Survey of American Colleges and Universities (1969–70; 1970–71)* (Baltimore: The Johns Hopkins University Press, 1972), as summarized in William A. Glenn and Louise G. Richards, *Recent Surveys of Nonmedical Drug Use: A Compendium of Abstracts* (Rockville, Md.: National Institute on Drug Abuse, 1974), p. 22.

Stimulants and Sedatives.   According to the figures in Table 11-2, 4 per cent of the adults and more than 3 per cent of the youth had used cocaine at least once, but 14 per cent of the young men had tried it. For stimulants and sedatives, 27 and 20 per cent, respectively, of the young men reported they had tried them. Similarly, in the previously cited study of college students, Peter Rossi found that 17 per cent had tried amphetamines, and 4 per cent were regular users. For sedatives, Rossi reports that 15 per cent of the college students had tried them, but less than 2 per cent were regular users. Although 3 per cent of the college students had tried cocaine, only one tenth of 1 per cent were classified as regular users.

Opiates.   Of the drugs shown in Table 11-2, heroin had the lowest incidence rate. In Rossi's study, the incidence figures were: heroin, less than 1 per cent; opium, 4 per cent; other narcotics, 5 per cent; and narcotic cough syrups, 38 per cent.

In the United States, illicit opiate use largely involves heroin. From reports submitted by police agencies, the Bureau of Narcotics maintains a file of the names of active opiate addicts. At the end of 1965, there were 57,199 opiate addicts listed, of whom 52,793 were heroin addicts. According to these records, more than half of all known heroin addicts lived in New York, with smaller concentrations in urban areas in California, Illinois, Michigan, New Jersey, Maryland, Pennsylvania, Texas, and the District of Columbia. "Within the cities it is largely found in areas with low average incomes, poor housing, and high delinquency. The addict himself is likely to be male, between the ages of 21 and 30, poorly educated and unskilled, and a member of a disadvantaged ethnic minority group."[23] This picture may have been essentially correct for the mid-1960s, but in the following decade heroin use spread to young persons from middle-class families and to smaller cities and towns. The number of heroin users—and addicts—increased substantially. In the study of 20- to 30-year-old men, it was estimated that 950,000 of the 19 million men in this age range had tried heroin (see Table 11-2).

In the early 1970s, the number of addicts was estimated at over 500,000. In 1974, Robert L. DuPont, Director of the National Institute on Drug Abuse, argued that as a result of Turkey's ban on poppy growing in 1971 the addict population in the United States had dropped to about 200,000. Consistent with DuPont's position is the fact that overdose deaths dropped 30 per cent

[23]*Narcotics and Drug Abuse,* op. cit., pp. 2–3. As far as one can judge from persons in treatment facilities, about 80 per cent of the addicts are black and male, but addicts who seek treatment may be unrepresentative.

between 1972 and 1973. Although narcotics-related deaths dropped 21 per cent in New York City in the same period, the number of deaths in 1973 attributable to illicit methadone exceeded those from heroin by almost two to one. One interpretation is that when heroin became scarce, addicts shifted to other drugs.

Turkish farmers resumed the planting of poppy seeds in 1974 and a new heroin epidemic was predicted. However, in a sense Turkey serves as a convenient scapegoat, for the bulk of the world's illicit opium is produced in Burma, Thailand, and Laos. In this country, Mexican heroin provides at least 60 per cent of the current supply. There are at least 40 countries with the required soil and climate to cultivate the poppy plant, and enough heroin for 500,000 addicts in this country could be derived from the poppy grown in 9,600 acres (15 square miles) of fields.[24]

Hallucinogens and Inhalants. Use of inhalants is more common among youth than adults, but about one in twenty youth and adults report having tried LSD or a similar hallucinogenic drug. Of the college students surveyed by Rossi, 9 per cent had used hallucinogenic drugs. Perhaps more than with any other class of drugs, figures on "ever use" are of limited value, for less than 2 per cent of the students were regular users. Apparently, many young persons experiment with LSD and other hallucinogens but do not continue use. One possible explanation is that the effects of LSD are inconsistent—one's trip may be ecstatic, uneventful, or horrifying. Erich Goode offers another possible explanation. Marihuana users claim they can "get straight" in order to face an emergency through such means as a shower, but LSD users never say that they can function normally or "come down" at will.[25]

DRUGS AND CRIME

It is essential to distinguish between drug-related offenses and other crimes committed by addicts. Except for physicians who are allowed to possess opiates for professional use, the possession, sale, or purchase of heroin (and

[24] *Lexington Herald-Leader* (December 1, 1974), p. F-4. Hunt estimates that there are 750,000 heroin addicts in the United States or a rate of 3 per 1,000. He concludes that if heroin is available, approximately 200,000 young persons in communities of half a million or less *could* become heroin addicts in the next few years. See Leon G. Hunt, *Recent Spread of Heroin Use in the United States: Unanswered Questions* (Washington, D.C.: Drug Abuse Council, Inc., 1974), pp. 16–17.

[25] Erich Goode, *Drugs in American Society* (New York: Alfred A. Knopf, Inc., 1972), p. 120.

other drugs) is a criminal offense. It is also illegal to possess syringes and needles for nonmedical use of drugs.[26] In some states, it is illegal to associate with known addicts or to be present where there are illicit drugs. Consequently, an addict is almost constantly in violation of one or more criminal laws. Addiction itself, however, is not a crime, and California's effort to so designate it was declared unconstitutional.

Addicts also commit a variety of other crimes, not because of the effects of heroin but, rather, to obtain money. Heroin is smuggled into this country and distributed by organized crime as an enormously profitable venture. An addict usually is unable to support his or her habit through legitimate pursuits. At least one third of the current heroin addicts engaged in criminal activities prior to using drugs, and nearly all of them continue to engage in crime because of the cost of heroin on the street. The 1,271 addicts arrested in one month in 1965 in New York City indicated that they spent an average of $14 a day for heroin; with inflation, heroin, like everything else, has become more expensive.[27] Many addicts now spend $50 to $100 a day for heroin.

An addict who discontinues heroin use experiences withdrawal symptoms within 10 to 12 hours. Consequently, an addict will go to great lengths to obtain drugs. Although they are not prone to commit violent crimes as a result of their drug use, addicts sometimes engage in armed robbery or mugging to obtain cash to purchase drugs. However, Mark Moore estimates that only about 20 per cent of the money used to purchase heroin is raised by street crimes such as mugging. Other sources are dealing in the drug, 45 per cent; prostitution, 17 per cent; and shoplifting, 12 per cent.[28] Unless cash is obtained from criminal acts, an addict has to steal three to five times the cost of the daily habit plus living expenses because stolen merchandise is sold for one fifth to one third of its retail value. In New York, 38 male addicts reported they had committed 6,766 offenses in a period of four years; 93 per

[26] The most recent statement of the federal policy regarding drugs is found in A Report to the President from the Domestic Council, Drug Abuse Task Force, *White Paper on Drug Abuse* (Washington, D.C.: U.S. Government Printing Office, 1975).

[27] *Narcotics and Drug Abuse,* op. cit., p. 10. Packets of heroin vary in purity, usually from 1 to 10 per cent; the addict does not know the exact strength of the heroin he purchases. This raises the possibility of an overdose, which may lead to coma, respiratory failure, and death. Another danger is that a person suspected of informing to the police may be given or sold a "hot shot" in which heroin is laced with a lethal quantity of strychnine.

[28] Mark Moore, "Economics of Heroin Distribution," *Policy Concerning Drug Abuse in New York State,* Vol. III (Croton-on-Hudson, N.Y.: Hudson Institute, Inc., July 20, 1972), as cited in George F. Brown, Jr., and Lester R. Silverman, *The Retail Price of Heroin: Estimation and Applications* (Washington, D.C.: Drug Abuse Council, Inc., 1973), p. 34.

cent of their offenses were against property, with burglary the most common. The ratio of arrests to offenses was 1 to 120.[29]

Alcohol also figures prominently in the nation's crime picture. Approximately one half of all homicides and one fourth of all suicides are alcohol-related and account for about 12,000 deaths annually. Alcohol is involved in many assaults, and persons arrested for a variety of other offenses claim to have been intoxicated. One third of the 9 million arrests yearly are directly related to the misuse of alcohol. Drunkenness accounts for 1.2 million arrests, and disorderly conduct and vagrancy account for another 790,000 arrests. Arrests of intoxicated drivers numbered 950,000 in 1975. Research based on the blood-alcohol concentration of drivers shows that alcohol plays a part in half of the 60,000 annual highway fatalities.

UNDERSTANDING DRUG USE

Cultural Attitudes

As previously noted, the United States is a drug-using society. However, there are various cultural attitudes toward drug use. For example, four cultural attitudes affect rates of problem drinking: (1) abstinence—some religious groups forbid the use of alcohol; (2) ritual drinking in religious ceremonies; (3) social or convivial drinking; and (4) utilitarian drinking, or use to further self-interest or to reduce tension. Ritual drinking produces a low incidence of problem drinking; social drinking is related to moderate levels of problem drinking; and the utilitarian attitude toward drinking is most likely to lead to problem drinking.[30]

Parental Influence

Not only cultural attitudes but the patterns of drinking and drug use of one's parents are also influential. The similarity between students' drinking patterns and the drinking practices of their parents was noted in an early survey of college students.[31] Goode cites a study in Toronto in which it was found that

---

[29] James A. Inciardi and Carl D. Chambers, "Unreported Criminal Involvement of Narcotic Addicts," *Journal of Drug Issues*, 2 (Spring 1972): 57—64.

[30] Robert F. Bales, "Cultural Differences in Rates of Alcoholism," *Quarterly Journal of Studies on Alcohol*, 6 (March, 1946): 480–499.

[31] Straus and Bacon, op. cit.

of the grade-school and high-school students whose mothers used tranquilizers daily, 32 per cent had tried marihuana and 15 per cent had used an opiate, whereas among the students whose mothers never used tranquilizers, only 12 per cent had tried marihuana and 2 per cent had used one of the opiates. Commenting on this generational continuity in drug use, Goode observes: "Parents who use legal drugs—cigarettes, alcohol, and prescription drugs such as barbiturates and amphetamines—are more likely to have children who use illegal drugs, marihuana included."[32]

Impact of Friendship Groups

Social scientists view drinking and other drug use as learned behavior. Learning occurs largely within the context of primary groups, particularly friendship groups. Recalling their own experience, most Americans would laugh at the suggestion that tobacco distributors or owners of liquor stores secretly provide cigarettes or alcohol to youth. Yet, such a view is as factual as the idea that peddlers of drugs introduce young persons to marihuana. Nearly all marihuana smokers first "turn on" in the presence of one or more experienced users. Marihuana smoking is typically a group activity, not a solitary pursuit. "One's friendship network is the 'intervening' variable between one's background and one's pattern of drug use."[33] Parental drug use and other background variables are influential, but the crucial factor in marihuana smoking is friendship with those who use marihuana. In certain social circles, drinking martinis is expected at the cocktail hour, whereas in other social groups, marihuana use is expected.

Participants in drug-using groups are thus taught that conventional notions about illicit drugs do not apply to marihuana, and they acquire rationalizations and justifications for its use. Common justifications are that the drug's effects are beneficial or that use of alcohol is a more harmful practice than marihuana smoking. One also learns to recognize the effects of marihuana and to define them as pleasurable in much the same way that one acquires a taste for scotch or dry martinis. Unless the drug's effects are considered enjoyable, its use will be discontinued.[34]

[32] Goode, op. cit., p. 34.
[33] Ibid., p. 39.
[34] Howard S. Becker, "Becoming a Marihuana User," *American Journal of Sociology,* 59 (November 1953): 235–242.

Regular marihuana use often requires a connection with someone who sells drugs; this increases the chances that one will develop a friendship with a person who uses other drugs or sells them. In addition, many regular users purchase their own supply and deal (sell) marihuana on a small-time basis. In a study of 204 marihuana smokers, Goode found that more than 90 per cent of the daily users had bought and sold marihuana. He suggests that regular marihuana use among middle- and upper middle-class youth is linked to experimentation with such psychedelics as LSD or mescaline, because buying leads to contacts with dealers who peddle these drugs, rather than heroin. For persons in the lower class, however, regular marihuana use increases the chances of using heroin: "In the slums and the ghettos, marijuana use often involves the user in heroin-associated activities and peers. Often marijuana use 'leads to' experimenting with the narcotics in a working class urban area not because of the search for an even-bigger and better 'kick,' but because the associations one makes as one's use level moves upward are increasingly also likely to experiment with the narcotics." [35]

In a study of college students in the New York metropolitan area, Bruce Johnson reports that less than 1 per cent of those who had never used marihuana had tried heroin, whereas 17 per cent of the regular users (once a week or more) had done so. Of the regular marihuana users, only 5 per cent of those with no heroin-using friends had tried heroin, whereas 45 per cent of the persons with at least one heroin-using close friend had done so.[36] Thus, it is not only use of marihuana that is spread within the context of friendship networks. Exposure to heroin-using friends links frequent use of marihuana to experimentation with heroin.

Alan Sutter describes how social contacts may lead to heroin use. He refers to young persons who purchase their own supply and deal in marihuana on a small-time basis as "pot heads." Some pot heads, attracted to the money that can be made by dealing, become "players" or the intermediaries for the flow of drugs and stolen merchandise from adult hustlers (thieves) to adolescents. A player on his way to a career in hustling (stealing by means of armed robbery or shoplifting, pimping, pool hustling, or dealing drugs) will come into contact with heroin. According to Sutter, young drug users "have a magical belief that one can 'chippy around' (use heroin intermittently)

---

[35] Erich Goode, "Multiple Drug Use Among Marijuana Smokers," *Social Problems,* 17 (Summer 1969): 59.

[36] Bruce D. Johnson, *Marihuana Users and Drug Subcultures* (New York: John Wiley & Sons, Inc., 1973), pp. 104, 226.

without getting hooked [addicted]. The firmness of this belief is communicated to players."[37]

Addict Subculture

An *addict subculture* involves interaction in which a neophyte learns from experienced addicts methods of acquiring and using drugs, beliefs about the benefits of drugs and justifications for their use, negative attitudes toward the drug laws, and a specialized vocabulary.[38] An important part of the addict subculture is its "reproduction" system. Committed to the ideology of the addict subculture and needing to sell drugs to support their habits, addicts recruit new users. Although the evidence is limited, it has been suggested that persons who have used heroin for less than a year are the ones most likely to "infect" others—their enthusiasm is contagious. Thus, heroin use spreads like an epidemic in which a "carrier" infects persons in his or her friendship network.

Because addicts do not conform to the expectations of conventional society, drug use has been viewed as a form of retreatism. Although they do not pursue legitimate jobs and seek material success, street addicts do not see themselves as withdrawing or retreating from life. Rather, heroin use provides an image of the addict as bold, reckless, and criminally defiant, which from a street perspective are praiseworthy qualities. It is a challenge to "hustle" enough money to maintain a heroin habit, and the size of a person's habit and success as a hustler are measures of prestige. Sutter notes that, in private, older addicts admit they are miserable with their habit, but these same individuals, when observed with their associates, "pretended to be satisfied and even proud of their addiction."[39] Edward Preble and John Casey suggest:

> Their behavior is anything but an escape from life. They are actively engaged in meaningful activities and relationships seven days a week. The brief moments of euphoria after each administration of a small amount of heroin consti-

[37] Alan G. Sutter, "Worlds of Drug Use on the Street Scene," in Donald R. Cressey and David A. Ward, eds., *Delinquency, Crime, and Social Process* (New York: Harper & Row, Publishers, 1969), p. 820.

[38] Edwin M. Schur, *Crimes Without Victims: Deviant Behavior and Public Policy* (Englewood Cliffs, N.J.: Prentice-Hall, Inc., 1965), p. 140; John A. O'Donnell, *Narcotic Addicts in Kentucky,* Health Services and Mental Health Administration (Washington, D.C.: U.S. Government Printing Office, 1969), p. 84.

[39] Sutter, op. cit., p. 822; see Harvey Feldman, "Street Status and Drug Users," *Society,* 10 (May–June 1973): 32–38; Alan G. Sutter, "The World of the Righteous Dope Fiend," *Issues in Criminology,* 2 (Fall 1966): 177–222.

tute a small fraction of their daily lives. The rest of the time they are aggressively pursuing a career that is exacting, challenging, adventurous, and rewarding. They are always on the move and must be alert, flexible, and resourceful. The surest way to identify heroin users in a slum neighborhood is to observe the way people walk. The heroin user walks with a fast, purposeful stride, as if he is late for an important appointment—indeed, he is. He is hustling (robbing or stealing), trying to sell stolen goods, avoiding the police, looking for a heroin dealer with a good bag (the street retail unit of heroin), coming back from copping (buying heroin), looking for a safe place to take the drug, or looking for someone who beat (cheated) him—among other things. He is, in short, *taking care of business*.[40]

LEGAL CONTROLS

Estimates of the size of the opiate-dependent population at the turn of the century vary but a total of approximately 250,000, divided equally between "medical" and "street" addicts, is generally accepted.[41] At that time, among the medical addicts there were more females than males and more whites than blacks. They were not restricted to cities or to a particular geographic region, and were predominantly middle class. The response of society to these medical addicts was nonpunitive. The medical profession paid greater attention to addictive drugs, and pharmacists adopted stricter prescription practices. In 1906, Congress passed the Pure Food and Drug Act, which required labeling of all preparations containing "habit-forming" drugs. With the exception of codeine-based cough syrups, patent medicines containing sizable amounts of opiates soon disappeared.

The Legislation of Morality

In the early 1900s, law-enforcement officials, physicians, and clergymen also focused attention on the street use of opium, morphine, and cocaine in the nation's cities. Some writers suggest that they waged a crusade against the street use of drugs.[42] In any event, society's response was punitive. Every

[40] Edward Preble and John J. Casey, Jr., "Taking Care of Business—the Heroin User's Life on the Street," *The International Journal of the Addictions,* 4 (March 1969): 2–3.
[41] Charles E. Terry and Mildred Pellens, *The Opium Problem* (New York: Bureau of Social Hygiene, Inc., 1928), p. 1.
[42] Charles Reasons, "The Politics of Drugs: An Inquiry in the Sociology of Social Problems," *Sociological Quarterly,* 15 (Summer 1974): 381–404.

state passed antinarcotics legislation, and in 1914 the federal government enacted the Harrison Narcotic Act. This legislation restricted the production and distribution of narcotics to registered producers, pharmacists, and physicians. Any other production, distribution, or possession of these drugs was defined as criminal. In effect, the Harrison Act transformed addicts into criminals.[43]

In 1919, in the case of *Webb* v. *the United States,* the Supreme Court ruled that it was illegal according to the Harrison Act for a physician to prescribe morphine to keep a user comfortable. Facing fines or imprisonment, physicians abandoned the practice of writing prescriptions to support addicts' habits. A temporary expedient was the establishment of clinics where addicts could obtain their supply. A total of 44 clinics operated in various cities from 1918 to 1922, when unfavorable publicity forced their closing. A system of illegal drug traffic has flourished ever since.

Prohibition: The Noble Experiment

The temperance movement, already underway when the early narcotics legislation was enacted, was a separate effort aimed at the problems resulting from the use of alcohol. The temperance movement led to the adoption in 1920 of the Eighteenth Amendment to the Constitution, which imposed a nationwide prohibition against the manufacture, sale, or transportation of beverage alcohol. People defied this "noble experiment" to suppress alcohol consumption by legislation. Prohibition produced widespread contempt for the law and corruption of law-enforcement agents. It also led to the expansion of organized crime. After 13 years of unsuccessful efforts to enforce the law, Prohibition was repealed by the Twenty-first Amendment to the Constitution. In the ensuing years, organized criminal syndicates turned to the distribution of heroin to replace the revenue that the distribution of alcoholic beverages had produced during Prohibition.

All of the states have had laws prohibiting public intoxication, drunkenness, or disorderly conduct. However, in the mid-1960s public intoxication statutes were successfully challenged in the *Easter* and *Driver* cases on the basis of "a fundamental principle of criminal responsibility"—that criminal sanctions may be applied only to voluntary action. It was argued that as a

[43] Troy Duster, *The Legislation of Morality: Law, Drugs, and Moral Judgment* (New York: The Free Press, 1970), pp. 3–28.

result of his disease, an alcoholic drinks involuntarily and therefore cannot be criminally punished for his intoxication. In addition to the District of Columbia, a number of states, including Florida, Hawaii, Maryland, Massachusetts, and North Dakota, have revised their statutes to eliminate public drunkenness as a criminal offense.

Pot Luck: Changing the Law

For a number of years, marihuana smoking was ignored by authorities. According to Richard Lingeman, Congress passed the Marihuana Tax Act in 1937 as a result of a highly publicized "crime wave" in New Orleans involving students using marihuana and the testimony of the Commissioner of Narcotics, Harry Anslinger, that marihuana caused criminal activity.[44]

Federal efforts are directed primarily at control of importation and sale of drugs, and the number of arrests by the Bureau of Customs and the Bureau of Narcotics and Dangerous Drugs increased tremendously in the late 1960s, because a new kind of drug user had emerged. "To a substantial degree, the narcotics policy had from the beginning been identified with underprivileged minorities, criminals and social outsiders in general. . . . However, the drug problem of the 1960s was clearly identified with the children of the middle and upper classes."[45]

Along with more widespread drug use came new life styles, communal living, defiance of the Establishment, campus unrest, antiwar demonstrations, and political protests. Although changes in the activities and attitudes of youth in the 1960s were far-reaching, public attention was focused on marihuana.

Primary responsibility for enforcing possession laws lies within the states. From 1965 to 1970, arrests for possession of marihuana increased from 18,815 to 188,682. As evidence accumulated that marihuana does not cause aggressive behavior or crime, the courts adopted a more lenient approach. From 1965 to 1970, the proportion of defendants convicted and incarcerated declined, as did the average length of sentences. In 1970, Congress passed the Comprehensive Drug Abuse Prevention and Control Act: "Possession of all drugs, including marihuana, was reduced to a mis-

---

[44] Richard R. Lingeman, *Drugs from A to Z: A Dictionary* (New York: McGraw-Hill Book Company, 1969), pp. 144–145. In hearings on narcotic laws in 1951, Commissioner Anslinger shifted his argument, proposing that marihuana is dangerous because it inevitably leads to use of heroin.

[45] *Drug Use in America,* op. cit., p. 17.

demeanor. Special treatment for first offenders was provided, allowing expungement of the record upon satisfactory completion of a probationary period. Casual transfers of marihuana were treated in the same manner as possession.'' [46] Today most states classify possession of small amounts of marihuana as a misdemeanor. For example, in Oregon the maximum penalty for possession of less than one ounce of marihuana is a $100 fine; violators receive citations similar to parking tickets. There is a continuing campaign for the decriminalization (removal of criminal penalties) of marihuana. The health hazards of tobacco and alcohol are now recognized, but these substances are subject only to minimal control, such as the age of the purchaser and the hours alcohol may be sold. However, for other types of drugs, the major goal of control efforts in this country is the elimination of nonmedical drug use. Whether this is possible or desirable has rarely been questioned. Prohibition of alcohol did not succeed, nor have legal controls stopped use of marihuana and other drugs.

WHAT CAN BE DONE?

Currently, alternatives to incarceration are being sought to handle persons with drug-related problems. In a number of localities, detoxification centers have been established as replacements for the "drunk tanks" in jails. Various clinics and hospitals also offer individual treatment for problem drinkers. Halfway houses, located between the alcohol subculture and the larger society, offer a place for skid row alcoholics to live during the transition to conventional society. Marshall Clinard believes that the group pressure from staff members, who often are recovered alcoholics, and other group members is the most important rehabilitative force in halfway houses. [47] Other alternatives include Alcoholics Anonymous, civil commitment, Synanon, and methadone maintenance.

Alcoholics Anonymous

Alcoholics Anonymous (AA), a fellowship of problem drinkers who have joined together in an effort to abstain from alcohol use, consists of some

[46] *Marihuana: A Signal of Misunderstanding,* op. cit., p. 135.
[47] Marshall B. Clinard, *Sociology of Deviant Behavior,* 4th ed. (New York: Holt, Rinehart and Winston, 1974), p. 486.

10,000 chapters with a membership of approximately 300,000, of which 28 per cent are women. Although there is a central office in New York that publishes the *AA Grapevine,* and a national board of trustees, there are no national officers, professional staff, or dues. Each chapter supports itself financially through members' contributions and without fund-raising campaigns.

Members join AA voluntarily and continue their previous living arrangements. A new member is assigned a sponsor who has dealt with his or her own drinking problem and who is available at any time to help a member abstain from alcohol use. The AA program involves four principles: (1) relying on a power greater than oneself and admitting one is powerless to deal with alcoholism; (2) making an inventory of one's problems; (3) making amends, if possible, to persons one has harmed; and (4) carrying the message of AA to other alcoholics.[48]

AA not only provides group support but also involves the problem drinker, who often has experienced social isolation, in an accepting group. Status is awarded for expression of antialcohol attitudes, and AA redefines members as ex-alcoholics who cannot tolerate liquor.[49] AA successfully relabels the alcoholic as an ex-alcoholic or sober alcoholic. In the absence of records, the overall effectiveness of the organization cannot be assessed, but regular AA membership validates an individual's claim to be "off the bottle," and more alcoholics have managed to remain sober through AA than from the combined efforts of all other treatments.

Federal Hospitals and Civil Commitment

Until recently, treatment for opiate addicts was confined largely to two federal hospitals, at Lexington, Kentucky, and Fort Worth, Texas. Research in these facilities led to the development of a gradual method of withdrawal that posed no serious danger to the patient. Psychiatric treatment was provided, but such therapy, if it is to work, requires some motivation on the patient's part, and many addicts had little desire to give up their use of drugs.

Federal prisoners were committed to these hospitals, which had a striking resemblance to federal prisons. Others were admitted on a voluntary basis as space was available. Over the years, there have been approximately 80,000 admissions (including many readmissions) to these facilities. The

---

[48] Ibid., p. 489.

[49] Edwin M. Lemert, *Social Pathology* (New York: McGraw-Hill Book Company, Inc., 1951), p. 367.

relapse rate was high—85 to 95 per cent—when relapse was defined as some subsequent opiate use. George Vaillant did a follow-up study that focused on the drug use of the patients at the end of 12 years. That study showed more positive results. Although 90 of the 100 heroin addicts had used drugs at some time after leaving the hospital, 46 of them were not using drugs at the time of death or the investigator's last contact with them. Among the 30 persons Vaillant considered to have made the best adjustment, the average time they had abstained from opiate use was 7 years.[50]

In the 1960s, California, New York, and the federal government began civil commitment programs similar to the commitment of mentally ill persons or those with contagious diseases. In these programs, criminal proceedings against addicts were dropped on the condition that the person enter a rehabilitation program involving about six months of hospitalization, followed by supervision. A relapse rate of 87 per cent in terms of some subsequent drug use, however, was reported.[51]

Synanon

A form of treatment that offers a dramatic departure from psychiatric therapy is Synanon. Founded in May, 1959, in Santa Monica, California, by a member of Alcoholics Anonymous, Synanon is an organization of former drug addicts that does not rely on the help of experts. The group's purpose is to keep addicts off drugs, and the antidrug message is continually reinforced through daily conversation and evening therapy sessions. In contrast to Alcoholics Anonymous, Synanon offers a residential program. Like AA, entrance into this program is voluntary, but admission is restricted to those who express willingness to submit to the authority of this antidrug society.

In an evaluation of the program, it was found that of 215 persons who remained at Synanon for at least one month, 103 (48 per cent) were still off drugs; of the 143 who remained for at least three months, 95 (66 per cent) were nonusers; of the 87 who remained at least seven months, 75 (86 per cent) were nonusers.[52] One of the criticisms of Synanon is that it encourages

[50] George E. Vaillant, "Twelve-Year Follow-up of New York Narcotic Addicts. II. The Natural History of a Chronic Disease," *New England Journal of Medicine*, 275 (December 8, 1966): 1282–1288.

[51] Richard Stephens and Emily Cottrell, "A Follow-Up Study of 200 Narcotic Addicts Committed for Treatment under the Narcotic Addict Rehabilitation Act (NARA)," *British Journal of Addictions*, 67 (1972): 45–53.

[52] Rita Volkman and Donald R. Cressey, "Differential Association and the Rehabilitation of Drug Addicts," *American Journal of Sociology*, 69 (September 1963): 129–142.

dependence on the organization. According to Donald Louria, "In a ten-year period, an average of no more than twenty persons per year has been returned to the community drug-free."[53]

Although modeled after Synanon, Daytop Village and the Phoenix Houses in New York City and other drug-free therapeutic communities offer more encouragement to the ex-addict to return to the larger society. Most of them are staffed by ex-addicts who have little interest in record-keeping, so their claims of 90 per cent success are essentially guesses.

Methadone Maintenance

Treatment of heroin addiction through methadone maintenance has gained widespread acceptance. The first program was initiated in 1964 by Vincent Dole and Marie Nyswander in New York. By February, 1973, approximately 73,000 persons were involved in methadone maintenance programs in various localities.

Methadone maintenance usually involves three phases. In a hospital or clinic, selected volunteers are stabilized on methadone at a dosage sufficient to permit normal functioning. Next, the addicts become outpatients but return to a center daily for their methadone. Finally, the patients are encouraged to become self-supporting.

Initially, Dole and Nyswander were highly selective; they accepted only men between 21 and 29 years of age who had used heroin for at least five years and had a history of failure in other treatment efforts but were highly motivated to quit using heroin. Some programs now accept persons who have used heroin for only six months and have no record of treatment failure. Persons with major health complications and histories of mental illness are now accepted, the upper age limit has been removed, the minimum age is 18, and women are no longer excluded.[54]

Although substitution of addiction to methadone for heroin addiction poses ethical questions, methadone has some advantages. It costs about $2 a week, in contrast with a $100 a day heroin habit. "Since it is longer lasting, the addict can take his methadone in the morning—usually dissolved in fruit

[53] Donald B. Louria, *The Drug Scene* (New York: McGraw-Hill Book Company, 1968), p. 183.

[54] Paul Danaceau, *Methadone Maintenance: The Experience of Four Programs* (Washington, D.C.: Drug Abuse Council, Inc., 1973), p. 103; Harrison M. Trice and Paul M. Roman, *Spirits and Demons at Work: Alcohol and Other Drugs on the Job* (Ithaca, N.Y.: Cornell University, School of Industrial and Labor Relations, 1972), pp. 227–233.

juice—and then work comfortably all day, unlike the heroin addict who may need several fixes in that time."[55] Because it is inexpensive and legal, users do not have to steal to support their habits, nor are they automatically considered criminals. Taken orally, methadone is supposed to block the euphoric effect of heroin without producing similar effects. Administered intravenously, it produces a high, and extensive cheating among methadone patients has been reported.

Methadone maintenance appears to work with some, but not all addicts. In one program in New York, the careers of 2,200 patients were followed for five years. For those who remained in treatment, the use of heroin dropped sharply, jail sentences were infrequent, and employment increased substantially. The patients were primarily over 30, white, and highly motivated. In a Philadelphia treatment center, where the majority of the clients were under 30 and black, the dropout rate was 70 per cent.[56]

Because the general population of addicts has not flocked to the methadone programs, the possibility of heroin maintenance, along the lines of the British system, has been suggested. In Great Britain, addiction is viewed as an illness and is handled in a manner similar to other sicknesses. Heroin is prescribed in regulated clinics, and addicts purchase their daily supply in a pharmacy at a cost comparable to what many Americans spend for cigarettes. In Britain, criminal syndicates are essentially unknown, and British addicts are not crime-prone. Continuous hustling to obtain sufficient funds to purchase drugs is unnecessary, and many addicts hold regular jobs.

There is a need for change in our public policy toward drugs, particularly marihuana. Our present policy has the effect of facilitating users' progression to more dangerous drugs, which has led to the realization that the legal penalties for possession and use of marihuana should be removed. The treatment of users of some drugs as criminals has complicated, rather than solved the drug problem.

Additional Readings

Agar, Michael. *Ripping and Running: A Formal Ethnography of Urban Heroin Addicts*. New York: Seminar Press, 1973.

[55] Walter R. Cuskey and William Krasner, "The Needle and the Boot: Heroin Maintenance," *Society*, 10 (May-June 1973): 48.
[56] Ibid.

Austin, Gregory A., and Dan J. Lettieri. *Drug Users and the Criminal Justice System*. Rockville, Md.: National Institute on Drug Abuse, 1977.

Bean, Philip. *The Social Control of Drugs*. New York: Halsted Press, 1974.

Blum, Richard H., and associates. *The Dream Sellers: Perspectives on Drug Dealers*. San Francisco: Jossey-Bass, Inc., 1972.

Bourne, Peter G., ed. *Addiction*. New York: Academic Press, Inc., 1974.

Chein, Isidor, Donald L. Gerard, Robert S. Lee, and Eva Rosenfeld. *The Road to H: Narcotics, Delinquency, and Social Policy*. New York: Basic Books, Inc., Publishers, 1964.

Danaceau, Paul. *Pot Luck in Texas: Changing a Marijuana Law*. Washington, D.C.: Drug Abuse Council, Inc., 1974.

Fiddle, Seymour. *Portraits from a Shooting Gallery: Life Styles from the Drug Addict World*. New York: Harper & Row, Publishers, 1967.

Gellman, Irving P. *The Sober Alcoholic: An Organizational Analysis of Alcoholics Anonymous*. New Haven, Conn.: College and University Press, 1964.

Gould, Leroy C., Andrew L. Walker, Lansing E. Crane, and Charles W. Lidz. *Connections: Notes from the Heroin World*. New Haven, Conn.: Yale University Press, 1974.

Gusfield, Joseph R. *Symbolic Crusade: Status Politics and the American Temperance Movement*. Urbana, Ill.: University of Illinois Press, 1963.

Kornetsky, Conan. *Pharmacology: Drugs Affecting Behavior*. New York: John Wiley & Sons, Inc., 1976.

Lennard, Henry L., Leon J. Epstein, Arnold Bernstein, and Donald C. Ransom. *Mystification and Drug Misuse: Hazards in Using Psychoactive Drugs*. San Francisco: Jossey-Bass, Inc., 1971.

Lindesmith, Alfred R. *Addiction and Opiates*. Chicago: Aldine Publishing Company, 1968.

Marihuana and Health. Second Annual Report to Congress from the Secretary of Health, Education, and Welfare. Washington, D.C.: U.S. Government Printing Office, 1972.

Miller, Loren L., ed. *Marijuana: Effects on Human Behavior*. New York: Academic Press, Inc., 1974.

Musto, David F. *The American Disease: Origins of Narcotic Control*. New Haven, Conn.: Yale University Press, 1973.

Nimmer, Raymond T. *Two Million Unnecessary Arrests: Removing a Social Service Concern from the Criminal Justice System*. Chicago: American Bar Foundation, 1971.

Smith, David E., and George R. Gay, eds. *"It's So Good, Don't Even Try It*

Once": Heroin in Perspective. Englewood Cliffs, N.J.: Prentice-Hall, Inc., 1972.

Wells, Brian. *Psychedelic Drugs.* Baltimore: Penguin Books, Inc., 1973.

World Health Organization. *Evaluation of Dependence Liability and Dependence Potential of Drugs.* Technical Report No. 577. Geneva: World Health Organization, 1975.

Yablonsky, Lewis. *The Tunnel Back: Synanon.* New York: Macmillan Publishing Co., Inc., 1965.

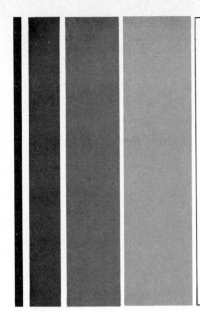

sexual deviance

Inevitably, there is one question which every customer puts to a prostitute—what might be called the sixty-four-dollar question: "How did you get into this business?" As a rule men ask it, expecting to hear a tale of woe, but the sort of answer they would prefer to hear is implicit in a well-known joke. According to this story a man sleeps with a beautiful girl who, though a prostitute, is rich, well-bred, well-educated, and intelligent. Amazed that a girl with all these endowments and advantages should stoop to whoring, he asks how she got into the business. "Oh, I don't know," is the tart answer. "I'm just lucky, I guess."

Men particularly relish this joke because it feeds their egos, and also because it would lessen their pleasure to think that a girl was submitting to them strictly from necessity. Actually, of course, despite all the feigned transports of ecstasy (for purposes of increasing the tip), to ninety-nine out of a hundred girls going to bed with a customer is a joyless, even distasteful, experience. Nothing could be farther from the truth than the "just lucky" explanation—unless the girl meant bad luck.[1]

The preceding statement was made by Polly Adler, a well-known madam in the years prior to World War II. Continuing, she attributes the entrance of many girls into prostitution not only to poverty but to a lack of love, educa-

[1] Polly Adler, *A House Is Not a Home* (New York: Popular Library, 1953), pp. 98–99.

tion, and hope. In addition to prostitution, sexual deviance covers a wide variety of activities, including forcible rape, incest, premarital intercourse, voyeurism (peeping Toms), exhibitionism, obscenity, nudism, co-marital sex (swinging), and homosexuality. All of these activities have only two things in common—they involve sexuality and are generally disapproved by law or by conventional morality.

SEX AND THE LAW

Although the laws vary from state to state, in most of the country the only forms of sexual behavior that are not prohibited are petting, solitary masturbation, and intercourse between husband and wife in private. According to a noted criminologist, the laws are designed to control four aspects of sexual relations: degree of consent, nature of the object, nature or the sexual act, and the setting in which sexual activity occurs.[2] The use or threat of force is prohibited, and the punishment for forcible rape has been as severe as for murder. The partners must be of legal age to consent to sexual relations, and laws pertaining to indecent liberties or child molestation prohibit noncoital sexual contacts with children. The only legitimate sexual object is an adult of the opposite sex to whom one is legally married. Sexual acts are to be restricted to normal heterosexual intercourse, and sexual activity is to occur only in private settings.

Perhaps as many as 90 per cent of the adults in the United States have at one time or another engaged in illegal sexual activities.[3] These include fornication—intercourse between two unmarried individuals of the opposite sex; adultery—intercourse between persons of the opposite sex when one or both are married, but not to each other; homosexual acts—sexual acts between persons of the same sex; unorthodox relations between husband and wife, particularly oral-genital contact; and statutory rape—nonforcible intercourse with a willing girl who is under the age of consent. The age of consent varies from 7 in Delaware to 21 in Tennessee but is usually 16 or 18. Co-marital sex, or swinging, which involves two or more married couples or three or more individuals, violates the laws on fornication and adultery. Nudity in public and the possession or sale of pornographic material are also against the law.

[2] Stanton Wheeler, "Sex Offenses: A Sociological Critique," *Law and Contemporary Problems,* 25 (Spring 1960):258–259.
[3] Fred Rodell, "Our Unlovable Sex Laws," *Trans-action,* 2 (May–June 1965): 36–39.

However, there is considerable variation from society to society in what specific behavior is defined as sexual deviance. Virginity prior to marriage has been upheld as a cultural ideal in American society, but in the Scandinavian countries there is considerably less emphasis on premarital chastity. The extent of family relationships covered by the incest taboo varies not only from society to society, but within societies. First cousins cannot legally marry in Iowa, but if they move to the neighboring state of Minnesota, they can. Laws that prohibit marriage between close relatives make sense from a genetic standpoint in terms of what we know about recessive genes, but the law frequently has been extended to other family members such as in-laws and step-children. Extension of the law beyond close relatives reflects not genetic concerns, but a particular conception of morality.

Many of the specific laws pertaining to sexual behavior are either unenforceable or enforced in a discriminatory manner. Laws that attempt to regulate the behavior of consenting adults in private cannot be enforced unless law-enforcement agents engage in illegal entrapment or invasion of citizens' privacy. Enforcement of the laws pertaining to exhibitionists, voyeurs, and frotteurs (who enjoy physical contact with others in crowded places such as elevators or subways) tends to be discriminatory because they are applied primarily to males. On the other hand, the female is the object of law-enforcement efforts designed to control prostitution. The prostitute's customer is rarely arrested.

BASIC CONCEPTS AND A TYPOLOGY

Basic Concepts

To clarify the nature of sexual deviance, it is necessary to define three concepts: sexual behavior, sexual attraction, and sexual identity.[4] *Sexual behavior* involves a continuum. In terms of their behavior, persons who have sex relations only with members of the opposite sex are *heterosexuals*. Individuals who have sex relations only with persons of the same sex are homosexuals; *gay* is the term homosexuals prefer and apply to themselves. Those who have sex relations with both sexes are *bisexuals*. The latter term is misleading because it implies they they divide their attention equally between the sexes.

[4] The discussion of these concepts is based on Barry M. Dank, "The Homosexual," in Erich Goode and Richard R. Troiden, eds., *Sexual Deviance and Sexual Deviants* (New York: William Morrow & Co., Inc., 1974), pp. 176–178.

This is seldom the case. Another relevant dimension involves *sexual attraction*. A person may be attracted solely to persons of the same or opposite sex or to both sexes. Most humans at times experience sexual fantasies, and an important criterion of sexual attraction is the sex of the person in these fantasies. However, attraction does not necessarily mean that the person will engage in sexual behavior consistent with his or her attraction to others. Finally, a person's *sexual identity* may be heterosexual, bisexual, or homosexual. The concept of sexual identity refers to a person's self-definition, not what others think of the individual. Thus, a person with a bisexual or homosexual identity may pass as a heterosexual in most settings to avoid legal, occupational, or social liabilities.

A Typology

John Gagnon and William Simon divide sexual deviance into three broad categories: normal deviance, pathological deviance, and deviance that produces a specific form of social structure.[5] The term *normal deviance* applies to masturbation, premarital coitus, and oral-genital contacts. These acts are generally disapproved, but they occur frequently, and few persons are punished for them because of their low social visibility. Extramarital affairs, co-marital sex, and obscenity are also included in the normal deviance category.

Pathological deviance includes incest, sexual contact with children, exhibitionism, voyeurism, and aggressive or assaultive offenses. In contrast with the large numbers of persons in American society who engage in normal sexual deviance, pathological deviance involves few people. Further, with the exception of gang rapes, there is usually no more than one offender involved in a particular incident.

Another type of sexual deviance is *socially structured deviance*. This includes prostitution and homosexuality. Many homosexuals are dependent upon their contacts with others in a homosexual subculture. Similarly, most prostitutes participate in an occupational culture, which includes specialized knowledge, language, and a network of social relations consisting of other prostitutes, pimps, the police, and customers. Like the homosexual subculture, the prostitute's network facilitates his or her activities.

[5] John H. Gagnon and William Simon, eds., *Sexual Deviance* (New York: Harper & Row, Publishers, 1967), pp. 7–11.

NORMAL SEXUAL DEVIANCE

Kinsey Studies

A few studies of normal sexual activities, focusing particularly on college students and married couples, were conducted prior to World War II, but it was the Kinsey studies that made human sexual behavior a legitimate area for scientific investigation. Alfred Kinsey, Wardell Pomeroy, and Clyde Martin, whose respective fields were zoology, psychology, and statistics, published their studies of the sexual behavior of the American male and female in 1948 and 1953.[6]

Kinsey and his associates relied on volunteers from a variety of groups. Among others, they interviewed members of college classes, fraternities and sororities, PTA groups, women's clubs, church congregations, unions, detention home residents, prison staffs, and even hitchhikers. While the use of volunteers resulted in a large sample (5,940 white females and 5,300 white males), it was not representative of the adult population of the United States. For example, blacks were excluded, and most of the lower-class males in the sample were prisoners. "The groups that Kinsey's sample most closely represented were the white, urban, Protestant, college-educated people from the northeastern quarter of the country."[7]

Premarital Intercourse. Kinsey and his associates reported that nearly 50 per cent of the women they studied who had ever married had had premarital coitus. Of these females, about one half had premarital intercourse with only one partner. Only 13 per cent of the females had had premarital sexual relations with six or more partners. Comparable figures for males were not reported. Approximately one half of the women who engaged in premarital sexual relations did so only with the male they later married, and many of the others had intercourse within the context of courtship. Only 13 per cent of the females reported coitus with a male who was not their fiancé. In the Kinsey studies, educational achievement was highly related to premarital coitus, but the differences were in opposite directions for males and females. For females reporting premarital coitus, the percentage distribution by educational

[6] Alfred C. Kinsey, Wardell B. Pomeroy, and Clyde E. Martin, *Sexual Behavior in the Human Male* (Philadelphia: W. B. Saunders Company, 1948); Alfred C. Kinsey, Wardell B. Pomeroy, Clyde E. Martin, and Paul H. Gebhard, *Sexual Behavior in the Human Female* (Philadelphia: W. B. Saunders Company, 1953).
[7] Ira L. Reiss, *The Family System in America* (New York: Holt, Rinehart and Winston, 1971), p. 130.

level was grade school, 30; high school, 47; and college, 60. For males, the comparable figures were grade school, 98; high school, 84; and college, 67.[8]

Masturbation. In Kinsey's samples, 58 per cent of the females and 92 per cent of the males had achieved orgasm at least once through masturbation. Masturbation (self-stimulation to produce sexual arousal) was a common sexual outlet for many unmarried persons, and prior to marriage it was the chief sexual outlet for college-educated males.

The incidence of masturbation was also related to education. Among females who had masturbated, the percentages ranged from a low of 34 per cent of those with a grade school education to 63 per cent of those who entered graduate school. Of the males with grade school education, 89 per cent reported masturbation, as did 95 per cent of the high school and 96 per cent of the college-educated males.[9]

Premarital Sex in the 1970s

In an important study of sexual behavior completed in the early 1970s, Melvin Zelnik and John Kantner obtained interviews from a representative sample of 4,240 never-married, 15- to 19-year-old females.[10] Of these unmarried females, 28 per cent had had intercourse. Not surprisingly, sexual experience was related to age. Of the 15-year-olds, one third of the black and one tenth of the white females reported coitus whereas, among the 19-year-olds, 80 per cent of the black and 40 per cent of the white females were no longer virgins.

Of the sexually experienced young women, three fifths had only one partner, and about half had relations only with the man they intended to marry. The whites were slightly more promiscuous than the blacks: 16 per cent of the white and 11 per cent of the black females had had four or more

[8] Kinsey et al., *Sexual Behavior in the Human Female,* op. cit., pp. 286–293; Kinsey et al., *Sexual Behavior in the Human Male,* op. cit., p. 552.

[9] Kinsey et al., *Sexual Behavior in the Human Female,* op. cit., pp. 142, 148; Kinsey et al., *Sexual Behavior in the Human Male,* op. cit., p. 499.

[10] Melvin Zelnik and John F. Kantner, "Sexuality, Contraception and Pregnancy Among Young Unwed Females in the United States," in Charles F. Westoff and Robert Parke, Jr., eds, Commission on Population Growth and the American Future, Research Reports, Vol. I, *Demographic and Social Aspects of Population Growth* (Washington, D.C.: U.S. Government Printing Office, 1972), pp. 355–374. Their respondents included 2,839 white and 1,401 black females. In 1976, these investigators interviewed a comparable sample of 2,200 women; 35 per cent of the women said they had had intercourse, which is an increase since 1971. Most first sexual encounters occur in the home while the parents are absent. *The Courier-Journal,* Louisville, April 8, 1977, p. A-5.

partners. The white girls also reported having intercourse somewhat more frequently than the black girls: "While proportionately more blacks than whites have had intercourse, it is the white nonvirgins who have sex more frequently and are the more promiscuous."[11]

One of the possible consequences of nonmarital coitus is unwanted pregnancy. Of the respondents who had had intercourse, 41 per cent of the blacks and 10 per cent of the whites had become pregnant. In fact, fully half of the sexually active, 19-year-old black respondents reported having been pregnant. The reasons for these pregnancies included misinformation about physiological processes, such as the period of greatest risk of conception during the menstrual cycle, and limited knowledge about contraceptive devices. A majority of the sexually active females either never used contraceptives or sometimes failed to do so.

Morton Hunt reports the results of a study, sponsored by the Playboy Foundation, that includes 982 men and 1,044 women in 24 cities.[12] Unfortunately, since residents of rural areas and small towns were not included in the sample, it may not be representative of the national population.[13] Hunt concludes that among the young in the study premarital intercourse is almost universal (see Table 12-1). Oral-genital sex is also now more common. In the Kinsey study, the percentages of males who reported experience with fellatio

Table 12-1. Per Cent Who Report Ever Engaging in Premarital Coitus (Total Married Sample) by Age: 1972

Age	Males	Females
18–24	95%	81%
25–34	92	65
35–44	86	41
45–54	89	36
55 and over	84	31

SOURCE: Morton Hunt, *Sexual Behavior in the 1970s* (New York: Dell Publishing Co., 1975), p. 150.

[11] Ibid., pp. 365–366.

[12] Morton Hunt, *Sexual Behavior in the 1970s* (New York: Dell Publishing Co., 1975).

[13] The questionnaires were completed after group rap sessions, which could have influenced the answers. Ibid., pp. 16–17.

and cunnilingus from adolescence to age 25 were 33 and 14, respectively; the comparable percentages for males 18 to 24 in the Playboy survey were 72 and 69. According to Hunt, the percentages of single respondents who reported that in the previous 12 months they had practiced cunnilingus or fellatio were white females, 67; black females, 48; white males, 72; and black males, 35.[14]

The Playboy survey shows that coitus and oral-genital contact frequently occur in the dating process, but the dominant sexual pattern is neither casual nor indiscriminate. As in the Kinsey study, about half of the females reported having had intercourse only with their fiancés. Hunt concludes that casual coitus is more common among single persons over 25 than it was a generation ago, but that the sex ethic of most young people today is essentially romantic: "For the great majority of Americans at the present time, the recreational philosophy of sex is viable only for brief periods; to meet their deeper needs for enduring love, security and intimacy, they turn to the romantic philosophy of sex."[15]

Marital and Extramarital Sex

Currently, marital sex involves a wider range of sexual practices than in the past. Married couples now experiment with a variety of coital positions and engage in prolonged foreplay and extended intercourse. There has been a striking increase in the incidence of oral-genital sex. More than four fifths of the married males and females under 35 years of age engaged in such oral practices in the previous year.[16]

Although a great deal of attention has been focused on such things as swinging and open marriages, extramarital sexual behavior has not changed drastically in the past 25 years. Kinsey's studies showed that about half of the men and a fourth of the women had extramarital intercourse during their marriages. The change in extramarital sexual activity has been confined largely to the young. Comparison of the figures reported by Kinsey and those of the recent Playboy survey suggest that for wives under 25 years of age, the incidence of extramarital sex has increased from 8 to 24 per cent, with a current figure of 32 per cent for husbands under 25 years of age. Kinsey did not inquire about the phenomenon of swinging, but recent research shows

[14] Ibid., pp. 166, 198.
[15] Ibid., p. 155.
[16] Ibid., p. 199.

that relatively few adults are involved in this form of sexual behavior. Only 2 per cent of those in the Playboy study said they had ever participated in swinging, and most of them had done so only once.[17]

Obscenity

With respect to obscenity, another form of normal sexual deviance, there has been a virtual revolution in attitudes. *Obscenity* is a legal term that has been defined as material without redeeming social value that excites lustful thoughts. In recent decades a more tolerant view of explicitly sexual materials has emerged; what formerly was clandestine is now publicly available in the form of erotic books, films, and magazines. For example, magazines that feature color photographs of well-endowed young females as well as nude photos of male athletes and actors are now available at newsstands.

Until recently, it was thought that sexually provocative material was linked to deviant sexual behavior. However, the findings of the Commission on Obscenity and Pornography suggest that exposure to pornographic material has less effect on behavior than many people thought. Experimental studies showed that exposure to erotic materials did not affect established patterns of sexual behavior. Some respondents reported short-term increases in masturbational or coital behavior, but these effects disappeared within 48 hours.[18] Further, evidence linking the availability of sexually erotic material to criminality in general and to sex offenses in particular is lacking. In a study conducted in Denmark, the investigator concluded that after pornographic materials became widely available to the public, there was a substantial decline in sex offenses against females, particularly exhibitionism, voyeurism, child molesting, and physical indecency toward women.[19]

PATHOLOGICAL DEVIANCE: THE CASE OF FORCIBLE RAPE

Forcible rape involves attempted or actual sexual intercourse with a woman through the use or threat of force. In the past, 11 states permitted the execu-

[17] Ibid., p. 271.

[18] Commission on Obscenity and Pornography, *The Report of the Commission on Obscenity and Pornography* (Washington, D.C.: U.S. Government Printing Office, 1970), p. 25.

[19] Berl Kutchinsky, "The Effect of Easy Availability of Pornography on the Incidence of Sex Crimes: The Danish Experience," *Journal of Social Issues,* 29, No. 3 (1973): 163–181.

tion of rapists, and from 1930 to 1959, 499 convicted rapists were executed in this country. In 1977, the Supreme Court ruled that it is cruel and unusual punishment to execute a convicted rapist if he does not kill his victim.

There are rarely witnesses in cases of rape. Except for tangible evidence in the form of a medical report, bruises, or torn clothing, a decision must be reached primarily on the basis of the male's and female's testimony. Extraneous factors such as the woman's reputation may be introduced by the defense attorney. Although both virgins and nonvirgins can be the target of a rapist, such irrelevant information is often noted in an effort to discredit the rape victim.

Sexual intercourse involves rape if it is against a woman's will, that is, without her consent. A recurring problem is that the male often claims the woman gave her consent. Consent is an intangible mental act, which is difficult to assess in a court of law. As a consequence, the courts often emphasize the amount of resistance, and conviction of a man for forcible rape often depends on interpretation of this factor. Some states require that a female must resist by kicking, biting, scratching, and screaming to the limits of her physical strength, whereas in other jurisdictions, it is necessary to demonstrate only that the male used some force or threat of force and that the woman did not agree to coitus. Although the crucial issue is consent, in the pursuit of tangible evidence, greater attention is often devoted to the secondary question of resistance.

Extent

In official statistics, rape is reported less frequently than are aggravated assault and armed robbery, but its importance cannot be judged solely by numbers because forced "intercourse entails a violation of 'private' property. It is an encroachment on or into one's body space, that most intimate of personal environments."[20] As noted in Chapter 10, victim surveys uncover three and one half times more rapes than are officially reported. According to the FBI, in 1975, 51 of every 100,000 females in this country were known to the police as rape victims. There were 56,090 forcible rapes or attempted rapes reported to the police in 1975. Of these offenses, 74 per cent involved rape by force, and the remainder were attempts or assaults to commit rape.

---

[20] Richard R. Clayton, *The Family, Marriage, and Social Change* (Lexington, Mass.: D. C. Health & Company, 1975), p. 236.

By way of comparison, in 1960 there were 7,000 rapes reported, and in 1965 there were 22,500 attempted or actual forcible rapes reported to the police. The increased number of such reports may reflect the occurrence of more attacks on females or the greater willingness on the part of women to file complaints, or both.

Studies of Forcible Rape

Research on forcible rape and other violent crimes is usually confined to a single city. In the most extensive study of forcible rape to date, Menachem Amir examined the information in the Philadelphia police files on cases of forcible rape.[21] In the crime of rape, both the victims and the offenders are usually young persons. In Amir's sample, half of the rape victims were between 15 and 29 years of age. The offenders were even more highly concentrated in terms of age; 66 per cent were in the 15 to 24 age range, and few offenders were over 35. Of the offenders, 54 per cent were employed as unskilled laborers and an additional 28 per cent were unemployed. Men employed in professional, managerial, clerical, and skilled jobs accounted for only 1 per cent, and 7 per cent were students.

Slightly more than 80 per cent of the victims and offenders were blacks. The population figures for Philadelphia show that 24 per cent of those age 15 and over were blacks. Rape is generally intraracial—of the 646 cases, 77 per cent involved black victims and offenders, and in an additional 16 per cent, the victims and assailants were white. Only 7 per cent of the rapes were interracial.

According to Amir, 71 per cent of the rapes were planned. Most rapes involved assailants who were strangers (52 per cent), acquaintances (14 per cent), or neighbors (19 per cent). More than two fifths of the 646 victims were raped by two or more assailants. Such multiple rapes almost always involved strangers, and two thirds of these victims met their assailants on the street.

Amir concluded that most rapists have been exposed to a subculture of violence, in which aggressive and exploitative behavior toward women is common and, therefore, considered by the assailant as acceptable. On the other hand, Amir described 19 per cent of the forcible rapes as "victim precipitated" in the sense that the female agreed to have intercourse but changed

---

[21] Menachem Amir, *Patterns in Forcible Rape* (Chicago: University of Chicago Press, 1971).

her mind before the act, did not strongly reject the suggestion of coitus by the offender, or through language and gestures invited sexual relations. There is, however, reason to question his classification of nearly one fifth of the cases as victim precipitated. The National Commission on the Causes and Prevention of Violence collected a 10 per cent random sample of offense and arrest reports from 17 cities.[22] Using essentially the same definition as Amir, the Violence Commission classified only 4 per cent of the forcible rapes as victim precipitated.

Sexual Assaults

Another form of pathological deviance involves men who are not sexually attracted to men but engage in homosexual behavior when women are not available. Sexual assault is a significant problem in jails and prisons. Unfortunately, prison authorities have generally ignored prisoners' sexuality. Consensual homosexual liasons are not uncommon, but often a young man in prison agrees to such a relation in return for protection against gang rape. Others are bribed by provision of scarce commodities, such as cigarettes, or are required to pay off gambling debts by providing sexual service.

On the basis of interviews with 3,300 inmates in three correctional facilities in Philadelphia, Alan Davis estimates that 2,000 of the 60,000 inmates who passed through these facilities in a 26-month period were sexually assaulted.[23] Excluding consensual homosexuality, he documented 129 incidents of sexual assaults involving 164 aggressors and 103 victims. In 20 cases, the aggressors and victims were white, and blacks were involved in 37 incidents. In none of the incidents did whites attack blacks, but 56 per cent of the assaults involved black aggressors and white victims. About 80 per cent of the inmates in the three Philadelphia institutions are black. Davis infers that the phenomenon of sexual assault in penal institutions often reflects current racial tensions and hostilities, rather than sexual deprivation, and that the goal of the aggressor is the conquest and humiliation of the victim. Sexual assaults parallel the rape of females in the use or threat of force, but a striking difference is the interracial factor.

[22] Donald J. Mulvihill and Melvin M. Tumin, *Crimes of Violence*, Staff Report Submitted to the National Commission on the Causes and Prevention of Violence, Vol. II (Washington, D.C.: U.S. Government Printing Office, 1969), pp. 207–258.

[23] Alan J. Davis, "Sexual Assaults in the Philadelphia Prison System and Sheriff's Vans," *Trans-action*, 6 (December 1968): 8–16.

SOCIALLY STRUCTURED DEVIANCE: MALE HOMOSEXUALITY

Extent

In forcible rape and sexual assaults, one can clearly differentiate between the victims and aggressors. However, in socially structured deviance such as male and female homosexuality and prostitution this is not the case. According to Kinsey's research, 60 per cent of all preadolescent boys engaged in some form of homosexual activity. After the onset of adolescence, some 37 per cent of American males had at least one homosexual contact resulting in orgasm, and another 13 per cent were physically attracted to other males without having overt homosexual experience. Between the ages of 16 and 55, only 4 per cent of the males were exclusively homosexual—they never had sexual contact with women and were not aroused by them.

Kinsey's findings and the recent Playboy survey differ somewhat regarding the extent of homosexuality. Kinsey reported that about a quarter of the males had more than incidental homosexual experience or reactions for at least three years, with 10 per cent more or less exclusively homosexual for that length of time. According to the Playboy survey, about 10 or 11 per cent of the males have had any homosexual experience after the age of 15, and only 1 per cent of the males said they were primarily homosexual. Attempting to reconcile these differences, Hunt estimates that the correct figure for males who are "more or less exclusively homosexual" is 3 per cent.[24] Kinsey's figures may be inflated, but in any event, there is no reason to suspect that there has been an increase in homosexual behavior in the past 25 years.

Homosexual Subculture

Sociologists use the concept of subculture to reflect immersion in a specific social scene. There are three ways in which homosexuals form a subculture: "(a) Its members interact with one another more frequently and more intimately than they do with members of other social categories; (b) its members' way of life, and their beliefs, are somewhat different from members of other social categories; (c) its members think of themselves as belonging to a specific group, and they are so defined by those who do not share this trait."[25]

[24] Hunt, op. cit., pp. 312–313; for the data from the Kinsey survey, see Kinsey et al., *Sexual Behavior in the Human Male,* op. cit., pp. 168, 650–651.
[25] Goode and Troiden, op. cit., p. 152.

In a homosexual subculture the novice learns justifications for the gay life, a special language, varieties of sexual acts, and how to recognize vice squad officers.

Some gays are immersed in a homosexual subculture involving gay bars, parties, clubs, coffee houses, and homophile organizations.[26] In fact, many males, puzzled by their sexual attraction to other men, discover that they are homosexuals when they meet others in gay bars. Gays refer to the public acceptance of a homosexual identity as "coming out"—the person identifies himself to other homosexuals as a homosexual. Among the 386 self-identified homosexuals who completed questionnaires for Barry Dank, the mean age for coming out was 21, with the following distribution by age: 8 to 14, 12 per cent; 15 to 19, 35 per cent; 20 to 24, 31 per cent; and 25 and over, 22 per cent.[27]

Gay bars serve as sexual marketplaces, where one-night stands (sex without obligation and commitment) are arranged, and as centers for social activities. As social institutions, they serve functions similar to neighborhood bars. Friends meet and exchange news and gossip; people are invited to parties, and information about police activity is shared. Other meeting places include homosexual bathhouses and "tearooms" (derived from the British slang for urine—*tea*—hence, men's restrooms), as well as particular coffee shops, restaurants, movie theaters, beaches, gyms, street corners, and sections of parks.

Passing

There are men with homosexual identities who have minimal contact with a gay community, largely because of their occupations. They may be government officials, ministers, physicians, lawyers, and teachers. These men prefer to keep their sexual identity secret and pass in the conventional world as heterosexuals. Because most males are exposed to heterosexual socialization, these men can present themselves as heterosexuals with little or no difficulty. For covert homosexuals, contacts with the gay world are limited and usually occur in restrooms or with male prostitutes.[28] Such contacts are not without risk of exposure. A number of years ago the career of a presidential advisor

---

[26] The term *homophile* refers to homosexuals, bisexuals, or heterosexuals who are sympathetic to and supportive of homosexuals and their problems.

[27] Dank, op, cit., p. 182.

[28] David J. Pittman, "The Male House of Prostitution," *Trans-action,* 8 (March–April 1971): 21–27.

was destroyed following his arrest in a YMCA men's room. It is fear of this kind of public exposure that creates psychological problems for passers.

In a study of the psychological problems of homosexuals, Martin Weinberg and Colin Williams found that homosexuals who attempt to pass have more psychological problems than those who do not.[29] The psychological problems associated with passing are caused by worry about exposure and anticipation of sanctions, rather than by the fact of passing. Homosexuals with high occupational status are more secretive but have fewer psychological problems than those with lower occupational status. High-status homosexuals are more likely to identify with persons in their social class than with homosexuals. Social position, therefore, affects the manner in which a person deals with his homosexuality. "The fact that homosexuals have a sexual identification in common does not erase their economic, political, religious, ethnic, and educational differences."[30]

Impersonal Sex

Other self-identified homosexuals are not sexually integrated into a gay community. Rather, they seek young, nonhomosexual ("straight") males as sexual partners. Albert Reiss asserts that these young delinquents did not consider themselves to be either hustlers or homosexuals—their involvement, as passive recipients of the homosexuals' attention, was simply a way to obtain money with little risk.[31] The assessment of risk in this instance is in comparison with other kinds of delinquent activity.

In a study of tearoom participants in a midwestern city, Laud Humphreys found that a slight majority (27 of 50) of the men in his sample were married and living with their wives, who were unaware of their tearoom activity.[32] Of the 50 men, 19 were "trade" in homosexual slang, or persons with heterosexual identities; 17 of them were married, and 2 were divorced or separated. A dozen of the participants were bisexuals who recognized their dual sexual orientation; 10 of these men were married and 2 were divorced.

---

[29] Martin S. Weinberg and Colin J. Williams, *Male Homosexuals: Their Problems and Adaptations* (New York: Oxford University Press, 1974).

[30] Dank, op, cit., pp. 186–187.

[31] Albert J. Reiss, Jr., "The Social Integration of Queers and Peers," *Social Problems,* 9 (Fall 1961): 102–120.

[32] Laud Humphreys, *Tearoom Trade: Impersonal Sex in Public Places* (Chicago: Aldine Publishing Company, 1970).

Only 7 of the tearoom participants were gay men with extensive involvement in a homosexual subculture. Finally, there were 12 *closet queens,* a term Humphreys used for married or unmarried homosexuals who are secretive about their homosexual activity. The term is more commonly applied to men who are sexually attracted to males and may engage in homosexual acts but have not developed a homosexual identity.

In a similar study, Richard Troiden studied homosexual encounters in a highway rest stop.[33] Rest-stop encounters took place either in wooded or secluded areas or in cars, rather than in restrooms, as in tearoom sex. Troiden conducted informal interviews with 50 of the participants. The sexual identity of 24 of the 50 men was bisexual. All of them were married and 21 of the 24 had children. Their wives were unaware of their activities. Seven informants had wives or girl friends and conceived of themselves as heterosexual. They supplemented their heterosexual activity with rest-stop sex. Fourteen men identified themselves as gay or homosexual, and the investigator met five closet queens. "Although these men have arrived at homosexual self-definitions, and their sexual activity is predominantly, if not exclusively, confined to same-sex members, the scope of their involvement in the homosexual community is extremely limited."[34] As was the case in Humphreys' study, none of the gay respondents or closet queens had ever been married.

Both Troiden and Humphreys use the term *closet queen* to refer to men who are aware of their homosexual orientation, but who remain covert and do not participate in a gay community. Because these men had homosexual identities, they might better be viewed as passing. According to the usual definition of the term, the sexual attraction and sexual identity of closet queens are at odds; because they continue to identify themselves as heterosexual, they may attempt to resolve their dilemma through marriage, often with disastrous results. In the questionnaire survey cited earlier, Dank found that 25 per cent of the self-identified homosexuals had previously been married, and these men tended to be ex-closet queens.[35]

In any event, it is important to recognize that a majority of the participants in tearoom sex do not identify themselves as homosexuals, yet homosexual behavior in men's rooms produces the majority of arrests for homosexual offenses, including such misdemeanors as solicitation, disorderly

[33] Richard R. Troiden, "Homosexual Encounters in a Highway Rest Stop," in Goode and Troiden, op. cit., pp. 211–228.
[34] Ibid., p. 220.
[35] Dank, op, cit., p. 182.

conduct, and indecent behavior. Many gays believe, rightly or wrongly, that persons who express strong antihomosexual attitudes are long-term closet queens who express such sentiments in an effort to hide their own homosexual desires.[36]

While persons not involved in the gay subculture often experience marital disruption and are subject to arrest in public places, participants in gay communities face a number of other problems. Paramount among these is jealousy among homosexuals, which may result in threats of blackmail or exposure to an employer. In one study, almost 10 per cent of the homosexuals reported having been blackmailed. An additional problem is robbery, frequently associated with "trade" contacts. Over 25 per cent of those interviewed had been robbed, often after they had been physically assaulted.[37]

Gay "Marriages"

Although the number of such unions is unknown, some men establish relationships similar to marriage. The participants "are married in the sense that they feel they have a permanent love and sexual and social commitment toward each other, and in the sense that they regard themselves as a couple and prefer to be regarded by other homosexuals as a couple."[38] There is, however, little social or cultural support for such relationships, and unless the couple withdraws from the gay bar scene and other homosexual meeting places, the relationship is likely to fail because of problems of promiscuity and jealousy.

SOCIALLY STRUCTURED DEVIANCE: FEMALE HOMOSEXUALITY

Just as there have been few studies of gay "marriages," female homosexuality, or lesbianism, has been the object of little research. It has been incorrectly assumed that conclusions about male homosexuals apply equally to females.

[36] Ibid., p. 183; Humphreys, op, cit., p. 141.
[37] William Simon and John H. Gagnon, "Homosexuality: The Formulation of a Sociological Perspective," in Ralph W. Weltge, ed., *The Same Sex: An Appraisal of Homosexuality* (Philadelphia: Pilgrim Press, 1969), p. 18.
[38] Dank, op, cit., p. 187.

Extent

According to Kinsey's research, 28 per cent of the females surveyed had at some time in their lives recognized an erotic response to other females.[39] After adolescence, 13 per cent of the females had at least one homosexual experience resulting in orgasm; an additional 7 per cent had one or more homosexual experiences after adolescence without achieving orgasm. Kinsey found that approximately 2 to 3 per cent of the females were exclusively homosexual, and were neither sexually aroused by men nor had sexual contact with them.

The Playboy survey, conducted some 25 years later, suggests that there has been no change in the incidence of homosexual experience among women, although Hunt reports his figures on a somewhat different basis. He estimates that over the course of their lifetime, approximately 9 per cent of the married women and 15 per cent of the single women have had at least one homosexual experience. Most of these experiences occur early in life. After the age of 19, only 7 per cent of the single women and 2 per cent of the married women have any homosexual experience.[40]

Many women who identify themselves as lesbians have at least some heterosexual experience. In a study of 57 lesbians, it was found that 95 per cent had dated and 79 per cent had experienced heterosexual coitus.[41] Most of these women had intercourse while they were in their late teens or twenties as a form of experimentation to test their sexual orientation or preference for females. As a measure of heterosexual desirability, the investigators asked about marriage proposals. Three fourths of the homosexual women *and* heterosexual controls reported one or more serious proposals for marriage, so the lesbians' identity cannot be explained by their lack of attractiveness to males.

Lacking heterosexual outlets, some women prisoners, like their male counterparts, have sexual relations with their fellow inmates. Prisoners distinguish between these "penitentiary turnouts" and lesbians who prefer same-sex relations. Women who engage in homosexual behavior during confinement do not identify themselves as homosexuals and resume heterosexual activity upon release.[42]

[39] Kinsey et al., *Sexual Behavior in the Human Female,* op. cit., p. 453.
[40] Hunt, op. cit., pp. 311–312; for the data from the Kinsey survey, see Kinsey et al., *Sexual Behavior in the Human Female,* op. cit., pp. 488–499.
[41] Marcel T. Saghir and Eli Robins, *Male and Female Homosexuality: A Comprehensive Investigation* (Baltimore: Williams & Wilkins Co., 1973), pp. 242–250.
[42] Rose Giallombardo, *Society of Women: A Study of a Women's Prison* (New York: John Wiley & Sons,

Lesbian Relationships

Lesbians usually recognize their sexual orientation at a later age than do gay males. Women are often in their late teens or early twenties when they become aware of their sexual attraction to females. According to Denise Cronin, the average time interval between a woman's first desire for another woman and the decision that she is a homosexual is five years.[43] Most of her respondents reported awareness of their sexual attraction to females between the ages of 15 and 19, but they did not develop lesbian identities until their early twenties. This generally occurred in the context of an intense affectionate relationship.

On the basis of interviews with 150 males and females with more than incidental same-sex experience, Philip Blumstein and Pepper Schwartz note that when women learn to love one another in a sisterly fashion in women's groups, the foundation is laid for them to love one another sexually. Some women adopt the bisexual label to avoid the stigma of homosexuality, but Blumstein and Schwartz indicate that among lesbians "a bisexual is often defined simply as a homosexual who has not yet been able to accept her true identity," and the lesbian community did not accept with good humor the slogan "If gay is good, bi is better."[44]

Gay Subculture

The homosexual community serves many of the same functions for male and female homosexuals. It provides social support and an ideology to combat the view of the larger society that homosexuals are depraved and shameful. Just as the male homosexuals can find a temporary partner or initiate a brief affair, a lesbian, after termination of a relationship, can select a prospective new partner from within this restricted community.[45] However, the proportion of lesbians involved in the public aspects of gay life is considerably smaller than is the case for male homosexuals. Lesbians are more likely to socialize in informal gatherings in the homes of friends than in gay bars.

Inc., 1966); David A. Ward and Gene G. Kassebaum, *Women's Prison: Sex and Social Structure* (Chicago: Aldine Publishing Company, 1965).

[43] Denise M. Cronin, "Coming Out Among Lesbians," in Goode and Troiden, op, cit., pp. 268–277.

[44] Philip W. Blumstein and Pepper Schwartz, "Lesbianism and Bisexuality," in Goode and Troiden, op. cit., pp. 291, 292.

[45] William Simon and John H. Gagnon, "The Lesbians: A Preliminary Overview," in Gagnon and Simon, op. cit., pp. 247–282.

Like most heterosexual women, lesbians consider a sexual relationship without romantic or emotional involvement unattractive. Consequently, they are less likely to cruise in public places in a search for a sexual partner. Not only are relations between lesbians more romantic and affectionate, but they are also generally longer-lasting and monogamous in contrast with those of male homosexuals. Some lesbian couples adopt the sex roles in heterosexual marriage; in gay terminology the husband and wife roles are referred to as "butch" and "femme."

SOCIALLY STRUCTURED DEVIANCE: PROSTITUTION

Prostitution is defined as the sale of sexual favors on a promiscuous basis in which the prostitute is emotionally indifferent to the customer. With the exception of some parts of Nevada, prostitution is outlawed in every state. Arrests may be made for soliciting, for violating health regulations, for disorderly conduct, or vagrancy. The double standard of sexual morality is reflected in the law; it generally is illegal for a woman to solicit or offer to sell her sexual favors, but it is not usually illegal for a man to accept such propositions. Recent revisions of the statutes in Illinois, Wisconsin, and New York made customers of prostitutes subject to prosecution, but the police usually ignore the patrons. Of the 508 convictions under New York's revised law, less than 1 per cent were for patronizing a prostitute.[46]

Extent

Estimates of the number of women who earn at least half of their annual income from prostitution range from 100,000 to 500,000. Arrests are not a reliable measure of the number of prostitutes because one woman may be arrested several times in a year; moreover, streetwalkers or "hookers" (a term derived from the camp followers of General Joseph Hooker in the Civil War) are more likely to be arrested than are call girls. In 1975, there were 68,200 arrests for prostitution, and some of the 100,000 female arrests for disorderly conduct and vagrancy undoubtedly involved prostitution.

Earlier in this century, most of the prostitutes were recruited from recent immigrants and worked in houses of prostitution. A major change in recent

---

[46] Pamela A. Roby, "Politics and Criminal Law: Revision of the New York State Penal Law on Prostitution," *Social Problems*, 17 (Summer 1969): 97.

years has been the heavy involvement of women from ethnic minorities, especially blacks and Puerto Ricans, in prostitution. Charles Winick and Paul Kinsie conclude that brothels or organized houses of prostitution are rapidly disappearing and are being replaced by less organized forms of prostitution such as street hookers or hustlers and call girls.[47]

Types

Types of prostitutes may be distinguished by the way they obtain customers. Status among prostitutes reflects these differences. Lowest status is assigned to street hookers, who find customers in bars, hotel lobbies, and on the street. Occupying somewhat higher status are those who work in houses. Girls who work in such establishments pay half or more of their earnings for their opportunity, for police protection, and for other services. Another type of prostitute operates in conjunction with legitimate businesses. In bars, "B girls" encourage men to drink and to buy drinks for them. Although they may define themselves as hostesses or waitresses, the sale of sexual favors is not unknown. Similarly, girls employed as go-go dancers or strip-tease entertainers may increase their earnings through prostitution.

A fourth type of prostitute is the call girl, who occupies the top rung on the status ladder. She may be an independent operator or she may have a manager. The latter may be a pimp or a madam, who in a former day, presumably, would have operated a house. Arrangements vary, but managed call girls give 40 to 70 per cent of their fees to their managers as payment for referrals and an apartment in which to work. A manager may have a list of 20 to 30 girls with whom contacts may be made by telephone. This arrangement facilitates part-time prostitution. Girls with full-time legitimate jobs may supplement their incomes by entertaining out-of-town businessmen or men attending conventions.

Apprenticeship

James Bryan has observed that an apprenticeship period is required to develop a clientele.[48] The training of a call girl centers on such matters as when

---

[47] Charles Winick and Paul M. Kinsie, *The Lively Commerce: Prostitution in the United States* (New York: Quadrangle, The New York Times Book Co., 1971), p. 5; Also see Polly Adler, *A House Is Not a Home* (New York: Holt, Rinehart and Winston, 1953); Xaviera Hollander, *The Happy Hooker* (New York: Dell Publishing Co., 1972).

[48] James H. Bryan, "Apprenticeships in Prostitution," *Social Problems,* 12 (Winter 1965): 287–297.

and how to obtain the fee, how to converse with a client, how to solicit a customer by telephone, and matters of sexual hygiene. The primary purpose of an apprenticeship is to develop a "book" or list of telephone numbers of prospective clients. All of the call girls Bryan studied made arrangements with clients exclusively by telephone.

With one exception, all of the call girls he interviewed had personal contact with other call girls or a pimp prior to entry into "the life." In some instances, the relationship with a pimp was strictly a business arrangement; in others, the pimp and the call girl were lovers. Even among the girls recruited by pimps, the apprenticeship period was commonly served under the supervision of another call girl.

Pimps

Many street hookers and even some call girls have what Americans call a pimp, who controls the girl's life and also serves as a source of emotional support. In the pimp's world, the men are dominant but the women are the economic providers. Polygamy is common. Most pimps have two or three ladies, although the number ranges from one to 20.[49]

Occupational Hazards

Professional prostitutes face a number of risks. In addition to fear of physical abuse by customers and the possibility of contracting venereal disease, exposure to alcohol and other drugs is an occupational hazard. Prostitution is also an occupational hazard for addicts. It has been suggested that in recent years drug use has increased among prostitutes in large cities.[50] In interviews with addicted females at the federal hospital in Lexington, Kentucky, Harwin Voss found that although approximately half of the women were involved in prostitution before they used illicit drugs, the women identified themselves primarily as addicts, not prostitutes, and justified their involvement in prostitution as a consequence of their addiction.

[49] Christina Milner and Richard Milner, *Black Players: The Secret World of Black Pimps* (Boston: Little, Brown and Company, 1972).
[50] John H. Gagnon, "Sexual Conduct and Crime," in Daniel Glaser, ed., *Handbook of Criminology* (Chicago: Rand McNally College Publishing Co., 1974), p. 260.

A PRIMER FOR PROSTITUTES

For whatever reason women stay with pimps—charisma, drugs, fear—they allow their men to have enormous control over their lives.

Pimps tell women what to say to "tricks," how long to spend with them, how much to charge, and how to show proper respect to the pimp.

Women who forget are routinely beaten.

Here, in material seized by police from a pimp's apartment, are examples of a pimp's hold over his women:

Prostitute's Code of Conduct

This article is being written for the purpose of informing ladies of leisure of the basic principles of courtesy and conduct while on the road and at home. It is to be adhered to strictly by the ladies of "Sugar Daddy," and can be applied to anyone's ladies who have the mentality to deal with it.

You are to remain as inconspicuous as possible while traveling between destinations. By this, I mean, you are not to let it be known whose ladies you are, and if staying in hotels, ladies are to register together, thereby leaving the men out of the picture.

You are to give your man unquestioned respect and courtesy in front of host macks [pimps] and whores.

You are never to indulge in conversation with other macks, even if they be associates of your own mack.

You are never to speak when other macks are present. You are always to agree with your man when you are asked to speak.

You are to pay close attention to your man's instruction so that it is not necessary for him to repeat himself or call you down while you are working.

You are only as sweet to the john as his money is to you. You never divulge your real name to the john.

You are to put no mortal man above your own. Your primary concern is for your man's safety and freedom and nothing else matters to you.

Whenever anyone speaks against your man, you are to defend his name in whatever manner possible.

Source: *The Washington Post*, October 11, 1977, P. A-6.

UNDERSTANDING SEXUAL DEVIANCE

Socialization and Sexual Behavior

Many Americans incorrectly believe that what humans do sexually is biologically determined. Humans have a sexual drive or appetite, but they do not have sexual instincts in the sense of predetermined behavior patterns. It is only among humans that sexual activity is given social meaning. Arguing that heterosexuality is not the biological destiny of all humans, Erich Goode and Troiden indicate that humans can respond to a wide variety of sexual stimuli. "In short, our basic biological equipment, both anatomical and hormonal, potentiates and sets limits on what we can and cannot do sexually. But it does not determine what we do, with whom we do it, why we do it, when we do it, how often we do it, or even if we do it at all." [51] Although one's sex is genetically determined, one's sexual identity as heterosexual, homosexual, or bisexual is a product of social experience. Norms, attitudes, and values about sexual acts are not inborn, but socially acquired. The desired outcome of the socialization process in American society is for a normal sexual identity as a heterosexual male or female. These identities usually develop from the generalized conception of self as a male or female that is provided the young child by parents and other persons.

In view of the importance of social influences in the development of patterns of sexual behavior and sexual identity, it is unfortunate that the experts on sexual matters have been almost exclusively physicians and biologists who have emphasized the biological aspects of sexuality and have neglected sociocultural influences. Sexual behavior cannot be understood solely in terms of physiology and human anatomy because it usually is a form of social activity.

Some homosexuals believe they were born as homosexuals, but many of them point to familial influences in their early lives as determining their sexual preference.[52] An isolated instance of homosexual behavior, if discovered and reacted to, may be significant in leading a person to identify as a homosexual. However, the crucial factor usually is the person's recognition of his or her sexual preference for persons of the same sex.

Attitudes regarding some forms of sexual behavior are undergoing change, but prostitution is still generally condemned in American society. Clearly, prostitutes do not represent a random sample of American women. Some call girls are drawn from middle- or upper-class backgrounds, but Gagnon and Simon suggest that the largest number of women who turn to prostitution are from working- or lower-class backgrounds and are females who were extensively involved in heterosexual activity as early

---

[51] Goode and Troiden, op. cit., p. 16.

[52] Further, they see limited possibilities for shifting to a heterosexual pattern. In a sensitive account of his experiences, Donald Cory notes his initial dismay when he recognized that therapy was helping him to overcome his feelings of guilt and shame but was not affecting his sexual attraction to males. Donald W. Cory, *The Homosexual in America: A Subjective Approach* (New York: Greenberg, 1951).

as 12 to 15 years of age. Those who enter the profession are often alienated and isolated from their families and the larger community: "For young women who have few interpersonal or familial resources during adolescence, repeated sexual contacts with males becomes a device for gaining acceptance and social status." [53]

Prostitutes have to cope with society's negative definition of them. Thus, it is not surprising that in one study of prostitutes, every one of the women expressed some guilt feelings. [54] Some of them rationalized their activities by saying they were no worse than other people and certainly were less hypocritical. Others justified their activities as essential to provide financial support for their children or other dependents. For many women, prostitution is degrading, boring, and frightening, and their lives are meaningless and empty.

While the influence of socialization is important, Gail Sheehy, a reporter who studied prostitution in New York City, offers another explanation for its existence: it is a multibillion dollar business. [55] At the minimum price of $20 per customer, 200,000 prostitutes would, with only six customers or "tricks" a day, earn about $9 billion dollars a year in untaxed income. A pimp may demand that each of his girls bring in $200 to $250 a night. [56] An independent call girl may earn $1,000 or more a week.

WHAT CAN BE DONE?

Normal Deviance

The Sexual Revolution.   Many commentators suggest that we are living in the midst of a sexual revolution that will alter what is defined as normal sexual deviance. [57] In other words, some currently deviant sexual activities will not be considered deviant in the future. If the goal of such a revolution is complete sexual freedom, then for the vast majority of the population the revolution has not succeeded, at least not yet, although considerable change has

---

[53] John H. Gagnon and William Simon, as cited in Goode and Troiden, op. cit., p. 108.
[54] Norman R. Jackman, Richard O'Toole, and Gilbert Geis, "The Self-Image of the Prostitute," *Sociological Quarterly*, 4 (Spring 1963): 150–161.
[55] Gail Sheehy, *Hustling: Prostitution in Our Wide-Open Society* (New York: Delacorte Press, 1973), p. 4.
[56] Ibid., p. 9.
[57] Clayton, op. cit., pp. 227–228; see also Editors of Playboy, *The Sexual Revolution* (Chicago: Playboy Press, 1970) and Edwin M. Schur, ed., *The Family and the Sexual Revolution* (Bloomington: Indiana University Press, 1964).

occurred in the past 25 years. In terms of normal deviance, change has been largely in attitudes and willingness to discuss sexual behavior.

As might be anticipated, greater change in attitudes and behavior has occurred among the young. Ira Reiss has shown that the change in attitudes and standards has been in the direction of greater egalitarianism and toward a norm of permissiveness within affectionate relations.[58] The double standard, in which sexual activity is permissible for males but not for females, has not completely disappeared, but women are asserting their right to sexual equality and the changes in premarital and extramarital behavior reflect greater equality between the sexes.

Legal Definition of Obscenity. In the United States, a number of legal battles have been waged concerning the definition of obscenity. They undoubtedly will continue because there has been little success in efforts to define obscenity without including some of the world's great literature and art. Nevertheless, some Americans find erotic materials to be offensive and believe that their distribution should be prohibited. In 1973, the Supreme Court handed down five decisions that suggest movement away from the rather tolerant view it had previously adopted. According to these decisions, states and communities can establish their own standards regarding what constitutes obscenity. Further, it was ruled that the guarantee of free speech is not violated by prohibitions on the sale or exhibition of obscene material, and the earlier defense in terms of redeeming social value was discarded. The Supreme Court also ruled that it was unnecessary to demonstrate a connection between obscene material and antisocial behavior. Yet, the provision of local option may produce chaotic results with a patchwork quilt of variable laws through the country. What is needed is a definition of obscenity that is applicable in all jurisdictions.

Sex Education, Contraception, and Abortion. Another change relevant to normal deviance is the development of sex education programs in the schools. The need for these programs is a reflection of the unwillingness or inability of many parents to provide their children with information about human sexuality. Unfortunately, in American society, sex is often defined as dirty and is not a topic for open discussion: ''Given this framework of repression and avoidance by parents, it is not surprising that the child gets the bulk

---

[58] Ira L. Reiss, *The Social Context of Premarital Sexual Permissiveness* (New York: Holt, Rinehart and Winston, 1967).

of his sexual information, though not his attitudes, through peer relationships.''[59] In some places, sex education programs have been opposed by concerned parents, but as long as parents are given the option of having their offspring quietly excluded, programs designed with the age of the students in mind deserve citizen support. One of the indirect benefits of such programs is that a channel of communication may be opened between parents and children for discussion of a previously taboo topic.

In view of the number of unmarried young females who become pregnant each year, there is a need to provide them not only with information about contraception, but also access to contraceptive devices. For females who do not use or have access to such devices, one alternative to an unwanted pregnancy is abortion. Until recently, a female with an unwanted pregnancy faced the prospect of furtive meetings and an illegal, often dangerous, and expensive operation if she wished to have an abortion. According to a 1973 Supreme Court ruling, a woman could legally obtain an abortion. However, opponents of nontherapeutic abortions initiated a Right to Life movement, and in some parts of the country, physicians who performed abortions were charged with criminal violations on technical grounds. A further victory was won by the antiabortion forces in 1977 when the Supreme Court ruled that states did not have to expend Medicaid funds for abortions.

Decriminalization of Sex Offenses. As noted earlier, most forms of sexual expression are legally prohibited in the United States. A variety of proposals have been made for the removal of criminal penalties or decriminalization of sexual acts involving consenting adults in private. Two law professors, Norval Morris and Gordon Hawkins, argue that the purpose of the criminal law is to protect individuals and property.[60] They refer to the application of the criminal law in the sphere of private activities as the overreach of the criminal law. They propose removal of criminal sanctions from a number of sex offenses—adultery, fornication, illicit cohabitation, bigamy, incest, statutory rape, bestiality, homosexuality, prostitution, pornography, and obscenity. Further, they suggest that the only sex acts that should be punishable are those involving the use or threat of force, adults taking advantage of juveniles, and sexual acts in public.

Although a strong case can be made that the criminal law should not be used to regulate the consensual private sexual activities of adults, it can be

[59] John H. Gagnon, ''Sexuality and Sexual Learning in the Child,'' *Psychiatry,* 28 (August 1965): 223.
[60] Norval Morris and Gordon Hawkins, *The Honest Politician's Guide to Crime Control* (Chicago: University of Chicago Press, 1970), p. 2.

argued that the penalties for statutory rape should not be totally removed. Rather, the age limit should be reduced from 18 to 15, the age of consent in most of Europe. By the age of 15, females are aware of the nature of sexual activity and its potential consequences.

Pathological Deviance

Rape is a distinctive crime because the victim is subject to almost as much stigma as the aggressor. Consequently, many rapes are not reported. It is humiliating to be interrogated repeatedly by policemen and to be examined by a physician in the presence of a policeman. To overcome the unwillingness of victims to report rapes, some police departments have established rape squads composed of policewomen. In many jurisdictions, there is also a financial penalty in that the victim is required to pay for the medical examination conducted to obtain evidence against her attacker. In a society that provides a public defender for the accused rapist, some governmental mechanism is needed to cover medical costs for the victim.

In many localities, women's groups have opened rape crisis centers to provide counseling, as well as medical and psychiatric help. In these centers, the victim "is not regarded as a culprit or challenged about the length of her skirts or the thickness of her eye make-up; her word is believed, as the first step to reconstituting an ego damaged by sexual misuse."[61] Rape squads and rape crisis centers may help to alleviate the suffering of the rape victim, but forcible rape will continue to be a major problem for women in American society until males' attitudes toward females are changed. As long as females are viewed as sex objects for males to conquer, rape will remain a fundamental problem.

Socially Structured Deviance

Attitudes Toward Homosexuality. A major change in the response to homosexuality in this society has been an increased willingness to discuss the subject. One reflection of this change in attitudes is that we now speak of homosexuality as a form of sexual deviance, whereas in the past it was considered a perversion. Homosexuality is still not acknowledged as simply a

---

[61] Germaine Greer, "Seduction is a Four-Letter Word," in Goode and Troiden, op. cit., p. 343.

variation in sexual orientation. A "live and let live" attitude is gaining acceptance among younger Americans who are more likely to view homosexuality as an alternative life style. Nevertheless, in a nationwide random sample of 3,018 adults (aged 21 and over) conducted by researchers at the Institute for Sex Research at Indiana University in 1970, 65 per cent of the respondents regarded homosexuality as obscene and vulgar, and 59 per cent thought there should be a law against homosexual acts.[62]

Organizations. In recent years, a number of homophile organizations, including the Mattachine Society, the Daughters of Bilitis, One, Inc., and the Gay Liberation Front, have come into existence. Another product of the Gay movement is a newspaper entitled the *Advocate*. Several churches for homosexuals also have been organized. These organizations have served as a basis for political action. They also provide group support for homosexuals.

The Law. Although homosexuality has been viewed as unnatural in the Judeo-Christian tradition, legal penalties for homosexual acts involving consenting adults in private have been removed in Great Britain and Canada with no apparent harmful effects. In this country, a number of states—Colorado, Connecticut, Hawaii, Illinois, Ohio, and Oregon—have made similar legal changes. In recent court decisions it has been ruled that the federal government cannot dismiss a homosexual from his job without showing how his sexual orientation interferes with his work. In California, school teachers cannot be dismissed simply because they are homosexuals. Nevertheless, the deportation of a homosexual who immigrated to the United States was upheld, and efforts to declare as unconstitutional the laws regulating homosexual behavior have failed. In a widely publicized case in 1977, voters in Miami rejected an ordinance outlawing discrimination against homosexuals in housing and employment.

Viewpoints. There has been vigorous debate on the question of whether homosexuality is a reflection of psychological abnormality or is an alternative life style. Most of the research on homosexuality has been conducted by psychiatrists and psychologists who viewed homosexuality as a form of mental illness. However, in one study, Evelyn Hooker administered the Rorschach and other projective tests to 30 homosexual males who had never sought psy-

---

[62] Eugene E. Levitt and Albert D. Klassen, "Public Attitudes Toward Sexual Behaviors: The Latest Investigation of the Institute for Sex Research," paper presented at the annual convention of the American Orthopsychiatric Association, 1973, as cited by Blumstein and Schwartz, op. cit., p. 295.

Gay organizations serve as a basis for political action and also provide group support for homosexuals. (Courtesy of Magnum; photo by S. Seitz.)

chological help and to 30 heterosexual controls, matched on age, education, and IQ.[63] With all identifying information except age deleted, two clinicians classified the men on the basis of the Rorschach tests. One expert rated 18 homosexuals and 18 heterosexuals as superior or above average in psychological adjustment. The other clinician gave similar ratings to 17 of the homosexuals and 10 of the heterosexuals. When they were given matched pairs to classify, the experts did no better than chance (guessing). Similar results were found for the other projective tests. Hooker's study allows the inference that heterosexuality is not necessarily essential for mental health.

Consequently, an emerging view of homosexuality is that it is not by definition abnormal, but is a variant form of sexual expression. As Hooker concludes, "Homosexuality may be a deviation in sexual pattern which is

[63] Evelyn Hooker, "The Adjustment of the Male Overt Homosexual," *Jouranl of Projective Techniques,* 21 (March 1957): 18–31.

within the normal range, psychologically.''[64] In 1973, the American Psychiatric Association dropped its classification of homosexuality as a mental disorder. This reflects a change in the attitudes of one group of experts which may eventually affect many other Americans.

Prostitution.   Morris and Hawkins include prostitution in the list of acts they believe should not be subject to criminal penalties, but the authors of *The Lively Commerce,* Winick and Kinsie, conclude that most Americans are unwilling to legalize it.[65] If Americans seriously wish to eliminate prostitution, it will be necessary, as an essential first step, to change the law to make the prostitute's customers equally liable to criminal penalty. Some people believe that prostitution should be legalized. This view is consistent with the idea that if a form of behavior cannot be eliminated, then the government should regulate it and perhaps even collect taxes on transactions. However, those who propose legalization of prostitution should recognize the alienation and degradation experienced by many prostitutes.

The importance of the sexual revolution, particularly the changes in attitudes toward sexual behavior, cannot be emphasized too strongly. Until some 25 years ago, sexual behavior was not considered an appropriate topic for polite conversation. Today it is permissible to discuss sexual conduct. Most forms of sexual behavior are still defined as criminal in American society, but efforts to remove criminal penalties from acts involving consenting adults in private are being made. A more tolerant view of deviant forms of sexual behavior has emerged, although one may anticipate that opposition will appear whenever the issue of decriminalization is raised.

Additional Readings

Alvarez, Walter C., and Sue March. *Homosexuality and Other Forms of Sexual Deviance; Gay Liberation—A Confrontation Doublebook.* New York: Pyramid Books, 1974.

Brecher, Edward M. *The Sex Researchers.* Boston: Little, Brown and Company, 1969.

Browmiller, Susan. *Against Our Will: Men, Women and Rape.* New York: Simon and Schuster, 1975.

---

[64] Ibid., p. 30.
[65] Winick and Kinsie, op. cit., pp. 285–286; Morris and Hawkins, op. cit.

Dank, Barry M. "Coming Out in the Gay World." *Psychiatry,* 34 (May 1971).

Ford, Clellan S., and Frank A. Beach. *Patterns of Sexual Behavior.* New York: Harper & Row, Publishers, 1970.

Gagnon, John, and Bruce Henderson. *Human Sexuality: An Age of Ambiguity.* Boston: Little, Brown and Company, 1975.

Gagnon, John H., and William Simon, eds. *The Sexual Scene.* Chicago: Aldine Publishing Company, 1970.

Gagnon, John H., and William Simon. *Sexual Conduct: The Social Sources of Human Sexuality.* Chicago: Aldine Publishing Company, 1973.

Geis, Gilbert. *Not the Law's Business? An Examination of Homosexuality, Abortion, Prostitution, Narcotics, and Gambling in the United States.* Center for Studies of Crime and Delinquency. Washington, D.C.: U.S. Government Printing Office, 1972.

Gover, Robert. *One Hundred Dollar Misunderstanding.* New York: Ballantine Books, 1972.

Henslin, James M., ed. *Studies in the Sociology of Sex.* New York: Appleton-Century-Crofts, 1971.

Hoffman, Martin. *The Gay World: Male Homosexuality and the Social Creation of Evil.* New York: Basic Books, Inc., Publishers, 1968.

Holmes, Ronald M., ed. *Sexual Behavior: Prostitution, Homosexuality, Swinging.* Berkeley, Calif.: McCutchan Publishing Corp., 1971.

Humphreys, Laud. *Out of the Closets: The Sociology of Homosexual Liberation.* Englewood Cliffs, N.J.: Prentice-Hall, Inc., 1972.

McCaffrey, Joseph A., ed. *The Homosexual Dialectic.* Englewood Cliffs, N.J.: Prentice-Hall, Inc., 1972.

Palson, Charles, and Rebecca Palson. "Swinging in Wedlock." *Society,* 9 (February 1972).

Perry, Troy D. *The Lord Is My Shepherd and He Knows I'm Gay: The Autobiography of the Reverend Troy D. Perry.* Los Angeles: Nash Publishing Corp., 1972.

Scarpitti, Frank R., and Ellen C. Scarpitti. "Victims of Rape." *Society,* 14 (July–August 1977).

Storaska, Frederic. *How to Say No to a Rapist and Survive.* New York: Random House, Inc., 1975.

Warren, Carol A. B. *Identity and Community in the Gay World.* New York: John Wiley & Sons, Inc., 1974.

Williams, Colin J., and Martin S. Weinberg. *Homosexuals and the Military: A Study of Less than Honorable Discharge.* New York: Harper & Row, Publishers, 1971.

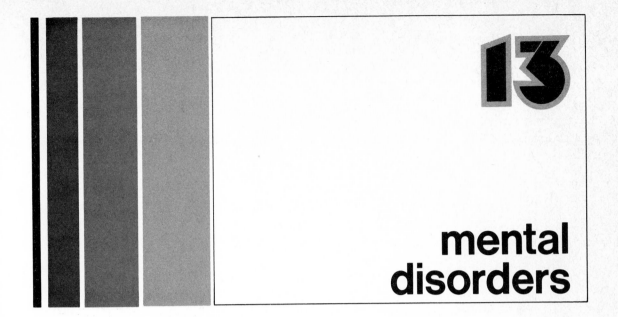

mental disorders

Hobbs was a little brutal sometimes, but it was more than that. He was frightened of the craziness he saw around him because it was an extension of something inside himself. He wanted people to be crazier and more bizarre than they really were so that he could see the line which separated him, his inclinations and random thoughts, and his half-wishes, from the full-bloomed, exploded madness of the patients. McPherson, on the other hand, was a strong man, even a happy one. He wanted the patients to be like him, and the closer they got to being like him the better he felt. He kept calling to the similarity between them, never demanding, but subtly, secretly calling, and when a scrap of it came forth, he welcomed it. The patients had merely continued to give each man what he really wanted. There was no injustice done.[1]

Americans generally are sympathetic toward persons who are physically ill, but an individual with a mental disorder is regarded as "crazy." Most citizens realize they have been physically ill at one time or another, but they do not recognize themselves as having suffered from psychiatric conditions, and they do not necessarily accept the idea that people like themselves can "become mentally ill."[2] Further, few people believe that an individual inten-

---

[1] From Joanne Greenberg (Hannah Green), *I Never Promised You a Rose Garden* (New York: New American Library, 1964), p. 66.
[2] David Mechanic, *Mental Health and Social Policy* (Englewood Cliffs, N.J.: Prentice-Hall, Inc., 1969), p. 25.

tionally gets tuberculosis or some other physical illness. Yet, there is a tendency to see mental patients as personally responsible for their condition, which helps to explain the stigma associated with mental disorders.

The difference in the public's attitudes toward physical illness and mental disorder is also related to the general conception of mental disorder in terms of its most serious forms. A common stereotype of mental patients pictures them as raving maniacs restricted in strait jackets or confined to padded cells.[3] It is true that psychologically disturbed individuals *sometimes* behave in unpredictable ways and may be threatening or frightening. Yet most Americans believe that *all* mentally disordered persons look different and act in strange ways. In one study, a sample of women were given brief descriptions of persons exhibiting symptoms of mental illness. It was found that unless the person was described as consulting a psychiatrist or entering a mental hospital, their unusual behavior was considered as merely eccentric or odd, rather than as an indication of mental disorder.[4] This implies that the public employs a narrow conception of mental illness. In contrast, many mental health professionals—psychiatrists, clinical psychologists, and psychiatric social workers—define mental disorders broadly and consider any form of social maladjustment as a psychiatric problem.

Before the advent of modern psychiatry, persons exhibiting deviant behavior (including mental disorders) were thought to be possessed by the devil or his agents. Through prayer or torture, an effort was made to drive out these demons. During the Renaissance, "madmen" were confined to boats, or the "ships of fools." In the nineteenth century, medical pathologists discovered a relationship between some forms of psychoses and brain damage; syphilis, alcoholism, and arteriosclerosis not only caused impairment of behavior but also produced identifiable physical changes. From this came the assumption that all forms of mental disorders constitute disease.

Consequently, physicians applied the disease model to mental disorders. This medical model involves four basic components: cause, lesion, symptoms, and outcome. Whether attributed to a genetic defect, injury, germ, or virus, a single cause for a disease is sought. There is also a basic lesion or an abnormal change in an organ or part of the body due to injury or disease. A disease involves uniform signs and symptoms. Signs (for example, a fever) are observable by a physician, whereas reports of discomfort (for example, pain) are symptoms. Finally, a disease involves a regular outcome—damage

---

[3] Jum C. Nunnally, Jr., *Popular Conceptions of Mental Health: Their Development and Change* (New York: Holt, Rinehart and Winston, 1961).

[4] Derek L. Philips, "Rejection: A Possible Consequence of Seeking Help for Mental Disorders," *American Sociological Review,* 28 (December 1963): 963–972.

ASYLUMS IN THE NINETEENTH CENTURY

The late Lord Shaftesbury, in the very interesting evidence he gave before the Commission on Lunacy, stated that "in the 'forties' he used to see as many as thirty, forty, or fifty patients chained to the wall. I never knew, he continued, an attendant go about who had not leg-locks and hand-locks to his waist, which were applied without remorse. A madman was in their opinion a creature so devoid of sense and feeling that he might be treated not only as a beast, but worse than a beast. At one Asylum in Bethnal Green, every Saturday night, over two hundred were chained down in their cribs, and never visited again until Monday morning. A crust of bread and a cruse of water were put beside them, and there they were left to pass their dreadful lives in a place no better than a filthy stable." Treatment little better than this being the rule rather than the exception down almost to the middle of the present century, it was no wonder that no one who had a spark of affection for their unfortunate friends would send them to such an inferno.

John Milson Rhodes, "On the Increase of the Certified Insane," in *Poor Law Conference Held in the Year 1900–1901* (London: P. S. King & Son, 1901), p. 9.

to the body or death, unless medical treatment is received. The definition of mental disorders as diseases clearly implies medical responsibility for diagnosis and treatment of mental disorders.

In recent years some social scientists and psychiatrists have challenged the idea that all kinds of mental disorders involve disease or a condition *within* the individual. In fact, many human problems reflect *external* or interpersonal difficulties. For example, Thomas Szasz, a psychiatrist, argues that the concept of mental illness is a myth and that the disease perspective should be discarded because it implies that the source of all psychological problems lies in persons, rather than in interpersonal relations.[5] An important aspect of this emerging perspective is an emphasis on the humanness of mental patients and their similarities to nonpatients.

THE NATURE OF MENTAL DISORDERS

The Conventional Psychiatric Perspective

Definition of mental disorders as diseases has validated treatment of mental patients by medical personnel. As a reflection of their training in medicine,

[5] Thomas S. Szasz, "The Myth of Mental Illness," *American Psychologist,* 15 (1960): 113–118.

psychiatrists tend to seek a physical or genetic cause for behavioral disorders. A variety of tests are often employed to determine whether a patient's problems are organic in origin. Some psychiatrists believe that genetic or chemical processes lie at the root of certain mental disorders such as schizophrenia, yet no physical test has been developed that differentiates schizophrenics from persons not so diagnosed.

If no sign of a disease is discovered, a patient's behavioral disorder is viewed as nonorganic in origin. Many mental health professionals view such nonorganic mental disorders in terms of Sigmund Freud's psychoanalytic perspective in which early childhood experiences are emphasized in the explanation of behavior and mental states. "The cardinal principle of this perspective is that behavior is dominated by unconscious processes which can contribute to inappropriate social functioning and psychological distress."[6] According to Freud, even in the behavior in which they believe themselves to be most rational, humans are moved by unconscious impulses beyond their control; thus, Freud emphasized the irrational, not the rational nature of human beings.[7]

In Freud's view, personality develops largely through identification and displacement. A child identifies with the parents initially and models his or her behavior after them. Although Freud believed that the personality was essentially formed by the end of the child's fifth year of life, he recognized that an adult's personality reflects an accumulation of various identifications, usually with the mother and father as the most important figures.

Freud saw expression of the sexual drive as an important, if not the primary, source of mental conflict. He believed that all children have sexual desires for the parent of the opposite sex. In his view, this problem is never fully resolved, but in addition to identification with the parent of the same sex, there is repression of incestuous desires and displacement to a substitute. With maturity, the object of one's sexual attraction becomes a person of the opposite sex other than one's parent.

In psychiatry, theorists have extended Freud's work. Among such neo-Freudians, greater emphasis is placed on the rational than the irrational aspect of human behavior. Nevertheless, psychiatric theories consistently emphasize the importance of early childhood experiences in the development of personality, and in this sense, one can speak of a conventional psychiatric perspec-

---

[6] Mechanic, op. cit., p. 8.

[7] Sigmund Freud, *Collected Papers,* Vol. IV, trans., Joan Riviere; 3rd ed. (London: Hogarth Press, 1946), p. 355; see Frank E. Hartung, "Manhattan Madness: The Social Movement of Mental Illness," *Sociological Quarterly,* 4 (Summer 1963): 261–272.

tive. In fact, such early family influences have been emphasized to the virtual exclusion of the effect on personality of subsequent experiences outside one's family. Thus, minimal emphasis is given to educational experiences, marital relations, or one's occupation. The effects of broader social influences such as poverty, unemployment, racial discrimination, and international tension also tend to be ignored.

Psychiatrists place little emphasis on interpersonal relations and generally locate the source of nonorganic problems in the individual, particularly in personality development. In other words, they make little attempt to distinguish between problems due to childhood experiences and those reflecting current problems of social adjustment. Utilizing Freud's views to explain human behavior and mental states, whether normal or disturbed, psychiatrists generally do not make an effort to determine whether a patient is mentally ill. The psychiatrist "tends to assume the existence of mental illness or personality disturbance by the fact that the patient is suffering and has come for help or by the fact that the patient's social behavior is sufficiently inappropriate to lead others to bring him to the attention of psychiatric facilities."[8] It is on this basis that they accept as patients persons who have difficulties or are dissatisfied with their jobs or school performance, persons experiencing marital difficulties, or problems with alcohol, as well as individuals with some kind of neurosis.

Are "Problems in Living" Psychiatric Problems?

The trend within psychiatry to define all human problems, including problems in living, as forms of mental illness has led to serious criticism. A leading psychiatrist, Fuller Torrey, argues that much of what is called mental illness has little to do with medicine in general or with brain disease in particular.[9] Such a view does not deny that some people have serious psychological problems. Neither does it discount the problems people have in getting along with others or with themselves.

Szasz argues that use of the terminology appropriate for disorders reflecting identifiable genetic defects and neurological damage when discussing human troubles misleads laypersons regarding the nature of mental illness.[10]

[8] Mechanic, op. cit., p. 21.
[9] E. Fuller Torrey, *The Death of Psychiatry* (Radnor, Pa.: Chilton Book Company, 1974).
[10] Szasz, op. cit.

Use of disease terminology means that human conflicts are disguised as diseases just as in former times devils and witches were considered responsible for human troubles. For example, paranoia begins with persistent interpersonal difficulties and often develops from real issues threatening the individual's status, such as loss of a job or failure to obtain a promotion. The individual is hostile, aggressive, insulting, arrogant, and otherwise disagreeable. Initially, the person may be tolerated by family members, friends, and fellow workers. With continued interpersonal difficulties, others begin to exclude the potential paranoid. Thus, paranoia is a product of persistent interpersonal difficulties between the potential paranoid and others. As the person "earns" the reputation of being unreliable, untrustworthy, or difficult, others react by avoiding the individual.[11] Such human conflicts are not diseases. Thus, many of the persons classified as having a mental disorder have no illness according to the medical definition of a disease.[12]

Szasz further observes that, unless there is evidence of genetic defect or neurological damage, the psychiatrist's judgment that a person is mentally ill must be made on the basis of some set of norms. "Since medical action is designed to correct only medical deviations, it seems logically absurd to expect that it will help solve problems whose very existence has been defined and established on nonmedical grounds."[13]

The Labeling Perspective

Proponents of the labeling perspective are critical of the conventional psychiatric perspective on several grounds. Psychiatrists can be faulted for their failure to differentiate between nonorganic mental illness and other problems in living and to recognize the diversity of norms in a multigroup society such as the United States. They judge a person's behavior according to their own middle-class norms. Another criticism is that the conventional psychiatric perspective is too individualistic because it assumes that there is something abnormal in the individual. This leads to the idea that individual treatment is the key to the problem of mental illness and other human problems. Individual treatment frequently is indispensable, but it is likely to be ineffective

[11] Edwin M. Lemert, *Human Deviance, Social Problems, and Social Control* (Englewood Cliffs, N.J.: Prentice-Hall, Inc., 1967), p. 198.
[12] Marie Jahoda, *Current Concepts of Positive Mental Health* (New York: Basic Books, Inc., Publishers, 1958), p. xi.
[13] Szasz, op. cit.

unless changes take place in the individual's social situation and in the personal relationships that support changes in his or her personality. Further, in the medical model it is assumed that, without intervention, there is a sequential development or unfolding of a disease. This is appropriate for illnesses that have a physical basis, but many human troubles reflect nothing more than situational stress or temporary difficulties.

A key factor in mental illness involves the reaction of others to unusual behavior, whether attributed to situational stress or other psychological difficulties. The person is labeled as one who is mentally ill and, as a consequence, may adopt the role of a mentally ill person.

Thomas Scheff has summarized this perspective on mental illness in terms of the following propositions:

1. Residual rule breaking arises from fundamentally diverse sources (that is, organic, psychological, situations of stress, volitional acts of innovation or defiance).
2. Relative to the rate of treated mental illness, the rate of unrecorded residual rule breaking is extremely high.
3. Most residual rule breaking is "denied" and is of transitory significance.
4. Stereotyped imagery of mental disorder is learned in early childhood.
5. The stereotypes of insanity are continually reaffirmed, inadvertently, in ordinary social interaction.
6. In the crisis occurring when a residual rule breaker is publicly labeled, the deviant is highly suggestible and may accept the label.
7. Among residual rule breakers, labeling is the single most important cause of careers of residual deviance.
8. Labeled deviants may be rewarded for playing the stereotyped deviant role.
9. Labeled deviants may be punished when they attempt to return to conventional roles.[14]

The concept of *residual rule breaking,* central to the labeling perspective, refers to those norm violations for which there is no explicit category in everyday language and which sometimes lead to labeling the violator as mentally ill. These norms fall in the area of what everyone in American society

---

[14]Thomas J. Scheff, "Schizophrenia As Ideology," in Thomas J. Scheff, ed., *Labeling Madness* (Englewood Cliffs, N.J.: Prentice-Hall, Inc., 1975), pp. 9–10.

presumably recognizes as proper behavior. Many norm violations are classified as crime, perversion, drunkenness, or bad manners. A person who steals an item from a store is a thief. One who is insulting to a clerk shows bad manners. However, after the familiar categories are exhausted, there is a residue of diverse norm violations. For example, a professor who places cigarettes in his or her ears does not fit the familiar categories. The professor might be attempting to amuse the students or defying the "No Smoking" signs in the classroom, but the students may define such behavior as a reflection, not of eccentricity, but of mental illness. Thus, residual rule breaking refers to the violation of norms for which there is no explicit label.

Most people at times violate residual rules. They "fly off the handle," withdraw, imagine strange occurrences, have premonitions of dire events, or even hear voices. The most common response to residual rule breaking is denial. That is, the person's behavior is explained in terms of stress, temporary upset, or the fact that he or she is "nervous." The person's behavior is defined as falling within the category of normal behavior by his or her associates and thus has limited significance. Such norm violations do not alter a person's self-concept or interfere with functioning in conventional social roles. Of itself, a brief episode of residual rule breaking is not important, especially if it is not taken as an indication of mental illness by one's family and friends.

If family members or friends suspect that one is mentally ill because of some unusual or even bizarre behavior, the individual may turn to a physician or psychiatrist for help. The result may be the public labeling of a person as mentally ill. In this encounter the rule breaker is confused, anxious, and ashamed. Lacking any other alternative, he or she may accept the mentally ill role. This possibility is enhanced when prestigious individuals such as physicians or psychiatrists suggest that the person is mentally disturbed. Acceptance of the mentally ill role is viewed as the first step in a "career" as a mental patient. In contrast with the usual meaning of the term, the "career" of a mental patient is not one of successive promotions, but a series of demotions. A person who begins to play the mentally ill role is viewed by others as "sicker" than one who does not, and the reactions of others intensify the person's identification with the mentally ill role. In other words, the concept of career is used to designate a person's progressive engulfment in the mentally ill role.

When persons who have been labeled mentally ill attempt to return to conventional roles, they are likely to find their entry systematically blocked.

As a result of the stigma attached to their status as former mental patients, they may face difficulties in occupational, marital, and social relationships.

TYPES OF MENTAL DISORDERS

The types of mental disorders presented here are essentially descriptions of certain clusters of symptoms. Mental health professionals often disagree on which of these labels should be applied to a particular person. In the following discussion, attention is focused on four types of mental disorders: psychosomatic illnesses, neuroses, organic psychoses, and functional psychoses.

Psychosomatic Illnesses

Emotions affect bodily functions and can be measured in terms of changes in blood pressure, pulse rate, and glandular secretions. If an emotional response continues without relief, the physical reactions continue and this can produce injury to body organs.[15] It is thought that this occurs through repression of such emotions as fear or hate. Conditions caused by emotional or psychological states are called *psychosomatic illnesses*. They are real and not imaginary illnesses. Currently, physicians suspect that hypertension (high blood pressure), peptic ulcer, ulcers of the colon, obesity, rheumatoid arthritis, migraine headache, asthma, and diabetes have a psychosomatic basis.

Neuroses

Unfortunately, many Americans confuse the terms neurotic and psychotic and even use them interchangeably. In contrast with psychoses, the severe forms of mental disorders, the *neuroses* are generally mild or moderate disorders. They do not involve delusions, hallucinations, or a radical break with reality. A neurotic response may be triggered by an emotionally difficult situation that threatens a person's emotional security. While a neurotic response may interfere with a person's efficiency, neurotics usually cope with the world and do not require hospitalization. If they seek or obtain treatment, it is usually

[15] Harry Milt, *Basic Handbook on Mental Illness* (New York: Charles Scribner's Sons, 1974), p. 57.

on an outpatient basis, commonly with a general medical practitioner. Classification of neuroses is based on the predominant symptom. The American Psychiatric Association lists six types: anxiety, depression, phobias, obsessive-compulsive reaction, conversion, and dissociation.

Anxiety involves a state of apprehension that something unpleasant is going to occur, but there is no apparent cause for the concern. This may take the form of hypochondria in which one has unfounded fears about the general status of one's health or of a particular condition such as cancer, or one may imagine that one has a variety of illnesses. Anxiety may be accompanied by tension and irritability as well as physical symptoms such as indigestion, headache, and fatigue.

Mild, short-term depression is not indicative of illness. As a form of neurosis, however, psychiatrists use the term *depression* for relatively mild forms of dejection in which the person may, without apparent cause, feel inferior, inadequate, or unloved. As in anxiety, increased irritability and physical symptoms may accompany depression. *Phobias* or inexplicable fears may center on objects or situations, as in fear of certain animals, fear of confinement (claustrophobia), or fear of heights (acrophobia). A person with an *obsessive-compulsive reaction* feels the need to do things repeatedly or in a particular way, without a rational basis. The person experiences discomfort if the pattern or order is not followed. Thus, one may step on cracks in the sidewalk or avoid them, wash the hands repeatedly, or demand meticulous order.

In *conversion,* the senses, vocal cords, arms, legs, or other muscles may be affected. In addition to paralysis and facial tics, the person may experience blindness, deafness, and muteness for which no organic basis can be discovered. As the term *dissociation* implies, a part of the person's life is blocked from consciousness. In somnambulism, or sleepwalking, a person walks in his or her sleep. The person is in a ''dream state'' and if someone speaks, answers are given in terms of this dissociated state. Although amnesia may be caused by a physical injury, a painful emotional experience may lead to memory loss.

Organic Psychoses

Whereas the neuroses involve emotional or psychological disturbance and have no physical basis, the organic psychoses are caused by injury to or impairment of brain tissue. These disorders, sometimes referred to as organic brain syndromes, are linked to infection, intoxication, or disturbance in physiological processes. The senile (old age) psychoses, paresis, and alcoholic psychoses are numerically the most common organic psychoses. The *senile psychoses* are classified as organic on the assumption that their cause lies in the physiological processes associated with aging, but social scientists suspect that the social isolation of aged individuals is also a factor.[16] Senile individuals experience a loss of memory, especially for recent events, and a limited span of concentration, but the severity of these impairments is quite variable. *Paresis* is caused by untreated syphilitic infection which leads to progressive deterioration of brain tissue. The cause of *alcoholic psychoses* is poorly understood. One possibility is prolonged dietary deficiencies, as some heavy drinkers live on the calories contained in alcohol and consume little food that provides essential vitamins and minerals.

Functional Psychoses

In functional mental disorders, there is no identifiable change in the brain, and no physical or chemical tests are available to identify them. There is a pervasive belief, however, that they are caused by some hereditary defect or undiscovered physiological problem. If an organic basis cannot be found for a person's behavior, it is diagnosed as a functional disorder. The major types are: manic-depressive psychoses, paranoia, and schizophrenia.

Only about a quarter of the persons diagnosed as manic-depressive alternate between feelings of dejection and brooding in a depressed state and a manic or agitated state.[17] Most of the patients labeled *manic-depressive* are deeply depressed. Manic-depressive patients, in contrast with many schizophrenics, maintain contact with reality. Although delusions are relatively common, neither memory nor place-time orientation is impaired.

Paranoia is characterized by delusions of grandeur or persecution but does not involve hallucinations. Some years ago, a social psychologist, Milton Rokeach, discovered that in the several mental institutions in Michigan there were three individuals who believed they were Jesus Christ.[18] Using all

---

[16] Marshall B. Clinard, *Sociology of Deviant Behavior*, 4th ed. (New York: Holt, Rinehart and Winston, 1974), pp. 571–572.

[17] Thomas A. C. Rennie, "Prognosis in Manic-Depressive Psychoses," *American Journal of Psychiatry*, 98 (May 1942): 801–814.

[18] Milton Rokeach, *The Three Christs of Ypsilanti: A Psychological Study* (New York: Alfred A. Knopf, Inc., 1964).

the Latin he knew, one of the men called himself *Dr. Domino Dominorum et Rex Rexarum, Simplis Christianus Pueris Mentalis Doktor* (Lord of Lord, and King of Kings, Simple Christian Boy Psychiatrist).[19] When Rokeach arranged transfers so that these individuals were all in the same ward of one hospital, they did not shed their individual delusions, but merely agreed to portray Christ on alternate days. Paranoid individuals interpret real or imagined slights as evidence of an organized plot. As a result, they engage in defensive or vengeful activity. This brings about reactions from others in the form of restraint or retaliation. Unfortunately, this only serves to convince the person that his or her initial interpretation was correct.[20]

Schizophrenia refers to the disintegration of personality organization; it is incorrect to speak of a schizophrenic as a "split personality." Cases of split or multiple personality, as in *The Three Faces of Eve* or *Sybil,* are extremely rare. The primary symptoms of schizophrenia involve the "4 As": affect, association, ambivalence, and autism. In everyday language, affect is called emotion. Distortion in affect is reflected in a passive or indifferent emotional response or by inappropriate action—the person is crying in a situation that calls for laughing, or vice versa. Association refers to the use of disconnected words or phrases. For example, in response to the question, "Why are you in the hospital?" a patient replied: "I'm a cut donator, donated by double sacrifice. I get two days for every one. That's known as double sacrifice; in other words, standard cut donator."[21] Ambivalence refers to continued uncertainty or changing one's mind repeatedly. Autism involves an apparent preoccupation with an internal fantasy life and withdrawal from interpersonal relationships.

Benjamin Braginsky, Dorothea Braginsky, and Kenneth Ring, a team of social psychologists, suggest that psychiatrists share a conception of schizophrenia that consists of three ideas. The basic idea is that a schizophrenic differs from other people in a fundamental way. This does not mean simply that a schizophrenic is a disoriented, forlorn individual who is one of the most maladjusted persons in the society; rather, a schizophrenic "is supposed to inhabit an unreal world governed by fantastic images and a pervasive illogi-

---

[19] Ibid., p. 5.

[20] Norman Cameron, "The Paranoid Pseudo-Community," in Arnold M. Rose, ed., *Mental Health and Mental Disorder: A Sociological Approach* (New York: W. W. Norton & Company, Inc., 1955), pp. 180–189; see Lemert, op. cit.

[21] Norman Cameron, *The Psychology of Behavior Disorders: A Biosocial Approach* (Boston: Houghton Mifflin Company, 1947), p. 466.

cality."[22] In this sense, psychiatrists commonly assert that a schizophrenic appears to be retreating or withdrawing from reality or is out of contact with reality.

Schizophrenia is also viewed as a disintegrative disease that essentially reverses the process of socialization so that the person progressively loses human qualities. Finally, it is believed that a schizophrenic is an involuntary victim of his "illness" and has virtually no control over his personal life. As a consequence, schizophrenics are characterized as passive, dependent, acquiescent, weak, and too ineffectual to pursue rational goals. Braginsky and his associates argue that this psychiatric conception serves both to deprive schizophrenics of their humanness and to justify their confinement in mental institutions.

If a person is so disturbed that communication is not possible, laypersons can recognize the disorder, but often even the experts cannot agree on a diagnosis of schizophrenia. Only diagnosis of the organic disorders is based on objective chemical or physical tests. For the other types of mental disorders, diagnosis reflects clinical judgment. Collectively, such judgments determine the extent to which people are diagnosed as mentally ill and in need of treatment.

THE EXTENT AND DISTRIBUTION OF MENTAL DISORDERS

In the past, the extent of mental disorders was estimated by the number of persons in mental institutions, but the population in such facilities does not accurately reflect the extent of mental disorders any more than the number of prison inmates reflects the extent of crime. In this country, there are approximately 500 mental hospitals, and they contain 28 per cent of all available hospital beds. Until recently, admission to one of these facilities was the usual response to psychological distress, but significant changes have occurred in the past two decades. Many general hospitals have opened psychiatric wards. Having medical insurance, individuals who experience an acute (short-term) disturbance often seek admission to these facilities. The number of mental health centers and outpatient clinics attached to hospitals has also expanded. Further, the number of psychiatrists has increased from about 9,000 in 1956 to over 25,000 today.

[22] Benjamin M. Braginsky, Dorothea D. Braginsky, and Kenneth Ring, *Methods of Madness: The Mental Hospital as a Last Resort* (New York: Holt, Rinehart and Winston, 1969), pp. 30–35.

Episodes of Patient Care

The number of persons receiving treatment for psychological problems from physicians and psychiatrists is not known, but estimates of patient care episodes in resident and outpatient facilities are available.[23] *Patient care episodes* involve the sum of two numbers: patients resident at the beginning of the year or on the active rolls of outpatient clinics plus admissions during the year. While the first figure does not involve duplication, a patient may be admitted to a service more than once in a year or to two or more different services. It is estimated that of the patients admitted to inpatient and outpatient services, 19 per cent were admitted to more than one service. The total number of patient care episodes increased from 1.7 million to 3.4 million between 1955 and 1968, the latest year for which information is available.

In the same period, there was also a dramatic shift from inpatient to outpatient services. In 1955, outpatient services accounted for only 23 per cent of the episodes, but in 1968, 45 per cent of the episodes involved outpatient treatment. As may be seen in Table 13-1, the number of episodes handled in

Table 13-1. Estimated Number of Patient Care Episodes by Type of Facility in the United States, 1968

Facility	Patient Care Episodes
Inpatient	
State and County Mental Hospitals	791,819
Private Mental Hospitals[a]	118,126
General Hospitals	558,790
VA Hospitals	133,503
Outpatient	
Hospital Psychiatric Services	1,507,000
Community Mental Health Centers[b]	271,590
Total	3,380,818

SOURCE: *Statistical Note 23,* Office of Program Planning and Evaluation, Biometry Branch, Health Services and Mental Health Administration (Washington, D.C.: U.S. Government Printing Office, 1971), p. 3.
[a] Patients in Residential Treatment Centers for Children are included in these figures.
[b] Inpatient and outpatient services are included in this category.

[23] *Statistical Note 23,* Office of Program Planning and Evaluation, Biometry Branch, Health Services and Mental Health Administration (Washington, D.C.: U.S. Government Printing Office, 1971).

general hospital inpatient psychiatric units was also large; this figure reflects a twofold increase over 1955. As a consequence, public mental hospitals handled only a quarter of the yearly episodes in 1968, in contrast with half of them in 1955.

Many of the persons receiving mental health care are children (under 18 years of age). According to a Committee on Child Mental Health, "In 1968, 437,000 children were seen in outpatient psychiatric clinics, 33,000 were patients in public and private mental hospitals, 26,000 were in residential treatment centers, 13,000 in day/night services, and 52,000 were patients in community mental health centers."[24] This totals 561,000 juveniles, and the Committee noted that "almost 10 percent of our young people will have had at least one psychiatric contact by the time they reach 25 years of age."[25] The Committee further observed that for persons under the age of 25, the number of admissions to mental hospitals had doubled in the preceding 10 years.

Mental Hospitals

Although other facilities are increasingly being utilized by persons seeking help for psychological distress, mental hospitals still occupy a prominent place in the handling of troubled people. The resident population in these institutions has declined each year from a high of 559,000 in 1955 to 338,000 in 1970, but the number of admissions to mental hospitals has actually increased. The explanation for this apparent inconsistency lies in the average length of time patients remain in the hospital. Until the mid-1950s, many of the patients admitted to mental hospitals remained on a relatively permanent basis. Today, government reports define long-term confinement as a period of more than six months.

Of the 400,000 admissions to public mental hospitals in 1971, 87 per cent were released within six months, 3 per cent died, and 10 per cent remained in the hospital for more than six months.[26] The deaths were concentrated among the older patients; 58 per cent of the deaths of persons 75 years of age and over occurred within a month after admission. Of the total number of ad-

---

[24] Ad Hoc Committee on Child Mental Health, *Report to the Director, National Institute of Mental Health* (Washington, D.C.: U.S. Government Printing Office, 1971), p. 1.

[25] Ibid.

[26] *Statistical Note 74,* Office of Program Planning and Evaluation, Biometry Branch, Health Services and Mental Health Administration (Washington, D.C.: U.S. Government Printing Office, 1973), p. 2.

missions, 61 per cent were released within two months; an additional 14 per cent left in the third month; and 12 per cent were released in the fourth to the sixth month following admission.

Admissions.   As shown in Table 13-2, more than half of the persons admitted to mental hospitals and released within six months were diagnosed as schizophrenic or were experiencing difficulty with alcohol. Those admitted because of their use of other drugs (usually young persons), remained in the hospital a short time. Persons diagnosed with organic brain syndromes or schizophrenia remained in the hospital the longest number of days. Nevertheless, their average stay was only about two months. The obvious inference is that mildly disturbed persons and those suffering an acute episode of schizophrenia (a "nervous breakdown") are likely to be discharged within a month or two.

Table 13-2.   Number of Admissions to Public Mental Hospitals Released Alive by Diagnosis and Age, and Median Days of Stay, United States, 1971

Diagnosis [a]	Number of Admissions	Median Days of Stay
Organic Brain Syndromes	35,988	70.2
Schizophrenia	120,492	60.4
Depressive Disorders	45,180	36.1
Neuroses	10,548	37.1
Personality Disorders	20,400	28.8
Alcohol Disorders	105,216	31.8
Drug Disorders	26,004	17.8
Mental Retardation	9,888	37.0
Age		
Under 24	103,152	44.3
25–44	159,084	41.1
45–64	110,760	44.4
65 and over	34,644	59.1
Total	407,640	43.5

SOURCE: *Statistical Note 74,* Office of Program Planning and Evaluation, Biometry Branch, Health Services and Mental Health Administration (Washington, D.C.: U.S. Government Printing Office, 1973), pp. 7–8.
[a] Because not all diagnostic categories are shown, the numbers do not add to the total.

Residents. The population residing in mental hospitals at the end of the year reflects a mixture of short-term patients and chronic cases (Table 13-3). Approximately four fifths of the resident population at the end of 1970 were in the diagnostic categories of organic brain syndromes and psychoses, and nearly half of these patients were diagnosed as schizophrenic. Presumably, the 30,000 retarded persons confined in mental hospitals were there because space was not available in other specialized facilities. An additional 200,000 mentally retarded individuals were confined in specialized institutions not classified as mental hospitals.

Mental hospitals have cared for more than just the mentally ill. Aged and indigent persons, and those who are lonely and unwanted or without social ties often enter these facilities voluntarily. Hospital personnel recognize that

Table 13-3. Estimated Number of Resident Patients at End of Year in Public Mental Hospitals by Diagnosis, United States, 1970

Diagnosis	Number
Organic Psychoses Associated with:	
Alcoholism	10,620
Syphilis	6,571
Drug or Poison Intoxication	557
Cerebral Arteriosclerosis and Senile Brain Disease	40,377
Other	21,079
Functional Psychoses	
Schizophrenia	162,970
Major Affective Disorder	14,237
Psychotic Depressive Reaction	1,884
Other Psychoses	4,665
Neuroses and Other	
Depressive Neurosis	4,119
Other Neuroses	2,226
Personality Disorders	6,581
Alcoholism Disorders	9,186
Drug Dependence	1,952
Other	20,256
Mental Retardation	30,339
Total	337,619

SOURCE: *Statistical Note 72,* Office of Program Planning and Evaluation, Biometry Branch, Health Services and Mental Health Administration (Washington, D.C.: U.S. Government Printing Office, 1972), p. 7.

as the weather turns cold and snow falls, the number of indigent alcoholics increases.[27]

Social Class and Mental Disorders

Some years ago, a sociologist, August Hollingshead, and a psychiatrist, Fredrick Redlich, set out to determine whether mental disorders are related to social class and whether a person's position in society influences how he or she is treated.[28] They collected information on all residents of New Haven, Connecticut who were being treated by private psychiatrists or in public and private psychiatric hospitals and clinics. Of the 1,891 patients, 68 per cent were in state hospitals and less than 2 per cent were in private hospitals; the remainder were drawn from Veterans' Administration (VA) hospitals, public clinics, and private psychiatrists. They also selected a 5 per cent sample of the general population for comparative purposes.

The investigators found the highest rates of diagnosed mental disorders in the lowest social-class level. Three times as many persons in Class V (lowest) as in Class I (highest) were under treatment for mental disorders. The highest class comprised 3 per cent of the general population, but only 1 per cent of the mental patients. In contrast, the lowest class, with 18 per cent of the population, had 38 per cent of the patients. Even with statistical controls for sex, age, race, marital status, and religious affiliation, class remained an important factor.

The investigators also found that class position influenced the kind of treatment a person obtained. Of the neurotics, 86 per cent of those from the two highest classes (I and II) were treated by private practitioners, whereas 90 per cent of those from Class V were treated in public clinics, military or VA hospitals, or state hospitals. Because all of the individuals from Class I were treated for their neuroses exclusively by private psychiatrists or in private clinics, Class I does not appear in some parts of Figure 13-1.

Similarly, among those diagnosed as psychotic, two thirds of the persons from Class I received treatment in private hospitals and one fourth from private practitioners. In contrast, nine tenths of the persons in Class V went to a state hospital, with most of the remainder treated in public clinics, as shown in Figure 13-2.

[27] David Mechanic, "Some Factors in Identifying and Defining Mental Illness," *Mental Hygiene,* 46 (January 1962): 70.
[28] August B. Hollingshead and Fredrick C. Redlich, *Social Class and Mental Illness: A Community Study* (New York: John Wiley & Sons, Inc., 1958), p. 11.

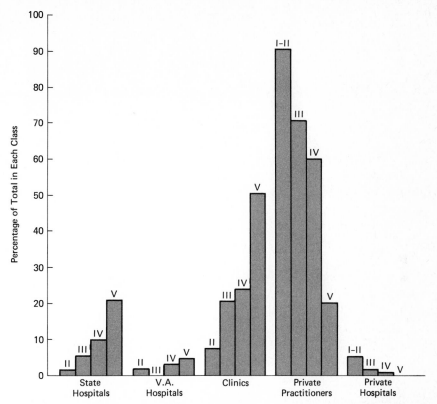

FIGURE 13-1. Percentage of neurotic patients in different treatment agencies by class (New Haven, 1950). [Source: August B. Holingshead and Fredrick C. Redlich, *Social Class and Mental Illness: A Community Study* (New York: John Wiley & Sons, Inc., 1958), p. 265.]

Social Class and Outcome.   A follow-up study was conducted a decade later to determine the treatment status of the 1,563 persons who had been patients in either outpatient psychiatric clinics or hospitals.[29] Of the 1,563 patients, 99 per cent were located. Of these, 49 per cent were still hospitalized, 29 per cent had died, and 22 per cent had been discharged from the hospitals and were living in the community.

The investigators examined records in treatment agencies and interviewed the 387 discharged patients and family members or friends to assess the former patients' mental status and social adjustment in the community.

---

[29] Jerome K. Myers and Lee L. Bean, *A Decade Later: A Follow-up of Social Class and Mental Illness* (New York: John Wiley & Sons, Inc., 1968).

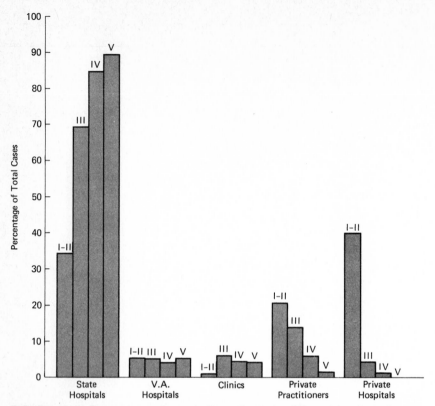

FIGURE 13-2. Percentage of psychotic patients in different treatment agencies by class (New Haven, 1950). [Source: August B. Hollingshead and Fredrick C. Redlich, *Social Class and Mental Illness: A Community Study* (New York: John Wiley & Sons, Inc., 1958), p. 283.]

Death had claimed about the same percentage of persons from each class, but evidence again emerged that social class influenced the subjects' current status. A decade later, some 40 per cent of the former patients from the three highest classes were living in the community, in comparison with 25 per cent of those from Class IV and 15 per cent of those from Class V (the lowest level). These differences could not be attributed to differences in initial diagnosis, type of treatment, type of hospital, or age.

A possible explanation for this difference was discovered in the interviews. Of those who had been released and were living in the community, the investigators found that lower social status was linked to better mental health. Patients from the lower classes had to be mentally healthy before their families would accept them or they could obtain release from the hospital. Having limited resources, some lower-class families were unable to undertake even minimal supervision of a patient if it were needed, and others had little interest in taking on the burden of caring for the patient, although able to do so. In contrast, many of the patients from the higher social classes continued to exhibit some psychiatric symptoms, and thus their mental health was rated as poorer. However, their families had greater resources to provide care and supervision as needed. In addition, their families and former associates welcomed them and involved them in social activities.

Manhattan Madness.   In another study, a random sample of 1,660 adults between the ages of 20 and 59 residing in midtown Manhattan were interviewed.[30] Questions were asked about experiences of nervousness, restlessness, and other forms of emotional disturbance, lapses of memory, and difficulties in interpersonal relations. The respondents were also asked whether they had ever had a "nervous breakdown" or sought psychiatric treatment. This information was abstracted from the interviews and rated by a team of psychiatrists in terms of the apparent degree of impairment in functioning. For the entire sample, the ratings, in percentages, were: well, 18.5; mild symptoms, 36.3; moderate symptoms, 21.8; marked symptoms, 13.2; severe symptoms, 7.5; and incapacitated, 2.7. Grouping the last three categories, the investigators considered 23.4 per cent of the sample as impaired.[31]

Although the ratings of psychiatric conditions were made independently of treatment status, the findings concerning the relationship between social class and psychiatric rating were consistent with the results of the New Haven study. For example, 30 per cent of the persons in the highest class were rated well, whereas less than 5 per cent of the respondents in the lowest class were so rated. And in the highest and lowest classes 12 per cent and 47 per cent, respectively, were classified as impaired.

The investigators also reported that of the persons rated as impaired, involvement in treatment was related to social status. In the higher status levels, one fifth were receiving outpatient therapy, and more than half of the persons rated as impaired had had psychiatric treatment earlier, primarily on an outpatient basis. At the lower status levels, only 1 per cent of the individuals considered to be impaired were receiving treatment, and another 20 per

---

[30] Leo Srole, Thomas S. Langner, Stanley T. Michael, Marvin K. Opler, and Thomas A. C. Rennie, *Mental Health in the Metropolis: The Midtown Manhattan Study* (New York: McGraw-Hill Book Company, 1962).

[31] Ibid., p. 138.

cent had earlier been patients, usually in mental hospitals. Thus, those in the highest social class were more likely to receive treatment.

The Manhattan study reveals that a sizable proportion of persons in this particular population experienced a wide array of problems in living—nervousness, worry, upset stomach, poor spirits, shortness of breath, trembling hands, and frequent headaches. Apparently, Manhattan is not as unique as one might expect, for comparable studies in other areas have produced similar results.[32]

However, in a review of 44 field studies of untreated and treated cases of psychological disorder, Bruce and Barbara Dohrenwend found that the reported prevalence (extent) varied from less than 1 per cent to 64 per cent.[33] This suggests that the estimates are unreliable, particularly in view of the Dohrenwends' comment that the median rate in studies completed after 1950 was seven times higher than the median in the studies done before 1950. Hollingshead has succinctly stated the underlying problem: "Currently, psychiatry does not have a standard test which researchers may use to diagnose any of the functional mental illnesses. A standardized, valid, diagnostic test would enable a researcher to determine the presence or absence of functional mental illness in individuals. Until this problem is solved, research into mental illness will continue to be hampered."[34]

TREATING MENTAL DISORDERS

Psychotherapy

There are various kinds of psychotherapy, but with a few important exceptions, all rely heavily on verbal interaction between patient and therapist. The model for this form of therapy is found in psychoanalysis, the perspective in psychiatry that is uniquely linked with Freud.

Freud emphasized unconscious processes in the explanation of human behavior and believed that "only by repeated and intensive exploration be-

---

[32] Dorothea C. Leighton, John S. Harding, David B. Macklin, Allister M. Macmillan, and Alexander H. Leighton, *The Character of Danger: Psychiatric Symptoms in Selected Communities,* Vol. III, The Stirling County Study of Psychiatric Disorder & Sociocultural Environment (New York: Basic Books, Inc., Publishers, 1963).

[33] Bruce P. Dohrenwend and Barbara S. Dohrenwend, *Social Status and Psychological Disorder: A Causal Inquiry* (New York: John Wiley & Sons, Inc., 1969), pp. 170–171.

[34] August B. Hollingshead, "Some Issues in the Epidemiology of Schizophrenia," *American Sociological Review,* 26 (February 1961): pp. 10–11.

tween therapist and patient using the psychoanalytic method can these basic unconscious processes be discovered and remedied."[35] In psychoanalysis, there is some reliance on the analysis of dreams because Freud believed they reflect wish fulfillment. Hypnosis is also used at times, but the primary therapeutic technique is verbalizing thoughts by free association.

Most psychiatrists do not attempt to probe as deeply into childhood experiences as do psychoanalysts; nevertheless, psychiatric treatment is a time-consuming process. Consequently, a therapist can handle only a limited number of patients. Their high fees and their stress on verbal skills restrict their clientele largely to well-educated, relatively affluent persons. Most psychiatrists in this country are in private practice and deal with persons who are moderately neurotic or experience some difficulty in their lives.

Supportive therapy is a form of psychotherapy that does not attempt to uncover unconscious motivation or help a patient achieve insight into the causes of his or her neurosis.[36] Rather, supportive therapy is employed on a short-term basis to help a person through an emotional crisis involving divorce, death of a family member, or occupational problems. There are also various forms of group therapy in which the range of interactions extends beyond the patient-therapist relationship. Group therapy participants benefit from recognition that their problems are not unique.

The greatest change in the practice of psychiatry in the past two decades has been the use of drugs—particularly tranquilizers, anti-depressants, and psychic energizers—in the treatment of many human troubles and types of mental disorders. Tranquilizers are used to combat anxiety, hallucinations, and delusions, and powerful doses of tranquilizers are used with patients diagnosed as schizophrenic or manic-depressive. With drug therapy, many patients who in earlier decades would have required hospitalization are now able to function in society. On the other hand, some experts suspect that psychiatrists and general medical practitioners are prescribing drugs too readily. Although not widely recognized as yet, the problem of drug dependence among housewives and other conventional citizens is apparently widespread.

Many persons who experience psychological distress either receive no treatment or are treated by general medical practitioners. Psychiatry is increasingly emphasized in the training of physicians, and doctors recognize that many of their patients—one authority cites a figure of 60 per cent as generally accepted in the medical profession—suffer from anxiety or other neuro-

---

[35] Mechanic, *Mental Health and Social Policy,* op. cit., p. 8.
[36] Milt, op. cit., pp. 79–86.

ses, not physical illnesses.[37] Others have psychosomatic complaints, or physical illnesses related to psychological problems. Some persons who experience interpersonal difficulties turn to clergymen, friends, or relatives for assistance.

Mental Hospitals

Many chronic mental patients are still confined in state mental hospitals. Most of these facilities were constructed in the latter part of the nineteenth century or early in this century. They are overcrowded and poorly staffed; many of them have over 1,000 patients and a population of 2,000 is not uncommon. Living conditions in many of these mental hospitals have bordered on the inhumane, and the condition of long-term patients often deteriorates. Most of the patients' contacts with staff members involve the nurses and aides, not psychiatrists or physicians, because the latter are in short supply.

Prior to the introduction of tranquilizers in the mid-1950s, a common form of treatment in mental hospitals was electroshock therapy in which electric current produced loss of consciousness and a convulsion. Although its use has also declined, another technique was lobotomy, in which an incision was made in the frontal lobes of the brain. This operation eliminated symptoms of mental disorder, but in many instances the patient was reduced to little more than a human vegetable.

The major innovation in the care of patients in mental hospitals has been the use of psychoactive drugs, particularly tranquilizers. While they do not cure mental disorders, they control disturbing symptoms and facilitate handling of patients. According to David Mechanic, the use of drugs increased the ability of hospital personnel to work with patients; more importantly, they ''gave the staff greater confidence in its own efficacy . . . [and] gave impetus to administrative changes such as eliminating constraints, minimizing security arrangements, and encouraging early release.''[38]

Admission Procedures and Labeling. A less optimistic view of the operation of mental hospitals is provided by a psychologist, David Rosenhan.[39] He wanted to determine whether normality (or sanity, to use the legal term) and

---

[37] Henry L. Lennard, Leon J. Epstein, Arnold Bernstein, and Donald C. Ransom, *Mystification and Drug Misuse: Hazards in Using Psychoactive Drugs* (San Francisco: Jossey-Bass, Inc., 1971), p. 41.

[38] Mechanic, *Mental Health and Social Policy,* op. cit., pp. 61–62.

[39] David L. Rosenhan, ''On Being Sane in Insane Places,'' *Science,* 179 (January 1973): 250–258.

abnormality are distinguished on the basis of characteristics *in* patients or according to the context in which patients are observed. He hypothesized that if sane persons cannot be distinguished from insane persons in a mental hospital, then psychiatric diagnosis is more a result of the hospital setting than of the characteristics of the patients.

Eight persons who had never had symptoms of serious psychiatric disorder independently gained admission to 12 psychiatric hospitals on the East and West Coasts. The pseudopatients included Rosenhan, two other psychologists, a psychology graduate student, a pediatrician, a psychiatrist, a painter, and a housewife. In the admission interview, the pseudopatients complained that they heard voices, described as unclear, and saying only "empty," "hollow," and "thud." However, as soon as the pseudopatients were admitted to a psychiatric ward, they quit pretending to hear voices. Yet they had difficulty in gaining release and spent from 7 to 52 days—an average of 19 days—in the hospital. The hospital staff treated the pseudopatients as nonpersons; only the other patients suspected that they were not really patients at all. Rosenhan comments:

> Despite their public "show" of sanity, the pseudopatients were never detected. Admitted, except in one case, with a diagnosis of schizophrenia, each was discharged with a diagnosis of schizophrenia "in remission." The label "in remission" should in no way be dismissed as a formality, for at no time during any hospitalization had any question been raised about any pseudopatient's simulation. . . . Rather, the evidence is strong that, once labeled schizophrenic, the pseudopatient was stuck with that label.[40]

Why have individuals been so readily admitted to mental hospitals? According to Scheff, the answer lies in an unwarranted extension to mental disorders of the medical approach in physical illnesses. Regarding physical illnesses, physicians are taught a simple decision rule: when in doubt, diagnose illness. For physical illness, the procedure may cause inconvenience and expense for the patient, but does no long-term harm. However, Scheff argues that this rule is inappropriate for mental disorders. In his view, the appropriate rule, regularly upheld by the courts, is that "there should be a presumption of sanity. The burden of proof of insanity is to be on the petitioners, there must be a preponderance of evidence, and the evidence should be of a 'clear and unexceptionable' nature."[41]

[40] Ibid., p. 252.
[41] Thomas J. Scheff, "The Societal Reaction to Deviance: Ascriptive Elements in the Psychiatric Screening of Mental Patients in a Midwestern State," *Social Problems,* 11 (Spring 1964): 403.

The fact that this is frequently not the case is revealed in an experimental study conducted by Maurice Temerlin.[42] Using a recorded interview with a professional actor who portrayed a normal, healthy man, Temerlin established four conditions and had groups of psychiatrists and clinical psychologists diagnose the interviewee. Included in the first group were graduate students in clinical psychology as well as practicing psychiatrists and clinical psychologists. They were told that the interviewee was "a very interesting man because he looked neurotic but actually was quite psychotic." In contrast, another group was told that their task was to select a scientist for industrial research, whereas a third group was told the interviewee was "a very rare person, a perfectly healthy man." A fourth group made diagnoses with no prior comment about the man's condition.

In the latter three groups, no one diagnosed the interviewee as psychotic, and the majority diagnosed him as mentally healthy. However, in the first group, none of the 25 psychiatrists, only 3 of the 25 clinical psychologists, and 5 of the 45 graduate students diagnosed the interviewee as mentally healthy. This research shows that suggestion has a marked influence on psychiatric diagnosis. An important implication is that appearance at a psychiatric facility strongly suggests that a person is "ill."

Why is this the case? In the admission interview, a psychiatrist does not have time to make an adequate diagnosis or even to determine whether illness exists. Laypersons assume that their conception of mental illness is unimportant because "the psychiatrist is the expert and presumably makes the final decision. . . . On the contrary, . . . persons are brought to the hospital on the basis of lay definitions, and once they arrive, their appearance alone is usually regarded as sufficient evidence of 'illness.' "[43]

Hearing the results of Rosenhan's study, the staff in one hospital doubted that pseudopatients could gain admission to their facility. Therefore, Rosenhan arranged another experiment. He informed the staff members—attendants, nurses, psychiatrists, physicians, and psychologists—that over the next three months, one or more pseudopatients would attempt to gain admission, and staff members were asked to rate each new admission for whom they were responsible. Judgments were obtained regarding 193 patients. Although Rosenhan sent no pseudopatients to the hospital, at least one staff member was highly confident that 41 of these persons were pseudopatients;

---

[42] Maurice K. Temerlin, "Suggestion Effects in Psychiatric Diagnosis," *Journal of Nervous and Mental Disease,* 147 (October 1968): 349–353.

[43] Mechanic, "Some Factors in Identifying and Defining Mental Illness," op. cit., p. 69.

23 were suspected by at least one psychiatrist; and 19 were suspected by one psychiatrist and one other staff member.[44]

Involuntary Confinement.   In this country, a person may be committed to a mental institution for short-term (ranging from 3 to 60 days) observation on the basis of a court order. All that is needed to obtain such an order is an affidavit signed by a complainant in which evidence of mental illness is stated. However, involuntary confinement for a longer period is presumably surrounded by a number of legal safeguards. In addition to an admission interview at the hospital, a prospective patient commonly has to be examined by two court-appointed psychiatrists and represented by legal counsel in a judicial hearing.

These safeguards are not as protective as they might appear. Scheff interviewed the judges in the four courts that handled the largest volume of mental cases in one state. The judges said that the criteria they used to establish a person's mental condition were "appropriateness of behavior and speech, understanding of the situation, and orientation." Yet, in 86 of the 116 judicial hearings that were observed, it was not established that the persons were mentally ill according to these criteria. However, in none of the hearings did the psychiatric examiners recommend the release of the person.

In another study, Dorothy Miller and Michael Schwartz observed 58 judicial hearings.[45] Commitment was recommended in nearly every case; when it was not, the defendant was termed emotionally disturbed and in need of psychiatric care on an outpatient basis. However, in 22 per cent of the hearings, the defendant was released. Most of those seeking voluntary commitment and those who remained silent or were bewildered by the proceedings were committed, but one third of those who resisted commitment were released. Of the resisters, all who attacked the doctors' testimony were committed; only those who questioned the complainant's action were freed.

According to Scheff, the legal safeguards are essentially inoperative because they screen out few, if any, persons who do not meet the statutory requirements for involuntary commitment. He argues that at each decision point there is a strong tendency to define a person as mentally ill. Inadequate amounts of time are devoted to crucial stages of the proceedings. Observing 26 examinations by court-appointed psychiatrists (who were paid only ten

---

[44] Rosenhan, op. cit., p. 252.

[45] Dorothy Miller and Michael Schwartz, "County Lunacy Commission Hearings: Some Observations of Commitments to a State Mental Hospital," *Social Problems,* 14 (Summer 1966): 26–35.

dollars per examination), Scheff reported that the average examination lasted nine minutes. Timing 22 judicial hearings, he indicated their average length to be 1.6 minutes.[46] In the study by Miller and Schwartz, the average length of the hearings they observed was 4.1 minutes, and they were tempted to infer that the court hearings were merely a ritual to rubber stamp a decision made earlier.[47]

Scheff indicates that a judge would be severely criticized if an individual was released and subsequently injured someone; consequently, judges rely on the psychiatrists' testimony, but the psychiatrists readily assume illness. The implication is that the layperson (often a family member or relative) who was the initial complainant is, in essence, the one who diagnoses mental illness.

Hospitalization: The Impact of Stigma. In one study of stigma associated with hospitalization, Howard Freeman and Ozzie Simmons conducted interviews with 649 relatives living in households with former mental patients.[48] The interviews were completed shortly after the patients were released from the institution; most of the patients were hospitalized less than six months. Overall, 24 per cent of the relatives reported problems of stigma. However, the feeling of stigma was clearly related to the severity of the former patient's current symptoms. If the former patient had either no symptoms or minor symptoms, 14 per cent of the relatives reported feelings of stigma, whereas the percentages were 22 and 45, respectively, among relatives of ex-patients with moderate or severe symptoms. The problem of stigma, thus, is not simply a reflection of the presence of a former mental patient in the household, but is related to the perception by family members that the person is still abnormal. Freeman and Simmons' study shows that in order to understand the feelings of stigma among relatives, the severity of ex-patients' current psychiatric symptoms cannot be ignored.

Walter Gove and Terry Fain analyzed a sample of persons one year after their admission to a mental hospital.[49] Of the 429 subjects, only 51 were still institutionalized. Most of the patients who were in the community had received intensive treatment and had been hospitalized an average of 21 days.

---

[46] Thomas Scheff, *Being Mentally Ill: A Sociological Theory* (Chicago: Aldine Publishing Company, 1966), p. 135.

[47] Miller and Schwartz, op. cit., pp. 28, 34.

[48] Howard E. Freeman and Ozzie G. Simmons, "Feelings of Stigma Among Relatives of Former Mental Patients," *Social Problems*, 8 (Spring 1961): 312–321.

[49] Walter R. Gove and Terry Fain, "The Stigma of Mental Hospitalization: An Attempt to Evaluate Its Consequences," *Archives of General Psychiatry*, 28 (April 1973): 494–500.

These former patients generally saw their period of hospitalization as helpful, rather than harmful; 19 of them said they had been harmed, but only 7 of these noted problems of stigma. The investigators suggested that although the public has a negative stereotype of the mentally ill, when face to face with someone who has been labeled mentally ill, they do not seriously discriminate against them.

It seems reasonable to expect that ex-patients may be ambivalent both about their own identity and about others' views of them. One implication of the labeling perspective is that the expectations communicated to a mental patient are important. Patients may either be led to believe that they are helpless and incurable, or that they can soon resume conventional roles in society. An expectation that they will behave normally would be consistent with the definition of their difficulties as problems in living, rather than as a disease or illness. Family members should be counseled that the returning patient can assume, and should be expected to assume, responsibilities.

The finding that few of the ex-patients interviewed by Gove and Fain noted problems of stigma suggests that the labeling perspective overemphasizes the importance of temporary occupancy of the mentally ill role. Gove observes that studies supportive of the labeling perspective are focused largely on chronic patients; he claims that short-term hospitalization avoids such problems.[50] Reliance on outpatient care at community mental health centers or on short- rather than long-term hospitalization tends to avoid the problem of stigma.

WHAT CAN BE DONE?

Commitment Procedures

Commitment procedures deserve attention. In the process in which a person is involuntarily committed to a mental hospital, there is clearly a need to follow established legal procedures designed to protect a citizen's civil rights. The provision of two court-appointed psychiatrists to examine a person is an adequate safeguard only if they make an extensive evaluation of the person prior to offering a clinical judgment. The provision of legal counsel is of little help if the attorney does not attempt to defend the client's interests. Nor

---

[50] Walter R. Gove, "Societal Reaction As an Explanation of Mental Illness: An Evaluation," *American Sociological Review,* 35 (October 1970): 880.

should judges rely exclusively on the recommendations of the psychiatric experts. If the court is incapable of making a reasonable judgment concerning a person's mental status, then the courtroom setting for what is essentially a clinical judgment is inappropriate.

Community Mental Health Centers

In 1956, Congress established the Joint Commission on Mental Illness and Health to evaluate the needs of the mentally ill and the resources available for their treatment. In 1961, the Commission published its report, *Action for Mental Health,* in which increased public expenditures for mental health services were proposed.[51]

Attacking the existing system of state mental hospitals, the Commission recommended against construction of additional large institutions and proposed the establishment of a community mental health center for every 50,000 persons. The Commission's argument for the concept of community mental health care was based on recognition that large mental hospitals were essentially custodial and served to isolate patients from the community. Implementation of this proposal outside the mental hospital system "implicitly endorsed the viewpoint that mental illness is not inherently different from the larger range of psychological difficulties common in the community."[52]

In 1963, Congress passed the Mental Health Centers Construction Act and as of June 1972, there were 493 federally funded community mental health centers in the United States. To qualify for federal funding, a center had to provide at least five essential services, such as inpatient service, outpatient service, day care service, 24-hour emergency service, and educational services to community agencies and professional personnel. A community center could qualify through administrative arrangement with other health facilities, and the inpatient or emergency services could be provided by a general hospital. As a result, many general hospitals have opened psychiatric units for short periods of inpatient treatment.

In addition to the 493 federally funded centers, in 1969, the latest year for which information is available, there were 833 outpatient psychiatric services attached to hospitals, and 1,109 outpatient clinics that were not supported by the federal government. The largest professional group represented

---

[51] *Action for Mental Health,* Final Report of the Joint Commission on Mental Illness and Health (New York: Basic Books, Inc., Publishers, 1961).
[52] Mechanic, *Mental Health and Social Policy,* op. cit., p. 60.

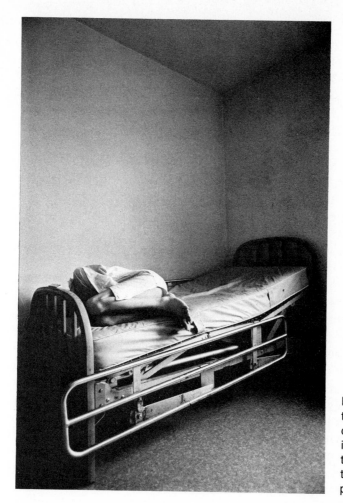

Large mental hospitals are essentially custodial and serve to isolate patients from the community. (Courtesy of Magnum, photo by E. Uzzle.)

among the employees of the 1,109 clinics were social workers—5,461 or 27 per cent of the professional and technical personnel. In addition, there were 3,412 psychiatrists and 3,778 psychologists; each of these professional groups represented approximately 18 per cent of the 20,675 staff members.[53] The remainder were nurses, therapists, and other professionals.

[53] *Health Manpower and Health Facilities, 1972–73,* Health Services and Mental Health Administration, National Center for Health Statistics (Washington, D.C.: U.S. Government Printing Office, 1973), p. 514.

Antipsychiatry

A small, but vocal antipsychiatry movement has developed in recent years, and these critics of contemporary psychiatry adopt a more radical perspective than Szasz, Scheff, and others discussed here. There are two schools of radical psychiatry, the American and English, with somewhat different objectives.[54] The American antipsychiatry movement rejects conventional psychiatric theories and therapeutic practices. These critics note the apparent lack of concern of the medical establishment for the plight of deprived groups—the poor, blacks, the emotionally disturbed, homosexuals, and women. Applying the ideas of Marx, they locate the cause of these deprived groups' troubles in the nature of capitalistic society. American radical psychiatrists emphasize encounter groups, in which participants develop awareness of their oppression and work through the resulting anger. They also suggest the establishment of therapeutic communes and stress the importance of providing inexpensive or free treatment in the community.

These critics of conventional psychiatry argue that therapy can be provided by laypersons. Claude Steiner, a therapist practicing in Berkeley, states that "Psychiatry is the art of soul healing. Anyone who practices the art is a psychiatrist. The practice of psychiatry has been usurped by the medical establishment. Medicine has done practically nothing to improve psychiatry since it assumed control over it. As practiced today, [medical] psychiatry is a step sideways, into pseudoscientism from the state of the art in the Middle Ages, when it was the province of elders and priests as well as physicians."[55] If Freud were alive today, he would probably support these critics. According to his biographer, in his later years Freud asserted that "The internal development of psychoanalysis is everywhere proceeding contrary to my intentions away from lay analysis and becoming a pure medical speciality, and I regard this as fateful for the future of analysis."[56]

The English school of radical psychiatry combines traditional psychoanalytic theory and therapeutic practices with political radicalism and existentialism.[57] The movement is based largely on the ideas of Ronald Laing and

[54] Hendrik M. Ruitenbeek, *Going Crazy: The Radical Therapy of R. D. Laing and Others* (New York: Bantam Books, Inc., 1972), pp. 3–4.

[55] Claude Steiner, "Radical Psychiatry: Principles," *The Radical Therapist*, 1 (January 1971): p. 2.

[56] Ernest Jones, *The Life and Work of Sigmund Freud* (New York: Basic Books, Inc., Publishers, 1955), p. 297.

[57] Existentialism is a philosophy that centers on the existence of human beings. According to this position, human existence cannot be understood solely in scientific terms, particularly experiences of anxiety, guilt, dread, and anguish. Also, the freedom and responsibility of the individual is stressed.

David Cooper, and attention is focused primarily on schizophrenics.[58] They emphasize individual therapy in their practice of psychiatry. In this sense, they are less radical than their American counterparts, but their writings are politically radical in that mental illness is seen partly as a reflection of social and political conditions. Their explanation of mental disorders is based on existentialism and the psychoanalytic or Freudian framework. Consistent with Freudian views, they believe the causes of schizophrenia are located primarily in family relationships.

According to Laing, the condition clinically diagnosed as acute schizophrenia "may be a resource a human being calls upon when all else seems impossible."[59] In Laing's view, a schizophrenic episode reflects a breakdown of a precarious balance between an outer false self, composed of others' intentions and expectations, and an inner true self. Schizophrenia is a voyage in which a person attempts to heal the division between true and false selves that deforms his or her life. Laing proposes that whether a *metanoiac* (metanoia means change of mind) voyage is defined as good or bad depends on the setting in which it occurs. In a psychiatric clinic or mental hospital, the orientation or set is one in which a schizophrenic epsode is defined as a pathological process. But to Laing, this voyage or trip may be a potentially healing one. Schizophrenia may be the only available avenue of escape from "crazy" or disturbed relationships, especially within the family.

Without denying that the person is disturbed, radical psychiatrists argue that the mental hospital is a maddening place. For example, what is called regression (reversion to behavior appropriate to an early age) may be a natural attempt at self-healing, but the nurses and staff attempt to halt the process, often through use of drugs. This does not alleviate the person's suffering, but perpetuates it.

The implication of Laing's view is that alternatives to hospitalization must be sought. At Kingsley Hall, formerly a settlement house in London, Laing and other therapists put his ideas into practice; persons diagnosed as schizophrenic lived communally with therapists and did not receive formal medical treatment. The psychiatrists in residence served as guides and guardians of persons experiencing psychotic episodes, rather than in the traditional role of therapist. There were no distinctions made between staff and patients,

---

[58] Ronald D. Laing and Aaron Esterson, *Sanity, Madness, and the Family: Families of Schizophrenics* (Baltimore: Penguin Books, 1970); David G. Cooper, *Psychiatry and Anti-Psychiatry* (London: Tavistock Publications, 1967).

[59] Ronald D. Laing, "Metanoia: Some Experiences at Kingsley Hall, London," in Ruitenbeek, op. cit., pp. 11–12.

and anyone's actions could be challenged by anyone else. Three fourths of the patients had been diagnosed as schizophrenic, and over half of them had previously been hospitalized. However, after leaving Kingsley Hall, only 9 of the 65 patients were subsequently hospitalized.[60]

Retreats and Organizations

In America, persons who can afford it visit hunting lodges, cottages near bodies of water, or resort areas to "get away from it all." There are no comparable facilities available for the less affluent. As a result, some contend, the mental hospital serves as a temporary refuge for persons with problems in living. The research of Braginsky and his co-workers suggests that some patients use the hospital as a retreat from a world in which they are reluctant to be social participants. Their research demonstrates that mental patients are anything but ineffectual; according to these investigators, patients inhibit symptoms if they wish to be discharged and exaggerate them if they wish to remain in the hospital.[61] It can be argued that rather than assigning individuals the status of patients so as to provide them relief from social pressures, an alternative would be to establish retreat areas for citizens, regardless of their economic position.

With the exception of patients' usual primary group contacts and Recovery, Inc., a small self-help organization of former mental patients, there is little group support for most persons released from psychiatric facilities. What is needed is a large-scale organization comparable to Alcoholics Anonymous or Synanon in which alcoholics and addicts receive group support for a new identity as sober alcoholics or ex-addicts.

There is a need for basic research concerning mental disorders and evaluation of the new efforts to provide mental health care. More than anything else, the concept of mental illness, with its implication that a person's entire personality is disordered, needs to be discarded. "To impose such a definition on a person may force him to redefine himself and subject him to redefinition by others. Moreover, it may so undermine his confidence in his abilities that his limited strengths are further retarded."[62] Assistance can be

---

[60] James S. Gordon, "Who Is Mad? Who Is Sane?" in Ruitenbeek, op. cit., p. 77; one resident's experiences are described in Mary Barnes and Joseph Berke, *Mary Barnes: Two Accounts of a Journey Through Madness* (New York: Ballatine Books, 1971).

[61] Braginsky, Braginsky, and Ring, op. cit.

[62] Mechanic, *Mental Health and Social Policy,* op. cit., p. 148.

provided to those who need help without requiring that a person accept a self-definition as mentally ill.

Not all persons who are labeled mentally ill are normal, nor are mental hospitals filled with people who are essentially sane. But, before an act is even tentatively labeled abnormal, three points must be considered. The first is motivation. The difference between compulsive hand-washing and normal washing depends on the motivation for the act. Second, the context in which the act occurs is important. Laughter in response to a television comedian is not the same as giggling at a funeral service. The third point concerns the question: Who is to make the judgment? If psychiatrists and the general public agree on the judgment that a person is disturbed, there is little reason to challenge the expert. However, the concept of mental illness has been expanded to include a wide array of human troubles. Concern about examinations, unemployment, or the education of one's child—even if expressed verbally as worry—are common *normal* experiences, not symptoms of mild mental disorder.

Another important consideration is that there are degrees of mental health. A patient with a broken leg expects a physician to set the bone so that within a matter of weeks he or she can walk normally, but not necessarily win an Olympic medal in the 100-meter dash. Similarly, if a person can function in social roles in society, he or she must be viewed as meeting the minimal requirements for definition as normal or healthy, even if the person is not perfectly happy or serenely content. Finally, it is important to recognize that persons who are psychologically disturbed should be seen, not as mentally ill, insane, or schizophrenic, but as *human beings* who require assistance in coping with the problems involved in living in a complex society. Only in this way will the essential humanness of mental patients be recognized.

Additional Readings

Angrist, Shirley S., Mark Lefton, Simon Dinitz, and Benjamin Pasamanick. *Women after Treatment: A Study of Former Mental Patients and Their Normal Neighbors.* New York: Appleton-Century-Crofts, 1968.

Cumming, Elaine, and John Cumming. *Closed Ranks: An Experiment in Mental Health Education.* Cambridge, Mass.: Harvard University Press, 1957.

Eaton, Joseph W., and Robert J. Weil. *Culture and Mental Disorders: A Comparative Study of the Hutterites and Other Populations*. New York: The Free Press, 1955.

Jaco, E. Gartly, ed. *Patients, Physicians and Illness: A Sourcebook in Behavioral Science and Health*. 2nd ed. New York: The Free Press, 1972.

Goffman, Erving. *Asylums: Essays on the Social Situation of Mental Patients and Other Inmates*. New York: Doubleday & Company, Inc., 1961.

Goldhamer, Herbert, and Andrew W. Marshall. *Psychosis and Civilization: Two Studies in the Frequency of Mental Disease*. New York: The Free Press, 1949.

Gove, Walter R., and Patrick Howell. "Individual Resources and Mental Hospitalization: A Comparison and Evaluation of the Societal Reaction and Psychiatric Perspectives." *American Sociological Review,* 39 (February 1974).

Gurin, Gerald, Joseph Veroff, and Sheila Feld. *Americans View Their Mental Health: A Nationwide Interview Survey*. New York: Basic Books, Inc., Publishers, 1960.

Hughes, Charles C., Marc-Adélard Tremblay, Robert N. Rapoport, and Alexander H. Leighton. *People of Cove and Woodlot: Communities from the Viewpoint of Social Psychiatry*. Vol. II. The Stirling County Study of Psychiatric Disorder and Sociocultural Environment. New York: Basic Books, Inc., Publishers, 1960.

Kittrie, Nicholas N. *The Right to Be Different: Deviance and Enforced Therapy*. Baltimore: The Johns Hopkins University Press, 1971.

Laing, Ronald D. *Self and Others*. Baltimore: Penguin Books, 1971.

The Mental Health of Urban America: The Urban Programs of the National Institute of Mental Health. Health Services and Mental Health Administration. Washington, D.C.: U.S. Government Printing Office, 1969.

NIMH Research on the Mental Health of the Aging. National Institute of Mental Health. Washington, D.C.: U.S. Government Printing Office, 1972.

Riessman, Frank, Jerome Cohen, and Arthur Pearl, eds. *Mental Health of the Poor: New Treatment Approaches for Low Income People*. New York: The Free Press, 1964.

Rokeach, Milton. *The Open and Closed Mind: Investigations into the Nature of Belief Systems and Personality Systems*. New York: Basic Books, Inc., Publishers, 1960.

Rubington, Earl, and Martin S. Weinberg, eds. *Deviance: The Interactionist Perspective*. 3d ed. New York: Macmillan Publishing Co., Inc., 1978.

Scheff, Thomas J. "The Labelling Theory of Mental Illness." *American Sociological Review,* 39 (June 1974).

Shore, Milton F., and Stuart E. Golann, eds. *Current Ethical Issues in Mental Health.* Washington, D.C.: U.S. Government Printing Office, 1973.

Spitzer, Stephen P., and Norman K. Denzin, eds. *The Mental Patient: Studies in the Sociology of Deviance.* New York: McGraw-Hill Book Company, 1968.

Stanton, Alfred H., and Morris S. Schwartz. *The Mental Hospital: A Study of Institutional Participation in Psychiatric Illness and Treatment.* New York: Basic Books, Inc., Publishers 1954.

Szasz, Thomas S. *The Myth of Mental Illness: Foundations of a Theory of Personal Conduct.* New York: Harper & Row, Publishers 1961.

Weinberg, S. Kirson, ed. *The Sociology of Mental Disorders.* Chicago: Aldine Publishing Company, 1967.

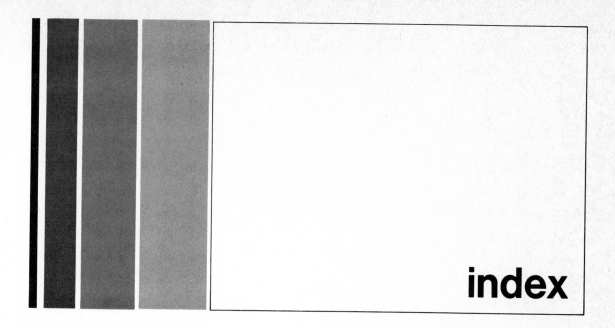

index